Moving Pictures/
Stopping Places

£51.95

Moving Pictures/ Stopping Places

Hotels and Motels on Film

Edited by David B. Clarke,
Valerie Crawford Pfannhauser,
and Marcus A. Doel

LEXINGTON BOOKS

A division of
ROWMAN & LITTLEFIELD PUBLISHERS, INC.
Lanham • Boulder • New York • Toronto • Plymouth, UK

LEXINGTON BOOKS

A division of Rowman & Littlefield Publishers, Inc.
A wholly owned subsidary of The Rowman & Littlefield Publishing Group, Inc.
4501 Forbes Boulevard, Suite 200
Lanham, MD 20706

Estover Road
Plymouth PL6 7PY
United Kingdom

British Library Cataloguing in Publication Information Available

Library of Congress Cataloging-in-Publication Data

Moving pictures/stopping places : hotels and motels on film / edited by David B. Clarke,
    Valerie Crawford Pfannhauser, and Marcus A. Doel.
      p. cm.
    Includes bibliographical references and index.
    ISBN 978-0-7391-2855-8 (cloth : alk. paper)
    eISBN 978-0-7391-3227-2
    1. Hotels in motion pictures. 2. Motels in motion pictures. I. Clarke, David B.,
    1964– II. Pfannhauser, Valerie Crawford, 1965– III. Doel, Marcus A.
    PN1995.9.H68M68 2009
    791.43'6559--dc22

                                                                    2009011547

Printed in the United States of America

♾ ™ The paper used in this publication meets the minimum requirements of American
National Standard for Information Sciences—Permanence of Paper for Printed Library
Materials, ANSI/NISO Z39.48-1992.

Contents

Checking In   1
*David B. Clarke, Valerie Crawford Pfannhauser, and
Marcus A. Doel*

1 Revisiting the Grand Hotel (and Its Place within the Cultural
Economy of Fascist Italy)   13
James Hay

2 Floating Hotels: Cruise Holidays and Amateur Film-making
in the Inter-war Period   49
Heather Norris Nicholson

3 Vacancies: Hotels, Reception Desks, and Identity in
American Cinema, 1929–1964   73
Jann Matlock

4 The Swiss Hotel Film   143
Roland-François Lack

5 Cinematic Topographies in Time–Space:
Wim Wenders' Hotels   183
Stan Jones

6 *The Decay of Fiction* and the Poetics of Pastness   209
Asbjørn Grønstad

7 'Now, where was I?'—Memories, Motels, and Male Hysteria   219
Stuart C. Aitken

8 'Just an Anonymous Room:' Cinematic Hotels and Motels as Mnemonic Purgatories 235
Katherine Lawrie Van de Ven

9 No Sympathy for the Devil, or, Lobby Music: Spaces of Disjunction in *Barton Fink*, *The Shining* and Muzak 255
Greg Hainge

10 Parallel Hotel Worlds 277
Yvette Blackwood

11 No Quarter(s), No Camel(s), No Exit(s): *Motel Cactus* and the Low Heterotopias of Seoul 297
David Scott Diffrient

12 Off the Highway: Some Notes on Stopping Places in Cinema 325
Rob Lapsley

13 The Real of the Screen: Atom Egoyan's *Speaking Parts* 353
Maria Walsh

Departures: The 21st Century Hotel—Your Media/Home Away from Home 371
James Hay

Index 381

Contributors 391

Checking In

David B. Clarke, Valerie Crawford Pfannhauser, and Marcus A. Doel

What is extraordinary begins at the moment I stop.

Maurice Blanchot

Edmund Goulding's (1932) *Grand Hotel*; Alfred Hitchcock's (1960) *Psycho*; Alain Resnais' (1961) *Last Year in Marienbad*; Chantal Akerman's (1972) *Hôtel Monterey*; Stanley Kubrick's (1980) *The Shining*; Sofia Coppola's (2003) *Lost in Translation*; and so on. It is relatively easy to bring to mind instances where hotels, motels, hostels, and the like have been immortalized on celluloid—and, not infrequently, entered into popular consciousness as iconic moments of cinematic history. Of all the manifold spaces and places that lend themselves to cinema, 'stopping places' would seem to hold a privileged position. Across virtually every genre, most national cinemas, and the most disparate of filmmakers, one is actually hard pressed to think of cases where such places fail to make an appearance. Yet the intense and enduring relationship between moving pictures and stopping places has rarely received explicit acknowledgement, let alone been subject to detailed scrutiny. The purpose of the present volume is, accordingly, to explore this elective affinity in all its manifold dimensions. There are, no doubt, as many reasons for the screen presence of this particular species of space as there are films that rely on such *mises-en-scène* to carry the narrative forward, to evoke or heighten some particular sensation in the viewer, and so on. Yet there is also something about stopping places that lends them this potency, some definitive quality or set of qualities that grants them their particular resonance. Ultimately, perhaps, it is the sense in which the distinction between belonging and being out of place—and the distinction between public and private space (McNeill, 2008)—breaks down in such liminal environments that ultimately

1

provides stopping places with their seductive fascination. The essays gathered together here seek to delineate the contours of such spaces through a wide variety of films and film genres, for it is through film that the qualities of stopping places have been explored in the most sustained and compelling manner. Indeed, one of the principal contentions of the book is that filmmakers have, for some time, been the prime theorists of such places, offering an immensely fertile series of insights through their cinematic conceptions and practices. They have, moreover, assumed this role where cultural commentators and social theorists have—with a few notable exceptions—remained largely silent.

Social theory has only relatively recently begun to grapple with a dramatic increase in mobility across the face of the globe (Urry, 2000; Sheller and Urry, 2006). "Nowadays we are all on the move," writes Bauman (1998, 77). Indeed, a new nomadism has taken its revenge on sedentary society (Urry and Rojek, 1997). We move out of choice or compulsion. "Some of us enjoy the new freedom of movement *sans papiers*. Some others are not allowed to stay put for the same reason" (Bauman, 1998, 87). This emphasis on mobility, however, has sometimes been neglectful of the places that serve to facilitate it: the fixed locations that are dedicated to ensuring smooth passage. As Cresswell (2006) notes, flow requires fixity; travel entails points of transit, terminals, and so on. "Social life . . . seems full of multiple and extended connections often across long distances, but these are organized around certain nodes" (Sheller and Urry, 2006, 213). A society in motion necessitates a vast array of places to serve as still points around which the world can be made to turn. In Augé's (1995) terms, such places may more accurately be described as 'non-places,' characterized—in contrast to the organic solidarity of 'anthropological places'—as "spaces where people coexist or cohabit without living together" (Augé, 1999, 110). Such non-places, Augé maintains, are characteristic of our age. Yet Augé's contention, which he explicitly associates with a new era of 'supermodernity,' is entirely consistent with Kracauer's Weimar-era observations on the modern metropolitan hotel lobby as a "space of unrelatedness" (Kracauer 1995, 179). Likewise, Jameson's (1984) invocation of John Portman's Bonaventure Hotel, in downtown Los Angeles, as a paradigmatic postmodern space gestures towards Kracauer (Katz, 1999). What is striking, however, is that Augé, Jameson, and Kracauer are more or less exceptional amongst the ranks of social and cultural theorists in affording the attention they do on the qualities of (non-)places devoted to facilitating motion. There are, of course, some highly insightful written texts that have taken hotels and motels as their object of study (Albrecht with Johnson, 2002; Denby, 1998; Groth, 1994; Jakle et al., 1996; Lamonaca, 2005; Margolies, 1995; Wharton, 2001). Yet the appearances made by hotels and motels in social and cultural theory are, to say the least, dwarfed by the roles they play in film. Artistic and creative endeavours have more willingly embraced what Koestenbaum (2007) terms the 'hotel mode.' One thinks of Sophe Calle's attempts (in 'The Hotel,' 1986) to imagine the identities of hotel guests by way of their unmade beds and scattered belongings (see Calle with Auster, 1999); Robert Coover's (2002) interpretation of Joseph Cornell's 'Grand Hotel' box-sculptures; or Koestenbaum's (2007) *Hotel Theory* itself, which offers a meditation on the nature of hotel space alongside the parallel world of a simulated dime novel, 'Hotel Women.' If stopping places are disorientating places, they nonetheless open themselves up to untold possibilities.

It is, one might propose, the aporetic nature of a fixed place dedicated to movement that underlies the particular interest that filmmakers and other artists and writers have found in hotels and motels. Such places, where circulation pauses to recharge itself, are marked by a vertiginous intensity, which expresses itself in a bewildering variety of ways: simultaneously disrupting and securing mobility; halting yet enabling movement; translating passage into the passage of time (Tallack, 2002); heightening emotion as much as fostering motion (Bruno, 2002); provoking transition as much as smoothing transit (Morris, 1988); registering identity whilst promoting anonymity. Paradoxically, therefore, stopping places are always already in motion, deriving their consistency from the unending sequence of arrivals and departures, the ceaseless flux of reservations, occupations, and vacancies that is their very *raison d'être* (Urry and Sheller, 2004). In Heideggerian mode, hotels and motels acquiesce to a way of being that amounts to a permanent state of transience. Hotels and motels thus create their own disadjusted temporality, erasing the traces of previous occupants on a daily basis, whilst reappearing ready-and-waiting for each and every new arrival. It is unsurprising, therefore, that the hotel or motel, as a 'home from home,' should so frequently register an uncanny (*Unheimlich*) screen presence—virtually the sole theme of a film like Jessica Hausner's (2004) *Hotel*. Places of sanctuary are prone to catastrophic inversion, to become demonic places, spaces of abjection, derangement, violence, and horror. The proximity of salvation and damnation and their susceptibility to inversion is related, by Freud (*SE xvii* [1919], 235), to the way in which the "primary narcissism which dominates the mind of the child" projects repressed thoughts onto the primitive image of a double. The double (or multiple) personalities the child constructs, Freud suggests, initially serve as an assurance against its extinction. "But when this stage has been surmounted, the 'double' reverses its aspect. From having been an assurance of immortality, it becomes the uncanny harbinger of death" (Freud, *ibid.*). This mechanism has been played out in numerous films, from Alfred Hitchcock's (1960) *Psycho* to James Mangold's (2003) *Identity*, all of which render stopping places as scenes of violent murder, perpetrated as a consequence of multiple-personality or disassociative-identity disorders. Yet stopping places, like the uncanny itself, are anything but non-contradictory. They may equally be figured as places of hospitality, compassion, and tenderness—less commonly, perhaps, but beautifully exemplified in films like Wong Kar-wai's (2004) *2046*, Sofia Coppola's (2003) *Lost in Translation*, and Hayao Miyazaki's (2001) *Sen to Chihiro no kamikakushi* (*Spirited Away*). If filmic stopping places already feature incidentally in the small number of books dedicated to road movies (Cohan and Hark, 1997; Sargeant and Watson, 1999; Laderman, 2002; Williams, 1982), in scattered works on film noir, detective films, and so on, there has nonetheless been surprisingly little sustained engagement with the near omnipresence of stopping places in film. Remedying this lack of attention is the principal aim of this book. As a path-breaking volume, it incorporates a dazzling range of themes, issues, films, genres, and directors, serving to map out a new field, orientate the reader to its potential, and provide the direction and impetus for further research. Each chapter develops a possible approach to the theme of cinematic hotels and motels, a particular take that may resonate with or contradict that offered in other chapters. Our intention is not to impose some kind of theoretical straightjacket onto this diversity, but to allow different approaches to occupy their own space, in a manner that may prove hospitable to future occupants.

Given that every hotel occupation is always already a reoccupation, it is fitting to begin with James Hay's 'Revisiting the Grand Hotel' (Chapter 1). Returning to a theme first considered in his (1987) *Popular Film Culture in Fascist Italy*, Hay begins with Fellini's (1974) *Amarcord* (*I Remember Fondly*) and proceeds to present a panoramic assessment of the myth of the Grand Hotel in the cultural economy of Fascist Italy. This myth taps into powerful currents that worked to articulate diverse aspects of a national-popular culture: class, scale, politics, architecture, commerce, and so forth. In tracing these connections, highlighting yet refusing to privilege the Grand Hotel's cinematic manifestations, Hay provides a sophisticated mapping of the Grand Hotel and its association with an ineffable *bel mondo*. Taking in Edmund Goulding's (1932) *Grand Hotel*, German 'Hotelfilms' of the 1920s, films set aboard luxury liners, the escapist themes of Mario Camerini's (1929) *Rotaie* (*The Rails*), and the identity dramas of Camerini's (1937) *Il Signor Max*, amongst others, Hay concludes with a reading of Augusto Genina's (1939) *Castelli in aria* (*Castles in the Air*) that reinforces his central message. If escapist fantasies were intimately connected to the democratization of leisure as a political project in Fascist Italy, the mobilization of considerable resources this necessitated was projected onto the Grand Hotel by harnessing cinematic resources alongside all the others.

Developing the suggestive parallels Hay notes between hotels and cruise-liners, in Chapter 2, 'Floating Hotels,' Heather Norris Nicholson considers British amateur filmmaking in the period between the two World Wars. The record left by a class of ciné-enthusiasts who made Mediterranean cruise-liners the prime site of a new genre of home-movie provides a powerful means of reflecting on visual, cultural, and tourism histories. In undertaking precisely this task, Norris Nicholson is particularly sensitive to the complexity of the relations between those behind and in front of the camera. The on-screen appearances of filmmakers' families, friends, and other tourists dramatize a kind of voyeuristic tourist gaze (Urry, 1990), later to be repeated by the audiences of home screenings. Meanwhile, others caught on camera—whether the native inhabitants of foreign lands or Lascars aboard ship—serve as representatives of the exotic 'other:' as objects of the tourist gaze. Elucidating these complex power relations, Nicholson Norris excavates a selection of largely forgotten films from the archive, including those of George Warburton, a representative of the then new middle class, who focused on recording the pleasures of foreign travel, and the films of the Preston brothers and of Dr. John Barker Scarr, which, although representing more ambitious aesthetic accomplishments, ultimately embodied similar social sensibilities.

In Chapter 3, 'Vacancies: Hotels, Reception Desks, and Identity in American Cinema, 1929–1964,' Jann Matlock offers an engaging study of American films, beginning in the same time-period as Norris Nicholson but reaching into the 1960s. Matlock's account reflects on the hotel register, the reception desk, and the questions of identity raised by their use in a wide variety of films—from the quintessential example of *Grand Hotel* to such films as Frank Capra's (1933) *Lady for a Day*, Gregory La Cava's (1936) *My Man Godfrey*, Arthur Lubin's (1949) *Impact*, Rudolph Maté's (1950) *D.O.A.*, John Huston's (1948) *Key Largo*, George Marshall's (1946) *The Blue Dahlia*, and Orson Welles's (1958) *Touch of Evil*. Shades of Kracauer and overtones of *noir* cast their influence over Matlock's painstaking piecing together of the clues afforded by such films into the hotel's status as a paradigmatic modern space, its refraction in microcosm of the city at large, and the vexed question of identity, as she demonstrates the variety of social, asocial, and even sociopathic tendencies that render the hotel far more than merely a place for pernoctation (Berens, 1997). Matlock isolates a wide range of features that have become classic cinematic tropes, allowing her to develop an account of the hotel as a space marked by misidentification and traversed by desire.

One of the most iconic images of the hotel is surely provided by the Swiss hotel. In Chapter 4, Roland-François Lack concentrates on 'The Swiss Hotel Film,' demonstrating the complex ways and means by which the Swiss hotel has become a cinematic icon. Lack's selection of films takes in an extraordinarily broad sweep, from 1890s documentary shots of Geneva, to Méliès's (1904) *Voyage à travers l'impossible*, to over fifty twentieth- and twenty-first-century fiction films: from Hitchcock to Disney to Bollywood to—in Lack's words, 'the *Swiss* hotel filmmaker'—Jean-Luc Godard; as well as films by Claude Chabrol, Alexander Kluge, Riccardo Signorell, and Daniel Schmid, in memory of whom Lack dedicates his essay. Given the ambition of this undertaking, Lack nonetheless manages to develop an intimate account, attending to the actual hotels that served as locations for filming as closely as he attends to the films themselves, their narratives, themes, characterizations, and cinematography. Lack brings together actual and diegetic cinematic geographies to disclose the close relation between film locations and filmic locations, and between filmmakers and hotels, as exemplified by such cases as the Hotel Waldhaus in Sils-Maria. In addition to its empirical documentation, Lack's chapter offers a series of suggestive insights with respect to the meaning of hotels and the reasons behind their cinematic significance.

If Lack's chapter is framed by a single country, in Chapter 5, 'Cinematic Topographies in Time–Space,' Stan Jones offers an assessment of the work of a single director, Wim Wenders—whose interest in hotels is, as Jones demonstrates, exemplary. Drawing on Gardies' (1993) cinematic conceptions of space, Bakhtin's (1981 [1933]) notion of the chronotope, and Foucault's (1986 [1967]) remarks on the heterotopia, Jones examines the time-space composition of Wenders' work, explicating the attraction Wenders finds in hotels. Jones focuses on three films in particular: *The State of Things* (1982), filmed on location in Sentra on the northwest coast of Portugal; *Wings of Desire* or *Der Himmel über Berlin* (1987); and *The Million Dollar Hotel* (1999), shot in downtown Los Angeles; and draws on a range of other work in Wenders' *oeuvre*, notably *Alice in the Cities* (1973), *Paris.Texas* (1984), and Wenders' joint venture with Michelangelo Antonioni, *Beyond the Clouds* (1995). Jones perceptively elucidates Wenders' fascination with the transience of time; his attentiveness to a sense of place as the site of historical memory; and his concern with the nature of cinematic memory. The potent mnemonic ambivalence of hotels—already alluded to above and developed further in a number of other chapters—is revealed as vital to Wenders' work.

In an evocative chapter devoted to an evocative film, Asbjørn Grønstad's '*The Decay of Fiction* and the Poetics of Pastness' (Chapter 6) takes Pat O'Neill's (2002) melancholic paean to the faded glories of Los Angeles's Ambassador Hotel as the basis of a meditation on memory, place, and the past. Just as the previous chapter reflects on the disruption of linear time in Wim Wenders' work, Grønstad detects a profound disturbance in the notion of linearity in O'Neil's experimental piece. As Grønstad's analysis makes clear, the shifting, ethereal, kaleidoscopic array of allusions to the erstwhile connections between Hollywood and the Ambassador Hotel dissolves the teleological into a hypertelic montage: ontology decomposes into a spectral hauntology in this particular hotelic setting. Yet this decomposition, Grønstad suggests, echoes the destiny of cinema as much as it encapsulates the memory of place. Consequently, Grønstad contemplates additional 'memory films,' notably Christopher Nolan's (2000) *Memento* and Michel Gondry's (2004) *The Eternal Sunshine of the Spotless Mind*, as a way of broaching the significance of *The Decay of Fiction* to a broader cultural sensibility, tapping into the question of cinematic memory. Perhaps *The Decay of Fiction*, like *Last Year in Marienbad*, also bears traces of Adolfo Bioy Casares' (2003 [1940]) reflections on the price of immortality: a state of permanent transience forces us to rethink everything that is valued when life is viewed as a merely transient state of permanence.

Christopher Nolan's (2000) *Memento* provides the focus of Chapter 7, '"Now, where was I?" Memories, Motels, and Male Hysteria,' by Stuart Aitken. *Memento* receives mention in several chapters, because it neatly encapsulates the disadjusted temporality and attendant questions of memory that take on particular charge in relation to stopping places. These issues reach a state of crisis in *Memento*, where the central protagonist suffers from 'anterograde memory dysfunction,' causing him to inhabit a world in which memory-traces are effaced rather than accumulated—paralleling the serial erasure of traces left by occupants of a hotel or motel room, and recalling Derrida's (1991) coinage of the term *seriasure* [*sériature*] to convey the disjointure of space-time. This lack of short-term recall sees memory displaced, externalized, most spectacularly onto the protagonist's body, as a series of tattoos meant to prompt recollection of an event and a sense of purpose stemming from it. Yet, Aitken argues, the protagonist's disassociation does not involve a confusion of interiority and exteriority. Reflecting on the gendered nature of what is too often regarded as a universal condition, Aitken insists that the film's protagonist constantly rekindles the desire for control that marks out men as men: a man's gotta do what a man's gotta do—even when he struggles to recall what that is, and falls back on a self-reinforcing and self-destructive fantasy construct.

In Chapter 8, on 'Cinematic Hotels and Motels as Purgatories,' Katherine Lawrie Van de Ven offers a wide-ranging discussion that seeks to understand why it is that filmic stopping places have come to accommodate the particular issues that they stage so effectively. Beginning with an explication of the purgatorial qualities of hotels and motels, Lawrie offers an initial exemplification by way of Mike Figgis's (1995) *Leaving Las Vegas*, providing a close reading of the moral ambiguity of the protagonist's self-destructive path.

This paves the way to further pertinent examples that address morally ambiguous themes. Revenge provides the first of these, with *Memento*, Patrick Stettner's (2001) *The Business of Strangers*, and Richard Linklater's (2001) *Tape* providing exemplars. A further issue Lawrie raises considers what we might call—borrowing Yvette Blackwood's (Chapter 10) terminology—the 'parallel worlds' of hotel or motel rooms, and the opportunities for multiple narratives they afford. David Weaver's (2001) *Century Hotel*, Ethan Hawke's (2001) *Chelsea Walls*, and Oxide Pang Chun's (2003) *The Tesseract* exemplify this tendency. Finally, Lawrie closes by reflecting on cultural transition in an era of globalization, drawing on Stephen Frears' (2002) *Dirty Pretty Things* and Wong Kar-wai's (2004) *2046*. Ambivalence is the abiding theme of Lawrie's analysis, insofar as the cinematic treatment of hotels and motels may signify both 'home deferred' and 'homesickness deferred.'

Lawrie Van de Ven's notion of the hotel or motel room as purgatory also underpins Greg Hainge's contribution, 'No Sympathy for the Devil or Lobby Music' (Chapter 9), which hinges on the inversion of places of salvation into places of damnation. Setting out from Kracauer's reflections on the hotel lobby as a 'negative church,' and focusing on the Coen brothers' (1991) *Barton Fink* and Kubrick's (1980) *The Shining*, Hainge offers a sharply suggestive theorization of hotels as spaces of disjunction—where time, space and sociality are all out of joint. Thus, the motto of *Barton Fink*'s Hotel Earle—'A Day or a Lifetime'— readily turns from the happy convenience of any desired duration to the endurance of an eternity. The film is redolent of Borges' Swedenborg-inspired (1998 [1954]) story, 'A Theologian in Death,' where the eponymous theologian is unwittingly transported to Hell. If *Barton Fink* evokes Arendt's banality of evil, The Hotel as Hell has never been more disturbingly rendered than in *The Shining*, where the transformation of the *Heimlich* into the *Unheimlich* assumes the full-blown proportions of a descent into madness. Both films, Hainge suggests, reveal how hotels camouflage a disjunctive synthesis as a conjunctive identity, echoing the genetic formula of elevator music, which, to borrow a phrase from Baudrillard (1993), might be conceived of as 'The Hell of the Same.'

As previously noted, the structure of hotels and motels lends itself to the idea of parallel worlds and multiple narratives. In Chapter 10, 'Parallel Hotel Worlds,' Yvette Blackwood draws out this theme in an analysis that uses a variety of films to understand this phenomenon. Initially, Blackwood discusses the 'hotelization' of narrative (i.e., the way in which cinematic hotels and motels are able to accommodate multiple narratives), using Jim Jarmusch's (1989) *Mystery Train* and Sofia Cappola's (2003) *Lost in Translation* as examples. Blackwood then moves her attention to the work of David Lynch, including his 1990s *Twin Peaks* television series and his 1997 film, *Lost Highway*, to consider how hotels have been used as a means of exploring postmodern questions of identity, text, location, and subjectivity—which, Blackwood suggests, no longer accord to a metaphor of reflection (*à la* Lacan's mirror stage) but to one of proximity (*à la* Vidler, 2001). Blackwood makes use of a number of recent theoretical approaches that relate changes in subjectivity to spatial transformations—the work of David Harvey, Marc Augé, Slavoj Žižek, and Franco Moretti—but makes particular use of Deleuze. Hotels and motels are multiplicities, and Deleuze sensitises us to the folded nature of space.

The convergence of multiple lives enfolded into a single space is considered in a different national-cultural context in Chapter 11. In an essay entitled 'No Quarter(s), No Camel(s), No Exit(s): *Motel Cactus* and the Low Heterotopias of Seoul,' David Scott Diffrient combines contextualized analysis with close reading to elucidate the role of 'love motels' in South Korean cinema. These curiously ambivalent spaces retain a marginal position, despite their centrality to the reproduction of patriarchal society in many East Asian countries. The cinematic resonance of such spaces is approached via what Diffrient terms 'situational poetics,' which offers an oblique critical commentary on social conditions at a particular conjunction, functioning in something like an allegorical mode. His central example is Pak Ki-yong's (1997) *Motel Cactus*, a film largely set within the confines of one motel room but which features six main characters who form four couples. The sense of emotional crisis and frustration their encounters express, Diffrient suggests, ensures that the spectator is affected by a sense of tension, which reflects an image of a nation caught between opposing forces. This sensibility, perhaps, accounts for the film's transnational success, which Diffrient relates to an increasingly complex dialectic of reception in a globalizing world.

The penultimate chapter—Chapter 12, 'Off the Highway,' by Rob Lapsley—seeks to account for the tensions and sensibilities conjured up by stopping places by drawing on a more theoretical apparatus, particularly Lacanian psychoanalysis but also the work of Deleuze. Beginning with Heidegger's observations on our metaphysical homelessness and the distinction—deriving from Lévinas— between Homeric and Abrahamic journeys, Lapsley draws on a wide range of films to elucidate the qualities that make stopping places so central to cinema. Lapsley initially pays particularly close attention to Hitchcock, but eschews the obvious tack of dwelling on *Psycho* alone, considering *Vertigo*, *North by Northwest*, *The Birds*, and *Marnie* as well. This is only part of a more expansive treatment, however, which touches on Nolan's (2000) *Memento*; the work of Wong Kar-wai; and concludes with a consideration of three films by Claire Denis: *Beau Travail* (1991); *Trouble Every Day* (2001); and *Vendredi Soir* (2002). Lapsley's take on stopping places provides an assessment of the possibilities and impossibilities presented and negotiated by filmic hotels and motels, which is taken up once more in the final chapter of the book, which also develops the significance of some of the Deleuzean themes intimated by Lapsley's analysis.

In Chapter 13, 'The Real of the Screen,' Maria Walsh provides a detailed analysis and assessment of Atom Egoyan's (1989) *Speaking Parts.* Egoyan, like Wenders, is a filmmaker for whom hotels have a particular potency. Indeed, before becoming a filmmaker, Egoyan worked in a hotel and is sensitized to the labours it involves. Yet beyond the parallels between the creation of a habitable space within a hotel and on the screen, Egoyan's affinity for hotels has a more profound bearing. As Walsh reveals, Egoyan's work explores the complexity of hotels as the empty meeting grounds of intimate strangers in an increasingly mediated and mediatized social world. As a means of understanding Egoyan's seeming preoccupation with the distanciation of social relations wrought by video technologies and the role of media images in the process of memorialization, Walsh mobilizes a number of concepts from Deleuze, especially his rendition of the ideas of Henri Bergson, focusing not only on the haptical qualities of Egoyan's cinema but also on the nature of 'creative emotion' as a transindividual force; on the role of the image as a site of emotional intensity; and the extensive nature of the surficial. Walsh thus demonstrates that *Speaking Parts* works by way of excess, promoting an encounter with points of intensity that escape the confines of a media-saturated environment.

In an afterword, James Hay highlights the fact that it is not only that hotels, motels, and the like feature in films; films also feature in hotel and motel rooms. As Hay points out, referring to certain suppositions made about a classic moment from media/cultural studies, it is often assumed that hotel rooms can be turned into private theatres for the viewing of films – from mainstream Hollywood to pornography. Tracing the historical development of entertainment networks that see 'homes' and 'homes from home' entangled in complex webs that constitutively transform both, Hay closes the volume by encouraging us to explore further the transitivity of moving pictures and stopping places. This again signals the central paradox of the necessity of stopping places for a society in motion. It is apposite to end with the words of Italo Svevo (2002, 157): "The earth turned, but all other things stayed in their proper place." Illuminating the spaces that accommodate this paradox is what moving pictures featuring stopping places allow us to do.

ACKNOWLEDGEMENT

We would like to express our sincere thanks to the Kraszna-Krausz Foundation for providing the financial support necessary to bring this publication project to fruition.

REFERENCES

Albrecht, Donald with Johnson, Elizabeth (eds). *New Hotels for Global Nomads.* New York: Merrell, 2002.

Augé, Marc. *Non-places: Introduction to an Anthropology of Supermodernity.* London: Verso, 1995.

———. *An Anthropology for Contemporaneous Worlds.* Stanford, CA: Stanford University Press, 1999.

Bakhtin, Mikhail Mikhailovich. *The Dialogic Imagination: Four Essays* (ed. Michael Holquist.; trans. Caryl Emerson, and Michael Holquist). Austin: University of Texas Press, 1981.

Baudrillard, Jean. *The Transparency of Evil: Essays on Extreme Phenomena* (trans. James Benedict). London: Verso, 1993.

Bauman, Zygmunt. *Globalization: the Human Consequences.* Cambridge: Polity, 1998.

Berens, Carol. *Hotel Bars and Lobbies.* New York: McGraw-Hill, 1997.

Borges, Jorge Luis. *A Universal History of Iniquity.* Harmondsworth: Penguin, 1998.

Bruno, Giuliana. *Atlas of Emotion: Journeys in Art, Architecture, and Film.* London: Verso, 2002.

Calle, Sophie with Auster, Paul. *Double Game.* New York: Violette Editions, 1999.

Casares, Adolfo Bioy. *The Invention of Morel.* New York: New York Review Books, 2003.

Cohan, Steven and Hark, Ina Rae (eds.). *The Road Movie Book.* London: Routledge, 1997.

Coover, Robert. *The Grand Hotels (of Joseph Cornell).* Providence: Burning Deck Books, 2002.

Cresswell, Tim. *On the Move: Mobility in the Modern Western World.* London: Routledge, 2006.

Denby, Elaine. *Grand Hotels: Reality and Illusion. An Architectural and Social History.* London: Reaktion, 1998.

Derrida, Jacques. *Between the Blinds: A Derrida Reader* (ed. Peggy Kamuf). Hemel Hempstead: Harvester Wheatsheaf, 1991.

Foucault, Michel. 'Of Other Spaces' *Diacritics* 16 no. 1, (January 1986): 22–27.

Freud, Sigmund. 'The Uncanny.' pp. 219–252 in *The Standard Edition of the Complete Works of Sigmund Freud, Volume xvii,* edited by James Strachey London, Hogarth Press/Institute of Psychoanalysis, 1953–1974.

Gardies, André. *L'Éspace au Cinéma.* Paris: Meridiens Klincksieck, 1993.

Groth, Paul. *Living Downtown: The History of Residential Hotels in the United States.* Berkeley: University of California Press, 1994.

Jakle, John A., Sculle, Keith A., Rogers, Jefferson S. *The Motel in America.* Baltimore: Johns Hopkins University Press, 1996.

Jameson, Frederic. 'Postmodernism, or the Cultural Logic of Late Capitalism' *New Left Review* 146 (July–August 1984): 53–92.

Katz, Marc. 'The Hotel Kracauer' *differences: A Journal of Feminist Cultural Studies* 11 no. 2 (July 1999): 134–152.

Koestenbaum, Wayne. *Hotel Theory*. New York: Soft Skull Press, 2007.

Kracauer, Siegfried. 'The Hotel Lobby.' pp. 173–185 in *The Mass Ornament: Weimar Essays*. Translated by Thomas Y. Levin. Cambridge: Harvard University Press, 1995.

Laderman, David. *Driving Visions: Exploring the Road Movie*. Austin: University of Texas Press, 2002.

Lamonaca, Marianne (ed). *Grand Hotels of the Jazz Age: The Architecture of Schultze and Weaver*. Princeton: Princeton Architectural Press, 2005.

McNeill, Donald. 'The Hotel and the City' *Progress in Human Geography* 32 (June 2008): 383–398.

Margolies, John. *Home Away from Home: Motels in America*. Boston: Little, Brown and Co, 1995.

Morris, Meaghan. 'At Henry Parkes Motel' *Cultural Studies* 2 no 1 (January 1988): 1–47.

Sargeant, Jack and Watson, Stephanie (eds.). *Lost Highways: An Illustrated History of Road Movies*. London: Creation Books, 1999.

Sheller, Mimi and Urry, John. 'The New Mobilities Paradigm' *Environment and Planning A* 38 (February 2006): 207–226.

Svevo, Italo. *Zeno's Conscience* (trans. William Weaver). Harmondsworth: Penguin, 2002.

Tallack, Douglas. '"Waiting, Waiting": The Hotel Lobby, in the Modern City' pp. 139–151 in *The Hieroglyphics of Space: Reading and Experiencing the Modern Metropolis* edited by Neil Leach. London, Routledge, 2002.

Urry, John. *The Tourist Gaze: Leisure and Travel in Contemporary Societies*. London: Sage, 1990.

———. *Sociology beyond Societies: Mobilities for the Twenty-first Century*. London: Routledge, 2000.

Urry, John and Rojek, Chris (eds). *Touring Cultures: Transformations of Travel and Theory*. London: Routledge, 1997.

Urry, John and Sheller, Mimi (eds). *Tourism Mobilities: Places to Stay, Places in Play*. London: Routledge, 2004.

Vidler, Anthony. *Warped Space: Art, Architecture, and Anxiety in Modern Culture*. Cambridge, MA: MIT Press, 2001.

Wharton, Annabel Jane. *Building the Cold War: Hilton International Hotels and Modern Architecture*. Chicago: University of Chicago Press, 2001.

Williams, Mark. *Road Movies: The Complete Guide to Cinema on Wheels*. London: Proteus, 1982.

Chapter One

Revisiting the Grand Hotel (and Its Place within the Cultural Economy of Fascist Italy)

James Hay

The Grand Hotel. Always the same. People come. People go. And nothing ever happens.

> Dr. Otternschlaz, *Grand Hotel* (d. Edmund Goulding, 1932)

THE POPULISM OF THE GRAND HOTEL'S REVOLVING DOOR TO THE *BEL MONDO*[1]

In Federico Fellini's *Amarcord* (1974), the Grand Hotel is a recurring setting—a stage—for performance and spectacle in the town.[2] For the adolescent protagonist, Titta, the hotel is almost a sacred shrine whose façade conceals exotic characters (a Prince or a Caliph) and erotic mysteries (the Caliph's harem or Titta's uncle dancing till dawn with a voluptuous Nordic vacationer). For Titta's provincial community, the Grand Hotel is a touchstone with a more cosmopolitan set—with that which comes from beyond. As a representation of the town's sense of self-importance and connectedness in the world, the hotel is majestic and even monumental. In that sense, the hotel is akin to the imperious and luminous luxury liner, the Rex, which the town's inhabitants venture in small boats to witness pass just off its shore one foggy night. The Grand Hotel and the Rex are not only gateways to the Great Beyond (ethereal in that sense) but coordinates for everyday life in the town.

Across these and other sites, *Amarcord* not only 'remembers' life in the town as a nexus of intersecting paths and coordinates, it also emphasizes that these coordinates provided a map through which Titta and the townspeople understood the world and their changing place in it. The film is, in this sense, a cultural history as well as a cultural geography. The daily rhythms and the

special *events* of life in Fascist Italy (what Fernand Braudel or Henri Lefebvre might describe as the little and big cycles of history) both produced and
were produced by the centers and borders, the sacred and profane ground,
the familiar and unfamiliar zones of everyday activity.[3] And as cinematic
reconstruction (a 'personal' record or recollection by a film director), it is
significant that through these rituals and coordinates the town's Grand Hotel
is linked to the town's only movie theater. In Fellini's attempt to represent
through the movie theatre the *coscienza* (the lived and spatially bounded
awareness/consciousness) of Italy during the 1920s and 1930s, it is no small
coincidence that the Grand Hotel was one of the most prominent icons or
settings in movies during the time that this movie is set—the late 1920s and
early 1930s.[4] To the extent that Fellini's film is an account of life under Fascism, the film represents politics and government as embedded in the rituals
and regularities along the path between the movie theater and the Grand
Hotel.

I begin with (or return to) Fellini's *Amarcord* particularly because it locates the town's Grand Hotel and movie theatre—along with the policies,
programs, and events of Italian Fascism—within the intersecting networks of
rituals and routes in daily life. This essay acknowledges that understanding
the relation between the cinema and the hotel can teach us something that fo-
cussing only on cinema may overlook. As much as this essay is motivated by
the intriguing possibilities of rethinking film history through the hotel, the essay is not just about developing an alternative perspective on cinema. Rather,
the essay focuses on how the cinema and the hotel developed and mattered
interdependently and how considering the cinema and the hotel through their
convergence teaches us something about the networks upon which political,
economic, and cultural formations have depended.

This essay is interested in a fairly specific historical and geographic conjuncture—between cinema, the Grand Hotel, and Fascism in Italy during the
late 1920s and 1930s. However, before discussing how the Grand Hotel, the
movie theatre, and Italian Fascism developed through one another, this section suggests reasons why this conjuncture deserves attention, and three general implications of their intersection. One implication concerns the Grand
Hotel's and cinema's intertwined representation of social *hypermobility*—the
rapid rise and fall of fortunes as well as a new regime of mechanized transport. A second concerns the Grand Hotel and movie theatre as *stages* for
enacting or performing a 'popular' culture—a modern formation that under-
went a period of intense mobilization politically and economically, nationally
and internationally during the 1920s and 1930s. And the third concerns the
Grand Hotel's and the movie theatre's relation to global networks and the
importance of locating them within an internationalism of the 1920s and

1930s. After all, as Otto Krengelein asserts with great certainty at the end of the MGM's *Grand Hotel* (1932), "there are Grand Hotels everywhere in the world." Collectively these three implications underscore that the cinema–Grand Hotel nexus was part of a geography, economy, and technology for travel and transport as 'popular' activity, and for *mobilizing* popular culture commercially and politically, nationally and internationally.

In the early 1930s, both the rarity (the 'grandness') and the ubiquity/regularity which Krengelein attributed to the ethos of the Grand Hotel was partly linguistic. The English term 'grand hotel' only partly connotes the status and opulence suggested by the French *hôtel de luxe* and the Italian *hotel di lusso*—hotels of luxury and ethereality, light and resplendence, hotels as lit stages and spectacle, hotels as objects of fascination and prohibition about being seen. During the 1920s and 1930s, both terms were common in Italy. That the anglicized term, 'grand hotel,' became widely accepted underscores the extent to which these hotels had become icons and 'meeting places' in the internationalization of Italy's cultural and political economy. Within these economies, movie theatres and luxury hotels comprised networks of an interurban as well as an increasingly international flow and exchange that were shaping Italy's national identity and transforming its cultural, political, and economic geography.[5] The status and modernity of cities and nations depended partly on their place within these economies.

To say that the term Grand Hotel was imbricated in these economies, networks, and geographies is also to recognize cinema's role not merely in the linguistic but also the visual construction and dissemination of the Grand Hotel's identity, meaning, and reality—the filmic world of the Grand Hotel. The Grand Hotel and the cinema developed interdependently as technologies and sites of *touring* and *transport*—as 'rooms with a view' to which audiences temporarily escaped. The 'motion picture' and 'moving image,' the conveyance of faraway places through filmic recordings (evident in the earliest cinematographic experiments by the Lumière brothers), mounting cameras on moving vehicles, and staging narratives about moving bodies and vehicles such as speeding cars and trains all connected the movie/theatre to a modern *regime* of travel, transport, and tourism in which the Grand Hotel was also situated and mobilized.[6] Arguably, the iconography and mythology of travel and tourism—luxury hotels, trains, and 'transatlantics'—greatly contributed to cinema's transcultural appeal and to a 'world' of the Grand Hotel that cinema helped sustain. In Italy, as in other Western nations, the luxury hotel and the cinema were points of interface between the international networks/economies of *touring* and a nation's cosmopolitanism (its cultural, economic, and political modernity in that sense). As an interface between the international and national, the movie theatre also helped *popularize* forms of tourism. Cinema was becoming a *vehicle* and medium for travel and tourism as an activity no longer restricted to the wealthy, but rather as a 'popular' enterprise—one that was decidedly commercial and that in Europe was increasingly organized and sponsored by national government.

As structuralist film criticism has shown, certain places or settings (such as a hotel) acquire significance and meaning within a film's 'narrative economy.' This would include how a hotel has functioned within the sequence and logic of film as narrative, but also how hotels or other sites have been conventionalized through film genres and how audiences' familiarity with the hotel through these conventions has informed the making and watching of films. In this latter sense, film genres have contributed to audiences' mental maps of a world comprised of places made familiar through popular representations. The Grand Hotel became mythic through the regularized iconography of cinema, novels, magazines, and brochures, and its mythic potential was in turn articulated to the identity of cities, regions, and nations (e.g., Berlin *as* Grand Hotel in MGM's eponymous film). Complicating the Grand Hotel as cinematic myth is its malleability and fungibility during this period—its adherence and articulation, as mobile signifier, to various cities and nations 'anywhere in the world' through national cinemas.

As mobile signifier and myth, the Grand Hotel acquired significance particularly through its difference from myths of Home—that is, from representations of a household, neighborhood, city and even nation as 'home.' In this respect, many films involving the hotel were narratives about the desire to leave and/or renew 'home.'[7] The Grand Hotel often was about negotiating home away from home or was an object of intense desire for a social mobility restricted by ties to home (particularly as that model of home was opposed to the hotel, as too provincial or culturally and economically restricted). In this way, the Grand Hotel became a conventionalized sign of—a place-marker on the road to—a cosmopolitanism and an otherworldly, mobile, and less restrictive domain. Against the backdrop of Home, the Grand Hotel's rarified atmosphere was inseparable from its capacity to represent aesthetic value—as something that comes from beyond the familiar and everyday, as modernism's internationalism, as a *bel mondo* (a beautiful world).[8] For the young Titta in *Amarcord*, the Grand Hotel is emblematic of a worldliness, leisure, mobility, and romance that is inaccessible but never far from everyday life and the town's movie theatre. It is off limits to him but alluring to him for the same reason. It is very much at the center of his own perception of the world, since the leisure, playfulness, and spectacle that it embodies pervade his own adolescent world and deepen his restlessness with the limitedness of his household and town.

The Grand Hotel emerged not only as a mythic world *in* movies; its currency, value, and mattering as a 'chronotope' (a time-space configuration) developed in the world—within the design conventions of actual Grand Hotels, within the historically and geographically situated production of space, within economies as temporalized and spatialized networks of resources and exchange, and within the regularity and paths of daily life.[9] For instance, the internationalism of the filmic Grand Hotel was the culmination of a relatively energetic building of large luxury hotels from the late nineteenth century through the first four decades of the twentieth century. Some of these hotels helped establish remote towns as destinations in a circuit of tourism for an upper class. Similar to and contemporaneous with this variant of Grand Hotel was the luxury ocean liner, the number and size of which grew rapidly during this period.[10] The luxury liner (e.g., France's Normandie, Italy's Rex, Germany's Europa, Britain's Queen Mary during the 1920s and 1930s) reinforced the link between Europe and North America through an economy of exclusive tourism, even as the liner was rapidly becoming available to tourism as popular activity. The liner was a vehicle—the international currency—of the nation-state's international dominion and prowess at a time when empire was being ratified in the name of the national-popular. And the names of the European luxury liners attested to both their regal and their national-popular genealogy as cultural currency.

The extra-urban Grand Hotels imparted an urbane aura to their towns and villages due to the increasing importance of Grand Hotels to metropolitan centers and life. During this period, the metropolitan luxury hotels helped anchor and represent (to their cities and to the world) the political, economic, and cultural capitals in the West (e.g., the Hotel Excelsior and the Adlon Hotel in Berlin, the Hotel Napoleon in Paris, the Plaza Hotel in New York City). Between 1927 and 1932, many of the earlier Grand Hotels were dramatically enlarged (e.g., the Hotel Excelsior in Berlin; the Palmer House in Chicago), and many new luxury hotels were constructed (e.g., the Dorchester, Grosvenor House, the Mayfair, the Park Lane, and the Strand Place in London; the Barbizon Plaza, the Hotel Carlyle, and the current Waldorf-Astoria in New York City). The opening of Grand Hotels in the early twentieth century were social and civic events that were widely covered in newspapers and magazines in these countries and abroad. Grand Hotels were semi-public (neither entirely elite nor popular) stages for varieties of entertainment. By the late 1920s, therefore, the metropolitan luxury hotels were not simply places represented *in* movies, newspapers, or magazines; they belonged to networks of civic, cultural, and entertainment centers, such as galleries and museums (since paintings and statuary often bedecked their lobbies), concert halls, fine restaurants, casinos, sporting clubs, and movie theatres. As elements of a city's modernity and its status as international capital and stopping point for an elite class of traveller/tourist, the Grand Hotels thus operated as gateways between the public life of specific cities and the international movement of culture, entertainment, and celebrity. In Europe, these hotels often sought to emulate and keep pace with ones in the United States, while the ones in the United States often sought to achieve an Old World pedigree.

This point also underscores that during the 1920s and 1930s, the currency of the Grand Hotel in movies, and the linkage between Home and Grand Hotel as filmic chronotopes in orbit around one another, were predicated upon the economies and lived pathways between households, movie theatres, and hotels. The difference or distance between home and hotel, in this sense, was mediated through the movie theatre—not only through the representation of Home and the Grand Hotel on the movie screen but through the theatre as site of commercialized leisure, recreation, and escape, as a site of certain freedoms and regulations, as a site mobilized and acted upon governmentally, and as a node in changing economies of value. If the Grand Hotel and Home were *represented* as different (even opposites), the movie theatre as 'popular' space helped make the everyday and the domestic commensurate with the vacation and helped make the hotel a stopping place that was rarified and Grand as well as familiar and ordinary for particular classes of audience. In this sense, the movie theatre served as a conduit and stage for mediating a relation between home(land) and that which stretched beyond the domestic and familiar temporality and spatiality of daily life. The internationalism of the Grand Hotel was not simply an escapist fantasy (a flight of false consciousness) but a lived and physically travelled relation to a sphere beyond the borders of everyday life and domestic life. It was an encounter with the international circulation of film and celebrity from the place where one lived (i.e., from one's homeland).

Considering the Grand Hotel in this way involves recognizing its relation to the circulation of national popular cultures during the 1920s and 1930s, particularly to cinema's emergence both as a profoundly national (often a 'homeland'-centric and nationalistic) enterprise/network and as an enterprise/network for inserting national-popular forms into these migrations and translations, redefining their national and international space of consumption. As Gramsci emphasized, the idea of the 'popular' was articulated to the 'national' with particular energy during the 1920s and 1930s, in Italy and the West. However, producing and mobilizing a 'popular culture' was not only integral to the formation of national culture, the nation-state, and nationalism; the 'national-popular' formed around international economic and cultural models (such as Fordism and the French detective novels to which Gramsci referred in his account of Italy).[11] During the 1920s and 1930s, protectionist governmental rationalities and policies became complexly intertwined with internationalist aspirations to export national culture as 'popular culture.' The tension between domestic and internationalist cultural economies already was inscribed in the literary and theatrical forms that circulated internationally for an educated and elite class of consumer/patron. Films that represented Grand Hotels during the 1920s and 1930s necessarily navigated this tension. The project of designing and disseminating a 'popular' form involved not only articulating the 'popular' as a new, modern culture that was not strictly for elite classes (the nineteenth-century economies of literature and theatre) but also articulating the national through the international, and vice-versa.

The European *hôtel de luxe* thus developed as a setting in films through the narrative economies of national-popular cultures in the West, even as national film styles circulated across national borders. As noted above, the Grand Hotel particularly cemented a network of cultural exchange between Europe and North America. While over the 1920s the hotel was a setting in films produced in different Western nations, there is a distinct pedigree of (sometimes converging) U.S. and German cinema, particularly in the latter's development of an Expressionist style that contributed to the hotel's image as a dark refuge, as a heightening of (in Georg Simmel's sense) the anonymity, freedoms, rootlessness, and loneliness accompanying modernity,[12] as a space of risk (sometimes associated with the casinos in luxury hotels) and of lurid, often tragic and deadly, sexual escapade. The Grand Hotel is a central setting in the films that German director Erich von Stroheim made in Hollywood— films such as *Blind Husbands* (1919) and *Foolish Wives* (1921), both of which concern an American couple on vacation in Europe whose marriage is nearly wrecked by a beguiling foreigner. *Hotel Imperial* (1927) was another example of the convergence between Europe and Hollywood—a Hollywood film that adapted a Hungarian play and was directed by Swedish transplant Mauritz Stiller. Though *Hotel Imperial* is set in a relatively small hotel, the hotel is a stage for a multinational cast of characters, including a heroine who is an aristocrat masquerading as a chambermaid. Films produced in Germany that are set in hotels include Siegfried Dessauer's *Hotel Atlantik* (1920), Eward Andre Dupont's *Das Grand Hotel Babylon* (1920), F.W. Murnau's *The Last Laugh* (1924), Johannes Guter's *Ihr Dunkler Punkt* (*The Beauty Mark*, 1928), and G.W. Pabst's *Pandora's Box* (1929)—films whose noir-ish intonations shaded their representation of the hotel.[13]

During the 1920s, the Grand Hotel as a point of convergence between cinema's dual strains of nationalism and internationalism, and of populism and elitism, helped attach a transposable set of connotations to the Grand Hotel but also complicated its significance and meaning within different parts of the world. In one sense, certain dimensions of the Grand Hotel in feature-films made it available for popular exhibition in various nations. For 1920s North American and European audiences, for instance, a Monte Carlo hotel was paradigmatic of an urbane yet slightly jaded and decadent lifestyle—one tainted by the values of an elite class and culture, yet fascinating for the same reason.[14] Though the elite class may have been depicted as 'foreigners' for certain national audiences (e.g., Stroheim's character's seducer of innocent U.S. vacationers in Europe), the foreignness of wealthy characters was also a matter of their relation to spheres that were class-exclusive and thus anathema to a 'popular culture.' Unlike the movie house, the exclusivity of a Grand Hotel ran counter to the everyday loci of activity comprising early twentieth-century 'popular' culture in Europe and the United States.[15]

Also, because the Grand Hotel's place in international circuits of travel and tourism (its distance from home and homeland) situated it in a realm 'bordering' the national and the popular, its border status both facilitated and problematized the 'national-popular.' As a cultural site for representing en-counters with foreigners/strangers, it restricted the foreign usually to White, Western ethnicities who could pay to enter. As the *Berliner Morgenpost* remarked in 1929 about one of the city's Grand Hotels, the Hotel Aldon, "In the foyer of the Hotel you can hear the languages of all civilized countries."[16] As a cultural site for regulating foreignness, and for enacting ambivalence about strangers, the filmic representations of the Grand Hotel depicted the boundaries of (even the threats to) the national-popular, and they affirmed the national-popular in this way.

Acknowledging, however, the Grand Hotel's place within transnational and transcontinental economies, and at the border of national economies, makes it difficult to generalize about its effectivity. For U.S. audiences during the 1920s and 1930s, a European Grand Hotel could be a setting for extensive leisure and (as Hollywood film-vacation) a remote stage for temporarily act-ing on temptations and acting out alter egos. Despite its potential mysteries, perils and perversities associated with Europe (in part through cinema), the Grand Hotel's setting in Europe assured the proper protocols and propriety underpinning 'civilized' and segregated social interaction. For European audi-ences, the authenticity of Hollywood cinema's representation of the European Grand Hotel was also a matter of how it operated as a point of intersection between 'old Europe' and a modernity associated with the United States.[17] As discussed below, the international popularity and acclaim of MGM's *Grand Hotel* rested partly upon MGM's strategy of filling the guest-registry of its luxury hotel with the most famous Hollywood movie stars and plugging its hotel/film into circuits of international distribution, thus supporting the perception that the Grand Hotel existed as an enclave of the rich and famous, somewhere between Hollywood and Berlin—or 'anywhere in the world.'

While the Grand Hotel emerged as a conventional setting in literature, theatre, and cinema, it also was conceived through the modernist 'internationalism' of design styles and architectonics. Art Deco and Bauhaus, styles that informed the design of vehicles of travel and leisure (hotels, movie theatres, telephones, liners, planes, and cars), were particularly suited to representing the modern circuit of transnational travel and tourism associated with the Grand Hotel. For instance, Pathé's *What a Widow!* (1930), a substantial part of which is set on a luxury ocean liner, featured the art direction of Paul Nelson, a young U.S. architect who was trained in modernist design in Paris and who was billed in the film's credits as 'Paul Nelson, Paris.'[18] Since the early 20th century, the architecture of movie theatres (their facades, lobbies, and auditoriums) and the design motifs of spaces in film informed and exploited one another; for instance, the monumental, exotic, and retro styling of early large movie theatres (those with neo-classical or Art Nouveau motifs) developed through the design of sets in the early silent historical spectacles such as *Cabiria*, *Quo Vadis?*, and *Intolerance*.[19] By the late-1920s, however, the openness and airiness of modernist architecture particularly enhanced the spaciousness of big-screen movie projection. The openness of modernist architectural styling in films contributed to the illusion of three dimensions on a two-dimensional screen and to staging simultaneous planes of action—a practice consonant with the use of hotels as settings. Through this style of set design, films from this period departed from the drawing room in nineteenth-century theatrical productions and from the relatively depthless interiors in the first silent features. The film genres that most used the Grand Hotel as setting, particularly Hollywood's romantic melodramas, comedies, and musicals, emphasized the lightness, brightness, and (racialized) whiteness of luxury hotels and liners. The styling of the Italian luxury hotel in RKO's *Top Hat* (1932) is an example of how the Art Deco set design in a particular studio's films inflected its representation of Italy as an ultra-modern, international resort for an elite class of White tourists and performers.[20]

While William Everson is right to point out that Art Deco was most vividly and powerfully realized through cinema,[21] this view simplifies somewhat the relation between the materiality of the Grand Hotel and the movie theatre, and their relation to the Deco-styling of sets in films. The observation also simplifies the material passage of this style from architecture to cinematic art direction (e.g., Nelson at Pathé in 1930). And the observation does not quite acknowledge how cinema and the historical trend away from 1920s 'movie palaces' toward less embellished, modernist-designed theatres occurred in a period when the Grand Hotel was a stage for enacting the popular through escape, leisure, and transport. In Italy, as 1930s film actress Laura Nucci has noted, Art Deco set designs corresponded less to actual interior designs of most Italian homes than to a popular view of modernity.[22] As shown in the next section, this is a significant and complicated matter since modernist, so-called Rationalist, architecture in Italy during the 1920s and 1930s became the dominant coda of civic buildings constructed by the Fascist government—a practice that linked the design/identity of the Grand Hotel, the movie theatre, and the civic/monumental space of Italian Fascism.

The architectonic of twentieth century hotels and movie theatres (particularly the exclusive ones) also adhered to modern principles of management—as technologies for classifying and spatially arranging customers. The exclusivity, propriety, and 'grandness' of first-class hotels and movie theatres depended on the protocols and staged courtesies of their customer services. However, the Grand Hotel (like the first-class movie theatre) was also 'grand' by virtue of its size, and hence its capacity to manage efficiently a large number of rooms and clients. The rooming in large modern hotels, trains, and liners (like the seating in large movie theatres) were organized numerically and symmetrically in long corridors and aisles. Hotel patrons were registered, counted, and verified—sometimes with passports and always with tickets in liners, trains, and theatres. This lent a formality and propriety to all of these sites but also served to regulate or make rational (to discipline in the Foucauldian sense) leisure activities.[23] In this respect, both the Grand Hotel and the movie theatre exploited a tension between escaping one's routine and the ordering of identity and behaviour, between the anonymity and the counting of individual customers within the bureau-mentality and the architectural rationalism of modern life. This tension linked the narratives (and narrative economy) of movies set in Grand Hotels to the space and activity of movie-watching in complicated ways—with respect to the gradation of exclusivity among 'popular' movie houses, and to ways in which the circulation of these films transported viewers out of their neighborhood theatres while reinforcing the spatial segregation of social classes.

Besides being the result of changing sensibilities in spatial modelling, the Grand Hotel was constructed within the intersecting development of sound film and radio. As numerous film historians have pointed out, feature-length silent comedies, adventure and 'strongman' spectacles, and Westerns during the 1920s dealt primarily with individual action—with "heightened essences, archetypes of certain kinds of human behaviour."[24] The use of sound, however, enabled filmmakers to foreground human communication (as opposed to mime or gesture) and social intercourse—conversation, eye contact, 'vibrations' between two or more people. By the 1930s, the hotel became an ideal space for conversational melodramas and comedies whose narratives involved more complex and multiple interactions among characters. In this way, sound enabled cinema to transpose to the screen some of the complexity of interrelationships in literary narrative; and thus, the twenties' *hôtel de luxe* also became a convenient diegetic model for exploring themes through the plurality of voices one finds in novels. MGM's *Grand Hotel*, as a relatively early sound film, begins with a long, intricately choreographed and edited scene of guests and employees of the hotel conversing by public telephone with individuals outside the hotel.

The conversion to sound contributed to the emergence of the Grand Hotel's importance to cinema in other, relatively less formalistic ways. In particular, this conversion compelled national film industries to develop facilities for producing multiple language versions of individual films. Hollywood's global dominance of film distribution during the 1920s led its major studios to establish units for making different versions of the same film or to open dubbing facilities. These initiatives also involved hiring cinema professionals and technicians from Europe. Some of these operations were located in the United States (as was the case with MGM) and some in Europe (Paramount's facility in France). Not only did sound therefore contribute to the convergence of national film styles, it also contributed to the design of vehicles, such as the Grand Hotel, that could circulate within this international economy and that could represent spaces of internationalism (meeting places for international casts of characters) as a central stage in these films.

The conversion to sound in movie theatres also forged a material and technological linkage between the Grand Hotel and the movie theatre during the late 1920s and early 1930s. The conversion to sound film and the emergence of the film musical intersected, for instance, with the emergence of radio broadcasting, as networks of national territory and of a new relation between the public and private sphere. Not only were elite hotels settings for radio broadcasts of musical performances, Hollywood-based cinema and radio exploited their interconnection through venues such as *Hollywood Hotel* (d. Busby Berkeley, 1937)—a film musical set in the hotel where the actual eponymous radio series was set. The connection between radio, cinema, and luxury hotels during the 1930s not only mythologized the identities of certain hotels such as the Rooftop Terrace of New York's Waldorf-Astoria Hotel and the Cocoanut Grove in Los Angeles's Ambassador Hotel, but also reinforced the perception that a certain class of hotel served as haunts for entertainment celebrities. This synergy in the United States helped fashion Hollywood's version of the luxury hotel and ocean liner during the 1930s through the generic conventions of screen comedy and the musical—for example, the Honeymoon Hotel sequences in *Footlight Parade* (d. Lloyd Bacon, 1933), *Transatlantic Merry-go-Round* (d. Ben Stoloff, 1934), *Broadway Gondelier*

(d. Lloyd Bacon, 1935), and *Shall We Dance?* (d. Mark Sandrich, 1937) all
as lighter and brighter representations of the Grand Hotel than was typical in
1920s and particularly German cinema.

The use of sound and its relation to broadcasting were integral to the
emergence of cinema and the luxury hotel as spaces for mediating elite and
popular entertainments, cultures, and citizenry. A public who could not afford
to be paying customers of a luxury hotel often gathered outside to view its
celebrity patrons. Charlie Chaplin reportedly lost the buttons to his trousers
amidst the frenetic crowd in front of Berlin's Hotel Adlon in the late 1920s.
Movie premiers, particularly at the most lavish, first-run movie theaters in
metropolitan areas were just as significant events for a city's elite. And radio
broadcasting carried the unseen and thus imagined entertainments from the
inside of luxury hotels to a popular audience at home. Struggling performers
were discovered at these hotels, as was Marlene Dietrich at the Hotel Adlon
in the late 1920s. By the mid-1930s, film directors began using the hotels as
sets for a popular cinema—e.g., Jean Gabin's use of the Hotel Napoleon in
Paris, or Busby Berkeley's *Hollywood Hotel.*

Because the value and aura of the Grand Hotel were established through
the *economies* of movie-distribution, movie-going, travel, and tourism (as
'popular' enterprises in and across nations), the film-hotels became stages
not only for enacting class difference as differences of mobility and access
(i.e., social mobility as access to restricted enclaves) but also for articulating class difference to differences between exclusive and popular cultures/
entertainments. Within these economies and their performance spaces, the
Grand Hotel—as extended leisure—was a goal and reward of modern work
routines—an immense complex for various leisure activities (spas, restaurants, casinos). The exclusivity of an actual luxury hotel, compared with the
movie theatre, contributed to making the movie version of the Grand Hotel a
popular stage for performing class difference. However, as mediations of the
Grand Hotel, movies also emphasized the anonymity, impersonality, and thus
the populism of the hotel as leisure time and space. A central paradox of cinema's representation of the Grand Hotel is that the hotel is both a popular and
a hierarchical/restricted realm, whose equalizing technology is anonymity,
the roulette wheel and games of chance (as in *Grand Hotel*), or a character's
ability to perform popular entertainment (as in *Hollywood Hotel*).

Gaming and 'popular' entertainment, as well as the 'popularization' of
luxury accommodations through advertising, all had become material features
of elite hotels in Europe and North America by the 1930s,[25] but the rapid rise
and fall of fortunes at the hotel casino or cabaret also provided a powerful and
timely way for movies to channel the ripple effects of economic depressions
in Europe and North America during the late 1920s and early 1930s. In the

immediate aftermath of these national (collectively international) depressions, the surge in building Grand Hotels increasingly made these hotels, and the increase in films that represented them, technologies in the mobilization of popular cultures. Channelling these repercussions through cinema was possible because of cinema's emergence as a space and network for *democratizing leisure*, and for enacting a popular culture in that way. The 1930s film version of the Grand Hotel as a 'popular' space and technology of social mobility certainly distinguished it from the boudoirs and drawing rooms of earlier bourgeois comedy. It appears 'open' to anyone who can pay for a room and hence serves as a promise and a lure to working-class and petit-bourgeois audiences: it is out of reach and yet attainable. The elite inhabitants of the Grand Hotel simply seem to have more leisure time. In Italian films, as in their American counterparts, the Grand Hotel functioned as a *liminal*, sometimes *carnivalized*, space for encounters and masquerades between upper- and lower- class characters. As the subject and place of post-depression popular entertainments, the hotel offered a powerful *mythos* and *ethos* of social mobility, not only as extended leisure time but as a *destination* (and ideal objective) within a modern, increasingly populist regime of travel, tourism, and transport. As a performance stage (a stage within the proscenium of the movie theatre), the cinematic Grand Hotel was a cultural technology of social mobility—a structure designed for passing and passages. The Grand Hotel was simultaneously about the freedoms and limits of social mobility and access. The cinematic Grand Hotel was a potentiality—a promise—for democratizing leisure as 'popular' pursuit and as fundamental requirement for enacting a 'popular culture.'

Many of these threads of the modern utility of the Grand Hotel came together in Vicki Baum's 1929 internationally bestselling novel and subsequent play, *Menschen im hotel* (*People in a Hotel*), which MGM re-titled and adapted in 1932 as the internationally acclaimed *Grand Hotel*. The film's production underscores how the value and utility of the Grand Hotel was shaped through an economy of *international* adaptation and media conversion. After the immediate success of Baum's novel and play, an English-language adaptation of the play was staged with great success in New York City in the early 1930s. MGM's Irving Thalberg bought the rights to this English adaptation, in part as a relatively unprecedented vehicle for a large cast of the studio's most popular actors and actresses: a movie star in every room of its Grand Hotel. The film's reinvention of the novel and play as a showcase for Hollywood celebrities also marked a historical strategy for marketing Hollywood films in Europe and elsewhere, and (in this way) for representing the grandeur of Hollywood's place within an international cultural economy.

The hotel in *Grand Hotel* is 'grand' by virtue of both its exclusivity (as self-enclosed space) and its relation to the ultra-modern regimes and networks of

transportation and communication flows linking its various rooms and interior
to places beyond Berlin. *Grand Hotel* is the quintessential *film as hotel* in both
respects: a stage/world enclosed within the walls of the hotel-film, and a world
whose various spaces are linked to one another and to an outside through modern transportation and communication media. Three recurring motifs in the film
are the hotel as telephonic network, as a gateway to travel by car, and as a space
that is both open and compartmentalized through an architectural rationalism.
Although nearly all of the film occurs inside the hotel, the intermittent scenes at
its threshold tie the hotel to a network of privatized, relatively exclusive travel
and tourism—the city's taxis, personal limos, and the flamboyant young couple
who arrive at the end in a long, expensive, convertible sports car wearing
leather aviator caps and goggles. Another index of the hotel's extrovertedness
is its relation to a telephone grid. In the opening scene, the hotel and central
characters are introduced through the intercutting of local and long-distance
conversations of employees and guests. Throughout the film, the many rooms
of the hotel are connected by telephone conversations—to other guests and to
places beyond the hotel. And several times the film exhibits the hotel's immense and vibrant telephone switchboard. The Grand Hotel's architecture as
an open space of flow and movement (frequently scored musically as a Strauss
waltz) accentuates patterns of circulation. An overhead shot toward the beginning of the film represents the hotel's floors as spiralling, concentric circles of
movement—an image that links the hotel's modernist/rationalist architecture
to its revolving door and to the roulette wheel and the game of chance that
change the fortunes of the central characters. As regulated circulatory system,
the corpus of the Grand Hotel is busy, in motion, and always a bit overheated
(hence the film's fundamental irony; that "people come and go, but nothing
ever happens").

Particularly in this latter respect, the film also attests to the salience of
Baum's and MGM's construction of the Grand Hotel in the wake of an international economic depression that made the Grand Hotel emblematic of the
contingencies of social status (the rapid rise and fall of fortunes), albeit in a
regulated, ordered space. The film's fatalism (its murders, deaths, and the
uncertain future of its petit-bourgeois protagonists) may have had something
to do with its formal relation to a German Expressionist literary, theatrical,
and cinematic style but it also attests to an unresolved crisis of social mobility in the West—a crisis around which the 'popular' cultures, movements,
and governmental programs in Western nations developed during the late
1920s and 1930s. The global economic depression, crisis of social mobility,
and formations of 'the popular' also occurred through the protectionist policies that targeted, among other commodities, the increasingly international
circulation of film.

In that the representations of the hotel during the 1920s and 1930s occurred through the 'escapism' of popular entertainments, all of the versions of *Grand Hotel* (albeit from different national cultural styles) dwelt upon the relation between money, difference, and social mobility—but social mobility (and thus 'escapism') in two interrelated senses. In the film, the hotel is a meeting place for representatives of a social hierarchy—the uniformed and thus dignified working class of waiters, bellhops, maids, operators, and chauffeurs, the petit-bourgeois private secretary and book-keeper, the haut-bourgeois factory manager, and a bankrupt aristocrat. The possibilities for characters' vertical social mobility, however, have to do with their potential for *passing*, often as someone they are not, through the hotel.[26] In this respect, changing social status (the vertical social mobility of money and class difference) is tantamount to the lateral mobility of the characters (and, as discussed above, to the audience's access to movie theatres where the film circulated). In this period, 'social mobility' involves opening up and making available the Grand Hotel, gaining access to and inclusion in the hotel as an emerging sphere of popular culture, and from the hotel to the world. This makes the film's/hotel's revolving door a metonym and a technology of social mobility in both senses, for passing between a formerly elite cultural enclave and an emerging popular culture—between Home and the world beyond.

The Grand Hotel as the penultimate setting for worldliness rests upon the film's use of some of the most internationally recognized Hollywood stars playing against their ethnic backgrounds (e.g., U.S. actors playing Germans, and the Swedish Garbo playing a Russian). *Grand Hotel*'s dramatization of class difference also is achieved by MGM's having cast an ensemble of its most prestigious and well-paid stars, thus reaffirming the public perception of Grand Hotels as celebrity haunts. As both a product of a global economic depression and a stage for masquerade—a play of differences and mistaken identities, of passing as someone else, and of interconnecting rooms and secret encounters—the film's hotel emphasizes the rapid rise and fall of financial fortune, which both affirms and dismisses the hotel's material limits. Money is everything and nothing in the Grand Hotel. In this way, the film represents the hotel both as a reward of capital and as the democratization of luxury. All of the characters are preoccupied with their financial and social status, but only one of the characters (the brutish manager-industrialist played by Wallace Berry) is driven by greed or even materialism. For the petit-bourgeois characters, the book-keeper Otto Kringelein (Lionel Barrymore) and the stenographer Frauline Flaemmchen (Joan Crawford), the Grand Hotel is an escape from the rational and ordered drudgery of the modern workplace. For Baron Felix von Gargern (John Barrymore) and the Russian prima-ballerina Grusinkaya (Greta Garbo), who are wealthier and more cosmopolitan, the hotel is simply 'a way of life;' their status results from their dwelling in a domain that is in some ways divorced from the routines and rules of the daily lives of their audiences. When the petite-bourgeois characters (Kringelein and Flaemmchen) pass through the hotel's revolving door at the film's end, they envisage a future, together but unmarried, in other hotels—living within the hotel's contradictory ethos of economic freedom and rootlessness, of transcendence and alienation.

In an essay published the same year as Baum's novelistic version of *Grand Hotel*, Siegfried Kracauer viewed this contradictory ethos of the hotel as profoundly modern—a space of transcendence (the hotel lobby as like a church, God's station) and of relatively arbitrary belonging (the hotel as the anti-church, a place of alienation and spiritual nothingness, "the coming and going of empty forms") watched over by the hotel management.[27] For Kracauer, the modernity of the hotel lobby is not its replacement of the church but its potentiality for being mobilized as a sanctuary (a space of mysteries and belief) in its emptiness, abstraction, and rationality. The critical game that Kracauer plays with the hotel lobby is about the double-bind of modern abstraction and rationality—about making the Something, one might say 'the grandness,' of the hotel lobby symptomatic of a pervasive rationality-cum-mystery in all corners of modern life. While Kracauer's rumination about the historical relation between church and hotel lobby emphasizes the 'inessential foundation' of membership and belonging in an age of rational architecture, managerialism, and socialization, it also recognizes that the lobby had become one of many, insignificant meeting places for staging and performing a popular (or in his terms, 'mass') culture in these terms. Referring to *Death Enters the Hotel*, a German detective novel set in an urban hotel, Kracauer notes that breaking the codes, abstractness, and banality of hotel-space lies in considering the mysteries (both the ordinariness and the exaltedness) upon which it is built and managed.

My own perspective about the (in)significance of the Grand Hotel in the cultural economy of Fascist Italy builds upon Kracauer's insights but pulls them in the direction of other theorists, particularly Henri Lefebvre's writing about a philosophy and politics of 'everyday life' and the 'production of space,' and Michel Foucault's writing about the microphysics of power and the many rationalities of governance in modern societies. Linked to this chapter's consideration of the Grand Hotel, Kracauer's rumination about the hotel lobby is as much a coordinate in my own theoretical compass as an element in the historical conjuncture that this chapter examines. Particularly, Kracauer's account of the hotel's (in)significance in modern, Western life doesn't go far enough in acknowledging how the hotel mattered or materialized within the differential mobility of social relations (to whom was the hotel lobby available?) and how that figured into the formation of a popular culture in Weimar Germany. The mobilization of the cinematic *hôtel de luxe* during the late 1920s and 1930s occurred within an emergent regime of travel, tourism, and transport as popular activity and culture, within commercial and state efforts to represent tourism as 'national-popular' practice, and within ways that the international paths/networks of travel, communication, and culture both bolstered and problematized national-popular designs and constructions of the cinematic hotel. The hotel was designed—in physical space and on the movie screen—as a gateway to travel, tourism, and transport (and to communication in this sense). Its utility as a stage for enacting popular culture was both profoundly national and international, and the cinematic hotel represented and mediated this tension. In these respects, the Grand Hotel was a potentiality for mediating and regulating a modern relation between Home or Homeland and its Other—between the *utopia* of a national-popular and the *heterotopia* of the foreign and rootless.

MOBILIZING CINEMA IN FASCIST ITALY
ALONG THE ROUTES OF THE GRAND HOTEL

One reason to consider the cinematic Grand Hotel's relation to a regime of travel, tourism, and transport is to provide an alternative way of thinking about popular cinema generally, and Italian cinema during the late 1920s and 1930s specifically, as 'escapist.' In Italian cinema during the 1930s, the Grand Hotel was a visual leitmotif of an escapism that post-World War Two Italian film critics and historians roundly dismissed as 'white telephones'—a class of films whose fetishization of luxury was most powerfully and regularly signified by the prominence of a white telephone. For these film critics and historians (particularly those in Italy who championed a 'neo-realist' film style), 'white telephone' was the most disparaging attribution of these films' inability to address the real predicaments of 'the people,' and thus of the films' perpetuation of a false consciousness that 'distracted,' 'captivated,' and 'concealed something from' their audience.[28] While the 'white telephone' became a key concept in a lexicon and discourse that understood 1930s Italian films purely as Fascist ideology and culture, this connection is complicated by the fact that Hollywood films from the 1920s and 1930s also contributed to the pattern of 'popular' and 'escapist' cinema in Italy. Hollywood films were decidedly the majority of films watched in Italy during the period of Fascism, and therefore making and watching films in Italy during the 1920s and 1930s was always situated between the networks of international distribution and a nationalist protectionism/mobilization of an indigenous popular culture. The post-war favoritism toward the neo-realist canon may have rejected pre-war cinema as 'Fascist culture,' but it too was oriented toward an 'Italian cinema' over Hollywood cinema.

The historical conjuncture that this chapter examines was pivotal to the 'rebirth' of cinema as a national industry and a national-popular cultural form in Italy—both of which were imbricated in but not coterminous with Fascist policy. After a period of relatively robust film production before World War One, the number of films produced by Italian companies declined precipitously during the 1920s—from over 130 in 1920 to less than 20 three years later, and to less than ten each year between 1926 and 1929. The decline in Italian film production during the 1920s cannot be reduced to but certainly was exacerbated by the dominance of Hollywood cinema in Italy. From 1922 through 1927, the percentage of Hollywood films exhibited in Italy rose from roughly forty percent to over seventy percent, a percentage level that remained fairly constant through the 1930s. The turning point in Italian film production occurred in 1929, with film production steadily increasing throughout the 1930s.

As many historians have noted, *Rotaie* (*The Rails*) was one of the few Italian films that was produced in 1929 and that made that year a watershed for the beleaguered Italian film industry.[29] The film's director, Mario Camerini, was one of several Italian directors who had worked abroad during the 1920s but who had returned to Italy to make films in the late 1920s. In certain respects Camerini, who had worked at Paramount's Joinville studios producing Italian-language versions of Hollywood films, brought to Italy a new kind of internationalist style (a style that partly borrowed from and competed with Hollywood film genres that had begun to dominate European theatres over the 1920s). *Rotaie* converted some of the stylistic elements of French, German, and Hollywood films, and it was produced for distribution in four languages. It is no small coincidence therefore that *Rotaie* is structured as a journey/vacation/tour along a route (as the title suggests, a modern rail system) to a Grand Hotel.

As a harbinger of what post-war critics would describe as 'escapist' cinema, it is noteworthy that *Rotaie* is about escapism as an activity performed through the intersecting technologies of cinema and transportation—along the routes and tourist vehicles of the Grand Hotel. *Rotaie*'s story develops over three sites/stages—each connected by train travel, and each imparting significance to the other two sites. The film begins in a third-rate urban hotel where a young, unmarried, apparently unemployed couple have withdrawn to commit suicide. The audience is never provided with an exact motivation for their self-destructive feelings, though their lack of material resources and their association with the city's and the hotel's bleak environment heighten their sense of futility. The first scenes in front of and within the cheap hotel are shot in very dim lighting since it is night and raining. The only light in the street where the audience first encounters them emanates from an electric sign that reads HOTEL, and the shadowy hotel interiors seem anything but a sanctuary. Just after the young man drops the lethal potion into a glass of water in their room, the audience views them, sitting quietly apart but for touching hands, through the glass's fizzing contents.

Just before they reach for the poison, however, the vibration created by a train rumbling and whistling loudly just under their window overturns the glass. (The third-class hotel's proximity to the rail network underscores both its relation to an undesirable part of the city and its relation to the technology of social mobility for escaping that place.) From this point, the train becomes a recurring and almost cosmic sign for the lovers and the audience. When the young man runs to the window to watch the train pass, the musical score changes from solemn chords to a much more gay jazz rhythm, and the sky is suddenly filled with light, followed by a phantasmagoria of electric lights and signs that are superimposed as a collage. The spectacle of the couple's epiphanic moment climaxes with the word LUNA (moon) spelled out in the midst of electric lights that are made to resemble stars in the urban night sky. Inspired by their new vision of their environment, the couple steals out of the hotel, and (as if gravitating toward the epicentre of urban life and its engine of escape) they are drawn to the city's train station.

The film's contribution to a popular iconography of the modern passenger train station and railway travel resembles Walter Ruttman's *Berlin: Symphony of a City* (1928) or a slightly later Italian documentary *Ritmi di stazione* (*Railway Station Rhythms,* 1933), wherein the shapes and activities (the kinesis) of rail travel are synchronized to a musical accompaniment.[30] However, unlike these documentaries, *Rotaie* plays upon the spectacle, romance, and allure of the vacation—of being able to escape. At the station, the couple marvels at an array of posters advertising exotic hotels, vacations in Capri, and transatlantic voyages. On screen, the collage of posters is captured through fade-in and fade-out editing; and then a close-up of one poster, an Art Deco rendition of train rails, which fills the screen to form an enormous, Expressionistic sign. In the bustle of the station, a well-dressed and portly man rushing to catch a train drops a wallet stuffed with money. The young man retrieves it and unsuccessfully attempts to hail the man. After ogling a shiny train and its fashionable passengers about to depart, they quickly board and find seats in a first-class compartment. "Where are we going?" the young girl asks her lover. "Where the others go," he replies. And so their escape from all that brought them to the first, squalid hotel is converted at the station into a vacation and tour to an alternate world—the *bel mondo* of the Grand

Hotel—whose pathway is a combination of the 'moving image' and modern networks of transportation.

The second part of the film occurs at a Grand Hotel in Sanremo, a Mediterranean resort along the Italian Riviera, adjacent to the international tourism of the French Riviera and Monte Carlo. The hotel is an Art Deco spectacle of ultra-modern leisure, recreation, and sport: speed boats, fashionable swim- and lounge-wear, etc. As in the Von Stroheim films, characters and forces at the resort test the couple's ability to perform outside their social class, and momentarily cause them to lose touch with their commitment to one another. At the center of their hotel-seduction is an entourage around the Marquis Mercier, who resembles one of Von Stroheim's decadent interlopers and who leads the young couple to the hotel's inner sanctum—the casino's wheel of fortune. In the young man's delirium at the casino, Camerini uses an overhead shot of the whirling roulette wheel (an image obliquely articulated to the spinning wheels of the train earlier in the film), followed by a dizzying, refracted vision, from the young man's perspective, of the game board and chips. The couple's commitment to one another is shaken by the Marquis's attempts to seduce the girl and by the young man's failure at the roulette wheel; the fact that the Marquis begins to lend the young man money (to buy the girl) only hastens their circle of despair. As in the film's first scene, the lovers again find themselves alienated and unfulfilled in their hotel existence. Unable to communicate with her withdrawn lover, the girl goes to the Marquis's room to 'repay' him for enough money to leave the hotel. At the same time, the young man gazes from his hotel window at families in apartments across from his room. His late-night vision of social stability and productivity through family life (an architect working at his drafting table, a middle-class family seated around the dinner table, a father reading his newspaper, a mother sewing, and a young boy asleep) abruptly compels him to return the Marquis's money, retrieve his fiancé, and flee the hotel.

The young man's epiphany—his view of the serenity of middle-class life in the adjacent apartment *from* his room at the Grand Hotel—leads the couple outdoors, to a public park. Here, they wake to experience the natural pleasures of washing their faces (and removing the girl's make-up) at a simple, public fountain. And as they embrace, puffs of smoke from a train appear just over a hedge. On the way back to their city, they ride in one of the train's economy cars which is filled with working-class travellers. This scene is replete with point-of-view shots of the weathered faces, the unabashed and unselfish demeanors of these working people: a mother nursing a baby, a little girl sharing her apple with the young lovers, and the young man sharing his cigarette with the little girl's father. The film closes with a shot of the lovers embracing outside a factory at the end of a working day, the sound of the factory's whistle conjuring the whistle of the train throughout the movie. Having discovered their 'true' place in family/social relations and in a *popular* culture, and having found value in a work-regimen and a 'different' view of leisure (the factory having an ambiguous correspondence with the previous hotels), the couple walk arm-in-arm down a street at sunset, gradually surrounded by a throng of other workers—a massing of 'the people.' Although the couple is presented as walking toward their leisure time (i.e., after a day's work), leisure is oriented toward home life rather than toward the world of the Grand Hotel. The film never makes clear what kind of job they have in relation to this work-complex (factory laborer, clerical staff, homemaker), only that their path away from the Grand Hotel and toward Home organically connects them to an amorphous social body, the People.

Central to the film's rationalization of the popular through the couple's journey/tour (from the first two hotels to the factory and an unseen home life) is its paradoxical relation to the formation of a popular culture in (or from) Italy. How does the film's representation of the factory, and the path homeward, occur outside the popular and commercial iconography of travel and tourism that the couple encounters early in the film, at the train station, where their conversion from their suicidal pact (their reason to live) is represented through a phantasmagoria of travel posters and logos? The latter are integral to the couple's dreams and desires to escape—to find new vehicles of social mobility. While the film's conclusion may gesture toward a realism that is not depicted through travel brochures, the couple presumably knows 'the way home' because of their passage through the Grand Hotel. In this sense, the film offers a potentially less bleak vision of their future than is the case with the petit-bourgeois characters at the end of *Grand Hotel*—a couple on the road to another Grand Hotel. But with respect to the internationalism of the cultural economy in which *Rotaie* was launched from Italy, the way Home is certainly about articulating the popular and the national—of launching a 'national-popular' culture/economy.

The centrality of train travel in *Rotaie* is not merely a narrative device that links various acts of the narrative, it is an instance of cinema and train-travel's intersecting technology for 'democratizing leisure' as 'popular' pursuit and for representing the popular in Italy as oriented toward the national and international cultural economy of cinema/travel. In their first-class compartments, on their way to the Grand Hotel (to 'where the others go'), the movie uses various techniques to convey a sense of the train's power (through whistles and sound effects) and its speed (through shots of the rails and of the wires and cables above that are superimposed to create the image of a metal web). The pejorative use of the term 'escapism' to describe Italian cinema as 'Fascist culture' fails to recognize not only how film-going and travel/tourism occurred through interdependent technologies but also how the technology of cinema and transport were integral to the conversion of Italy into a national network and utopia that was connected/articulated through popular *media*: the motorized sprockets of the camera and projector, in motion with the wheels of trains; the movement of film/image through those sprockets synchronized with the movement of the train over the parallel rails and their cross-ties; the moving image of the snaking rail accomplished by the mobile camera atop the moving train; the national economy of film distribution laid over the more exclusive, internationalist routes to the Grand Hotel.

As a motorized vehicle within the 'rebirth' of Italian cinema around 1930 (a period when the programs of Italian Fascism had begun to act upon and through the cultural economy of which film-making and -watching were part),[31] *Rotaie* helped mobilize a decade of films in Italy oriented toward representing and rationalizing a national-popular in no small measure along the routes of the Grand Hotel. In one sense, these routes were through other feature-length films during the 1930s that situated the Grand Hotel as a central stage and problematic in advancing a national-popular in Italy.

One of the most celebrated and successful films that Camerini made during the 1930s was *Il Signor Max* (1937), which embellishes some of the elements from *Rotaie*. *Il Signor Max* is structured as a rite of passage for a young, Roman newspaper vendor, Gianni (Vittorio DeSica), who has saved and borrowed enough money to embark on an odyssey 'to learn about the world' and thus to become a gentleman (a *signore*). As in *Rotaie*, a passage through the ethos of the Grand Hotel leads him to don the costumes and trappings accompanying luxury and leisure, and to learn the conduct befitting a gentleman, even as this conversion leads him to value elements of his life that initially had compelled him to see the world and to embrace the paths of social mobility that it represented.

The narrative arc of *Il Signor Max* follows Gianni's upward social and geographic mobility since his path to the Grand Hotel and to becoming a gentleman involves a journey/tour from Rome (the capital of the nation-state and the Fascist state) to Sanremo. On this trip, he takes a single suitcase, a borrowed camera, and some American magazines (which he tells his uncle should help him appear to be more of an English journalist and adventurer). At a station in Naples (a southern Italian city with a vibrant tourist economy), Gianni observes a group of affluent vacationers deboard a luxury bus. As he drops his *Time* and *Esquire* magazines, a couple of young women from the bus note the magazines and the American brand-name of his camera, and, after he acknowledges them in rather broken English (which he has also learned from reading foreign magazines), they assume he too is a world-traveller: '*prestigioso quel signore.*' They invite him to a party on board their liner which is sailing for Sanremo, and thus begins Gianni's brief masquerade as Signor Max.

Living beyond his means, Gianni quickly exhausts the limited stipend he has allotted for his journey, and he returns to his family, who are shocked to realize that he got no further than Sanremo. His return home marks a deepening of the film's ambivalence about the road to the Grand Hotel. Gianni is both cast out of the *bel mondo* and pulled back to where he belongs—to home, family, and his job at the newsstand. On one hand, he desires to prove to his family that he is *familiare* (familiar/family) and not a child, spendthrift, snob, poseur, or vagabond—any of the qualities that his family associates with the lifestyle and 'loose morals' of the highly mobile leisure set. On the other hand, he misses the fun and esteem of playing Signor Max. This middle part of the narrative essentially concerns his desperate attempts to overcome his alienation. Like the lovers in *Rotaie*, whose desires are first realized through popular mythologies, he turns to popular images that surround him every day at the newsstand. In fact, his transition here is cinematically charted by bridging shots of magazine covers (all English) from consecutive months. This part includes match cuts from Gianni's perception of a magazine image—a tennis match, for instance—to a scene wherein he attempts to emulate the image. Thus, Gianni tries his hand at tennis in July, at golf in September, etc. In this fashion, the film dramatizes the allure of a social mobility represented through the international circulation of photographic/cinematic images in popular texts. The film progressively becomes about performing the behaviours and protocols of a leisurely lifestyle; being comfortable in one's leisure involves mastering the 'rules of the game.' Max, Gianni's grand delusion, is an alter ego-cum-collage of popular images, and Gianni (at the center of the film) is thus doubly a subject of an international cultural economy that links tourism and a popular iconography and performance of social mobility.

Like *Rotaie*, *Il Signor Max* ridicules upper-crust snobbery as much as Gianni's unfamiliarity with its rules and with his futile pursuit of Max and the *bel mondo*. Much of the ironic humour in the film results from Gianni's awkwardness at the bridge table, on the golf course, on horseback, and so on. When Donna Paola and her entourage arrive at the Grand Hotel in Rome and notice Gianni/Max at his newsstand, his efforts to maintain his double identity and to consummate his relationship with Donna Paola and her world become more hectic and, consequently, more humorous and painful. In the midst of this comedy of confused identities, Donna Paola's maid servant, Lauretta, suddenly recognizes Gianni's 'true' self; they are, after all, cut from the same social fabric. As Max, Gianni continually deflects her queries about his identity, but as a magazine vendor he develops a more intimate relationship with her. She, who is constantly on the road, admires his family, his valuing of home life, and his singing in a local Dopolavoro group—even though when they finally kiss, it is obvious that the intensity of her emotion is sparked by her inability to dissociate Max's image (as *signore*) from the lesser Gianni.

The film's staging of the young couple's attraction for one another at the intersection of the Grand Hotel and the Fascist Dopolavoro program in Rome is significant for several reasons. The rest of the film charts the erosion of Gianni's foothold in the hypermobile social echelon of luxury hotels and first-class tourism, as well as his gradual recognition that he belongs instead with Lauretta (intertwined movements that culminate when Gianni abandons his Max persona in the first-class section of a train to find Lauretta in the second-class section). In the last part of the film, Lauretta's attraction to Gianni/Max has to do with his mediation of a cosmopolitanism and orientation to domesticity—in part a domesticity whose civic virtues are exhibited through the Dopolavoro (or 'after work') activities. The Opera Nazionale del Dopolavoro, formed in 1927, was one of the earliest programs by the Fascist state to organize national life through leisure activities and to mobilize the Italian population through a national network of local Dopolavoro services and events. The Dopolavoro thus was primarily rationalized as an initiative for democratizing leisure (particularly among salaried employees). It was one of many fronts (albeit one of the most expansive agencies) for administering popular culture as social welfare and civic reform in daily life. Through the Dopolavoro, leisure and recreational activities became instrumental in enacting the 'national-popular' and in instituting Fascism at a local, communal level of sociality.

Film exhibition, alongside associations such as the choral group represented in *Il Signor Max*, were kinds of leisure activities supported by Dopolavoro programs. By 1937, when eighty percent of salaried employees in Italy participated in some kind of Dopolavoro activity (compared to only twenty percent of industrial workers and seven percent of peasants),[32] *Il Signor Max* could invoke the Dopolavoro (e.g., Gianni's choral group) as an alternative to the Grand Hotel, even as the cinematic Grand Hotel's potentiality for democratizing leisure informed the film's representation of Dopolavoro. Conversely, the Dopolavoro initiative (like other Fascist institutions of a national-popular culture) expanded through and depended upon media such as cinema. The Dopolavoro initiative was not only about organizing/mobilizing leisure activities for the lower classes, it also involved educating citizens about *how* to perform leisure activities—about the rules of the (citizenship) game in Fascist Italy. This point is significant because Italian cinema's programmatic relation to the Dopolavoro (as 'popular' activity) also mediated between the internationalist circulation/economy of culture and the national(ist) programs of social uplift/welfare through leisure. Thus, seven years after *Rotaie*, *Il Signor Max* could invoke the Dopolavoro as a basis for mediating the *bel mondo* and Home (or homeland)—the popular cultural iconography of Gianni's newsstand (particularly its foreign images) and Fascism's programs of a national-popular culture.

Though discussing the numerous other Italian films from the 1930s that contributed to a cinematic ethos of the Grand Hotel lies beyond the limitations of this chapter, it is worth noting briefly certain trends to which these films contributed. By the late 1930s, a spate of Italian films—e.g., *Ai vostri ordini, signora!* (*At Your Service, Madam!*, d. Mario Mattoli, 1938/39), *La dama bianca* (*The Lady in White*, d. Mario Mattoli, 1938), *Ho perduto mio marito!* (*I've Lost My Husband!*, d. Enrico Guazzoni, 1937), *Una donna tra due mondi* (*A Woman Between Two Worlds*, d. Goffredo Alessandrini, 1938)—used the Grand Hotel as their primary setting.[33] No longer did the effort to build a national-popular cinema culture and economy occur *on the way* to the Grand Hotel (as in *Rotaie*); building and maintaining them occurred instead primarily or entirely on the terrain of the Grand Hotel. Some of these films (such as *Una donna tra due mondi* and *Ai vostri ordini*) involved characters masquerading as members of another economic class, but these films were less about access to the hotel than about the hotel as an ubiquitous and generic environment. Compared to Italian cinema during the early 1930s, these films were part of a more concerted effort by the Fascist state to distribute Italian films and culture abroad. The Grand Hotel thus had become a basic *premise* (a cultural site/sight and political-economic logic) for confronting the internationalist cultural economy in Italy, for reterritorializing its dominion in the world, and for rationalizing an Italian national-popular culture. Also, as a narrative convention for accentuating the fluidity of identity (masquerades and plays of double identities), the Grand Hotel became an artefact of the requirements for mediating Italy's national-popular and internationalist economies. Within an internationalist cultural economy, how else might cinema represent the national-popular *except* as/through the play of doubling identity?

FASHIONING A FASCIST ITALY AS GRAND HOTEL

Italian cinema's role in mediating international and national-popular cultural economies propelled it along the route of the Grand Hotel—a route that crossed through places in films, movie screens, the sites of filmmaking, the networks of film distribution and adaptation, and even the festivalization of cinema (the launching of the Venice Biennale Film Festival). Mapping this route is an ambitious project that lies beyond the scope of this chapter, but a few of the intersections along this route are worth mentioning.

One of these intersections involves the relation between studio versus location filming. The former is most often associated with cinema during the Fascist era (and the development during the 1930s of two film studios in Rome—Cines followed by Cinecittà), while the latter is most often associated with a post-war Italian film style (a neo-realism whose defenders often rejected the studio-film as symptomatic of a Fascist cultural production). However, recognizing the linkage between studio- and location-filming during the 1930s (i.e., complicating this binary) leads to recognizing the relation between feature-length filmmaking and the documentary 'tourist film,' or to recognizing the relation of fiction *and* documentary films to transport and tourism. There were numerous documentaries produced just prior to and after the formation of LUCE (the Fascist state's entity for producing newsreels, documentaries, and educational films) that were classified as 'tourist films.' These films not only showcased Italian cities, towns, and resort areas but adopted techniques for mounting cameras on moving vehicles to represent these places as moving panoramas and as tour. *Rotaie* is significant for its having filmed/staged many of its scenes on location—at Rome's two passenger train stations, onboard trains, and at a casino in Sanremo. These examples attest to how the route and passage to the Grand Hotel developed through an emerging cultural geography/economy of the nation during the Fascist era.

This cultural geography/economy was mapped onto a set of political programs and initiatives (such as the Dopolavoro) for mobilizing the national-popular as a space of citizenship—a political-cultural geography into which Fascism inserted itself and was represented. One example of the relation between studio and location filming at an intersection between the Grand Hotel and Fascist programs for democratizing leisure are the instances in *Ho perduto mio marito!* when the haut-bourgeois protagonists, who never seem to work and who are mostly situated in the film's Grand Hotel, twice visit the outside world—once in an encounter at a rural *osteria,* and another time at a factory. The couple is taken on a tour not of the factory's work-spaces but of its recreational facilities—a commodious bar, huge swimming pool, adjacent gymnasium, and child-care unit. Not only are these facilities consonant with the government's Dopolavoro initiatives, their amenities are represented through documentary footage—viewed through the protagonists' leisurely lifestyle and the film's audience as a kind of Grand Hotel. In this way, the film also links popular entertainment and popular education.

Another example of location filming that mediated cultural geography/ economy and the political programs for achieving a national network of tourism was *Treno popolare* (*The People's Train*, d. Raffaelo Matarazzo, 1933).

The 'popular train' refers to the Fascist state's discounts for weekend train travel in second-class compartments and to the excursions into the provinces sponsored during the 1930s by the Dopolavoro. This travel project was initiated just over a year before the film was made, and during its first years was taken advantage of by hundreds of thousands of urban residents.[34] As a feature-length narrative-cum-documentary, many of the film's scenes were filmed at the train station in Rome, onboard train cars, or in the countryside, and the film integrates long expository sequences of rural panoramas and of crowds of passengers who were not trained actors. *Treno popolare* travels a path away from the Grand Hotel, but in so doing it casts the Italian countryside as the authentic (cinematically documented) setting of popular cultural citizenship—the environ most open and available for democratizing leisure. As object and objective of popular cinema-cum-popular train tour, the Italian countryside is a spacious, non-exclusive resort—a popular *bel mondo*—whose *raison d'etre* is the Grand Hotel and whose political rationality is Fascism's Dopolavoro.

While *Treno popolare* propels Italian cinema moving along the routes for converting the Italian countryside into a Grand Hotel for state-engineered tourism, another branch of Italian cinema during the 1930s that extended these routes were the films set and/or made across Italy's colonies and territorial claims in North Africa. As cultural forms that were politically mobilized in the tracks to and from the Grand Hotel, these films mediated the internationalist aspiration of Italian empire-building and the efforts to secure the Homeland as national-popular territory. While they are examples of filmmaking's relation to expansionist militarism, they also were instrumental in efforts by Italians to domesticate/tame Africa, partly through campaigns that encouraged Italians to settle there. Africa's domestication occurred through cinematically documenting an Italian presence beyond its national borders and through distributing Italian films to Italian settlements and outposts. These films accomplished this in various ways. *Squadrone bianco* (*The White Squadron*, d. Augusto Genina, 1936), for instance, contrasted the exclusive arenas of haut-bourgeois masquerade (typical of the cinematic Grand Hotel) with the open spaces and remote military outposts of the African desert—the outpost as a counter-Grand Hotel. Or in *Sotto la croce del sud* (*Under the Southern Cross*, d. Guido Brignone, 1938), the characters' labor to establish an outpost of Western commerce, rationality, and *civilization* in the African jungle overlaps with the film's provision of a touristic document about the fringes of Italian empire.[35] And *Il grande appello* (*A Call to Arms*, or literally *The Highest Calling*, d. Mario Camerini,1936) involves a young man's journey from his home in Italy to Africa, where he works as part of a company of Italian laborers/settlers. There he finds the father who abandoned his mother

and him years before and who now presides over a seedy hotel in Djibouti—
a hotel that is a sanctuary for unscrupulous businessmen, international arms
trafficking, mercenaries, and prostitutes. While the father enjoys listening on
the radio to news about Italian victories in Africa, he also is involved in selling arms to Abyssinian troops fighting against Italians. In the film's conclusion, the father recognizes his allegiance to the homeland (and the son that
he had abandoned), sacrificing himself for Italy's imperial project and thus
redeeming Africa as a site (as the film's title suggests) for a 'grander' hotel
than the one he has operated.

The corpus of Italian films made in or about Africa underscores a final
point about the cinematic Grand Hotel's utility within a political and cultural
economy that was both internationalist and national-popular. Both the recovering Italian film industry and Italian Fascism's programs for democratizing
leisure through the Dopolavoro and other mobilizations of a popular culture
tapped into the potentiality of the Grand Hotel to mediate their internationalist and national-popular orientations. Several examples offer ways of thinking
about this economy's significance in organizing Fascist Italy along the interface between internationalism and the national-popular (i.e., along the route
of the cinematic Grand Hotel).

One example has to do with the creation of the Venice Biennale Film Festival in 1932. In the wake of a recovering Italian film industry, the festival was
conceived as a state initiative for showcasing a new wave of Italian cinema,
and Italian cinema's new relation to (if not competitiveness with) other national cinemas. As the first international film festival in Europe, the Venice
Biennale operated at the interface between internationalist and national-
popular cultural economies. Throughout the 1930s, the festival (whose directors had been approved or appointed by the state) attracted and bestowed
awards upon films from Europe, but it also included awards for domestic
films, such as the Mussolini Cup for best Italian Film. In this sense, the festival acted upon the popularity of foreign, particularly Hollywood, films in
Italy to establish a pedigree for domestic production, while using the international network of distribution to promote abroad Italy's national-popularity.

The Venice Film Festival is also worth mentioning because of its material
formation through the routes of the Grand Hotel. The first screenings of the
festival occurred on the terrace of the magnificent Hotel Excelsior on Venice's Lido, located on a boulevard of exclusive hotels which accommodated
the celebrities attending the event. The festival thus helped establish Venice's
and Italy's identity as a meeting place for international film celebrities, with
some of Hollywood's most prestigious stars present in the early years of the
festival.[36] Furthermore, the Grand Prize in the festival's first year went to
MGM's *Grand Hotel*—an award that publicly recognized the link between

the physical terrain of Grand Hotels and a cinematic world. And while the Venice Film Festival's formation upon the terrain of the Grand Hotel acted upon the internationalist networks of film production that Italian film professionals had worked within during the 1920s, the festival also represented the return Home of some of these directors (such as Camerini and Genina) and their relation to a domestic popular culture.

In 1937, the festival moved into the Palazzo del Cinema (The Palace of Cinema) designed by Italian Luigi Quagliata in the Rationalist architectural style that had become the public facade of the Fascist state's civic buildings. The Palazzo del Cinema not only was constructed through the pedigree of the Grand Hotel (the festival's initial location at the Excelsior Hotel) but also through the maturity of Fascism's promise to democratize leisure (to turn Grand Hotels into sites of populist entertainment and tourism). Designing a 'cinema palace' also became a site for *rationalizing* the state's efforts to link the civic networks of Italian popular culture to the international cultural economy of cinema.

By the late 1930s, the route to and from the Grand Hotel in Italy, and this route's mediation of Italy's national-popular and international cultural economies, continued and even deepened Italian cinema's preoccupation with its cosmopolitanism, particularly as that cosmopolitanism pertained to its international alliances. Italian cinema's navigation of the crossroads of international and national-popular political and cultural economies continued the practice of adapting European novels, plays, and films for Italian audiences. In the late 1930s, some Italian films set their Grand Hotels in other countries; *Ai vostri ordini, signora!* and Camerini's *Batticuore* (*Heartbeat*, 1939) both are set in French luxury hotels. The latter film's displacement of its Grand Hotel outside Italy is particularly significant because France doubles as Italy (at least as a *state* invented by Italian cinema), and because the film's Parisian hotel is a stage for comic and romantic intrigues and masquerades among diplomats and dignitaries from various fabulated nations—Stivonia, Nirvania, and Lucrazia. While the film's coding of these fictitious nation-states may have had something to do with the political ensnarements of designing a comic farce about international politics, it certainly attests to how complicated traversing the route to the Grand Hotel and the *bel mondo* had become on the eve of World War Two. *Batticuore* is also an example *par excellence* of the extent to which the Grand Hotel had become a conventional stage for performing the masquerades and plays of double identities for mediating Italy's national-popular and internationalist economies/alliances on the eve of World War Two.

One (albeit temporary) solution to this dilemma or 'play' of double identities had to do with Italian popular culture's alignment with a German political and cultural economy during the late 1930s. *Una donna tra due mondi,* for instance, was one of two filmic adaptations of a German romance (*Die weisse Frau des Maharadscha*)—the French version directed by Arthur Rabenalt, and the Italian version by Alessandrini. However, a more remarkable outcome of the Italian-German alliance that was cemented the year that Adolf Hitler made his celebrated trip through Italy in 1938, was *Castelli in aria* (*Castles in the Air*, d. Augusto Genina, 1939)—a film made in German and Italian versions. This film cast Italy as Grand Hotel for German tourists, and paired the German film star Lilian Harvey with Italian film star Vittorio DeSica (the protagonist of *Il Signor Max*) as tourist and tour-guide through Italy as *bel mondo*. The film begins as the couple are brought together on a train from Germany to Italy. Harvey's character (Annie, a young seamstress and wardrobist for costumes in a German theatre) has accepted an offer by an elderly, wealthy German industrialist to accompany him to Capri, but on board the train, the industrialist hires DeSica's character to play the role of an Italian aristocrat and to accompany them on their tour/vacation. The three stops along the route of the Grand Hotel are Venice, Florence, and Naples— arguably the most fabled tourist destinations in Italy during the early twentieth century, and prime locations of Italian Grand Hotels. The film concludes in a theatrical performance in Naples, as Harvey's and DeSica's characters each recognize the true social status of the other. So not only does the film formalize a pathway—a political and cultural economy—between Germany and Italy, it represents a point of intersection between these separate national-popular cultures on a performance stage located along the route of the Grand Hotel.

I conclude with a reference to 'castles in the air' to underscore several points. One has to do with the governmentalization of the relation between location and studio filming in Italy during the 1930s. *Castelli in aria* borrows heavily from the conventions not only of the film musical (a genre more rooted in German than Italian cinema) but also of the European operetta. The title's reference to the 'aria' has as much to do with building 'castles in the air' as with the harmonic potential between two national-popular cultures exhibited in the 'arias' performed by the German–Italian couple, on the stages of various Italian Grand Hotels. The hotels in these films are the sound-castles of a period when the elitism and classicism of national musical culture is both conjured and popularized through performance stages such as the luxury Hotel and the movie theatre, and through radio broadcasting's relation to both.

However, this point leads to a second connotation of the title. 'Castles in the air' also suggests the most pure flight of fantasy through an absolute leisure—an 'escapism' in that sense. *Castelli in aria* does not engage in the mixing of location and studio production that typified Italian cinema's relation to the routes of the Grand Hotel over the 1930s. In many respects *Castelli in aria* is the antithesis of documentary realism; it is replete with scenes of magic, mysticism, and the occult that have more in common with German than Italian film culture—two lower-class characters acting as if they were aristocrats in pre-modern settings where the old aristocracy appears as phantasms and 'special effects.' But as a fiction film that was made in the immediate aftermath of Hitler's celebrated first train-tour of Italy in 1938, *Castelli in aria* became a fictional counterpart of the German and Italian newsreels that recorded and celebrated Hitler's train-tour—part of the cultural economy of tourism and film distribution upon which government acted.

An alternative way of thinking about the 'escapism' of both filmic records of the German–Italian, North–South 'axis' is in terms of their mobilization of national-popular cultures through a regime of transport linking cinema, train travel, and the routes of luxury hotels. Casting Italy as central to the routes of the Grand Hotel also contributed to defusing the problematic perception in Nazi Germany of the South as not sufficiently White and Aryan—the ethos and *lightness* of the Grand Hotels (castles in the air) being steeped in the elite vehicles of travel by White tourists.

The tendency to understand the filmic Grand Hotel as pure fantasy and 'escapism' in fact requires that we suspend attention to the material paths and technological vehicles through which the tour and transport linked the movie theatre and the civic/monumental spaces of Fascism. This perspective also requires us to ignore how the mobility and mobilization implied by the term 'escapism' pertained to the Grand Hotel's utility, in a historical conjuncture, for mediating the internationalism and national-popular orientations of cultural economies. While I would concur with Ernesto Laclau's statement that "populism is the royal road to understanding something about the ontological constitution of the political,"[37] the populism of the Grand Hotel's revolving door to the *bel mondo* was not simply a filmic representation (a castle in the air) but a material and technical achievement of building royal roads as popular routes. While 'the popular' may have been an abstraction, an empty signifier for political mobilization in different nations, its utopian aspirations, mobilization, and circulation (e.g., the 'democratization of leisure' in Fascist Italy) have occurred through sites where the popular is *rationalized* (in Foucault's sense, an object of governmental reflection) and through the kinds of technologies and networks of communication and transportation that this chapter has considered.

NOTES

1. This chapter's title refers to the author's return to '*Castelli in aria:* The Myth of the Grand Hotel,' in James Hay, *Popular Film Culture in Fascist Italy: The Passing of*

the Rex, Bloomington, IN: Indiana UP, 1987. The current chapter poses a slightly different set of questions about the relation between cinema, hotels, and Italian Fascism.

2. *Amarcord* (*I Remember Fondly*) is set in a town that loosely represents Rimini, where Fellini was reared during the 1920s and 1930s. The Grand Hotel Rimini opened in 1908 and was the town's largest hotel. A fire during the 1920s destroyed part of the hotel's roof-design and was never replaced. After significant damage from bombings during World War Two, the hotel was refurbished during the 1950s. In the 1970s the street and park in front of the hotel were renamed after Federico Fellini, and the hotel's touristic value remains tied in part to its mythologization in this film. Fellini frequently stayed in the hotel (always in the same room), and in 1993 he suffered a stroke there that led to his death two months later. In 1994, the hotel was designated as a National Monument.

3. Fernand Braudel, *The Structure of Everyday Life: Civilization and Capitalism: 15th–18th Century, Vol. 1*, New York: Harper Row, 1982. Henri Lefebvre, *Everyday Life in the Modern World*, New Brunswick, NJ/ London: Transaction Publishers, 1971/1994.

4. Corrado Augias, 'Ho inventato tutto. Anche me: conversazione con Federico Fellini,' *Panorama* (January, 14, 1980), p. 95. The Preface to *Popular Film Culture in Fascist Italy* begins with a discussion of Fellini's discussion of *Amarcord*'s representation of Italy during the 1920s and 1930s.

5. For more on cinema's place within the changing cultural, political, and economic geography of Italy, see James Hay, 'Placing Cinema, Fascism, and the Nation within a Diagram of Italian Modernity,' *Re-viewing Fascism: Italian Cinema, 1922–1943*, ed., Jacqueline Reich and Piero Garofolo, Bloomington, IN: Indiana UP, 2002.

6. Although I discuss how the Grand Hotel became an international sign circulating though international political and cultural economies, it is worth acknowledging that this circulation (the mobility of the 'moving image') was predicated upon a regime of transportation. See James Hay, 'Toward a Spatial Materialism of the "Moving Image:" Locating Screen Media within Changing Regimes of Transport,' *Cinema and Cie: Internation Film Studies Journal*, no. 5, Fall 2004.

7. To the extent that the Grand Hotel is situated away from Home, particularly away from a *popular*, middle-class and lower-middle-class domesticity, the early filmic representations of the Grand Hotel often are about the restrictiveness of home, family, occupation, and daily life and about the threats to the comforts, security, and respectability of home life. For a national audience, for whom images of family offer indispensable models of collective identity, and for the petit-bourgeois sensibility that stresses the value of monogamy and the nuclear family, the Grand Hotel represents a realm in which family ties and, hence, values become arbitrary and often suspended. On vacation (staying at a hotel), one is not obliged to conduct oneself in a manner determined by the social and familial identity from which one has come. Presumably, the inhabitants of a hotel are strangers, with whom one can form a more transient bond. Given the deeply rooted practice of aligning women with the domestic sphere ('a woman's place is in the home'), and men with the open road ('a man makes a place for himself in the world'), this paradox plays out differently for male and female characters in films during the 1930s, as well for male and female audiences who en-

joyed different degrees of access to public places such as movie theatres and hotels. As shown below, this paradox also makes film narratives about the distance between Home and Grand Hotel a framework for representing both as stages for enacting the 'homeland' (the nation)—a mythic territory whose borders mark the difference between the domestic and the foreign.

8. As mentioned throughout this chapter, the Grand Hotel's association with an ineffable *bel mondo*—as a rarified place of beauty—was easily articulated to its racialization of exclusivity and even beauty as a Light or White space of leisure.

9. This term is derived from Mikhail Bakhtin, *The Dialogic Imagination*, ed., Michael Holquist, Austin: University of Texas Press, 1981. I have inflected the term in a slightly different way in order to discuss what I have termed a 'spatial materialism' of cinema and other media. See James Hay, 'Piecing Together What Remains of the Cinematic City,' *The Cinematic City*, ed., David B. Clarke (London: Routledge, 1997), p. 217.

10. While the history of the luxury liner dates from the mid-nineteenth century, the most energetic building of luxury liners occurred during the first decades of the twentieth century, and particularly during the period with which this essay is most concerned (the late 1920s and 1930s). The expansion of luxury liners, and the competition among national companies to make the largest and swiftest liners, attests to a historical conjuncture when an elite form of travel was articulated to tourism as a 'popular' activity.

11. On Fordism, see Antonio Gramsci, 'Rationalization of Production and Work,' and on foreign novels in Italy, see Gramsci, 'Various Types of Popular Novel,' *An Antonio Gramsci Reader: Selected Writings 1916–1935*, ed. David Forgacs, New York: Schocken Books, 1988.

12. Georg Simmel, 'The Metropolis and Mental Life,' *Simmel on Culture: Selected Writings*, ed. David Frisby and Mike Featherstone, London: Sage, 1997, pp. 174–186.

13. There also were early twentieth-century German novels and plays set in Grand Hotels and resorts—Thomas Mann's *Death in Venice* (1911) and *The Magic Mountain* (1924), Sven Elvestad's detective novel *Der Tod kehrt im Hotel ein* (*Death Enters the Hotel*, 1928), and Vicki Baum's novel and play (*People in a Hotel*, 1928/29) which was adapted to become the MGM film, *Grand Hotel* (1932).

14. The Grand Hotel in film borrowed and distanced itself from the theatrical set design of late nineteenth- and early twentieth-century bourgeois comedies and dramas, which (though sometimes involving a multi-ethnic cast of characters) occurred indoors in boudoirs or drawing rooms and involved characters from an aristocratic or upper middle-class milieu. The films in the twenties whose events transpired in a luxury hotel, at a resort, or on a transatlantic liner invariably included upper-crust characters, though often (as discussed below) in stories about a conflict between socioeconomic classes and/or between characters from different parts of the world who are brought together in the hotel as a space of chance encounter and tourism.

15. This statement recognizes that, for different social classes in Italy, there were different tiers of movie theatres—just as there were different categories of hotels. (See Hay, *Popular Film Culture in Fascist Italy*, op cit.) However, while Grand Hotels may have excluded social classes that were unable to afford them, and while

different tiers of movie theatres did not *always* exhibit the same films, public/popular access to films such as MGM's *Grand Hotel* was greater than to one of Italy's Grand Hotels.

16. Quotation found on the website for the Hotel Aldon Kempinski: http://www .hotel-adlon.de/en/hotel/index.htm.

17. The international fascination and valuing of the Grand Hotel in Europe was complexly interwoven with ways that the U.S. was imaged and imagined through Hollywood. Mario Baffico, an Italian director who returned to Italy from making pictures abroad, stated in 1933 that "the enormous fortune that has befallen the American cinema in the last few years should not be attributed solely to its early financial organization but also to the widespread acceptance of the product itself which has piqued the interest of the world because it reveals the passions, the feelings, the character and the customs of American men and women in all those manifestations of their way of life that no book, play, or journalistic report could document with such exactness" (*Il cinematografo*, May 17, 1933, p. 2). And as Robert Sklar has contended: "It would be fair to say that Europeans did not go to American movies to see themselves, nor did they consider Gloria Swanson or John Gilbert 'Europeans' no matter what nationality they were presumably portraying" (*Movie-made America*, New York: Vintage Books, 1975, p. 102). For more on the uptake of Hollywood cinema in Italy during the 1920s and 1930s, see James Hay, 'Cose dell'altro mondo: American Images in Fascist Italy,' *Popular Film Culture in Fascist Italy*, Bloomington, IN: Indiana UP, 1987.

18. For more on Nelson's relation to this film, see Donald Albrecht, *Designing Dreams: Modern Architecture in the Movies*, New York: Harper and Row, 1986. The employment of a professionally trained architect as art director for a Hollywood film underscores that the filmic Grand Hotel was a setting introduced through the interplay not just between European and U.S. filmmaking but between European architectural modernism and Hollywood filmmaking during the late 1920s and early 1930s. As Albrecht notes, by the mid-1930s, Hollywood filmmaking had so internalized this style that it no longer needed professionally trained architects such as Nelson to design film sets.

19. This is slightly different than saying that the movie theatre was a generalizable 'ideological apparatus' or Platonic Cave (as Jean Baudry once argued); the design-style of movie theatres was materially practised through the built environment as well as film codes and conventions.

20. A vivid example of the link in Hollywood cinema between the racial identities of the Western tourist-class and the brightness and airiness of their elite settings is RKO's *Shall We Dance?* (1936), in which Fred Astaire's character dances amidst the sweaty, dark-skinned workers in the engine room of a luxury liner.

21. William Everson, *The American Silent Film*, New York: Oxford University Press, 1978.

22. Francesco Savio, *Cinecittà anni trenta* (Rome: Bulzoni, 1979) p. 861.

23. It is worth thinking about how this phenomenon develops through Vicki Baum's account of the Nazi regime in the final stage of World War Two Berlin in her *Hotel Berlin* (1945).

24. Gerald Mast, *The Comic Mind* (Indianapolis: Bobbs and Merrill, 1973) p. 203.

25. As sites of popular entertainment and gambling, the 1930s films set in Grand Hotels are part of the lineage of late-20th-century hotel casinos (the MGM Grand in Las Vegas) and of TV game shows and more recently Reality TV formats such as *The Next Joe Millionaire* (whose games were set in a Tuscan villa).

26. As an adaptation, the film was an example of how early sound film exploited the multi-character narrative of the novel, and it converted the dystopic and cynical shadings of 1920s German film styles through Hollywood stars.

27. Siegfried Kracauer, 'The Hotel Lobby,' *The Mass Ornament*, trans. and ed. Thomas Y. Levin, Cambridge, MA: Harvard UP, 1995, p. 183.

28. For an alternative perspective about the 'white telephone' films, which focuses on the relation between cinema and telephony, see Hay, 'Placing Cinema, Fascism and the Nation in a Diagram of Italian Modernity,' op cit.

29. *Rotaie* was filmed in 1929 but not released until 1931, after sound had been added to the original silent version.

30. The young Italian director Corrado D'Errico worked as an assistant director on *Rotaie* and *Ritmi di stazione*

31. The emergence of Fascism in Italy is most often associated with the November 1922 'march on Rome' that installed Benito Mussolini as head of the Fascist party and of Italy. Most historians concur that the programs of Fascism, particularly its ability to act upon and through the formation of a 'popular culture,' did not make popular culture a civic objective until the late 1920s. In this sense, the 'rebirth' of Italian cinema, while not determined solely or even primarily by Fascist policy, became integral and instrumental to a rapidly emerging linkage between government, economy, and culture, and to the contradictions of policy that both sought to protect Italian culture from the onslaught of foreign (particularly Hollywood) culture and to install Italian popular cultural forms (particularly cinema) within an international economy.

32. Victoria DeGrazia, *The Culture of Consent: Mass Organization of Leisure in Fascist Italy*, Cambridge/New York: Cambridge UP, 1981.

33. For more on these films, see Hay, *Popular Film Culture in Fascist Italy*, op cit.

34. As DeGrazia has contended, the state discounts had two objectives: "to boost mass transit, thereby reducing the huge deficit of the state railroads as revenues declined during the depression; at the same time they provided the urban unemployed and poor brief respite from the dismal depression atmosphere of the cities," (op cit., p. 180).

35. As in Hollywood studios' jungle-films during the 1930s, *Sotto la croce del sud* integrates footage obtained from travel and expeditionary documentaries.

36. For more on the transformation of the Venice Film Festival over the 1930s and early 1940s, see Marla Stone, 'The Last Film Festival: The Venice Biennale Goes to War,' *Re-viewing Fascism*, op cit., pp. 293–314.

37. Ernesto Laclau, *On Populist Reason*, London/New York: Verso, 2005, p. 67. Laclau posits that 'the people' is primarily a discursive construction—an 'empty' or 'floating' signifier that has been articulated to various political objectives.

Chapter Two

Floating Hotels: Cruise Holidays and Amateur Film-making in the Inter-war Period

Heather Norris Nicholson

A cruise on an ocean liner. This surely is the cameraman's paradise now.

(Brunel, 1936, 99)

According to Paul Fussell (1980, see also 1992, 71–72), the idea of travel became practically equivalent to the idea of ships during the inter-war period. Professional and non-professional filmmakers from the same period also display a fascination with sailing and sea-related images, particularly in relation to passenger ships. Commercial films set on cruise-ships date from the early 1900s but by the 1920s, passenger vessels had become distinctive filming locations that, like hotels, were well-suited to murder, mystery, intrigue, romance or comedy and often very popular with audiences eager for escapist relief from prevailing economic conditions. British and American studios produced a number of such cruise-ship films including *Isn't Life Terrible* (McCarey, 1925), *The Floating College* (Crone, 1928), *Rich and Strange* (*East of Shanghai*) (Hitchcock, 1932), *Melody Cruise* (Sandrich, 1933), *Trouble* (Rogers, 1933), *Seeing is Believing* (Davis, 1934), *Transatlantic Merry-Go-Round* (Stoloff, 1934), *The Captain Hates the Sea* (Milestone, 1934), *Black Sheep* (Dwan, 1935), *All at Sea* (Kimmons, 1935) and *Night at the Opera* (Wood, 1935). While newsreels featured transatlantic super-liners and luxury cruises for the rich and famous, Thomas Cook and other providers of organised travel widened the social appeal of pleasure cruising. Such popularity (Brendon, 1991; Henniker Heaton, 1935; Green, 1944; Stock, 1922) also coincided with a surge of amateur interest in filmmaking. As a result, cruise-holidays soon featured in the repertoire of early non-professional filmmakers and now offer us a fascinating contemporary gaze upon the floating hotel during the interwar years.

This discussion situates amateur Mediterranean cruise-holiday films made by British ciné enthusiasts within a specific stage of modernity that clearly reflects wider issues of visual, cultural and, as discussed elsewhere, tourism history (Norris Nicholson, 1997; 2002; 2003a; 2004; 2006a; 2006b). For filmmakers and their subsequent viewers, each ship is a floating hotel that binds, severs, and regulates social practice within clearly differentiated spaces for passengers and crew. Deck activities, shore visits, and entertainment diversify the recognisable rituals of hotel service. People, like different parts of the ship, assume different identities and roles over time, albeit within prescribed roles as guest, host, and servant. The cruise-ship as floating entity travels through, defines, and connects space as a series of places on an itinerary. Emblematic of globalizing travel trends, floating hotels were part of modernity's "homeless technologies" (Lamprecht, cited in Kern, 1983, 230) that combined a new sense of ubiquity with home comforts. Like railways and telephones, they expanded horizons within motionless journeys. Rather like the passport—long resented after its introduction in 1915—and its mimetic grasp of an unchanging self, cruise-ships combined the possibility of travel whilst also controlling the kinds of transformative encounters conventionally associated with the process of journeying. Their protective bubble transported passengers enabling them to experience sites/sights safely with minimal exposure to exoticism or danger.

During the 1920s, amateur interests in cinematography coincided with unprecedented opportunities to see and be seen elsewhere albeit in changing geo-political and societal contexts. New patterns of recreational mobility and (in)activity, as well as changing ideas about the relationship between work, fatigue, and modernity (Rabinbach, 1992, 274) and different attitudes toward sunshine following the publication of Auguste Rollier's influential *Heliotherapy* (1923), situate pleasure-cruise footage as a distinctive component of interwar visual and cultural practice. Holiday footage helps to illuminate wider relationships between mobility and modernity found within other filmic imagery. Accordingly, the following discussion positions depictions of cruising holidays within a broader system of cinematic hotel/motel stopping and moving places. This exploration of the cruise-ship as transport, accommodation and an integral part of the recorded holiday experience refers to black-and-white archival travel footage, made between 1928 and 1934, and now held at the British Film Institute and North West Film Archive. Ideas form part of my continuing research on visual and tourism histories in relation to Britain's amateur film movement although this volume's specific focus on hotels and motels in cinematic representation permits more speculative exploration of modernity, mobility, and forms of amateur visual practice. Further aspects of twentieth-century holidaying afloat and the critical neglect of the relationship between shipping and broader cultural patterns in a contested and postcolonial era, as identified by Quartermaine (1996, 27), are developed elsewhere (Norris Nicholson, 2006c).

FLOATING HOTELS AND MODERNITY

The boat, as Foucault reminds us (1998, 244), "is a floating piece of space, a place without a place, that exists by itself, that is closed in on itself. . . ." At the same time, it has the capacity, on leaving its moorings, for mobility and, paradoxically, given its restrictive form, for freedom to cross "the infinity of the sea . . . from port to port, from tack to tack . . . ." The cruise-ship, in particular, is simultaneously a means to move between places and also a stopping place for passengers who spend their vacation time afloat. This "self-contained environment" (Pizam and Mansfeld, 1999, 376) crosses time zones whilst being dependent upon tidal movements. For its passengers, leisure time assumes a distinctive shipboard logic, determined by diverse routines and prescribed activities and itineraries. Promoted as an effortless, efficient, and safe means of group travel and yet lacking, when out of sight of the coast, any constant external measures to define distance, the cruise-ship experience represents a multi-nuanced focus for issues of mobility, time, and space.

Understanding the socio-cultural, economic and ethnic processes that helped to determine the micro-geographies evident in cruise-ship footage situates issues of spatiality and social relations within a distinctive milieu that reflects a specific phase in both maritime and cultural history. Speed and motion became synonymous, for some commentators, with modernity (Conrad, 1998, 91–109; Kern, 1983, 109–130). The sleek and competitive streamlining of new turbine-driven motor vessels evinced new levels of efficiency and velocity, even as they promoted the pleasure of effortless travel.[1] Scenes of mechanised motion and personal stasis, filmed during holidays afloat, seem to capture amateur delight in recording an experiential paradox for vicarious consumption back home. Such hints at the observational detachment and whimsical propensity for visual reflection found in amateur material may be likened briefly to Kracauer's suggestion of the detective's centrality as a figure of modernity (Koch 2003, 22–24). Pushing simplistic analogies too far would be inappropriate but, as with his reflections upon contemporary metropolitan hotels, some comments seem germane to this examination of cruise-ship imagery.

Most obviously there is a temporal relevance as Kracauer's essay on the hotel lobby appeared in print just as shipping companies were modernising their passenger vessels for a wider leisure-orientated travel market (Hyde, 1971, 156–159; see also Louden-Brown, 2001). If large hotels seemed, to contemporary commentators, to be the metropolis in microcosm, cruise-ships also involved socially diverse people co-existing in close proximity. Offi-cers, crew and 'guests' were able, like hotel visitors, to maintain distance by disappearing behind their "social masks" (Kracauer, 1995, 181) of civility and professional duty. Admittedly, the host's incognito status among hotel visitors contrasted with passengers' expectation to fraternize with senior crew members and the master of the ship through dining at the captain's table and visiting the bridge. Nonetheless, Elvestad's evocation of the large hotel, quoted by Kracauer (1995, 184), transfers readily to floating hotels: indeed, the ambiguous sense of how "guests here roam about in their light-hearted, careless existence without suspecting anything of the strange mysteries circulating among them" captures the carefree and pleasure-seeking mood captured in much interwar footage of holidays afloat.

Differences abound too: hotels, for Kracauer, epitomised opportunities for brief encounters in which freedom from normal constraints was possible—metaphorical as well as spatial or sexual. Anchored to a particular location and served by interconnected networks of established urban or national route systems—pavements, streets, railways and subways—modern metropolitan hotels, in reality or on film, were primarily passing places associated with their guests often anonymously moving on. Thus they differ from the floating hotel where commitment and social interaction with other passengers were requisite features of group travel. Essentially, the fleeting, arbitrary, and tem-porary nature of human contact within modern hotel settings, as discussed by Clifford (1997, 17ff), contrasted with the inescapably collective experience of being guests at sea. Moreover, unlike the fixity of the motel/hotel through which flows of people pass at differing speeds, circulation remains the *raison d'être* of the cruise-ship: immobility, as shown by the £30 million bill for compensation facing P. and O. after cancelling a much delayed luxury cruise on the *Aurora*, can be a commercial and public relations disaster.[2] Mobil-ity is thus embodied by the ship, but those on board participate in a kind of motionless trip that requires their voluntary confinement in a shared setting (Hughes, 1998, 21).

If staterooms and cabins approximate to the private atomized spaces of the hotel/motel, then various public spaces, especially upper decks where most amateur filming occurs, are the equivalent to Kracauer's lobby. In ei-ther instance, access may be under surveillance (Pizam and Mansfeld, 1999, 376) but while sliding, swing or revolving doors offer conventional forms of exit from the lobby, only a removable gangway or launch re-connects those aboard with the wider world. Once removed, of course, the absence of opening and the invisible maze of different deck levels hidden within a sheer steel exterior evoke the glass-sides, materially different but functionally analogous, of more contemporary hotels, epitomised by Jameson's (1984) seminal comments on the Bonaventure Hotel in Los Angeles. Cruise-ships and hotels share the capacity to seem adrift and isolated from their surroundings. Both distinctive settings frame the travel encounters that occur within and beyond their physical form (Figure 2.1).

Confined aboard between shore excursions, amateur attention typically focuses upon the immediate filmic possibilities of the ship. The camera captures the informality of people at ease with each other enjoying socially permitted freedoms of vacation time and space (Figure 2.2).

Their needs are pampered by a tightly controlled system of service that ensures 'others,' whether on the basis of gender, occupation or ethnicity, stay in their own place. Scenes onboard disclose how social interactions inhabit various kinds of shipboard space. Social relations captured in moving form thus help us to understand the scopic regime of the interwar period (Lukinbeal, 2004, 249).

Figure 2.1. *Royal Mail Line. M. V. Asturias (22,500 tonnes) to Spain, Madeira, and the Canary Islands* **(Preston brothers, 1928)**
Still supplied by the North West Film Archive at Manchester Metropolitan University, UK

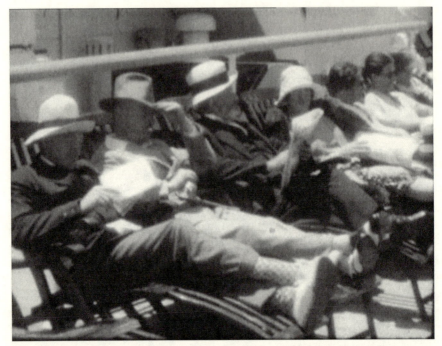

Figure 2.2. *Line SS. Orama Cruise. Tetuan and Ceuta* **(Preston brothers, 1932)**
Still supplied by the North West Film Archive at Manchester Metropolitan University, UK

As the amateur lens appropriates and domesticates unfamiliar places, the cruise-ship's bulk, towering over foreign quaysides or reassuringly filmed at anchor offshore, dominates foreign space. The passenger vessel's formative role in widening the modern tourist periphery is apparent yet, as its protective bubble transports tourists safely to 'exotic' places, it is also a refuge. Belonging to a ship's "short-lived society" (Foster, 1986, 216) confers an associative identity upon its passengers (Figure 2.3).

This characteristic is fundamental to the plot dynamics of mystery-based cruise films in which passengers remain under suspicion until the moment of detection. In amateur footage, posed shots beside the ship's name may also hint at how strength and status accrue from being part of a larger entity that carries its title on bows, stern, and much on-board equipment. The recurrence of more distant views of the parent-ship viewed from land, similarly, suggests that the vessel's visible presence and recognisable company livery offered valuable orientation during excursions ashore. These visits often involved free wandering that was regulated only by when the launch would return passengers to the ship. The cinematic flânerie that results from seemingly unstructured strolls through old-town areas at different destinations suggests

Figure 2.3. *Royal Mail Line. M. V. Asturias* (22,500 tonnes)
Still supplied by the North West Film Archive at Manchester Metropolitan University, UK

uninhibited exploration. While the resultant footage details now transformed urban social contexts and is imbricated with the power geometries of insider/ outsider relations, the images, as well as their subsequent editing, also hint at levels of self-assurance and authority that perhaps conflict with other aspects of the filmic holiday record.

Let us now consider how filmic sightseeing evoked the pleasures of a holiday afloat for subsequent recollection and sharing with family, friends and wider audiences. The making and screening of non-professional footage did not occur in a visual vacuum and should be understood within a wider context of prevailing visual meanings and representations then in circulation. Amateur imagery, no less than its professional counterpart, helped to valorise specific moments, feelings, and situations. Less sophisticated than feature film undoubtedly, its gaze now offers often compelling visual historical evidence. Attention first turns to consider examples of archival material that detail aspects of cruise-ship life for passengers and, more rarely, members of their crew. Next, the filmic portrayal of life onboard is contrasted with a wider gaze beyond the ship's rail. The resultant montage of panoramic, aerial views, and filmic vignettes found in these scenes filmed from the ship, frequently disclose a filmmaker's subjectivities as well as a densely textured sense of unfamiliar places and urban space. The concluding section returns to a broader analysis of the cruise-ship's significance in cinematic and societal terms during the interwar years and, more speculatively, in recent times.

FLOATING HOTELS AS
DIVIDED AND CONFINED SPACE

The value of movement and travel-related metaphors, in recent social and cultural analysis, is frequently predicated upon differences in access and patterns of mobility through and within space (Cresswell, 1997; Clifford, 1992, 111; 1997, 17–46; Mitchell, 2000, 256ff). Similarly, pleasure cruises during the interwar period required that passengers and their attendant crew members functioned within carefully defined social and physical space that replicated structural inequalities at a wider level. The unrestricted gaze of privilege and access to sight-see were reliant upon 'others' being in their putative, hierarchical places, delineated by ethno-cultural, material, or spatial boundaries. When captured on camera for later viewing, such images now seem double-edged: they function like visual invitations beckoning vicarious participation while simultaneously reducing and distancing anything unfamiliar. Moving imagery literally offers safe distance to its audience just as filming physically separates and emotionally liberates the filmmaker from the scene in front of the camera. As onlooker and witness, the filmmaker's own non-intervention selectively discloses the actions of others onboard and elsewhere.

Passengers typically spent longer aboard than did their equivalents confined within the grounds and buildings of a metropolitan hotel, so entertainment was a key component of pleasure cruising. Recreational activity was popular during sea passages and helped to offset the "sight-seeing ennui" (Foster, 1986, 235) that became associated sometimes with shipboard lectures and shore visits. Organised sports contrasted with the crew's own physical exertion but occasionally, as detailed below, involved passengers and crew in unlikely levels of proximity and shared space. Through reference to George Warburton's silent, 17 minute film in black-and-white aboard the *SS. Lancastria*, and also to imagery of Asian seamen filmed aboard the cruise-ships, *SS. Orama* and *Moldavia*, this section highlights many of the distinctive and divisive spatialities associated with being guests afloat.[3]

Warburton's hobby of making and showing ciné films was sustained by family prosperity founded on the development of a thriving regional bakery.[4] The Warburtons were characteristic of the new, moneyed middle classes that held influential social positions in the industrial parts of England during the interwar years. *Sunshine, Sea Breezes and Strange Places* (1932) details a fourteen-day cruise of the western Mediterranean undertaken with his wife and son.[5] Although George Warburton films extensively during shore visits, his chief interest seems to lie in recording what he describes as "the pleasures of cruising" and these detailed scenes provide the focus in subsequent paragraphs. As with many early ciné enthusiasts, it seems that, for Warburton, the portrayal of other people's enjoyment of activities possibly already made familiar by contemporary feature films, ensures audience appeal and prompts much of the filmic focus during the cruise.

Warburton's film opens with embarkation from Liverpool on the evening high tide. Images of supplies and luggage being swung aboard are inter-cut with shots of the river-front buildings and activity on the water. Flanked by tugs, another massive cruiser decorated with flags and bunting approaches the quayside through mist. It dwarfs a rowing boat briefly framed between bow and stern of two nearer moored vessels. Well-wishers' white handkerchiefs flutter against the monotones of a Merseyside skyline. Warburton's eye for detail and contrast, together with the different dates of film stock, suggest that this introductory sequence may have been filmed separately and spliced to the adjacent footage. The film continues with medium and long-distance shots from an upper deck. They capture the receding waterfront, gulls overhead, and passing vessels framed by the darkening forms of rigging and spars as the vessel heads out to sea.

Shots are well-composed, held steadily and, importantly, given the frequently moving subject matter, often quite long. Sharply defined images of shadows on bulkheads, shapes, the mix of verticals and horizontals found in rails, decking, stowed ropes, chains, and other gear evoke the ship's form and provide cut-away shots from sequences involving people and views beyond the ship's rail. The visual competence and semi-abstract quality is neither particularly unique nor highly original as it recurs in other early amateur material. Nevertheless, it establishes the *SS. Lancastria* as setting and exemplifies the stylistic qualities and perceptions of different visual opportunities that help to individualise the work of different filmmakers. Warburton's interest in the passengers starts with his sequence of a safety drill shortly after embarkation. The caption, 'Safety first,' introduces the passengers reporting to muster stations with life jackets and taking part in a lifeboat drill. As the first cruise activity likely to involve all passengers (Pizam and Mansfeld, 1999, 392) it combines novelty, excitement, and interaction with each other and crew members. As safety equipment is tried on, inhibition gives way to humour, seemingly untroubled by concerns about accidents at sea.

Following the catastrophic loss of the *Titanic*, improving ship stability was essential to the interwar expansion of recreational pleasure cruising. Despite various technical improvements, some aspects of cruise-holidays remained problematic. "A really up to date ship has every advantage over a hotel except stability and fresh meat," quipped Waugh (1930, 37). Meals rarely feature in cruise-holiday films, perhaps because of seasickness, although eating together was a significant routine. Waugh observes that, "It seems one of the tenets of catering on-board ship that passengers need nutrition every two and a half hours" (1930, 38). Clearly, meals regulate time in many social settings as in Foucault's (1998) heterotopia and dining with senior officers was an essential aspect of shipboard social relations. Did rules exclude ciné cameras from the dining room or was it just considered unacceptable? The absence is curious, given that a hotel meal eaten alone or in company on screen has long been a form of coded, visual shorthand. Moreover, ciné footage of service on deck does occur, as do meals eaten in restaurants or hotels ashore, and, occasionally, film sequences portray musicians silently playing to accompany after-dinner drinks.

Staterooms or cabins are also absent from the amateur filmmaker's holiday record. The simplest of tracking shot goes no further than the cabin door.[6] This contrasts with commercial cinema and also with ciné films of package holidays in the early 1950s in which the delight in disclosing the hotel room plus balcony and wash basin, and the lavish self-service buffets, a few years later, seems palpable as unfamiliar levels of vacation comfort and lavishness are recorded to share back home.[7] But the pre-war film enthusiast afloat observed greater discretion in how he captured the social character of the ship's public and private spaces. Warburton was no exception in his focus upon activities in public areas, particularly the promenade and boat decks where deck space was designated for deck quoits, table tennis, and other ball games. Group sessions in physical exercise occur as do the occasional shot of a solitary passenger skipping.

Promenading was popular and easy to film. Generally at sea guests had access to more public areas than their equivalents in an urban hotel although deck space became congested during settled weather. Flânerie assumes a more hybrid character than on land although it remains at strolling pace. Women and men, of different ages, take part, usually in pairs or small mixed groups. Heads inclined, as if in conversation, suggests that talking is as important as observing although contact with passing officers and seated passengers hints at a mobilised gaze that contrasts with the more sedentary viewing from deck chairs. Away from the shore, inevitably, attention turns to other passengers, or crew as discussed later, unless birds overhead, passing ships or marine life offer visual distraction. The gendered nature of deck promenading varies according to the overall passenger composition of different cruises although the scenes of young women seemingly engaged in reading concur with social comment (and satire) on cruise participants and may disclose other gendered patterns of tourist behaviour (Norris Nicholson, 2004a).

Organised entertainment converts places on deck into performance spaces. *SS. Lancastria* was not unique in offering model horse-racing and a variety of competitive games in which passengers race to complete ridiculous tasks. The cruise-ship is more like a holiday camp than a hotel in such sequences, although the transgressive opportunities offered by the cinematic hotel/motel also occur in highly modified form. Some passengers seem to perceive the ship as a space that legitimises and, at times, requires behaving differently (Graburn, 1983, 21; Gottleib, 1982; 168–170; Lett; 1983; Foster, 1986; 232). Without detailed knowledge of passengers' backgrounds, freedom from home conventions remains speculative and, of course, the programme only replicates activities found to be popular on previous cruises. Moreover, as cruise-ship comedy films reveal, such holidays are expected to be amusing. Although amateur footage does not record the excesses of some passengers' antics parodied by Sitwell (1927) or Waugh (1930; 1943) it reflects prevailing attitudes and assumptions. Public performance confers acceptability on levels of physical proximity and bodily contact between sexes and particularly between younger female passengers and crew members during deck games that cut across conventional norms of social identity and class relationships (Hughes, 1998, 22–23). Crew members, for instance, join in with tug-of-war competitions or as guides or assistants in other races. They administer ties and blindfolds for obstacle races, retrieve equipment and wandering participants who stray off-course. They also stand alongside people pillow-fighting on greasy poles and during other kinds of game; ready to catch those who lose their balance or succumb to laughter (Figure 2.4).[8]

Small canvas swimming pools held taut by ropes and often positioned in the stern away from the gaze of deck hands also offered easy opportunities for filming.[9] They symbolized luxury at a time when bathrooms were still innovative additions to the design of much suburban housing in Britain. These crowded scenes of men and women in shoulder-length woollen bathing suits and rubber skull caps, set alongside people under parasols or awnings, also illustrate a transitional phase in attitudes towards sunbathing evidenced by interwar writers, although Fitzgerald's (1939, 69–73) distinction between "raw whiteness" and tanned bodies does not clearly show in monochrome. The pool acts as a performance space for burlesque and physical playfulness that contrasts with the restraint and formality of some other passengers. Cut-away shots to the ship's surging wake or, more occasionally, to white-uniformed officers upon an upper deck, are reminders of the vessel's steady onward movement and broader rhythms of work. Despite its unsophisticated design,

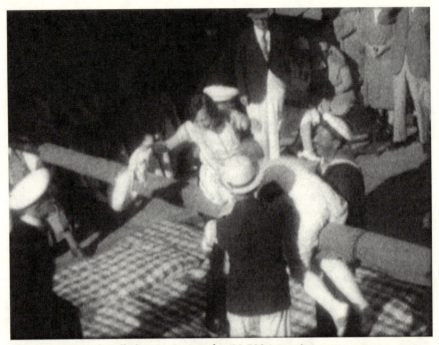

Figure 2.4.   *Royal Mail Line, M. V. Asturias* (22,500 tonnes)
Still supplied by the North West Film Archive at Manchester Metropolitan University, UK

the pool's presence and associated sunbathing approximate to levels of hotel elegance found in contemporary colour advertising and film. One filmmaker, Dr. John Barker Scarr, even includes a separate pool sequence on colour-stock edited in with the rest of his black-and-white film.[10]

Behaving differently, like dressing up or performing for the camera, briefly changes identity. Shipboard life, as with excursions ashore, offered some opportunities for identity-shifting and perhaps approximate more to the masked ball than to modern metropolitan hotel stays. Cross-dressing in a borrowed sailor's suit connotes pleasurable and sexualised risk-taking in putting on the clothes of a working man (Waugh, 1943, 17). A 'Clothes of the Empire' procession, filmed aboard *SS. Lancastria*, includes passengers as peasants, clowns, Russians, and 'Chinese coolies' in costumes probably brought from home or borrowed from the purser or other passengers. Its embedded notions of superiority occur elsewhere in amateur footage and the depiction of 'foreigners' through comedy seems particularly inappropriate on vessels often crewed by non-European seamen. Yet its perceived harmlessness also illustrates the acceptable face of racism that permeated upper- and middle-class British life during this period and, arguably, persists into the present.[11]

Significantly, the distinctive garments of Lascars, the East African and Asian crew members employed by British shipping companies, are absent from such masquerades.[12] Asian seamen, however, provided considerable visual interest for different amateur filmmakers. Described by one commentator (Mitton, 1913, 57–58) as being part of "the picturesqueness of the steamer, with their red sashes and turbans, and the quaint adornments that they love," imagery of Asian crew members in holiday ciné footage also concurs with the documentary and ethnographic interests espoused by many amateur filmmakers. From contemporary comments (Jones, 1931, and see also 'Lighterman,' 1957; Burton 1998), it seems that clothing was emblematic of culture, racial identity and colonial relationships.[13] Unlike the adoption of western dress that, according to Collingham (2001, 186) often helped to blur "the distinction between colonizer and colonized" in India under British rule, on-board ship amateur footage emphasizes visible difference. Perhaps amateur interest was also prompted by then prevalent media coverage of recurrent unrest prompted by discriminatory legislation, payroll practice, strained union relations and the continuing rise of Indian nationalism (Sherwood, 1991, 229–244; Lahiri, 2002, 169ff). Undoubtedly, just as imperial epics flourished through the thirties (Aldgate and Richard 1999, 21), cruise footage also places specific colonial encounters centrally in the camera gaze.

Asian deck hands are the most visible crew members in amateur footage, featuring more frequently than higher-ranking officers although rarely in posed shots.[14] Such footage is often in medium range and in profile or from behind when unloading supplies from rope nets. Transfers by launch between boat and shore also enable filmmakers to film in close up, dwelling on clothing or an individual's face or side profile, although acknowledgement of such portraiture is rare. As in the unquestioning acceptance of a helping hand, social interaction is usually minimal and emphasizes the unequal exchange of photography. The launch's bounded space replicates the cruise-ship's hierarchies in microcosm and the socio-cultural separation, despite spatial proximity, is striking in these sequences. It reminds us of another distinctive contemporary stopping place—John Ford's western boarding house—in which spectator positioning and exotic dress transposed from Mexico into Monument Valley affirm prevailing ethnocentric perspectives.

Cruise-ship imagery exemplifies the contradictory power relations of subalternity: aboard the launch, Asian sailors are responsible for safety. The silent mouthing of their seated passengers contrasts with their own watchful, silent vigilance as they stand in the bows. Their anonymous authority derives from long-established social structures as well as modernity and consumerism: just as the institutionalization of travel led to new levels of trust and paid service between tourist and guide (Lash and Urry, 1994), the infrastructures of pleasure-cruising necessitated an ever-widening circle of professionalized support to transport, accommodate and care for its customers. A pre-paid ticket ensured all-inclusive service "with no one expecting tips" and a "Jeeves-like standard of courtesy and efficiency" (Waugh, 1937, 38). "There is an integrity and decency about a ship," Waugh observed, "which one rarely finds on land except in very old-fashioned and expensive hotels" (Waugh, 1937, 37). Such service, however, has always relied on low-paid workers who, like the exploited floating underclass of today's luxury-cruise industry, typically remain out of sight.[15]

GAZING OVER THE RAIL

Simultaneously evoking a place of refuge and the power of surveillance, the hotel window's gaze upon the street is a visual device that recurs across many film genres to advance plot, character, atmosphere or psychological insight. Distance lends perspective, permits focus and careful aim. A ship's upper decks provided amateurs with an equivalent vantage point that combined observation with convenience and safety. Gazing from the rail gave scope for jostle-free and uninhibited camerawork of adjacent activities. Close-ups contrast with long- or medium-length panning shots that typically provide initial shoreline panoramas prior to anchoring or mooring alongside a quay—as well as some final views of different ports of call. The outdoor position contrasted too with the more restricted focus adopted by some amateurs who framed establishing shots through portholes or from one of the lower covered decks. Footage broadly contemporary with Warburton's films permits us to analyse specific views over the deck rail. Attention now turns to imagery by Sidney and Harold Preston, two enthusiasts from Stockport, who made and showed material in their own home-based cinemas, and the films of Dr. John Barker Scarr, a physicist and chemist from Preston.[16]

Unlike Warburton's principal although not exclusive concentration upon recording leisure pursuits during his holiday afloat, Barker Scarr and the Preston brothers took possibilities of amateur cinematography further. They all tried night filming and the twin brothers also combined information, humour, and aesthetic effect very successfully. Their cruise films place greater emphasis upon travel as self-improvement but their material also evinces contemporary responses to unfamiliarity encountered beyond the boat. Watching landfall from the deck was popular among passengers and ciné enthusiasts generally recorded their first impressions from the ship's rail. Such all-encompassing, establishing images may be understood differently from those deck-side views filmed after returning from a shore excursion. Returning from encounters ashore, like retreating from the external world to the privacy of a hotel room, offered distance for reflection. Unlike the private balcony, public deck space may mean other people enter the view but the retrospective filmic gaze was often more controlled and focused. It provided a chance for revisiting, and sharing with later audiences, places that featured on an itinerary or discoveries made alone. Being able to visually locate landmarks in an alien setting made more knowable through going ashore with a guide or alone perhaps imposed order and also conferred authority when subsequently screened. As successive frames retrace a route or piece together topographical clues, the amateur filmmaker's visual navigation again evokes Kracauer's detective searching for contemporary meaning.

Labelling, however erroneously, seeks to impose order too. The caption, 'Tangier: The Fancy Dress Town of Morocco,' introduces Barker Scarr's first close-up impression of North Africa and comes from *Mediterranean Cruise: SS Arandora Star, May 1933,* the first of two films made on holidays on the same cruise-ship in two successive years.[17] Described as a progressive thinker by Barker Scarr's daughter in a recent interview, the intertitle echoes the shipboard parodies discussed earlier and captures his response to the local people that fill his scenes of activity ashore. His repeated views of veiled women seem like scopic signifiers of foreign territory and link to the long tradition of reductive stereotyping prompted by the colonial gaze (Alloula, 1998, 319). Much of his shore footage depicts people and donkeys as they disappear into courtyards, alleyways or under arches. In contrast, sequences filmed from deck while at the quay-side in Tangier, Casablanca, or in the port of Algiers the following year, seem to offer a more manageable form of encountering North African 'exoticism.'

If orientalism may be detected in the iconography of contemporary advertising, its presence in much amateur travel filming is unsurprising.[18] Passenger expectations, let alone prevailing opinions mediated by other forms of text and image, pre-disposed ciné enthusiasts to search out visual difference. Equally, local traders deliberately sought out passengers and cruise ships. Just as a cinematic hotel doorstep often represents a real contested and regulated space adjacent to a city street, a contact zone forms where gang plank meets quay-side. Vendors patiently cluster to hawk leather wallets and jewellery, and become easy prey for the filmmaker in search of ethnographic detail.[19] Postcard sellers draped in readymade views attract attention; their own fixity contrasting with their wares and the mobility of the camera-touting tourist. While an urban hotel generates its own associative ring of regular shoe-shiners, taxi ranks, and errand boys, a cruise-ship's cyclical stops attract more ephemeral forms of enterprise.

For the amateur, no less than the professional, such quay-side activities connote distinctive place identity and atmosphere.[20] They delineate abutting and interdependent social worlds. Penetration of guest space without permission constitutes a violation that is crucial to narrative tension in different cinematic hotel/motel settings. Safe on deck, amateurs film social difference with impunity. At times it seems that local activity compensates for their own restricted movements and becomes an essential ingredient of their own travel narratives. A quay-side tussle or aerial view of tumblers, musicians or snake charmers combines novelty with human interest and sometimes humour. Amateurs capture impromptu markets and relish the visual opportunities when traders sell from boats piled high with tourist souvenirs of cloth, leather, pottery, and wood. Scenes that depict how boys and young men dive to amuse watching passengers and clamber onto mooring chain or companion steps until detected and dislodged with apparent good humour by members of the crew particularise the floating holiday record and strengthen its appeal with subsequent viewers. Other people's economic imperatives, however performative, become stock ingredients for the tourist gaze.

The disruption of underlying routines aboard ship or in a hotel/motel location frequently signals abnormality and heightens suspense, as in such screen classics as *Psycho*. Cruise-ship itineraries also enabled amateurs, occasionally, to juxtapose scenes of physical chaos with shipboard order as illustrated by the Preston brothers who filmed earthquake devastation in the Sicilian city of Messina and framed Stromboli's rugged craters in between the gleaming polished surfaces of ship's pulleys, spars and handrails.[21] Rough seas were more predictably unsettling in various senses and harder to film. While crossing the Bay of Biscay was an unavoidable but recognised travellers' rite of passage, instability and difficult shore landings within the Mediterranean itself only feature occasionally in amateur footage. When such conditions permitted filming, the resultant imagery denotes a visual excitement and quite literally a sensation of movement that more typically was absent from the floating hotel. Indeed, Conrad describes (1998, 92) how interior design on Cunard liners seemed to compensate for the apparent absence of speed. Aboard the *Queen Mary*, for instance, Art Deco motifs combined mythic centaurs and winged horses with streamlined images of planes and trains that would appeal to passengers "addicted to motion" and "the thrill of acceleration." Unlike the transatlantic liners, Mediterranean cruises rarely were out of sight of land for long and numbers of passengers who lined the rail awaiting each new headland, coastline, and shore approach tended to dwindle until the final home-coming. The appetite for travel could apparently diminish even during a motionless journey.

CONCLUSION

Foucault (1998) suggested that "the ship is the heterotopia *par excellence.*" Floating hotels approximate particularly well to his notion of a distinctive and unique self-contained space and temporal locus of hybridity that simultaneously relates to other spaces and times. Their characteristics, functions, and the experiences they provide for the varied people aboard offered amateur filmmakers, like their professional counterparts, diverse subject matter that now contributes to our own understanding of relationships between modernity, mobility, and identity during the early decades of the last century. Just as some audiences enjoyed the fictive relationships of imaginary screen or stage characters variously played out amid the sophisticated settings of luxury travel, amateur film facilitated both personal reminiscences and more personalised vicarious participation in someone else's travel experiences. Whether viewed on screen or from the shore, passenger cruise-ships represented ludic spaces where unreal lifestyles could be indulged briefly. Holidays afloat were time out of daily routines in settings where technology re-configured distance and speed. Essentially escapist fantasies for those able to afford overseas vacations, cruise vessels were also a product of tight discipline, exacting labour, and wider uncertainties over company survival during years of commercial insecurity and economic depression. Exploring these nuanced meanings with reference to the work of individual filmmakers has clarified the significance of particular sequences and images.

By the early decades of the last century, notions of modernity, for some people, offered new ways of representing a universe that, according to Conrad (1999, 286), had "lost its fixity and anchorage." Central to the project of modernity were concerns about time, change, and novelty. In the aftermath of war, changed circumstances prompted the questioning and challenging of older certainties and existing structures—conceptual, ideological, material, and societal. People's lives, hopes, and fears interwove innovation and insecurities. New social and spatial freedoms opened vistas of mobility and opportunity unimaginable in pre-war and wartime conditions. While commercial cinema confronted audiences with endless variations upon "the everyday socio-cultural and geopolitical imaginaries and realities of everyday life" (Lukinbeal, 2004, 247) during the twenties and thirties, new travel possibilities permitted the means for more individual encounters with being elsewhere. If cinematic fascination with hotels/motels was emblematic of modernity's tempo, alienating effects and endless mobility, cruise-ships combined new spatial and sight-seeing possibilities with modes of travel and hierarchical service provision of an earlier era. The vicarious enjoyment of armchair travel, watching someone else's pictures of journeying within a floating hotel equipped with home comforts, seems to encapsulate contradictory desires for novelty and reassurance.

Such duality echoes the modern metropolitan hotel's role as mass provider of individualised private stopping spaces. Arguably, the passenger liner epitomised human technological achievement and also, after the sinking of the *Titanic*, its inherent weakness. Notwithstanding public response to loss of life on such a scale, doubtless understood differently in the aftermath of wartime casualties, Mies van der Rohe, in 1924, on behalf of modern architects, envisaged the turbine rather than religion as a determining influence of the age (Conrad, 1998, 276). Less obvious perhaps than aeroplanes and cars as symbols of life's changing tempo, the sleek streamlining of new vessels evinced new levels of efficiency, velocity, and endeavour. Sitwell's (1927) preamble to *All at Sea*, a vitriolic farce that parodies cruise passenger behaviour, expresses the prevailing ambivalence.[22] As a symbol of "swift and constant movement in every direction," the cruise-ship is a "thing of beauty" kept afloat by hard labour: "a crowd of people engaged in pointless movement, conveyed in suffocating and unnecessary luxury from place to place by an army of sweating and grimy workers." Despite their "loveliness," these "rusty hulks . . . like the cast shells of some great crustacean fallen from another planet . . . will one day seem the supreme monument which this age has left . . . " (Sitwell, 1927, 96–102). Such contemporary apocalyptic tones merge science fiction with the imagery of disaster movies. Modernity's eventual eclipse is paradoxically symbolised by their antediluvian bulk. Even as passenger-ships vie for coveted trophies (Conrad, 1998, 92), the possibility of obsolescence gains recognition too.

Among box-office successes too, the implied vulnerability of modern maritime technology seems unavoidable, even if cruise fiascos and flawed relationships afloat were usually treated lightly. Hints at wider aspects of societal instability occur within the numerous plots based on fraught relationships, duplicity, and estrangement, escapes from suburban ennui, misuse of inheritances, exposed identities or disappearance and murder. Unsaddled by commercial narrative conventions, the realism of much amateur reportage offers sometimes very direct testimony to social difference through its depictions of life on-board ship and the material evidence of ethno-cultural difference in every port of call. The enthusiasm, among some regional filmmakers, for filming liners at sea and also in dock at Liverpool and elsewhere is also understandable given such contemporary British documentaries as *Liner Cruising South* (Wright, 1933), *Shipyard* (Rotha, 1935) and others. For professional and amateur alike, as well as for some members of the public, watching the gradual construction of a "huge edifice towering over the town and its people" was compelling to observe, even if most amateurs were more interested, ultimately, in the associative vision of "the cruise life [than] the bloke that did the blinkin' rivet" (Low (1979, 96) on Paul Rotha's *Shipyard*). Perhaps even amateurs were not completely unaware of the economic context as their own filming opportunities mirrored the decline in building contracts and celebratory launches during the interwar years.

Despite cruise liners' iconographic status as symbols of modernity, travelling by sea essentially was slow. Turbine-driven vessels were undoubtedly faster than in the past but the widening social appeal of cruise holidays, as well as their enjoyment on screen, may also be understood as a reaction against modernity. Did cruise holidays represent a desire for less rather than greater acceleration and a preference for a different tempo among those able to afford leisure time? Innovation paradoxically sustains tradition, or rather invents a variant in which traditional routes convert from sea passages into passenger experiences predicated on travelling slowly and, in terms of energy expended, remaining relatively immobile. Privilege permits periodic escape from rapidity. If not completely motionless forms of travel, the seemingly carefree holidays afloat recorded by the moneyed classes of interwar Britain and elsewhere, denote a caution and confinement perhaps borne of wider uncertainties at home and abroad.

Did the pleasurable indulgence of slowness, to borrow Kundera's words (1995, 4), offer an antidote to anxiety, whether mediated by the cinematic screen or through direct experience? It is tempting to question whether the revival of interest in cruising holidays and the continuing popularity of films with cruise-related themes may equate with more contemporary global and societal uncertainties. Currently, over 50 million people worldwide book holidays afloat. The cruise industry is the fastest growing sector of global tourism and is dominated by the North American market. In one sense, modern cruises are the ultimate form of footloose and all-inclusive holiday, where even the marketing brand of a specific destination is jettisoned in favour of photo-opportunities in different stopping places stitched together by the ship's motion. Too much diversity occurs within today's industry to suggest its vacationers are searching solely for a reassuringly safe retro-chic trip out of place and modern time but, like its interwar antecedents, the promise and representation of an idyllic experience remains widespread.

Cinematic interest, within the past decade, meanwhile reveals that free-floating forms of paradise, even as they offer distance from terrestrial threats, can themselves become inescapable hellish nightmares as shown by *Speed 2* (De Bont, 1997), *Deep Rising* (Sommers, 1998), *Final Voyage* (Wynorski, 1998) and *Ghost Ship* (Beck, 2002) while Oliviera's *A Talking Picture* (2003) engages with the anxieties of contemporary life on existential rather than psychological levels. For almost a century, the floating hotel has been a potent symbol and versatile lens through which to expose societal concerns and behaviours. The gentility and restraint of amateur film material may be more oblique than commercial cinema in addressing interwar uncertainties, but its determined positioning of self and others at home and abroad for later viewing was, itself, a way of dealing with changing times and places. Arguably, so too was the decision to bring home travel footage of a motionless trip.

ACKNOWLEDGEMENTS

Sincere thanks are due to staff at the British Film Institute and the North West Film Archive (NWFA), Manchester Metropolitan University, England. This work is based on research funded by the British Academy and the Krazsna-Krausz Foundation.

NOTES

1. 'The Royal Mail Steam Packet Company. Motor-ships versus Steamships' *The Times*, 20 May 1925, p. 20; Richardson, Sir A. and Hurd, A., (eds) *Brassey's Naval and Shipping Annual*. Reviewed in *The Times*, 8 November 1927, p. 19.

2. 'P. and O. scraps Aurora's world cruise' *The Guardian*, 20 Jan 2005.

3. Northwest Film Archive (hereafter NWFA), Preston Collection: *Orient Line Cruise on SS Orama*. Accession nos. 1894, 1960D, 1964D, 1967D, RR481/21; British Film Institute (hereafter BFI), Finlay Personal Collection, Accession nos. 576251, 576256, 576258, 576635, 576643.

4. NWFA, Warburton Collection, *A Modern Bakery* (1931/32), Accession no. 707.

5. NWFA, Warburton Collection, *Sunshine, Sea Breezes and Strange Places: A Cruising Holiday*, Accession no. 1019.

6. NWFA, Preston Collection, *Orient Line Cruise*, Accession no. 1894.

7. NWFA,Weiner Collection, *Weiner Holiday to Ibiza*, Accession no. 4161.

8. See, for example, NWFA, Preston Collection, Accession nos. 1187D, 1961D, 1964D, RR481/21; Barker Scarr Collection, Accession nos. 229/14, 229/16.

9. NWFA, Barker Scarr Collection, Accession nos. 229/8, 229/13, 229/19. See also NWFA, Barker Scarr Collection, *Mediterranean Cruise: SS Arandora Star, May 1933*, Accession no. 3803.

10. NWFA, Barker Scarr Collection, Accession no. 229/19.

11. See, for example, the discussions prompted by society fancy dress partying trends in contemporary Britain; 'Renegade royal flouts the rules' *The Guardian* 13 January 2005; 'Royal family caught up in Nazi row' *The Guardian*, 13 January 2005;

'The very nasty party' *The Guardian*, 15 January 2005; 'Harry's crew' *The Observer*, 16 January 2005.

12. National Maritime Museum, Lascars – able seamen, Frequently asked questions: www.mmm.ac.uk/server/show/conWebDoc.17863 (accessed 24 May 2005); also, www.lascars.co.uk

13. NWFA, Preston Collection, *Orient Line Cruise on SS Orama*, Accession nos. 1894, 1960D, 1964D, 1967D, RR481/21; BFI, Finlay Personal Collection, Accession nos. 576251, 576256, 576258, 576356, 574798, 576635, 576643.

14. NWFA, Preston Collection, Accession nos. 1967D, RR481/21; BFI, Finlay Personal Films, Accession nos. 576251, 576256, 576258, 576356, 574798, 576635, 576643.

15. Deardon, N. (October 2002) 'Secret film exposes reality of working life on luxury cruise ships' *Red Pepper Archive*. Available at www.redpepper.org.uk/intarch/x-cruiseships.html (accessed 23 May 2005).

16. NWFA, Preston Collection, Accessions nos. 1187D, 1944D, 1945D, 1960D, 1964D; Barker Scarr Collection, Accession no. 3803.

17. NWFA, Barker Scarr Collection, Accession no. 229/14.

18. See, for instance, the arabesque arch framing a street scene of people in local dress against minaret towers and mosque dome, printed in black and white to accompany text advertising 'Blue Star Cruises by Britain's Wonder-Ship, "Arandora Star"' *The Times*, 22 August 1930, p.14.

19. NWFA, Barker Scarr Collection, Accession no. 229/10.

20. NWFA, Preston Collection, *Palma and Mallorca 1933*, Accession no. 1958D; Barker Scarr Collection, Accession nos. 229/13 and 229/14.

21. NWFA, Preston Collection, *Orient Line Cruise on SS Orama*, Accession no. 1894.

22. 'Arts Theatre Club, "First Class Passengers Only"' *The Times*, 28 November 1928.

REFERENCES

'Lighterman.' 'A Pattern of Loyalty' *PLA Monthly* (December 1957) www.lascars .co.uk (accessed 24 May 2005).

Aldgate, Anthony and Richards, Jeffrey. *Best of British: Cinema and Society from 1930 to the Present*. London: I. B. Tauris, 1999.

Alloula, Malek. 'The Colonial Harem' pp. 317–322 in *The Visual Culture Reader* edited by Nicholas Mirzoeff. London: Routledge, 1998.

Burton, Antoinette. *At the Heart of the Empire. Indians and the Colonial Encounter in Later Victorian Britain*. Berkeley: University of California Press, 1998.

Clifford, James. 'Travelling Cultures' pp. 96–112 in *Cultural Studies* edited by Lawrence Grossberg, Cary Nelson and Paula Treichler. London: Routledge, 1992.

——. *Routes: Travel and Translation in the Late Twentieth Century*. Cambridge, MA: Harvard University Press, 1997.

Collingham, Elizabeth M. *Imperial Bodies*: *The Physical Experience of the Raj, c. 1800–1947*. Cambridge: Polity, 2001.

Conrad, Peter. *Modern Times, Modern Places*. London: Thames and Hudson, 1998.

Cresswell, Tim. 'Imagining the Nomad: Mobility and the Postmodern Primitive' pp. 360–379 in *Space and Social Theory*: *Interpreting Modernity and Postmodernity* edited by Georges Benko and Ulf Strohmeyer. Oxford: Blackwell, 1997.

Fitzgerald, F. Scott. *Tender is the Night*. Harmondsworth: Penguin, 1939.

Foster, George M. (1986) 'South Seas Cruise: A Case Study of a Short-lived Society' *Annals of Tourism Research* 13 no. 2 (Summer 1986): 215–238.

Foucault, Michel. 'Of Other Spaces' pp. 229–236 in *The Visual Culture Reader* edited by Nicholas Mirzoeff. London: Routledge, 1998

Gottlieb, Alma. 'Americans' Vacations' *Annals of Tourism Research* 9 no. 2 (Summer 1982): 165–187.

Graburn, Nelson. H. H. 'The Anthropology of Tourism' *Annals of Tourism Research* 10 no. 1 (Spring 1983), 9–33.

Green, Alfred J. *Jottings from a Cruise* s. n., 1944.

Henniker Heaton, Rose. *The Perfect Cruise and Other Holidays*. London: Nicholson and Watson, 1935.

Hughes, George. 'Tourism and the Semiological Realization of Space' pp. 17–32 in *Destinations*: *Cultural Landscapes of Tourism* edited by Greg Ringer. London Routledge, 1998.

Hyde, Francis E. *Liverpool and the Mersey*: *The Development of a Port, 1770–1970* Newton Abbott, David and Charles, 1971.

Jameson, Frederic. 'Postmodernism, or the Cultural Logic of Late Capitalism' *New Left Review* 146 (July–August 1984): 53–92.

Jones, J. P. 'Lascars in the Port of London' *PLA Monthly* (February 1931) www .lascars.co.uk (accessed 19 May 2005).

Kern, Stephen. *The Culture of Time and Space, 1880–1918*. Cambridge, MA: Harvard University Press, 1983.

Koch, Gertrud. *Siegfried Kracauer: An Introduction*. Princeton: Princeton University Press, 2003.

Kracauer, Siegfried. 'The Hotel Lobby.' pp. 173–185 in *The Mass Ornament*: *Weimar Essays*. Translated by Thomas Y. Levin. Cambridge, Harvard University Press, 1995.

Lahiri, Shompra. 'Contested Relations: the East India Company and Lascars in London' pp. 169–181 in *The Worlds of the East India Company* edited by Huw Vaughan Bowen, Margarette Lincoln and Nigel Rigby. Suffolk: Boydell Press, 2002.

Lash, Scott and Urry, John. *Economies of Signs and Space*. London: Sage, 1994

Lett, James W. 'Ludic and Liminoid Aspects of Charter Yacht Tourism in the Caribbean' *Annals of Tourism Research* 10 no. 1 (Spring 1983): 35–56.

Louden-Brown, Paul. *The White Star Line*: *An Illustrated History, 1869–1934*. Indian Orchard, Titanic Historical Society, 2001.

Low, Rachael. *Films of Comment and Persuasion of the 1930s*. London: Allen & Unwin, 1979.

Lukinbeal, Chris. 'The Map that Precedes the Territory: an Introduction to Essays in Cinematic Geography' *GeoJournal* 59 no. 4 (April 2004): 247–251.

Mitchell, Don. *Cultural Geography: A Critical Introduction*. Oxford: Blackwell, 2000.

Mitchell, Timothy. 'Orientalism and the Exhibitionary Order' pp. 293–303 in *The Visual Culture Reader* edited by Nicholas Mirzoeff. London: Routledge, 1998.

Mitton, G. E. 'An Amusing Extract from *Peeps at Great Steamship Lines – The Peninsular and Oriental*" Published by Adam and Charles Black, London, 1913' www.lascars.co.uk (accessed 19 April 2005).

Norris Nicholson, Heather. 'Moving Memories: Image and Identity in Home Movies' pp. 35–44 in *The Jubilee Book. Essays on Amateur Film* edited by N. Kapstein, Charleroi: Association Européene Inédits, 1997.

———. 'Telling Travellers' Tales: the World through Home Movies, 1935–1967' pp. 47–66 in *Engaging Film: Travel, Mobility and Identity* edited by Tim Cresswell and Deborah Dixon. Lanham, Rowman & Littlefield, 2002.

———. 'British Holiday Films of the Mediterranean. At Home and Abroad with Home Movies, c.1925–1936' *Film History* 15 no. 2 (Summer 2003a): 152–165.

———, (ed.) *Screening Culture. Constructing Image and Identity*. Lanham: Lexington, 2003b.

———. 'At Home and Abroad with Ciné Enthusiasts: Regional Amateur Filmmaking and Visualizing the Mediterranean, c. 1928–1962' *GeoJournal* 59 no. 4 (April 2004): 323–333.

———. 'Sites of Meaning: Gallipoli and Other Mediterranean Landscapes in Amateur Films (c. 1928–1960)' pp. 167–188 in *Landscape and Film* edited by Martin Lefebvre. London, Routledge, 2006a.

———. 'Through the Balkan States: Home Movies as Travel Texts and Tourism Histories in the Mediterranean, c.1923–39' *Tourist Studies* 6 no. 1 (2006b): 13–36.

———. 'Shooting in Paradise: Conflict, Compassion and Amateur Filmmaking During the Spanish Civil War' *Journal of Intercultural Studies* 27 no. 3 (2006c): 313–330.

Pizam, Abraham and Mansfeld, Yoel (eds.). *Consumer Behaviour in Travel and Tourism*. Binghamton: Hawsworth Hospitality Press, 1999.

Rabinbach, Anson. *The Human Motor. Energy, Fatigue and the Origins of Modernity*. Berkeley: University of California Press, 1992.

Ringer, Greg (ed.) *Destinations. Cultural Landscapes of Tourism*. London: Routledge, 1998.

Sherwood, Marika. 'Race, Nationality and Employment Among Lascar Seamen, 1660–1945' *New Community* 17 no. 2 (Summer 1991): 229–244.

Sitwell, Osbert and Sitwell, Sacheverell. *All at Sea. A Social Tragedy in Three Acts for First-class Passengers Only*. London: Duckworth, 1927.

Stock, Ralph. *The Cruise of the Dreamship*. London: Heinnemann, 1922.

Waugh, Evelyn. 'Cruise (Letters From a Young Lady of Leisure)' pp. 15–21 in *Work Suspended and Scott-King's Modern Europe*. Harmondsworth: Penguin, 1943.

———. *Labels: A Mediterranean Journal*. London: Duckworth, 1930.

Chapter Three

Vacancies: Hotels, Reception Desks, and Identity in American Cinema, 1929–1964

Jann Matlock

"Do you have a vacancy," she asks.

"Oh, we have twelve vacancies. Twelve cabins, twelve vacancies," he answers, rifling through a large black volume that he places before her. "They, uh—they moved away the highway." The tired traveler, rain-drenched and hungry, stands expectantly, pen in hand. On her side of the counter is a register awaiting her signature. "Marie Samuels," she will inscribe in the book, as if for posterity, and when cued to give a home address ("just the town will do," he says, apologetically, as though he'd asked for something a little too private), she'll offer up the one on her newspaper, "Los Angeles" (Figure 3.1).

He is turned away from her now, picking a key from the pegboard that holds twelve of them: twelve keys, twelve vacancies. They are not actually cabins—not separate "housekeeping units" in a neat row divided by miniature "yards"—but rather just rooms, adjoining single-storied, basic bed-and-bath set-ups with desk, chair, and chest of drawers, with all the amenities of modern life: toilet, bathtub and shower spigot.[1]

His hand hovers over the keys, choosing, as if the rooms might have real variations between them—say, prettier wallpaper in one or a newer mattress in another. As she speaks her city name, his hand moves from above the third key to the one on the far left. "Number one," he'll say, pointing out the convenience of it being right next to the office: "If you want anything, just tap on the wall."

The kind of travel experience that Janet Leigh's character enjoys in *Psycho* belonged, in 1960 when the film was made, as thoroughly to the past as the highway that once furnished the Bates Motel with regular clients—and by this, I don't mean Marion's rendez-vous with the fateful shower. I am, instead, thinking about the encounter at the reception desk of the traveler's way station, about the process of registering writ large, but also about a

Figure 3.1. *Psycho*
PSYCHO ©1960 Shamely Productions Inc. Courtesy of Universal Studies Licensing LLLP

myriad of engagements that occurred at that front desk in the various spaces that welcomed transients—from palace hotels to residential hotels, from roadside taverns to small-town boarding houses, from cabin camps to motels. The reception desk marked the moment where travel stopped if only for a night, where a "space" was transformed, if ever so briefly by means of shelter and privacy, into a "place." The reception desk of the hotel is the space of identity, but it is also the place of a crisis over what identity might imply in modern society.

The hotel represented modernity in the nineteenth century, and it did so, historians have shown, from its foundations in that most "modern" of countries, the United States, and in the cities poised as leaders in a new market economy (Philadelphia, New York, Boston, Washington, D.C., and soon after, Chicago and San Francisco). Andrew Sandoval-Strausz points to the perfect suitability of the hotel to "a metropolitan age in which strangers, rather than being seen as threatening and warned off, were considered a normal part of the routine of the day" (2002: 6).[2] From its origins in the 1790s, the hotel had maintained a peculiarly ambivalent relationship to those "strangers" it housed. It collected their names in public registers and at times reported their data to the local and state police, but it nevertheless superficially promised them discretion and privacy—a haven from the outside world as well as from the moralistic gaze of social standards. At the same time, hotels served as the center point for towns large and small, bolstering their own reputations through their service as a social venue for the local society's elite. One read the hotel register, in fact, to know just how elite the society a hotel entertained, or to gauge the significance of the events — such as marriages and debutante balls — staged there.[3] One even read the register to pick up on information about places one might visit down the line or to see if another traveler had left news from one's home (Williamson 1975: 82–3).[4] One commentator, wistful about the fading of such practices, remarked on how the register had served to position travelers in relation to all those others who had passed that same way:

Down at the left-hand corner [the register] was always rumpled, where the inscribed leaves had been turned over as the years went oozing by. M. Bertillon, the well-known authority on Who Stole the Jam, could have spent a month in sheer ecstasy transcribing all those thumb prints. The pen was rusty, and as you entered your name, there was a squeak and a splatter appropriate to the importance of the occasion. Unraveling the mysterious chirography of your predecessor, you learned that J. Blennerhasset Oofendorffer at French Lick, Indiana, had also sat in the red plush sofa beside the potted plant. (Williamson 1975: 191)

This nostalgic paean to the hotel register evokes not just the lost age of traveling salesmen passing from town to town, identified as who they said they were because they said so (or at least because they were willing to sign something saying so). It also figures the very technological wizardry that by the end of the nineteenth century was already transforming how identity was understood — if not actually *produced*: first, the police surveillance techniques called anthrometry, those measurements of criminals' faces and bodies put into practice by Alphonse Bertillon in Paris beginning in the 1880s; and second, fingerprinting, which was not, in fact, Bertillon's discovery but rather what would come, in the 1910s, to replace the time-consuming and scientifically questionable techniques vaunted by the French police.[5] Hotel registers, like files in local and state bureaus tasked with registering foreigners, were regularly culled by authorities throughout Europe for information for the surveillance of foreigners,[6] but such data were used far less in the United States for keeping bureaucratic watch on outsiders than for advertising the appeal of a city as a destination, in the way that today statistics on foreign visitors might be reported to demonstrate a city's healthy self-marketing in the tourist industry.[7] New York City kept a "Stranger's List" in 1835 that recorded the names of all 59,970 "transient guests" registered in the hotels of the city in the period between February and September, but such information is a rare exception. Although this registration list gives a good idea how hotel travel already was transforming one of the most important cities of the nineteenth century, such data collection seems not to have been pursued beyond this brief moment in any systematic way in any American town. Hotel registration information was not even legally mandated by authorities in most states (Williamson 1975: 29, 180; Sandoval-Strausz 2002: 206–10).[8] The most scrupulously reviewed identification data seems, in fact, to have been that of women who were not admitted, according to the *New York Tribune* in 1885, to any hotel unless they could produce a letter of introduction or other evidence demonstrating "respectability" (Williamson 1975: 127).

Just as the hotel experience is one with a relatively short history, dating from the turn of the eighteenth to the nineteenth century in the United States and Europe, the processes engaged by hotel reception desks—ranging from checking in and out to collecting mail, from depositing luggage and valuables to arranging meals and further travel—are part of a bureaucratization of the hotel business that dates from an even more recent moment, the end of the nineteenth century. And just as identification cards—imitators of the passport "invented" in France at the time of the 1789 Revolution—have given way to retinal scans, handwriting analysis to fingerprinting, and eyewitness testimony to DNA typing, the processes that might occur at a hotel reception desk have increased, since World War II, in their technological sophistication as well as in their complexity and scope. Most remarkably, the kind of "signing in" that we witness in *Psycho*, the creation of a registration document without external verification by phone, telex, or credit card, was already obsolete by 1960 when Hitchcock's film premiered. Before technology made it hard to hide under a false name or behind a fake driver's license, Americans regularly walked into hotels and offered up a fantasy identity without anyone batting an eye. The period between the creation of rapid cross-continental travel—by train, car, and plane—and the jet age of lightning-speed verifications was not only an era of enormous mobility for Americans, but one of fluid identity. And that fluidity of identity was nurtured and even underwritten by hotels.

The cinema shared this fascination with both changing places and changing names. From its first decade, the cinema exploited the spaces of the hotel to suggest the surprising new worlds and new people that moving pictures could transport viewers to encounter. Biograph's 1903 *A Search for Evidence* accompanied a detective and a neglected wife on a journey of keyhole-peeping in hotel corridors in a successful attempt to catch her adulterous spouse *in flagrante* (Gunning 1988: 38). The early narrative cinema elaborated plots around the very conspiracies possible when strangers may turn out to be people other than those they seem at first glance: Feuillade's *Fantômas* begins, for example, in 1913 in a grand hotel—in fact, at the reception desk of the fictional Royal Palace Hotel in Paris. By the time of the early sound cinema, the hotel had itself transformed the world both for travelers and for city residents, and this is reflected in cinematic exploitations of the glamour of that world—with *Grand Hotel* of 1932 as the quintessential example—in films fascinated with the myriad possibilities of encounters across class and other socially constructed boundaries.[9] This essay is primarily concerned with the

United States in the period running from the 1930s into the 1950s—from the Depression through the wartime years and their aftermath—a temporal frame marked by high geographical mobility, profound political anxiety, and also, quite concretely, deeply problematic housing conditions both for those who wanted to put down roots and for those who, because of social or economic difficulties, were temporarily without a permanent home. I explore here how the cinema became, like the hotel itself, complicitous with the slippages of identity at work in this period; I analyze how the cinema made possible crises of identity and how it exploited those crises. I am especially interested in how the cinema registered a certain kind of passing—not just passing *through* but passing *as*—and what that passing meant for the travelers who were transported into other worlds via cinematically thematized hotels. In order to explore the fluid identities registered in the films of these two decades, I will be looking at films that move into and through hotels and motels, but especially at the processes engaged through reception desks in these films.[10]

WARPED ETHICS

"[O]ne is verily tempted to ask if the hotel-spirit may not just *be* the American spirit most seeking and most finding itself," wrote Henry James in *The American Scene* (1968: 102). The place of seeking and finding in the hotel, for American as well as other national spirits, is its control-central, the reception desk. There, one might check in, check out, request reservations elsewhere, or secure travel arrangements within and beyond the city. One could complain about one's room and request improved amenities. One could check for messages and leave messages, collect mail and leave mail. One might look for someone who had already checked into the hotel. Luggage could there be deposited or collected. Meals and entertaining could be arranged. Jewels and other valuables might be safely stored in the hotel safe—or collected upon receipt of appropriate identification. One could pay for one's stay. One might seek there words of welcome or reassurance, even just idle chat. Like a barman, the desk clerk entertained those needing human contact (and even psychotherapy): the uprooted and the alienated, those whose very status as strangers increased their vulnerability if not also their eagerness for connections. Most important, the reception desk served to focus the desires channeled through hotels, such as those described modestly by Anthony Trollope on return from his American travels in 1862:

> The things wanted at a hotel are, I fancy, mainly as follows: a clean bedroom with a good and clean bed, and with it also plenty of water. Good food, well

dressed and served at convenient hours, which hours should on occasion be allowed to stretch themselves. Wines that shall be drinkable. Quick attendance.
Bills that shall not be absolutely extortionate, smiling faces, and an absence of
foul smells. (1951: 480)

Trollope's desiderata seem mundane by comparison with the kinds of services
associated with hotels by the cinema of the mid-twentieth century. Strikingly
absent from this list, of course, are the "secret" services, ranging from gambling games to prostitution (See Groth 1994: 46). Equally absent are the ethical expectations projected onto hotels, such as discretion about who registers
there (and with whom), an appearance of luxury or at least of homeyness, and
a fantasmatic framework that operates outside the "real" world.

Warped doppelgänger[11] of the city in which it rises almost as high as the
most prestigious office building, the urban hotel is more than just, in Rem
Koolhaas's words, "a plot" unto itself (1978: 124); it is the space for plotting.
And it is especially the space of disavowed plots. The cinema's complicity
with such conspiracies makes it a privileged extension of the hotel world.
More significantly, the cinema's complicity makes it a mirror in which one
can see the trouble disseminated by the warped ethics of this warped space.
In his attempt to define the counter-sites in which "all the other sites that can
be found within [a] culture are simultaneously represented, contested, and
inverted," Foucault designated the hotel as one example of such a heterotopia (Foucault 1986: 22–7). Film theorist Giuliana Bruno points out that the
cinema, both in its material spaces and in its workings, similarly operates het-
erotopically for it serves as a separate space—what Foucault called "outside
of all places"—even though existing in real architectural terms (Bruno 1993:
57). Like the mirror that Foucault uses as emblematic of the heterotopia, the
cinema "makes this place that I occupy at the moment when I look at myself
in [it] at once absolutely real, connected with all the space that surrounds it,
and absolutely unreal, since in order to be perceived it has to pass through this
virtual point which is over there" (1986: 25).

The reception desk, that place where one signs up for a move into that *het-
erotopos*, is the frontier on which these complicities get exposed in the most
explicit of ways. The cinematic hotel does not so much mirror the society that
watches its film. It problematizes the very kinds of watching—surveillance,
spectacles, sideshows, stripteases—that society deploys for political and cultural purposes. *Le Sang d'un Poète* (1930–32), with its voyeurism sequence
at the Hôtel des Folies Dramatiques, provides a stunning example of such an
interrogation of the uses of vision. As this film illustrates, seeing beyond the
surfaces in hotels often requires Herculean efforts well beyond routine hotel
practices—a discovery that promotes thinking about real hotels and their cinematic doubles in a broader context than that of the ocularcentric.[12] As Bruno

argues, cinematic viewers are far more *voyageurs* than they are *voyeurs*. Cinema transports us into diverse cultural, historical, and psychogeographic architectures, and not just into a "fixed optical geometry" (2002: 6). The hotel as an architectural space—and even more so the film in its hotel passages— prepares the way for the workings of precisely such voyages.

The most significant plots of hotels, in fact, surround the invisible: what happens behind closed doors or up guarded elevators, what happens with lights out in locked rooms down dark corridors. Registering for the hotel is the moment of gaining permission to be part of that shadowy world, to seek what one might be able to find there, or to find there what one does not necessarily seek. When a film deploys cinematic time and space around the registration desk (making it what Bakhtin called a chronotope), it elaborates possibilities for exchange in that shadow world.[13]

"All margins are dangerous," Mary Douglas has argued. "Any structure of ideas is vulnerable at its margins" (1966: 121, cited in Torpey 2000: 12). In this essay, I contend that the reception desk functions, both for the hotel and for the film that moves through the hotel, as a margin that articulates vulnerabilities as well as dangers. It is the place of acknowledgement of being "not-at-home."[14] As the geographic locale of entering and exiting, the reception desk is also the (architectural) structure of being positioned, even framed. Identity is given a narrative form at the registration desk, which is not to say that an individual gains a life story or even, in Lockean terms, that an individual can remember having the experience of someone who has the same name.[15] Identity takes narrative shape in the hotel lobby because it is exchanged—for space or services. Trollope claimed the moment of registration to be particularly unnerving because the American hotel was structured around giving refuge to people who did not actually reside there:

> To the office, which is in fact a long open counter, the guest walks up, and there inscribes his name in a book. This inscription was to me a moment of misery which I could never go through with equanimity. As the name is written, and as the request for accommodation is made, half a dozen loungers look over your name and listen to what you say. They listen attentively, and spell your name carefully, but the great man behind the bar does not seem to listen or to heed you. Your destiny is never imparted to you on the instant. (1951: 486).

The extremely public encounter with the hotel clerk further inspired Trollope's anxieties at the point where he was, at last, discussing his room request: "'What do you mean by a dressing-room, and why do you want one?'" he describes being asked "before five-and-twenty Americans with open mouths and eager eyes," despite the fact that this is "a conversation that might be more comfortably made in private" (1951: 487).

Trollope concluded that the problem of this show of discourtesy on the part of the hotel clerk (and those seemingly encouraged by that clerk to leer even more discourteously) was related to the clerk's "battle against the state of subservience, presumed to be indicated by his position." Trollope relates this rudeness not just to the clerk's paradoxical position in the hotel environment—as having power as well as lacking it—but especially to the very core of American political culture: "that want of courtesy which democratic institutions create" (1951: 487). In contrast to James's ebullient praise of the hotel world as "a gorgeous golden blur, a paradise peopled with unmistakable American shapes," where "everyone is . . . practically in everything, whereas in Europe, mostly, it is only certain people who are in everything" (1968: 105, 103). Trollope was horrified by the way individuals of uncertain classes intrude on his experience at the frontier of public and private space. James looked out into the lobby of the Waldorf-Astoria at "the hundreds and hundreds of people in circulation" and wondered "who they all might be, seated under palms and by fountains, or communing, to some inimitable New York tune" (1968: 103). Trollope surveyed the lobby of his antebellum urban hotel and agonized about his own identity being put so visibly on display for—and by—those of lower ranks.

The class tensions evoked by Trollope belong to a series of tensions depicted by travel writers as articulated at hotel reception desks. James likewise evoked "promiscuity," euphemistically summarizing with this moralizing language the sexual tensions that he construed the American hotel as managing to repress (1968: 103). Geographer Paul Groth describes the difficulties encountered by women travelers in the late nineteenth and early twentieth centuries, particularly the hostility visited in even the grandest hotels upon women arriving unaccompanied (1994: 46).[16] Sandoval-Strausz provides rich evidence of the tensions around race that accompanied the Jim Crow era in American hotels (2002: 351–93). By the early 1930s when the cinema began exploring the possibilities offered by the hotel for narrative, spectacle, and cinematic profitability, these tensions marked (and even defined) American modernity.[17] It is as if the hotel film of 1928–1962—the period between the coming of sound and the break-up of the studio system—offered a privileged space for exploring some of the key tensions of contemporary life. The reception desk, as Trollope indicates in his representation of class anxieties in the hotel, served to measure the topography of these tensions. In the filmic context, it worked out point of view and narrative position (in relation to narrative space). It established orientation and disorientation. Especially, it made way for the narratives of identity banked on by films that transpire primarily in hotels as well as by films where hotels served as way stations. Within the filmic diegesis, reception desks frequently served to codify a character's identity, but they even more often served to expose that character as operating under false pretenses. In what follows, I look at how these filmic moments at reception desks work, both in relation to the films in which they occur and in terms of the imbrication of these films in a broader spatial, social and political context.[18]

ZIGGURAT PROJECTIONS

Unlike the American hotel lobby populated by strangers idling away the afternoon, the ground floors of the two Berlin hotels in the great films of 1924 and 1932 emerged far more as spaces for *passing through* than for passing time. While the former, Murnau's *Der letzte Mann*, does situate a lounge area off to the side of its cavernous lobby, it depicts movement within that ground-floor space as primarily centrifugal: the camera follows individuals going out much more frequently than it follows them coming in, a movement that parallels that of the hero in the comic version of the film (which ends with him riding away from the hotel in a carriage) while reflecting a greater preoccupation in the film as a whole with the doorman's departures—including the metaphoric one of the tragic ending—from the hotel. Similarly, the brilliant set designed for the Hollywood MGM studio shoot of *Grand Hotel,* plotted a circular space through which characters revolved, as through the famous spinning door,[19] itself repeatedly focalized as the frontier of the fantasmatic space occupied by the film. While Murnau's earlier work took us to the tenement of the doorman as well as into the streets in front of its Atlantic Hotel, *Grand Hotel* operates as if the building were impervious to the incursions of the city. Art historian Annabel Wharton describes its extraordinary Art Deco interior as "hallucinatory": "a vortex that entraps the spectator as well as the characters" (2003: 540). Wharton is correct in signaling the dazzling quality of the film's interior space, but she is wrong, I think, in imagining that the film closes both characters and viewers into that space. Like the Adlon-based Atlantic Hotel of *Der letzte Mann*, the fictional Berlin palace hotel achieves its Hollywood-incarnation tragedy by whirling its visitors out and away, whether in a wicker casket or in a taxi carrying them on to other destinations (as, for example, Kringelein and Flämmchen toward Paris). The class-based anxieties inherent to both these films can only be fully expressed if there is a danger of expulsion from the fantasy of belonging to this hotel world. In that respect, the space of *Grand Hotel* is best understood not as a vortex but as a ziggurat, a spiraling honeycomb tower modelled on that of Babel—with all the discursive confusion and especially all the danger implied by that model (Figure 3.2).[20]

Figure 3.2.   *Grand Hotel*

"The Grand Hotel. . . . People come. People go. Nothing ever happens," Dr.
Otternschlag famously announces at both the opening and closing of novel
and film, but with one significant difference. The novel makes the disfigured
Great War veteran depressive from the outset: "This is no life. No life at all.
. . . Nothing happens. Nothing goes on. . . . The world was a crumbling affair

not to be grasped or held. You fell from vacancy to vacancy." In the novel, what especially does *not* move Otternschlag is modernity in its diverse— even Baudelairean—dimensions ("Ocean flights, speed records, sensational headlines. . . . The noise and bustle nowadays. . . . Pictures of nude women, of legs, breasts, hands, teeth" [Baum 1948: 10, 11]). The world moves *around* him, however, in both novel and film. This modernity is more than just "morally emptied by the economic depletions of the depression," as Wharton suggests (2003: 540). This is a world that turns on all kinds of vacancy.

The hotel of the nineteenth and early twentieth century transformed the salon space of previous eras into a lobby. *Grand Hotel* literally whirls that lobby around its control center. The cinematic world of *Grand Hotel* (as well as the imaginary world for which it doubles) is, therefore, *moved by* a reception desk. And that reception desk is uniquely panoptic (cf. Foucault 1977: 195–228). While the panopticism of *Grand Hotel* stands alone in relation to actual hotel architecture of its era as well as by comparison to other filmic architectural space, it is suggestive of the power networks that underwrite the ideological workings of the reception desk in both real hotels and their filmic twins, an issue to which I return later in this essay.

The fantasmatic space of *Grand Hotel* is equally *moved* by the relation of that reception desk to the domed ziggurat that rises above it, a hotel design that mimicked the dome of the Printemps (1882–83) and Galeries Lafayette (1907) department stores in Paris, the Umberto I Arcade in Naples (1887–91), or Gropius' 1920s theater projects, building designs singularly unlike any hotels extant before 1932. The filmic hotel's corridors are organized like a beehive looking down onto the lobby but also visible from below by all who occupied that reception round-about.[21] The prototype for the kind of atrium hotel imagined by Goulding's 1932 film was the Brown Palace in Denver, opened in 1892 which, like its glamorous predecessor the San Francisco Palace Hotel (1875–1906), had a glass-roofed lobby with galleries, constructed around a hexagon that looked down over the lounge area (Denby 1998: 232). Unlike the fantasy space built for Garbo's entrances and exits, the actual early atrium hotels charted a space meant for stasis: sitting, waiting, watching.[22]

What does it mean for the great hotel film of the Depression to have centered, quite literally, its space around the reception desk? For one thing, the central desk gave the characters a convenient location to meet, as do, elsewhere in the film, other circular structures such as the round balcony-like galleries and the curvilinear bar. It provided, as well, a space for upper-class characters to interact with those not necessarily of their class, both those working in the hotel and those calling on hotel residents. In this way, the reception desk operated as a social leveler and, significantly, as the pivot for coincidences of fate, themselves central to the hotel-film cycle. Perhaps more

importantly, the pivotal position of *Grand Hotel*'s reception bureau obtains
the centrality of the *desires*—thematized and imaginary—of guests, with the
implication that the center-desk puts into circulation all potential demands
made on the cinematic space of the hotel: it spins forth those desires capable
of being satisfied and those desires quite thoroughly insatiable. Through this
mechanism, the film is capable of evacuating what is a threat to the order
established by the registration desk's invisible management, for example,
the broken side of war-wounded Otternschlag's face, or the little dachshund
who is literally swept out of the door at the film's conclusion, evicting any
reminder of the baron's scandalous murder. In all hotels, the reception desk
circulates guests' needs in order to recycle visitors: sent their way satisfied,
patrons will return. For *Grand Hotel*, that return will not occur in the film's
two-hour playing time, but rather only in the hotel's imaginary future, a
temporality evoked to inflame film spectators with a wish to belong to that
future. It is for them a future that requires an infinite projection in order for
the proclamation of "nothing happens" to seem plausible and not just ironic.
After all, one wishes that what happens in the space of a two-hour film to be
"nothing" in order that it distract from the events of the lackluster world outside the cinema. But one cannot escape a retrospective awareness of the irony
of the contrast of the distracting melodramas played out by Garbo, Crawford,
and the Barrymores, with what was happening outside hotels and cinemas in
1932–33, the year of the film's U.S. and European distribution (Hall 1932;
Kracauer 1933), as Hitler rose to power in Germany.

FRAMING PROXIMITY

The melodramas of *Grand Hotel*, preoccupied with what Kracauer called
"the gruesome proximity in the hotel" (1933: 1), nevertheless served for decades, along with Murnau's film, as the touchstones for what might occur in
filmic hotels. What made these dramas so powerful in the period between the
Crash of 1929 through to the beginnings of World War II was the way they
problematized (socially as well as spatially) the class relations that modernity
had allowed tenuously to endure. If the cinema is, as Vanessa Schwartz has
argued, the pinnacle of a kind of troubled and troubling modernity born of the
late nineteenth century and procuring its magic through technological prowess as well as fake intimacy (1998: 177–99), then the hotel film of the early
sound era forcefully emblematized that modernity by displaying the spaces
through which the urbanity of the modern had been made possible: department stores, palace theaters, and, of course, hotels themselves. By showing
the inner workings of the hotel world, films like the Marx Brothers' *Cocoa-*

nuts (1929) and *Room Service* (1938), *Blonde Crazy* (1931), *Gold Diggers of 1935*, and *Stage Door* (1937), and, in slightly lesser ways, *The Broadway Melody* (1929), *Trouble in Paradise* (1932), *Lady for a Day* (1933), *Dinner for Eight* (1933), *The Thin Man* (1934), *Top Hat* (1935), *My Man Godfrey* (1936), *Topper* (1937), *Midnight* (1939) and *Ninotchka* (1939) threatened to explode the values of modernity by problematizing the prestige accorded to the places through which the modern was mediated. By establishing the hotel as a space of coincidence, these films opened up a potential site of ideological tension in which class, sexual, and gender conflicts were negotiated.[23]

Both *Lady for a Day* and *My Man Godfrey* broach in explicit ways the problems of rootlessness and even homelessness born of the economic conditions of the Depression that will become, as we shall see, significant themes for the film noir cycle during the war decade of the 1940s. Both Capra's and LaCava's films begin by circulating around a grand hotel, the former because that is where a high-society scavenger hunt is taking place and the latter because the protagonist Apple Annie pretends to reside there. The latter film will substitute, for the hotel reception desk of the fictional "Waldorf-Ritz," a judge's bench (Figure 3.3), a useful reference point for thinking about the

Figure 3.3.   *My Man Godfrey*
MY MAN GODFREY © 1957 Universal Pictures Company Inc. Courtesy of Universal Studios Licensing LLLP.

potential workings of the hotel desk since no one participating in the game needs a room for the night—with the single exception of the "forgotten man" who is on the list of "things" required to be collected by the winners. The earlier film turns on two central sequences at the reception desk of the Hotel Marberry where street-vendor Annie has been receiving her daughter's letters for two decades but where, coincidentally, her ruse has been exposed just as her daughter sails toward New York with her fiancé and his father Count Romero. Without an address at the Marberry, Annie is terrified that she will not be able to make the show necessary to the Count's approval of this marriage. Without the pretense of a life like those whose financial and social standing lets them reside year-round in grand hotels, Annie risks failing to ensure her daughter's ascent into Spanish royalty. The improbable scenario of the screwball comedy ensures that the homeless "forgotten man" Godfrey can be transformed into a gentleman first through a job then through the love of the rich Bullock daughter. Similarly, the Capra twist on a comedy of manners procures a Cinderella story for mother and daughter alike through the intervention of the gangster Dave "The Dude" and his make-over team who give Annie the social graces appropriate to the mother of a future countess. Dave's crew even manages to call in enough favors to put on a reception at the Marberry attended by the mayor and the governor.

The two films get to their fairy-tale endings in slightly different ways, however, and with different prognoses for the future. LaCava's film makes Godfrey redeemable in part because he has always been *other* than a city-dump tramp: scion of a prominent Boston family, the "forgotten man" of the opening is a Harvard graduate who hit the skids when a relationship soured. After saving the Bullock family finances through his astute financial management, Godfrey leaves his employers to start a bar/restaurant, called "The Dump," that will employ and house the homeless. Because Godfrey has always belonged to the upper classes despite his brief foray into tramp life, he can easily exploit old social connections to invest the money that now gives value to the less fortunate lives around him. The conclusion to the film shows him making a further social ascent by marrying Irene Bullock, screwball female character par excellence, who trusted him with a job as her family's butler. Capra's Apple Annie will have no such ascent because she is no more of the class of Godfrey and the Bullocks than of the imaginary hotel resident Mrs. E. Worthington Manville whom she impersonates. Her achievement, like many a Capra figure who follows her, is a fragile one: she manages not to be unveiled as a poverty-stricken apple vendor; she passes successfully as a high-society lady long enough to ensure her daughter's fine marriage; she even guarantees her daughter's fortune through a bet won by the pool shark playing her husband. Perhaps most important, Annie is able to keep up appearances because her story, including the story of her attempt to pass as an American aristocrat for her daughter's sake, has had currency with city notables just as it initially appealed to the gangsters. When Annie is nearly forced to tell her daughter's future family that her entire identity has been a masquerade, the crowd suddenly swells into a reception of well-wishers far grander than anything planned by Annie's gangster friends, ensuring that no truths need be revealed. A good marriage is secured not by class mobility but by the silencing of the dirty secrets about class that even the poorest members of this society are prepared to keep. There can be no class mobility in this world because even those poised on the edge of homelessness, like the hustler called "The Judge," believe there are strict boundaries that even the best appearances of theater cannot dissolve. Asked to play Annie's husband, he initially refuses, claiming that to do so would be "acting too much!" Annie is "a mere apple vendor, practically a mendicant!" he rails, evidence that this man—who stays out of the street by snookering his monthly rent in low-life pool joints—views *himself* as more than a notch above *her*. But this film gives an important role to all those who see themselves as *above* the social status of the street people. Both the upper-crust thematized in the film and the middle-class filmgoers on whose success Capra's film depended were invited to celebrate Annie's success as a mother. And the film lets them do so, without any cost besides a few choked laughs: the film's conclusion assures us that a woman like her will not soon be infiltrating their hotels and their receptions. Even if the title fibs a little by announcing she will have been a *Lady for a Day* only, her masquerade has no legs to last beyond that special week. American high society remains untouched—all the more so since Annie's daughter moves up in the world through a marriage into *European* society.

The interactions in each of these films around hotel "reception" desks further highlight how each film negotiates class relations. I have been suggesting that neither *My Man Godfrey* nor *Lady for a Day* allows any more social fluidity than had *Grand Hotel* before them. In one respect, however, these films are not quite so rigid. Both socially marginal figures in these films have plans for the future. Godfrey actually acts in his own future to run a project to help the homeless. Annie has similarly plotted a future for her daughter. The "reception-desk" moment in each film focalizes the crisis of Depression-era poverty and elaborates the terrible inflexibility through which that poverty was perceived. The films use these moments to identify not just the characters and their desires, but to transform social marginality into a problem for each film to solve. What the films cannot solve, however, are the underlying prejudices that marginalize the already marginalized. "Are you wanted by the police?" the scavenger-hunt reception man asks Godfrey after taking his address as "City Dump 32." "No," says Godfrey, "that's the problem": he is not wanted by anyone. To be unwanted by family or job is nearly Annie's plight—except that she is indeed wanted, through mail addressed to her at the Marberry Hotel, by her daughter. And although she has more of a "home" than does Godfrey, her tenement boarding house suggests an existence in which dreams about her absent daughter may well be the only thing standing between Annie and the gutter. Indeed, when Annie appears at the hotel to collect the letter that her inside man has been unable to retrieve, she cannot turn on an appearance of propriety as does Godfrey after only a proper night's sleep in a bed and a shave in a proper bathroom.[24] Annie looks in this scene every bit the "beggar" that her social station makes her. In the first scene where she appears in the hotel lobby, the manager of the hotel even comes out from behind the reception desk, not to create proximity with her, but rather to obtain a different relationship than that created by having a counter between them: he is not there to serve her but rather to intimidate her into leaving the hotel. In the second hotel-desk sequence, he relays that job to several lackeys handily primed to put unwanted visitors in the street. In both these scenes, despite the polite appearances embraced by the hotel staff, class difference is depicted as so thoroughly calculable that someone like Annie cannot be allowed to pass through the lobby even for a few minutes. While hotel visitors' memoirs have often depicted the lobby as a stomping ground for many more people than those actually staying in a hotel, Annie's haggard exterior—if not also her gender—marks her as incapable of passing through that space unnoticed. This is true, of course, because Annie is not just looking to pass time in the hotel but because she has been *passing as* belonging to its registered guests. The occupation of hotel detective, a profession that grew contemporaneously with the rise of the American hotel, depended on identifying and expelling, from the hotels they served, troublemakers like Annie: individuals who did not match the expectations of hotel management, people who were not registered, and people who did not plan on registering in the first place.

CHECKING OUT IDENTITY

The Waldorf in 1945 employed 33 private policemen for a total of 42 stories—26 uniformed men and seven plainclothes detectives. Although it is hard to know what percentage of the detectives employed by agencies like Pinkerton's worked in hotels, this New York palace hotel's staff roster suggests how widespread the use of private eyes had become for policing the liminal public sphere of the hotel world ("The Waldorf-Astoria," 1945: 103).[25] The American hotel detective would, in the 1930s and 1940s, serve as the surrogate for the authority of the front desk and its invisible management. Not surprisingly, his filmic stand-ins demonstrate just what kinds of authority may be wielded in the spaces of hotels.

"The detective wanders in the emptiness between characters," wrote Kracauer, who imagined that in the detective novel (the prototype for the filmic mystery thriller of the 1940s), the private police might represent reason in the halls of hotels (2001: 93). Marc Katz has astutely pointed out that in Kracauer's early thinking about popular culture, the hotel lobby functions as a key locus of fantasy, with the reception desk serving as a kind of police bureau (1999: 137). This grants perhaps more significance to the powers of that bureau than either real life or popular culture accorded it. It nevertheless recognizes the centrality of fantasies about policing to the hotel world. The cinema of the 1930s and 1940s indeed imagined detection occurring in hotels with the goal of preventing tragedies like the murder of the Baron in *Grand Hotel*. The 1945 remake, *Weekend at the Waldorf*, even has a secondary role played by a detective—and no murder.

The impossibility of policing in the hotel world is equally foregrounded as a central theme of American cinema in these years. Superficially, the hotel becomes a useful double for the city because it seems so potentially "rationalizable." Because rights accorded to individuals in the public sphere are not necessarily preserved in this private sphere, the hotel establishes the possibility of an alternative disciplinary framework in which a different kind of surveillance might be employed in the interest of protecting those with the most money to pay for it. And yet, the filmic representations of that surveillance suggest that policing practices are no more effective here than in the world where civil rights are most thoroughly preserved. Indeed, as is often the case in the detective novel of the nineteenth and early twentieth centuries, those authorized to police hotels are revealed ineffective (*The Maltese Falcon* and *Don't Bother to Knock*), ludicrously bumbling (*Topper*), dimwitted (*Spellbound*), and even corrupt—as in *The Blue Dahlia*, where the house detective in an exclusive residential hotel turns out to be the murderer of the adulterous wife of a returning serviceman. Alternative networks for policing, outside the hotel authority, prove far more successful in revealing the inner workings of hotels and the private affairs of hotel patrons. Striking examples include *Crossfire* and *The Street with No Name,* where the military and the FBI, respectively, manage to unveil corruption where the local police can't or won't. Even more effective are the private citizens who appoint themselves detectives, such as the poison victim of *D.O.A.*, the military buddy of *Dead Reckoning,* and the brother in *Killer Bait*. The film world of the 1940s and 1950s gives little reason to imagine the hotel gumshoe outside the framework proffered by Lauren Bacall's Mrs. Routledge in *The Big Sleep* when she growls to Bogart's character: "So you're a private detective. I didn't know they existed except in books or else they were greasy little men snooping around hotel corridors."

What exactly hotel private eyes had the job of detecting remains uncertain, but Pinkerton's memoir suggests that, as in *Lady for a Day*, the real-world detective had a job of protecting the management's interests, especially, by limiting hotel owners' liability in case of theft or other misfortune (1984).[26] In this respect, the reception-desk personnel acted as a first line of defense in the work of detection, checking over the appearance, the signature and identification papers (including the letter of credit), the luggage, and ultimately, the behavior of hotel guests. Cinema of the late 1930s and 1940s frequently show these moments, implicating viewers in that process of checking over the identity of characters poised to move through the cinematic hotel space. These sequences are marked by a complicated process that invites film viewers into shifting identifications not always parallel to those created by the film as a whole. Despite the fact that the person checking into a hotel is frequently the protagonist, it is extremely rare for the camera to look from the exact posi-

Figure 3.4.   *Dead Reckoning*

DEAD RECKONING © 1947, renewed 1974 Colombia Pictures Industries, Inc. All Rights Reserved. Courtesy of Columbia Pictures.

tion of the person checking into the hotel, with *My Favorite Wife* providing one example. Nearly so rare are sequences where the camera looks from the place of the reception clerk (Figure 3.4).[27]

In films of this era, especially when a guest is checking into the hotel, the encounter at the reception desk is achieved in one of three ways: (1) through an angled shot that lets us see both figures (Figure 3.5, *D.O.A.*; see also *Monkey Business, Somewhere in the Night*, and *Don't Bother to Knock*); (2) by means of a profile shot that uses the hotel desk to split the screen between the clerk and the patron (e.g. Figure 3.6 *Fallen Angel*; see also *My Favorite Wife*; *Killer Bait*) or (3) with over-the-shoulder shots and even, occasionally, in the manner of classical Hollywood narrative suture shots, shot–counter-shot exchanges[28] (Figure 3.7, *Impact*, see also *Dead Reckoning*).

Each film gives its own meaning to the way it frames these exchanges. One of the most complex sequences, containing almost every imaginable variation of point-of-view and shot framing, occurs in *My Favorite Wife*, a screwball comedy that revolves around the disappearance of Nick Arden's photographer wife at sea and her reappearance seven years later—a film made, not inconsequentially, in 1940, contemporaneous to Amelia Earhart's disappearance and when wartime was already eclipsing civilians along with

Figure 3.5. *D.O.A.*
Public Domain.

Figure 3.6. *Fallen Angel*

soldiers on the European front. Garson Kanin's film productively uses sutur-
ing point-of-view shots at the reception desk of a hotel where Arden is going
on a honeymoon with his new bride just as his "former" wife turns up alive
with hopes of reuniting. The camera also lets us look from the points of view
of the various individuals who are not in on the surprise as well as from
that of the one person who *is* in the know, returning wife Eve, in a way that
compares the experience of each individual as he or she comes to "get" what
is going on. In a similar way, a number of films noirs exacerbate the tension
around their characters' falsified identities by letting spectators look through
the eyes of, or over the shoulder of, a suspicious desk clerk—a prime example
being the exchange over Bogart's alias, "Allan Linnell," in *Dark Passage*,
which I discuss in the following section.

Manet's *A Bar at the Folies-Bergère* (1881–82) has long served art historians as a model for the way a picture can problematize point of view. As T. J.
Clark famously contended, the painting depicted an exchange that was so hard
to pin down perspectivally that it forced new questions about relationships—
both relationships in space and relationships in general (1984: 239–58; Collins
1996). The woman who stares over the counter at the painting's viewer cannot

Figure 3.7. *Impact*
Public Domain.

possibly be the same one who is leaning toward the man with the top hat. The point of view of the person who, like the painting's viewer, is engaging the barmaid's eye cannot possibly be the same one we see in the mirror cozying up to someone dressed just like the barmaid. "Little by little we lose our imagined location, and because of that . . . our first imaginary exchange of glances with the person in the picture is made to appear the peculiar thing it is," writes Clark. When we cannot take up the place of the gentleman mirrored behind the bar, the picture puts us in a "kind of suspended relation to the barmaid, to ourselves as viewers, to the picture itself as a possible unity" (1984: 251).

Something similar happens around reception-desk exchanges in films of the mid-twentieth century. A rare registration sequence, such as the ones in *Journey into Fear* and *Psycho*, will even use mirrors in a manner reminiscent of Manet's strategies. Filmic mirrors, of course, do more than just show the other side of what we are looking at. They remind us, as do painted mirrors, that we are not really there. Our absence from the filmic mirror jolts us as spectators into an awareness that our identifications with narratives are ficti-tious.[29] Mirror sequences like these do not just serve as *trompe-l'oeil*, tricking our eye into thwarted expectations; they serve as *trompe-désir*, taunting us that we cannot get here what our bodies lurch after through space.

Film achieves effects like those in Manet's painting through nuanced jolts to our expectations. Most of the complexity around perspective, space, and point of view devolves in the filmic sequences of our corpus from the way editing transforms our understanding of the possible places from which we, as spectators, can see. Those possible positions are not voyeuristic[30] anymore than the one of the man standing at the bar of the Folies-Bergère, but rather far more caught up in the movements of travel and the transports of masquerade.

The *voyageur* at the filmic reception desk is a traveler through space, but he or she is often also someone who passes. Just as the barmaid in Manet's painting is, in Clark's words, "detached" by her failure to appear in the mirror (1984: 254), reception-desk sequences in war-decade films have a remarkable way of intensifying the disconnections that marked so many interrupted lives on and off screen. The vacancy in the painting's mirror evokes a locus of incommensurable desire in exchanges like those of the café-concert bar (1984: 254–5).

The exchanges around the reception desk, especially in post-war thrillers, evoke other kinds of vacancy as well. First, at a superficial level, as for example in *Dead Reckoning*, they elicit our investments in characters who

Figure 3.8. *13 rue Madeleine*

might put faces on those lost either in the war or because they would not fit in at its conclusion. While the meeting between guest and clerk in these 1940s–1950s films usually makes us external witnesses to their exchange, the moment of registering frequently emerges, however, as a point-of-view shot in which the film spectator sees the signing through the eyes of the hotel client (Figures 3.8–3.12).

Second, sometimes there is enough of a disjunction between the registering guest's point of view and what we see on screen to introduce tension into our relationship to his quest. The point-of-view shot at Bogart's character's registration in the Southern Hotel turns out to be an impossible identificatory position, something we notice all the more when we see, explicitly from his point of view, the letter written to him by the wartime pal he seeks there.[31] Third, through their site-specificity (in a place of registering passage) and their sight-dependency (deploying point-of-view shots to establish spatial and narrative relationships), these exchanges transpire as *mises-en-abyme* for the anxieties around identity in a world where old forms of rootedness no longer function.

Troubling space as well as identity, these films set up moments of spying at registration desks that put pressure on spectators by asking them to take up

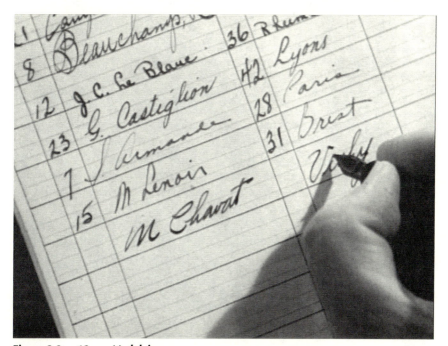

Figure 3.9. *13 rue Madeleine*

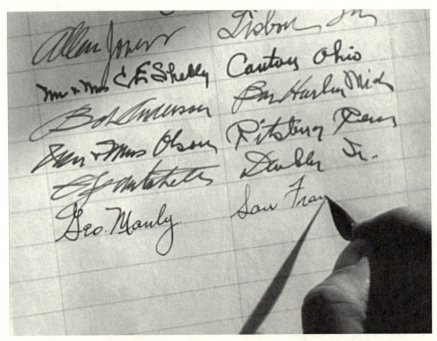

Figure 3.10. *The Street with No Name*

a place in relation to the story and its ideological implications. The moments where a character looks at prior registrations, either thumbing through the book to look at other signatures (as in *The Street with No Name*) or scrutinizing another character's signature (as for example do Constance in *Spellbound*, the desk clerk in *Impact,* the Nazi spy in *13 rue Madeleine*, and both Norman Bates and Inspector Arbogast in *Psycho*), insistently invite our identification with the person reading the register.[32] These point-of-view shots around registrations are significant since they position the film viewer as signatory as well as detective—authorized or not—of signatures. In doing so, the films that pass by the hotel reception desk manage to explore in exacerbated ways the meanings of identity.

BODY TRACES

The woman stands at the desk in a red cross-backed dress and an elegantly draped headscarf. She rings. The desk clerk emerges from where she has been watching television in the back parlor. "Is something wrong?" she

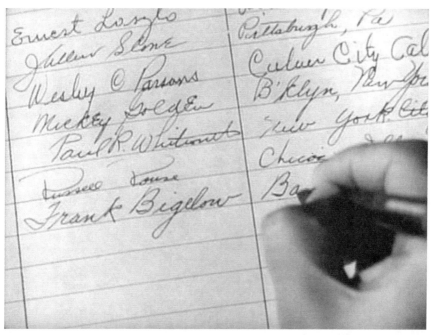

Figure 3.11. *D.O.A.*
Public Domain.

asks, then starts. "Oh, I'm sorry. I thought you were the other woman," she says, confused. "No, I'm me," announces her client. How can we be certain, as Moira Langtry in *The Grifters* pretends so self-assuredly to know, that we are who we say we are? How do we share this knowledge with others? What enables us to guarantee this knowledge? Sociologist Gary Marx delineates seven types of "identity knowledge" including "(1) legal name; (2) locatability; (3) pseudonyms that can be linked to legal name and/or locatability."[33] In addition to a person's name, address, and social security number, one might find aliases, behavior patterns, and social associations used as techniques of identification in Western societies. The signature in a hotel, combining a legal name and other identifying information, traditionally provided an "open sesame" for obtaining a place within: "If the customer can be accommodated," advised one hotel guide, "he is invited to sign the book, that is to enter his name and various particulars, concerning his residence and time of intended stay in the proper register. After which he is given the number of his room" (Meunier 1961: 21). According to Sandoval-Strausz, "The signing of the hotel register marked the creation of the relation between hotel and guest, with both parties establishing their

Figure 3.12. *Killer Bait*
Public Domain.

roles in written form." This signing had a "clerical" purpose, but it "also operated as a means of supervision" (2002: 215).[34]

The contract between a hotel guest and management was, significantly, not just one of trust regarding payment. It equally implied a spatial contract: the hotel management depended on the guest to tell the truth about who would occupy a particular space.[35] The efficiency of a reception department depended, claimed hotel guides, on the clerks' ability to provide information about guests (Meunier 1961: 21). Ostensibly this information had a function of helping others to find guests, but it served, as is obvious from one hotel writer's description of a particularly exemplary head of reception, far more purposes than keeping guests happy: "[He] could draw from memory a plan of every room, with every piece of furniture in it, . . . knew by sight and name and number every guest, and had a full record of every guest, including the dubious, with particulars of his sojourns, desires, eccentricities, rate of spending, payments (even to dishonored cheques)" (Meunier 1961: 194). The conjunction between being allowed to use space and the signature that authorized its use created a one-to-one relationship not just between a particular person and a particular space,[36] but between a particular identity and a place that would, temporarily at least, substitute a room number for that person's name.

"An effective system of identity depends on stabilizing personal identity," argues historian Jane Caplan (2001: 51). Writing who you are in a book alongside information about your address, your occupation, and the name of the person who referred you[37] creates an illusion of stable identity for the hotel that lets you take your place within it. A signature, according to Béatrice Fraenkel, "refers to absolutely every other thing. It belongs to that category of signs . . . of identity [that] indicate an individual's characteristics in such a way as to enable recognizing him. . . . The traced becomes a trace, charged with manifesting the presence of a unique body that is singular, inscribed on the page." One of the most interesting aspects of Fraenkel's treatment of the signature is her insistence on its relation to the body. Through gesturality, our signatures become extensions of our bodies. The signature is thus not just a metonymy, but a synecdoche: the determining detail (1992: 8, 10).[38]

The hotel registers signatures as a way of contracting the presence of individuals in its space. But its creation of these records is not, as the mid-twentieth-century cinema reminds us, just a matter of requiring a contract. Hotel registers serve as the archive for the hotel's transients, purporting to identify them well beyond their presence in its spaces. The registers serve as arms against the "empty forms" that Kracauer imagined in the hotel lobby, "ungraspable ghosts" who sink into the anonymity of the hotel space (1995: 183).[39] Like all signing of permanent records in the modern world, the signature in the register operates as a weapon against the manifold deceptions perpetrated in societies where transactions with strangers predominate. One could sign an alias in the register, but hotels seem to have taken a cue from Victorian graphologists in believing that the handwriting sample recorded there would betray the identity of guests even if the name was false.[40] As early as the 1850s, expert witnesses were engaged in legal proceedings to argue that handwriting, especially signatures, demonstrated that someone had been present (or absent) in a transaction with financial or moral consequences. Mid-twentieth-century films passing through hotels occasionally testify to the continuing belief in a human immanence conveyed by a signature, as we see when detectives pore over records in *Impact* or when Detective Arbogast compares Marion Crane's real signature with the one in the Bates Motel.[41] Most of the time, these signatures have a less-than-scientific status while nevertheless recalling that, in Diana Fuss's words, "identification . . . makes identity possible, but also places it at constant risk" (1995: 45).[42]

"You'll have to sign again," the clerk of *Grand Hotel* informs Kringelein when this demanding guest moves from his first to his second, much improved hotel room, but we only see that signing from a distance, over the clerk's shoulder, and amidst the swirling distractions of the hotel lobby. One of the earliest materializations I have found of a registration book in a film appears in Fritz Lang's *You Only Live Once* (1937), a proto-noir thriller that uses the characters' signing into a hotel to communicate that the couple has gone on their honeymoon: we are shown the sign for Valley Tavern, then the Valley Tavern Register with "Mr. and Mrs. Edward Taylor, Room 7," inscribed on the full screen, then the image of their marriage license (as if we need proof they are not just passing as a married couple—perhaps since, as the film will eventually demonstrate, they cannot *just pass* as ordinary citizens given Taylor's criminal history), and then the starstruck couple. Soon after, the film will show the process of identification engaged in by the hotel owners, behavioral determinists who pore over old detective magazines in search of the "real" identity of Taylor. According to the male proprietor, this is because "When he asked me for a room I asked him for his name and I looked him right in the eye and that young woman gave me a funny look!" The film cannot decide if the owners were, in the amateur detective's words, "right to be suspicious." On the one hand, it makes the events of the couple's fall partially the result of being thrown out of the hotel in the middle of the night for Taylor's being viewed as a "jailbird" (an assignation that he can never live down in the society of the 1930s depicted here, even though he has served his prison time for robbery and has been released for good behavior). On the other hand, the film seems almost as suspicious as the characters who refuse to give second chances to convicts, since it shows Taylor resorting to violence when fired from his job, consorting too easily with criminals from his past when the chips are down, and finally shooting the priest because he does not believe he could have been pardoned for crimes he didn't commit. The film has signed Taylor over to outsider status. The hotel register's early materiality gains thus another, more sinister, significance, for it marks this couple's position, from the moment of their marriage, as lacking a permanent home.

Just before the film's conclusion, Taylor poignantly tells his wife he imagines her "inside a house." He projects that at the end of their escape they will have the real home he has been seeking for them since the night they were thrown out of the Valley Tavern. Gunned down as they attempt to run away from a roadblock, they are given implicitly by the film a permanent home in death. The film's narrative framework is much more cynical, for we know that its appeal was to readers of detective fiction such as the hotel clerk. The film in effect fulfills a promise to put them where they belong rather than allowing them to linger in the heterotopia of the hotel.[43] Neither able to let its characters wander through hotels nor to allow them to steal away into imaginary domestic spaces, the film signs its characters over to non-places, first to the highway and then to the freeway of information that is the tabloid press. Is this perhaps paradigmatic of the way film characters escape hotel living—by engaging with the damning terms of filmic fate?[44]

Two films from the decade after World War II articulate in particularly complex ways the significance of signatures as legal touchstones, and they do so by thematizing hotel registrations. *Impact* and *D.O.A.* both turn on a character's signature, used in the former case to resolve the crime and exculpate the film's male protagonist, and serving in the latter case as the justification— quite literally—for the hero's murder. Films of the post-war period frequently show an interest in signatures, ranging from the graphological skills employed in *Spellbound* by Bergman's lovestruck psychoanalyst to find her patient/beloved in the Empire State Hotel[45] to those used by Detective Arbogast to determine that Marion did indeed stay in the Bates Motel under an assumed name. Others use the moment of signing into a hotel to articulate danger, as in *Dark Passage*, where the hotel manager has checked out the hero's luggage and appearance, but finds his name, Linnell, "very unusual"—a moment in the film that evokes an expression of alarm from Bogart's character who is seen there in one of the rare point-of-view shots from the vantage point of a hotel clerk.[46] The shift in *Dead Reckoning* from a false point-of-view shot when Murdock signs in, to a believable identificatory position when he reads his friend's message, evokes two relationships, one between the spectators and Murdock and another between the two men who fought together in World War II. Sometimes, as *Dead Reckoning* reminds us, the things we read at hotel desks are not only the signatures of guests, but messages sent for them to collect. The threatening anonymous message we read with Robie in *To Catch a Thief*, for example, relays the significant information that Robie is *not* the cat burglar while inviting the spectator's identification with the threatened Robie, thus heightening the anxiety of that threat and the need to keep it at bay by finding the real thief.

Impact similarly appeals to the viewer to identify with a process of detection, although always at a remove from the documents we peruse. In this film, the narrative lure consists of the protagonist finding proof that his wife conspired to kill him and that, furthermore, his wife's lover was charged with the task. Things become especially complicated when the hero is charged with killing the boyfriend. As is often the case in film noir, everything about the moral structure of the narrative encourages us to cheer when the murderous boyfriend perishes by his own fault. We cheer again when the naively trusting husband survives to fall in love with a war widow whose service station needs a real man to keep the local cars chugging along. But the law will have other views on the matter. If Walter Williams cannot prove the boyfriend was up to no good, he'll face the gas chamber for what the film has shown to be unadulterated self-defense. As in *The Postman Always Rings Twice*, an accident brings the "repressed," secret plotting to the surface of the text and into the courts. In contrast to the Cain plot where the conspiring adulterous killer was convicted of murder by accident, this protagonist is proven innocent by coincidence. By chance, his wife's lover exploded in a stolen car in the mountains. By chance, his wife forgot her boyfriend's checked luggage at the airport hotel and left the room key in her coat. By a stroke of luck, the servant is able to retrieve that key which unlocks the dark secrets of that baggage—and the untoward signatures—of the conniving wife.

Those signatures become the focus of the film's investigation in ways that reveal not only the wife's true identity but also her trajectory away from the marital home posited by the film as its ideal. The first time we see the wife signing something, we don't know why the hotel clerk pauses to give us a point-of-view look at her signature card. We know, of course, what he does not: that she has told her husband she is staying home with a toothache, which makes her signature under a false name all the more damning when she fills out that registration card in an airport hotel late the same night. The fact that the film dwells so long on her filling out this card suggests in a less-than-subtle way that her "signing" there will come back to haunt her. By the time we watch her, much later in the film, penning a telegram under that same alias, the film has primed us to expect a signature as a smoking gun. And indeed, this turns out to be the case. The hotel registration is not enough to prosecute the wife for conspiracy to commit murder. She may have checked into a hotel instead of nursing her dental woes, but adultery does not rhyme with murderous intent. The damning detail comes from her signature on two photographs, one given to her husband and the other to her boyfriend. Found in the luggage room of the hotel, the signed photograph of her lover in his unclaimed suitcase demonstrates conclusively for the court that she planned to meet him there the night he rode into the mountains with her doting spouse. The wife has set her husband up to be killed, planned to cash in on his estate with her beau, and has gone to the hotel to meet him—only to find the dead never come on time. Once she learns that her lover has died that night, she has vengefully sought to send her husband up for murder only to have that plot backfire too. Her signature in a series of unexpected places—the hotel register, the telegram, the photograph—ultimately ensures that she will pay for her evil ways.

Whereas *Impact* aspires for hotel signatures to reveal true identity, *D.O.A.* is far more anxious about the relationship between an individual's presence and the written performance of a name on official documents. *Impact* believes, albeit tenuously, in presence while *D.O.A.*'s documents testify only to absence. Rudolph Maté's 1950 noir depicts a heroine who is as good as the wife of *Impact* is evil. Paula serves as the film's archivist, unraveling at a distance the original location of the signature that has made her lover's life go awry: Bigelow has been poisoned, the film shows viewers early on, then traces in flashback his attempt to find out who did so and why. The murder turns out to be the result of a series of coincidences resulting from Bigelow's normal occupational activities. This accountant and notary has simply witnessed a bill of sale six months before for a stranger passing through his town: "All you did was authorize one little paper," says Paula. *D.O.A.* is the quintessential film about signatures and we see them materialize twice in point-of-view shots, once on a hotel register at the Alison Hotel in Los Angeles and again at the car rental where Bigelow's shaky signing shows his failing health and increases the tension about whether the self-authorized detective will find his own murderer before it's too late. The fact that Bigelow is a notary serves the plot in significant ways since it makes him extraneous to the machinations between gangsters and adulterers that led to the murder of one Eugene Philips and ultimately, as part of their murder cover-up, to his own poisoning. Because Bigelow had signed that "one little paper out of hundreds" one morning months before, he could prove that there had been a real bill of sale for goods that were later found to be stolen merchandise.

Notaries possess privileged witnessing capacity in the Western societies that have employed them since the middle ages as what Kathryn Burns calls "truth's alchemists." A notary's truth, explains Burns, was recognizable because of its "very regularity," through the use of formulaic templates that gave documents the force of "state-sanctioned 'official' writing." The notary could not make things true as such, but he made them true "in law" (Burns 2005: 352, 360, 352n11). Thus, *D.O.A.*'s casting Bigelow as a notary makes him function as guarantor—of the identity of the person whose contract he has witnessed with his signature.[47] That we see Bigelow sign into hotels twice, in San Francisco and in Los Angeles, underlines the role his signature plays in this film, not just an attestation of presence at the vacation's border-checkpoint, but the crucial gesture that has determined the course of his life.

Jacques Derrida has argued that for a signature to be "readable" it has to be "able to be detached from the present" and from that specific moment in which it was "intended" to "mark and retain" the presence of its author (1988: 20). The reiterability of a notary's signature represents the perfect example of a case where, as Derrida pointed out in his critique of Austin, a signature's value resides in its reproducibility—up to the dangerous point of seeming manufactured—recognizable precisely because always the same. Theorists of handwriting in the nineteenth century (contemporary to the rise of the hotel in America and Europe and to its use of the hotel register to hold its patrons' identities) argued that every man's handwriting was distinctive,

yet they also were firm in advising individuals to ensure their signatures
were not only distinctive but reproducible: Lord Chesterfield wrote his son,
for example, that all gentlemen and all men of business "write their names
always in the same way, that their signatures may be so well known as not
to be easily counterfeited" (cited in McGowen 1998: 406).[48] *D.O.A.* enlists
its viewers to reflect on what makes a signature "readable." It queries what
makes witnessing a signature valid and problematizes the "having been
there" of the notarial oath. It does this, in part, through spotlighting that
oath's uncanny double: the hotel clerk's witnessing of the guest's signing in.
D.O.A. enlists spectators in a riveting, tension-filled investigation that mo-
tivates our interest not through the revelations of its knotted plot but rather
through the charms and foibles of its main character whose struggle to learn
his murderer's name is paralleled by his struggle to decide if he loves his
girlfriend Paula.

One could argue that Paula is to blame for everything. After all, in the bar
scene just before his departure for San Francisco, the film has likened her to
Bigelow's murderer by having her switch her glass with his—just as the murderer will later do. Everything is especially her fault because she looks out for
her irresponsible boyfriend. Not only did she record, months ago, information
in the notarial ledger that her lover had himself "forgotten" to document, but
she has given information over the telephone to people who have used it to
locate, follow, and poison Bigelow. The pressure for marriage she has been
exerting on the jolly bachelor is, furthermore, depicted as his reason for flee-
ing their desert town of "Banning" for a San Francisco vacation.

But Bigelow is also represented as complicit in his own downfall. Flirt-
ing with every skirt that comes within inches, he is already exposed when
registering at his first hotel as gallivanting if not yet two-timing. In the
Fisherman's Club where he is poisoned, he loses track of his drink because
he has moved around the bar to seduce a pretty blonde. The barman's care
in "following" him with his drink might have been a useful service, but his
bourbon has been switched with a "luminous toxic matter" while Bigelow
is busy charming *his* prey. Bigelow gets responsible only when he is dying.
Only after he has been poisoned does he pay attention to the contents of his
notarial records and to the people with whom he has done business. Only
when he seeks his own killer does he care for detecting those people's real
names and real activities. Though his trade is in signatures, only too late does
he take charge of knowing the meaning of his own autograph.

His dying oath of love to Paula suggests that this film's protagonist has
changed—although with only the value that such a change can imply in an
obituary. *D.O.A.* thus operates retroactively, through its framed flashback
narration, to remember Bigelow as a brave, loving man. At the same time, its

narrative frame undermines this prospective memory. A document appears in the film's final sequence: a missing person's report filed by the San Francisco police at the request of the doctors who first diagnosed Bigelow's condition. "How shall I make out the report?" one of the detectives has asked the captain after they have listened to Bigelow's account of his murder. "Better make it 'dead on arrival,'" the captain has answered, providing an explanation to the film's title as well as the meaning of the letters that stamp the film's final frame: "D.O.A." does not just mark Bigelow's demise in the homicide detective's office; instead, it implies that the person who has just told his story for the previous seventy minutes is being "filed" as never having been present. This film signs its protagonist absent through death, both without a story (because none is recorded in the file we see) and with one—the film itself. In this respect, the film takes the notary's place, procuring for him the formulae that can structure an account of having been present.

Narratively, much of the noir cycle operates under terms that parallel the notary's gestures. Offering formulaic variants for recurring stories of betrayal and loss, these films frequently represent their dying protagonists testifying through flashbacks. The noir cycle thereby returns obsessively to crimes connected to characters' double identities, either metaphorical or literal. One might attribute this fascination with aliases, covert operations, and double lives to the narrative requirements of the thriller. As we see in the following section, however, the noir cycle's concern with slippery identity is emblematic of conditions in the wartime and immediate post-war era: geographic mobility, disrupted social relations, housing crises, and anxieties about foreignness and foreigners.

RUNNING OUT OF PLACE

"Give me an Eight o'clock call!" a man cavalierly demands of a young female usher in the movie-theater aisle next to where he is settling in for the night. A 1945 Goodyear Airfoam advertisement in *Life* magazine depicts the man in his pyjamas and slippers, so joyously comfortable in the Goodyear Airfoam Chair of his local cinema that he would prefer sleeping there (Airfoam Advertisement 1945: 11). The previous pages of the same year-end issue of the popular weekly showed some of the conditions of the world outside that imaginary movie theater. In caricature series, we see a veteran's return from the front, from his giddy discharge up through his return home—to posters announcing "Housing shortage worst in 100 years." Alarmist accounts of looming diplomatic crises, spiraling inflation, and severe unemployment (initial predictions in 1944–45 claimed that 3 million would be without work

Figure 3.13.   *D.O.A.*
Public Domain.

in the post-war economy) had indeed greeted the return of more than just the fictional soldier, "Sad Sack."(Baker 1945: 9–10).[49] Of these predictions, the one that had the most enduring effect on the post-war years was surely the housing crisis. As late as 1950, *D.O.A.* would show a San Francisco newsstand with headlines announcing the sale of thousands of new housing units—an indication that even five years after the war, the housing crisis still had such an enduring valence that news reports about the creation of homes could help define what the doomed man has lost (Figure 3.13).

The National Housing Agency reported that three and a half million new housing units were needed in 1946 just for returning veterans, but fewer than a half million could be accommodated. Want-ads showed desperate apartment seekers as well as ambitious entrepreneurs, such as the offer in an Omaha newspaper of a "Big icebox, 7 by 17 feet inside. Could be fixed up to live in" ("The Great Housing Shortage" 1945: 27). The Republicans campaigned in 1946 with the slogan, "Under Truman: Two families in Every Garage" (Bennett 1996: 5). Forty percent of returning soldiers were still living with families and friends in 1947. Even in 1950, 14.8 million Americans were living in substandard housing (Jezer 1982: 177; Kaledin 2000: 61–5; Bennett 1996: 280–7).[50]

Hotel settings serve a special function in working through these anxieties: First, because the housing crisis of the 1940s was overwhelming enough to serve as a powerful metaphor for the rhetorical and literal rootlessness of the era. Second, because the exchange at a hotel front desk made material a process of owning identity, therefore enabling these films to elaborate plots around the value/validity of the identity lodged in these moments. Third, hotel settings evoke tensions about belonging—to a class, a gender, a sexuality. Fourth, these moments explore the space around the practices of taking a place, and in doing so in the most filmic of ways, they make the site of the hotel into a mechanism for other kinds of motion—in the sense that Bruno evokes when she explains how cinematic movement elaborates structures for the passions (in her parsing of the word *cinema* and the word "e-motion") (2002: 6–7, 64). Films passing through hotels create frameworks for thinking about transience—especially for thinking about the kinds of transience we might associate with the post-war period—rootlessness, homelessness, and exile. Postwar films passing through low-end hotels tempt us to imagine that these kinds of transience are only fleeting occurrences, a function of a turn of hard luck or the current housing shortage. Yet these films also convey a looming anxiety about the endurance of these new ways of being out-of-place. Just as social scientists of the post-war period embraced for the first time a widespread discourse about "identity"[51] the popular discourse of the 1940s and early 1950s in mass-market magazines, advertising, and Hollywood cinema revolved strikingly around what it might mean to elaborate that identity in relation to a place.[52]

For many returning veterans, the warmth and comfort of a movie theater was likely to have seemed far preferable to the kinds of housing available. Indeed, Edward Dmytryk's *Crossfire* shows a veteran holed up in an all-night cinema while waiting to be proven innocent of murder.[53] And while films of the post-war years don't otherwise, to my knowledge, show veterans taking up residence in movie theaters, they do represent in extraordinary ways the crises around housing that *Life*'s advertisement implicitly evoked. The films of the forties and fifties reiterate the difficulty of having a place to belong, or even just of finding a place to sleep for the night, and in doing so, they reflect on what it means to be a transient or a stranger. While only a few films evoke literal foreignness as a key element of this marginality, nevertheless national and ethnic otherness—depicted as growing threats by the forties' popular press—emerge through these films' obsessions with outsiders.

Film thrillers of the post-war years evoked these anxieties in powerful ways, especially *Key Largo* (1948) and *Touch of Evil* (1958), both taking place almost exclusively in hotel spaces and each struggling with national identity, foreignness, and the expectations of individuals about what home can mean. One might equally point to the anxiety-producing representation of the post-war moment in *The Blue Dahlia*, a film whose murderer's identity had to be changed along the way away from the traumatized veteran to the slimy hotel detective (Naremore 1998: 107–11).[54] Moving through a series of high-, medium-, and low-priced hotels, this Alan Ladd vehicle shows the hero, recently discharged Lieutenant Commander Johnny Morrison, seeking a hotel room after the death of his wife: "We haven't had a vacancy in eight weeks," the desk clerk tells him, apologizing for being unable to direct him to any alternatives. When he at last finds a skid-row hotel on Santa Monica Boulevard with space, its comforts leave more than a little to be desired:

"You call this dump a hotel?"

"That's what the sign said. Clean sheets every day they tell me."

"How often do they change the fleas?"

The housing crisis has so jammed Los Angeles-area hotels that even this tenement with "Rooms by the Day or Week" demands the ten dollars rent *in advance*. After a scuffle with the men who brought him there, Morrison decides he still wants to take the room—"if you're sure nobody's dead in it," he tells the manager. This sleazy hotel seems to offer little respite to someone who returned from the front a hero, but there are no other options. Ironically, the worst aspects of the hotel's conditions will help Morrison break the case and free himself from police scrutiny. As a result of the manager's nosy ambitions to exchange safety for his fugitive resident, the framed photograph of Morrison's son breaks, revealing a message from his wife: "the charge is murder," reads Johnny who must now prove that the real culprit was the character the film calls the "hotel peeper," a man who claims that he was "tired of being pushed around by cops and hotel managers." Unlike the head-injured veteran, Buzz, who was the screenplay's original choice for the murderer, or nightclub owner Harwood who has been fooling around with Mrs. Morrison in her husband's absence, the detective can be made guilty without the film bearing ideological burdens. Except for one: the film lumps together all the places that rent short-term lodging to such an extent that the resort hotel of Malibu, the luxury hotel where Harwood lives with his unhappy wife, and the tenement hotel with peeling wallpaper all seem equally unsettling. Like the "Exclusive Wilshire Boulevard Hotel Bungalow" residence where Johnny is only barely admitted to his own wife's apartment without being announced, all these places bespeak a disrupted relationship to place. All these characters—both the veterans and the gangsters, the wives and the girlfriends, perhaps even the cops and the detective—seem to lack permanent roots, and they pay for their inability to find somewhere to belong. It seems only logical that Morrison's small son has died during the war, not of diphtheria as his wife claimed, but in a road accident. The child's death is only one element of this film's striking pessimism. Despite its happy resolution where the veteran is proven innocent, his old army buddies are freed from suspicion, and the new girlfriend relieved of her marital ties, much is amiss. Johnny has become a killer—even if in self-defense—strangling one of Harwood's goons and shooting Harwood. His nerve-jangled military pal seems likely to hurt someone in the near future. And the new couple still has a housing problem. Perhaps *The Blue Dahlia* offered as happy a plot for returning veterans as most audience members could have hoped for in 1946: the story of what might develop when you hitch a ride down the highway with a beautiful blonde who isn't afraid of strangers.

The war looms large in a number of other films that rotate their characters through grungy boarding houses and trailer camps: *The Killers* avoids explaining the Swede's lost years between the fatal night in a Baltimore hotel when he understood his lover's betrayal and his murder in a barebones rural boarding house, but the dates of his "disappearance," 1940 to 1945, suggest military service. *Cry Danger* puts its returning veteran and his "friend" the ex-convict in a trailer so rickety they comment, "It's a wonder it didn't fall down before we got here!" The film playing inside the theater where *Crossfire*'s Mitch hides, *Cornered*, is even a further filmic account of a post-war veteran's difficulties.[55] Those films that do not explicitly thematize their male characters' military service often raise questions about what these draft-age men did in the wartime years and what put them into a situation where run-down hotels were their homes, with examples including *Black Angel, Born to Kill, Where the Sidewalk Ends, Detour,* and *Fallen Angel.*

The war-era Hitchcock film that shows its protagonist living in a low-rent boarding house, *Shadow of a Doubt*, moves him from there into two other spaces, one fantasmatic—the luxury hotels where he has victimized bored, rich women—and the other idealized, the cheerful small town of Santa Rosa, California. When Charlie comes to visit his sister Emmie's home in this film that invites us to imagine its world as contemporary with its 1943 premiere, he is idealized by his family and the townspeople who eagerly invite him to speak to their civic group about the places he's traveled. But no account is provided to explain those travels—especially not the war. This is a film in which, strangely, the war seems almost to disappear, invisible except for the occasional presence of men in uniform in a few street scenes and war posters on a random wall.[56] Charlie is supposedly interesting to Emmie's club because he has seen far-flung places, as a veteran might have, but with the

implication that—unlike a soldier in a world at war—he has had a choice in
what lands he toured. And yet, what was he doing wooing widows without
husbands? Why so much interest in the heroism of travel except that other
heroes at the same time would have been more deservedly idealized? It is
as if *Shadow of a Doubt* creates a shadow *world* in which the war looms as
powerfully in its absence as the ideal of home operates in a parallel presence.
The fictive nature of the war's absence serves in turn to suggest that home is
perhaps just as fictitious. Later Hitchcock films will allude much more explicitly to the war and not without parallel investments in the anxieties about
home evoked by hotels. From *Spellbound*'s adventures in the Empire State
Hotel for traumatized war veteran Doctor John Ballantine who suffers from
amnesia, to French resistance fighter Robie's jaunt under an assumed name
through Monte Carlo's palace hotels to catch a real jewel thief and nab a rich
heiress played by Grace Kelly in *To Catch a Thief*, Hitchcock figured the war
as fathomable only through movement out of the home.

The noir hero's detachment from traditional bourgeois home comforts was
not just a metaphoric state, but a material condition of the period between
the worst years of the Depression and the early 1950s.[57] Beginning in the
Depression years, well over half of the renters in American moved annually,
a figure that would drop in the post-war years only because of the paucity of
places to move. The percentage of Americans in 1947 residing in the same
dwelling as in 1940 was barely one third, suggesting how much having a
home had been disrupted by the war (Tobey et al. 1990: 1402–3).[58] While
repatriation threw large numbers of returning veterans and their partners
into situations where they were obliged to stay with friends and family, it
also drastically increased the number of people living in residential hotels
or boarding houses. Mobility figures comparing periods before and after
the war show that people's geographic associations changed markedly. This
understates, however, an even more significant aspect of transience in the
1940s, the movement during the war of 15 million civilians (Adams 1994:
119). Women especially relocated, drawn by work in the war industries, with
seven million of them following their military spouses, or simply seeking an
alternative to the life they had before the war (Chafe 1972: 140).[59] World
War I had drastically increased Americans' uses of hotels of all levels: one
of twelve Americans was residing permanently in a hotel in 1920 (Groth
1994: 88). World War II would do this even more so, with occupancy rates
as high as 82%, as Groth has shown: "Wartime meant expanded employment. New hotels of all ranks were built or converted for war demands,
and each wartime boom stretched all existing hotels to their maximum potential—and sometimes beyond. War industry workers packed into lodging
houses and rooming houses while the better hotels did thriving business with

war-material brokers, production engineers, government officials, and military officers" (1994: 265, 181–2). Despite the expanded need for hotels and the booming variants of their services, the decades before and after the war also correlated with increasing questions about the propriety of hotel life. By the late 1930s, palace hotels had begun to seem decadent. Commercial hotels were associated with traveling salesmen's excesses, such as wild parties and debauchery (the marketers' convention in *D.O.A.* gives an idea of the myth). Residential hotels and boarding houses were connected, in Groth's words, with "people who symbolized social and personal failure" (1994: 196).[60] Anxieties revolved around the anonymity of residential hotels, but also about the ease with which people could pass there for someone they were not, as in the hotels Raymond Chandler described where "nobody except Smith or Jones signed the register" (*High Window*, cited in Groth 1994: 221).[61]

The extraordinary mobility of the wartime period made possible entirely new identities in ways that the noir cycle spotlighted. From *Dead Reckoning*'s war hero (operating under an alias to escape prison for a murder he didn't commit), to Mitchum's doomed gas station manager in *Out of the Past*, noir repeatedly invited its characters to take assumed names and reinvent their lives. While only a few of those operating covertly are represented explicitly as having served overseas, the men and women of post-war noir seem to thrive on the crises that made slipping from one identity to another easy if not profitable. Films in the post-war years (1945–52) with characters who pass at some point for someone else include *The Blue Dahlia* (Morrison), *Spellbound* (Ballantine), *Detour* (the voice-over narrator, Al, passes as the man he has accidentally killed), *The Killers* (Ole Anderson, "the Swede"), *The Stranger* (Welles's devious Nazi, Franz Kendler), *Notorious* (Alicia Huberman), *Born to Kill* (the psychopath Sam Wild), *Dark Passage* (Vincent alias Allan Linnell), *The Street with No Name* (the FBI agent), *Impact* (the wife, her lover, and later, her husband), *Killer Bait* (the brother of the femme fatale's dead husband), *D.O.A.* (Rekubian passing as Reynolds), *Cry Danger* (the false witness), *Macao* (the detective), *Don't Bother to Knock* (Nell, who pretends to be the woman for whose child she's babysitting).[62] The central conflict of a melodrama of the war's end, the 1944 *I'll Be Seeing You*, underlines the extent to which this filmic obsession with passing is a function of the war's often traumatic disruptions. In this film, Joseph Cotten's GI covers up his war-induced psychiatric disorder while the young woman he has met on a train likewise hides her obligation to return to prison to serve out her term for accidental manslaughter. While the film lets the characters hope for a future at the film's end, it also implies that the war will have disrupted the lives of many returning veterans' girlfriends and wives in ways that a happy ending cannot palliate.[63]

One might be surprised to find so few of the shadowy women of noir operating under assumed names, but the very nature of marriage, under most U.S. state laws until the 1980s, meant that it gave women a new alias, as was the case for "the Swede's" lover Kitty in *The Killers* or the two-timing bigamist Mrs. Cora Chandler in *Dead Reckoning*.[64] And one did not even seem, in many states, to need to be using one's real name when one married to gain the new name of one's husband, as Sean Connery's character would comment to the covert operator Marnie in Hitchock's 1964 film: "You can sign Minnie Q. Mouse on a marriage license. You're still married." What differs, I think, for noir characters is that the women's disconnectedness is less correlated to geography. Jayne Russell's Kitty tells Mitchum's wandering veteran in *Macao* that she doesn't know if she's looking for "a person or a place." His response: "there are lots of places," an oblique allusion to his New York City home from which he is uprooted because of a pre-war bar fight that left a man dead. Whereas Kitty is shown opportunistically seeking a good situation, a regular singing gig or a plantation to run, Cochrane wants to go home.

The GI Bill made going home in a material sense possible for record numbers of veterans and their families, particularly favoring male veterans and excluding anyone whose discharge implied propensities other than heterosexual.[65] Two million veterans took out loans under the GI Bill, although banks still required these individuals be good credit risks, as *The Best Years of Our Lives* anxiously reminded viewers with a scene where a veteran returning to his bank manager's job has his job threatened for being too trusting of a veteran loan-seeker. The radically increased accessibility of money to buy businesses and homes nevertheless allowed veterans to achieve, as historian Lizbeth Cohen argues, "substantially higher median incomes, educational attainments, home ownership rates, and net worths than non-veterans of comparable age" (2003: 138).[66] The implication was that for the men and women who were not among the 13 million GIs returning to civilian life after World War II, home ownership—and the income required to achieve it—remained out of reach. Rosie the Riveter got no housing loan. Neither did her compatriot, that woman who kept the gas stations and hotels of American running while the men were off at war.[67] If she was lucky, she got herself a veteran, as *Key Largo* demonstrates.

John Huston's 1948 thriller rewrote the gangster film, casting *Little Caesar* star Edward G. Robinson as a washed-up, deported gangster attempting a comeback as a counterfeiter. It also revised the political romance, recasting *To Have and Have Not*'s Bogart–Bacall team and presenting tough-guy Bogart with a conflict where, as in that 1944 account of the resistance in Vichy Martinique (or in the earlier *Casablanca*), he will have to decide between defending democratic principles or protecting his own personal interests.

Whereas those earlier wartime dramas showed Bogart's character's decision as a complex one, achieved at great personal sacrifice, *Key Largo* loads the dice. Frank McCloud (Bogart) is homeless, rootless, jobless, without family, without even the army buddies whose courage has bolstered him. When he walks into the well-appointed lobby of a Florida resort hotel during the off-season, he seems to be looking opportunistically for a fantasy he heard about from one of those pals, killed during the war, all the more so since the narrative gives him no official mission (he is not carrying any messages, letters, photographs, memorabilia, or medals, though he finds all of these, belonging to his dead friend, in every room of the hotel). A new battle, this one involving gangsters, Native Americans, disabled old men, and a comely war widow, looms quickly on the horizon. The traditional question of the hotel, "What's your name?," is here asked not at its registration desk but at the bar, its architectural double, and that question is asked not by the hotel management but by a gangster moll whose boyfriend has taken over the hotel. The owner of "Hotel Largo," "Dad" Temple, will be defined by his widowed daughter-in-law, as carrying a weight for the Native Americans as if "he's the United States of America," a formula that rhetorically frames the film's quest—protecting "Dad" and Nora Temple from harm—as an allegory. The events of the one long stormy night nuance what aspect of America needs protection, just as Frank's own position as hero is challenged. The official police are only too pleased to assassinate a couple of Native Americans whom they have wrongly suspected of killing one of their own. Rocco the gangster may well have a valid beef about having been deported despite thirty years on American soil—as if his Italian ancestry distanced him from the civil rights one would have assumed due a permanent U.S. resident. In fact, despite all their differences, Rocco shares with Frank a rootlessness that even predisposes the former to give the sheriff a false address ("Hotel Central, Milwaukee") even as it leads the veteran to answer the same question even more elliptically: "Frank McCloud, no address." "What's *he* doing here?" asks the sheriff about Frank despite having remarkably not inquired what Rocco, alias "Howard Brown," and his party from the Hotel Central were doing so far from Milwaukee. The answer, provided by Frank, "Passing through," underlines the extent to which this is a film about multiple kinds of vacancies.

Key Largo creates an emptiness at the core of post-war identity in order to present its protagonist as having, through a replay of his wartime heroism now on American turf, to achieve new fulfillment in the ideal of putting down roots, connecting to a new family, finding a partner, joining a community, and adopting a profession. But that profession, running a small resort hotel, is still one caught up in transience. That community, despite its connections to Native Americans whose ancestors "go back to the gods," still consists, as the hotel world always does, of a swirl of strangers. Despite the fact that the hotel is ready-made for an enterprising former army major, it will remain a space haunted by the brutality through which Frank has won the heart of the widow of his army pal. When Nora announces to "Dad" at the end, "He's coming back to us," the film tellingly does not show that home-coming, leaving our last image of this family's future as one without its hero present, and our last image of McCloud still at sea. The telephone lines are no longer dead, which is why Frank has managed to call "home," but the lobby of the previously well-kept fishing hotel is now littered with the damage wreaked by a hurricane, a half dozen gangsters, and a vigilante sheriff. The film lets us see McCloud acting violently only in self-defense— alone against the bad guys and with no alternative but to use his gun—but it also embraces a value structure in which one shoots gangsters to kill and asks questions later.

Key Largo nonetheless remains an immensely moving film because it does not boil the war down to a momentous past event that makes permanent heroes of those who fought. It powerfully questions growing Cold War demands for a politics of exclusion, first through the subplot of the revenge-killing of the Native Americans, and then through the out-of-character positions embraced by the otherwise kindly Temple when he rages that people like Rocco should be "exterminated," and by Rocco himself when he complains he was deported as if "I was a dirty Red or something." *Key Largo* also demands that the battles fought in World War II have a lasting value for the world inherited by its survivors. But it is nevertheless peculiarly optimistic about the world that it produces as a replacement: this broken hotel with the USO dance girl and a wheel-chair bound man who offer roots to the hero.[68] Their eagerness to have the veteran "regard [them] as [his] family" seems not only too convenient but immensely trusting. It is as if none of them has ever seen a film noir. At the film's end, as at its beginning, they seem not to have a clue what can happen when you take up with strangers.

"Movies have taught us to want buildings that bend to our desires," states David Thomson, imagining ways that cinema creates "challenging alternatives to fixed or built realities" (2000). When McCloud walks into the Hotel Largo, the film frame positions him in an interior space as expectant as the bus scene that preceded this sequence in which McCloud's face is reflected in the bus driver's mirror. It is as if this stranger, shot in the hotel lobby from the side of the reception desk, is waiting for another mirror to fragment his body. He seems to be waiting for something like the cinema frame itself to invite the curious gaze, tracking his relation both to ideal bodies and to the ideal architectural spaces constructed according to the classical tradition on the model of those bodies.[69]

Critics like to remember that Jacques Lacan visited the Czech spa town of Marienbad during a 1936 conference where he supposedly first delivered his mirror phase essay. While this anecdote has a humorous resonance in terms of the mirror-filled Resnais film in which the characters circulate anxiously through a spa hotel, it is perhaps most interesting for two other reasons: first, for articulating what Bruno has called "the geography of transience" (Lacan moving through a spa hotel); and, second, for evoking the soon-to-be lost world of those Czech spas. Edward Dimendberg has underlined the "breakdown of spatial and temporal convergence in the present [that] pervades film noir" (2004: 130).[70] Noir is the exploration through cinema of the late 1940s of what it might mean not to be able to use architecture to remember. This is partly a matter of not being able—yet?—to evoke a cinematic architecture of desire that will match the ideals of the post-war era. It is also about interrogating the kinds of ideals marketed as attainable and the conditions through which they may be attained.

The movement of soldiers "from foxhole to park bench to ranch house," as Todd DePastino describes the years between 1945 and 1950 (2003: 224) not only exacerbated the fantasmatic weight of "home," but it stigmatized those living outside that ideal. First elaborated in advertisements for consumer goods newly available after the war, "home" came to mean clean sheets, vacuum cleaners, and cars, described evocatively in one *Esquire* magazine publicity spread as "so much a part of home." Like so many of the advertisements that accompanied the veterans' return, this one showed an imaginary suburbia with couples walking their dog down streets lined with large houses, picket fences, lights in every window. The car in the driveway was billed as "part of home," even if it was designed, in fact, to take residents away from home (Studebaker Advertisement 1945).[71] Similarly, the publicity campaign of the Hotel Statler in December 1945 transformed a hotel suite into a perfect home for returning paratrooper Frank Lillyman—accompanied, notably, by his wife and toddler daughter. In the same *Life* magazine issue that depicted returning veterans struggling with unemployment in a "community not altogether ready for them emotionally or industrially," Lillyman "loll[ed] in the Pennsylvania's five-room George Rex suite" receiving free of charge "tea in bed every morning, candles on the table at dinner, a maid for his daughter, Strauss waltz records, dill-pickle midnight snacks" ("U.S. Normalcy" 1945: 30; "Soldier at Ease" 1945: 43–6).[72] "Some of us have idealized home and America," wrote Charles Bolté, author of a book about the veterans' dilemma much debated for its criticism of anti-communist propaganda: "We may be shocked when we see what the country really is" (1945: 57).

By checking its characters into hotels, post-war noir demanded that its spectators have a good look at the real conditions of those the GI Bill did not

launch into the new middle classes. The desk scenes in post-war noir repeatedly evoke anxieties about identity even as they position their protagonist, like
the film viewer, in relation to a window by means of which one might satisfy
desires. Behind the desks are frequently dozens of small cubby holes, each
one corresponding to a place for a key, messages, perhaps even cards (like the
one signed by *Dead Reckoning*'s Murdock) that allowed the representatives of
"control central" to prepare to provide those services that hotel-management
experts claimed would be "invaluable to travelers" (Sandoval-Strausz 2002:
167). Those frame boxes are the synecdoche of the dozens of identical rooms,
arranged in neat rows and stacked on top of one another, as were the private
spaces of most hotels from the early nineteenth century through to the standard-
ization of the luxury hotel by the Hilton Chain in the 1940s. Those frame boxes
represent both spaces of the imaginary (think of all the things happening in the
private rooms of a large hotel at the very moment when someone is checking
in) and spaces of transparency (like the cells of the panopticon, imagined by
Jeremy Bentham, the hotel management promises to see inside the individual
cubicles just as we see inside the boxes from outside the desk). Those boxes
also represent spaces of danger—with everything that we can't see now, everything that has been inside those boxes and their corresponding rooms at one
point or another, everything that may have been made to disappear here, from
stolen jewels to dead bodies, treated as if it had never taken place. In the words
of *Love in the Afternoon*, that archetypal Cold War romance about domestic
espionage in the Paris Ritz: "there are 7000 hotels in Paris and 220,000 hotels
rooms in them, and in approximately 40,000 of them, especially on a night like
this," there are things happening that could easily lead to crimes.

HAUNTED PLACES

One of the earliest films to represent a haunted space, Pathé's *Maison Ensorcelée* (*The Bewitched House*, 1907), shows a group of weary travelers stumbling into shelter where they discover that the monster living in the house's
painted portrait is not eager to have them sleeping in his bed. Before the night
is over, they will have been teased, shoved around, and finally, unceremoni-
ously dumped into the forest where, ostensibly, they will wind their nomadic
path toward better future lodgings. While the film's point is that the empty
house stumbled onto by the travelers was *not* a hotel, the anxieties about
sleeping out evoked here recall the very material hauntings of all hotels. No
matter how generic the furnishings, we always know that a stranger has been
living in this very space. No matter how clean the room, we always know that
someone else has been sleeping in our bed.

The hotel's inherent "unhomeliness" (the *Unheimlichkeit* of Freud's "uncanny") finds representation in the cinema, through far more than just seamy surroundings or anxiety-producing accounts of robbery and crime. Orson Welles's *Touch of Evil* expands these anxieties further than any other film of the Cold War years, taking viewers on a mesmerizing tour of three border hotels. In this chilling spectacle of frontier-crossings, no hotel is safe or comfortable—to recall terms evoked by Susie Vargas when she begs her husband to let her stay in a motel on the American side of the border. At the Mexican St. Mark's Hotel where the couple has been on honeymoon, there are no shades on the window, making it easy for someone to trap her in a flashlight beam and watch her undressing from across the way. At the Mirador Motel, nobody even bothers to register guests in the bound volume dedicated to that purpose, but the "nightman" has known about Susie's visit just as he has let Grandi's hooligans drug themselves and the sleeping American (whom we also assume they also violate in other ways). Finally, visits to the sleazy Ritz Hotel bookend this honeymoon with horror. Susie has been first taken there just after the bombing by Grandi's messenger boy, ostensibly to intimidate her into calling off her husband whose high-level government position makes his meddling anathema to this brood of small-time gangsters. After the Mirador "party," Police Inspector Quinlan will have her brought back to Grandi's tourist hotel on the Mexican side of town where he stages a murder for which she can be framed. When she awakens from her drug-induced haze, Grandi's bug-eyed head is hanging over the bedrail looking down at her from where Quinlan has strangled him.

The hotel will also serve as a space of ultimate violation to Quinlan's power over these frontier spaces of tourism and pleasure. "Stop. Forget anything. Leave key at desk," reminds the handwritten sign on the back of the door as Quinlan edges out into the night after killing Grandi. But he has forgotten his cane there, an object that will serve Vargas to frame the policeman and extricate his wife from the web of accusations surrounding her. The haunted spaces of the border hotels turn out to have material ghosts who can be set up to reveal their "crimes."[73]

The film's exploitation of hotel spaces has equally paradoxical implications for its government emissary and his wife who there pass as honeymooners. While the film repeatedly plays on the theme of foreignness, for example framing Vargas at one point below a sign that announces, "Welcome Stranger!", it launches their need to sleep in hotels into a kind of allegory for their inability to find a place where they belong. It does so through almost intolerable reminders of the dangerous unhomeliness of places we sleep while on the road. The scenes at the St. Mark's reception desk, like those in the terrifying Mirador, suggest that there may not be anyone who is, in

Susie's words, "in charge." When Susie calls the office at the motel to ask
not to be disturbed so she can sleep, the audience can see what she cannot:
the boy she has earlier slurringly called "Pancho" has taken over the reception desk. "Don't you worry, Mrs. Vargas," he purrs chillingly, giving her
reassurances that imply more promises than they literally deliver: "I'm the
one who's in charge . . . nobody's gonna get through to you—unless I say
so." And so he will indeed say that a whole troop of Grandi's lackeys can get
through to her. The person who has been "in charge" of this border area for
the last few decades is, of course, the corrupt police officer Quinlan, played
by Welles himself in a role that exploits the monstrosity of the character's
physicality while simultaneously excusing that obesity with tragic stories
about Quinlan's inability to save his wife or to catch her killer. When the film
demonstrates that, despite his longstanding penchant for framing people he
believes guilty, he has been right about the car bomber all along, the filmic
narrative ultimately functions like the convenient fictions used by Quinlan. It
frames Vargas as wrong despite his being right. The film thus cast aspersions
on its violated honeymooners, making them guilty if not of addictions and
murder, then at least of naiveté, racism, and xenophobia. Vargas's inability
to recognize the logic in the laws of this border town has brought about the
death of the "good" policeman as well as the "bad one." And even if the
Mexican notable can head home to Mexico City with his American wife's
reputation intact, one suspects that no government-protected compound will
keep safe this woman who cannot speak a word of the language of her husband's homeland.

Touch of Evil portrays hotels as dangerous, haunted places not just to recall
the difficulty of crossing borders culturally and socially but to evoke a modern world in which it is no longer clear who is "in charge." This is a world in
which hotel registers do not even record those who have stopped over. One
might imagine that Welles's film, like Hitchcock's nearly contemporaneous *Psycho*, exploits that moment of anxiety around the hotel registration
book, to evoke the difficulty of keeping track of strangers passing through.
A democratic state cannot, of course, restrict its citizens' freedom of movement. It cannot impose police checks on identity at every doorstep. And yet,
of course, modernity by the late twentieth century had begun to opt for just
such restrictions. "Before the war, nobody asked you for a passport," wrote
B. Traven, author of *Treasure of the Sierra Madre*, in a 1926 novelistic dia-
tribe against identification cards for travelers (cited in Torpey 2001: 270). By
the time Marion Crane checked into the Bates Motel, it had become possible
to run radio police checks, telex wires, and even proto-faxed fingerprint identifications in a flashing moment. The registration desks of hotels, both real
and filmic, had by the 1960s become haunted by the specter of surveillance.

The Cold War, already brewing at the close of the Pacific front in August 1945, informed the anxieties reflected by post-war noir films by suggesting that in an atomic age, there could be no completely safe place. "There's no place to hide," concluded one girl whose glimpse of *Life* magazine's coverage of mushroom clouds left her anxious throughout the 1950s (Kuznick and Gilbert 2001: 21).[74] A respected Harvard physician and executive director of the American Hygiene Association warned that an atomic bomb explosion would break down "normal family and community life" (cited in May 1989: 154). The rootlessness evoked in films like *The Blue Dahlia* and *Key Largo* may have come to an end within the films' frames, but the fifteen years between the war's end and Kennedy's election brought the architecture of home selectively to American citizens.

The hotel films of the noir era were displaced by another kind of film, depicting innocents abroad. And few of those films made the dangers of haunted hotel rooms as palpable as *Touch of Evil*. Amidst the post-war confusion about what kind of place was safe in the modern world, hotels now provided fantasy environments not just for the wealthy (as between 1880 and 1929), but for the growing middle classes as well. Advertising in the *Saturday Evening Post* in 1945 suggests something of the fantasmatic potential for the large American urban hotel. According to the Statler Hotel advertisement, you can expect the same things from every one of their hotels: comfortable mattresses, strategic locations, great meals, a laundry service, and radios in every room to bring the news (Statler Hotel Advertisement 1945: 47).[75] The heterotopic potential of the hotel expanded as it grew away from serving as a potential place of residence for the wealthiest and poorest members of society, and began to offer a dream to those in between.[76] Air travel, to Europe and beyond, could only stretch the world of filmic hotel travel into all reaches of the globe: in the 1950s and early 1960s, film guests registered in several Paris palaces (*Gentlemen Prefer Blondes*, *Funny Face*, *Love in the Afternoon*, *Charade*, *Paris When It Sizzles*), on the French Riviera (*To Catch a Thief*), in a Venice *pensione* (*Summertime*), and at a grand hotel in the Bahamas (*That Touch of Mink*). The American cinema had traveled since the earliest Edison films, but it rarely did so with such a preoccupation to demonstrate that what lay abroad could be domesticated and made familiar through a cinematic projection of American values triumphing in the spaces of hotels.[77]

Touch of Evil sustains a blistering critique of that cinematic projection, just as it raised complex questions about how one governs in a modern world. Like most of the films considered in depth in this essay, it sidesteps the ideological frameworks that much of popular culture uses to frame identity and leaves its audiences, even decades later, anxiously wondering what kinds of values one should embrace when crossing borders—into hotels, into cities,

into countries. When Michel de Certeau argued that "haunted places are the
only ones people can live in," he surely meant that places become livable
through the spatial practices that give meanings to them (1990: 162). I want
to suggest that haunted places have a less reassuring valence in cultural
representations: they pressure us into anxious positions in our imaginary as
well as geographic travels. Films such as *Grand Hotel, My Man Godfrey,
Lady for a Day, D.O.A., Impact, The Blue Dahlia, Key Largo,* and *Touch of
Evil* established precisely such haunted spatial practices for their eras, first
through their widespread diffusion and also through their problematizing of
the fictions on which public spaces like hotels were dependent. I am arguing
that several dozen films—that took as a central thematic their characters'
movement through spaces where they were not at home—used the practices
of hotel space to problematize the meaning of having a fixed domicile and
a fixed identity to go with it.[78] The reception desk moments in these films
repeatedly magnified the anxieties around passing through since, as I have
argued, they simultaneously focalize the myriad possibilities for passing as
inherent to being on the road. They expose the paradoxes that mark the slip-
periness of identity that accompanies rootlessness. Haunted places may be the
only ones people can live in, but they render that living anxious, as we learn
in films that thematize such ghostings. They also allow critical perspectives
that enable us to grasp the way our histories have been made, by popular
culture, into fictions. It is up to us to exploit the potential for those critical
perspectives to learn how, in our turn, to haunt popular culture with its own
anxieties.

Hotels are always haunted places, because even if we are at home in them,
our passing there is always registered as outside Western mappings of belonging. "Home is a fragile system, easy to subvert," Douglas has argued. The
hotel that she views as its "perfect opposite" is subversive because of the
anxiety it provokes about the kinds of privacy that can be bought there (1991:
301, 304–05). DePastino similarly points to the ways that the hotel might
answer some of the central modern anxieties about the constraints of home:
"More than mere shelter or the means of social reproduction, home provides
a well of identity and belonging, 'a place in the world.' In exchange, home
demands subordination to prescribed roles and routines, exercising a tyranny
over its members and a vigilant defense against the encroachments of outsiders" (2003: vii). Like the movie theater, the hotel produces a semblance of a
place where one might belong, where one could take up the option to become
noticeable in its public spaces or to pretend to invisibility in its private ones.
Like the films that played in those theaters, the hotel proffers an imaginary
space for identification, intimacy, nostalgia. And like most of the hotel films
of the 1940s and 1950s, from the ones that check their characters into skid-row

hotels to those that more optimistically promise comfortable hotel surroundings, the space of the thematized hotel operates to trouble, fragment, and warp the imaginary spaces imagined as home. The mid-twentieth-century cinema moves its characters into hotels to produce vacancies that nothing can fill.

POSTSCRIPT

As I wrote the last section of this essay, Hurricane Katrina brought homelessness and rootlessness to hundreds of thousands of Gulf Coast residents. As the faces of those suffering and dying flashed across my computer screen, as New Orleans palace hotels disintegrated into chaos, as the architecture of houses collapsed under the weight of flood waters, I realized that the kind of dislocation wrought by the Depression and World War II over a period of more than a decade was occurring in 2005 in the space of little more than a week. It is too early to imagine how American politics or culture will assimilate this tragedy, far too soon to imagine how New Orleans will reclaim its central position in American tourism, perhaps even too optimistic to imagine how the historic city can welcome its citizens back home. I have been repeatedly reminded in these past days by DePastino's argument that homelessness has long underwritten American values. The tragically meager response by federal and state authorities to the Katrina tragedy in New Orleans suggests that it is high time Americans reflected on what it might mean to have a right to a safe place. Haunted place par excellence, New Orleans registers the tragedy of a society in which home is still something, to borrow a formula from Robert Frost's poem, you have "to deserve" (1915).

NOTES

1. On the transformations in architectural styles of roadside hotels, see Jakle et al. (1996: 63, 71, 77), who show examples of "cabin"-style motels, typical of the 1930s and 1940s. Such motels are depicted in *It Happened One Night*, *You Only Live Once*, *High Sierra*, *Niagara*, and *That Touch of Mink*.

2. Important studies on the relationship of the hotel to modernity include Boorstin 1965; Berger 1999; Berger 2005. Unless otherwise indicated, I use the word "hotel" in this essay to designate the generic form of temporary housing that might include all classes of hotels and motels. I usually differentiate boarding houses when they operate as long-term housing. For nuances in hotel terminology, see Groth 1994.

3. Williamson calls reading the register "one of America's most popular indoor sports" and cites H. Rhodes as saying, "Another of the common people's inalienable rights is to know who is staying in a hotel" (1975: 180–1).

4. Sandoval-Strausz cites evidence of travelers leaving messages in hotel registers geared toward arranging meetings and locating one another (2002: 156–57).

5. On techniques of identification, see Cole 2001. On Bertillonage, see Kaluszynski 2001; and Cole 2001: 32–59. Fingerprinting was first used forensically in the 1850s, frequently praised as a technique in the 1890s, and legally persuasive by the first decade of the 1900s (Cole 2001: 169, 101–3, 159–60). For the displacement of the questionable anthropometric techniques by fingerprinting and for Bertillon's engagement with the new forensics of dactyloscopy, see Cole 2001: 140–70, 201.

6. See Torpey 2000, as well as essays in Caplan and Torpey 2001, esp. Noiriel and Lucassen.

7. Since so few documents were required by local and state authorities, few hotel registers seem to have survived World War II: registers were victims of hotel fires and hard times, perhaps even destroyed to hide scandals, or simply not valued beyond the era of the hotel's glory (Williamson 1975: 90–91).

8. Williamson says that only "four or five states" required this information, but does not say which ones or in what period (1975: 180). By contrast to the freedom of movement guaranteed by the U.S. Constitution, hotels in European countries were often asked to provide data to the state or local governments on visitors. For example, recounts Torpey, as of the end of World War I, hotels in Great Britain were obliged to report on aliens staying there (2000: 116). A French guide for hotel trainees provided this advice in its chapter on "Hotel Law": "The hotel keeper has certain obligations, for instance he must keep a register and require every guest to sign it and state his nationality. Those registers are open to police inspections" (Meunier 1961: 137).

9. Katz claims the "Hotel film" even became a genre in 1920s Germany (1999: 139). Arns perceives films set in hotels rather as part of the growing genre of detective films (1999: 32–41). I think films set in hotels in the 1920s and 1930s have too few common traits to be considered bound generically, though one could plot the emergence of a loosely linked series, a hotel-film cycle, on the model of the successful 1932 Best Film Oscar winner, culminating in *Weekend at the Waldorf* (1945), written by the same Vicki Baum behind *Grand Hotel*.

10. The 115 American films in my corpus deriving from the period framed here (defined as 1929–1964) are primarily comedies and thrillers (especially works from what Dimendberg [2004, 11–12] defines, following Borde and Chaumeton [1955], as the "film noir cycle"); there are also a few spy films and melodramas. 83 of these films have a reception desk sequence. I arrived at this corpus through a preliminary list created by running keyword searches in film databases (looking for all American films from any period known to represent hotels, motels, and reception desks), then watched all the films from my focus period that were available in VHS and DVD while also seeking copies of other harder-to-find films containing sequences that dovetailed with my concerns. Although I have given much thought to European (especially English, French, German, and Italian) films engaging similar issues, my corpus here is explicitly American for methodological reasons. One of my goals in this essay has been to demonstrate how historical research can provide a rich framework for thinking about the imbrication of cultural, social, and political concerns. By concentrating on the period that is, in my view, the golden age of filmic representations

of hotels and motels in the country that has served for two centuries as the innovator in services to travelers, I have been able to explore the material conditions of passing through hotels, the architecture of these spaces, and the social as well as political contexts for those stays.

11. My formula here cites Vidler's theorization of "warped space." Vidler defines spatial warping as produced, in one conception, by the imagination of space as a projection of the subject, a projection that makes that space a repository of disturbing objects and forms. Warped space is created, in a second conception, says Vidler, by "the forced intersection of different media . . . in a way that breaks the boundaries of genre" (2000: vii).

12. See Bruno's critique the over-dependence on looking as a paradigm for film studies in 2002: 6–7, 15–16. A historicized approach to vision has been advocated by Silverman (1996, 125–61), and by my work on nineteenth-century vision in Matlock (forthcoming), chapters of which have appeared as Matlock 1995 and 1996.

13. On the concept of the chronotope, defined as "time space"—"the intrinsic connectedness of temporal and spatial relationships that are artistically expressed in literature," see Bakhtin 1981, 84–258, esp. 84–85. Sobchak (1998) makes fascinating use of the concept as a touchstone for reading film noir.

14. See Wigley (1997) on Jameson (1991: 39–44). Reed (1996) offers further reflections on "not-at-home"-ness.

15. See Perry (2002: 84), citing John Locke's *Essay concerning human understanding* (1694): "as far as this consciousness can be extended backwards to any past action or thought, so far reaches the identity of that person."

16. See also Williamson 1975: 127. Groth notes that women staying in palace and middle-priced hotels were treated contemptuously because some conservatives saw those stays as giving women too many liberties (1994: 208–12). On views of women staying in urban residential hotels in the early twentieth century, see Meyerowitz 1993: 43–71 and Groth 1994: 107ff, who discusses Richardson 1972. Gilfoyle analyzes the prostitution trade and Raines laws intended to stem it in urban hotels (1992: 243–7).

17. Hotels made an ideal, cheap cinematic environment because they eliminated the high costs of shooting exteriors, had easily built sets, and allowed for simplicity of shooting in either stage-lot structures or real hotels.

18. While I am interested in this essay especially in the period 1932–1958 (bookended by *Grand Hotel* and *Touch of Evil*), which I see as the key epoch for the cinematic uses of the hotel to articulate tensions about identity, one needs to see this period in the larger context of Hollywood narrative cinema. We can codify three distinct moments in the period of 1929–1962 for the uses of reception desks in Hollywood narrative cinema: the 1930s "hotel" film and its offshoots—films that crossed genre boundaries or veered toward comedy and melodrama; the 1940s to early 1950s, characterized by film noir (called mysteries and thrillers in their time), spy films, and, occasionally, comedy; and the reworking of the hotel film in the tourist cycle of the 1950s and early 1960s, films that veered again toward comedy, but which also included a number of films about spying where the innocents abroad turned out to be less-than-innocent or where their very innocence enabled them to

conquer Cold War bad guys. In the next section of this essay, I consider hotel films of the 1920s and 1930s in order to give a context to problems in the middle period of the century. The 1950s-early 1960s Cold War cycle will serve in my essay's conclusion as a touchstone for the endurance of certain representational problems from earlier periods.

19. The last line of Vicki Baum's *Menschen im Hotel* (1929), on which the film was based, is memorable pulp-fiction allegory: "The revolving door turns and turns — and swings . . . and swings . . . and swings . . . . " (1948: 255).

20. Wilson credits one critic of the era with calling this a "honeycomb set," though she believes he was only remarking on how the set was constructed out of "interlocking spaces that create the illusion of an entire building whereas it was actually composed of several unconnected sets constructed on sound stages" (2000: 107).

21. On the structure of related buildings see Pevsner 1976. One could see this film's architecture as a sort of proto-Guggenheim Museum (1943–59) with a police bureau on the ground floor. Frank Lloyd Wright's earliest design in this ziggurat mode dates, in fact, from the same decade as Gibbons's *Grand Hotel* set: the Gordon Strong project for Sugarloaf Mountain, Maryland, 1924–25 (see Riley [1999: 221, 298] for this project as well as for a completed Wright ziggurat building, the Morris Gift Shop in San Francisco [1948–49]). Absolutely nothing resembling a hotel operated in this way at the time of Gibbons's project: Keck notes that nineteenth-century hotels resembled palaces and castles of the aristocracy whereas post-war hotels "looked, albeit unintentionally, like hospitals." The pre-war hotels, he accurately describes as "large boxes" "pleasantly ornamented on the outside and furnished with magnificent spatial sequences on the inside" (1999: 42).

22. This function of hotel space as a world unto itself is also embraced by the radical 1970s architectural shift represented by the Portman hotel atrium, itself based on department store, arcade, and railway station spaces. The Portman atrium has two functions, Keck argues, the first "permit[ting] open spaces to be slipped into the dense infrastructure of the city, ... as if the hotel had been turned outside in, as if the exterior urban space . . . had been transferred to the interior of the hotel"; and the second, serving "as a distributor for access to the rooms, . . . the one space from which the entire complex can be seen at once, . . . provid[ing] for a better sense of orientation than in conventional hotel corridors" (1999: 48). Vidler suggests that "a certain strain of modernist architecture . . . was intent on transforming the world into . . . a gigantic hotel atrium" (2000: 79). Tallack (2002) offers a further view of the hotel lobby.

23. I think it is significant that the hotel seems *not* to have served as a locale in films of the 1920s and 1930s for the negotiation of racial conflicts. Although blackface plays a central, disturbing role in Hitchcock's English-made *Young and Innocent*, and black characters occasionally appear as servants in films set in hotels dating from this period (e.g., a black maid in the hotel in *Blonde Venus*, a black bellboy in *Dead Reckoning*) — though far less frequently than they would have appeared in the real-life hotel worlds of the segregation era where white clients frequently were waited upon by blacks — the cinema represents hotels of Depression-era America as shockingly white spaces. Sandoval-Strausz discusses the application of Jim Crow laws in hotels,

evoking anxieties about racial mixing in the pre-Civil Rights era (2002: 351–93); Armstead studies the black hotel visitor in this same period (2005: 136–59). One of the few spaces of racial mixing possible in most mass-market Hollywood films prior to the 1960s was the nightclub where black musicians, bartenders, and waiters "served" the white audiences represented in the films as well as those watching in the movie theaters. A particularly remarkable (and racist) example of the appearance of blacks in a space patronized by whites, occurs in the Fisherman's Bar sequence of *D.O.A.* Although the bartender who poisons the film's protagonist is white, the film creates an atmosphere of danger and excess by means of a series of close-ups of the black musicians' faces covered with sweat and transported by their music. Racial and ethnic tensions emerged repeatedly in film noir, such as in the bar sequence of *The Blue Dahlia* where a returning veteran starts a fight with another soldier over music he criticizes with racial epithets, in the Chinese-mockery sequence of *Clash by Night*, in the film *Crossfire* which revolves around an anti-semitic killing, and in *No Way Out* and *Odds Against Tomorrow* which explicitly engage civil rights by representing racial bigots.

24. Godfrey's transformation serves the purpose of demonstrating, in his words, that "The only difference between a derelict and a man is a job."

25. The size of the new Waldorf, opened in 1931, is from Denby (1998: 226). Groth provides a roomcount from the 1930s for the new Waldorf-Astoria, of 2253 guest rooms and 500 luxury suites (1996: 43). Hotel advertisements demonstrate powerfully the investment hotels had, even as late as the 1930s, in preserving an elite population: "Frankly Conservative," read the headline to the Devon Hotel publicity that depicted a group of people in seventeenth-century French costumes, either an allusion to the elitism of the world of salons or a suggestion that one could expect chic masquerade balls there. The ad copy even more poignantly evokes the hotel's desired public: "A tradition of quiet reserve marks the atmosphere of The DEVON [that] offers you a protective haven in the spirit of a luxurious private house . . . AND you will be in good company" (Devon Hotel Advertisement, *Harper's Bazaar*, February 1932, 120).

26. See Groth (1996: 46, 53), who discusses the advice of trade journals such as *Hotel World* to hotel management. Groth views the detectives' roles as being particularly significant to the policing of class relations in late nineteenth-century society: "The lobbies, dining halls, and hallways of palace hotels were public only to those people in the upper and middle class whose clothing and decorum passed the unobtrusive inspection of a phalanx of hotel detectives and floor clerks who, if necessary, were ready to quietly interview and eject people who looked out of place" (1996: 53). On hotel detectives, see also Sandoval-Strausz 2002: 232–39.

27. The lion's share of exceptions I have found are comedies: In *Mr. and Mrs. Smith* we see the clerk from the point of view of the couple checking into the lodge. In *My Favorite Wife*, we see both Nick Arden and his long-lost wife Eve from the point of view of the clerk; we also see the clerk from the point of view of each main character, especially that of Nick. *Topper* procures a logical point-of-view shot over the reception desk, but there is no one registering at that moment and the space from which we look at the clerks does not jibe with the location of the ghost although it

does recall other point-of-view shots that position her as present although absent to the camera eye. The major film noir exceptions to these strategies of avoiding reception-desk point-of-view shots are *Dark Passage* and *Dead Reckoning*, each of which shows us Bogart's character from the desk clerk's viewpoint, and *The Strange Love of Martha Ivers*, where the clerk's point of view invites judgment of the couple checking in.

28. I take the infrequency of shot-counter-shot exchanges to be the result of the hotel clerk's relative lack of significance as a touchstone for identification. Most of the cases where we see characters shot over their shoulders (inviting but not requiring our assimilation of their point of view), that person is the clerk, as in *Impact*—unless the film is spotlighting the clerk's reaction to something the already established principal character says or does, as in *My Favorite Wife* (which for this reason likewise has point-of-view shots from the checking-in character's point of view). On the workings of shot-counter-shot cutting in establishing identification, see Oudart, 1977/8; Heath 1981; Silverman 1983: 194–236; and Penley 2000.

29. Cf. Borges cited by one of Manet's analysts: "What disturbs us most about such paradoxical instances of *mise-en-abyme*, such as Don Quixote being a reader of the *Quixote* and Hamlet a spectator of *Hamlet*, is that 'these inventions suggest that if the characters of fictional work can be readers or spectators, we, its readers of spectators, can be fictitious" (Flam 1996: 183).

30. I am here drawing on Bruno's formula, cited earlier, that the cinematic viewer is more of a *voyageur* than a *voyeur* (2002: 6). Compare Armstrong's description of the painting's "place in which spectatorship is defined by dislocation." She claims the reflected male customer "dramatizes this imaging of the space of the Folies-Bergère as one in which spectatorial fixture is converted, by a series of dislocations, into spectatorial mobility" (1996: 37–8).

31. In *Dead Reckoning* we do not see the Bogart character's registration card from his point of view at all, despite the close-up, but rather from the side. What we see from Bogart's point of view is the message he finds, to his surprise, left at the desk for him by his war buddy "Preston" signed under the alias of "Geronimo." Such an impossible identificatory position would suggest that we are seeing through the eyes of the character when in fact we are seeing from an angle that would not accurately replicate that of someone signing. Another example of this occurs in *Topper* when both the eponymous hero and his ghostly companion sign into the Seabreeze.

32. An exception is *The Street with no Name* where we see a believable point-of-view shot of the FBI covert operative's signature but a faked point-of-view shot of his rifling through the book looking for the signature of the man whose death he is investigating.

33. The other kinds of "identity knowledge" described by Marx are: "(4) pseudonyms that cannot be linked to other forms of identity knowledge . . . ; (5) pattern knowledge; (6) social categorization; and (7) symbols of eligibility/non-eligibility" (2001: 311–26).

34. Sandoval-Strausz contends that even if a false name was given, the handwriting sample was taken to be solid "evidence" of the contract entered into between hotel and guest (2002: 217).

35. See Sandoval-Strausz: "When a guest was entrusted with control over a private space of his or her own, it was with the understanding that the hotel staff would know the exact location of that space and the identity and appearance of the person who would be occupying it" (2002: 217).

36. Sandoval-Strausz defines the contract of the hotel as establishing "a one-to-one relationship between a particular person and a particular space" (2002: 217).

37. These are pieces of information collected by the Ritz in Paris in the 1930s, according to registration cards reproduced in Étienne and Gaillard (1992: 147). The cards reproduced here show hotel patrons' various visits over time, the numbers of rooms and people housed, the number of days stayed, and the price paid.

38. On nineteenth-century theories of the signature's gesturality, see also Thornton (1996: 83).

39. Kracauer opposes this anonymity to the status of those in a church congregation who "outgrow their names because the very empirical being which these names designate disappears in prayer" (182). In the hotel lobby, Kracauer claims, "the name gets lost in space" (182).

40. Sandoval-Strausz 2002: 217. On graphological belief in the signature's revelation of true character, see Thornton, 1996: 91–99, esp. 95.

41. Although it does not contain hotel scenes, Alfred Werker's police procedural *He Walked by Night* (1948) also has a sequence where handwriting analysis is used to procure absolute certainty about a criminal's identity.

42. My reflections in this essay on identity have also been informed by Gleason 1983; Appiah and Gates 1995; Bhabha 1997; and Brubaker and Cooper 2000, as well as the participants in the conference that became Garber et al., 1993, particularly the late Michael Rogin whose influence my own work gratefully embraces.

43. Foucault puts forward the honeymoon hotel as an exemplary heterotopia (1986: 25). I am grateful to Tom Gunning for reminding me of the significance of the hotel register in this film.

44. Another example of such an escape from hotels into damnation would be the nightmarish *Detour*. My reference to "non-place" here is indebted to Augé 1992. I see the mid-twentieth century real and filmic hotel as very much distinct from a "non-place" as Augé defines it. Citing Michel de Certeau, Augé reminds us that the practices of space allow individuals to be "in a place, *to be other*, and *to pass to the other side*" (*"être dans le lieu, être autre* et *passer à l'autre"*) (Certeau 1990: 164, cited by Augé 1992: 107). If as Certeau argues, "Every story is a travel story" (1990: 171), the hotel is a primary locale for turning space into place. The non-places of postmodernity are places of transit without being plausibly topographies of performing the self. They are the locales of passing through as opposed to the places, as in the hotel tradition, of *passing as*. Although Augé assimilates his "non-places" to Foucault's heterotopia (1992: 141), to do so underestimates, in my opinion, the crucial political interrogations made possible by movements through heterotopic spaces.

45. Once the hotel detective has used her description of her "husband" to narrow the field of possibilities who checked in under an alias the previous morning, Elsa picks his registration card from a small stack through his handwriting and learns that "John Brown" is staying in room 3033.

46. Bogart's character Vincent—operating under the alias "Allan Linnell" given to him by his savior, Irene, with a given name she has called "quiet"—seems to respond in alarm not to the hotel clerk's saying his name is unusual, but simply to being called by that name in the first place. By making the film spectator identify with the clerk's viewpoint of seeing "Linnell's" anxiety when his name is pronounced, *Dark Passage* creates tension around whether Vincent can successfully pass himself off as someone else—despite his new face and despite his alias. "Linnell" seems less unusual than the clerk suggests, which made me wonder if it had a resonance lost since the film was made: John Linnell was the poet Blake's patron, but no other Linnells emerged from my searches.

47. The document—a bill of sale for the purchase of a nuclear material—which was witnessed by Bigelow, never materializes in the film, of course, having been disappeared from the private possessions of the man, Philips, who bought the substance. The iridium has been discovered to be stolen, placing Philips at risk of prison unless he can prove he bought it from someone else. When it becomes apparent that the notary's expert testimony, backed up by his notarial ledger, can demonstrate that the iridium was indeed purchased legally from the now-dead "Reynolds" alias Rekubian, others involved with the iridium sale, including Philips's wife and her lover, kill Philips and then poison Bigelow to cover their tracks. Bigelow's signature does not exist anymore but the fact that records exist proving it once existed gives it a power that ultimately rebounds to kill the notary himself. It is as though the chain of coincidences has transformed Bigelow from signator to author—of his own postmortem tale—in part because the contract had more than just a guarantor. In making this suggestion, I am thinking of Foucault's account of these relationships: "a private letter may well have a signator—it does not have an author; a contract may well have a guarantor—it does not have an author" (1979: 148).

48. On nineteenth-century American anxieties over counterfeit signatures, see Thornton 1996: 99–107.

49. On the conditions for returning veterans, see Adams 1994; and Severo and Milford 1989. Unemployment rates remained much lower than predicted after the war in part thanks to the high numbers of veterans enrolling in universities through the GI Bill (Bennett 1996: 2, 12–13, 195).

50. DePastino reports that 6 million families were doubling up in the late 1940s and a half million were living in makeshift shelters (2003: 228). Clark views the housing crisis as already brewing in the Depression when "housing starts fell by over ninety percent" (1989: 172). Press coverage of the housing crisis includes "The Great Housing Shortage" 1945: 27–36; Bolté 1945; "No Vacancies" 1946; "Homesteading Veteran" 1947. On the recurring crises of homelessness in the United States, see DePastino 2003; Cresswell, 2001; and essays in *Home* 1991.

51. Gleason notes that the word "identification" takes on new meanings in this period as well. "Identity," he shows, was thoroughly absent as a keyword until the 1950s, while "identification" was hitherto used for thinking about the likes of Bertillonage (1983: 910).

52. Jakle and Sculle define "place" as "meaningful contexts for behavior" (1999: 12). My thinking about "place" has been influenced by Foucault 1986; Casey 1997; Lefebvre 1991; Vidler 2000; Wigley 1997; and de Certeau 1990.

53. Groth notes that all-night movie theaters that opened beginning in the 1920s in inner-city areas "added to the urban landscape a variant of the flophouse" (1994: 147). Like the substandard locales—an example of which is shown in *Sullivan's Travels*—that provided the homeless a dry place on the floor to throw a bedroll or curl up in newspapers, the all-night movie theater gave shelter to those without anywhere else to go.

54. A clue to the explosiveness of the film, even in its watered-down form, emerged in the violent reaction of the *New York Times* review that described the film as cynical and of questionable tact, and suggested it would appeal "to those lovers of the brutal and bizarre" (Crowther 1946, 27:3).

55. One might add to this list the female police guard in *The Tight Spot* who is free to work nights in a downtown hotel guarding a state's witness because she has lost her husband in the Normandy Landings. The gardener's daughter is staying with him in *Without Warning* because her husband is overseas. *The Strange Love of Martha Ivers*, *The Crooked Way*, *Somewhere in the Night*, and *Shock* check returning war veterans into hotels rather than homes.

56. Polan likewise notices the peculiar distance this film puts on the war, remarking that *Shadow of a Doubt* seems almost to allegorize the war (1986: 227).

57. MacCannell 1993 promises more about homelessness in noir than it delivers given its very limited film corpus. Sobchak likewise critiques MacCannell for overdetermining the metaphoric aspects of noir's transient environments, which she perceptively explores by analyzing noir's depiction of various spaces off the beaten track of the bourgeois home—hotels, boarding houses, cocktail lounges, and nightclubs.

58. Vacancy rates in the post war years, as low as 4.4% in 1950 (Tobey 1990: 1406) drastically lowered mobility for renters as well as homeowners in the immediate post-war years. On wartime and post-war migration, see Gilbert, 1981: 107–109; Daniel 1990; and Kuznick and Gilbert 2001: 5–6.

59. See also Crawford 1995; and the classic account, Hartmann 1982. By 1944, nineteen million women were working, up from 11.5 million in 1940 (Adams 1994: 123–4).

60. Hotel life, argues Groth, was the most vigorous between 1880 and 1930 (1994: x). On the loss of prestige of the palace hotel, see Groth, who notes that by the Depression expensive hotels often had below 60% occupancy (1994: 265). On commercial hotels' reputations, see Spears 1995: esp. 100–102, and Boorstin 1965: 143. Groth cites the research of a number of social scientists of the pre-World-War II period, including Chicago sociologist Harvey Warren Zorbaugh (*Gold Coast and Slum* [1929], a study of Chicago tenement residential hotels), as exacerbating the hostility toward hotel dwellers (221–31). Daniel cites accounts of wartime migrants that range from those depicting their new horizons to others expressing anxieties about their refusal to live in apartments in favor of trailer parks and tents (1990: 902).

61. Groth points out that for many people the anonymity of cheap hotels may have been ideal: "Landladies might not remember or even know a new tenant's name. The frequent change of address possible at hotels, perhaps with a corresponding change in name, helped runaways elude their parents, reformed people escape their past, and criminals evade the police. For anyone who wanted to melt into the physical maze of

the city, such anonymity and the large number of rooming houses offered the perfect setting" (1994: 120).

62. The major spy films of this era, *The Lady Vanishes, 13 rue Madeleine* and *Five Graves to Cairo* (like the wartime espionage send-up, *To Be or Not to Be*), also show villains and heroes operating under assumed names.

63. Divorce rates grew at war's end to levels never before witnessed in the United States, around one in four marriages. *Life* provided an alarmist account of the post-war divorce boom in Rodell 1945. Marriage rates also soared after the war: in 1946, 2.2 million couples wed, "twice the number who had married in any single year before World War II" (Chudacoff 1999: 255). Courtwright further nuances divorce and marriage rates in this period (1996: 203–7).

64. Alicia in *The Big Combo* operates under a falsified identity because her husband, Mr. Brown, committed her to a mental asylum after she witnessed him killing his boss. Apparently, the private hospital was prepared to accept his word for who he is and therefore to register her under the false name Anna Lee Jackson.

65. See Canaday 2003, as well as Bennett 1996 and Cohen 2003: 137–46.

66. Home ownership increased from 44% in 1940 to 64% in 1950 (Adams 1994: 136).

67. On the displacement of women workers after the war, see Honey 1984. Of the six million women who had worked during the war, nearly four million were fired or left voluntarily. Women's proportion in the civilian labor force dropped from 35.4% in 1944 to 28.6% in 1947. Their earnings proportionate to men's wages dropped from 62% in 1939 to 53% in 1953 (Kaledin 2000: 65, 21). Historians have recently demonstrated that these statistics, while disturbing relative to the high mobilization of women in the work force during World War II, neglect the upturn in women's participation in the work force in a peacetime economy. After the war, although women were initially strongly encouraged by the press and by advertising to return home, competing accounts of women's options—and the strong need in many households for a woman's wages—found more women entering the labor force in the late 1940s than ever before. Chafe, an early proponent of this revisionist view of the narrowing options for wartime women workers, argued that the number of women newly hired after the war was sufficiently high that women's net loss of jobs was only 600,000 (1972: 180). Meyerowitz (1993) has nuanced our understanding of the post-war domestic ideology by means of her analysis of the popular press which she claims endorsed more diverse roles for women than just those of homemaker. While I do not think the ideological thrusts visible in the cinema of the post-war period are consistent with Meyerowitz's findings for periodicals like *Ladies Home Journal* and *Reader's Digest*, her discoveries suggest that we need to re-evaluate our account of how popular culture framed women's options after World War II. Particularly problematic, therefore, is the account of film noir as a misogynous genre that condemned women who take initiatives. In fact, the women who work in noir are precisely the ones who turn out to be trustworthy, whereas those who seek to marry often do so for money and those who spend their days around the house tend to be rotten to the core. Meyerowitz (1996) and Westbrook (1990) offer rich frameworks in their work on pin-ups for rethinking post-war cinematic obsessions with female sexuality.

68. The film has a peculiar relationship to mothers who are either absent (McCloud says he has "no folks"; Nora says she "never had much of a home and what [she] had [she] didn't like much"; no mention is ever made of George Temple's mother, "Dad" Temple's wife, despite several accounts of his childhood; we see the little girl born in the hotel lobby during the last hurricane, but not anyone identified as her mother) or only euphemistically cast in that role, as is the case with the elderly Native American woman who is described as having a son older than she claims to be.

69. That reception desk, unlike any other I have seen in a film of this era, has a divider behind it made of window panes. I initially thought this divider was a mirror, but realised that it operates instead both to reflect and to allow light through to the bar area behind it.

70. Polan associates this aspect of modernity with the motel, which he calls "the figure of furtiveness and a life dominated by the endless but transitory interaction of people all with something to hide" (1986: 232–3).

71. On the marketing of the domestic ideology of "home," see Clark 1989: 172; and Cohen 2003. DePastino evokes E. May's argument that Americans fought the cold war "through the analogue of home," concluding that "homelessness potentially threatened not only gender and family norms, but national security itself" (2003: 230).

72. *Life* published photographs of the unemployment lines, citing predictions (that turned out to be overstated) that 6,200,000 would be out of work by December ("Peace Brings Temporary Unemployment" 1945: 30–1). Effective pressure to get women to leave jobs attenuated this expected direness as did the return of 2 million men to tertiary education by fall 1946.

73. Heath's path-breaking analysis pays strikingly little attention to the spaces the film traverses (1975).

74. A *Saturday Evening Post* cartoon showed a man being told, during a loan interview: "Since the atom bomb we require ten co-signers, each living in a different part of the world" (1946: 50).

75. This account of Statler hotels takes a new twist in late 1946, when the *Saturday Evening Post* ad depicts a tour guide showing his group the hotel and remarking on the lobby where we are "surrounded by the friendly atmosphere, the feeling of old-fashioned hospitality" (Statler Hotel Advertisement 1946: 163). While Statler promised that *all* its company's hotels would provide the same high-quality services, it also now sought to bank on notions of homeyness that are hard to imagine in mass-produced corporate services.

76. On European and other international travel in relation to the hotel world of the post-war period, see Endy 2004; Wharton 2001; Blume 1992; Silver 2001; Kanigel 2002.

77. In this respect, Roman Polanski's Reagan-era thriller *Frantic* (1988), about an American doctor and his wife drawn into a terrorist plot because of mistaken luggage, provides a prophetic rethinking of the genre for the twenty-first century world. Harrison Ford's character will triumph—finding his wife and keeping nuclear materials out of the hands of terrorists—because he learns to respect the foreignness of the environment in which he is a guest rather than expect it to function like a carbon copy of the world he left behind.

78. I am not arguing for the transformative power of these films, for I think the press of the 1930s through 1950s gives us too small a basis through which to understand their uses.

FILMOGRAPHY

Films, 1929–1964, that formed the basis of this research, listed in chronological order. All have sequences that occur in hotels (a designation broadly construed to include hotels of all classes, residential hotels, boarding houses, and motels). An asterisk marks those films with at least one scene at a hotel reception desk. Hitchcock films produced in the UK are listed here in brackets because of their connections to the American films to follow.

Cocoanuts (Robert Florey, 1929)
The Broadway Melody (Harry Beaumont, 1929)
Man of the World (Richard Wallace, 1931)
Blonde Crazy (Roy Del Ruth, 1931)
Grand Hotel (Edmond Goulding, 1932)
Blonde Venus (Josef von Sternberg, 1932)
Trouble in Paradise (Ernst Lubitsch, 1932)
Dinner at Eight (George Cukor, 1933)
Lady for a Day (Frank Capra, 1933)
It Happened One Night (Frank Capra, 1934)
Sadie McKee (Clarence Brown, 1934)
The Thin Man (W. S. Van Dyke, 1934)
Gold Diggers of 35 (Busby Berkeley, 1935)
[*The Thirty-Nine Steps* (Alfred Hitchcock, 1935)]
Top Hat (Mark Sandrich, 1935)
The Great Ziegfeld (Robert Leonard, 1936)
Desire (Frank Borzage, 1936)
[*Secret Agent* (Alfred Hitchcock, 1936)]
My Man Godfrey (Gregory La Cava, 1936)
You Only Live Once (Fritz Lang, 1937)
Topper (Norman McLeod, 1937)
Stella Dallas (King Vidor, 1937)
Stage Door (Gregory La Cava, 1937)
[*Young and Innocent* (Alfred Hitchcock, 1937)]
The Amazing Dr. Clitterhouse (Anatole Litvak, 1938)
Room Service (William Seller/Marx Brothers, 1938)
[*The Lady Vanishes* (Alfred Hitchcock, 1938)]
Midnight (Mitchell Leisen, 1939)
Ninotchka (Ernst Lubitsch, 1939)
Rebecca (Alfred Hitchcock, 1940)

My Favorite Wife (Garson Kanin, 1940)
High Sierra (Raoul Walsh, 1941)
Mr. and Mrs. Smith (Alfred Hitchcock, 1941)
The Maltese Falcon (John Huston, 1941)
Sullivan's Travels (Preston Sturges, 1941)
To Be or Not To Be (Ernst Lubitsch, 1942)
This Gun for Hire (Frank Tuttle, 1942)
Shadow of a Doubt (Alfred Hitchcock, 1943)
Journey Into Fear (Norman Foster with Orson Welles, 1943)
Five Graves to Cairo (Billy Wilder, 1943)
Since You Went Away (John Cromwell, 1944)
Arsenic and Old Lace (Frank Capra, 1944)
To Have and Have Not (Howard Hawks, 1944)
I'll Be Seeing You (William Dieterle, 1944)
Without Love (Harold S. Bucquet, 1945)
Weekend at the Waldorf (Robert Leonard, 1945)
Fallen Angel (Otto Preminger, 1945)
Spellbound (Alfred Hitchcock, 1945)
Detour (Edgar Ulmer, 1945)
Cornered (Edward Dmytryk, 1945)
Shock (Alfred Werker, 1946)
Spiral Staircase (Robert Siodmak, 1946)
Gilda (Charles Vidor, 1946)
The Blue Dahlia (George Marshall, 1946)
The Stranger (Orson Welles, 1946)
Somewhere in the Night (Joseph L. Mankiewicz, 1946)
The Strange Love of Martha Ivers (Lewis Milestone, 1946)
Black Angel (Roy William Neill, 1946)
The Big Sleep (Howard Hawks, 1946)
The Killers (Robert Siodmak, 1946)
Dead Reckoning (John Cromwell, 1947)
13 rue Madeleine (Henry Hathaway, 1947)
Born to Kill (Robert Wise, 1947)
Crossfire (Edward Dmytryk, 1947)
Golden Earrings (Mitchell Leisen, 1947)
Dark Passage (Delmar Daves, 1947)
Nightmare Alley (Edmund Goulding, 1947)
Out of the Past (Jacques Tourneur, 1947)
T-Men (Anthony Mann, 1947)
Raw Deal (Anthony Mann, 1948)
The Street with No Name (William Keighley, 1948)
Key Largo (John Huston, 1948)
Impact (Arthur Lubin, 1949)
The Set-Up (Robert Wise, 1949)

The Crooked Way (Robert Florey, 1949)
Killer Bait (Byron Haskin, 1949)
The Third Man (Carol Reed, 1949)
Holiday Affair (Don Hartman, 1949)
Whirlpool (Otto Preminger, 1949)
Gun Crazy (Joseph H. Lewis, 1949)
D.O.A. (Rudolph Maté, 1950)
Where the Sidewalk Ends (Otto Preminger, 1950)
Born Yesterday (George Cukor, 1950)
Cry Danger (Robert Parrish, 1951)
Fourteen Hours (Henry Hathaway, 1951)
The Day the Earth Stood Still (Robert Wise, 1951)
On Dangerous Ground (Nicholas Ray, 1952)
Without Warning! (Arnold Laven, 1952)
Don't Bother to Knock (Roy Ward Baker, 1952)
Monkey Business (Howard Hawks, 1952)
Niagara (Henry Hathaway, 1953)
Gentlemen Prefer Blondes (Howard Hawks, 1953)
Vicki (Harry Horner, 1953)
The Big Heat (Fritz Lang, 1953)
Bad Day at Black Rock (John Sturges, 1955)
The Big Combo (Joseph Lewis, 1955)
Mr. Arkadin (Orson Welles, 1955)
Tight Spot (Phil Karson, 1955)
Kiss Me Deadly (Robert Aldrich, 1955)
Summertime (David Lean, 1955)
To Catch a Thief (Alfred Hitchcock, 1955)
Killer's Kiss (Stanley Kubrick, 1955)
The Man Who Knew Too Much (Alfred Hitchcock, 1956)
Funny Face (Stanley Donen, 1957)
Love in the Afternoon (Billy Wilder, 1957)
Kiss Them for Me (Stanley Donen, 1957)
Touch of Evil (Orson Welles, 1958)
Vertigo (Alfred Hitchcock, 1958)
Some Like It Hot (Billy Wilder, 1959)
North by Northwest (Alfred Hitchcock, 1959)
Odds Against Tomorrow (Robert Wise, 1959)
Psycho (Alfred Hitchcock, 1960)
The Bellboy (Jerry Lewis, 1960)
The Thousand Eyes of Doctor Mabuse (Fritz Lang, 1960)
Pocketful of Miracles (Frank Capra, 1961)
That Touch of Mink (Delbert Mann, 1962)
Charade (Stanley Donen, 1963)
Paris When It Sizzles (Billy Wilder, 1964)
Marnie (Alfred Hitchcock, 1964)

Other Films Cited—from Outside the Geographical or Temporal Frame of this Study

(Films in double brackets are cited but do not have hotel sequences.)

A Search for Evidence (Biograph, 1903)
La Maison Ensorcelée (*The Bewitched House*, Segundo Chomón, Pathé, 1907)
*Fantômas (Louis Feuillade, 1913–1914)
*Der Letzte Mann (*The Last Man*, F. W. Murnau, 1924)
Le Sang d'un poète (*The Blood of a Poet,* Jean Cocteau, 1930–32)
[[*Notorious* (Alfred Hitchcock, 1945)]]
[[*Best Years of Our Lives* (William Wyler, 1946)]]
[[*The Postman Always Rings Twice* (Tay Garnett, 1946]]
[[*He Walked By Night* (Alfred Werker, 1948]]
[[*No Way Out* (Joseph L. Mankiewicz, 1950)]]
[[*Clash by Night* (Fritz Lang, 1952)]]
*Frantic (Roman Polanski, 1988)
*The Grifters (Stephen Frears, 1990)

REFERENCES

Adams, Michael C. C. *The Best War Ever: America and World War II.* Baltimore: Johns Hopkins University Press, 1994.

Airfoam Advertisement, *Life*, (31 December 1945), 11.

Appiah, Kwame Anthony and Gates, Henry Louis Jr., (eds) *Identities.* Chicago: University of Chicago Press, 1995.

Armstead, Myra B. Young. 'Revisiting Hotels and Other Lodgings: American Tourist Spaces Through the Lens of Black Pleasure-travelers, 1880–1950', *Journal of Decorative and Propaganda Arts* 25 (Spring 2005):136–59.

Armstrong, Carol. 'Counter, Mirror, Maid: Some Infra-thin Notes on *A Bar at the Folies Bergère*', pp. 25–46 in *Twelve Views of Manet's Bar* edited by Bradford R. Collins. Princeton: Princeton University Press, 1996.

Arns, Alfons. 'Hotel as Motion Picture/Hotel As Film', *Daidalos* 62 (March 1999): 32–41.

Augé, Marc. *Non-Lieux: Introduction à une Anthropologie de la Surmodernité*, Paris: Seuil, 1992.

Baker, S. G. 'Speaking of Pictures', *Life* (31 December 1945), 8–10.

Bakhtin, Mikhail Mikhailovich. 'Forms of Time and the Chronotope in the Novel' pp. 84–258 in *The Dialogical Imagination.* Austin: University of Texas Press, 1984.

Baum, Vicki. *Grand Hotel* (Basil Creighton trans.). London: Pan Books, 1948 [1930].

Bennett, Michael J. *When Dreams Came True: The GI Bill and the Making of Modern America.* Washington, D.C.: Brassens, 1996.

Berger, Molly W. 'The American System: The Nineteenth-Century American Luxury Hotel', in *Voyageurs et Voyages*, Aix-en-Provence: Publications de l'Université de Provence, 1999.

———. 'The Rich Man's City: Hotels and Mansions of Gilded Age New York', *Journal of Decorative and Propaganda Arts* 25 (Spring 2005): 46–71.

Bhabha, Homi K. 'Minority Maneuvers and Unsettled Negotiations', *Critical Inquiry* 23 no. 3 (Spring 1997): 431–59.

Blume, Mary. *Côte d'Azur: Inventing the French Riviera*. London: Thames and Hudson, 1992.

Bolté, C. 'The New Veteran', *Life* (10 December 1945), 57–66.

Boorstin, Daniel J. 'Palaces of the People' in *The Americans: The National Experience*. New York: Random House, 1965.

Borde, Raymond and Chaumeton, Étienne. *Panorama Du Film Noir Américain*. Paris: Minuit, 1955.

Brubaker, Rogers and Cooper, Frederick. 'Beyond "Identity"', *Theory and Society* 29 no 1 (February 2000): 1–47.

Bruno, Giuliana. *Streetwalking on a Ruined Map: Cultural Theory and the City Films of Elvira Notari*. Princeton: Princeton University Press, 1993

———. *Atlas of Emotion*. London: Verso, 2002.

Burns, Kathryn. 'Notaries, Truth, and Consequences', *American Historical Review* 110 no. 2 (April 2005): 350–79.

Canaday, Margot. 'Building a Straight State: Sexuality and Social Citizenship under the 1944 G.I. Bill', *Journal of American History* 90 no. 3 (December 2003): 935–57.

Caplan, Jane. '"This or That Particular Person": Protocols in Identification in Nineteenth-Century Europe' pp. 49–66 in *Documenting Individual Identity: The Development of State Practices in the Modern World* edited by Jane Caplan and John Torpey. Princeton: Princeton University Press, 2001.

Caplan, Jane and John Torpey (eds). *Documenting Individual Identity: The Development of State Practices in the Modern World*. Princeton: Princeton University Press, 2001.

Casey, Edward S. *The Fate of Place*. Berkeley: University of California Press, 1997.

Certeau, Michel de. *L'Invention Du Quotidien, I*. Paris: Seuil, 1990.

Chudacoff, Howard P. *The Age of the Bachelor*. Princeton: Princeton University Press, 1999.

Chafe, William Henry. *The American Woman: Her Changing Social, Economic, and Political Roles, 1920–1970*. Oxford: Oxford University Press, 1972.

Clark, Clifford Edward, Jr. 'Ranch-House Suburbia: Ideals and Realities', pp. 171–193 in *Recasting America: Culture and Politics in the Age of Cold War*, edited by Lary May. Chicago: University of Chicago Press, 1989.

Clark, Timothy James. *The Painting of Modern Life*. New York: Knopf, 1984.

Cohen, Lizabeth. *A Consumer's Republic: the Politics of Mass Consumption in Postwar America*. New York: Knopf, 2003.

Cole, Simon A. *Suspect Identities: A History of Fingerprinting and Criminal Identification*. Cambridge: Harvard University Press, 2001.

Collins, Bradford R. (ed.). *Twelve Views of Manet's Bar*. Princeton: Princeton University Press, 1996.

Courtwright, David T. *Violent Land: Single Men and Social Disorder from the Frontier to the Inner City*. Cambridge: Harvard University Press, 1996.

Crawford, Margaret. 'Daily Life on the Home Front: Women, Blacks, and the Struggle for Public Housing', pp. 90–143 in *World War II and the American Dream: How Wartime Building Changed a Nation* edited by Donald Albrecht, Cambridge, MA: MIT Press, 1995.

Cresswell, Tim. *The Tramp in America*. London: Reaktion, 2001.

Crowther, Bosley. 'Review, *The Blue Dahlia*', *New York Times* (9 May 1946), 27: 3.

Daniel, Pete. 'Going Among Strangers: Southern Reactions to World War II', *Journal of American History* 77 (December1990): 886–911.

Denby, Elaine. *Grand Hotels: Reality and Illusion. An Architectural and Social History*. London: Reaktion, 1998.

DePastino, Todd. *Citizen Hobo: How a Century of Homelessness Shaped America*. Chicago: Chicago University Press, 2003.

Derrida, Jacques. 'Signature Event Context' pp. 1–24 in *Limited Inc.* translated by Samuel Weber and Jeffrey Mehlman, Evanston, IL: Northwestern University Press, 1988.

Dimendberg, Edward. *Film Noir and the Spaces of Modernity*. Cambridge, MA: Harvard University Press, 2004.

Douglas, Mary. *Purity and Danger*. London: Routledge, 1966.

Douglas, Mary. 'The Idea of a Home: a Kind of Space', *Social Research* 58 no. 1 (Spring 1991): 288–307.

Endy, Christopher. (2004) *Cold War Holidays: American Tourism in France*. Chapel Hill: University of North Carolina Press.

Étienne, Bernard and Gaillard, Marc. (1992) *Palaces et grands hôtels: ces lieux qui ont une âme*. Paris: Atlas.

Flam, Jack. 'Looking Into the Abyss: The Poetics of Manet's *A Bar at the Folies Bergère*', pp. 164–188 *Twelve Views of Manet's Bar* edited by Bradford R. Collins, Princeton: Princeton University Press, 1996.

Foucault, Michel. 'Of Other Spaces' *Diacritics* 16 no. 1, (January 1986): 22–27.

——. *Discipline and Punish*, Trans. Alan Sheridan. New York: Vintage, 1977.

——. '"What is an Author?"' pp. 141–160 in *Textual Strategies: Perspectives in Post-structuralist Criticism* edited by Josué Harari, Ithaca: Cornell University Press, 1979.

Fraenkel, Béatrice. *La Signature: Génèse d'une Signe*, Paris: Gallimard, 1992.

Frost, Robert. (1915) 'Death of the Hired Man', in *The Norton Anthology of American Literature*, 5th ed., edited by Nina Baym, New York: (W. W. Norton, 1998), 2:1120–24 [1915].

Fuss, Diana. *Identification Papers: Readings on Psychoanalysis, Sexuality, and Culture*. New York: Routledge, 1995.

Garber, Marjorie B., Matlock, Jann and Walkowitz, Rebecca L. *Media Spectacles*. New York: Routledge, 1993.

Gilbert, James. *Another Chance: Postwar America, 1945–1968*. Philadelphia: Temple University Press, 1981.

Gilfoyle, Timothy J. *City of Eros: New York City, Prostitution, and the Commercialization of Sex, 1790–1920*. New York: Norton, 1992.

Gleason, Philip. 'Identifying Identity: A Semantic History', *Journal of American History* 69 no. 4 (March 1983): 910–931.

'The Great Housing Shortage' *Life* (17 December 1945): 27–36.

Groth, Paul. *Living Downtown: The History of Residential Hotels in the United States*. Berkeley: University of California Press, 1994.

Gunning, Tom. "What I Saw from the Rear Window of the Hôtel Des Folies-Dramatiques, or the Story Point of View Films Told" pp. 36–38 in *Ce que je vois de mon ciné: la représentation du regard dans le cinema des premiers temps*, edited by André Gaudréault. Saint-Étienne: Méridiens Klincksieck, 1988.

Hall, Mordaunt 'Review, *Grand Hotel*', *New York Times* (13 April 1932), 23: 3.

Hartmann, Susan M. *The Home Front and Beyond: American Women in the 1940s*, Boston: Twayne, 1982.

Heath, Stephen. 'Film and System, Terms of Analysis, Parts 1 and 2', *Screen* 16 nos. 1 and 2 (Spring and Summer 1975): 7–77, 91–113.

Heath, S. 'On Suture' pp. 76–112 in *Questions of Cinema*. Bloomington: Indiana University Press, 1981.

Social Research 58, No. 1 Special Issue, *Home: A Place in the World*. 1991.

'Homesteading Veteran', *Life*, (20 January 1947), Cover.

Honey, Maureen. *Creating Rosie the Riveter: Class, Gender, and Propaganda During World War II*. Amherst: University of Massachusetts Press, 1984.

Jakle, John A. and Sculle, Keith A. *Fast Food: Roadside Restaurants in the Automobile Age*. Berkeley: University of California Press, 1999.

Jakle, John A., Sculle, Keith A. and Rogers, Jefferson S. *The Motel in America*. Baltimore: Johns Hopkins University Press, 1996.

James, Henry. *The American Scene* (ed. Leon Edel). Bloomington: Indiana University Press, 1968 [1907].

Jameson, Frederic. *Postmodernism or, the Cultural Logic of Late Capitalism*. Durham, NC: Duke University Press, 1991.

Jezer, Marty. *The Dark Ages: Life in the United States, 1945–1960*. Boston: South End Press, 1982.

Kaledin, Eugenia. *Daily Life in the United States, 1940–1959: Shifting Worlds*. New York: Greenwood Press, 2000.

Kaluszynski, Martine. 'Republican Identity: Bertillonage as Government Technique', pp. 123–138 in *Documenting Individual Identity: the Development of State Practices in the Modern World* edited by Jane Caplan and John Torpey. Princeton: Princeton University Press, 2001.

Kanigel, Robert. *High Season: How One French Riviera Town Has Seduced Travelers for Two Thousand Years*. New York: Viking, 2002.

Katz, Marc. 'The Hotel Kracauer' *Differences: A Journal of Feminist Cultural Studies* 11 no. 2 (July 1999): 134–152.

Keck, Herbert. 'The Profitable Void: The Atrium hotel', *Daidalos* 62 (March 1999): 42–51.

Koolhaas, Rem. *Delirious New York: A Retroactive Manifesto for Manhattan.* London: Academy Editions, 1978.

Kracauer, Siegfried. 'The Hotel Lobby.' pp. 173–185 in *The Mass Ornament: Weimar Essays.* Translated by Thomas Y. Levin. Cambridge: Harvard University Press, 1995 [1922–25].

———. *Le Roman Policier*, Gustav and Rainer Rochlitz (trans.) Paris: Payot, 2001 [1922–25].

———. 'Berliner Nebeneinander', *Frankfurter Zeitung* (17 February, 1933), 1–2.

Kuznick, Peter J. and Gilbert, James Burkhart. *Rethinking Cold War Culture.* Washington D.C.: Smithsonian Press, 2001.

Lefebvre, Henri. *The Production of Space* (translated by) Donald Nicholson-Smith, Oxford: Blackwell, 1991.

Lucassen, Leo. 'A Many-Headed Monster: The Evolution of the Passport System in the Netherlands and Germany in the Long Nineteenth Century', pp. 235–255 in *Documenting Individual Identity: the Development of State Practices in the Modern World* edited by Jane Caplan and John Torpey, Princeton: Princeton University Press, 2001.

MacCannell, Dean. 'Democracy's Turn: On Homeless Noir', pp. 279–297 in *Shades of Noir: A Reader* edited by Joan Copjec, London: Verso, 1993.

Marx, Gary T. 'Identity and Anonymity: Some Conceptual Distinctions and Issues for Research', pp. 311–327 in *Documenting Individual Identity: the Development of State Practices in the Modern World* edited by Jane Caplan and John Torpey, Princeton: Princeton University Press, 2001.

Matlock, Jann. *Desires to Censor: Spectacles of the Body, Aesthetics, and Vision in Nineteenth-Century France.* (forthcoming)

———. 'Censoring the Realist Gaze' pp. 28-65, in *Spectacles of Realism: Gender, Body, Genre*, edited by Margaret Cohen and Christopher Prendergast, Minneapolis: University of Minnesota Press, 1995.

———. 'The Invisible Woman and Her Secrets Unveiled', *Yale Journal of Criticism* 9 no. 2 (Summer 1996): 175–221.

May, Elaine Tyler. 'Explosive Issues: Sex, Women, and The Bomb' pp. 154–170 in *Recasting America: Culture and Politics in the Age of Cold War*, edited by Lary May. Chicago: University of Chicago Press, 1989.

McGowen, Randall. 'Knowing the Hand: Forgery and the Proof of Writing in Eighteenth-Century England', *Historical Reflections* 24 no. 3 (Fall 1998): 385–414.

Meunier, H. *The Hotel and Catering Trades: Ouvrage à l'Usage Des Élèves Des Écoles Hotelières et Du Personnel de l'Hotellerie.* Paris: n.p., 1961.

Meyerowitz, Joanne. 'Sexual Geography and Gender Economy: The Furnished Room Districts of Chicago, 1890–1930', pp. 43–71 in *Gender and American History Since 1890* edited by Barbara Melosh. London: Routledge, 1993.

———. 'Beyond the Feminine Mystique: A Reassessment of Postwar Mass Culture, 1946–1958', *The Journal of American History* 79 no. 4 (March 1993):1455–82.

——. 'Women, Cheesecake, and Borderline Material: Responses to Girlie Pictures in the Mid-Twentieth Century U.S', *Journal of Women's History* 8 no. 3 (Fall 1996): 9–35.

Naremore, James. *More Than Night: Film Noir in Its Contexts*. Berkeley: University of California Press, 1998.

'No Vacancies' *Life (International Edition)*, (9 December 1946), 12–13.

Noiriel, Gérard. 'The Identification of the Citizen: The Birth of Republican Civil Status in France', pp. 28–48 in *Documenting Individual Identity: the Development of State Practices in the Modern World* edited by Jane Caplan and John Torpey, Princeton: Princeton University Press, 2001.

Oudart, Jean-Pierre. 'Cinema and Suture', *Screen* 18 no. 4 (Winter 1977–78): 35–47.

'Peace Brings Temporary Unemployment', *Life* (3 September 1945): 30–31.

Penley, C. 'Feminism, Film Theory, and the Bachelor Machines' pp. 456–473 in *Film and Theory: An Anthology* edited by Robert Stam and Toby Miller. Oxford: Blackwell, 2000.

Pevsner, Nikolaus. *A History of Building Types*. London: Thames and Hudson, 1976.

Pinkerton, Allan. *Thirty Years a Detective*. New York: Dillingham, 1884.

Polan, Dana. *Power and Paranoia: History, Narrative and the American Cinema, 1940–1950*. New York: Columbia University Press, 1986.

Reed, Christopher (ed.) Not *at Home: The Suppression of Domesticity in Modern Art and Architecture*. London: Thames and Hudson, 1996.

Richardson, Dorothy. 'The Long Day [1905]' pp. 1–303 in *Women at Work* edited by William O'Neill. Chicago: Quadrangle, 1972.

Riley, Terence (ed.) *Frank Lloyd Wright: Architect*. New York: Museum of Modern Art, 1994.

Rodell, Fred. 'Divorce Muddle' *Life* (3 September, 1945): 86–96.

Sandoval-Strausz, Andrew K. 'For the Accommodation of Strangers: Urban Space, Travel, Law, the Market, and Modernity at the American Hotel, 1789–1908'. Chicago: University of Chicago (Ph.D. Dissertation; Order No. DA3070204) 2002.

Schwartz, Vanessa R. *Spectacular Realities: Early Mass Culture in Fin-de-Siècle Paris*. Berkeley: University of California Press, 1998.

Severo, Richard and Milford, Lewis. *The Wages of War: When America's Soldiers Came Home—From Valley Forge to Vietnam*. New York: Simon and Schuster, 1989.

Silver, Kenneth E. *Making Paradise: Art, Modernity, and the Myth of the French Riviera*. Cambridge, MA: MIT Press, 2001.

Silverman, Kaja. *The Subject of Semiotics*. New York: Oxford University Press, 1983.

——. *Threshold of the Visible World*. New York: Routledge, 1996.

'"Since the Atom Bomb"' (Cartoon), *Saturday Evening Post*, (19 October 1946), 163.

Sobchak, Vivian. 'Lounge Time: Postwar Crises and the Chronotope of Film Noir', pp. 129–170 in *Refiguring American Film Genres: History and Theory*, edited by Nick Browne. Berkeley: University of California Press, 1998.

'Soldier at Ease: New York Hotel Treats Paratrooper Veteran', *Life*, 3 December 1945, 43–6.

Spears., Timothy B. *One Hundred Years on the Road: The Traveling Salesman in American Culture*, New Haven: Yale University Press, 1995.

'Statler Hotel Advertisement', *Life*, (26 November 1945), 47.

'Statler Hotel Advertisement', *Saturday Evening Post*, (19 October 1946), 163.

'Studebaker Advertisement'. *Esquire* (19 December, 1945), n. p.

Tallack, Douglas. '"Waiting, Waiting": The Hotel Lobby, in the Modern City' pp. 139–151 in *The Hieroglyphics of Space: Reading and Experiencing the Modern Metropolis* edited by Neil Leach. London: Routledge, 2002.

Thomson, David. 'Review, Lamster, Ed. *Architecture and Film*', *Metropolis Magazine* www.metropolismag.com/html/content_0500/review.htm 2000 (accessed 11 August 2005).

Thornton, Tamara Plakins. *Handwriting in America: A Cultural History*. New Haven: Yale University Press, 1996.

Tobey, Ronald, Wetehrell, Charles and Brigham, Jay. (9909) 'Moving Out and Settling In: Residential Mobility: Home Owning, and the Public Enframing of Citizenship, 1921–1950', *The American Historical Review* 95, no. 5. (December 1990): 1395–1422.

Torpey, John C. *The Invention of the Passport: Surveillance, Citizenship, and the State*, Cambridge: Cambridge University Press, 2000.

——. 'The Great War and the Birth of the Modern Passport System', pp. 256–270 in *Documenting Individual Identity: The Development of State Practices in the Modern World* edited by Jane Caplan and John Torpey, Princeton: Princeton University Press, 2001.

Trollope, Anthony *North America*, New York: Knopf, 1951 [1862].

'U.S. Normalcy', *Life*, (3 December 1945), 27–35.

Vidler, Anthony. *Warped Space: Art, Architecture, and Anxiety in Modern Culture*. Cambridge: MIT Press, 2000.

'The Waldorf-Astoria: Most Famous U.S. Hotel Thrives on Sumptuous Efficiency', *Life*, (24 September 1945), 98–103.

Westbrook, Robert B. '"I Want a Girl Just Like the Girl That Married Harry James": American Women and the Problem of Political Obligation in World War II', *American Quarterly* 42, no. 4 (December 1990): 587–614.

Wharton, Annabel Jane. *Building the Cold War: Hilton International Hotels and Modern Architecture* Chicago, University of Chicago Press, 2001.

——. 'Two Waldorf-Astorias: Spatial Economies as Totem and Fetish', *Art Bulletin* 85, no. 3 (September 2003): 523–543

Wigley, Mark. 'Lost in Space', *Archis* 12 (1997): 8–18.

Williamson, Jefferson. *The American Hotel: An Anecdotal History*, New York: Arno Press, 1975 [1930].

Wilson, Christina. 'Cedric Gibbons: Architect of Hollywood's Golden Age', pp. 111–116 in *Architecture and Film* edited by Mark Lamster. Princeton: Princeton Architectural Press, 2000.

Chapter Four

The Swiss Hotel Film

Roland-François Lack

Pour Daniel Schmid (1941–2006)

The recent closure of the Grand Hôtel de Locarno-Muralto was a blow to the international prestige of Swiss hotel-keeping, and also to Swiss film culture. When it opened in 1874, it was the first of its kind in Ticino and, like most of the grand hotels then proliferating elsewhere in Switzerland, became a draw for international celebrities. Already a part of History, as site of the 1925 Locarno Conference, the hotel became part of cinema history in August 1946 as first home of the Locarno Film Festival, premiering *Rome Open City* and accommodating Ava Gardner. It has remained the glamorous heart of the Festival: for a certain kind of visitor to Switzerland, it is *the* Swiss film hotel.[1]

Under four headings ('Grand Hotels', 'Tourists', 'Locals' and 'The Swiss Hotel Film'), this essay explores several comparable conjunctions of Switzerland, cinema and *hôtellerie* (Figure 4.1).[2] The hotels featured cover the range identified by Henry James in 1879: "from the 'grand hotel' of the newest fashion, with a chalk-white front, a hundred balconies, and a dozen flags flying from its roof, to the little Swiss *pension* of an elder day" (James 1988, 47), plus a variety of twentieth-century additions, from glass and steel high-rise hotels to concrete, low-rise motels. The films range from 1890s' documentary views of Geneva, both visitor and local, through eighty or so twentieth-century fictions, by both outsiders (including Méliès, Hitchcock, Lang, Bergman, Sirk, Disney, Bogdanovich, Eastwood and Chabrol) and insiders (especially Tanner, Soutter and Godard), to several Swiss-hotel-related films made this century, including Plattner's *Les petites couleurs* (2001), Signorell's *Nocturne* (2004), both Swiss, Rai's *Asambhav* (India 2004) and Sorrentino's *Consequences of Love* (Italy 2005).

143

Figure 4.1. The Grand Hôtel des Salines, Bex, which features in Soutter's *Repérages* (1977)
Public Domain

Asambhav is a Ticino-set Bollywood thriller with sequences shot at Locarno's Grand Hotel, displaying well the splendour of its interiors and exterior. If, as may happen (D'Urso 2003), the hotel is demolished or remodelled beyond recognition, it will persist more vividly in Rai's film than in our fading memories. Before the dilapidated Grand Hotel in nearby Brissago was demolished, Swiss filmmaker Isa Hesse-Rabinovitch commemorated the building and the spirit of those it had housed in her film *Geister und Gäste—In memoriam Grand Hotel Brissago*. The ghosts were not only those of past guests (among them Paul Klee, Thomas Mann, Hemingway, Nabokov and Hermann Hesse, the filmmaker's father-in-law); Hesse-Rabinivitch had also retrieved the hotel's ciné-memories, with footage from *Stresemann*, a 1957 German film on the Locarno Conference,[3] shot at the hotel in Brissago. The ruins of the hotel are now gone, replaced by Aurelio Galfetti's Villa Bianca, a block of private residences, and Hesse-Rabinovitch's film is almost alone in remembering the lost hotel (see Nestler, 1993).

The selection of *Asambhav* to open the 2004 Locarno Festival signalled this memorial function of cinema, and in more localised terms celebrated the growing enthusiasm of Bollywood for Swiss locales, as well as Switzerland's continuing readiness to have foreign cinema exploit its familiar landscapes. Indian filmmakers come to Switzerland for the mountains and lakes but, like other such tourists before them (like Hitchcock, Disney and Clint Eastwood), they stop at and film in Swiss hotels.[4]

If other films were made at this Locarno hotel before *Asambhav*, memories thereof are also fading and, like the hotel itself, may eventually be lost. The archivists of the Festival seem not to have extended their remit beyond records of guests invited, films shown and prizes awarded. It would have fallen to the archivists of the hotel itself to preserve the memory of its associations with cinema, but the decline in the hotel's prestige and the struggle for actual survival made the retrieval of its ciné-memories a lesser priority.

To be fair, ciné-memories are rarely a hotel's priority. Films remember hotels better than hotels remember films. Too often the places occupied by cinema are what Alexander Kluge (1998, 138) calls "Flecken ohne Erinnerung" (spots without memory), though right next to them will be the "highly-concentrated, memory-laden places" that were occupied by literature, or philosophy, or politics. This essay has concentrated, accordingly, on what in cinema there is of hotels, while occasionally discovering in hotels the traces of cinema. These last can most often be found in the memories of the grander type of hotel, which is where we begin.

GRAND HOTELS

> From our heritage of the last three centuries, we will take into the 21st century: the stock exchange, human rights, paper money, genocide, the difference between light and serious music, the rule of law, national constitutions and the grand hotel.
>
>   Kluge (1998, 139)[5]

Kluge's eclectic list, compiled in honour of, and in the comfort of, one of Switzerland's grandest hotels, connects the grand hotel with the big things of history. The smaller-scale history of particular grand hotels is regularly related in the Swiss press, as part of a national heritage, and several hotels have commissioned their own celebratory volumes for the coffee-table.[6] In these accounts are normally foregrounded their associations with politics, aristocracy, high society, sporting endeavour and culture. The cinema has its place in this display of prestige, most commonly in the mention of film stars who have been guests (Errol Flynn and Roger Moore at Geneva's Beau Rivage, for example, Douglas Fairbanks and Brigitte Bardot at St Moritz's Palace Hotel, or Walt Disney and Audrey Hepburn at the Grand Hotel Zermatterhof). A recent collective publication vaunting the merits of Geneva's hotels reproduces pages from the *livre d'or*, the guestbook, of several of the most prestigious: we learn, for example, that Alain Delon has stayed at the Bergues (as well as presidents Aristide Briand and Valéry Giscard d'Estaing), Sophia Loren at the Intercontinental (alongside Egyptian and U.S. presidents), and that guests at the Beau Rivage have included not only De Gaulle and the Aga Khan, but also Michel Piccoli.[7] Cinema's best Swiss hotel joke is, incidentally, delivered by Michel Piccoli (as the President of the Committee to Celebrate the Centenary of Cinema) on leaving the 'Hôtel du Lac' in Jean-Luc Godard's essay-film *2x50 ans de cinéma français* (1995).[8] A hotel employee rushes to bring him the guestbook to sign: "le livre d'or, Monsieur, le livre d'or", to which Piccoli replies: "Mon ami, laissez-le dormir" ("let it sleep, my friend", as if the other had said, "le livre dort", "the book is sleeping").

The Hotel Waldhaus in Sils-Maria (GR), 'Historic Hotel of the Year' for 2005, is one of the best served by commemorative publications, with a study by an architectural historian (Flückiger, 2005), a history written by the owners, descendants of the hotel's founder (Kienberger, 1984), and a photographic portrait (Schaefer, 1998). This last was published to celebrate the ninetieth anniversary of the hotel's inauguration, with accompanying texts by eminent signatories of the Waldhaus's *livre d'or*, including the filmmakers Alexander Kluge, Daniel Schmid and Claude Chabrol.

Kluge's contribution, cited above, theorises on the grand hotel in general, and evokes the Waldhaus's associations with literature (Hermann Hesse and Thomas Mann) and with philosophy, through T.W. Adorno:

> Places are defined by what happened there, by collective memory. Civilised places are receptacles as they concentrate *subjective* relationships. Among the thousand dessert forks at the *Waldhaus*, said Theodor Adorno, there are seven forks, washed thousands of times, which Thomas Mann once used to eat his plum cake. Adorno continues, 'There are no places for people without imagination.' (Kluge 1998, 139)

Schmid, a great imaginer of hotels, also theorises, as he writes of his childhood in a hotel in the same canton. He connects personal memories to the history of Swiss hotel-keeping, like the stories, told by his grandmother, of his grandfather who had waited on Sarah Bernhardt while working for César Ritz at the Savoy in London:

> In their retelling her stories never stayed quite the same and often took surprising, unexpected turns in the exuberance of the telling and later especially in my oblique memories. It is not the facts that are crucial but what one makes of them. This, in turn, builds on the 'vibrating screen of forgetting' as a component of

the process of remembering, with the various possible strands of a story meeting, seemingly contradicting each other and expanding on each other. (Schmid 1998, 31)

Chabrol provides an excerpt from the script of *Rien ne va plus*, a 1996 thriller with scenes set and shot at the Waldhaus. Revised editions of this commemorative volume will no doubt also feature Riccardo Signorell, whose *Nocturne* (2004) was set and shot entirely at the Waldhaus. Signorell draws, indeed, on the 1998 book for elements of his script, evoking Kluge's account of waiting for sleep in grand hotels. The difference in how the Waldhaus is represented by the outsider Chabrol and by the local Signorell comes down not so much to the latter's use of black and white, where Chabrol uses colour, but rather to the peculiar intensity in Signorell's use of the locale. For *Rien ne va plus* the Waldhaus is just one picturesque stage in the criminals' itinerary (which includes a hotel in Savoy and a villa in Guadeloupe), whereas *Nocturne* begins by arriving at the hotel and ends by leaving it. The outside world (outside the hotel and outside of Switzerland) hardly impinges, is confined to records of Schubert lieder and to quotations from Celan and Nietzsche (who anyway is thought of as a local in the Grisons). The hotel's collective memories are embodied in the manager, whose quoting of Hesse trivialises this cultural stock. The Waldhaus becomes a space occupied entirely by the suicidal protagonist's broodings, forgetting all else, including the collective memory of the hotel. *Nocturne* cannot be *the* Swiss film about the Swiss hotel, since the Swiss hotel is above all, for Switzerland, *the* memory-laden place. *The* Swiss hotel film, this essay will conclude, is a film by Daniel Schmid, one that "builds on the 'vibrating screen of forgetting' as a component of the process of remembering".

The Swiss hotelier was César Ritz, 'hôtelier des rois' and 'roi des hôteliers', according to Edward VII. He is briefly remembered in Schmid's *Zwischensaison*, but there is no film biography of Ritz to commemorate on screen the finest hours of Swiss hotel-keeping.[9] Perhaps any scene set at a hotel associated with him—at the Savoy, Carlton or Ritz, for example—can be read as cinema's acknowledgement of that pre-eminence. See, for example, in the work of cinema's pre-eminent maker of hotel scenes, the sequence in *Foreign Correspondent* where the protagonist takes a taxi from the London Carlton to a party at the Savoy.

The Swiss hotel would not be one of Ritz's since, though he established his reputation as manager of the Rigi-Kulm and the Grand Hotel National in Lucerne, the great hotelier created no hotels in his homeland. The Swiss hotel *par excellence* would be, rather, one of those luxurious lakeside or alpine palaces for which Switzerland is equally famous, one of those I have already mentioned, or else the Suvretta Haus in St Moritz, the Palace in Gstaad, the Mont Cervin in Zermatt, the Bergues or the Richemond in Geneva, the Beau Rivage in Lausanne or the Montreux Palace.

With appearances in several European comedies and Indian melodramas, the Gstaad Palace is probably the most frequently filmed Swiss hotel,[10] but few establishments of this kind have been displayed on screen more fully than the Trois Couronnes in Vevey, location and setting for Peter Bogdanovich's 1974 film of *Daisy Miller*. Henry James wrote and set the novel there in 1879, and—as the recent director's commentary makes clear—Bogdanovich revelled in the preserved authenticity of the locale, though in fact the hotel was extensively remodelled in 1890, creating a façade and interior features that are lovingly framed by the film but which do not belong to the hotel James knew and wrote about. The film also did its own remodelling (importing period furniture and candelabras from Rome, adding gravel to the surrounding paths), and after a period of decline new owners completely restored the hotel's 'belle époque' splendour, winning the 2003 'Historic Hotel of the Year' award as a consequence. It now trades on its association both with James's novel and Bogdanovich's film, as well as on the usual display of shahs, tsars and stars.[11]

Bogdanovich's *Daisy Miller* is a period fiction that documents the present aspect of Switzerland's palace hotels, while sharing their interest in constructing authenticity. It is not, however, *the* Swiss hotel film, which really should spend more time in the relevant locale (after twenty minutes at Vevey *Daisy Miller* moves on first to the castle at Chillon and then to Rome), should give a fuller picture of the life of the hotel (Bogdanovich's film focuses only on the guests), and should perhaps offer a view of this Swiss particularity from the inside. Bogdanovich claims an affinity with James's Europe as himself a descendant of Europeans, but his film's fixation on a postcard image for tourists—his determination, for example, to frame Cybill Shepherd on the hotel terrace with the Alps behind her—represents an outsider's view of Switzerland, and of its hotels.

Bogdanovich's *Daisy Miller* is a faithful adaptation, but what the film only shows the novel can discourse upon eloquently and—for our purposes—usefully, as in its opening paragraph:

At the little town of Vevey, in Switzerland, there is a particularly comfortable hotel. There are, indeed, many hotels; for the entertainment of tourists is the business of the place, which, as many travellers will remember, is seated upon the edge of a remarkably blue lake—a lake that it behoves every tourist to visit. The shore of the lake presents an unbroken array of establishments of this order, of every category, from the 'grand hotel' of the newest fashion, with a chalk-white front, a hundred balconies, and a dozen flags flying from its roof, to the little Swiss *pension* of an elder day, with its name inscribed in German-looking lettering upon a pink or yellow wall and an awkward summer-house in the angle of the garden. One of the hotels at Vevey, however, is famous, even classical, being distinguished from many of its upstart neighbors by an air both of luxury and of maturity. (James 1988, 47)

Even still, *Daisy Miller* is not *the* Swiss hotel novel, no more than are two other famous Swiss-set American novels, Hemingway's *A Farewell to Arms* (with only brief scenes in an anonymous hotel in Lausanne) and Fitzgerald's *Tender is the Night* (with glimpses of hotels in Caux and Gstaad). Films of these novels by Charles Vidor and Henry King respectively are lesser items in the Swiss-hotel-film canon, but Frank Borzage's 1932 adaptation of *A Farewell to Arms* adds to Hemingway's story material a highly charged Swiss hotel scene. Catherine is alone in Brissago and in a letter to Frederic describes her surroundings: "I've taken a suite in the best hotel and I'm fairly wallowing in luxury. [. . .] There's a divine view of the lake shimmering in the moonlight." As we hear this description the camera explores the room to reveal the truth, a truth she confesses aloud to a photograph of Frederic: "It's mean, cheap and horrible."

The *Swiss* hotel novel is either Dürrenmatt's little known *Durcheinandertal* (1989), or Martin Suter's *Le Diable à Milan* (2005), neither of which has yet been filmed. The better-known Swiss hotel novels are outsider fictions, Anita Brookner's Léman-set *Hotel du Lac*, for instance (1984, adapted for television in 1986), or better still Thomas Mann's Davos-set *The Magic Mountain* (1924). When adapted by Hans Geissendorfer in 1982, Mann's novel can seem to have become a viable Swiss hotel film. But though Geissendorfer's set is an authentic reconstruction, the setting of both novel and film is not a hotel but a sanatarium, an institution of a quite different order (and the matter of a quite different essay from this one[12]). It is true that the distinction is collapsing now the sanataria have almost all been converted to hotels, available to tourists wanting to relive the past in authentic locales without having to contract authentic diseases. The book *The Magic Mountain* has been co-opted by Davos's hotel industry as a promotional tool: at least two hotels trade on being Mann's model (the Waldhotel Bellevue and the Berghotel Schatzalp), and the film has played regularly at the local cinema (and on occasion at the Schatzalp).[13]

The *Swiss* hotel film might be found in the pages of Hervé Dumont's *Histoire du cinéma suisse*, a complete listing of fiction films produced in Switzerland between 1896 and 1965. Dumont signals the recurrence of topographical stereotypes in the corpus, notably mountain, village, lake and frontier settings, and identifies, out of Switzerland's 217 full-length features made in this period, some fifteen with a significant hotel setting. One of the

earliest is Choux's 1925 *La Vocation d'André Carel*, filmed on Lake Geneva
and framing its image of the lake as frontier by movement between two hotels, one in Switzerland (Glion) and one in France (Evian). (Seventy years
later *Le Parfum d'Yvonne* will move as freely across this frontier from hotel
to hotel, also using the Hôtel Royal in Evian.)

Other strong candidates are *Kleine Scheidegg* (1937), filmed at the Hotel
Bellevue there, at the foot of the Jungfrau, and *Der Hotelportier* (1941),
set in a fictional hotel in a fictional resort, but the strongest is *Palace Hotel*
(1952), set and shot in Badrutt's Palace Hotel in St Moritz. The set designer
Jean d'Eaubonne gives the film a visual allure, but the replacement at the last
minute of Max Ophuls as director, apart from depriving Ophuls of a subject
well suited to his opulent style, also deprived *Palace Hotel* of the chance to be
canonised internationally as a memorable Swiss hotel film. It ended up being
directed by less accomplished locals, and is now forgotten. (The hotel's chief
association with the cinema is now to be made in room 501, the favoured
suite of Alfred Hitchcock, and a key site for the ciné-tourist.)

Dumont points out that the Palace Hotel's complicity with the interests of
the Swiss hotel trade makes it a slightly embarrassing paean to the virtue of
the humble hotel worker. It is as if the filmmakers had noted the press comments (cited by Dumont) on *Der Hotelportier*, expressing the anxiety that
the caricatural portrait of a hotel director might "harm our hotel trade [. . .].
Make farces if you must, but don't use them to endanger our healthy Swiss
mentality." It is hard to imagine any palace-centred hotel film not serving
the interests of the hotel, and of the tourist industry more generally. Literary
representations of the Swiss hotel are less bound to the exigencies of tourism.
No hotel would, for example, accommodate the making of a film that shared
the views of the novelist Jacques Chessex, who in his *Portraits des vaudois*
delivered the most scathing critique of the palace hotel and its place in Swiss
culture, castigating its snobism, its ugliness, and the protection it offers the
privileged against the ravages of time. The film of *The Magic Mountain* is
perhaps different from the book in this respect exactly, in not holding the
place represented responsible for the sickness it houses.

The Magic Mountain, *Palace Hotel* and *Daisy Miller* were made with the
cooperation of the hotels featured, and all are excellent advertisements for
them. Even so bleak a hotel-centred film as Riccardo Signorell's *Nocturne*—a
monochrome brooding on metaphysical angst and the prospect of suicide—
displays the luxurious aspect of the Hotel Waldhaus as lovingly as A. T.
Schaeffer's commissioned photographs of the same hotel. (And just in case
the film missed something, the DVD of *Nocturne* has as a bonus a short film
documenting the real staff of the hotel, each smiling in his or her setting, in
colour.)

The circumstances of production prohibit such films from developing a discourse hostile to the grand hotel and its cultural prestige. Nor are we likely to find such a critique in the body of films discussed in the next section. Very few ciné-tourists have gone home from ciné-Switzerland complaining of their accommodation.

TOURISTS

We're only passing through.[14]

Swiss hotels are familiar sights in foreign films, beginning in 1896 with a Lumière view showing the Hôtel de la Balance in Geneva's Place Bel-Air, continuing through travelogue-type documentaries and into fiction films. In 1903, a British company's reconstruction of a spectacular motoring exploit (known as 'Captain Deasy's Daring Drive'), showed a (Swiss-made) motor vehicle driving up the cog railway from Caux to the Rochers de Naye. The film also shows the Palace Hotel at Caux, not incidentally since, as Roland Cosandey points out (2005, 101), in Switzerland "cinematic travelogues follow the many international tourist rail networks established between 1880 and 1914—lines offering multiple means of access to spectacular Alpine sites", and hotels were an integral part of the "tourism-designed facilities" exploited by these films. (Cosandey also suggests that the director of the Caux Palace may be identified at one point as a passenger in the vehicle.)

The following year saw the cinematic record of a yet more spectacular exploit, Méliès's *Voyage à travers l'impossible*. This appears to be the first fiction film to visit Switzerland, bringing curious travellers from Paris through a picturesque (indeed painted) landscape of mountains, valleys, waterfalls and lakes, to Interlaken (according to the signpost on the painted set of the railway station). There the vehicle in which they are travelling destroys the dining room of an inn (transposing an incident in 1901 in Germany, when a train crashed through buffers to enter the station restaurant at Frankfurt-am-Main). After the crash Méliès's tourists reassure those in the inn with a remark emblematic thereafter of the ciné-tourist in Switzerland: "Nous ne sommes que de passage"—"We're only passing through."

After time spent recovering in hospital (initiating thereby convalescence as another recurrent motif in Swiss-set films), Méliès's tourists move on to the Jungfrau, using its slope as a launch pad for their train's take-off into space. This particular choice of locale for the exploit signals the actuality of the Jungfrau railway then under construction, a complex feat of engineering that would, when completed in 1912, bring rail travellers to the Jungfraujoch, reaching spectacular Alpine sites hitherto accessible only to climbers. A film of the genuine Jungfrau railway was shown at the 1914 National Exhibition in Berne, among dozens of other local views (Cosandey 2000, 106), and by 1937 the Jungfraubahn is instrumental in the denouement of a marital melo-drama in Schweizer's *Kleine Scheidegg* (see Buache 1998, 80). The site was made spectacularly accessible to cinemagoers in Clint Eastwood's 1975 film *The Eiger Sanction*, and today Indian ciné-tourists are catered for by the 'Bol-lywood' restaurant there, 'the highest Indian restaurant in Europe'.

The hotel-restaurant destroyed by Méliès's tourists is incidental to the main action. As much is true of the many Swiss hotels seen on screen thereafter. In foreign fictions especially, Switzerland is a place of passage, traversed by a predictable if varied set of strangers, all of whom are likely to be filmed near mountains and lakes, and in hotels. By the nineteen-thirties, German, English and American cinema had begun to litter Switzerland with its tourists—with honeymooners and adventurers, sports enthusiasts and convalescents, dip-lomats and travelling salesmen, criminals, detectives, spies, anarchists and other miscellaneous strangers.

The Berlin-based production *Der Springer von Pontresina* (aka *Liebe in St. Moritz*) is a comedy filmed in February 1934 during a ski-jump competition in which, according to Dumont's description, "St. Moritz and its hotels are omnipresent". The same year, Hitchcock's *The Man Who Knew Too Much* also featured winter sports in St. Moritz (perhaps using footage of the same competition?). Hitchcock and Alma Reville had honeymooned in St. Moritz in the twenties, and this is the first of two Swiss-set thrillers that place his tourists and spies in those familiar surroundings. *The Man Who Knew Too Much* spends its first ten minutes in Switzerland, beginning with a pre-credits prologue showing piled-up holiday brochures, from which a hand selects, firstly, a 'Guide to Swiss Hotels, 1934', then guides to various resorts, includ-ing Arosa, Griesalp and St. Moritz. Though Hitchcock and Reville had first thought of making this film while staying at the Palace Hotel, the studio-built hotel interiors do not seem to be directly modelled on that locale, and the resort's exteriors are supplied by secondary footage.

Two years later, his other Swiss film derived its authenticity from clichés ("What do they have in Switzerland?", asked Hitchcock: "mountains, lakes, folk dancing and chocolate"), but also drew on reminiscences of his regular Alpine holidays. *Secret Agent* mixes studio reconstruction with location foot-age but, unlike *The Man Who Knew Too Much*, the specific Swiss locale is not fixed. The spies reside at a Hotel Excelsior in an anonymous resort that is, according to a signpost, somewhere near the Niesen mountain, so just south of the Lake of Thun (though there was no actual Hotel Excelsior in that vicinity at the time[15]). They visit the church at Langenthal, apparently nearby but actually some sixty kilometres away, and later climb the 'Langen Alp', the name of a mountain not in Switzerland but somewhat further away, in Austria. In one sequence, the images of a Swiss lake projected behind the actors in a London studio were, according to the star John Gielgud, footage of Lake Como (which is in Italy).

German productions such as Trenker's *Love Letters from the Engadine* (1938) could easily access authentic Swiss settings but, given the availability of stock footage and, for Hollywood at least, the proximity of alternative mountainous regions, nothing requires that a Swiss-set film be shot in Switzerland. The landscape around the Swiss hotel in *Thin Ice* (1937), a Sonje Henie vehicle, is Mount Rainier National Park, Washington;[16] in *Stolen Holiday* (1937) and *Swiss Miss* (1938) it is Big Bear Valley, California, but both locales pass for authentic Alpine settings, as does Idaho's Sun Valley in *I Met Him in Paris*. *Swiss Miss* makes an effort to be precise about where it is set (in the Grisons, somewhere near Pontresina), and the 'Alpen Hotel', the film's studio-built setting, is, as James might have described it, a "little Swiss pension of an elder day, with its name inscribed in German-looking lettering upon a pink or yellow wall". But it is doomed to inauthenticity by the plot premise that the staff should all wear local costume to create a Tyrolian atmosphere, since a composer who is a guest there is writing a Tyrolian opera. (The Tyrol is in Austria and Italy, not in Switzerland.[17])

In *Magnificent Obsession* (1954), Douglas Sirk seems wilfully to be playing on the inherent facticity of the Swiss hotel and its cinematic construction when he accesses the Swiss-set passage of the film via a picture-postcard received in the United States, postmarked Lucerne. The still photograph of the Lucerne Schweizerhof becomes a moving image before our eyes, a topographically redundant transformation of absence into presence, since the city and hotel made present are not otherwise a setting for the film. The Swiss-set action is centred on another hotel, the 'Alpen Ruhe' in or near Zurich, which is also picturesque, studio-built, and has its name inscribed in German lettering on a yellow wall.

For Fritz Lang's spy thriller *Cloak and Dagger* (1946), footage of mountain tops seen from a plane authenticates Gary Cooper's flight to Zurich, with the Swissness of the studio-confected airport marked by posters recommending local resorts.[18] An exterior shot of a certain Hotel Bristol suggests location work, but this is not the hotel of that name in Zurich: it looks like stock footage of a Hotel Bristol in another, as yet unidentified, European city. At the desk, the hotel is named on the registration form as the Neues Posthotel, which was not a Zurich hotel, but from this point the Swiss-hotel based action is all studio confection, made authentic more by the exotic manner of the international guests and the obsequiousness of the local staff.

Switzerland's airports and hotels receive similar filmic treatment twenty years later in the thriller *Kaleidoscope*, a European-based production enjoying spectacular London and Monte Carlo locations, with a ten-minute episode in Geneva. Warren Beatty's arrival is marked by an unconvincing sign reading 'Geneva Airport', but the real streets and real hotel ('the Alexandra') that follow restore verisimilitude. Beatty later leaves his hotel room by the window, and plunging views of the real streets below are offered as he crosses from rooftop to rooftop. These real streets are not Geneva, however, but Monte Carlo, which properly, according to the story, is Beatty's next destination. And Geneva's 'Hotel Alexandra' is in fact the Monte Carlo hotel of that name: its exterior is recognisable to locals and habitués, for whom *Kaleidoscope* accordingly fails the test of verisimilitude.[19]

Kaleidoscope borrows plot elements from Ian Fleming's novel *Casino Royale*; Bond films from the same period are only a little more careful in their depiction of Switzerland. A shot of the emblematic bears means, for instance, that there is no mistaking Berne in *On Her Majesty's Secret Service* (1969), but that city's distinguished Schweizerhof Hotel is then made to pass as an office building. A glimpse later of the Hotel Oberland in Lauterbrunnen is a rare sight of a Swiss hotel in the Bond corpus, though a good opportunity was missed in *Goldfinger*. Fleming's novel had Bond stay at the Bergues, one of Geneva's palace hotels. Perhaps to avoid the expensive studio-reconstruction of the Bergues's distinctively luxurious interiors, or simply to omit a setting where nothing happens, the film has Bond drive straight on in pursuit of his prey, into the distinctly natural and authentic setting of the Furka Pass (driving past Seiler's famous Hotel Belvedere on the way).

Bond films went to Switzerland in the sixties for the picturesque landscapes. The mountains shown in *Goldfinger* and *On Her Majesty's Secret Service* are authentically Swiss, an advance not only on Méliès in 1904, but also on Hitchcock in the 1930s, who combined real Swiss mountains with studio-built fakes, on Sirk in the 1950s, who in *Magnificent Obsession* projected authentic-looking Alpine footage behind Rock Hudson and Jane Wyman in the studio, on *The Trollenberg Terror* (1959), where location work for scenes in the valley and for some panoramic views is combined with unconvincing back projection and studio constructions, and even on Disney's *Third Man On the Mountain* (1959), which achieved its 'high altitude thrills' through painstaking and dangerous location shooting on the Matterhorn, but still used painted mattes for some panoramic views (Maltin 1985, 165). In 1948 David Lean's *The Passionate Friends*, opening with "a sunlit lake and snow-capped mountains and a holiday in Switzerland," had taken great pride and achieved great beauty in its authentic Alpine locations, even if the actual locations were not Switzerland but the mountains, lake and hotel of Annecy, in French Savoy.

Seventy years after Méliès destroyed a plasterboard hotel-restaurant against a painted Alpine backdrop, the anxiety of authenticity was felt at its deepest by another director-star, Clint Eastwood in *The Eiger Sanction*. As well as authentic stunts performed by Eastwood himself, this film had a real mountain, the Eiger (only a short distance from Méliès's Jungfrau), and, in this picturesque setting, a real hotel, the Hôtel Bellevue des Alpes—the hotel that had provided the setting for the 1937 Eiger film, *Kleine Scheidegg*.[20]

In his 1930 essay on the beauty of mountains, the Swiss novelist Ramuz (1968, 360) argued that the subject was particularly suited to cinematic representation, arguing that the cinema alone, thanks to its mastery of scale, can fully express that beauty: "The cinema is not at all troubled by the Cervin" (the French name for the Matterhorn). Ramuz could have cited in evidence *La Croix du Cervin* (1922), *Der Kampf ums Matterhorn* (1928) or *Der Bergführer* (filmed on the Eiger in 1917),[21] local instances of a genre preoccupied with the authenticity of locale, at least as far as filming up real mountains is concerned (any contiguous hotels can more readily be studio constructions, as in the 1923 *Appel de la montagne*). Later, Disney's Matterhorn-set *Third Man on the Mountain*, with its studio-confected hotel,[22] and Eastwood's *The Eiger Sanction* revived a tradition that local filmmakers had abandoned.

It is the tourist film especially that has continued to realise the cinematic potential of mountains, above all in those films made by ciné-tourists from India. Among the first was Raj Kapoor, whose 1964 film *Sangam* has a honeymoon sequence filmed in several Swiss locales, including Kleine Scheidegg, which is at the foot of the Jungfrau, Monch and Eiger mountains. The Hôtel Bellevue can be glimpsed from the train the honeymooners take up to the Jungfraujoch, the same hotel and railway seen later in *The Eiger Sanction*, and seen again in Anil Sharma's *The Hero: Love Story of a Spy* (2004). Unlike Eastwood's film, however, Bollywood's Swiss-shot productions cannot be seen as continuations of the indigenous *bergfilm* tradition, if only because they lack the concern for topographical exactitude that underscores the authenticity of the filmed experience. Bollywood's Switzerland is a composite fantasy in which the passage from lakeside to mountain top to hotel bedroom is the visualisation of desire, not the representation of displacement. Many such productions do not even seek to represent Switzerland, but simply present its mountains and lakes as local, i.e., Indian, or as other locales. (In Sharma's *The Hero*, so distinctive a Swiss tourist site as the Jungfrau and its railway is transformed by the story into a mountain and railway in Canada.)

The tourist films discussed so far, if not all from Holly- or Bollywood, have all been studio-based or sanctioned productions that have reconstructed or actually visited Switzerland because of the contribution Swiss elements might make to the envisaged spectacle. Though the sense of spectacle tends to be somewhat muted, the same impulse is evident in more independent European works from an art-cinema tradition. The first is probably the British avant-garde film *Borderline* (1930), centred dramatically and symbolically on the arrival at and departure from a small lakeside town (a composite of Lutry, Territet, Aigle and Saint Maurice) of an emblematic stranger, played by Paul Robeson. He and his wife are pictured against the wide open spaces of the landscape as a harmonious couple, and in the claustrophobic spaces of the town's small hotels as fatally separated. This spatial opposition is a cliché in the indigenous mountain films of the same period, but it also, as we shall see, informs the structure of films by later Swiss filmmakers such as Godard and Tanner. The emblematic stranger is also recurrent in their work.[23]

Ingmar Bergman's *Törst* (1949) exploited the same claustral motif in its Swiss hotel setting, but there the contrast is with landscapes beyond Switzerland, evoked in memory. After four shots that establish the place as Basel and the space as a hotel on the banks of the Rhine, the next twenty-five minutes are spent with the bored married couple in a small room, an intense atmosphere relieved only by flashbacks to Sweden and a brief glimpse of the street (not the river) outside when the man buys a newspaper. The exterior is a location shot of a famous hotel (the Krafft-am-Rhein, where Hesse wrote *Steppenwolf* twenty years before). The interior is a studio construction, where nothing marks the setting as Swiss except the narrative context that this is a place of passage, an intermediary between Sicily and Sweden, and a preliminary to crossing the ravaged landscape of Germany: untouched by history, the Swiss hotel room is a non-place at the centre of the film's topography.

A similar void at the centre of things is signified in one of the more recent Swiss hotel films to be distributed internationally, Sorrentino's *The Consequences of Love* (2005). Apart from an excursion to Naples (to the Hotel New Europe), almost all of the action is centred on what the press release and reviews identify as 'an anonymous Swiss hotel' in an unidentified Swiss town, which in fact is a composite of Lugano, Mendrisio, Chiasso and Bellinzona (all Ticino). The reception desk, foyer, bar, restaurant, corridors, and rooms of the hotel are shown, as well as the view from its windows, but nothing dispels its anonymity. Nor could a match among the hotels of those four towns be found, for the simple reason that the hotel we see is actually in Treviso, Italy (the filmmaker's home town).

The story's representation of this Italian hotel as Swiss suits its preoccupation with money: the hotel resident on whom the plot centres deposits mafia money every week in a Swiss bank, where of course no awkward questions are asked (the Swiss-banking motif is a stereotype not discussed in this essay, though it occasionally connects with the Swiss-hotel motif). The actual location of the bank shown is Chiasso, on the Swiss–Italian border,[24] and this precarious position connects thematically to that of the protagonist, just as the hotel's anonymity connects to his self-effacement.

Consequences of Love would perhaps be better discussed in an essay on the Italian Hotel Film, but it belongs here too, surely, alongside Tyrolean operettas, Bollywood travelogues and other outsider confections, because the anonymity of its hotel is not only stereotypically Swiss (as in *Secret Agent*), but also authentically Swiss, very like the anonymity of hotels in the work of certain local filmmakers. Both anonymous and recognisable hotels in Swiss-made films are discussed in the following section, chiefly through two opposed cases: one, Jean-Luc Godard, a director of international reputation, only a fifth of whose output can be called Swiss; the other, Michel Soutter, hardly known outside of Switzerland, every one of whose ten films is Swiss. (Also discussed are hotels of both types in films by Patricia Plattner and Alain Tanner.[25])

LOCALS

It's beautiful from here. You can see all of Switzerland.[26]

Jean-Luc Godard is the *Swiss* hotel filmmaker—parsed as the Swiss film-maker who films hotels. Hotels figure significantly in at least half of his thirty-six feature-length films,[27] and five different films feature Swiss hotels (*Le petit soldat, Sauve qui peut (la vie), Passion, King Lear, 2 x 50 ans de cinéma français*). The first of these, from 1960, played on and played down the glamour of the spy thriller ("You're really mysterious—Yes, I'm a secret agent") which had recently been given literary prestige and a Swiss setting in Fleming's *Goldfinger* (1959) and Hergé's *L'Affaire Tournesol* [*The Calculus Affair*] (1956).[28] *Goldfinger* was in 1960 only a literary pretext, but in what is effectively the first feature film of the Swiss New Wave, Jean-Louis Roy's *L'Inconnu de Shandigor* (1966), cinematic Bondisms are exploited in, again, a Geneva-set spy thriller. Both Godard's film and Roy's add to the conventional features of the spy genre a de-glamorised representation of the city's topography, which in both implicates hotels. When Godard's 'little soldier' arrives in Geneva, the visual accompaniment to the narrator's commentary on the city's aspect includes two brief, low-angled, tracking shots from car level of the luxury hotels along the Quai du Mont Blanc (including the Beau Rivage). Spatially the film opposes urgent movement around and out of the city (by car, bicycle, boat, train, plane and on foot, running) with drawn out interior sequences, notably in two apartments and a hotel room.[29] The two apartment buildings and the hotel, the Century, were newly built at the time of the shoot, fitting the film's contrast between Geneva's traditional aspect—including its luxury hotels—and its architectural newness.

The walls of the room at the Century are covered with photographs, mostly tear-sheets of news stories: "A few snapshots from the four corners of the world paraded before me, like in a bad dream." They represent in microcosm the political and cultural references that give an international frame to the local story of neutral Switzerland, and connect with the supra-local name of the Hôtel Century, first seen as an isolated neon at night. (His modern hotel residence contrasts also with that of the fellow agents assassinated by Algerian militants at the old-world Hôtel Bristol.)

The name of the hotel in *Le petit soldat* ironises the playing out of history in a city out of time. 'Hôtel Century' is transnational, whereas 'Hôtel Beau Rivage' is more clearly a sign of Swissness, used for grand palaces and more modest hotels or restaurants, but almost always for a lakeside setting, as in Godard's *King Lear* (1987).[30] When Nyon's Beau Rivage is shown in this film (identified by a neon sign), the name of this old-world hotel (parts of which date from 1481) joins other signs of place to contrast with the post-nuclear setting of the narrative, in a country out of time. In one of the three other films by Godard featuring Swiss hotels, the hotel is given a generic pseudonym, the Hôtel du Lac, and the exact locale is obscured. In the other two, the hotels' names are not given as signifiers, and the locales (Geneva, Lausanne, and two Vaudois villages, Le Pont and Etoy) are allowed to preserve a limited anonymity. The hotels enter, thereby, a signifying system of generic locales, each opposed to an idea of home: workplace, marketplace, place of leisure.

There are three hotels in *Sauve qui peut (la vie)* (1980), all three anonymous and generic.[31] One is in a rural setting, but only its dining room is shown. Another is in a big city, but all we see is a bedroom and a corridor. The third is shown almost in full: bedrooms, corridors, stairways, foyer, entrance and car park. This composite of spaces is part of a larger composition that opposes domiciles (hotel, rented room, apartment, house . . .), places of work (hotel, café, television studios, farm, factory . . .), places of commerce (hotel, supermarket, garage . . .) and places of leisure (hotel, café, restaurant, cinema, sportsfield . . .), all connected by modes of displacement (foot, bicycle, motorcycle, car, racing car, lorry, train, yacht, aeroplane), and framed by landscape (lakes, fields, hills and sky). The interlocking of these generic topoi overlaps with the arrangement of specific Swiss locales (Geneva, Nyon, Lausanne, the lac de Joux) that are distinct on paper but less so in the mise-en-scène. Nyon is the only place that is named (by signs at the railway station), marking it as the point of junction between the other three. The vallée de Joux is the highland region in the Jura identified as the countryside to which the city worker Denise Rimbaud (played by Nathalie Baye) escapes, and localised in published preliminary notes to the film as a village actually named *Le Lieu* (the place). Near Le Lieu, the city dweller stops for coffee at a hotel in another generic locale turned proper name, Le Pont (the bridge). In these Joux-valley sequences it is barely specified where the traveller is (in gossip overheard in the hotel-restaurant the village Les Bioux is mentioned), and the general identification as countryside suffices for the film's topographical arrangement. The city, as further opposed to the small town Nyon, is represented by Geneva and Lausanne, recognisable in the distinctive Les Grottes district behind Geneva's Cornavin station, and by the sight of Lausanne's Grand Pont and distinctive steep streets. The strongest motif connecting countryside, small town and city is the prostitute, but between the cities her movements confuse their differentiation. More precisely, it isn't made clear in which city are the hotels in which we see her at work. Her hotel sequences are the bearers of the urban anonymity and indifferentiation that are the film's thematic premise.

Thirty minutes into *Sauve qui peut* Isabelle (Isabelle Huppert) visits a client in room 510 of the Hôtel Continental (opposite Lausanne station). Only the room and the corridor outside are shown. No exterior enables identification and only one element in the mise-en-scène allows us to place her: the client gives the hotel's telephone number, which has a Lausanne code. The client (the emblematically named 'M. Personne', played by the emblematically named actor Fred Personne) is a football club executive or agent whose telephone conversations mention known French players as well as Dutch and Swiss clubs, a microcosmic suggestion of the film's localised, 'continental' topography. This is a scaled-down variant of the international frame created in *Le petit soldat* by photographs in the hotel room at the Century. While the client is outlining his requirements she is positioned at the window, looking out, trousers down ("Are you admiring the landscape?" she asks as he contemplates her backside). A point-of-view shot shows the perspective from the window: a landscape, more exactly an expanse of lawn with lake and mountains beyond. This shot is reproduced exactly towards the end of the film and identifiable there through the mise-en-scène as the view from the apartment in Nyon that Isabelle will eventually take on. The proleptic insert in the hotel room disrupts the topographical coherence of the mise-en-scène—you don't get the same view from a window in Nyon and a window in Lausanne—and marks the hotel room as a space of the imaginary, detached from its exact locale. This imaginary space turns out to have multiple occupants: Isabelle's voice-over reverie recites a Charles Bukowski story of a beach-picnic idyll; the client's requirements involve a fantasy scenario of happy families with hints of voyeurism and incest; and at the end overheard dialogue reveals there to have been a third party to the scene, an observing woman whose desires the client has failed to realise ("You always mess things up").

Two other sequences show Isabelle at work in another city hotel, firstly with the film's male protagonist, Paul, as client. We only see his room at night, while they are having sex, and then the morning after. Again the room is a space for the imaginary, with Isabelle's reverie (during coitus) again taking the form of a voice-over reciting a Bukowski story, followed the morning after, in bathetic diminuendo, with Isabelle telling Paul that she'd had bad dreams: "Yes, dreams are always terrible. Even in a dream you can't help looking for solutions."

Isabelle's second liaison in this same hotel, the Geneva Intercontinental, is the much-commented set-piece where a businessman arranges a *ménage-à-quatre*, a clumsy male's fantasy about composition and control, acting out one more Bukowski text. The sequence begins with Isabelle in the hotel foyer and follows her to the suite where her client and his minion await her. Internationalism at the Intercontinental is signalled in the real by a football match on the television (Geneva's Servette versus the East German team Dynamo Berlin) and a long distance phone call to Montreal, and in the imaginary by the Californian Bukowski-pretext and Isabelle's voice-over reverie, quoting Conrad's tale of the Belgian Congo, *Heart of Darkness*.

Nothing in the story connects the location for this sequence with Isabelle's night spent earlier with Paul at the same hotel, and nothing in either sequence makes meaning out of the fact that this is Paul's home, a fact elaborately established in the first ten minutes of the film, recalled at intervals throughout and insisted upon at the end when Paul informs the hotel manager that he is staying another six months. That Denise and Isabelle change homes (Isabelle from a flat in Lausanne to one in Nyon, Denise from the flat in Nyon to lodgings in a farm near the lac de Joux) while Paul stays put in his hotel is more or less the narrative shape of the film. The difference between the narrative connections made (Paul moves out of Denise's home, Paul sleeps with Isabelle at his hotel, Isabelle moves into Denise's home) and the unconnectedness of the scenes at the Intercontinental shapes the thematic disparity of scale between human love and commerce.

The Geneva Intercontinental (built 1964) is anonymous in aspect, distinguished chiefly by its proximity to the buildings of the United Nations and by the ease with which it can be made secure for high-level politicians (the 1985 Reagan-Gorbachev summit took place there, and Pérez de Cuellar, Moubarak, Carter and Bush senior are among other signatories of the hotel's guest book). Its representation in *Sauve qui peut* offsets this anonymity with the anecdotal quirkiness of its minor characters. First, a diva in the room next door disturbs Paul by rehearsing the 'suicide aria' from Ponchielli's *La Gia-*

conda, with the punchline that when we cut to a general shot of the hotel's foyer, she is still to be seen and heard singing at the top of her voice as she descends an escalator. Second, a hotel employee appears to be stalking Paul, from the corridor outside his room, through the foyer to the driveway outside, where he finally declares his love for Paul, his desire that he fuck him, and kisses Paul on the lips. As Paul drives away the employee shouts "city of the devil," signalling the anecdote's origin in the hotel-centred Bukowski story 'An Evil Town.' The third of these humanising anecdotes (also derived from Bukowski) is the orchestration of sex by the businessman in the famous set-piece, which ends on the human frailty of his lip-sticked smile.

The vastness of the Intercontinental's foyer space, made broader still on film with a wide-angle lens, is a synecdoche for the hotel's breadth of reference, accommodating disparate characters and anecdotes, international business deals and football matches, intercontinental encounters and inter-texts (Ponchielli and Bukowski). Nonetheless, the film's referential breadth subordinates its hotels to a bigger opposition: urban and rural, cityscape and landscape. A similar subordination is evident in Godard's next Swiss hotel film, where the signifying system of generic locales is at its most schematic. *Passion* is composed around types of workplace: film studio, factory and ho-tel. The village where these are situated (Etoy) and its background landscape are, within the same limits, anonymous; that is, they are not identified by place names or other such signs, though they would be known and familiar to habitués of the region. The Hotel Lunika (unnamed in the film) is in fact in two parts, motel and hotel, each with its own sign to that effect, but only one sign is shown in the film, a neon reading 'MOTEL': a hybrid word for a space represented as hybrid. The film opposes a drinking and eating area, no different from an ordinary café (with counter, pinball machine and diurnal customers—no different from ordinary cafés in other Godard films), and the corridors, stairways and bedrooms of the living area, no different from those of any other functional hotel. The hotel in *Passion* embodies in its ordinary functions the film's ordinary thematic concerns (work, love, leisure) and, through the presence at the hotel of the aesthete filmmaker and the militant worker, incorporates the film's extraordinary themes: art and sacrifice.

A topographical coincidence allows us to appreciate more exactly the com-plexities played upon in *Passion*. In the same small village, a few hundred me-tres further up the highway from the Lunika, is another early '60s motel, which features in Patricia Plattner's 2002 film *Les petites couleurs*, a road movie that has come to a happy halt by the roadside.[32] The picturesque but somewhat rundown Motel des Pêchers is transformed for the film into the Galaxy Motel, an idealised space of refuge for the transient, imbued with the personality of its owner (played by Bernadette Lafont), of the characters who fetch up there,

Figure 4.2.   The remains of the *Motel des Pêchers* (Etoi VD), demolished 2008.
Photograph by Isaac Letterhead

and indeed of the original Motel des Pêchers itself (before it was destroyed by fire in 2004) (Figure 4.2). The film opposes not only anxious mobility and happy rest, but also the violence of hetero marriage and the comfort of female solidarity. The contrasts with *Passion* are striking: the transients in *Les petites couleurs* are all Swiss, and its motel accommodates restlessness as a national characteristic: it is situated emblematically on the 'Route Suisse'; in *Passion* the motel's residents are French, German, Polish or Italian, and the motel itself is emblematically situated at the frontier with France. In *Passion* no one at the motel is happy or restful, and solidarity is only the name of a revolutionary movement in Poland, not an option for more local human endeavours. Briefly, *Les petites couleurs* is happy to be *the* Swiss motel film, whereas *Passion* aspires to something more transcendent, and less happy.

The occupants of Godard's Swiss hotels are almost all strangers, whether as characters in the fiction or as the actors who play them: Michel Subor in *Le petit soldat*, Jacques Dutronc and Fred Personne in *Sauve qui peut*, Michel Piccoli in *Passion* and in *2 x 50 ans* are all French; in *Passion* Hanna Schygulla is German and Jerzy Radziwilowicz is Polish; in *King Lear* Burgess Meredith, Peter Sellars, Molly Ringwald and Norman Mailer are all American. An exception is Roland Amstutz, a distinctively Swiss actor who, to play the orchestrating businessman at the Intercontinental in *Sauve qui peut*, is shorn of his Swissness and made to say 'soixante-dix-neuf' in the French manner, rather than the Swiss 'septante-neuf'.

To find foreigners in hotels is of course hardly surprising,[33] and though it would be possible to see the strangers in Godard's Swiss hotels as emblematic of the filmmaker's own ambiguous relation to his homeland, we might be obliged then to discern an analogous anxiety of identity in other filmmakers who put strangers in hotels. Alain Tanner, for example, whose surname signals his family's American origins, would be seen to be signalling his not-quite-Swissness when he lodges a Mauritian woman in an anonymous Swiss hotel in *La Femme de Rose Hill* (1989), and more generally whenever his Switzerland is peopled with foreigners (see Olimpia Carlisi in *Le Milieu du monde* and Laura Morante in *La Vallée fantôme*, both Italians, and the Portuguese Maria Cabral in *No Man's Land*).

Reading these as identifications wouldn't quite work, not so much because of the gender line crossed, but rather because the big hotel-related identification with a foreigner in Tanner's work, in *Dans la ville blanche*, is polarised the other way: the hotel is foreign and the stranger is Swiss.[34] *Dans la ville blanche* is *the* hotel film by any Swiss filmmaker, and also—in my view— the most beautiful Swiss film of all: a sailor, another 'Suisse errant' still tied to the homeland,[35] jumps ship in Lisbon and fetches up in a small hotel. At the westerly edge of Europe, as far from Switzerland as he could have got by land, the sailor (played by the Swiss-Italian Bruno Ganz) expresses this separation by sending super-eight footage home to his wife in Bâle, and by falling in love with a worker in the Portuguese hotel.

The beauty of *Dans la ville blanche* is the beauty of Lisbon, discovered from the paradoxical viewpoint of the sailor in his hotel room:

> Even if at times he refuses to leave his hotel room, the character played by Bruno Ganz is attracted by the city. He is attracted by its climate. For me it's a city that's nostalgic, but very sensual. A city where, if you listen, if you sniff the air, if you open your eyes, you are drawn by an immense beauty.[36]

Dans la ville blanche reads the hotel and the spaces around it with more intensity and more complexity than does any outsider film in a Swiss hotel.

The intensity is contingent, a function of Tanner's method,[37] but the relative complexity is relational. The outsider filmmaker *in* Switzerland, filming in hotels, is not encouraged by the hotel's relation to its environs to present the one as the key to the enigma of the other, and almost always relates to the hotel in terms dictated by the official handbook of cinematic cliché. In visitor cinema the hotel is a sign of Swissness, at best because it is simply part of the landscape (Méliès, Eastwood) or cityscape (Lang, Sirk), but often, worse, because it is one of a set of localised signs that are familiar to foreign audiences, a cliché alongside mountains, lakes, clinics, banking, neutrality, anarchism, cheese, chocolate, folk-dancing, cuckoo clocks and Tyrolean kitsch.[38] Whereas, for the indigenous filmmaker, the hotel is a sign of Swissness only to the extent that visitors lodged in hotels have made the meaning of Switzerland, for an international public but also for the Swiss themselves.

This argument, I confess, reduces the signification of the Swiss hotel on screen to a simple opposition and discounts those films, native and visitor, where the hotel is not positioned in these terms. The Geneva hotel, as yet unidentified, seen briefly in Soutter's *L'Amour des femmes*, is shown only as an adjunct of the film's *amour* motif (as scene of a sexual encounter). Philip Kaufman's *The Unbearable Lightness of Being* has all the potential to be a hotel-centred visitor film on the meaning of Switzerland for the Czech exiles it welcomes, and it does show sex at Geneva's Hôtel de la Cigogne, but though distinctive and recognisable this location does not signify alongside the film's other, even more recognisable signs of Swissness, chief among which is the national flag. Moreover, the film suppresses from Kundera's novel not only a significance attaching to the particular city in which this hotel-room sex takes place—in the novel the woman has travelled from Geneva to meet the man in Zurich, and it has already been specified that 'Geneva is not Zurich'—but suppresses also the resonance of this incident within an internationalised sex-based thematic, captured in the man's comment that he had made love to the woman "in fifteen hotels in Europe and one in America".

The international frame in which the Swiss hotel is positioned is a motif as strong in native as in visitor films: we have seen this in Godard's Swiss hotel films, and will see it again in readings of hotel films by Soutter and Schmid. Narratives of displacement *within* Switzerland, including stops in hotels, are a stronger motif for the locals, at their strongest perhaps in Tanner's *Messidor* (where the protagonists are warned to "stay within the frontiers: beyond lies catastrophe"). His women on the run through Switzerland stay first in a cheap anonymous hotel, then in an expensive anonymous hotel, and in front of a third they resolve: "No more hotels . . . no more money . . .", precipitating their descent into lawlessness. (They still pass time in hotel bars, and their last act before they are arrested is to shoot dead a bystander—in another hotel.)

From its opening montage of aerial shots over Switzerland, *Messidor* presents itself as a vision of the country's landscape: lakes, mountains and motorways. Soutter's *L'Escapade* (1974) is a less travelled film, but when its protagonist moves by train from Geneva to a grand hotel near Sainte-Croix, it is to a location known as the 'balcon du Jura', offering an embracing viewpoint over the Alpine landscape to the south. In his hotel room, this aspect is hyperbolised by the woman who joins him there: "It's beautiful from here. You can see all of Switzerland." Actually when this is said in the film, no one is looking out of the window. While the man and the woman have sex on the floor, the camera takes in the hazy landscape beyond and, as the published script puts it, we, the spectators, "see all of Switzerland" (Boujut 1974, 23).

Michel Soutter was one of the 'Groupe 5' who, with Tanner, Claude Goretta, Jean-Louis Roy and—later—Yves Yersin, contributed to "the burgeoning of Helvetic fiction cinema" (Schüpbach 1973, 13). He made Swiss films, two of them in Swiss hotels. *L'Escapade* spends about half of its time at the Grand Hôtel des Rasses, actually next door to Soutter's family home and itself loaded with associations that personalise *L'Escapade*. His next film, *Repérages* (1977), comes via a far more circuitous route towards the autobiographical, taking Jean-Louis Trintignant, who had been in *L'Escapade* and has become an alter-ago, and loading the film with references to Russia, whence Soutter's family had come to Switzerland after the Revolution. The hotel location at Bex-les-Bains is not a personal memory but a collective one, a vestige of the grand hotel tradition that brought to Switzerland and deposited there the history and culture associated with its visitors from abroad. To Bex, to stay at the Grand Hôtel des Salines, came monarchs, politicians, film stars and—more significantly for Soutter's film—famous Russians like Tolstoy, Rimsky-Korsakov and Nabokov.[39]

The opening sequence shows Viktor (Trintignant), a film director, telling his Russian language tutor (played by Soutter's godfather Gabriel Arout), in Russian, that he is going to Bex to prepare a film of Chekhov's *Three Sisters*. For the rest of the film we are at Bex and its environs, and mostly at the Hôtel des Salines, with Viktor and his cast. The use of non-Swiss actors (Trintignant, Valérie Mairesse and Delphine Seyrig are French, Léa Massari is Italian), apart from ensuring international audiences for a local product, is a device for signifying Swissness differentially that is used, as we have seen, by Godard, but also by Tanner (e.g., *Le Retour d'Afrique*, *Le Milieu du monde*, *La Vallée fantôme*) and Schmid (*Violanta*, *Zwischensaison*, *Berezina*). Delphine Seyrig, moreover, carries into this hotel film associations with the archetype of spa-resort cinema, *L'Année dernière à Marienbad*.

There are other intertextual connections between Soutter's and Resnais's film—both, for example, have a theatrical intertext, Chekhov in the one, Ibsen in the other—and *Repérages* takes from *Marienbad* the figure of the spa-hotel as repository of cultural memory, but the significant difference lies in the locale, as motif in each film and as a place that has been *mis-en-scène*. There is no actual Marienbad in Resnais's film, it is only a memory of last year, remembered in another, unnamed place. And there is no single, specific place on screen, since the hotel filmed is a composite of actual locales (the Bavarian palaces Schleissheim, Nymphenburg and Amelienburg) and studio constructions. In *Repérages* the relation between place as motif and actual locale is less complicated. The hotel is named as destination from the beginning, with motif-related explanations on how the place-name Bex should be pronounced (the 'x' is silent), and an establishing shot then shows us the hotel framed in the Vaudois landscape. The hotel is situated thereafter within a number of specific topographical differentiations that frame the film's Swissness. The hotel is just outside the town of Bex, and the opposition between town and hotel is most clearly signalled by the movement of a character from a café in Bex—the Café Suisse,[40] complete with its standard painting of *the* Swiss mountain, the Cervin (Matterhorn)—to the hotel, by contrast a more internationalist space.

A set of broader distinctions isolates Bex and its hotel from the world beyond, in the first place from the rest of Switzerland (from Geneva, explicitly), from France (after an excursion to nearby Evian and flashbacks to a remembered sentimental liaison in Paris), and then more broadly from the rest of Europe, with a flashback to Belgrade (though shot at Bex railway station) and the acting out of the death of Chekhov at the German spa town of Badenweiler (at the Hotel Sommer, to be precise). The broadest of these contrasts is of course with Russia, not only through the central Chekhov intertext, but also through the memory of Dostoevsky, invoked in the course of an excursion to nearby Saxon-les-Bains, also a health resort, but famous above all for Joseph Fama's casino (1855–1877), where Dostoevsky had gambled and lost in 1867. The parochialism of present-day Saxon, where Viktor and one of his actresses drop in on a local *dancing*, contrasts with the international glamour of the resort in the days when it competed with Monte Carlo to be the gambling capital of Europe.

The imagined flashbacks to the death and burial of Chekhov modify the pro-filmic realism of the grand hotel, which is topographical, in favour of a place in time. Setting *Three Sisters* there does the same, favouring a correspondence of time—the play dates from 1901, the heyday of the hotel's fame—over a disparity of place: though Bex-les-Bains is somehow Russian because Tolstoy and other Russians stayed there, it cannot stand in for the Russia of the three sisters. This applies more broadly: be they tourists, exiles, convalescents or economic migrants, for all of the Russians who came to Switzerland—Gogol, Tolstoy, Dostoevsky, Bakunin, Kropotkin, Lenin, Nijinsky, Stravinsky, Chagall, Nabokov and Soutter's father included—Switzerland was, precisely, *not* Russia.

The layered chronology of *Repérages* may adjust our perception of the place represented, but a grand hotel, as edifice composed of accretions over time, can easily accommodate a reading that sees it as a *lieu de mémoire*. The site of memory that concerns us here is *Repérages* itself. The buildings and grounds of the Grand Hôtel des Salines, Bex-les-Bains, are better documented by Soutter's film than is perhaps any other hotel in any other fiction film. Which is just as well, because only four years after Soutter had celebrated it as vestige of a fading cultural history—it had ceased to be commercially viable the year before the shoot, in 1976—chance overcame history and the Grand Hôtel was completely destroyed by fire. Absolutely nothing remains but a few ruined greenhouses, a crumbling pavilion in the grounds and a dilapidated swimming pool.

Or rather, all that survives of the hotel is Soutter's film. It has become evidence of the Swiss hotel industry's decline, but it was from the outset something bigger, a poetic brooding on a national theme, the loss of a grandeur embodied in hotels. As such, for the nostalgia-prone Swiss, *Repérages* may be *the* hotel film. If it is not, that is because in 1992 Daniel Schmid made *Zwischensaison*.

ZWISCHENSAISON: THE SWISS HOTEL FILM

Mais ici il n'y a pas de mer, maman.[41]

Hotel-keeping and film-making in Switzerland are most strongly associated in the person of Daniel Schmid, born and raised in a family-run hotel,[42] his imagination fuelled by those he saw pass through, and by stories told to him of earlier encounters there (Douglas Sirk had been a guest) and in other hotels (the story of Sarah Bernhardt and his grandfather at the Savoy, for instance). His favourite childhood reading included an Italian magazine called *Grand Hotel*, an early model for his cinematic storytelling. In 1982, his contribution to a collective volume on his work was a forty-page photographic montage of stills from his films, which he called 'Grand Hotel'. This visual essay-form was reprised by Schmid in a later volume on his work, the 2001 picture book called *A Smuggler's Life*, using images from his films and from his personal photo-album and postcard collection. In these illustrations, ciné-memories mix with memories of life, which of course includes hotels: not only "The Hotel Schweizerhof, Flims, built in 1903, where Daniel Schmid was born in room no. 11"; or the "Grand Hôtel des Bains, Venice, 1972" where his friend Werner Schroeter is pictured; or the Alhambra Hotel, Nice, where his grandmother's brother had worked (represented by a still from *La Paloma*, the film Schmid shot there in 1974); or the Palazzo Salis in Soglio (where Schmid made *Violanta* in 1977); or the Palace Hotel, Curia (from *Zwischensaison*,

1992); or his room at the Hotel del Norte, Puerto Barrios, photographed in 1995; but above all, photographed on the same trip to Guatemala as an emblematic image for any book about hotels and cinema, the Palacio del Cine, an edifice combining hotel and movie house, built in 1948 and a Guatemalan national treasure.

In a 1984 picture book, Schmid was the historian of more than just his life and films. *L'invention du paradis* is a visual history of the image of Switzerland in five acts, from Rousseau's *La nouvelle Héloïse* to the end of the First World War, told through archive images, with a text commenting on the spectacle. Central to this history is the creation of tourism and the development of Switzerland's hotel industry. The images collected by Schmid represent many of the great hotels I have mentioned, including the family hotel at Flims, and the anecdotes tell of visitors who stayed in Swiss hotels and became thereby a part of this history: Ludwig II of Bavaria, Kaiser Wilhelm II, Queen Victoria, Sissi, Tolstoy, Nietzsche, Nijinsky, Sherlock Holmes.[43] He tells again the story of Sarah Bernhardt and his grandfather (also called Daniel), but relocates it to the Grand Hotel National in Lucerne. In an interview published in 1978 he set the story at the Savoy in London, as he did in his contribution to the Waldhaus commemorative volume in 1998 and in the family history he wrote as a booklet for the guest rooms of the Hotel Schweizerhof. (In 2004 Schmid also published *Excitation Bizarre*, a visual essay on romantic exultation as expressed in the hotels of Flims between 1870 and 1945.)

Schmid was a historian of hotels who also made films. As well as in *Les Amateurs*, a compilation of footage from between 1905 and 1930 showing leisure in Switzerland, hotels feature regularly in his fiction films. Swiss hotels appear in *Zwischensaison*, in *Violanta*—shot at the Palazzo Salis, Soglio ('Historic Hotel of the Year 1998')—and in *Heute Nacht oder Nie*, shot at the family hotel in Flims, though the setting is a chateau in Bohemia (in fact the only instance I have found of a Swiss hotel passing as a location outside of Switzerland).

The Swiss hotel film is *Zwischensaison*. The narrator returns to the hotel in which he was born and raised, having learned that it is due for demolition. This narrative pretext positions Schmid's fictional locale at a key juncture in the history of the Swiss hotel's decline, alongside the real Grand Hotel in Locarno (see *Asambhav*), and positions it also in the symbolic space occupied by lost hotels like the Grand Hôtel des Salines at Bex (see *Repérages*). There is room in that space too for the more modest Motel des Pêchers at Etoy (see *Les petites couleurs*), destroyed by fire, and room also, I would hope, for the lost interiors of remodelled hotels, like the grand two-floor reception area

Figure 4.3.   The impossible sea, from the end of Daniel Schmid's *Zwischensaison*

of the Geneva Intercontinental (as seen in *Sauve qui peut*), reshaped beyond recognition five years ago.

In the deserted hotel, present and past overlap as he encounters his deceased relatives and then himself as a child. Remembered scenes from the hotel's past are played out before him, alongside anecdotes he remembers being told, from the history of this and other hotels. In 1906, for example, in the dining room of Interlaken's Victoria-Jungfrau (run by the brother of Schmid's grandmother), the Russian anarchist Tatiana Leontieva shot and killed a tourist, mistaking him for Durnovo, the former Russian Minister of the Interior. This scene is re-enacted in the film, as, of course, are the two anecdotes relating to Schmid's grandfather at the Savoy in London.

The use of these (and other) anecdotes in Schmid's personal reminiscences and in *Zwischensaison* leads to the reasonable conclusion that the film is autobiographical. Amongst much that could be invoked to undercut that conclusion, central to our purpose here is the presentation of the hotel itself. It should not be assumed, following the autobiographical premise, that the hotel filmed in *Zwischensaison* is, as in *Heute Nacht oder Nie*, the family hotel in Flims. When the narrator arrives at the hotel, the exteriors we are shown are of Brunnen's Grand Hotel Axenstein, on Lake Lucerne, a different type of hotel in a quite different type of locale. This may seem to direct the discourse of the film towards Swiss hotels more generally, but the movement into the fictional space takes us further afield. The interiors on display are a splendidly luxurious representation of the Swiss hotel's bygone splendour, and an entirely appropriate frame for the behavioural excesses of the hotel's guests. But these are not Swiss interiors at all: these sequences were filmed at the Palace Hotel in Curia, Portugal. Furthermore, the expansion of the narrative frame to include the Victoria-Jungfrau in Interlaken shows the assassination of the tourist not in a Swiss hotel but in another Portuguese location, the Hotel das Termas in Curia. Unsurprisingly, then, the Savoy in London where the Sarah Bernhardt story is depicted is actually yet another Portuguese treasure, the Busacco Palace Hotel, Coimbra.

Portuguese interiors were not used simply because comparable luxury has not been preserved in available Swiss hotels. They signify, rather, if by quite different cinematic means, the same displacement central to Tanner's *Dans la ville blanche*. Portugal, in this argument, is the place in Europe least like Switzerland, even if the salons, bars and dining rooms of grand hotels in the one country can pass as those of grand hotels in the other. The move out from the confines of the snow-bound Alpine resort to the boundless vistas of the Atlantic seaboard is an expressive one, expressing at a different level the same frustration with the landlocked Swiss hotel evident in this exchange from *Zwischensaison*. A female guest is complaining to her son about the weather and the situation of the hotel:

—They'd have much to learn from the Hotel Quisisana at Capri. There, not a day without sunshine. And every room has a view of the sea.

—But here there is no sea, maman.

—Exactly my point.

In *L'Invention du paradis*, Schmid described Switzerland's palace hotels as "strange isolated objects, as mysterious as an ocean liner in the night, carrying within it a world cut off from the world". *Zwischensaison* represents just such an isolated world, and hints at an allegory of something larger still from which we are separated (the past, possibly). The film ends with an allegorical expression of the power of cinema to override topographical difference, troping on the suggestion that Swiss hotels should be more like hotels in Capri. The narrator walks down a deserted corridor in the family hotel and stops at a shuttered window. He unfastens it and, in the single most expressive representation of the Swiss hotel among the eighty or so films I have watched for this essay, the film's last shot reveals what, impossibly, he sees: the sea, the sea (Figure 4.3).

In December 2005, Schmid was on Spain's Atlantic coast shooting *Portovero*, but was forced to abandon the film through illness. He died on August 6, 2006.[44] This essay is dedicated to his memory, to the memory of Switzerland's grand hotels.

NOTES

1. At least it was until 2000, when Jean Nouvel's cinema-themed The Hotel opened in Lucerne: projected images from the architect's favourite films are incorporated into the décor of each of the 25 rooms. Films by Wenders, Fassbinder, Antonioni, Fellini, Bertolucci and Oshima are among those featured. The only Swiss hotel film on show is Buñuel's *Cet obscur objet du désir*, though the brief images from the beginning of the Beau Rivage in Lausanne are not among those sampled by Nouvel in Lucerne.

2. I would like to thank the following for help with the research for this essay: Felix Aeppli, Marie-Lise Blum, Sandrina Cirafici and Pierre-Yves Pièce (Musée historique du Chablais), Marguerite Collomb (Motel des Pêchers), Hervé Dumont (Cinémathèque suisse), Leonhard H. Gmür (Unicorn Media), Lucette Grieshaber, Françoise Guinand, Tim Hale, Christian Hallstein, Philip Horne, Cyril Jost (Film Location Switzerland), Jean-Jacques Jost, Daniel Kletke (RW Fassbinder Foundation), Vérène Lack-Grieshaber, Daniel Lehmann (Hôtel de la Truite), Colin MacCabe, Jann Matlock, Daniela Mettler (The Hotel), Francesco Mismirigo, Pierre Monsciani (Hôtel Lunika), Daniel Schmid, Sangita Shah.

3. Very similar footage is used at the beginning of a 1959 French comedy, *Le petit prof*, where the hero's pregnant mother is in a cinema watching newsreel of the Locarno Conference just before she goes into labour. A history of a child of the century is then inaugurated by this world historical event.

4. Perhaps the most famous Swiss-shot Indian film is *Dilwale Dulhania Le Jayenge* (1995), with its notorious 'Swiss hotel room' scene (discussed in Shakuntala Banaji 2005, 180–185), but Swiss-shot (and sometimes set) Bollywood productions number in the hundreds. See *Bollywood: The Indian Cinema and Switzerland* (2002), website for an exhibition at the Museum für Gestaltung in Zurich. See also the official brochure produced by the Swiss tourist agency, *Switzerland for Movie Stars*. (All website addresses are listed at the end of this essay.)

5. The English translation of Kluge's text, by Nancy Kienberger, is given in an insert in the book *Das Waldhaus, Sils Maria*.

6. A recent example of these is *Le Montreux Palace, ans 100*, a volume celebrating the centenary of the self-styled 'pearl of the Swiss Riviera', published by the hotel itself. A resident of the Montreux Palace, Peter Ustinov, shot scenes there for his 1965 film *Lady L*.

7. See Senarclens et al (1993, 76–78). The Intercontinental, a relative parvenu among Geneva's grand hotels, included pages from its *livre d'or* in the volume commemorating its first twenty-five years of existence, see Pottier (1989).

8. Actually the Hostellerie du Château in Rolle, and no relation to the Vevey hotel in Anita Brookner's novel, though it too is on the shores of Lake Geneva.

9. To my knowledge, the only other eminent Swiss hotelier represented on film is Alexander Seiler, twice, in *The Challenge* and *Berg Ruft* (1938), English and German parallel productions, using the same exterior footage, about Whymper's attempt to climb the Matterhorn. Exterior shots show Seiler's Hotel Riffelberg, though Whymper actually stayed at the Monte Rosa (a location for *Love and Bullets*

in 1979; another Seiler hotel, the Belvedere on the Furka pass, can be glimpsed in *Goldfinger*).

10. See for example *The Return of the Pink Panther*, *Christmas in Love*, *People— Jet Set 2* and *Jodi No. 1*.

11. The Tsarina Alexandra stayed for a whole summer in 1859, the Prince of Wales came a few months later, and the Shah of Persia dined with the King of Holland there in 1873; Tchaikovsky, Thomas Mann, Chaplin and W.E.B. Dubois are all mentioned, and more recently French film star Nathalie Baye is cited as an habituée. No mention is made, however, of the scenes shot there in 1980 by John Avildsen for *The Formula*.

12. For which the corpus would be smaller: the only other Swiss-sanataria films I know of are *Mutter, dein Kind ruft* (also in Davos) and *Brennendes Geheimnis* (both Swiss-set versions of Stefan Zweig's Austria-set sanatarium-novel), *The Other Love* and *Bobby Deerfield*. If spa-hotels are included then *Repérages* and *Journey of Hope* can be added, as well as the footage from 1912 of the Grand Hôtel des Bains at Yverdon from the compilation film *Il était une fois . . . la Suisse*.

13. The closure in 2004 of the Valbella Clinic, one of Davos's last surviving sanatoria, was greeted in England with the headline: 'Alpine sanatorium that provided backdrop for classic novel falls victim to economic slowdown'; a spokesperson for the clinic affirmed: "It's our south-facing view Mann writes about" (see website Harding, 2004).

14. From Georges Méliès's commentary text for his 1904 film *Voyage à travers l'impossible*.

15. The town has a Kursaal Casino, so suggests a memory of Arosa, which also had a Hotel Excelsior, but Arosa is some 400 kilometres from the Niesen.

16. Sonja Henie's first film, *One in a Million*, also had a Hollywood-made Swiss setting, with a St. Moritz hotel.

17. A similar confusion arises regarding Dorothy Arzner's 1937 hotel film *The Bride Wore Red*, sometimes thought to be set in Switzerland but actually set in the Austrian Tyrol, and Clarence Brown's *Idiot's Delight* (1939), set in a Tyrolean hotel in Italy (though near the Swiss border).

18. The real Zurich airport, exteriors and interiors, can be seen in *Asambhav*.

19. A similar transposition occurs in the 1979 thriller *Avalanche Express*, where the distinctive Hotel Senefelder in Munich is supposed to pass, name unchanged, as a hotel in Zurich (and I suspect, furthermore, that the railway station in Munich is used to represent the railway station in Zurich). The other 'Swiss' hotel in this film is an anonymous alpine *gasthof*, a model of which is destroyed by the eponymous avalanche.

20. With appearances in *Kleine Scheidegg*, *Sangam*, *The Eiger Sanction* and *The Hero*, the Bellevue is the only rival to the Gstaad Palace for the title of most often filmed Swiss hotel. For then-and-now photographs of the Bellevue as used in *The Eiger Sanction*, see website 'The Eiger Sanction 1975'.

21. Though Ramuz was probably thinking of these when he complained that hitherto mountain-cinema had done little more than put on, "very badly (but in 'local' costume), some little love story, and to wallow in folklore: because, alas, though still new, the cinema already has bad, indeed very bad habits" (Ramuz 1968, 361). For a discussion of the Swiss *bergfilm*, see Pithon (2002).

22. While location shooting in 1959, and staying at the Grand Hotel in Zermatt, Disney had the idea to build a replica Matterhorn in his Anaheim theme park, cementing thereby its status as an international icon, the most famous mountain in Switzerland. As national icon, it is deconstructed in Yves Yersin's 1979 film *Les petites fugues*, when the protagonist, a peasant in his sixties, visits the mountain by helicopter and declares it to be "just a heap of stones".

23. Sixty years after the Robesons, Marie Gaydu arrives in Tanner's *La Femme de Rose Hill* as another unassimilable black person, and spends her share of time in small Swiss hotels.

24. What appears to be a lapsus shows the bank first, briefly, with its real name, 'Crédit suisse', then later with a false name, 'Crédit national'. The correction is perhaps an effort not to offend the Crédit suisse by associating it with the Mafia. Even with the name corrected, however, this visually distinctive edifice would be instantly recognisable both to Chiasso residents and students of contemporary Swiss architecture, and the offensive association would still be made.

25. Several more significant Swiss films with hotels were listed in the sequel to Dumont's *Histoire du cinéma suisse*, covering the period 1966–2000 (published after the research for this essay was completed). See especially: *Tauwetter* (Markus Imhoof, 1977); *Der Hunger, der Koch und das Paradies* (Erwin Keusch and Karl Saurer, 1981); *Kaiser und eine Nacht* (Markus Fischer, 1985); *Hammer* (Bruno Moll, 1986); *Der Wilde Mann* (Matthias Zschokke, 1988); *Quicker than the Eye* (Nicolas Gessner, 1989); *Das stille Haus* (Christof Vorster, 1995).

26. Said of the view from the Grand Hôtel des Rasses, in Soutter's *L'Escapade*.

27. Only the most notable of which are the Grand Hôtel, rue Scribe, in *Alphaville*, the InterContinental, rue Castiglione, in *Prénom Carmen* (also seen in *Eloge de l'amour*), and the Concorde Saint-Lazare, rue Saint-Lazare, in *Détective* (all Paris).

28. This Tintin adventure (Hergé 1956) features the most famous hotel room in Swiss-set literature: room 122 at the Hôtel Cornavin, Geneva, the one occupied by Tournesol (aka Calculus). Unfortunately, Ray Goossens's 1961 film (compiled from his earlier television adaptation) of *L'Affaire Tournesol* omits the hotel-room scenes, excluding it from the canon being drawn up in this essay. Bernasconi's 1991 version for television does include the famous room.

29. In *L'Intrus* (2004) Claire Denis takes this same actor, Michel Subor, whom in *Beau travail* she had already borrowed from *Le petit soldat*, and brings him back to where he started, a Geneva hotel room. The hotel is one of those that are glimpsed in an angled tracking shot in *Le petit soldat*, and the manner of that shot is replicated by Denis when she reveals the name of *her* Geneva hotel, the Beau Rivage.

30. There are lakeside 'beaux rivages' at, for example, Locarno, Geneva, Lausanne, Neuchatel, Bienne, Thun and Weggis. The Beau Rivage at Interlaken can be seen to advantage in Raj Kapoor's *Sangam* (1964).

31. This despite Godard's use of the distinctively luxurious Beau Rivage in Lausanne ('Historic Hotel of the Year, 1999') as a base for preparing the film.

32. Godard knew the locale, since as an adolescent (according to the motel owner) he would frequent the 'fruit bar' next door, apparently the first bar of any kind in Switzerland to be open twenty-four hours.

33. More surprising perhaps is the absence of foreigners from the Concorde St. Lazare, Paris, in Godard's principal hotel film *Détective* (1985).

34. "In all my films there's a character called Paul and it's always the one who represents me a little. That doesn't mean it's autobiographical. In *Dans la ville blanche*, it is a little more so, and the character is also called Paul" (see website Tanner 1996). In *La Vallée fantôme*, *No Man's Land* and *Le Milieu du monde*, the Paul character is each time played by a French actor (Jean-Louis Trintignant, Hugues Quester and Philippe Léotard respectively). The identification in *Dans la ville blanche* is stronger with the character (Tanner had also served in the merchant navy) and with the actor (Bruno Ganz, who is Swiss).

35. The expression is from an essay on Tanner's migratory characters by Maria Tortajada (2000).

36. Website Tanner 1996.

37. Website Tanner 1996: "Before beginning the shoot I shut myself up in a hotel room for a week. There was a bar-restaurant, so I could eat. But I didn't go out at all. I had no books, no newspapers, no radio. Try it: it's very difficult to stay on your own in a hotel room. I had a view over the Tagus, as in the film. [. . .] I had no building opposite, which would have made it even harder. I had the same perspective. I did this to get into the skin of characters, simply. And it's very difficult, because you fall back on yourself, on your own phantasms, on your own stories. And then, during the shoot, when the crew had Sundays off, I went out to take the Super-8 images myself. I remained constantly within this state of mind, in this painful solitude."

38. Cuckoo clocks (a German invention of the 1730s) have been erroneously associated with Switzerland, most notably and unjustly in Orson Welles's famous speech in *The Third Man* (1949). They are now to be found in all Swiss tourist shops and in many Swiss-set tourist films (e.g., Dario Argento's *Phenomena* and Yash Chopra's *Darr*).

39. Nabokov stayed only briefly, in 1968, his permanent Swiss residence being, between 1961 and his death in 1977, the Montreux Palace Hotel, now a place of pilgrimage for Nabokovians. He is also supposed to have stayed at Brissago's Grand Hotel.

40. In contrast to the assembly of foreigners at the hotel, the Café Suisse is the place to find Roger Jendly and Roland Amstutz, the Swiss actors of *Repérages*.

41. Said of the lack of a view from the hotel in Schmid's *Zwischensaison*.

42. A background he shares with Billy Wilder, raised in a family hotel in Cracow. In 1931, incidentally, Wilder wrote *Der falsche Ehemann*, set and shot in a hotel in St. Moritz, and the first of many hotel films he would write or direct.

43. Schmid mentions details of Conan Doyle's story 'The Final Problem', but invents the discovery of documents in Holmes's hotel room after his 'death' at the Reichenbach Falls. Holmes's stay at the 'Englischer Hof' in Meiringen may be represented in *Sherlock Holmes* (1922) (filmed partly in Switzerland) or in *The Final Problem* (1923), but I have not been able to see either to verify. *Sherlock Holmes and the Secret Weapon* (1943) has a Swiss setting, but no hotels.

44. Schmid died as the Locarno Festival was just getting underway. Antoine Duplan published this homage: "In 1999 he presented his last film, *Beresina*, a satire on

Switzerland, in the Piazza. He has given the Festival some of its finest moments, he has haunted Locarno, remaking cinema with his broken voice. In the rococo salons of the Grand Hotel, he felt at home. This year, the Grand Hotel has closed and Daniel Schmid has gone, in the middle of the Festival. *Portovero*, the film on which he was working, will not see the day. We are out of season . . . for ever."

FILMOGRAPHY

Swiss Hotel Films

A Farewell to Arms (Frank Borzage, US, 1932): a hotel room in Brissago (TI)

L'Affaire Tournesol (Stéphane Bernasconi, France, 1991): Hôtel Cornavin, Geneva (GE)

Agents secrets (Frédéric Schoendoerffer, France, 2004): Lausanne Palace, Lausanne (VD); Hôtel Beau Rivage (1861), Lausanne-Ouchy (VD)

L'Amour des femmes (Michel Soutter, Switzerland, 1981): unidentified Geneva hotel

L'Appel de la montagne (Arthur Porchet, Switzerland, 1923): hotel in Champex (VS)

Asambhav (Rajiv Rai, India, 2004): Grand Hotel de Locarno-Muralto (1874), Locarno (TI); Hotel Principe Leopoldo (1868), Lugano (TI); Hotel Eden Roc (1971), Ascona (TI); Hotel Carcani (1963), Ascona (TI)

Avalanche Express (Mark Robson, US, 1979): a hotel in Zurich (actually the Hotel Senefelder in Munich, Germany); a *gasthof* in an unspecified alpine location

Les bains de la jetée des Paquis (Casimir Sivan, Switzerland, 1896): exterior of the Beau Rivage (1865), Geneva (GE), on the Cinémathèque suisse DVD *Il était une fois . . . la Suisse*

Der Bergführer (Eduard Bienz, Switzerland, 1917): a hotel near the Jungfrau

Der Berg ruft (Luis Trenker, Germany, 1938): Hotel Riffelberg (1855), Zermatt (VS)

Beyond the Rocks (Sam Wood, US, 1922): 'an inn in the Swiss Alps'

Bobby Deerfield (Syndey Pollack, US, 1977): hotel-sanatorium, Loeche-les-Bains (VS)

Borderline (Kenneth MacPherson, UK/Switzerland, 1930): unidentified hotels in Lutry (VD)

Brennendes Geheimnis (Robert Siodmak, Germany, 1933): the 'Miramar' hotel in Ascona (TI)

Captain Deasy's Daring Drive (Emile Lauste and Walter Booth, UK, 1903): Palace Hotel (1900–1902), Caux (VD)

Cet obscur objet du désir (Luís Buñuel 1977): Hôtel Beau Rivage (1861), Lausanne-Ouchy (VD)

The Challenge (Milton Rosmer, UK, 1938): Hotel Riffelberg (1855), Zermatt (VS)

Christmas in Love (Neri Parenti, Italy, 2004): Palace Hotel (1915), Gstaad (BE)

Cloak and Dagger (Fritz Lang, US, 1946): 'Neues Posthotel', Zurich. Also seen is the exterior of a Hotel Bristol, somewhere in Europe and supposed to be Zurich

The Consequences of Love [*Le Conseguenze dell'amore*] (Paolo Sorrentino, Italy, 2004): Hotel Continental, Treviso (Italy); Hotel New Europe, Naples (Italy)

Daisy Miller (Peter Bogdanovich, US, 1974): Les Trois Couronnes (1842), Vevey (VD)

De ma chambre d'hôtel (Gérard Courant, France, 1979–2003): Hôtel Agora and Hôtel Astoria, Lausanne (VD); Hôtel Moreau, La Chaux de Fonds (NE); Hôtel des Tourelles, Geneva (GE); and 53 other hotels in France, Belgium, Germany, Italy, Bosnia, Serbia, Greece, Turkey, Ukraine and Canada

Despair (R.W. Fassbinder, Germany, 1978): hotel in Interlaken, probably the Victoria Jungfrau (BE)

Deux fois cinquante ans de cinéma français (Jean-Luc Godard & Anne-Marie Miéville, France/Switzerland, 1995): Hostellerie du Château (1735), Rolle (VD)

Dilwale Dulhania Le Jayenge [*The One with the Heart Takes the Bride*] (Aditya Chopra, India, 1995): hotel in Saanen (BE)

Eden (Riccardo Signorell and Samuel Schwarz, Switzerland, 1999): 'Hotel Eden', i.e., Hotel Waldhaus (1908), Sils-Maria (GR)

The Eiger Sanction (Clint Eastwood, US, 1975): Hôtel Bellevue des Alpes (1865), Kleine Scheidegg (BE)

L'Escapade (Michel Soutter, Switzerland, 1974): Grand Hôtel des Rasses (c.1890s), Les Rasses (VD); Chalet Beau Site, Les Rasses (VD)

Der falsche Ehemann (Johannes Guter, Germany, 1931): hotel in St. Moritz

La Femme de Rose Hill (Alain Tanner, Switzerland, 1989): unidentified hotel in the Vaud

Five Days One Summer (Fred Zinnemann, US, 1981): view of the Hotel Sonne, Fex (GR): actually a set built nearby (in the Roseg Valley), in the style of the Hotel Sonne. Another 'Alpine Hut' style hotel was also built as a set nearby (on top of the Diavolezza).

The Formula (John Avildsen, US, 1980): Les Trois Couronnes (1842), Vevey (VD)

Fräulein Else (Paulo Czinner, Germany, 1929): hotel in St. Moritz (GR)

Geister und Gäste (Isa Hesse-Rabinovitch, Switzerland, 1989): Grand Hotel (1906–1993), Brissago (TI)

Gilberte de Courgenay (1941): Hôtel de la Gare (1877), Courgenay (JU)

Goldfinger (Guy Hamilton, UK, 1964): Hotel Belvedere (1882), Oberwald (VS)

The Hero: Love Story of A Spy (Anil Sharma, India, 2004): Hôtel Bellevue des Alpes (1865), Kleine Scheidegg (BE), though supposed to be in Canada

Heute nacht oder nie [*Tonight or Never*] (Daniel Schmid, Switzerland, 1972): Hotel Schwiezerhof (1902), Flims (GR)

Hotel du Lac (Giles Foster, UK, 1986): Hôtel du Lac, Vevey (VD)

Der Hotelportier (Hermann Haller, Switzerland, 1941): the fictional 'Hotel Bellevue, Bäumlikon'

I Met Him in Paris (Wesley Ruggles, US, 1937): fictional hotel in Swiss mountain region (actually Sun Valley, Idaho, USA)

L'Inconnu de Shandigor (Jean-Louis Roy, Switzerland, 1966): unidentified Geneva hotels

L'Intrus (Claire Denis, France, 2004): the Beau Rivage (1865), Geneva

Jodi No. 1 (David Dhawan, India, 2001): Palace Hotel (1915), Gstaad (BE)

Journey of Hope (Xavier Koller, Switzerland, 1990)

Kaleidoscope (Jack Smight UK 1966): Hôtel Alexandra (c.1900), Monte Carlo, passing for Geneva

King Lear (Jean-Luc Godard, Switzerland, 1987): Hôtel Beau Rivage (1481, with additions c.1900), Nyon (VD)

Kiss of the Dragon (Chris Nahon, France/USA, 2001): the Montreux Palace, Montreux (VD)

Kleine Scheidegg (Richard Schweizer, Switzerland, 1937): Hôtel Bellevue des Alpes (1865), Kleine Scheidegg (BE)

Lady L (Peter Ustinov, France/Italy/UK, 1965): the Montreux Palace, Montreux (VD)

Liebesbriefe aus dem Engadin [*Love Letters from the Engadine*] (Luis Trenker, Germany, 1938): hotel in the Engadine (GR)

Love and Bullets (Stuart Rosenberg, UK, 1979): Hotel Monte Rosa (1855), Zermatt (VS); hôtel de Londres, Montreux (VD)

Magnificent Obsession (Douglas Sirk, US, 1954): the fictional 'Hotel Alpen Ruhe', somewhere near Zurich (ZU); view of the Hotel Schweizerhof, Lucerne (LU).

The Man Who Knew Too Much (Alfred Hitchcock, UK, 1934): unspecified hotel in St. Moritz (GR)

Merci pour le chocolat (Claude Chabrol, France/Switzerland, 2000): restaurant of Le Chateau d'Ouchy (1889–93), Lausanne-Ouchy (VD)

Messidor (Alain Tanner, Switzerland, 1979): Gasthof Rössli, now the Hotel Schwanden, Schwanden bei Schüpfen (BE); Hotel Steingletscher, Sustenpass (BE); three unidentified hotels

Mutter, dein Kind ruft (Rochus Gliese, Germany, 1923): hotel in Davos (GR)

Nocturne (Riccardo Signorell, Switzerland, 2004): Hotel Waldhaus (1908), Sils-Maria (GR)

Ohm Krüger (Hans Steinhoff, Germany, 1941): fictional 'Hôtel de Suisse', by lake Geneva (but not what is now the Villa Krüger in Clarens, where Paul Krüger lived in 1904)

On Her Majesty's Secret Service (Peter R. Hunt, UK, 1969): Schweizerhof Hotel (1859), Berne (BE), disguised as an office building; Hotel Oberland, Lauterbrunnen (BE)

One in a Million (Sidney Lanfield, US, 1936): fictional St. Moritz hotel

The Other Love (André de Toth, US, 1947): fictional sanatorium in the Alps (near the Jungfrau)

Palace Hotel (Emile Berna and Leonard Steckel, Switzerland, 1952): Palace Hotel (1896), St. Moritz (GR)

Le Parfum d'Yvonne (Patrice Leconte, France, 1994): unspecified Geneva hotel; 'Hôtel Hermitage', i.e., the Hôtel Royal (1909), Evian (France)

Passion (Jean-Luc Godard, Switzerland, 1982): Motel Lunika (1962) Etoy (VD)

The Passionate Friends (David Lean, UK, 1949): the 'Hotel Splendid', by an unspecified Swiss lake (actually the Lac d'Annecy in Haute-Savoie, France); mention is made of the Schweizerhof Hotel, Zurich

People—Jet Set 2 (Fabien Onteniente, France, 2004): Palace Hotel (1915), Gstaad (BE)

Les petites couleurs (Patricia Plattner, Switzerland, 2001): Motel des Pêchers (1964), Etoy (VD)

Le petit soldat (Jean-Luc Godard, France/Switzerland, 1960): Hôtel Century (1959), Geneva (GE); also seen are the exteriors of the Hôtel d'Angleterre (1872), the Beau Rivage (1865), the Hôtel de la Paix (1865), the Regina and the Hôtel de Russie (1852, demolished 1970), all Geneva (GE)

Place Bel-Air, Genève (Alexandre Promio for Lumière, France, 1896): view of the Hôtel de la Balance (now demolished), Geneva (GE), on DVD *Il était une fois . . . la Suisse* (Cinémathèque suisse, 2002)

La Princesse Lulu (E.B. Donatien, France/Switzerland, 1924): Hôtel Byron (1837; now a retirement home), Villeneuve (VD)

Repérages (Michel Soutter, Switzerland, 1977): Grand Hôtel des Salines (1868), Bex-les-Bains (VD)

The Return of the Pink Panther (Blake Edwards, UK, 1975): Palace Hotel (1915), Gstaad (BE)

Rien ne va plus (Claude Chabrol, France/Switzerland, 1997): Hotel Waldhaus (1908), Sils-Maria (GR); Park Hotel, Aix-les-Bains, France; Savoy Hotel, Aix-les-Bains, France

Sangam (Raj Kapoor, India, 1964): the Beau Rivage (1874), Interlaken; Hôtel Bellevue des Alpes (1865), Kleine Scheidegg (BE)

Sauve qui peut (la vie) (Jean-Luc Godard, Switzerland, 1980): Hotel Inter-Continental (1962–1964), Geneva (GE); Continental Hotel (1966), Lausanne (VD); Hôtel de la Truite (1780), Le Pont (VD)

Schneewitchen un die sieben Gaukler (Kurt Hoffmann, Switzerland, 1962): hotel in St. Moritz (GR)

Secret Agent (Alfred Hitchcock, UK, 1936): fictional 'Hotel Excelsior' in an unspecified resort

Der Springer von Pontresina (aka *Liebe in St. Moritz*) (Willie Morrie & Erich Frisch, Germany/Switzerland, 1934): Grand Hotel (1864), St. Moritz (GR), and other St. Moritz hotels

Stolen Holiday (Michael Curtiz, US, 1937): fictional 'Imperial Hotel', Geneva

Stresemann (Alfred Braun, Germany, 1957): Grand Hotel (1906–1993), Brissago (TI)

Swiss Miss (John G. Blystone, US, 1938): fictional 'Alpen Hotel', somewhere in the 'Swiss Tyrol'

Syriana (Stephen Gaghan, US, 2006): Hôtel President Wilson (1962), Geneva (GE)

Thin Ice (Sidney Lanfield, US, 1937): fictional hotel

The Third Man on the Mountain (Ken Annakin, US, 1959): fictional hotel 'Monte d'Oro' in fictional village 'Kurtal' near the Matterhorn (filmed in Zermatt, VS)

Törst [*Thirst*, aka *Three Strange Loves*] (Ingmar Bergman, Sweden, 1949): view of the Hotel Krafft am Rhein (1873), Basel (BS)

The Trollenberg Terror [aka *The Crawling Eye*] (Quentin Lawrence, UK, 1959): the fictional 'Hotel Europa' at the fictional 'Kleindorf zum Trollenberg'

The Unbearable Lightness of Being (Philip Kaufman, US, 1988): Hôtel de la Cigogne (18th-century building, a hotel since 1900), Geneva (GE)

Violanta (Daniel Schmid, Switzerland, 1977): Palazzo Salis (built 1630, a hotel since 1876), Soglio (TI)

La Vocation d'André Carel (Jean Choux, Switzerland, 1925): Grand Hôtel Bellevue (1885, now the Glion Hotel School), Glion (VD); Hôtel Royal (1909), Evian (France)

Voyage à travers l'impossible (Georges Méliès, France, 1904): unspecified inn somewhere near the Jungfrau (BE)

Waiting Room for Death [*I dödens väntrum*] (Hasse Ekman, Sweden, 1946): a sanitarium in Lugano (TI)

Der Zauberberg [*The Magic Mountain*] (Hans Geissendorfer, West Germany, 1982): 'Berghof Sanatorium', Davos

Zwischensaison [*Off Season*] (Daniel Schmid, Switzerland, 1992): Grand Hotel (1905), Brunnen (SZ); Hotel Astoria, Coimbra (Portugal); Hotel das Termas, Curia (Portugal); Palace Hotel (1926), Curia (Portugal); Bussaco Palace Hotel (1885), Coimbra (Portugal)

Other Films Cited

L'Affaire Tournesol (Ray Goossens, Belgium, 1961)

Alphaville (Jean-Luc Godard, France, 1965): Grand Hôtel (1862; now the InterContinental), rue Scribe, Paris

The Bride Wore Red (Dorothy Arzner, US, 1937)

La Croix du Cervin (Jacques Béranger, Switzerland, 1922)

Darr (Yash Chopra, India, 1993)

Eloge de l'amour (Godard, Switzerland, 2001): Hôtel InterContinental (1878; now The Westin), rue Castiglione, Paris

The Final Problem (George Ridgewell, US, 1923)

Foreign Correspondent (Alfred Hitchcock, US, 1940): studio reconstructions of the Carlton and Savoy hotels, London

Idiot's Delight (Clarence Brown, US, 1939)

Il était une fois . . . la Suisse (Cinémathèque suisse, Switzerland, 2002): compilation of archive footage from 1896–1934

Der Kampf ums Matterhorn (1928) (Mario Bonnard, Nuntio Malasomma, Switzerland/Germany, 1928)

Les Petites Fugues (Yves Yersin, Switzerland, 1979)

Phenomena (Dario Argento, Italy, 1989)

Prénom Carmen (Jean-Luc Godard, France, 1983): Hôtel InterContinental (1878; now The Westin), rue Castiglione, Paris

Sherlock Holmes (Albert Parker, US, 1922)

Sherlock Holmes and the Secret Weapon (Roy William Neill, US, 1942).

REFERENCES

Banaji, Shakuntala. 'Intimate Deceptions: Young British-Asian viewers discuss sexual relations on and off the Hindi film screen' *Journal of South Asian Popular Culture* 3 no. 2 (October 2005): 177–192.

Boujut, Michel. *L'Escapade ou le cinéma selon Soutter*. Lausanne: L'Age d'Homme, 1974.

Buache, Freddy. *Le Cinéma suisse 1898–1998*. Lausanne: L'Age d'Homme, 1998.

——. *Michel Soutter*. Lausanne: Cinémathèque suisse/L'Age d'Homme, 2001.

Cosandey, Roland. 'De l'Exposition nationale Berne 1914 au CSPS 1921: charade pour un cinéma vernaculaire', pp. 91–109 in *Cinéma suisse: nouvelles approches* edited by Maria Tortajada and François Albera. Lausanne: Payot, 2000.

——. 'Tableaux pour une expédition cinématographique au pays du panorama: *Captain Deasy's Daring Drive*' *Décadrages* 6 (2005): 98–110. (English translation from an earlier version published as '"Sensational Films. Ascent of the Alps by Motor Car": Mutoscope and Biograph in Switzerland, 1903' *Historical Journal of Film, Radio and Television* 15 no. 4 (October 1995): 475–495).

Dumont, Hervé. *Histoire du cinéma suisse: films de fiction 1896–1965*. Lausanne: Cinémathèque Suisse, 1987.

—— and Maria Tortajada. *Histoire du cinéma suisse, 1966–2000*. Hauterive: Editions Gilles Attinger, 2007.

Flückiger-Seiler, Roland. *Hotel Traüme zwischen Gletschern und Palmen: Schweizer tourismus und Hotelbau, 1830–1920*. Baden: Hier und Jetzt, 2001.

——. *Hotel Waldhaus, Sils Maria: canton des Grisons*. Berne: Société d'histoire de l'art en Suisse, 2005.

Guide to Swiss Hotels. Basle: Swiss Hotel Proprietors' Association, 1934.

Hergé *L'Affaire Tournesol*. Tournai: Casterman, 1956.

James, Henry. *Daisy Miller*. Harmondsworth: Penguin, 1988 [1878].

Kienberger, Rolf and Kienberger, Urs. *Le Waldhaus 1908–1983: Scènes de la vie d'un grand hôtel*. Sils-Maria: Hotel Waldhaus, 1984.

Kluge, A. 'Notizen im Waldhaus' pp. 138–142 in *Das Waldhaus, Sils Maria* edited by A. T. Schaefer. Mönchengladbach: Kühlen, 1998.

Maltin, Leonard. *The Disney Films*. Hyperion: New York, 1985.

Le Montreux Palace, ans 100. Montreux: The Raffles Montreux Palace, 2006.

Nestler, Monica. *Grand Hotel Brissago 1906–1989*. Brissago: Editions Scala, 1993.

Pithon, Rémy. 'Le *Bergfilm* ou l'obsession alpine' pp. 41–54 in *Cinéma suisse muet: lumières et ombres* edited by Rémy Pithon. Lausanne: Editions Antipodes/ Cinémathèque Suisse, 2002.

Pottier, P. *Livre d'Or, Hôtel Intercontinental Genève 1964–1989: Un quart de siècle de l'histoire du monde*. Geneva: Herbert A. Schott, 1989.

Ramuz, Charles-Ferdinand. 'La Beauté de la montagne' pp. 352–362 in *Oeuvres complètes*. Lausanne: Editions Rencontre, 1968 [1930].

Schaefer, A.T. *Das Waldhaus, Sils Maria: Insel mit Brücken*. Mönchengladbach: Kühlen, 1998.

Schmid, Daniel. '"Grand Hôtel" roman-photo' pp. 9–76 in *Daniel Schmid* edited by Iréne Lambelet. Lausanne: L'Age d'Homme, 1982.

——. 'Bericht eines Hotelkindes' pp. 26–33 in *Das Waldhaus, Sils Maria*, edited by A. T. Schaefer. Mönchengladbach: Kühlen, 1998.

——. *A Smuggler's Life*. Zurich, Edition Dino Simonett, 1999.

——. *Romantik Hotel Schweizerhof*. Schweizerhof: Flims-Waldhaus, n.d. (Also at http://www.schweizerhof-flims.ch/e/history.htm)

Schmid, Daniel and Bener, Peter C. *L'Invention du paradis*. Lausanne: Editions Hebdo, 1984.

Schmid, Daniel and Simonett, Dino. *Excitation Bizarre*. Zurich: Zyloc, 2004.

Schüpbach, Marcel. 'Groupe 5: le bon ménage du cinéma et de la télévision suisse' *Travelling* 35/36 (1973): 12–13.

Senarclens, Jean de, van Berchem, Nathalie and Marquis, Jean. M. *L'Hôtellerie genevoise*. Geneva: Société des Hôteliers de Genève, 1993.

Tortajada, Maria. 'Le suisse errant. Fantasme et réalité du voyage dans le cinéma d'Alain Tanner', pp. 362–370 in *Les défis migratoires* edited by Pierre Centlivres and Isabelle Girod. Zurich: Seismo, 2000.

Websites

'Bollywood: The Indian Cinema and Switzerland' (2002), Zurich: Museum für Gestaltung, http://www.museum-gestaltung.ch/Htmls/Ausstellungen/Archiv/2002/Bollywood/ (14 April 2006)

D'Urso, G. 'Si les vieilles pierres pouvaient parler . . .', (2003) http://www.swissinfo.org/sfr/swissinfo.html (14 April 2006)

'The Eiger Sanction, 1975' http://www.cinema-astoria.com/cinematography/filminglocation/eigersanction/ (14 April 2006)

Harding, L. 'Inspiration Leaves Mann's Mountain' (2004) http://books.guardian.co.uk/news/articles/ (14 April 2006)

'Les hôtels de légende', *Le Temps*, http://www.letemps.ch/dossiers/2005hotels/ (14 April 2006)

Icomos, 'Hôtels et restaurants historiques', http://www.icomos.ch/histhotel_f.html (14 April 2006)

Schmid, Daniel 'Daniel Schmid Filmmaker' http://www.daniel-schmid.com/ (14 April 2006)

Switzerland for Movie Stars, 'MySwitzerland'http://www.filmlocation.ch/uploads/indian_films.pdf (14 April 2006)

Tanner, A. (1996) *Dans la ville blanche*: presentation at the 'Rencontres du Cinéma en Beaujolais', perso.wanadoo.fr/cine.beaujolais/tanner.htm (14 April 2006)

Chapter Five

Cinematic Topographies in Time–Space: Wim Wenders' Hotels

Stan Jones

. . . a painter of space engaged on a quest for time.[1]

(Graf, 2002, 63)

Wim Wenders recognizes in himself what he calls a "weakness" for places: "Ich habe einfach ein Faible für Orte. Im vorigen Jahrhundert wäre ich Reiseschriftsteller geworden" ["I've simply a weakness for places. In the previous century, I would have been a travel writer"—all translations by SJ] (Kilb, 2000, 27). The collections of Wenders' writings on cinematic topics and related matters, such as his *Emotion Pictures* (1986), *Die Logik der Bilder/ The Logic of Images* (1988) or *The Act of Seeing* (1992), the books-of-the-film which frequently accompany his work, and particularly his collections of photographs, such as his *Bilder von der Oberfläche der Erde/Images of the Earth's Surface* (2001) and *Einmal/Once* (2001), all reinforce his 'weakness' for places, his conscious response to space and place, occurring before him. And he recognizes a particular, personal response to hotels: "Ich habe kein tolles Gedächtnis für Namen oder Dialoge, aber ich kann mich an jedes einzelne Hotelzimmer erinnern, in dem ich je gewohnt habe" ["I haven't got all that fantastic a memory for names or dialogue, but I can remember every single hotel room in which I've ever stayed"] (Kilb, 2000, 26).

Identity and its politics, as expressed through space, place, location, in film, inevitably underpin any discussion of Wenders and his work. As he says: "Myself, as much as I am a storyteller—and as such time-driven—I always tried to anchor my films in a particular place. It is important for me that the audience understands the space of the film and is able to find orientation in it."[2] He offers narrative topographies, which invite audiences to navigate them. David Harvey goes beyond this cinematic context to allot considerable relevance to Wenders' films by citing two of them, with the aid of Charles Newman of the *New York Times*, in his *The Condition of Postmodernity:*

> Excessive information, it transpires, is one of the best inducements to forget-
> ting. The qualities of postmodern fiction—'the flattest possible characters in the
> flattest possible landscape rendered in the flattest possible diction' . . . —are
> suggestive of exactly that reaction. The personal world that Wenders depicts
> in *Paris, Texas* does likewise. *Wings of Desire*, though more optimistic, still
> replies in the affirmative to the other question which Newman poses: 'Have the
> velocities of recent change been so great that we do not know how to trace their
> lines of force, that no sensibility, least of all narrative, has been able to articulate
> them?' (Harvey, 1989, 350)

In the wide-ranging context of his survey of postmodernism, Harvey affirms Wenders' films as documents of contemporary cultural history. However, he inevitably fails to show how they work as films to secure their relevance. The more specialist studies of Wenders' output, like those of Ibrahim (1986), Grob (1991), Kolker and Beicken (1993), Cayla (1994), Cook and Gemünden (1997) or Graf (2002) enable more detailed insight into the way his films work and justify his reputation, or otherwise. Naturally, they refer to the use of the hotel/motel as setting and motif in specific films and make general points about it in circulation throughout Wenders' work, but they do not investigate the topic systematically.[3] Something of an exception is Winkler-Bessone's study, *Les Films de Wim Wenders*, which takes a psychoanalytical approach to what it sees as archetypal imagery. Where he focuses on the hotel/motel, he offers a useful insight:

> The character of these places *of passage* is at once open and closed and makes of
> hotels and motels veritable spaces of transition, which simultaneously express
> the desire to flee out of this world, the origin of wanderlust, and the incessant
> fear of enclosure, of imprisonment. (Winkler-Bessone, 1992, 120)

The notions of transition and of the interaction of interior and exterior mark all Wenders' filmmaking. However, as Winkler-Bessone stops at 1991, he has nothing to offer on the subsequent work. On the motel/hotel motif, he also compromises his interpretation by falsely locating the hotel scenes in one film he deals with extensively. In *Der Himmel über Berlin/Wings of Desire* (1987) he attributes them to a former café in Berlin-Kreuzberg (Winkler-Bessone, 1992, 130), whereas they were shot in a far more significant location, as this study will demonstrate in some detail: the quondam Grand Hotel Esplanade on the Potsdamer Platz. Similarly, press reviews of Wenders' films do fre-quently describe the hotel/motel settings, but as an aspect of a general assess-ment, which is itself often located in the director's work as a whole.

The hotel/motel figures as a recurring motif indicating location, setting, identified place, cinematic mise-en-scène, symbol, metaphor, allegory, with the aesthetic, cultural, even political and also, closely connected to the notion of the 'authenticity' of a fiction in its setting, the ethical implications of those functions. Naturally, this study cannot hope to trace all the implications Wenders' concept and construction of space/place in his films, but it will attempt to investigate how the hotels/motels figure and to form some assessment of their overall importance for his work. To that end, I shall concentrate on three main works: *Der Stand der Dinge/The State of Things* from 1982 (subsequently referred to as '*State*'), *Der Himmel über Berlin/Wings of Desire* from 1987 ('*Wings*') and *The Million Dollar Hotel* from 1999 ('*Million$*'). As supplementary examples, I shall refer to *Alice in den Städten/ Alice in the Cities* from 1973 (*Alice*), to *Paris.Texas* from 1984, and to his cooperative venture with Antonioni, *Au-delà des Nuages/Beyond the Clouds* from 1995 (*Clouds*). I shall refer to Wenders' abiding concerns with the nature of memory, both in what we generally call history and specifically as it is constructed and used in the cinema. Here Zygmunt Bauman's (1997, 86) suggestion that linear time has been imposed on the cyclical—"Modernity furnished time with certain traits which only space possesses 'naturally': modern time had direction, just like any itinerary in space"—is a useful approach to the workings of Wenders' topographies. I shall examine how they incorporate the nature of perception, notions of 'home' *vs.* the nomadic existence, the relations between the sexes, and the tension between image and narrative in filmmaking. I shall also cite biographical and historical connections and influences and aspects from Wenders' creative history, such as his fascination with American culture and specifically with the painter, Edward Hopper. With *State* and *Million$*, I will examine how these films become their own subjects (Figure 5.1), with particular implications for the hotel setting as theme: the former illustrates in its narrative and thematic structure a programmatic High Modernism, and the latter integrates the music used on its soundtrack with its imagery and displays its own production through the 'making of' reports that accompany it on the commercially released DVDs. These offer the spectator documentary structures with a further range of viewpoints on the film and its setting in the hotel.

To approach questions of space and place raised by the hotel/motel motif in Wenders' films, a premise from Gardies's *L'Éspace au Cinéma* provides a wider context: " . . . does not every narrative, regardless of which medium accommodates it, tell, either explicitly or allusively, openly or subliminally, the story of humanity in its relations with space?" (Gardies, 1993, 142–43). For cinema and its particular narrative constructions, Gardies offers analytical criteria, "here/there/elsewhere" to define space and place within a film and

Figure 5.1.   The film set as a stage before the Atlantic

how the spectator relates to them: "One will not fail to notice that there exist, despite their differences, some common traits between the here and the there, whilst the elsewhere bears no relation to the former" (Gardies, 1993, 36). "Here/there" he sees as belonging to the diegetic unity of any film, the former as the actual image and the latter as the virtual, incorporating the implications of the out-of-frame and the non-diegetic soundtrack. "Elsewhere" is the Other by definition, either indicated within a film's narrative and thematic structure or as a function of a film's production and consumption, both of which have implications for the position and function of the spectator, particularly in constructing what Gardies deems a "topography" for a film's entire narrative (Gardies, 1993, 108).

To identify and interpret the wider cultural implications of the space/place in Wenders' films, I shall also apply two analytical schemas proposed by Harvey: firstly "a 'grid' of social practices" (Harvey, 1989, 220–1);[4] and secondly, to link this to the implications of Wenders' images in time via "Gurevich's [1964] typology of social times" (Harvey, 1989, 224–25).[5] With reference to Bakhtin's notion of the chronotope and Foucault's heterotopia, I shall then return to Gardies' conclusion:

> If one admits that it [space] confronts place like the virtual to the actual, it could not be reduced to its solely physical and geographical dimension, but rather considered as a constructive system . . . it does not barricade itself any more into a single, diegetic world; it reveals its structural and functional power in the entirety of filmic/cinematographic activity. It is probably in this way that it is

able to enter the general field of semiotic narratology and to bring some new light onto the theory of narration. (Gardies, 1993, 216)

THE FILMS

In Wenders' "filmic/cinematographic activity" what sort of hotel/motels appear and how do they function in the respective narratives?

In the three main texts, the settings are all hotels: none displays the unit layout typical of motels. In *State,* the entire topography of the hotel indicates it is a resort, and it forms the setting for the first two-thirds of the film. In *Million$*, the hotel as permanent residence dominates the entire narrative. In *Wings*, by contrast, it functions as a setting for performance and initially appears only briefly, as one location among many, but then forms the mise-en-scène for narrative resolution. The first two films depict entire hotels, whilst *Wings* restricts itself to two interiors, which are not, in fact, identified or recognisable as belonging to an hotel. What links all three hotel locations is their location in time: all are in some way 'relics', left over from a previous, more impressive existence.

Because each film is shot on location and not in studio sets, they use sites with geographical identities locatable on maps: Sentra on the northwest coast of Portugal for *State,* Berlin for *Wings* and downtown Los Angeles for *Million$*. This means they already have different sorts of implied 'elsewheres': the (unnamed) hotel in Portugal is on the European periphery, while the other two are geographically central to major cities, although historically and socially peripheral. As narrative settings, they provide the possibilities for mise-en-scène, which generate thematic implications from their locations for the identity of place. *State* and *Wings* are European, while *Million$* is, like the motels and hotels in *Paris.Texas*, unequivocally American. And then again, *State* and *Million$* share that symbiosis of Europe and America, which is fundamental to Wenders' entire imagining, as *Alice* already displays in its protagonist's journeyings, and which appears in *Clouds* through the star-aura of John Malkovitch playing the American director scouting Italian locations. The interiors of *Wings* contribute to the wider theme of Berlin and its history, only referring obliquely to anything American, as the film's penultimate scene borrows stylistically from Hollywood genre conventions to support the thematic development. Its "here/there" construction implies less a differentiated "elsewhere" as place, than a range of "elsewheres" in time, whilst the other two films imply "elsewheres" as geographical locations, but also in terms of the cultural, political and economic domination of space, as

one place 'appropriates' another by controlling the identity, or identities, that
are available from it.

The State of Things

> C'est dans un hotel plus qu'ailleurs que l'on se sent le plus seul. [More
> than anywhere else, you feel most alone in a hotel.]

(Ibrahim, 1986, 133)

The opening sequence of *State* ends with an abrupt reorientation of the spectator. The film opens with sci-fi imagery of a group of what look like survivors
of some ecological disaster struggling through a deserted landscape. They
arrive at what turns out to be an abandoned hotel right on the edge of the sea,
and one declares: "Now we have found a home." With that, the film's director, Friedrich, intrudes into the frame and ends what has been clearly a take.
With his image, the crashing of the surf that forms the background suddenly
replaces the sci-fi soundtrack. As they prepare the next shots, the cameraman reveals to Friedrich that they have run out of filmstock. Their American
producer, Gordon, has gone back to the States and not sent any more. So the
set is packed up, the crew and actors disperse, and the film begins to observe
them in the hotel, as they adapt to what the director assures them will be
merely a creative pause. To fill in the 'dead time,' some take to drinking; one
practices the violin and sleeps fitfully to the sound of a metronome; another
photographs himself as he lies in the bath before continuing a love affair with
one of his colleagues; the director tends to his children, drinks too much and
sleeps it off on the floor of his apartment, and his wife speaks a personal diary
into a dictaphone while observing herself in a mirror; one of the other actors
similarly writes a diary before a mirror, but then deliberately covers it to hide
her reflection; the cameraman falls asleep to the sound of a talking clock.
When news comes through of his wife's death in a Los Angeles hospital,
he takes himself off to Lisbon, and the scene shifts briefly, as several others
go there seeking a change of scene. After a bitter exchange with his writer,
Friedrich decides to go to Los Angeles to find Gordon. The setting shifts
radically, as he cruises the LA streets in vain, until by chance locating his
man hiding out in a mobile home. In a melancholic and blackly comic final
sequence, he learns that his film has been financed by money from the Mob
and that they now want their money back. Gordon is, then, on the run and the
entire project is over. After cruising the streets all night, the two are gunned
down the next morning as they take leave of each other in a parking lot.

With that, the rest of the characters in *State* are left, literally, stranded in
the hotel on the edge of Europe: the narrative makes no provision for their

further fates. It brings Wenders' film, in a sense, back to the origins of its own production. He became aware of the location when he heard that the director Raul Ruiz had actually run out of stock for his *The Territory* (1983) and decided to take him some supplies. As Wenders tells it, he came upon his location completely by chance after taking a wrong turn (Combs, 1983, 9). He found a hotel from the 1960s, built on the very edge of the coast and abandoned after inundation by a flood tide. Of this location he maintained: "Der Ort wollte mit Macht ein Film werden" ["The place wanted forcibly to become a film"] (Wenders, 2001, 26). So, he persuaded Ruiz's crew, and especially the cameraman, Henri Alekan, to sign up for his project. He raised the finance in less than two weeks and, having assembled what he called: "a most unlikely collection of people" (Combs, 1983, 9), Wenders set about his film by improvising *in situ* from a story he had devised some years before, a creative method he prefers to detailed planning, storyboarding and so on. From an almost *ad hoc* screenplay, he proceeded to shoot the story of an abandoned shoot in an abandoned hotel. *State* is, then, not so much a commercial project as an 'art film,' derived entirely from personal inspiration stimulated by the chance finding of an hotel with a 'genius loci' presenting a suitable location to realize his imagining.

Gilbert Adair's analysis reveals how his film works:

> . . . because the first challenge facing any movie (certainly any low-budget European art movie) is that of simply surviving its own shoot, it too may be made to function as a source of narrative, engendering its own stars (not necessarily in the same order of billing), its own dramas, conspiracies, love affairs, rhythms, moods, even mise en scène, so to speak. It's the reverse side, the verso of the tapestry. (Adair, 1983, 140)

It is the converse of the 'seamless' narrative of conventional, genre-based filmmaking, as it reflects ironically on the conditions of its own existence. Adair points to the widest possible "elsewhere" implied by the "here/there" of the hotel setting and its surroundings: the contrasting of Europe and America through their cultures of filmmaking. This contrast underlies *State* through its narrative, its characters and their dialogue and its mise-en-scène. It even appears as the most comprehensive "elsewhere" through the fact that Wenders shot his film in English, the international language of everywhere and nowhere, to accommodate his multinational team.

At one point, Friedrich declares to his cast and crew: "All of this is a fiction" and goes on to maintain that there are no stories in real life, only in films. When shooting stops, they cease to appropriate the space around them, turning it into the setting and mise-en-scène to create their film's fiction and express its implications. Instead, they try vainly to create some sort of community by

turning themselves into guests of the hotel, by the ritual of a semi-formal dinner, for example. But this turns out to be a 'fiction,' as they cannot get beyond
a collection of simultaneous personal spaces, an effect intensified by the film
omitting any sign of staff in the hotel or of nearby locals. What is actually
holding the film team together now is a centripetal force, the 'closed' nature
of a peripheral and inaccessible place—symbolized by the faltering telephone
link to the outside world, or, in the case of the "there" of Lisbon and the surrounding country, by a foreign language which none of them can use. As they
fail to make even a fiction of the place they are in, even as a community of
hotel guests, the film team succumbs to what Gurevich describes as "erratic
time," that is: "time of uncertainty and accentuated contingency in which
present prevails over past and future" (Harvey, 1989, 224). Their relation to
the place harks back to Phillip Winter's frustrated wanderings through various
hotels in *Alice* and corresponds to Gardies' use of "parcours" and "itinéraire"
(Gardies, 1993, 115ff) to describe the interaction of figures in a film narrative
with the space of that narrative and the way it constructs place. From being
governed by the latter, embodied in the schedule of a film, which makes the
hotel one place in a scheme of places visited, the 'guests' are travellers immobilized by forces literally beyond their horizons and hence caught in a state
of transient permanence, a 'Hotel Narcissus' as non-place with no points of
departure or arrival. It parodies any sense of 'home' and exists as a permanent
present closed in on itself. It is hence reminiscent, albeit here without any hint
of development, of the way all film narratives function in a permanent present
tense.

   To reinforce the significance of their fragmented pastimes, Wenders fashions his film's diegesis, the space of the hotel and its surroundings, through a
montage of interiors and exteriors, often with complex framing. He inserts at
various points disconnected shots of various pieces of filmmaking equipment
standing idle around the hotel's terraces and contrasts the claustrophobia of
the hotel's rooms, which are naturally designed for transience, with what here
concretely fates them to it, the relentless sea. He uses wide shots of the sea,
sometimes with small figures in the foreground, and has its roaring almost
permanently on the soundtrack, reminding the spectator that the "here" of the
hotel is not possible without the "there" of the sea. Such shots parallel careful
studies of it repeatedly washing over the hotel's balustrades and re-filling the
decaying basin of the swimming pool to create images of a limitless element
displaying a permanent transience in contrast to the situation of the people
marooned at its edge.

   Wenders also has one of the cast, ironically the Californian, reinforce the
location of the hotel by seeking it on an illuminated globe and spelling it out
to the spectator in a monologue. This same character muses aloud on the

immensity before his window and declares: "One big wave, and they all go phut, baby," commenting on the self-absorption of the people around him. This same figure also tries to fill in the dead time by learning Portuguese, but the film indicates this is to no avail by showing him emerging from a barber's in Lisbon nursing a shaving cut, despite frequenting the place regularly. His particular narcissism does not appear through the bitter images and exchanges that mark his companions, and it comes in for gentle mockery in a sequence using the pool as mise-en-scène. He sidles across it, pegging out washing on a line and all the while explaining to a companion his grotesquely unfortunate childhood back home. When he reaches the end of the line, the film broadens his context by cutting to a long shot showing him scampering away out of the pool to go to the city and calling to his companion to gather in the washing again, as the ever-present sea is threatening to overwhelm it.

The most radical irruption of the exterior into the interior carries a reference to American literature and to one of the most famous pieces of American cinema fashioned from it. As Friedrich sleeps off his drinking, the storm outside hurls the trunk of a small tree through the door of his apartment. What Marsha Kinder (1990, 77) rightly calls "This blatantly symbolic incident" directs us to the role of the novel, *The Searchers*, in the narrative and the implied parallels with John Ford's film adaptation. Friedrich carries the book with him, recommends it to one of the cast, and then uses it and his memory of the film adaptation (where the sight of a similar tree in both presages the death of the protagonist) to interpret it. The lead figure then joins the spectators in verbally constructing a symbolic, even allegorical, significance from the incursion of the exterior, the "there" of the place, just out of frame, into the interior, the "here" of this sequence, and bases his understanding on his knowledge of other fictions. At this point, *State*'s high-modernist self-reflexivity is acute.

A further refinement of the same process leads Friedrich to tell his wife on the phone from LA: "I'm not at home anywhere." This directly quotes the German director F. W. Murnau and signals, as does the director's very name, Munroe, the film's deliberate self-reflexivity, applied to the allegory for actual and spiritual homelessness it generates from its setting. In the last analysis, this allegory of the hotel on the edge of Europe is Wenders' meditation on the condition of filmmaking in Europe, for which, so *State* implies, there is certainly no 'home' of any kind but, at best, a contingent and peripheral existence. He constructs a "Hotel Melancholia," where his figures exist dependant on the support of the great "elsewhere," the American industry, and at the same time threatened by it. Wenders present them as a collection of foreigners with little connection to their surroundings, caught up in a place the location of which was always, at the least, unwise, and may cease to exist at any time. They are in all senses homeless, even as far as being unable to construct what Ganter (2003, 118) called in his application of Derrida's ideas to Wenders' work "eine Signifikantenkette" [a chain of signifiers], the gesture of a meaningful narrative out of their circumstances in that place, which might at least imitate the promise of a meaning behind the story they were constructing in their film.[6]

The only hint of a way out of the ennui comes, typically for Wenders, through the two children accompanying Friedrich. In contrast to the resentful question of one actor: "What are we supposed to do here?" when the shooting stops, they treat the hotel, the film location and the surroundings as a playground. They invent their own fantasy worlds, take pictures of the adults and interact spontaneously with them, all the while commenting sagely to each other on their observations of them. Hence, the children offer us, as spectators, another viewpoint on the action. In Gardies' terms they are fully in the 'here' of the place, both in place and time. They hint at the possibility of establishing Gurevich's category of "enduring time" expressed in "kinships and locality groupings," because they are not cursed by the (adults'?) pressure from, or desire for, any 'elsewhere.'

Wings of Desire

> Berlin ist das Letzte. Der Rest ist Vorgeschichte. Sollte Geschichte stattfinden, wird Berlin der Anfang sein [Berlin is the last thing. Everything else is pre-history. If history is to happen, then Berlin will be the beginning]
>
> (Heiner Müller; Mühlhaupt and Knödler-Bunte, 1986, n.p.)

Paris.Texas closes with the sequences at the Houston hotel and on the road out, after which *Wings* shifts the implications of the hotel setting radically. Wenders declared of the former:

> . . . initially the point of departure for that film was in the last thing we shot on *Paris.Texas*. It was the scene where the mother gets reunited with the little boy and Nastassja comes up to the room where he is waiting for her and he walks up to her and takes her in his arms. . . . Somehow I had got to a point, emotionally as well as a possibility for myself, where it would open up to something new for me, that I could tell another story. I knew that whatever I was going to do had to start at this point. (Hawker, 1987, 22)

Parallel to the 'here' of this hotel scene, Wenders shows, in frame compositions highly reminiscent of Edward Hopper, the husband and father, Travis, watching, from the corresponding 'there' of a carpark, the reunion he organized. Having chosen what will now be the (virtual?) 'there,' he then heads off back into the film's 'elsewhere,' from which he materialized at the beginning. So the director claims he made the decision then to return to Europe on the basis, if we accept his account, of a sort of 'epiphany,' experienced through creating the dénouement of *Paris.Texas* in its final hotel setting. He reached a point of conscious transition in himself, which he translated into physical relocation to make Berlin the 'here' of his next film and hence of the spectator, wherever they may be watching it. Its aesthetic, narrative and thematic complexity make it probably his most noted work, and it is probably his masterpiece so far.

Wings locates itself, in time and place, centrally in a city: the pre-reunification Berlin of 1987. It reflects much about the actual nature of its location and the city's history and has itself since become part of that history thanks to its images recording places that no longer exist or have changed radically. The Grand Hotel Esplanade and the Potsdamer Platz are two such. City maps show both, and the Platz itself has famously become a showcase reconstruction of part of the dead zone imposed on the city centre by the Wall. With such developments, the city as capital of Germany has sought architectural expressions for its desired identity as a world city.

The film depicts a city divided and still exhibiting empty spaces and scarring from 1945. It does this by offering its spectators one of the most remarkable viewpoints in all cinema, that of avatars. They are angels left behind in the city by a God who has departed in anger at their intercession for a humanity the Second World War has shown to be debased. Damiel and Cassiel are the lead figures among the metaphysical observers, who have recorded all history from the beginning of time and continue to do so. The first third of the film depicts the city and its inhabitants as a loosely structured montage of observations in black and white, up to the point where Damiel notices Marion, a trapeze artiste in a travelling circus. The sight of her stimulates his nagging desire to experience human temporal existence, so that, in a famous shift into colour imagery, he crosses over from limitlessness into place and time. With the aid of an ex-angel film star, Peter Falk from the United States, who happens to be filming in the city, he begins to learn to be human by seeking out Marion. She is seeking him as well, and the film comes to its climax as the two meet in the bar of the déclassé Hotel Esplanade. Marion explains to him the significance of their love, and by the next morning Damiel can declare she has given him his most important lesson in becoming human.

She offers a joint *Geschichte* (the German meaning both story and history), which will have ongoing significance, in contrast to the ennui of the characters left behind in *State*. Ganter sees the Esplanade as a setting for communication and the establishment of identity: "An example is the bar scene in *Wings of Desire*. There two self-determining partners are united,

Figure 5.2.   The hotel ballroom – "Now I know what no angel knows"

although Marion speaks in a monologue and paradoxically about solitariness as the condition for togetherness" (Ganter, 2003, 102). The setting is a filmic mise-en-scène writ large to enable the prospect of a story, of a coherent communication to establish, despite the apparent paradoxicality of the situation, a common understanding of what their situation means to them. And the next day, whilst he holds the rope on which Marion practises amid the faded prewar décor of one of the hotel's public-rooms, Damiel affirms that he now "knows something that no angel knows," and that he can look forward to having the memory of their first night right up to his moment of death—that is, that he will have a *Geschichte* with her as a human (Figure 5.2).

In Gurevich's terms, he is conscious of entering "cyclical time" (Harvey, 1989, 224), where the "past, present and future [are] projected into each other accentuating continuity within change."

By this point, the construction of the Esplanade's interiors as mises-en-scène has established this location as a particularly pure form of Bakhtin's chronotope: "the place where the knots of narrative are tied and untied."[7] To prepare this status, the setting shifts out of the random space of the city the angels patrol to create an intense experience of place. It means abandoning their vertical axis, along which they regularly descend from limitlessness to observe particular places, for the horizontal and for space compressed into a completely enclosed interior. Here Damiel's increasing fascination prompts him to seek out Marion in what is the venue for the self-conscious morbidity of '80s punk-rock performances. Any nostalgia for the decaying luxury from the '30s at once becomes ironic in the spectacle of its use as a setting for the cult music of 50 years on. In the black and white of the angel's dimension, and watched by his companion Cassiel, Damiel tries to go beyond the sight of Marion's sensual dancing and his sense of her emotional response, by touching her. His avatar existence means, however, that he can only ever exist in a virtual 'there' to the actual 'here' of humanity and hence only ever imitate human actions. And we, as spectators, share, at least indirectly, the virtual viewpoint of the angels, even though we apparently enjoy some position independent of them. So, observing the ritual of the punk-rock in the old hotel finally convinces him to cross over, and the mise-en-scène subverts its inherent irony by using its setting to prepare the identity of the place, which then generates the full chronotope, with all of its implications for this complex film.

For an audience viewing it post-reunification and post-millennium, *Wings* functions like a piece of archaeology, particularly as it displays the Hotel Esplanade. This location, like that of Sentra in Portugal, was available as a 'ready-made,' but it was hardly unknown and scarcely without connotations. Its status stands out in a major town-planning exercise carried out in 1985, namely an architectural competition to build a complete "Filmhaus" incorporating the site.[8] The Grand Hotel had sparkled in the glory days of German cinema between the wars in the Weimar Republic and had figured as setting for Bob Fosse's *Cabaret* from 1972. Then, one night in November 1989, events (Müller's 'History'?) overtook all of Berlin's town-planning, so that what is left of the hotel today has become a conserved relic, with pieces of its interiors and its facade shifted from its site to be incorporated into the Sony Centre, next door to the actual "Filmhaus," housing one of Berlin's film schools and the Stiftung Deutscher Kinemathek.[9] What is left of the settings Wenders used is now arguably a simulacrum. It is a 'retro' display offering visitors a setting as a sort of envelope into which they can insert themselves to 'perform' nostalgia in seeking the aura of an ostensibly glamorous aspect of the city's past. And all of it is enclosed (literally, by armoured glass outer walls) in the prodigious project to re-claim and re-assert the significance of the deserted space that was the Esplanade's neglected location.

In an interview from 1987 (Ciment and Niogret, 1984, 12), Wenders described how Berlin attracted him, because: "Tout la ville est sur une errance, bizarre" [All the city is on its wanderings, bizarre]; and "C'est une ville qui est sur un parcours" [It's a city that's on its travels]. It is a place, the very spatial structure of which displays acutely an unresolved past but also offers possibilities for development. Hence, he did not create any identity for the Esplanade in *Wings,* but made it the place where the film's account of its protagonists' desire receives expression in the 'here' of the interiors, and action, implied in the 'there' of the night spent between the meeting in the bar and the practice session under the glass roof the morning after. As a chronotope, its widest significance is that of a place where a possibility of redemption for the 'fallen' state of the divided city might materialize. The only way the setting might be considered as any sort of hotel in the conventional sense is that of a meeting place and brief refuge for the protagonists, where they leave the state of 'parcours' and 'errance' and 'erratic time' to determine some sort of 'itinéraire' in 'cyclical time.' It is the sort of cinematic portal *State's* narrative would have had to generate to allow its stranded souls to escape their transient permanence. Since the film was made, the entire city has gone through a phase of Gurevich's "time in advance of itself" (Harvey, 1989, 225) and must now appear as a place displaying "itinéraire." However, as to whether the sort of developments possibly manifested by *Wings'* Esplanade, both as a Berlin locality and as mise-en-scène, will materialise, that is a topic well beyond the scope of this study.

The Million Dollar Hotel

> Wenders instaure ici un rapport à l'éspace et au temps pertinent et brutal. [Here Wenders establishes a relation to space and to time that is pertinent and brutal.]
>
> (Piégay, 2000, 77)

When his film opened the first Berlinale film festival of the new millennium, Wenders responded to the showplace: "Nur einen Steinwurf vom roten Teppich entfernt sind wir im Niemansland herumgestolpert. . . . 'Das hier kann er doch nicht gewesen sein,' an diesen Satz von damals muss ich mich erinnern, wenn ich die Hochhäuser sehe, die Laserstrahlen. Dass mein Film hier gezeigt wurde, ist eine sehr emotionale Angelegenheit für mich" ["It was only a stone's throw away from the red carpet that we were stumbling around in no-man's-land . . . . 'All this here just can't have been it,' I have to think back to that sentence from those days, when I see the skyscrapers, the lasers. That they are showing my film here is a very emotional thing for me"] (Löser, 2000, 44).

Wenders' comments here reflect identity politics writ large, as he and his film contribute to a spectacle intended to attract global attention to a centre in Berlin as a stage for displaying the German 'Filmkultur' and film industry. However, the choice of *Million$* was not uncontroversial because of its location in LA, the centre of the filmmaking 'elsewhere' that dominates German screens, and because it was shot in English. Where *Wings* refers directly to questions of German identity, *Million$* shows Wenders reprising his role as the filmmaker with a "European way of seeing"[10] applied to the United States.

While the festival used the original version, the copy for German commercial consumption is displaced at least one degree from the original cut and displays the inevitable 'second-hand,' slightly surreal quality that comes with dubbing.

Where Wenders talks about it in press interviews and in the 'making of' accounts accompanying the DVD version,[11] the film becomes overtly its own subject and acquires another set of 'elsewheres.' The DVD's account, "One Dollar Diary," shows the director and crew working in his locations as figures in another film and also intercuts between the shooting on the sets and the post-production of the musical soundtrack carried out in Ireland. In the same way, Wenders' voiceover in the 'Audiokommentar' track suggests a viewing perspective some time and somewhere after the final cut, so that the director becomes his own spectator in order to explain his film to his audience.

Million$ originated with the reaction of a musician to the aura of its setting. Bono, from the Irish band, U2, apparently became fascinated with what is today called the Frontier Hotel in LA (with its companion, the Rosslyn, just across the street) whilst making a music video on its roof. He wrote a story using the location, turned that into a film treatment and persuaded Wenders to direct it. Paralleling the origin of *State*, the filmmaker affirms how the place played on his "weakness"—"Das Hotel hat uns seine Geschichte geradezu aufgedrängt" ["The hotel positively forced its history/story on us"] (Schnelle and Gansera, 2000, 19)—persuading him to direct, and he emphasizes how he sought consciously to capture its local identity in downtown Los Angeles. Despite the signage on its roof, the hotel changed its name sometime after 1945, when it lost its glamour as a haunt of filmstars and politicians together with the glamour of its neighbourhood (where Chaplin, for example, once had his offices) as Hollywood producers relocated their premises elsewhere. Wenders maintains that the area is today much photographed and used as a location for filmmaking but rarely presented in its own right (apparently the Schwarzenegger-vehicle, *End of Days* (2000), was being shot all around their sets). So, he claims for the way the film constructs the fictional setting of the hotel, a deliberate sort of authenticity of 'genius loci,' transmitted by the geographical location it used.

Like *State*, *Million$* starts with a surprise. Its establishing shot depicts a United States familiar from many of its movies: an aerial take drifting past the spectacle of central LA. The sequence cuts to the hotel roof, where it shows one of the leads, Tom Tom, jumping to his death. As he falls, the mise-en-scène shifts into subjective slow motion to depict his glimpses of events in particular rooms. Tom Tom's voiceover establishes his ownership of the narrative viewpoint, as it declares paradoxically that he never loved life more than in his last moments. Wenders stresses the stark restriction of his narrative: "And the time of this film is, of course, only the fraction of a second from the jump off the roof to hitting the asphalt. I have never had less 'room for manoeuvre' at my disposal. Yet I have never made a more tender film, even if the rules of play were brutal."[12] To derive such an effect from the drastically foreclosed narrative time, he does not let us experience the paradox of the dominant narrator exiting his own story with the extinguishing of his consciousness. Instead, Wenders uses a match cut, which simultaneously seeks to shock, showing a bottle breaking on the pavement outside the hotel as it slips from Tom Tom's hand. With that we are into flashback and the main story.

Two weeks previously, Skinner, an FBI agent, arrives in the hotel to investigate why another resident, Izzy Goldkiss, fell from the same roof. At the behest of Izzy's father, a powerful media tycoon who cannot allow his son's death to be publicly reported as suicide, he has to investigate a case the police would routinely ignore. Skinner's aversion translates into initial contempt for the residents, whom he badgers, photographs, bugs and even deluges with the hotel's sprinkler system in his violent attempts to secure one of them as a murderer. The murder motive supposedly lies in the fact that Izzy was a junkie, who had been stealing paintings and covering them, literally, with tar to pass them off as his own, avant-garde work. A group of the residents claim them as their inheritance and stage a media spectacle around the 'discovery' of a new talent, now tragically cut off. Skinner rapidly spots Tom Tom's fascination with Eloise and plays on his childlike nature to bring them together so he can eavesdrop on their conversation. As that fails, he eventually bullies Tom Tom into incriminating one of his friends. Tom Tom then videotapes a false confession for the TV news and kills himself to get his friend released. *Million$* closes its narrative circle with Skinner and Eloise comforting each other by the pool of blood in front of the hotel. Wenders pulls us up and out of the story and the place with a helicopter shot matching the introduction but finally tilting the camera up to the limitless sky over LA.

The detective thriller/love story structure incorporates reflections typical of Wenders on the nature of images and on the cynicism of the media industry, which it links with indirect commentary on the 'there' of the actual Frontier hotel, in which he constructed the 'here' of his fiction, with its own 'elsewhere' of LA and the possibly implied 'elsewhere' of the rest of the United States. The narrative also contains a further remove in time, in that its opening makes it clear who owns the story, but challenges viewers' identity with that figure by dis-locating us from the narrative's 'here/there' structures through a voiceover remembering from the film's ultimate 'elsewhere' in some hereafter. A narrator outside of our concept of time then relates for us, in the space of the film's running time, a story over a specific period in his former life. While Wenders may use the hotel setting to frame a thoroughgoing story, he makes the implications surrounding it complex by creating a complex position for his viewers. On the plot, our viewpoint is simple: we know its destination, but it becomes difficult because we do not know its itinerary, how and why it will get there, let alone what the bizarre suicide might mean.

The thematic implications of *Million$* are indeed brutal, but we see them through what one critic described as: "l'élégance un peu affectée de la mise-en-scène" ["the somewhat affected elegance of the mise-en-scène"] (J.-M. F., 2000, 20). The central group are not conventional 'guests' but transients permanently resident there because they have nowhere else to go. It is an eccentric ensemble: Tom Tom is a childlike, puckish figure, popping up all over the hotel and the surrounding area (Figure 5.3); his beloved Eloise is a whimsically self-destructive beauty addicted to reading as a defence against her surroundings; Dixie styles himself as the forgotten fifth Beatle, modelled on John Lennon and complete with Merseyside accent; Geronimo is a Mexican constantly slipping in and out of role as indigenous American; Jessica is a former actress capable of surprising with grandmotherly profanity; Shorty is a drunken ex-agent from Hollywood in an impossible wig; Vivien is an addict styling herself as Izzy's fiancée. They form a sort of extended family in the hotel because none of them has any alternative but the streets. Into this rejected class of American society, one aspect of the dominant culture, embodied by media tycoon Goldkiss, intervenes, using Skinner, expert in surveillance and discovery, as its tool. The tycoon is seeking to avoid the gaze

Figure 5.3. Tom Tom's world. The street and the hotel

he arrogantly governs, that of the media, being turned on him, but he fails as the residents take over the TV scenario for their few minutes of fame. They can do this thanks to a languidly English art critic, who is following the media reporting and descends into their world, where he declares he can validate Izzy's "garbage" and hence sell it. The hotel briefly becomes their scenario, as they shift themselves from the invisible periphery of society by staging a vernissage in the lobby, which in turn makes them visible for TV. Here they can perform their desired personas and have them validated by broadcasting. Tom Tom's particular performance is at one remove: his 'confession' on tape, which goes to the reporters to accompany the gala. The entire scheme collapses when Skinner literally uncovers the 'real' paintings underneath the tar, the tycoon is confronted with the truth of the son he did not want to know, the media spectacle is over, and *Million$*'s 'family' is left where it always was—except that Tom Tom has killed himself.

Why he has to do this emerges through the fantastical mise-en-scène presenting the death of Izzy. The camera revolves in slow motion around the two of them, as Tom Tom holds Izzy back from the brink, only to release him when his friend claims to have seduced Eloise just to demonstrate her worthlessness. Whether he did, we cannot know, but Tom Tom believed him, and he owns the viewpoint completely. This is, then, the memory and associated guilt he cannot escape, even in a successful relationship with Eloise. Everyone in *Million$* is a loser, except perhaps the ubiquitous TV crews, although they will now have to seek their next spectacle elsewhere.

Skinner is no exception. He links the dominant society and the underclass. He uses various forms of violence on the residents, but, as he at one point explains to Goldkiss, he knows them too well because he is a freak himself. Wenders could use the star image of Mel Gibson for this role as the actor had had an interest in the screen rights but not used it. He cast Gibson against type (except, perhaps, for overtones of the *Mad Max* series) as a scarred and suffering abnormality, self-consciously reminiscent of a 'Frankenstein' monster, rigidly held together by a metal corset and permanently wired in to his mobile phone and laptop. Perhaps the most important 'there' to the hotel's 'here' is Skinner's office, from where he monitors his suspects via his bugs and to which he retreats in pain after he has been attacked by a street gang. In excruciating scenes, he tries to learn what he needs by remotely manipulating Tom Tom and Eloise, while he grimaces at his own suffering reflection in a mirror and tries to reassemble the framework that holds him up.

After the attack on him comes one of the film's key scenes, when, slumped in a chair in an underground carpark, he tries to persuade Eloise to cooperate in nailing a culprit. He thinks he has rescued her from rapists, but she is actually debasing herself in her self-loathing. In a black-comic passage, she rejects his proposition and tells him, with a perverse pride in her certification of madness, what her fate is, namely to wind up back in the hotel regardless of what he might do for her. She does finally turn to him for comfort, however, after she bloodies his hands from the pool on the asphalt, and Tom Tom's voiceover, accompanied by a slight acceleration of the sequence by merging edits to simulate his perception, comments how he is really "one of us," although he does not know it. To leave the hotel in its downtown location, the film shows Eloise shedding a tear over photos of Izzy and Tom Tom, as she sits reading in her window overlooking the city. From his metaphysical vantage point, Tom Tom comments a last time on how wonderful life is, although we don't realize that when we are in it. For the final images of the LA panorama, the soundtrack then shifts its reference, although remaining in an indeterminate elsewhere, by fading in U2 singing "The Ground beneath her Feet." So *Million$* leaves us with a form of music video extolling the reconciliatory power of love to round off the "somewhat affected elegance" of Wenders' art film.

As a major influence on his images, he acknowledges in his 'Filmbuch' to *Million$* the influence of fictional constructions in a related medium from another observer of America, the painter Edward Hopper:

> The views from outside to inside,/through the window spaces,/but also in reverse, the bleak interiors with the perspectives/they opened into the streets and alleys/or onto the rows of windows opposite/there was for all that a great example: the painting of Edward Hopper./He was the godfather for many images in our film,/even though we never consciously set one up in imitation. (Wenders, 2000, 139)

Wenders has written of his admiration for Hopper in the German press (Wenders, 1996). In Hopper's work he sees a particular authenticity of response to a similar environment to the one he was using. Such painting is arguably cinematic before its time, as one critic pointed out:

> He repeatedly shows perspectives which only became possible with the use of camera cranes in film production; these suggest a viewer, who is situated high up in the air, without a really secure location and who is moving at the same time. Hence a sense of the danger to their own position is communicated to the viewer of the picture and, of course, the act of seeing becomes that much more patent. Observers suddenly become aware of themselves as observers. (Liesbrock, 1992, 25)

State's self-reflexivity certainly has this effect, and the film displays some shots reminiscent of Hopper, especially in its interiors. A similar, but not so pronounced, effect comes from *Million$*'s images of the media invading the hotel, and its camerawork and the composition of many shots shows the influence of Hopper. Wenders is constantly concerned with an interchange of interior and exterior, as he incorporates window frames with perspectives leading out over the cityscape into many shots. He also uses travelling shots that leave interiors by these windows to reveal a wide shot that places the hotel in its downtown context. The converse also features as the camera travels across the façade to enter one particular room and close down the frame. In this way, he constantly reminds the spectator that there is a 'there' just outside the 'here' of the image in the frame. Even when the interiors become most claustrophobic, as when the 'family' debates what to do about the paintings, the soundtrack maintains the same 'here/there' correspondence by conveying street sounds from outside. Yet it is probably in individual compositions that the painter's example becomes most obvious: Eloise viewed asleep in her window from several floors up outside the hotel and lighted by the morning sun, or her and Tom Tom in a diner highlighted by the neon and enclosed by a scheme of colour and shadow very reminiscent of Hopper's famous 'Nighthawks' of 1942.

In his director's audiocommentary, Wenders describes the final sequence as a "sad happy ending." Eloise is left, in a composition again reminiscent of Hopper, bereft in the hotel, but has learned the lesson about life from her lover's sacrifice of himself. This is Wenders' romantic and idealizing imagination applied in retrospect for any of his audience who care to take notice. Paralleling the way the plot shows the residents becoming briefly their own subjects for the media, so the 'making-of' reports provide the spectator with at least one other viewpoint. They demonstrate that the hotel in *Million$*, in contrast to that in *Wings* but paralleling that of *State*, is too large to be understood as a chronotope. There are too many narratives running through it simultaneously and it hence contains too many 'theres' and 'elsewheres.' The setting might be seen rather as something Foucault (1986) might have defined as a heterotopia: a space, fictional or actual, set aside from the dominant ordering of space and place and often functioning as a refuge, a site for ritual, for celebration and holiday, or as a prison. Arguably, the use of the hotel in the film allows at least three of these interpretations, as does its reality in LA.[13]

Wenders called the place: "ein Narrenschiff, ein Irrenhaus, Ersatz für die abgeschlossenen Asyle" ["a ship of fools, a madhouse, a substitute for the closed asylums"] (Köhler, 2000, 45). Constructing the setting for the film meant engaging very closely with the actual location in what was, despite the opening and closing sequences, a very 'closed' shoot, as he has affirmed: "Der RAUM, den dieser Film ausfüllt, ist ja winzig" ["The SPACE that this film occupies, is certainly tiny"].[14] The filmmakers rented the first two floors of the place, built a special set in its cavernous lobby and shot all other sequences but one in the streets immediately adjacent to the hotel block. The DVD's 'Production notes' illustrate this concentration on proximity, where Wenders talks about the way one of his production designers sought to recreate the location's authenticity by physically importing it into the fiction:

> Serrell added that his crew had taken great pains to construct the sets as realistically as possible by using materials they found in situ and using the hotel itself as reference point . . . . Fortunately, we were allowed to look into the rooms of some of the residents and furnish the rooms of some of the figures after their example. Jessica's room, for instance, is a combination of several authentic rooms.

Wenders describes the hotel as a holding place for the most destitute residents of LA, who otherwise have to live on the streets in the makeshift encampments that appear every night and are swept away each morning to free the daytime streets for business and tourism. He identifies such poverty as the result of the Reagan administration and comments in his audiocommentary that: "So ein Hotel könnte in Europa keinen Tag lang geöffnet bleiben" ["Such a hotel couldn't remain open a single day in Europe"]. At this point, he is closest to recognising the tension inherent in his fictional hotel as mise-en-scène. The 'One Dollar Diary' refers repeatedly to the difficulties of the location, such as the repulsive conditions in the actual hotel, or the hostility of some of its residents and of some neighbours to the film crew, which led to them wearing safety helmets to protect against the odd missile from above. Such a report carries a (self-reflexive) irony in the parallel between the intrusion of the TV crews depicted in the film and the film crew working in the actual location to create those images. To return to Gardies' notion of 'topography' as placing the spectator vis-à-vis a film, viewing the supplementary DVD edition of the film forces us to ask ourselves from where we view the film: whether we are not indulging in what one critic called the (brutal?) "Poetisierung des Elends" ["poeticising of misery"] (Kopold, 2000) as entertainment.

The sense in which this is a "poetics of space" (Harvey, 1989, 221) appears most acutely in Wenders' use of the hotel's signage, a huge gantry on its roof. It features in wideshot, in closeup, semi-abstract frame compositions and as the immediate context of Tom Tom's sprint to his death. It, therefore, labels the mise-en-scène as the vehicle for the story (a function that continues in the DVD tracks as the framework for the disc's menu). Like many of the interiors, the signage came in for a significant piece of post-production digital modification, when Wenders had its hundreds of lightbulbs restored, something technically impossible in situ. The filmic image as the dominant identity of the hotel, the 'here' we perceive, is, then, a purely virtual 'there.'

Wenders responds to the implications of fictionalizing the location by point-ing to the conflict between the fairytale quality of his work (in this sense a vir-tual 'there') and the "unbarmherzigen Realität" ["unrelenting reality"] (Ko-pold, 2000) of the actual place in the United States. He concedes, however, that engaging with the place is not possible: "Dennoch muss man diese Leute nach dem Drehen hinter sich lassen. Was soll man machen?" ["Nevertheless one has to leave these people behind after shooting. What is one supposed to do?"] (Westpahl and Jähner, 2000, 19). The ethics of filmmaking and the ethics of accepting its products as 'mere entertainment' surface through Wenders' use of this particular hotel for a filmic fiction.

CONCLUSION

In the framework of his abiding concern with narrative in cinema, Wenders' constructions of hotels in particular relate to Gardies's (1993, 216) specula-tion on the significance of filmic space/place as "it reveals its structural and functional power in the entirety of filmic/cinematographic activity" for the general theory of narrative. The way he uses his hotels makes us, as specta-tors, aware of the dynamic of fiction and actual location, and of our own activity in creating a 'topography' out of the images as site for the narrative. In turn, the locations as sites for fictions become chronotopes, which can then possibly develop the implications of the heterotopia.

   Million$ takes the significance of the three hotel settings the furthest in its implications for the nature of the actual place used for the fiction. Its 'elsewhere' is the United States in a broader, social/economic sense than this figures in *State*. Both films share a reference to a 'virtual elsewhere' in the media, although *Million$*'s reference to the tycoon and TV news goes way beyond the cynical melancholy of the Hollywood presented in *State*. Both films share Wenders' characteristic trait of constant reference to a 'there' as their style and technique point to an 'out of frame' surrounding the hotel setting. *Wings* is, as befits its concentration on the chronotope in its final setting, much more closed and conveys an 'elsewhere' though its dialogue rather than its imagery. By contrast, the hotel setting in *State* resists functioning as chronotope, in so far as it reinforces the film's self-reflexive theme about the impossibility of transferring the fictional narrative over into the 'reality' it suddenly takes on when it ceases to be a place to construct a series of filmic mises-en-scène. As any form of heterotopia, it is completely negative: the place where the stories stopped because they are no use to the dominant 'elsewhere.' *Wings*'s thoroughgoing chronotope works because it is fully embedded in the 'there' of Berlin, both in space and time. The Hotel Esplanade functions as a site for 'remembering forwards,' the complex narrative implications of which imply of the city as a sort of heterotopia where further narratives can demonstrate fundamental truths about nothing less than human existence itself. How far the subsequent fate of Wenders' hotel setting in this film bears out these implications remains to be seen. With *Million$*, the hotel setting for his narrative carries huge implications for the 'there' constantly constructed out of frame and for the narrative and thematic range of 'elsewhere' it implies. It is indeed ironic that the ethical implications of using the real setting of the hotel in this film lead Wenders back to the narrative implications of the abandoned 'guests' in *State*: when you have finished telling your story, can you simply check out of the hotel as if were a virtual space, a 'there', in contrast to your own existence in the actual 'here'?

The three hotels in these three films are all peripheral relics. In the first, it is the place where the story stops; in the second and third, they are places which offer to us as spectators a 'topography' to suggest that stories can go on, even beyond the film's own fiction. How Wenders uses them in his film-making indicates much about how his work has developed, ". . . engaged on a quest for time," and perhaps indicates something about the possibilities and the limitations of the locations created by this "painter of space."

ACKNOWLEDGEMENTS

I would like to thank the staff of the Bibliothek der Hochschule für Film und Fernsehen, Postdam and the Bibliothek der Stiftung Deutscher Kinemathek, Berlin, for their help in providing material for this study. I also thank Herr Wenders for responding to my questions and Dave Clarke for his advice.

NOTES

1. Wenders on his own development as a filmmaker.
2. Email to Stan Jones, 7 January, 2004.
3. See Roger F. Cook on the penultimate scene of *Der Himmel über Berlin*:

The evolving narrative reflects itself as cinematic love story at every step, without becoming self-parody, even when the climactic scene—from the lavishly decorated barroom, including a bucket of champagne on the bar [*sic*], to Marion's passionately red dress and matching lipstick—says to the spectator at every turn, 'This is a romantic scene in a movie.' Thus the film both draws attention to the way desire is generated in cinema and also induces the spectator to take the investment of desire seriously. (Cook and Gemünden, 1997, 177)

His essay, "Angels, Fiction, and History in Berlin," interprets the film convincingly but, despite its title, does not credit the function of this mise-en-scène sufficiently.

4. It sets "material spatial practices (experience)," "representations of space (perception)" and "spaces of representation (imagination)" against "accessibility and distanciation," "appropriation and use of space," "domination and control of space" and "production of space."

5. It sets eight forms of time: "enduring"; "deceptive"; "erratic"; "cyclical"; "retarded"; "alternating": "time in advance of itself (rushing forward)"; "explosive" each into four categories: "type; level; form; social formation."

6. In 2004, Herr Wenders commented, by contrast, positively on the existence in hotels: "Hotels offer a pronounced anonymity, of course. On the one hand, there is everything you need to live, and on the other you are released from all the responsibilities being at home brings with it. That is, naturally, an ideal state for creativity." See note 2.

7. From his 'Forms of time and of the chronotope in the novel' (quoted by Konstantarakos, 2000, 2).

8. See *Engerer Wettbewerb zur Errichtung eines Filmhauses. Protokolle der Preisgerichtssitzungen* [Selective Competition for the Construction of a Film House. Protocols of the Prize Jury] published by the Senator für Bau und Wohnungswesen, Berlin. Source: Staatsbibliothek Preussischer Kulturbesitz, Berlin.

9. See the website for the "Kaisersaal. Die Salons am Potsdamer Platz": www.kaisersaal-berlin.de

10. In *State*, the writer explains to the director why he got the job from an American producer, anyway (see Jones, 1996).

11. See, for example: Körte and Scholz (2000); DVD (Concorde Home Entertainment, Munich, 2001); and the website: http://www.milliondollarhotel.com/

12. See note 2.

13. See Kummer (2000): this report on the actual Frontier Hotel emphasizes the surveillance maintained by the hotel management over the crowded and often squalid conditions. Particularly ironic is Wenders' comment from his 'Audiokommentar' on how the poverty of the residents revealed itself in cinematic terms as they recognized Jimmy Smits from his TV roles but none knew Mel Gibson because they cannot afford to go to the movies (in LA!).

14. See note 2.

REFERENCES

Adair, Gilbert. "The State of Things" *Sight and Sound* 52 no. 2, (1983): 140.

Bauman, Zygmunt. *Postmodernity and its Discontents*. Cambridge: Polity, 1997.

Cayla, Denise. *Errance et Points de Repère chez Wim Wenders*. Bern/New York: Peter Lang, 1994.

Ciment, Michel and Niogret, Hubert. 'Entretien avec Wim Wenders' *Positif* 3 (September 1984): 8–15.

Combs, Richard "The Long Goodbye . . . Goodbye . . . Goodbye" *Sight and Sound* 52, no. 4 (1983): 9.

Cook, Roger F. and Gemünden, Gerd (eds.) *The Cinema of Wim Wenders*. Detroit: Wayne State University Press, 1997.

Foucault, Michel. 'Of Other Spaces' *Diacritics* 16 no. 1, (January 1986): 22–27.

Ganter, Matthias. *Wim Wenders und Jacques Derrida*. Marburg: Tectum Verlag, 2003.

Gardies, André. *L'Éspace au Cinéma*. Paris: Meridiens Klincksieck, 1993.

Graf, Alexander. *The Cinema of Wim Wenders: The Celluloid Highway*. London: Wallflower, 2002.

Grob, Norbert. *Wenders*. Berlin: Edition Film, 1991.

Gurevich, Georges *The Social Spectrum of Time*. Dordrecht: Reidel, 1964.

Harvey, David. *The Condition of Postmodernity: An Enquiry into the Origins of Cultural Change*. Oxford: Blackwell, 1989.

Hawker, Philippa. 'Wings of Desire' *Cinema Papers* 65 (September 1987), 22–23.

Ibrahim, A. F. *Analyse de l'oeuvre cinématografique de Wim Wenders* doctoral thesis, 1986, Université de Paris, Panthéon Sorbonne.

J.-M. F. 'Un rêve de mise-en-scène passé' *Le monde* (15 March 2000).

Jones, Stan. 'Wim Wender's *Paris, Texas* and the "European Way of Seeing"' pp. 45–52 in *European Identity in Cinema* edited by Everett Wendy. Exeter: Intellect, 1996.

Kilb, Andreas. 'Was reizt Sie bloß am Leben in Hotels, Herr Wenders?' (What is it about living in hotels that's so attractive to you, Mr. Wenders?) *Die Zeit* (10 February 2000): 27.

Kinder, Marsha. 'Ideological Parody in the New German Cinema. Reading the *State of Things*, *The Desire of Veronika Voss* and *Germany, Pale Mother* as Postmodernist Rewritings of *The Searchers*, *Sunset Boulevard* and *Blonde Venus*' *Journal of Film and Video* 12 (1990): 73–103.

Köhler, Michael. 'Mit dem Herzen sehen: Interview mit Wim Wenders zu THE MILLION DOLLAR HOTEL' *film-dienst* (September 2000): 44–46.

Kolker, Robert Phillip and Beicken, Peter. *The Films of Wim Wenders: Cinema as Vision and Desire*. Cambridge: Cambridge University Press, 1993

Konstantarakos, Myrto (ed.). *Spaces in European Cinema*. Intellect, Exeter, 2000.

Kopold, R. 'Alles anders, immer noch?' *Stuttgarter Zeitung*, 7 February 2000.

Körte, P. and Scholz, M. 'Berlin ist mir auf den Docht gegangen' ['Berlin got on my wires'] *Frankfurter Rundschau*, 7 February 2000.

Kummer T. 'Im Foyer der Melancholie' *Frankfurter Allgemeine* (9 February 2000).

Liesbrock, Heinz. 'Die Wahrheit des Sichtbaren. Edward Hopper und die Photographie' pp. 15–33 in *Die Wahrheit des Sichtbaren. Edward Hopper und die Photographie* edited by Költzsch Georg-W. and Liesbrock Heinz. Essen: Museum Folkwang, 1992.

Löser, Claus. 'Mit dem Herzen sehen' *film-dienst* 5 (2000).

Mühlenhaupt, F. and Knödler-Bunte, Eberhard (eds). *Mythos Berlin. Concepte. Katalog zur Werkausstellung* Berlin: Verlag Ästhetik und Kommunikation, 1986.

Piégay, Baptiste. 'Heartbreak Hotel' *Cahiers du Cinéma* 544 (March 2000).

Schnelle, Josef and Gansera, Rainer. 'Ein Kinderwelt in Los Angeles' *epd film* 2 (2000), 18–22.

Westphal, Anke and Jähner, Harald. 'Filmen ist Handwerk, keine Kunst' *Berliner Zeitung* (5 February 2000).

Wenders, Donata and Wenders, Wim. *The Heart is a Sleeping Beauty. The Million Dollar Hotel-Filmbuch*. Munich: Schirmer/Mosel, 2000.

Wenders, Wim. *Emotion Pictures*. Frankfurt am Main: Verlag der Autoren, 1986.

——. *Die Logik der Bilder*. Frankfurt am Main: Verlag der Autoren, 1988.

——. *The Act of Seeing*. Frankfurt am Main: Verlag der Autoren, 1992.

——. 'Der Sonnenfleck wandert' *Die Zeit* (29 March 1996).

——. *Bilder von der Oberfläche der Erde*. Munich: Schirmer/Mosel, 2001.

——. *Einmal*. Munich: Schirmer/Mosel, 2001.

Winkler-Bessone, Claude. *Les Films de Wim Wenders. La nouvelle naissance des images*. Bern/New York: Peter Lang, 1992.

Chapter Six

The Decay of Fiction and the Poetics of Pastness

Asbjørn Grønstad

This enormous, luxurious, baroque, lugubrious hotel . . .

X in L'année dernière à Marienbad[1]

Forgetting is a relation with that which is forgotten, a relation that, making secret that with which there is a relation, possesses the power and meaning of the secret.

—Maurice Blanchot (1997, 45)

3400 WILSHIRE BOULEVARD

SITE: *The Decay of Fiction* is an homage to the seductiveness of the forgettable. Although the film is hardly deprived of drama, it is the kaleidoscopic snippets of unspectacular life in a famous hotel that register the most. Honeymooners bicker, chambermaids gossip, sunbathers while away the hours by the pool, and dejected men make lackluster conversations with cocktail waitresses. Wistful, languorous, and surreal, the film's mood is immersed in the now patently oneiric paraphernalia of Tinseltown days gone by. Since it first opened in 1921 the Ambassador Hotel in Los Angeles has maintained an ineradicable relation to Hollywood history. Not only did it accommodate the glamoramania of the vintage movie elite, the hotel also subsequently served as a facility for hundreds of film productions. If ever a location has been "certified" by the movies, to use Walker Percy's phrase from his novel *The Moviegoer* (Percy 2002, 63), it is surely that of the Ambassador. The 500-room building hosted the first eight academy award ceremonies, and, more recently, the Ambassador's kitchen became the site of Robert Kennedy's assassination in 1968. In the 1970s the hotel fell into a state of decrepitude, and it eventually closed its doors to the public in 1989. After the Los Angeles Unified School District (LAUSD) acquired the property toward the end of 2001, opinion has been divided on the issue of whether the structure should be demolished or preserved as a city historical landmark. By tradition, history and Los Angeles have been implausible companions.

Experimental filmmaker Pat O'Neill's strangely ethereal ode to the 3400 Wilshire Boulevard site is a performative meditation on the subject of temporal corruption. As I shall argue in this essay, the film's form works to destabilize conventional relations of chronology, in the process engendering images of a durable past and a flimsy present. How may an ostensibly non-narrative film in fact be able to pose questions about the nature of temporality that cannot readily be answered by the recent spate of so-called 'memory films' such as *Memento* (Christopher Nolan 2000) or *The Eternal Sunshine of the Spotless Mind* (Michel Gondry 2004)? In *The Decay of Fiction*, the present seems to cave in as the spaces of the past progressively encroach upon it, an event which inevitably challenges the notion of linearity and ushers in a sense of perpetual pastness. Superimposing black and white images of actors over footage from the Ambassador, O'Neill fashions a self-reflexive exploration of the meta-history of the hotel, one that is neither fact nor fiction but something in-between. As both shooting location and the lair of the movie stars, the Ambassador can easily be construed as an intertextual morgue, or a spectral archive in the Derridean sense (Derrida, 1996)—a repository of fragments belonging to an ever more mythicized movie history. The film sets out deliberately to reconstruct that phantom decadence of which the dilapidated hotel itself is an iconographic epitome, and in doing so the director deploys a particular stylistic register. In *The Decay of Fiction*, much like in Stanley Kubrick's *The Shining* (1980) or Aleksandr Sokurov's *Russian Ark* (2002), the building itself is the chief protagonist. O'Neill's denarrativized, associative method, moreover, has repetition and serialization take precedence over chronology.[2] Overlain by a cacophony of voices from old motion pictures, these images suggest the unique architecture of a cinematic memory re-emerging even as it crumbles.

I JUST WANT TO TELL YOU SOMETHING[3]

TIME/IMAGE: In his college days at UCLA, Pat O'Neill would spend time in the library leafing through the pages of books and magazines which he selected arbitrarily. This aleatory behavior would one day yield up an article in a 1943 volume of *Life* magazine on a Salvador Dali exhibit. Glancing at the article he realized, all of a sudden, that he actually knew that particular issue of *Life*. At age four, as it turned out, he had been scrutinizing Dali's *Persistence of Memory* along with several other works by the illustrious surrealist (James 1997). The image thus provided both the occasion and the name for that ripple of temporality that was at the heart of O'Neill's experience. Dali's painting could also have provided an alternative name for *The Decay of Fiction*, a film whose logic seems to dictate a conflation of the spheres of memory and fiction. How does one account for this oblique and somewhat paradoxical title, one that more than anything else connotes some kind of theoretical, scholarly monograph? The inherent friction of fiction resides in its resistance to processes of putrefaction. Since the fictional already is a distortion of the 'real' it is in a certain sense incorruptible. Unlike people and events, narratives do not fade away. They might transmute, get modified, or fall intermittently into oblivion, but theirs is a peculiar longevity beyond the reach of the extra-fictional. In his most recent book W.J.T. Mitchell writes that "[t]he image cannot be destroyed," which is a feature they seem to share with narratives (Mitchell 2005, 84). Hence, the idea of a decaying fiction seems oddly preposterous. Or does it?

That the phrase *The Decay of Fiction* could have provided a felicitous title for a book of literary or film theory is no mere flippancy. Such a book does in fact exist. Its name is *The Death of Cinema: History, Cultural Memory and the Digital Dark Age*, authored by the curator Paolo Usai, who is also the director of the L. Jeffrey Selznick School of Film Preservation.[4] Perhaps incongruously, Usai seems to be both mourning and celebrating the ephemerality of film. Cinema, according to this preservationist, "arise[s] out of an intent to transform into an object whatever is forgettable and therefore doomed to decay and oblivion" (Usai 2001, 65). Usai's proclamation and his theorization of the moving image in *Death of Cinema* need to be appreciated as an endeavor to remind us of the fragile quality of film's materiality, the negligible number of films actually preserved, the cultural contingencies of such an impossible selection, and, finally, the oxymoronic patina that attaches to the very notion of successfully preserving something that is transient by nature. What is more, Usai thinks that our preoccupation with permanence is not only questionable but "deluded" and that the art of cinema is anchored in the destruction of its images (Usai 2001, 129; 7). Our delusions aside, what might also be said about permanence is that it is not only a state but an effect the cause of which is memory itself. The continuity of our experiences is enabled by a resistance to acts of forgetting. Usai's opinion that permanence is mostly undesirable, therefore, resonates to some extent with the emphasis on the necessity of forgetting in Marc Augé's *Oblivion*, where the author pinpoints the inseparability of memory and oblivion (Augé 2004). It is not only that something has to be blocked out in order for something else to be recapitulated (which, incidentally, is also one of the functions that Derrida attributes to the archive (Derrida 1996)) but also that oblivion facilitates the immersion in a fluid present. In O'Neill's film, as in Usai's study, the tenacious withering away of the image becomes oblivion's trope.

Having detoured around the melancholy ruins of Usai's curious concoction of elegy and theory speech we may be better equipped to confront the question put forward above. That is to say, the concept of decaying fictions now no longer appears that eccentric. It could very well be that O'Neill's movie is an unhinged, semi-narrative parable of the process by which filmic fictions evaporate due to an apparently imperceptible yet gradual corrosion of their material carrier. Both as a film and a title, then, the decay of fiction euphemistically invokes the specter of its own cause, the disintegration of film stock and the subsequent demise of cinema. *The Decay of Fiction* may thus be read as a form of imaging, as it were, of Usai's theory. In this respect the film is vaguely reminiscent of Bill Morrison's far more extreme essay on celluloid decomposition, *Decasia* (2002). A film made up of found archival footage in various stages of deterioration, *Decasia* relentlessly and hypnotically re-enacts the moment at which the image is about to become, or just has become, indecipherable. Among the debris one is able to delineate the ghostly figures of camels traversing a deformed desert, parachutes falling from a cracked sky, and a tarnished boxer striking the void. Inscribing into its very form and fabric the experience of fading vision, *Decasia* arguably also aestheticizes the process of decay.

What is particularly intriguing about *The Decay of Fiction* is that it stages the drama of decay as a temporal event which erases the boundary between the material and the allegorical, the indexical and the narrative. Insubstantial chronicles of material decay and social decadence morph into images that are themselves festering. O'Neill's sepulchral fantasia is a film in which images and fictions literally come apart. While allegorizing the narrative of its own decay, the film also undoes its allegorical provenance in the process. In this sense *The Decay of Fiction* negates—or at least resists—the Bazinian archivability of time that Mary Ann Doane problematizes in her 2002 monograph *The Emergence of Cinematic Time*. These time-images, unlike those of Gilles Deleuze (Deleuze 1989, 210), conjure not so much a direct experience of time as an explicit rendering of time's nasty work. As it does for Philippe Nahon's character in Gaspar Noé's *Irreversible* (2002), time in *The Decay of Fiction* seems to destroy everything, though not quite; what is beyond destruction is the recalcitrance of a memory engendered and sustained by an intertextual space. O'Neill's concern is the fragment, not any fragment, but the record of the forgettable.

YOU'LL NEVER GUESS WHO'S STAYING HERE

CITE: The aforementioned memory films by Nolan and Gondry propound a kind of recollection that is obsessively and neurotically teleological: what has to be retrieved or preserved is that which is decisive. And, no less importantly, the process of retrieval is itself decisive. For the Guy Pearce character in *Memento*, what has to be restored are the circumstances surrounding his wife's murder, whereas Jim Carrey's persona in *Eternal Sunshine of the Spotless Mind* is desperate to prevent the memory of his beloved from being erased. The act of remembering in these films is the act of remembering something pivotal. *The Decay of Fiction*, in part because it dispels the narrative conventions of even a film as narratively unconventional as *Memento*, eschews such a coalition of memory and psychic urgency. It flirts with oblivion instead, like Blanchot's narrator quoted in the epigraph. And the film prompts the viewer to consider the possibility that there are other memories besides the essential ones. There are, for instance, memories that are peripheral, or else inconsequential. But, insofar as the act of recollection entails an ethical readiness, even that which is ephemeral may warrant the gesture of memory. This may be the central insight of *The Decay of Fiction*'s contemplative images.

In the first of these images, we are inside an empty room, a room that has already fallen apart, tattered curtains fluttering in the breeze, the overwhelming sense of abandonment made even more palpable by a radiator in the corner. The room darkens, the screen goes black, and the text 'The Hotel Ambassador, Los Angeles' appears. This beige room, its state of disrepair made almost tactile by the juxtaposition of the quivering curtains and the general sense of temporal paralysis, denotes a space that continuously awaits oblivion. Prominently positioned as a kind of prologue to the film, the image distils a theoretically pregnant moment. What it fastens on is this: when fiction decays, what is left is neither reality nor the non-fictional, but philosophy, or thought. The implied movement in the film's title felicitously captures this textual slide, the inadvertent template for which may be a work already alluded to by the influential and often opaque French novelist and critic Maurice Blanchot. When as a viewer I find myself in *The Decay of Fiction*'s naked room, nondescript yet exposed, I am at the same time in that sparsely furnished hotel room that constitutes the ascetic setting for *Awaiting Oblivion*, Blanchot's perhaps most acute refraction of an aesthetics of the fragmentary. In this book, which could be described as a kind of aphoristic novel, Blanchot strives to transcend the opposition between creative and critical writing. The minimal narrative context there is takes the form of an encounter between a man and a woman, who spend an indeterminate stretch of time together waiting for something to transpire while unsuccessfully attempting to remember something that has possibly already happened to them. Like this text, *The Decay of Fiction* charts the terrain between narration and fragmentation; it draws on the fragment's capacity for condensation and metonymy. In Blanchot's own words this mobilization of the fragment leads to a rhapsodic mode of textuality, one in which the distinction between the theoretical and the creative blurs. For Blanchot, rhapsody involves

> that perpetual repetition from episode to episode, an interminable amplification of the same unfolding in place, which makes each rhapsode neither a faithful reproducer nor an immobile rehearser but the one who carries the repetition forward and, by means of repetition, fills in or widens the gaps, opens and closes the fissures by new peripeteia. (Blanchot 1993, 390)

In its play upon repetition and difference, this description of the rhapsody recalls the serialist pattern which undergirds *The Decay of Fiction*. Likewise stuck between narration and abstract form, fiction and theory, the film subscribes to that same Blanchotian desire to overcome discursive categories and to generate theory from aesthetics.

Visualizing that state of awaiting oblivion, which is also a cultural process, epitomizes one of the theoretical intuitions to which O'Neill's film gives rise. But there is more at stake. *The Decay of Fiction* reaches out for the transitory, which it tries to delineate, and this is its most compelling though frustrated gesture. If the filmic mummifies change, as André Bazin famously stated (Bazin 1967, 15), how can the medium at the same time record impermanence? Once committed to film, the transient is no longer impermanent. How then to spatialize it? As one may have come to suspect, this is a contradiction which the film attempts to resolve through its conceptual investment in the fragment. Its manifestations are all over the place in this film, from the mosaic of allusions to Hollywood history to the de-narrativized slices of life lived in the hotel.[5] As citations to the Ambassador's past, these fragments foreground the traces of the transitory even as the idea itself ultimately eludes them.

DON'T YOU LAWYERS HAVE TO BE SOMEWHERE?
USUALLY. TODAY IT'S HERE

SPACE: After the introductory shot of the empty room and the black screen, what ensues is a long shot of the hotel seen from outside. The lawn is green and the sky is blue, the sun reflecting in the windows. Then a woman unexpectedly materializes from somewhere to the left of the screen and walks toward the hotel, her shimmering, silvery outline an esoteric contrast to the charged tactility of the derelict room.[6] In the condensed space of the fragment, two temporalities merge; that of the ephemeral present, always already awaiting oblivion, and that of the enduring past, an apparition on the way to the lobby. The hotel room itself is of course a pre-eminent example of an evanescent space that, unlike one's bedroom, is to be inhabited only temporarily. As if to underscore the troping of the hotel room as a home to the transitory, O'Neill's camera moves restlessly in and out of the rooms while a murmur of indistinct voices is heard on the soundtrack. *Really, that seems incredible . . . We've already met, long ago . . . I don't remember very well. It must have been in '28 or '29.*[7] Alain Resnais' austere cadences suggest an evocative subtext for *The Decay of Fiction*, but O'Neill's sensibility is more modern than modernist, his aesthetic diction closer to the quintessentially American noir tradition than to the insular gravity of the French director's memory-soaked films. At times it may even appear as if O'Neill has somehow transplanted the vaporous spirit of the rural cosmology of Greil Marcus's 'old, weird America' to the notoriously ahistorical metropolis of 20th century L.A.[8]

Whichever room O'Neill's camera lets us peek into, sooner or later we end up back in the city. I mean this in the sense that the film invites a reading that plausibly posits the Ambassador as a metonym for L.A., according to some critics itself a city haunted by specters (Ethington 2001, 29).[9] Sometimes, especially in the beginning, the camera interrupts its ceaseless probing of the hotel's interior to cut away to shots of the nocturnal traffic outside on Wilshire. The film thus connects the physical space of the freeways with the less earthly, more metonymically fertile space of the Ambassador, thereby suggesting the latent isomorphism of two different yet interrelated infrastructures. No less than L.A.'s complex network of freeways and superhighways—exquisitely explored in Michael Mann's *Collateral* (2004)—the infrastructure of the hotel conveys an architecture of the transitory. A microcosm of the city, the hotel's spaces are also draped in a film noir iconography of fedora-clad detectives, giddy femmes fatales, and after-hours lighting. In its oscillation between the motifs of decadent leisure and noir murkiness, the film can be seen to embody aspects of both of the main artistic constructions of Los Angeles from the mid-60s and onward: that of the city as a "commodified Arcadia" and as a "pathological" metropolis (Carringer 2001, 246). Generically rarefied as it may be, *The Decay of Fiction*—in its emphasis on the architectonics of the transitory—persuasively consolidates the mounting engagement on the part of cinema studies with what has been referred to as the 'spatial turn.'

I'M SORRY BUT HE'S JUST NOT RIGHT FOR THE PART

SIGHT: Attendant upon this turn to geography, architecture, and urban studies[10]—unsurprisingly—is a reconfiguration of the terms within which questions of visibility may be framed. As a filmmaker working in the tradition of American avant-garde cinema, O'Neill has a distinctive affinity for the ramifications of that 'perceptual ambiguity' which characterizes that scene (James 1997). As William Wees has argued, avant-garde filmmaking gravitates by nature toward self-reflexive ruminations on the problem of vision and the difficulties of seeing (Wees 1992, 3). If there is an enactment of this concern in *The Decay of Fiction* it may be evidenced in the film's consistent embracing of the perspective of the eavesdropping flâneur as the hermeneutic center of the text.[11] Straying through what is conceivably the Ambassador's unconscious, this flâneur takes in the sights of a myriad of fractured perceptions, residues from a thousand movie performances.[12] This is how the film reconnects with the history of Hollywood history; by reassembling fragments of memory, by resisting linearity and closure, and by disrupting the "smooth continuities and psychic repressions of industrial cinema" (MacDonald 2002, 205). Such an approach to the past, to temporality, is a defining feature of the avant-garde, which, as Christof Decker points out, has tended to indulge "the psychoanalytic notion of re/inscribing a past that is in a state of constant change and subjected to interpretations, as in the figure of the palimpsest" (Decker 1998, 119). The property of 'deferred interpretation' [*Nachträglichkeit*] that Freud attributes to memory refers to the way in which memory is always narrated retrospectively (typically, for Freud, in narcissistic confirmation of the self-identity of the ego). The perpetual reworking of memories is, for Freud, their most consistent feature. The process of inscription, rhapsodic and repetitious, disseminates this sense of pastness that envelops *The Decay of Fiction*. You can check out any time you like, but you can never leave.

NOTES

1. Dir. Alain Resnais, Argos Films, 1961.
2. For a discussion of serialist film aesthetics, see Burch (1973).
3. This and subsequent captions are the flotsam and jetsam of overheard dialogue from O'Neill's film.
4. In the introduction, Usai divulges some of the preliminary titles for his book, one of which was *Decay Cinema*, another *The Last Spectator*. I particularly cherish the latter one, with its faint implications of the (allegorical) decay of the act of looking itself.
5. The Ambassador has been home to more than a thousand film projects, including *Pretty Woman* (Garry Marshall 1990), *Forrest Gump* (Robert Zemeckis 1994), *Fear and Loathing in Las Vegas* (Terry Gilliam 1998), and *Man on the Moon* (Milos Forman 1999). Among the hotel's long-term residents were Gloria Swanson, Jean

Harlow, Howard Hughes, and John Barrymore. And it was in the Coconut Grove nightclub that the likes of Joan Crawford, Carole Lombard, and Loretta Young reputedly were discovered.

6. An accomplished special-effects expert whose resumé includes *Return of the Jedi*, O'Neill made *The Decay of Fiction* using a combination of 35mm location shooting, digital overlay, and time-lapse photography. The eerie effect that suffuses the film stems in part from the director's decision to superimpose images of actors shot in black and white on a soundstage over footage from the Ambassador.

7. These are lines spoken in *Last Year in Marienbad* (Alain Resnais 1961).

8. See Marcus (1997).

9. For a filmic meta-dramatization of the city's shifting functions as background, character, and subject in film, see Thom Andersen's (2003) documentary *Los Angeles Plays Itself*. For a comprehensive treatment of the relationship between cinema and urban space in general, see Clarke (1997). See also Dimendberg's (2004) analysis of the relation between cinema and urbanism.

10. See for instance Penz and Thomas (1997); Rohdie (2001); Pallasmaa (2001); Bruno (2002); Barber (2002).

11. Why the flâneur, or eavesdropper, rather than the voyeur? As one struggles to make sense of the bewildering collage of images, in short, as one tries to come to terms with the discourse of the fragment, one tends to focus more on what is overheard in passing for anything resembling narrative information. An act of voyeurism seems to require a measure of persistence and duration that one never attains in *The Decay of Fiction*.

12. Roughly every fifteen minutes or so the film veers into surrealism, and what appears is a patchwork of disconcerting sights of flabby, naked men with oversized *papier mâché* heads and women in white who flap about ferociously. These sequences, along with one in which a young woman in a blue dress walks hurriedly down a maze-like basement corridor, seem to literalize the hotel's unconscious.

REFERENCES

Augé, Marc. *Oblivion* (trans. M. De Jager). Minneapolis, Minnesota, 2004.

Barber, Stephen. *Projected Cities*. London: Reaktion, 2002.

Bazin, André. 'The Ontology of the Photographic Image' in *What is Cinema? Volume 1* (trans. Hugh Gray). Berkeley: University of California Press, 1967.

Blanchot, Maurice. *Awaiting Oblivion* (trans. John Gregg). Lincoln: University of Nebraska Press, 1997.

———. *The Infinite Conversation* (trans. Susan Hanson). Minneapolis: University of Minnesota Press, 1993.

Bruno, Giuliana. *Atlas of Emotion: Journeys in Art, Architecture, and Film*. London: Verso, 2002.

Burch, Noël. (1973) *Theory of Film Practice* (trans. Helen R. Lane). Princeton: Princeton University Press.

Carringer, Robert. 'Hollywood's Los Angeles: Two Paradigms,' pp. 247–266 in *Looking For Los Angeles: Architecture, Film, Photography, and the Urban Landscape* edited by Charles G. Salas and Michael S. Roth. Los Angeles: Getty Publications, 2001.

Clarke, David B. (ed.). *The Cinematic City*. London: Routledge, 1997.

Decker, Christof. 'Interrogations of Cinematic Norms: Avant-garde Film, History, and Mnemonic Practices' *Amerikastudien* 43 no 1. (Spring 1998), 109–130.

Deleuze, Gilles. *Cinema 2: The Time-Image* (trans. Hugh Tomlinson and Robert Galeta). London: Athlone, 1989.

Derrida, Jacques. *Archive Fever: A Freudian Impression*. Chicago: University of Chicago Press, 1996.

Dimendberg, Edward. *Film Noir and the Spaces of Modernity*. Cambridge, MA: Harvard University Press, 2004.

Doane, Mary Ann. The *Emergence of Cinematic Time: Modernity, Contingency, the Archive*. Cambridge, MA: Harvard University Press, 2002.

Ethington, Philip J. 'Ghost Neighborhoods: Space, Time, and Alienation in Los Angeles,' pp. 29–56 in *Looking For Los Angeles: Architecture, Film, Photography, and the Urban Landscape* edited by Charles G. Salas and Michael S. Roth. Los Angeles: Getty Publications, 2001.

James, David E. 'An Interview with Pat O'Neill' *Millennium Film Journal* 30–31 (Fall 1997), http://mfj-online.org/journalPages/MFJ30%2C31/DJamesInterview.html

MacDonald, Scott. 'Professional Myopia: How American Academe is Failing Cinema' *Quarterly Review of Film and Video* 19 no. 3 (July–Sept. 2002): 201–207.

Marcus, Greil. *Invisible Republic: Bob Dylan's Basement Tapes*. New York: Henry Holt, 1997.

Mitchell, W. J. T. *What Do Pictures Want? The Lives and Loves of Images*. Chicago: University of Chicago Press, 2005.

Pallasmaa, Juhani. *The Architecture of Image: Existential Space in Cinema*. Helsinki: Rakennustieto, 2001.

Penz, François and Thomas, Maureen (eds). *Cinema and Architecture: Méliès, Mallet-Stevens, Multimedia*. London: BFI, 1997.

Percy, Walker. *The Moviegoer*. London: Methuen, 2002 [1960].

Rohdie, Sam. *Promised Lands: Cinema, Geography, Modernism*. London: BFI, 2001.

Scheib, Richard (2003). '*The Decay of Fiction*' The SF, Horror and Fantasy Film Review, http://www.moria.co.nz/fantasy/decayoffiction.htm

Shiel, Mark and Fitzmaurice, Tony (eds.). *Screening the City*. London: Verso, 2003.

Strathausen, Carsten. 'Uncanny Spaces: the City in Ruttmann and Vertov' pp. 15–40 in *Screening the City* edited by Mark Shiel and Tony Fitzmaurice. London: Verso, 2003.

Usai, Paolo Cherchi. *The Death of Cinema: History, Cultural Memory and the Digital Dark Age*. London: BFI, 2001.

Wees, William C. *Light Moving in Time: Studies in the Visual Aesthetics of Avant-Garde Film*. Berkeley: University of California Press, 1992.

Chapter Seven

'Now, where was I?'— Memories, Motels, and Male Hysteria

Stuart C. Aitken

A pause, a moment to recollect, a gathering of wits, a breath before a push forward. Or is it a pull backwards? The push/pull—ten minutes before the forgetting—is a calculating logic, the formulation of writhe coherency that is brutally connected to a single-minded purpose. Leonard Shelby closes his eyes and pushes to remember his murdered wife and his purpose in life: to find and punish Johnny G. The last thing he remembers is his wife's death. The year since, for Lenny, is composed of 10 minute intervals none of which he remembers. I am inside that calculating part of Lenny's mind, working with him to make the connections. We don't have that much time. Everything will fade in a few minutes. Bit by bit, facts are revealed through Lenny's notes and Polaroid pictures. Facts are faster than memory. And his body doesn't lie; the facts are there too, in tattooed text. This is good because we only have ten minutes to figure out what they mean. No hysteria here. An anonymous motel room. Cool. Calculating. Pragmatic. And then into action.

The façade presented to me by director Christopher Nolan's *Memento* (2000) is that Lenny has a memory condition; and the condition makes me sympathetic to his purpose. I want Lenny to succeed and, as the film proceeds, I sense at least part of his frustrations. He is framed as the classic victim, susceptible to everything from bar-room jokes, getting charges for two rooms in the same motel, to being conned into killing people. And he is not a killer. That is why he is so good at it. He always forgets. But I don't know that yet.

Lenny wakes and looks around. He is sitting up in bed scanning bland walls as light leaks in through half-drawn curtains. He is filmed from above (as if from a security camera) in stark-contrast black and white. This early scene of *Memento* is meant to give a sense of documentary, cinéma-vérité surveillance. Lenny's voice-over provides a further distance; a seemingly objective, second-person perspective: "So, where are you? You are in some

219

motel room. You are just waking up and you are in a motel room. There is the key. It feels like maybe it is just the first time you've been there and yet perhaps you've been there a week . . . three months. It is kind of hard to say. I don't know. It is just an anonymous room."

Lenny's first moments of consciousness are always frenetic as he tries to remember, as he searches what he knows to associate with his surroundings, to connect with his immediate context. He always connects and associates with the image of his murdered wife. It is the last thing he remembers. He is less able to associate with what has happened in the year since. Kirby (1996, 102) suggests famously that disassociation refers "not only to . . . detachment . . . from the world, but also to the deterioration of the internal ordering of subjectivity. . . . The internal-external relation breaks down, resulting in a degeneration of interior organization, and finally . . . in a confusion of external order too." More than detachment from the world, disassociation spirals those susceptible to its promises into schizophrenic geographies of chaos and confusion. What I want to show with this essay is that this is precisely what does not happen in the structure of *Memento*, and I end with the suggestion that the interior and exterior merge in this movie (structurally and existentially) in a delightfully unconfused way. Nonetheless, disassociation is an intriguing starting point for considering male hysteria in *Memento*, especially when it is countered with Silverman's (1992) admonition that patriarchy must be understood in terms of the adequacy of a male subject who is in place and taking responsibility. In *Memento*, I think, Lenny is ultimately and precisely in place and he is taking responsibility for his own, quite fearsome, adequacy.

I have argued elsewhere that male hysteria is a disassociation from hegemonic masculinity, and its allegory, the road movie, is a spatial performance of a redoubtably male disenfranchised spirit (Aitken and Lukinbeal 1997, 354). Of course, hysteria is the original female condition of Western society. As a disorder, it has its origins in early Egyptian and Greek medicine, where male practitioners attributed it to a disturbance of the uterus and its functions. This definition held sway through Freudian interpretations, but as Showalter (1993, 335) points out, "hysteria is no longer a question of the wandering womb; it is a question of the wandering story." And *Memento* is a story that wanders through plots, subplots and parallel narratives. The counter to this wandering is, as Clarke (2008) notes in his exploration of *Memento*, the narcissistic subject's attempt to maintain an imaginary sense of completion. The devising of coherent memory offsets to a degree the onslaught of hysteria. In his discussion of Wenders' classic road movie, *Paris, Texas* (1984), Corrigan (1991) argues that hysteria points to a crisis in male subjectivity. Chris Lukinbeal and I take this further to suggest that the road movie genre combines the hysterical and the disassociated in what might be thought of as disturbance of the phallus and its functions. I don't want to make much of that psychoanalytic point here—Clarke (2008) does an excellent job of connecting Freud's understanding of memory to *Memento*—except to use it as a conduit to speak about Lenny's condition and, particularly, how it is constructed in *Memento*. Indeed, Connolly (2002) argues that the dominance of psychoanalytic interpretative strategies in film studies has occluded questions about technique, which is what I really want to focus on with this essay. Connolly argues for an understanding of film in which interpretation remains and is coupled with a focus on techniques that foreground the affective aspects of filmmaking.[1]

Lenny's memory condition requires focus and association that is cognitive. Cognition is the action of a faculty of knowing. Behind the cognition, notes Clarke (2008), memory is deployed as defensive armory for the narcissistic ego. For Lenny, this defense is calculating and precise, it is about habit, conditioning and contexts. Anonymous motel rooms play a huge part in these contexts. In this essay, I want to look at *Memento*'s contexts and repetitions, and get at hysteria by 'shocking my thought' through the male self as it is expressed in Leonard Shelby. I use Massumi's (2002a) term 'shock my thought' to get at affect in *Memento*, and I use his contortions of the idea of 'expressionism' to elaborate to some degree the spaces of motels as an aesthetic for psychotic surrender, a respite before hysteria that never comes. I have a sense, at least at the moment, that expressions come together in the spaces of *Memento*, and motels are a fulcrum for those spaces. Rather than effacing the individual, I think, shockingly, that motel spaces contrive the psychosis of Lenny, etch his memory with purpose and give pause from hysteria. I try to get to memory in *Memento* through affect and Nolan's cinematic techniques. If motels are an important aspect of Lenny's context, his memory is produced through repetition, echoes and cycles.

In what comes next, I look more closely at how Nolan creates a memorable structure through *Memento*'s quirky sequencing. In the section following, I look more closely at the motel spaces of *Memento* to suggest a way that they contrive Lenny and me. The point by the end of both sections that I presage now is that motel rooms are memorable structures that offset hysteria. They are, quite precisely, stopping places that express the disturbed mind. The last section of the essay raises the specter of dubious narration and its relations to shock.

REPETITION, ECHOES AND CYCLES

For the half-thoughts that are synaesthetic images are memories of situated responses past, pressing to come again. They are has-beens to be. Future-pasts.

Minus the present, which has been submerged in mistimed tendencies. The present is only half-formed, not yet emerged from the variability, deformability, of the virtual (Massumi 1996, 399). Time slips sideways, space dissolves virtually, connections appear and are reified by facts: narrative pressures make concrete Lenny's notes, his Polaroid pictures, and the revelations on his body. Lenny needs his narrative to be driven by facts. Facts—indelibly etched all over his body—are more reliable than memory. As he tells Teddy (a crooked cop who befriends him, who may have set him up as a murderer and who Lenny kills in the first scene of the movie): "Memory's not perfect. It's not even that good. Ask the police; eyewitness testimony is unreliable. . . . Memory can change the shape of a room or the color of a car. It's an interpretation, not a record. Memories can be changed or distorted, and they're irrelevant if you have the facts." Facts rather than memory provide coherency, a seemingly pre-given structure. Mementos are facts: reminders, warnings, hints as to conduct or with regard to future events (*The Compact Edition of the Oxford Dictionary*, 1971). The movie, *Memento*, is in large part about imagined coherency, pre-given structures and the nature of their pre-givenness. For Lenny, memories are particularly problematic. He cannot make new ones: severe anterograde memory dysfunction, chronic and incurable. And yet he does not degenerate into hysteria because he has discipline and organization with which to structure the facts of his Polaroid pictures and his notes. This discipline and organization happens in motel rooms.

What *Memento* expresses is organic in the sense that I cannot apprehend it from within and I only vaguely hold on to it from without. This is intentional. Lenny's inability to convert short-term experience into long term memory is in part reflected in *Memento*'s quirky sequencing. Nolan wants me to feel what Lenny is feeling as I watch the film. How does it feel not to remember? How does it feel to experience emotions and not know why? How is that conveyed cinematically?

I do not think that *Memento* is the contorted, unhinged postmodern movie that a number of critics suggest (cf. Klein 2001). It is certainly about disturbing truth to a degree, but it is not a willfully disconnected narrative that unmoors truth from any kind of designation. *Memento*'s designation, I argue, is quite obviously patriarchal, focusing on romantic notions of Arthurial quests, the lonely hero (what can be lonelier than forgetting everyone you meet?), vengeance and dispatching the bad guys. Lacking a sequential referent or a preconceived meta-narrative, conditions of truth in postmodernism, at least in a Baudrillardian sense, languish indistinguishably from whimsy and the absurd. The re-ordering of sequence and time in *Memento* is not about quirky turnings that cleverly unhinge narrative and truth. Rather, it is very much about sequential references.

All the previews of the movie let me know that the story is told in reverse order, so there are no surprises there. Once I get the sequencing, and Nolan works hard with the movie's beginning to make sure that I get it, the narrative unfolds in a fairly ordered, albeit reversed, sequence of five minute segments. I see the last frame of the story first. Lenny kills Teddy in the first scene, and the film then moves backwards, in roughly five minute segments, from that point. Through the reverse narrative, I see how Lenny tracks Johnny G, how he kills the wrong guy, and how he meets that guy's girlfriend Natalie (a classic film-noir femme fatale). The film ends with what is, chronologically, the story's beginning, with Lenny driving along an anonymous small-town street: anywhere USA (and yet slightly peculiar). My certainty about Lenny's condition and his quest is revealed with the sequencing and then is held in question by a couple of one-second frames towards the end of the movie, but let me leave those points hanging for the moment. The point I want to make here is that *Memento* is not about occluding certainty, it is about articulating it through the self of Leonard Shelby. And this is a potently patriarchal, positivist certainty.

The seemingly reversed sequencing is, according to Nolan, to portray what it is like to live with Lenny's condition. It is about affect. So, how does Nolan drag me into Lenny's condition? How do I feel what he feels? Indeed, it is misleading to say that *Memento*'s plot runs in reverse. To bring us into Lenny's condition, Nolan does something much more complicated and clever. Rather than run in reverse, the story devolves as if being unrolled, slipping and sliding, down a precarious slope. And there is an order to this devolution. Certainly, I am surprised by seemingly new characters, as is Lenny. Time goes backwards and I meet characters as they leave the narrative, with no information on who they are. This, to a degree, mirrors Lenny's memory condition. Nor is *Memento*'s narrative structure wholly a plot in reverse. Rather, Nolan uses color and music to structure my narrative experience and pull it forward. The color and music turns out to be quite important for what I want to say. The opening scene—Lenny killing Teddy—literally runs backwards (and it is the only scene that does so), and it is in color. This beginning is immediately followed by the black-and-white, surveillance-camera, motel scene with documentary style, film noirish voice-over. This is followed by a color scene showing Lenny meeting Teddy at the motel vestibule and traveling to an abandoned building, whereupon Lenny shoots Teddy (again, but more graphically). The movie then proceeds with alternating black-and-white and color sequences. Nolan uses these alternate sequences to juxtapose cool, calculating forward-looking positivist empiricism (black and white) with unstructured, normative feelings and emotions (color). Nolan's sequencing, then, is all about affect.

Deleuzian affection-images in *Memento*'s color sequences not only highlight Lenny's visceral reactions to what is happening to him and his attempts
to exercise/exorcise the only memories he retains, they also say something
important about space and differentiated masculinities (see Aitken 2006).
Deleuze (1986, ix) suggests that movies often present "pre-verbal intelligible
content" that is not about story-lines, linguistically based semiotics, a universal language of film, or some existential or Lacanian lack in the viewer.
Rather, a *perception-image* moves me from total objective and indistinguishable knowledge at the periphery of my universe to a central subjective perception, an *action-image* grounds my perception of things here at the center
of my universe and then helps me grasp the 'virtual action' that they have
on me, and simultaneously the 'possible action' that I have on them. Finally,
something in-between perception and action, the *affection-image* "surges in
the center of indetermination" between the perceptive and the active, occupying it "without filling it in or filling it up" (Deleuze 1986, 65). Affection re-
establishes the relation between "received movement," as perception moves
me from the total objective to the subjective, and "executed movement" when
I grasp the possibility of action. Affect, then, alludes to the motion part of
emotion that sloshes back and forth between perception and action. In a rather
crude way, this is what happens as I move between the color and black and
white sequences in *Memento*. This movement of expression carries *Memento*
between different levels of articulation between the embodied and visceral,
and the abstracted and calculated.

The corpus of Deleuze and Guattari's work (1983, 1987) suggests a non-
representational and non-discursive way of knowing that relates affect to
ways that ordered spaces are disrupted in quirky and relational ways. The
objective positivism of the black-and-white segments is (under)scored by
music that is cold, abrupt and subversive. In color, Lenny is cast adrift, disrupted, sometimes awash in emotion, and the music is ambient, suggestive,
incoherent, wavy. In *Anatomy of a Scene* (2002), Nolan says that for the
color sequences he "wanted the music to suggest sadness and melancholy
without explaining it." *Memento*'s production designer, Patti Podesta, pur-
posefully produced a color palette of pastel blues, greys and browns to give
the film's color segments an 'anywhere and nowhere' feel to them. If the
black and white camera hovers over Lenny as if in surveillance; in the color
sequences the camera is always over Lenny's shoulder as he goes from point
A to point B. It is about movement, but not necessarily movement forward.
It is purposeful and intentional, but forgetful also because there is no forward
motion. This works at two levels. Lenny is limited in his capacity to appreciate a world in its fullness, and so the look of the film brings the viewer into
Lenny's point of view.

Summarizing a number of writers who are influenced by Deleuze's work, Harker (2005) points out that affect is about intense expression that exceeds representation and, by extension, the affection-image is a part of cinema that is felt and understood bodily rather than represented in a mechanistic or calculated way. But what happens when embodiment is scripted in a mechanistic way, as suggested by the sequenced revelations of the tattoos on Lenny's body? Perhaps Lenny's tattoos link the workings of language to a Deleuzian problematic of power. They are embodied indelibly and this gives them power, and they are repeated through the sequencing of the film. But with each repetition, their meaning changes.

We discover with Lenny the extent of his tattoos, which begin on his left arm with his own hand writing: 'Remember Sammy Jankis.' Directly below, covered by his sleeve, is the professional tattoo 'THE FACTS:' in gothic script. With shirt removed, Lenny's body reveals a plethora of hand written and professionally rendered facts. These writings are the contexts of his life that we get to glimpse and ponder, they are the important details left by himself and others we can only imagine. Prior unknown contexts written elaborately, written finely, written with care, written in haste. They suggest unknown connections, indelibly etched and coded conspicuously. This links the workings of language to power in a very Deleuzian way, insisting on the intrinsic connection between language and extra-linguistic forces. For Deleuze and Guattari (1987), representational models communicate because they mold and model, leaving us with expression as a faithful reflection of things as they are, a positivist mirror. Molding by language—the texts on Lenny's body—is different from the mirrored molding of the backwards text that reifies Lenny's purpose: "We all need mirrors to remind ourselves who we are." The mirror is a turning point for Lenny. The most important tattoo on his body is the one he writes backwards on his body. The tattoo reads 'John G. raped and murdered my wife.' For Lenny, there is no reality without this mirrored representation, and it urges his action, the primary action that drives the movie. Lenny's performative relation to this expression is different from the other texts, it is factual and representational, and it is also an emotive call to action. The tattoos on Lenny's body and the Polaroid images in his pocket, annotated importantly by his own writing (something he can trust), are facts that reflect the state of things, and are calls to immediate action. They are his empirical evidence. The power of the word made flesh, and the skin is faster than memory (Massumi 2002b, 495).

On the wall of his motel room, Lenny constructs his mind map, connecting the writing on his body with the images from his Polaroids, but the focus of the map is always just out of reach. Lenny is the Polaroid pictures in his pocket. He embodies the facts. He trusts only his experience. He makes conclusions that conspire to action. This is positivism. This enhances objective empiricism. A map for life hanging on a motel room wall. We see the map twice, once in a color segment and once in black and white. The repetition is important. Seeing the initial murder twice at the beginning is also important. The same seeing encounter re-adjusts and delimits the viewing. This is Lenny's world. More repetitions, half-remembered. An important clue. And then the forgetting.

This is the power of Nolan's structure. This is the power of Lenny's world. No matter how many times I see the movie, no matter which chapter I start at on the DVD, I cannot quite remember where I am. This Deleuzian recycling, repeating and forgetting is part of the devolutionary organism that is *Memento*. Nolan describes this affect in his commentary track on the DVD:

> The film is full of direct repetitions, but it is also full of echoes and cycles, and that is where the film starts to get very confused in the mind of the audience and in my mind as I watch it, and it is a deliberate confusion. It is a deliberate spinning of narrative . . . the idea was that it would live on in the mind a bit, the relationships between the different scenes, the black and white and color and so forth . . . It would become hard in the mind to distinguish between what you'd seen when . . . that the film would live on in the mind and so grow in the mind. I can come into the film, even although I've seen it a thousand times, and not know where I am . . . It is that organic in that sense, it is that messy even although it is tightly structured.

Out of the tightly structured segments that make up and devolve down Lenny's story, there is one recycling, returning that is quintessentially and traditionally spatial and without which the movie, this chapter and this book does not work. A continual return, the motel provides a space of being, a space of connection, a space of learning, a space of forgetting, a space to stop, and a space of duplicity.

SPACES OF EXPRESSION

The conventional wisdom on expressionism is that it is an aesthetic of unbridled and uncritical subjectivism. Expression suggests the image of a self-governing, reflective individual whose inner life is conveyed at will to effect an aesthetic that is communicable. Drawing on Deleuze and Guattari (1983, 1987), who argue that the notion of communication is severely tested by post-structural and post-postmodern thought, Massumi (2002a, xiii–xiv) notes that expression goes beyond the representations embedded in communication. Expression is not self-referential to some understood language, it does not simply represent or describe. The work of Deleuze and Guattari suggests that the subject is spoken by extra-linguistic forces of expression; like the tattoos on Lenny's body, which are in places scrawled in his own handwriting and in others professionally stenciled, there is something else going on and it is of consequence. Alternatively, communicative expression is problematically formative of, and anchored to, its own content: "the assumed solidity of the content transfers across the mirror-like correspondence or molded conformity, into a trustworthiness of the subjective expression. Molded, mirroring, expression faithfully conveys content: re-presents it at a subjective distance . . . the subjective distancing upon which communication is predicated enables deception no less than exchange" (Massumi 2002a, xv). Ultimately, whether John G. raped and killed Lenny's wife is of no consequence to the movie. What is of consequence is the deception that is Lenny's performative relation to his mirrored text.

There is nothing 'hidden' to uncover that has any consequence to my engagement with the movie. Rather, I am encouraged to pay attention to the ways in which film expresses relations between, within and beyond bodies. What is important is that the "force of expression . . . strikes the body first, directly and unmediatedly. . . . The body, fresh in the throes of expression, incarnates not an already-formed system but a modification—a change" (Massumi 2002a, xvii). This idea of expression as an event compels me in the powerful scene where Natalie removes Lenny's shirt to reveal to him (in the mirror) the full force of the power of his language, his words, his facts. And with each devolved segment of the movie I get the sense that this is not, in Massumi's (2002a, xviii) words, a "grid-locked positional system." Lenny, Teddy and Natalie all play parts in affecting change in the forces that compose the wandering story that is *Memento*.

Anonymous places, especially motels, collude with color and sound to contrive the stable story that is *Memento*. These are ordered spaces. The black-and-white, starker-contrast, segments provide a sequenced objective point of view. As the plot goes backwards, memory gaps are filled in and I get to piece together the duplicity of the puzzle in reverse, which is better than Lenny can do with his tattoos and Polaroid pictures. In black and white segments, and always in motel rooms, Lenny is an empiricist and a positivist. The motel in *Memento* is a fulcrum around which Lenny's experiences coagulate. He wakes up in different rooms to construct new sets of memories. To these ten minutes of memories he drags his facts, and his props. The facts propel him into action. Lenny is a pragmatist. He uses habit and routine to organize the facts of his memory-less experiences. Lenny brings out (as Nolan describes when I switch on the director's commentary on the DVD) "his props, his charts, his map for living." Lenny's map is crinkled and well-used. He's been here before. He is close again.

It is important that the movie does not describe where it takes place, that it is 'anytown' USA. For Nolan, anytown evokes the dead-end sensibility of classic film noir:

> We talked a lot about not referencing too obviously the cinematic idea of what film noir is. If you look at a film like *Double Indemnity* . . . it is actually set in a very ordinary reality. If you were to show that now you have to be very contemporary and not have guys in fedoras walking around. . . . [*Memento* is about] the kind of environment where you would wake up and it would be very difficult to know where you are, to be able to orientate yourself. So with the motel, for example, we spent a lot of time looking for something that was realistic and ordinary but in some way expressive of the story. (*Anatomy of a Scene*, 2002)

The importance of anytown realism for production designer Podesta is to not have a series of symbols but to have anonymous, peculiar, places. The anywhere peculiarity is about remembering and recycling. Lenny repeatedly looks in motel room drawers when he wakes up—"I read the Gideon's Bible religiously"—and then, later/earlier, he finds a gun on top of the Bible—"It can't be mine, who would give someone like me a gun." The recycled anonymity is also very precise in the design of the derelict building where Teddy is killed: cracking of plaster, leaking light, and other specific things that would remind me, the viewer, that we'd been there before at the beginning of the film.

Motel rooms are an organizing principle. In the story I am creating with *Memento*, they supply certainty and they provide routine. As organizing principles, the movie suggests to me that motels embody objectivity, positivism and empiricism. When Lenny is away from the motel rooms he is bewildered, reaching for memories of his wife. At Natalie's home he is comforted and deceived. In the restaurant with Natalie he remembers the beauty and perfection of his wife. Natalie gets Lenny to close his eyes: "Don't just recite the words. Close your eyes and remember her." He remembers the small details, the bits and pieces he never bothers to put into words. Putting all these together, he gets the feel of his wife. But the motel rooms are not about feeling, they are a space of contrivance. They are where he puts the facts of his life, imprinted on his body and mapped on his wall. The motel rooms and Lenny's body are repositories of facts. Ultimately, Natalie (or perhaps it is Lenny) contrives his facts for the final scenes of the movie when Lenny kills Teddy, thinking he is John G. But memory is also about feelings and stories.

Time slips sideways and space congeals. Lenny's coherency is a mechanistic logic borne from routine and habit. The space of coherence comes together in black and white in a motel room: a little bit peculiar but nonetheless recognizable as anywhere. A continual return, a forward sequence; the motel room provides a space of reflection, connection and duplicity. The duplicity emanates from the oddly parallel story of Sammy Jankis, who Lenny remembers from his previous life as an insurance investigator, before his wife's death. Sammy is the reason for Lenny's discipline and organization. Sammy's story is important.

DISCIPLINE, ORGANIZATION AND FIXING CONTEXT

Is hysteria a psychosis or is it simply a condition? If I accept Showalter's (1993, 335) admonition that hysteria is a flight from wandering stories, then I can accept further that it conditions past stories. And so, Lenny's condition is further conditioned—his hysteria is deluded and diluted—by discipline and organization. Lenny trusts his writing, his notes and his Polaroids; Lenny trusts his conditioning.

Samuel R. Jankis also suffered from anterograde memory dysfunction. Jankis wrote endless notes to himself but, unlike Lenny, he had no system of organization. Sammy was one of Lenny's clients in his previous life as an insurance investigator. Conditioning did not work for Sammy, but it works for Lenny. Habit and routine make Lenny's life possible. Conditioning is about acting on instinct. And Lenny is not faking. As an insurance investigator he wrote that Sammy's condition was mental, not physical. Sammy was not faking. Lenny is not faking. He should be physically capable of making the memories but isn't, so he creates them on his body. His body is not lying. It is real and physically capable of holding memories. Massumi (2002b, 495) characterizes an embodied move beyond, beneath and before representation with his suggestion that "the skin is faster than the word." Lenny's tattooing is, as he puts it: "all about context."

But Lenny's remembering is not only about conditioning and discipline, it is also about feeling and ritual. In several color segments, Lenny gives in to the sadness of losing his wife. In these segments, he does not remember facts but, rather, the small memories and silent details that are bittersweet and less than ideal. Memory is about the mementos of his wife—a hairbrush, a bunny, a book—that he places around his motel room so that she will be real, for a moment, when he awakes. He later burns these mementos to exercise/exorcise the memory. When he says "I've probably tried this before," Lenny refers to using a prostitute to help him exercise/exorcise the memories of his wife by paying the woman to place mementos around the motel room and then leave.

The truth that Lenny articulates towards the beginning of the film (the end of the story) is that he doesn't know anything. He feels angry and he doesn't know why. He feels guilt and he doesn't know why. Perhaps Lenny feels guilty because he, and not John G., killed his wife. For Sammy's wife, who could no longer live with his condition, a final test was to have him give her an insulin overdose. As Lenny recalls on the phone, "she knew beyond a doubt that he loved her so she found a way to test him. She really thought she'd call his bluff or she just didn't want to live through the things she'd been through." Perhaps Lenny's wife killed herself in a similar way. Perhaps Lenny is Sammy.

Ultimately, *Memento*'s statement about memory is that it is not reliable. Lenny fixes his context: he conditions himself to forget; he lies to himself to stay happy; he makes up his own truth; he creates a puzzle he cannot solve; and he creates his own sense of purpose through this puzzle. And this purpose enables him to believe in a world outside his own mind. Clearly, this is not about disassociation.

STORIES THAT ARE FELT THROUGH NARRATORS THAT ARE UNRELIABLE

Narrative is important for Lenny. And yet what he thinks he knows for sure are expressions that emerge, disappear, mutate and change with different composing forces. Other things he knows for sure—other pieces of empirical evidence—are about his experience of things. He knows what things sound like, he knows what things feel like when he picks them up. He knows these things for sure. They are certainties, the kind of memory he takes for granted. That Lenny's wife is gone is also his certainty (even when Teddy tells him that she survived the assault). Lenny communicates to himself facts that are immutable and trustworthy. But Lenny, the narrator of *Memento*, is unreliable because of his condition.

Massumi (2002a, xxi) notes that Deleuze and Guattari (1987) get to the primacy of expression by suggesting that there is an impersonal expressive agency that is not related to subjective aesthetics. Expression is not in a cognitive assessment of language, or in the speaking, remembering subject and its mementos. Nor is it rooted in an individual body or an institutional body. Deleuze and Guattari suggest that there is an impersonal trajectory to enunciation and that expression is abroad in the world; that there is an "autonomy to expression" (Deleuze and Guattari 1987, 317). In interpreting this, Massumi (2002a) suggests that because expression continues across experiences—like the authorship and meaning of Lenny's tattoos—it is too big to fit the contours of an individual human body.

Deleuze (1994, 138–140) avers that a body is "forced to think" rather than chooses to think, and this propulsion to the cognitive is a serial and self-propagating movement towards organization. Massumi (2002b, 22) notes that affect is about emotional intensity that is not directly accessible to experience and to facts and yet is not exactly outside of experience either. This elusive intensity is felt in my body rather than understood in my mind. Thought is shocking and, as such, it is felt. Lenny is organizing his life cognitively, but the subtle mixing of color and black and white at the end of *Memento* suggests an important conflation of thought, feeling, and action. The division between cognitive, thinking, black-and-white segments and emotive, affective color segments in *Memento* is purposeful, as is their dissolution. Brief color flashbacks to his wife's murder intrude in the black and white scenes. In a crucial black-and-white segment towards the end of the movie, Lenny takes a Polaroid shot of Jimmy, who he has just killed, and as he waves the photograph to hasten its development, the image slowly emerges in color as does the rest of the shot. The movie continues in color to its end/beginning.

Deleuze and Guattari (1987, 90) aver that "there is a primacy of the collective assemblage of enunciation over language and words." The meaning of *Memento* changes several years after its release, after the revelations on the DVD, and after I've read some more reviews, watched it again and again (with and without friends and their commentaries), and reread some work on Deleuze, on hysteria, and on road movies. And so, in closing, I get to own my personal enunciative position. Thought is owned as a process and as its own event. Even with his condition, Lenny cannot divorce his thoughts, his cognition, his black and white, from his color, his emotions, his remembering. Facts deceive; memories deceive. Like me, Lenny doesn't really need to know, he just needs *something to believe.*

And so, *Memento* might very well be about unhinging truth. If I take *Memento* to be about bridling hysteria, then perhaps Lenny is packaging his life in a way that makes sense to his own sense of self and security. And the space of that security is not an anonymous motel room but a psychiatric ward. As part of Lenny's flashback to the conclusion of the parallel Sammy Jankis story we see, for less than a second, Lenny taking the place of Sammy. If Lenny is, indeed, Sammy Jankis, then perhaps his life is lived in a psychiatric ward and the story we've just participated in is part of his hysterical delusions.

Alternatively, perhaps Lenny's condition is homicidal mania rather than severe anterograde memory dysfunction. In this story, Lenny not only kills Jimmy and Teddy, but also, originally, his wife and countless others in between. As Lenny strangles Jimmy in black and white I get a color flashback of 'someone' strangling Lenny's wife. This duplicitous, delusional story is suggested by another one second frame, this time in color, where Lenny is lying with his wife (who looks a lot like a younger version of Sammy's wife). In this frame, Lenny's body is tattooed and below the mirrored text 'he raped and murdered your wife' is 'I'VE DONE IT.' And on several occasions prior to this scene, I've seen a Polaroid of Lenny, grinning hysterically, pointing to this spot on his body.

So, where was I? Oh yes, I just need *something to believe*. Teddy reels off some platitudes in one of his last monologues in the movie, perhaps those will do: "So you lie to yourself to be happy. There is nothing wrong with that. We all do it. Who cares if there are a few little details you'd rather not remember. . . . You don't want the truth, you make up your own truth. . . . You're living a dream, a romantic quest . . . Come on, let's go down to the basement, you and me, and then you'll know who you really are." Alternatively, Lenny drives down an anonymous street as the movie rolls/devolves to a close. As he does so, he plays out an existential drama, shocking his/my thoughts. Perhaps that will do: "I have to believe in a world outside my own mind. I have to believe that my actions still have meaning, even although I cannot remember them. I have to believe that when my eyes are closed the world is still there." Flash to the frame of I'VE DONE IT. "Is it still out there? Yes? We all need mirrors to remind us who we are. I am no different. Now, where was I?"

NOTE

1. Lukinbeal and I offer an interpretative strategy to interrogate male hysteria in the classic road movie, *The Adventures of Priscilla, Queen of the Desert* (1994), in which Guy Pierce plays the part of Adam, a drag queen in search of his place in the world (Aitken and Lukinbeal 1997). If Pierce's portrayal of hysteria in that movie is circumscribed by movement away from the patriarchal norms elaborated through a road trip across the desert from Sydney to Alice Springs, his cure is perhaps a re-inscription into hegemonic space and place in *Memento*, where he plays the part of Lenny. The re-inscription is literally on his body.

REFERENCES

Aitken, Stuart C. 'Leading Men to Violence and Creating Spaces for Their Emotions' *Gender, Place and Culture* 13 no. 5 (October 2006): 491–507.

Aitken, Stuart C. and Lukinbeal, Christopher Lee. 'Disassociated Masculinities and Geographies of the Road' pp. 349–370 in *The Road Movie Book* edited by Steven Cohan and Ina Rae Hark. London: Routledge, 1997.

Anatomy of a Scene: *Memento*. A Sundance Channel Production, 2002.

Clarke, David B. 'Spaces of Anonymity' pp. 95–114 in *The Geography of Cinema: A Cinematic World* edited by Anton Escher and Stefan Zimmerman. Mainz: Geographisches Institut der Johannes Gutenberg Universität, 2008.

Connolly, William E. *Neuropolitics: Thinking, Culture, Speed*. Minneapolis: University of Minnesota Press, 2002.

Corrigan, Timothy. *A Cinema Without Walls: Movies and Culture after Vietnam*. New Brunswick: Rutgers University Press, 1991.

Deleuze, Gilles. *Cinema 1: The Movement-Image* (trans. Hugh Tomlinson and Barbara Habberjam). London: Athlone, 1986.

——. *Difference and Repetition* (trans. Paul Patton). New York: Columbia University Press, 1994.

Deleuze, Gilles and Guattari, Félix. *Anti-Oedipus: Capitalism and Schizophrenia* (trans Robert Hurley, Mark Seem and Helen R. Lane). Minneapolis: University of Minnesota Press, 1983.

——. *A Thousand Plateaus: Capitalism and Schizophrenia* (trans. Brian Massumi). London: Athlone, 1987.

Harker, Christopher. 'Playing and Affective Time-spaces' *Children's Geographies* 3 no. 1 (April 2005), 47–62.

Kirby, Kathleen M. *Indifferent Boundaries: Spatial Concepts of Human Subjectivity*. New York: Guilford, 1996.

Klein, Andy (2001). 'Everything you Wanted to Know About "Memento": A Critic Dissects the Most Complex—and Controversial—Film of the Year.' Salon Media Group Inc. http://archive.salon.com/ent/movies/feature/2001/06/28/memento_analysis/index.html

Lukinbeal, Christopher and Aitken, Stuart C. 'Sex, Violence and the Weather: Male Hysteria, Scale and the Fractal Geographies of Patriarchy' pp. 356–380 in *Places Through the Body* edited by Heidi J. Nast and Steve Pile. London: Routledge, 1998.

Massumi, Brian. 'Becoming-deleuzian' *Environment and Planning D: Society and Space* 14 no. 4 (1996): 395–406.

——. 'Introduction: Like a Thought' pp. xiii–xxxix in *A Shock to Thought: Expression after Deleuze and Guattari* edited by Brian Massumi. London: Routledge, 2002a.

——. *Parables for the Virtual: Movement, Affect, Sensation*. Durham, NC: Duke University Press, 2002b.

Showalter, Elaine. 'Hysteria, feminism and gender' pp. 286–344 in *Hysteria Beyond Freud* edited by Sander L. Gilman, Helen King, Roy Porter, G. S. Rousseau and Elaine Showalter (eds). Berkeley: University of California Press, 1993.

Silverman, Kaja. *Male Subjectivity at the Margins*. London: Routledge, 1992.

Chapter Eight

'Just an Anonymous Room:' Cinematic Hotels and Motels as Mnemonic Purgatories

Katherine Lawrie Van de Ven

> What do you do in the Grand Hotel? Eat. Sleep. Loaf around. Flirt a little. Dance a little. A hundred rooms leading to one hall. No one knows anything about the person next to them. And when you leave, someone occupies your room, lies in your bed. That's the end.
>
> Dr. Otternschlag (Lewis Stone) in *Grand Hotel*
> (d. Edmund Goulding, 1932)

The hotel and the motel—paradigmatic zones of transit and homelessness—have provided settings for a rich history of film narratives, most memorably those in which identity has proven to be a tricky thing—something complicated, obfuscated or anguished over, and only occasionally fixed or resolved in any traditional sense. Trading in weighty interrogations of souls in the balance, these are films of identity crisis. Many ask more complicated questions of their characters than 'Who are you?' though often that is a crucial starting point. Rather, they concern themselves with protagonists at the crossroads, torn between noble impulses and self-destruction; ready to move on yet plagued by past sins or missed opportunities. Where, if anywhere, are such characters headed? Hotels and motels offer space to work out the answers.

Focusing upon films from the past few decades, this study maps the qualities of these spaces that position the rented room as a privileged, symbolically charged cinematic site. The films under consideration are representative of a wider spectrum of narratives in which it is the hotel or motel room's function to assume strong parallels with popular conceptions of purgatory: a metaphorical or allegorical elsewhere reserved for the working through of crises of identity, morality, and memory. We begin with discussion of the mutual aspects that allow hotels, motels, and purgatory to share their symbolic bond. We follow with a reading of *Leaving Las Vegas* (d. Mike Figgis, 1995), a paradigmatic portrait of the lonely soul confined to motel purgatory. We then devote further consideration to the connection between hotel/motel space and the past by way of three films—*Memento* (d. Christopher Nolan, 2000), *The Business of Strangers* (d. Patrick Stettner, 2001), and *Tape* (d. Richard Linklater, 2001)—in which hotels/motels set the stage for revenge. Next, we look at the juxtaposition of rooms and isolated identities in three recent films: *Century Hotel* (d. David Weaver, 2001), *Chelsea Walls* (d. Ethan Hawke, 2001), and *The Tesseract* (d. Oxide Pang Chun, 2003). Finally, brief examinations of *Dirty Pretty Things* (d. Stephen Frears, 2002) and *2046* (d. Wong Kar-wai, 2004) will invite speculation on future developments for hotel/motel cinema.

The trip includes stops at dingy Las Vegas motels, a stately London hotel, a New York landmark, and a small hotel in Hong Kong, among others, to spy on amnesiacs, insomniacs, alcoholics, liars, and adulterers. The examples are recent highlights of a long cinematic hotel/motel history of characters strung out, on the lamb, out for revenge, running from their pasts, hiding from the inevitable or, in some in cases, hoping for nothing more than to speed its arrival.[1] As diverse as the sites/sights may be, the films connect in their narrative use of hotel or motel spaces as purgatorial stopping places where, even when in the company of an often-illicit lover, protagonists are alone with their deeds and self-doubt, future uncertain. No matter how elite or run-down, hotels and motels are the places where, paradoxically, "[e]veryone is alone with themselves."[2] Purgatory with color TV.

SPACES AND THEIR QUALITIES

What facilitates the use of hotels and motels as purgatorial spaces to study moral arcs and crises of identity? Cut free from a strictly doctrinal application and used pervasively in general discourse, purgatory is a powerful and flexible metaphor of marginal and transitory space and the alienated existence found there.[3] Popularly understood, purgatory retains the theological connotations of a 'condition or place of spiritual purging' but has dovetailed with the notion of limbo. It is a bleak elsewhere in which one endures an unwelcome stay as result of some wrong-doing or wrong turn; a space evoking questions of identity, morality, and memory. While Manichean binaries, or stark notions of good or evil, broadly infuse traditional forms of narrative (including both spiritual allegories and the majority of film genres alike), real life rarely unfolds along such simple dualities. Resisting easy conclusions and trading in the purgatorial grey areas of identity, hotel/motel films provocatively employ marginal, transitory spaces to speak to experiences of complexity or uncertainty. The soul in purgatory and the soul in the hotel or motel have much in common as a result of the spaces by which they are surrounded. These similarities may be discussed in terms of five discourses: location, duration, function, individuality, and morality.

In terms of location, both hotels/motels and purgatory are spaces apart, spaces between. The latter is conceived as a way-station or holding cell, one where the soul is cleansed or weighed in the balance awaiting a final verdict. It is a place to which people are banished, pending return—a nodal point in a flow. The hotel/motel is similarly a space apart. Even when located in the middle of a city, these sites are outside of its community and are frequently considered as conduits in a ceaseless flow of travelers, myriad points in the network of what anthropologist Marc Augé has termed non-places: "If a place can be defined as relational, historical and concerned with identity, then a space which cannot be defined as relational, or historical, or concerned with identity will be a non-place" (Augé 1995, 77—8). To be sure, ours is a transient society, traveling regularly and slow to put down lasting roots. However, transience and identity are surely not mutually exclusive. As used in films of this sort, rooms in even the most nondescript business hotel or clichéd roadside motel are precisely—almost excessively—connected to identity and therefore brim with meaning. They may be stopping places, but the stop is hugely significant.

Secondly, both types of space—hotels/motels and purgatory—are precisely understood in relation to duration: they exist to pass time. In his account of the significance of the concept of purgatory to contemporary spirituality and culture at large, theologian Richard K. Fenn has written: "Time, sheer duration, is therefore the medium through which the soul moves in its passage to God. If the medieval soul went on pilgrimages through space, the modern soul therefore takes up its trajectory through time" (Fenn 1995, 52). By their very nature, hotels, motels, and purgatory alike are defined by time and transience; neither home nor ultimate destination, they are stopping places en route to something else. Both are inhabited in a limited way, for a limited period, existing only in so much as they are arrived at and then departed from. In the hotel/motel, one's stay is gauged in terms of *nights*. In purgatory, it is gauged in terms of suffering and waiting: you do not pass time; rather it passes you by until wrongs have been worked through and forgiveness achieved.

Next, we arrive at the question of function. Hotels and motels emerged in a mobile, modern, frequently impersonal world in which travelers needed a space to call their own, if temporarily. As applied to their décor, this translates, as Peter Wollen has observed, into an emphasis "on providing an adequate set of functional articles (bed, closet, bathroom) which are replete with symbolic meaning" (Wollen 2002, 211). That meaning, largely, seems to be 'self-enclosure': providing everything the traveling soul requires. Similarly, the Catholic belief system from which the more salient concept of purgatory is inherited also *needed a space*, one between earth and heaven to solve that otherwise paradoxical dilemma of how the career sinner who repents on his death-bed can nonetheless arrive in the same paradise as the saint. The answer: an interstitial space functioning like a factory of forgiveness, where through an alloy of appropriate suffering and the prayers of the faithful, sin was purged. In effect, all narratives—whether films or spiritual allegories—need spaces of specific kinds and valences in which to stage events and, when dealing with such narratives of crisis of identity, morality, and memory, the marginal zones of hotels or motels are uniquely suited.

Furthermore, both hotels/motels and purgatory—while understood as housing (the word is ironic in both cases) countless souls through the unfolding of time—are conceived as functioning at the level of the individual: the traveler, or the soul in need of moral abreaction or isolation. Purgatory is designed to the measure of the man (or woman); a vastly lonely space where the punishment somehow fits the crime. The hotel/motel room also takes the individual (or at best the couple) as its basic unit. It is theoretically designed to be universal, or, put another way, to embrace any individual identity into its structure, but this is a slippery kind of individuality, in which the hotel/motel room's own mode of anonymity or sameness creates the possibility for individual space. Despite the presence of 'communal' areas such as pools, bars or lobbies—to which Marc Katz, following Siegfried Kracauer, has attributed a "particularly promiscuous energy"—in the end, every guest is really just a number, assigned an individual zone behind a closed and locked door (Katz 1999, 139).

As a result of these isolating structures, both hotel/motel spaces and purgatory are typified as ones of heightened emotional intensity. Purgatory, of course, is a space heavily coded with issues of morality. The same can be said for the terrain of hotels and motels experienced in film. From the registration desk—how many films depict characters checking in under false names?—through to the illicit encounters or tragic overdoses, even the grandest of hotels exist under the sign of moral ambiguity. This is perhaps a function of the *uncanniness* of the hotel space: it is consistently refreshed to meet each guest (whether vacationer, business traveler, or down-and-outer) with the same space, furnishings and services experienced by those that came before them and those that will come after (renovations notwithstanding). Whether possessed of the minimal amenities or fitted out in the trappings of decadence, the hotel/motel room is anonymous ground available to all at a price. A space that is capable of returning to a fresh state—*tabula rasa*-like—on a daily basis, it is perfect for trying to escape one's past or coming to terms with one's identity. We are both drawn to and unnerved by this deception: what secrets does the hotel keep?

THE HOLE YOU'RE IN

Leaving Las Vegas offers a provocative manifestation of the relationship between purgatorial space and the hotel/motel. Ben Sanderson (Nicholas Cage) has decided to check out early via a deleterious path of his own choosing. We meet Ben during a night of unbridled drinking that ends with a steamy encounter with a prostitute outside a neon-lit motel. Alcoholic, unemployable and estranged from his wife and son, Ben decides to burn what was left of his former life, take his generous severance package and drink himself to death in Las Vegas. When he leaves Los Angeles, he leaves his identity behind him: among the items he burns is his passport. He is nothing but a soul in transition.

If Las Vegas is hell—as is suggested by the opening sequence of *Casino* (d. Martin Scorsese, 1995)—then perhaps its countless motel rooms are the purgatories through which souls enter. Upon arriving in Vegas, Ben checks into the Whole Year Inn which his irrepressibly creative mind quickly re-configures as "The Hole You're In." It is noteworthy that supplemental definitions of 'purgatory' offered by the *Oxford English Dictionary* include a cavern, a swamp and "a hole under a fire-place"—its strictly spiritual connotation has long coexisted with material definitions pertaining to isolated, inhospitable sites. Ben's rented room, if not an actual hole, is certainly a 'hole in the wall'; it is a hyperbolic image of the anonymous, dimly lit, run-down motel space with the minor exception of four Vegas-kitsch aces painted on the wall.

He meets Sera (Elisabeth Shue), another prostitute, to whom he reveals his intention to die, but admits that he can no longer remember why (a telling example of the repression or refusal of memory that is so frequently exhibited by the protagonists of hotel/motel narratives). Over the second act of the film, Sera invites Ben to leave "that cheesy motel" and stay at her apartment. However, it is only a matter of time before the intense disparity between Ben's amicable personality and his avowed intentions to die overwhelm her. They leave town briefly to go even further into the realm of elsewhere, to another motel, this one in the middle of the desert. However, Ben's drinking reaches a critical new low-point (he literally drinks underwater in the swimming pool). Thereafter, Ben and Sera discuss his moving back to a hotel or motel on several occasions. The subtext to their conversations is, at root, about what constitutes the appropriate space to wait out his days in such fatal ambivalence. Her apartment, which Ben describes as "the home of an angel," is evidently too much of a site: one filled with at least minimal notions of identity, history and, by extension, a future. The film is not subtle on this point: "the home of an angel" is precisely heaven, a space which Ben is not, and may never be, ready to inhabit. He chooses the purgatory of the cheap motel, its allure lying in its dire anonymity and its symbolic appropriateness for the long, dark night of his soul.

Leaving Las Vegas is virtually transparent in its use of the motel room as ambiguous space for the moral/mortal crisis of a protagonist resigned to a process, indifferent as to whether it is one of redemption or damnation.[4] Many levels of complexity and conflicting meaning pervade the film; for instance, the clash between Ben's hellish experience and the often loathsome trappings of Las Vegas life, and the quasi-spiritual discourses structuring the plot and dialogue. Sera, as an example, is frequently positioned as an angel (both the soundtrack and several lines of Ben's dialogue explicitly liken her to one). However, her role in Ben's life is more complicated: she does not exclusively set out to save him, but rather insinuates herself into his crisis in the guise of a fantasy. As a prostitute, a woman whose time and body are rented, usually in the exact type of rented rooms in which Ben stays, her character takes on the same ambiguous qualities of the space with which she is tied. She offers Ben a complex enticement: on one side, to abandon his suicidal binge and re-join the world through a new romance; on the other, to go out in a languid abyss of sex and booze, a death which is, in itself, an ambiguous blend of ugliness and sensuality.

So what conclusions may be drawn about the use of motels to stage Ben's time in the balance? His decision to go to Las Vegas—a city founded on hotels—is a decision to embrace the grey area, as he seeks out a space where dramatic opposites may co-exist. His more sordid or self-destructive actions—hiring prostitutes, gambling and damaging property while plummeting into a morass of intoxication—commingle with his potential to care for others and the tragedy of his dis-ease. *Leaving Las Vegas* is propelled by an acute focus of the often-painful process of dealing with one's human weaknesses, a paradoxical kind of knowledge that manifests itself in the contrasts between Ben's ignominious motel death near the end of the film and the elegiac, slow-motion image of Ben, smiling happily, against the backdrop of the Vegas Strip that follows soon after. Such a profoundly uncertain character arc required the transitory and polyvalent spaces that motels offer.

ROOMS FOR REVENGE:
AMBIGUITY, IDENTITY, MEMORY

Revenge, much like the self-destruction discussed in relation to *Leaving Las Vegas*, is a morally ambiguous act which, in cinematic narrative at least, necessitates an appropriately marginal terrain. Here, again, hotels and motels have been employed in a powerful array of films built around revenge and, in particular, those interrogating that problematic question of whether it is ever justified. Notable examples include Christopher Nolan's *Memento*, Patrick Stettner's *The Business of Strangers*, and Richard Linklater's *Tape*.

There are several reasons why the hotel or motel is a symbolically appropriate space for characters out for revenge to incorporate into their plans or to simply be drawn toward, perhaps unconsciously. First, as already discussed, these rented rooms are coded as anonymous: while they may possess the basic amenities, they are never 'your things,' never your clock radio, your flowery bedspread, your ugly brown curtains. They facilitate the stealth and deception the would-be avenger requires but also enable such subjects to distance themselves from their past, from society and from its moral values. Through estrangement, they may encounter their violent, asocial impulses. Additionally, such spaces enable one to forget one's present situation because everyday, the discrete figure of the housekeeper will enter and return the room to a zero-degree standard, making beds, emptying ashtrays, cleaning spills, and erasing as much as possible any indication that anyone is in fact staying there. This phenomenon is commented on by *Memento*'s Leonard Shelby (Guy Pearce) who, 'coming to' after one of his moments of memory loss, looks around his motel room and tries, without luck, to deduce how long he has been staying there and exactly *where* there is: "it's just an anonymous room."

For those impelled to try to forget their past, the hotel or motel is a logical choice. However, characters in revenge narratives are never able to just forget and so continue on their morally ambiguous (at best) quests. The marginality of the hotel or motel room in relation to some boundary of settled society is thus also central to each narrative. These are, as discussed in relation to morality above, simply the kind of places where such things are *presumed* to occur.

Memento—which is discussed in great detail in the previous chapter—has been a defining film of recent times and continues to be analysed from many perspectives. Its use of space, that of the motel in particular, is equally provocative in relation to purgatory. In his perceptive analysis of the film, critic Andy Klein wrote: "Leonard has suddenly become an Everyman in a potentially infinite purgatory, blindly trying to revenge an act that has already been avenged, and finding himself manipulated, over and over, by people who would use a splendidly configured avenger for their own ends" (Klein, 28 June 2001). Klein's statement not only evokes the concept of purgatory as a description of a particular protagonist's experience but also uses the term to characterize—perhaps unintentionally—the physical landscape in which Leonard is mired (one coded by cheap motels, fading commercial boulevards, and abandoned warehouses) *and* the way in which revenge itself is frequently conceived of in symbolic spatial terms as a prison from which those who seek it cannot escape. Much as purgatory is a sequestering during which one has no alternative but to reckon with one's past, revenge is similarly a backwards- and inwards-turning process. In fact, the three films under consideration here markedly portray subjects that seek revenge, bound as they are in grief, regret or rage, as very much already stranded in a purgatory from which they can escape neither to the present nor the future, remaining trapped in a prison of past emotion, symbolically figured by way of the dead-end hotel or motel room.

This dire predicament is elegantly voiced by *Memento*'s Leonard who, unable to retain new memories after being the victim of an assault which, either directly or indirectly, also caused the death of his wife, asks: "How can I heal if I can't feel time?" The passage of time is crucial in purgatory, as it provides the medium through which souls earn redemption. However, Leonard introduces a nuanced take on that metaphorical experience: time is passing him by but his suffering comes precisely from the fact that he has no way of perceiving its progress, no reason to believe that he is moving closer to any salvation.

Leonard sets up camp at the Discount Inn, located in a vaguely defined corner of Southern California (possibly Los Angeles's Venice Beach) while trying to track and kill the man who he believes raped and murdered his wife. His inability to make new memories could render him useless as a detective (though, as Klein's words above suggest, ideal as an avenger). However, Leonard is proud of his "elegant system" for living, one built around being able to trust his own handwriting, tattoos and Polaroids of important facts, places and people. He functions on the most individual level imaginable—there is no permanent world for him beyond what he can physically carry *except* for his rented room. In fact, however, Leonard has at least two rooms—21 and 304—at the Discount Inn. The clerk owns up to the con, admitting he took advantage of Leonard's "condition"—severe anterograde memory dysfunction—to rent him a second room. The spaces are virtually indistinguishable, and the only reason Leonard discovers he is double-booked is because of a scrap of his handwriting. However, the film's careful construction of spaces suggests that the doubling is more significant than simply a comedic plot twist.[5] It is telling that his "stays" at the two rooms at the motel seem to correspond with the film's two stylistic halves (room 21 with the forward-moving black-and-white segments and room 304 with the backward-moving color sequences) and with the climatic act that finally unites their two trajectories. That is, with Leonard's murder of drug-dealer Jimmy G, after which he takes a Polaroid: while it develops, color bleeds into the whole of what had been a black-and-white scene. The killing is a fulcrum point in the film and may also be so for Leonard's moral identity. Leonard's killing of Jimmy is potentially the moment when his identity diverges from grieving husband on a quest to avenge his wife's death to tormented soul on an unending hunt for blood. *Memento* eventually opens the possibility that not only has Leonard already killed his wife's attacker, but that he has willfully reconstructed the facts in order to repeat the process again and again, to exact revenge on at least two people who were blameless in the attack, if not all together innocent. His memory, like the anonymous, ordinary rooms in which he stays, can be re-made daily, so no incriminating facts intrude to deter him from continuing along his path. Morally speaking, his strangling Jimmy may constitute a move from revenge to murder, a whole new space of reckoning. Does Leonard thus move from room to room as those souls in Dante's *Purgatory* moved from terrace to terrace? The question is largely academic, especially given that *Memento*'s much vaunted anti-chronological narrative structure brings the forward- and backward-moving portions of Leonard's tale into a grinding, and ultimately perpetual, collision. As we would expect of one cast into purgatory, he is getting nowhere fast.

In *The Business of Strangers*, Julie (Stockard Channing), a vice-president, and Paula (Julia Stiles), an AV assistant, are both stranded at a "claustrophobic" airport hotel when their flights are cancelled. Julie has just had Paula fired, and a fierce battle of nerves centered around age, power, and ambition erupts over late-night drinks, but the two women briefly transcend their animosity when they unite to exact highly physical revenge on Nick (Frederick Weller), a slick corporate headhunter whom one of them alleges to be a rapist. Despite adhering to a business-hotel standard for décor, the airport hotel—with its suites, lounge, soaring glass atrium, and well-outfitted gym—is nonetheless a marginal space suited to the asocial and destructive drives of the travelers to whom it caters. Notably, the culminating scene of this plot occurs in a space of the hotel that is even *more* marginal than the characterless, "demographically tested interior design"[6] of the rest of the establishment, as Julie and Paula's attack on Nick is carried out in a guestroom in an area under renovation, one that literally requires the women to cross a boundary to enter.

However, their cathartic act of vengeance never unites Julie and Paula in anything other than moral culpability, and no real bond can be formed between these transitory souls, trapped in distrust and disaffection that leaves them thoroughly and mutually isolated. Nor can the viewer identify with either figure. The plot nominally and briefly positions the horrifying attack on the headhunter as both retribution for a particular crime, and somehow a measure of retribution for an entire history of gendered violence and discriminatory corporate culture. However, even if we briefly accept such a challenging moral stance, the final scene of the film reveals that the rape allegations most likely had been false, a twisted machination. The ambiguous ground of the hotel had given space for characters to embrace and act upon uncertainty; for standards of truth and fact to be dismissed in favor of subjective memory and feeling.

Finally, in *Tape*—the most viscerally claustrophobic film discussed in this essay—three grown high-school friends reunite for an evening in a morbidly average motel room in Lansing, Michigan. The action is entirely set in room 19 of the Motor Palace, the cheap room rented by Vince (Ethan Hawke), in which he is joined first by his old friend John (Robert Sean Leonard) and then by the one-time object of both men's desires, Amy (Uma Thurman). During the evening, devastating but also contradictory allegations emerge, including one about a possible date-rape ten years in the past.

Waiting for John to arrive, a frenetic Vince paces like a caged animal around his room, stripping down to his boxers, chugging a couple of beers, and emptying a couple more into the sink but strategically placing the empties around, all in an effort to put John off-guard by creating the impression that he is more drunk than he actually is. It turns out that the evening is an ambush, as Vince, like *Memento*'s Leonard, has been unable to heal from a past hurt. Amy was Vince's first girlfriend. However, they never had sex and shortly after they broke up, she slept with John. Vince has concluded that the event was a rape and that it is up to him to resolve the unpunished crime. The fact that his life has been one of drift and limited success in the intervening decade (he is a drug-using, drug-dealing volunteer fireman), and that he stages this reunion out of the blue, classify his quest for vengeance as a prison that has prevented him from engaging in the present.

Things get complicated when Vince secretly records John making a confession, but one which is later disputed by Amy. The dynamics of which of the three protagonists are using the encounter as a trap become increasingly ambiguous while the question of who—if anyone—has the right to revenge becomes problematic. If Vince originally sets out to use the reunion to take pride-driven revenge on John, and John tries to shoehorn the scene into an opportunity for moral absolution, it is Amy who is ultimately able to turn the event into an occasion for judicious revenge, one which she did not need to plan herself, but simply arrive at and manipulate to her advantage. At points, the grim, drably furnished room suggests a spatialization of each character's besmirched memories. In the end, however, as Amy leaves, abandoning the two men to their respective failures, it provides a unique purgatory devoted not to revenge of a rape, but rather punishment for male possessiveness and competitiveness. This is just the latest forum in which Vince and John's destructive battle for moral, intellectual, and sexual superiority has played out, a prison in which regret and recrimination damage them both while leaving open the likelihood that their contest is not over. While a moral showdown leading toward some final verdict had *seemed* to be unfolding, the story ends, at least so far as the two men are concerned, in a purgatory of lingering doubt, guilt, and emotional torment.

These films witness all of the traits of the hotel or motel as purgatory, and exploit the ambivalence of this space to underscore the fundamental moral ambiguity of the quest for revenge. Their characters, collectively, are out to avenge heinous wrongdoings—rape, murder, betrayal. Yet, it is always difficult to argue the rationale of an eye for an eye, always dangerous to repay violence with violence, and the microscopic prisons and rent-by-the-day border zones to which these protagonists confine themselves provocatively situate this moral impasse where no choice can ever feel like the right one.

BEING ALONE—WITH EVERYONE ELSE

Another tendency of the hotel or motel in cinema has been the use of such spaces for a particular type of multi-linear narrative in which the multitude of rooms and guests creates the premise for studies of contrasting—and often conflicting—individuals. These are films of the *Grand Hotel* or *Four Rooms* (d. Allison Anders, Alexandre Rockwell, Robert Rodriguez, and Quentin Tarantino, 1995) variety. Shifting focus away from one strikingly solipsistic protagonist and their personal demons, these narratives explore the paradoxical individuality that rented rooms offer their guests by way of showing the often ironic interactions (or lack thereof) between the numerous subjectivities isolated in identical rooms behind an establishment's many doors, exploring what happens when they are positioned adjacent or slammed into each other. Recent films representative of this tendency, which is both structural and thematic, include *Century Hotel*, *Chelsea Walls*, and *The Tesseract*.

In *Century Hotel*, stories are contrasted through time, as opposed to through the walls, as the film interweaves seven distinct narratives set in room 720 at the fictional Century Hotel. Though grand when it opened, we learn that the fate of the establishment has risen and fallen over time and, on 31 December, 1999 (the 'present' of the narrative) it is found in a state of unfinished— perhaps abandoned—renovation. Editing its stories in a braided manner, as opposed to strictly sequentially, the film emphasizes the sharing of space by a flow of protagonists during different segments/decades, though the décor changes across the eras in which various stories unfold. In fact, much as purgatory is conceived as personally appropriate for each soul cast there, room 720 takes on trappings suited to each inhabitant's fate, ranging from claustrophobic splendor, to dismal cluttered mess, to ultraviolet-lit late-night luridness.

The story of a particular room, the film also offers a summa of the types of narratives that define hotel/motel cinema. In the 1920s, a young bride, unhappy on the night of her arranged marriage, has a fatal tryst with an intruder. In the 1930s, a Chinese mail-order bride faces doubt on the eve of her wedding, while discussion of commitment is even more problematic in the 1940s for a G.I. returning home to his sweetheart but being, deep down, attracted to his male best friend with whom he shares the room. In the 1950s, a milquetoast husband staying at the hotel while looking for his runaway wife falls victim to a vengeful scheme, as does an agoraphobic has-been rocker in the 1960s who is duped and exploited by the generally overlooked figure of the hotel's maid. Throughout the 1980s, a lonely businessman returns to room 720 for yearly assignations with a prostitute and, finally, in 1999, a young woman waits for a New Year's 'date' with whom she plans to carry out a millennial suicide pact. Both literally (by the ghost of the 1920s bride) and thematically, room 720 of the Century Hotel is haunted by many of the same themes ascribed to the purgatorial site of the hotel or motel over a century of narrative cinema. It has seen adultery, murder, self-destruction, theft, revenge, and betrayal unfold over many years, but the telling point is how little changes as the tropes of transience, marginality, and anonymity haunt the space and its guests.

Chelsea Walls adopts a similar approach but, setting events in New York City's fabled Chelsea Hotel, takes the venue's history as home to famed authors, musicians, and artists as a given as it contrasts stories set within the hotel's present, where it now functions, at least in part, as apartments.[7] Some of its newer residents, such as Terry (Robert Sean Leonard, again), an aspiring folk singer, are chewed up by New York almost instantly; others who have been there longer, like Bud (Kris Kristofferson), a tormented alcoholic author, are even less lucky and are abandoned there to wait, the love or peace they seek unlikely to ever arrive. The film languishes in the stylistic representation of a marginal space that is replete with the history of its own population of transients; one denizen opines "ghosts are our most valuable assets" and the space is portrayed as run-down, maze-like, a discomfiting mix of creaky old wood and unexpected linoleum floors (one wonders when they took the old carpets out of the halls).

The aspiring artists and jilted lovers (portrayed by actors also including Uma Thurman, Rosario Dawson and Vincent D'Onofrio) that now walk the Chelsea's halls are themselves little more than phantoms, seeking a place to hide from the rejection they experience at the hands of a world indifferent to their dreams. The purgatorial isolation prompts Terry to pen a ballad called "The Lonely One" while the waiting inspires Audrey (Dawson), a struggling poet tormented by her husband's mercurial commitment to their bond, to write: "Oh, may it come, the time of love, the time we'd be enamored of. I've been patient too long, my memory is dead."[8] As a narrative correlative of purgatorial time, very little happens throughout the characters' interwoven strands other than their visibly and verbally anguishing over their plights— broke, lovelorn, or self-doubting. Furthermore, the film begins with an introductory montage revealing that someone has overdosed in the Chelsea; as the film ends, we discover that the victim had been one of the individuals whose plotline the film had unraveled. Time, thus, moves cyclically here.

In his review of *Chelsea Walls*, Stephen Holden wrote: "Loneliness, misery, poverty, alienation and substance abuse, the movie implies, are part of being an artist" (Holden 2002). It seems more apropos to say that they are part of the marginal spaces to which artists are too often confined. The hotel/motel film here shows its adaptability, transiting seamlessly from tales of individual crises of identity to embrace the theme of the cultural purgatory of the artist, marginalized in a society that cherishes capital over inspiration.

A final example of the multi-linear structure available to the hotel/motel film is *The Tesseract*, a transnational perspective on the juxtaposition of identities. A young British drug courier (Jonathan Rhys-Meyers) checks into room 303 of the Heaven Hotel in Bangkok, where he soon dreams that time stops. Literally, in this purgatory, the hands of the clock cease moving. Meanwhile, a wounded female assassin (Lena Christenchen) checks into room 203, a British psychologist (Saskia Reeves) moves into 205, and an enterprising little boy (Alexander Rendel) both works at the hotel *and* steals the guests' belongings for resale on the black market. By now, the juxtapositions of the stories may be intuited: someone grieves a painful past loss, someone dies, someone winds up enmeshed in a double-cross. However, the film is notably concerned—in a way that those discussed thus far have not generally been—with the function of hotels as both marginal spaces *within* a culture, but also as access and meeting points *between* cultures; in particular, within the context of Thailand's role as a popular location for western monetary influence and tourists. In the film, the figures of global capital (in the guise of skyscrapers, Mercedes-Benzes, and a corporately modeled underground crime-world) are re-mapping Bangkok at the same time as its popularity as an exotic destination space in which to forget one's past troubles increases among western pleasure travelers. These factors come together in the ironically named Heaven Hotel with calamitous effects and, while the hotel is initially coded as a self-selected purgatory for the primary characters, it ultimately sees most of them leaving on even darker, more final paths, unable to extricate themselves from criminal activities or from past heartaches that prevent them from seeing the dangers of the present.

IDENTITY, CULTURAL TRANSITION, GLOBALIZATION

The movement through the corridors of cinematic hotels and motels has carried us from the tormented individual to communities of mutually isolated transients. We now arrive, finally, at the level of cultures in transition in the era of globalization. As suggested by *The Tesseract*, recent hotel/motel films are embracing the significance of these sites to travel and tourism, but also to the movement of cultural influence, power, and identities in the age of global capital.

Stephen Frear's *Dirty Pretty Things* has much in common with a typical hotel/motel film: the tortuous passage of time, devious schemes, and the contested value of individual identity. However, it focuses on the tales of several of its cinematic hotel's employees, that same community of largely immigrant service workers whose discretion is key to the shady goings-on of most other hotel narratives. As this hotel's manager says, "The hotel business is about strangers . . . they come to hotels in the night to do dirty things and in the morning it is our job to make things look pretty again."[9]

Dirty Pretty Things is chiefly set at London's middle-ranking Baltic Hotel, the very name of which, according to critic Philip French, "suggests that most inhospitable of inland seas, a silent, purgatorial place, like some no man's land between life and death" (French, 15 December 2002, 7). Okwe (Chiwetel Ejiofor) is an illegal Nigerian immigrant who drives a taxi by day and is the Baltic's desk clerk at night. For the rare hours that he sleeps, Okwe rents a couch from young Turkish immigrant Senay (Audrey Tautou), who works as a maid at the hotel. The two are drawn closer through the discovery of a vile conspiracy after a prostitute who frequents the Baltic tells Okwe to check on room 510; when he does, he finds the toilet stopped up by a human heart.

From here, the film explores how transient, undocumented service workers wind up stranded in a very real purgatory, pushed by personal or political reasons to leave their homelands, then harassed by the authorities and exploited by their bosses as they try to eke out a living, suffering for the sin of being 'illegal' in the eyes of the government and waiting for the break that will change their fates. However, this break rarely comes, as the economy is structured around such endless flows of cheap labor, enabling exploitative employers to wield the nuclear option of deportation as a weapon to push standards of living ever lower. *Dirty Pretty Things* uses its hotel narrative to interrogate this situation. When these workers can no longer endure the waiting, we learn, merciless exploiters are there to offer a devil's wager: fronted by the hotel's manager, a shady group is using passports and money to lure illegal immigrants into selling their organs to the black market. Room 510, it turns out, has been doubling as a fly-by-night operating room where the

Figure 8.1.   Employees trapped in a different world in the Baltic Hotel's imposing lobby
© Miramax Films; photo by Laurie Sparkham

organ-donor's fate is of little concern to those doing the harvesting. Even more so than the 'hotel guest' protagonists of other films, illegal employees such as Okwe and Senay are in a different world (Figure 8.1). Devoid of legal recourse, they have no avenue of exit other than the cooperation of a network of marginalized peers.

Dirty Pretty Things is the hotel-film counterpart to the work of sociologist Saskia Sassen (1998, 1999), and her critiques of outdated and hypocritical national immigration policies. The film mobilizes the long-established conventions of hotel narratives to offer a blankly metaphorical look at the purgatorial plight of immigrant workers in the new economy, critiquing the western world's exploitation of its multicultural service workers and its place atop a food chain gorging on the increasing traffic of migrant workers around the globe.

Lastly, we come to Wong Kar-wai's fascinating *2046*. The film involves two primary locations and temporal settings: Hong Kong's Oriental Hotel in the late 1960s and a time-traveling train hurtling towards the year 2046 on which one lonely passenger is served by a crew of robot attendants. The film follows Wong's *In the Mood for Love* (2000), sharing its themes of bitterly lost love, regret and frustratingly shared spaces.[10] It also putatively extends the plot of the earlier film, as pulp serial author Chow Mo-wan (Tony Leung Chiu-wai), heartbroken at the end of *In the Mood for Love*, returns to Hong Kong, a jilted shadow of his former self. He is drawn to the Oriental Hotel when a showgirl for whom he had shown guarded affection is murdered in room 2046. He moves into 2047 for several years at the end of the 1960s and winds up in several failed relationships with women, some of whom he meets in the hotel.

Wong has reportedly resisted attempts to position *2046* as an allegorical approach to the identity of Hong Kong between its initial return to China in 1997 and its last year of economic and cultural sovereignty in 2046. However, there is clearly something to be argued here—there is no way that the room numbers at the small, family-run Oriental Hotel naturally run that high!

So, how does one character's emotional purgatory play out in ways which may be considered allegorically? Chow is in love with a past that he cannot capture: his painfully frustrated romance with Su Li-zhen (Maggie Cheung) in *In the Mood for Love*. His heartbreak drives him into a purgatory of longing in which he, evidently, abandons himself to years of cynical womanizing only to discover that it takes away his ability to love. As he passes the time in room 2047, he writes a science-fiction tale—played out as the futuristic 'train' sequences—the essence of which is that a train leaves periodically for the year 2046 when, it is said, anyone can recapture lost love and recover memories. Clearly this complex film is about more than the hollow romances of hotel life. Chow figures a cultural identity near the beginning of a long transition, obsessed with the passage of time—with a romanticized past to which it can never return, and with an uncertain future that will be slow to arrive and that thus preoccupies the cultural imaginary. The erotics of memory and the frustrations of time rarely receive more intricate treatment than they do in Wong's films and in *2046*, he extends these questions from the individual to the cultural level. The hotel/motel film has thus come full-circle, beginning in the creation of spaces for a single character's identity crisis and culminating in use of that exact same image—the lone soul (here, Chow) in a room, waiting—to portray the cultural limbo of Hong Kong as it redefines itself in the space between being one of the last remaining outposts of Britain's once expansive empire and being part of China. For such small, anonymous rooms, the potential is startling.

CONCLUSION

Looking at *2046*, it is fascinating to note that the most conceptually progressive hotel film of recent years is a period piece, trading in an image of a motel from an explicitly bygone era. One wonders what film roles the hotel and motel will play as, increasingly, the paradigms discussed here are replaced in the 'real' world by structures more akin to Los Angeles's spatially implosive Bonaventure, or Vegas's mixed-use theme-park/casino/concert-venue/mall/ hotels such as Caesar's Palace. As we have observed, hotels and motels have offered potent narrative stages for purgatorial states of identity, morality, and memory precisely *because* of their anonymous functionality and marginality in relation to the more 'meaningful' spaces of rooted civic life. Since the early twentieth century, when "the modern urban dweller could rely only on spaces, like that of the hotel lobby, 'that bear witness to his nonexistence',"[11] such stopping places have offered ideal sites to work through moral ambiguity and marginal identities.

However as many commentators, like journalist Eleanor Curtis, have noted, "the most important and subtle turning point in the development of interior design trends for the contemporary hotel is the introduction of narrative into design, requiring that the designer view the project more as a film director, theatre set director, or author of fiction" (Curtis 2001, 8).

What will become of cinematic purgatories if their preferred spaces—hotels and motels rich in potential precisely because they offer blank canvases for personal prisons and identities in the balance—progressively come pre-packaged, the intended story already encoded in every detail from light switches to bathroom tiles? At the same time that life has become increasingly prefabricated and pre-scripted according to the laws of global capital and transnational commercial culture, it has ironically become more mobile (Albrect with Johnson, 2002). Questions of identity, morality and memory grow ever more persistent as the distinctions between settled homes and itinerant spaces become less clear, and as the division between individual and consumer risks disappearing all together. Yet how—or more precisely, where—can we contemplate identity in transition when the consumerist sublime attempts to use scripted space to mask or elide precisely the kinds of marginality and doubt symbolically associated with purgatory? How can identities be hashed out in the dark of night in a rented room when renters' roles in the hotel-as-spectacle is increasingly already scripted for them?

NOTES

My title, 'Just an anonymous room,' is taken from the words of Leonard Shelby (Guy Pearce) in *Memento* (d. Christopher Nolan, 2000).

1. Titles that come immediately to mind by way of an illustrious and illustrative hotel/motel film canon include *Grand Hotel*, *Psycho* (d. Alfred Hitchcock, 1960), *Last Year at Marienbad* (d. Alain Resnais, 1961), *The Shining* (d. Stanley Kubrick, 1980), and *Barton Fink* (d. Coen bros, 1991). These latter two titles and their relationship to conceptions of infernal spaces are thoroughly analysed by Greg Haines in the next chapter.

2. Vicki Baum (from *Hotel Shanghai*), quoted in O. Riewoldt (2002, 7).

3. It is important to distinguish between doctrinal or theological and popular conceptions of purgatory. In Roman Catholic belief, purgatory is a state "in which souls who depart this life in the grace of God suffer for a time, because they still need to be cleansed from venial sins, or have still to pay the temporal punishment due to mortal sins." (*Oxford English Dictionary*, Second Edition, 1989)

4. Fatalistic use of hotel space is taken to extremes in Figgis's 2001 film, *Hotel*. *Hotel* revolves around a three-layer plot: a multi-national Dogme-style film-crew stays at a Venetian luxury hotel while filming an adaptation of *The Duchess of Malfi*; a Hollywood entertainment reporter brings her crew for a making-of piece about the Malfi production; and the hotel's staff—seemingly a cannibal cult—dine on unlucky guests in the hotel's basement. The film explicitly positions the hotel as a site of sin followed by often self-initiated torture, culminating, by way of example, when the Malfi film's producer (played by David Schwimmer), dismayed over misdeeds he has perpetrated, walks knowingly into the basement.

5. For a complementary discussion of the significance of two motel rooms to Leonard's narrative, see Clarke (2008).

6. Paula (Julia Stiles) in *The Business of Strangers* (d. Patrick Stettner, 2001).

7. The hotel's noteworthy cinematic history dates back to Andy Warhol's infamously unenjoyable *Chelsea Girls* (1966).

8. Audrey (Rosario Dawson) in *Chelsea Walls* (d. Ethan Hawke, 2001).

9. Juan (Sergi López) in *Dirty Pretty Things* (d. Stephen Frears, 2002).

10. Thematically, *2046* is also in dialogue with several of Wong's even earlier films, including *Days of Being Wild* (1991) and *Happy Together* (1997), the latter of which is discussed in detail in Chapter 11 of this volume.

11. Siegfried Kracauer, quoted in Vidler (2000, 73).

REFERENCES

Albrecht, Donald with Johnson, Elizabeth (eds). *New Hotels for Global Nomads*. New York: Merrell, 2002.

Augé, Marc. *Non-places: Introduction to an Anthropology of Supermodernity*. London: Verso, 1995.

Clarke, David B. 'Spaces of Anonymity' pp. 95–114 in *The Geography of Cinema: A Cinematic World* edited by Anton Escher and Stefan Zimmerman. Mainz: Geographisches Institut der Johannes Gutenberg Universität, 2008.

Curtis, Eleanor. *Hotel: Interior Structures*. Chichester: Wiley, 2001.

Fenn, Richard K. *The Persistence of Purgatory*. Cambridge: Cambridge University Press, 1995.

French, Philip. 'Frears Finds the Heart of London's Underground' *The Observer* (15 December 2002): 7.

Holden, Stephen. 'Poor, Miserable, and Addicted? They Must Be Poets' *New York Times* (19 April 2002): E15.

Katz, Marc. 'The Hotel Kracauer' *differences: A Journal of Feminist Cultural Studies* 11 no. 2 (July 1999): 134–152.

Klein, Andy. (2001) 'Everything you Wanted to Know About "Memento": A Critic Dissects the Most Complex—and Controversial—Film of the Year.' Salon Media Group Inc. http://archive.salon.com/ent/movies/feature/2001/06/28/memento_analysis/index.html

Riewoldt, Otto. *New Hotel Design.* London: Laurence King Publishing, 2002.

Sassen, Saskia. *Globalization and Its Discontents: Essays on the New Mobility of People and Money.* New York: New Press, 1998.

———. *Guests and Aliens.* New York: W. W. Norton, 1999.

Vidler, Anthony. *Warped Space: Art, Architecture, and Anxiety in Modern Culture.* Cambridge: MIT Press, 2001.

Wollen, Peter. *Paris Hollywood: Writings on Film.* London: Verso, 2002.

Chapter Nine

No Sympathy for the Devil, or, Lobby Music: Spaces of Disjunction in *Barton Fink, The Shining,* and Muzak

Greg Hainge

It has been suggested, by Siegfried Kracauer, that the hotel lobby can be "conceived as the inverted image of the house of God [. . .] a negative church [. . .] the setting for those who neither seek nor find the one who is always sought, and who are therefore guests in space as such—a space that encompasses them and has no function other than to encompass them" (Kracauer 1995, 175–176). For Kracauer, then, the hotel lobby—for all of its similarities to a church-like structure—constitutes the antithesis of the house of God, affording none of the apparent trans-subjectivity bestowed upon the individual by religious ceremony in sacralised places of worship or, more generally, the religious experience in which 'those who stand before God are sufficiently estranged from one another to discover they are brothers [. . .] exposed to such an extent that they can love one another without knowing one another and without using names' (Kracauer 1995, 182). In the hotel lobby, according to Kracauer, whilst similarly dispossessed of one's name and self, 'we' do not access the commonality of this personal pronoun but become, instead, isolated anonymous atoms. He writes:

> Here [in the hotel lobby] profession is detached from the person and the name gets lost in the space, since only the still unnamed crowd can serve *Ratio* as a point of attack. It reduces to the level of the nothing—out of which it wants to produce the world—even those pseudo-individuals it has deprived of individuality, since their anonymity no longer serves any purpose other than meaningless movement along the paths of convention. But if the meaning of this anonymity becomes nothing more than the representation of the insignificance of this beginning, the depiction of formal regularities, then it does not foster the solidarity of those liberated from the constraints of the name; instead, it deprives those encountering one another of the possibility of association that the name could have offered them. Remnants of individuals slip into the nirvana of relaxation,

faces disappear behind newspapers, and the artificial continuous light illuminates nothing but mannequins. (Kracauer 1995, 182–183)

Kracauer's analysis here of the mechanisms operating on the individual distributed in the space of the hotel is utterly compelling even if the opposition between the hotel lobby and the church he outlines is perhaps less and less extreme, it being possible in our desanctified postmodern, postreligious (or post.*) present to formulate an objective response to religious faith. Thus, it has become possible to speculate that if the religious experience provides the impression of a higher form of organisation, a communality ordinarily beyond the reach of mortal man, then it is only able to do so within the space of a conjunctive synthesis in which an *impression* of communion is gained through the diversion of both terms of a relation through an abstraction exterior to both—a description which might even be thought of as an attempt at a definition of the Deleuzoguattarian concept of the conjunctive synthesis.[1] This is to say, then, that the faith that binds people together does so by creating a narrative which gives the impression of a shared reality even though the narrative in actuality bears no relation to the reality of any of the individual subjects held in this synthesis and this is ultimately no different to the work of the hotel lobby in Kracauer's analysis, a space in which individuals gain the impression of inhabiting a common space only at the expense of their individuality, which is to say their own reality. It is then significant that the hotel lobby constitutes the ideal space for a detective narrative according to both Kracauer (1995, 174) and Tallack (2002), since for Tallack—in his study "'Waiting, waiting,'" which analyses various instances of the hotel lobby in film and art subsequently to propose a "hotel-lobby-theory-of-the-novel" (Tallack 2002, 145)—"without being an artwork, the *detective novel* still shows civilized society its own face in a purer way than society is usually accustomed to seeing it" (Kracauer 1995, 174), as does the hotel lobby itself. This is to say, then, that the hotel lobby shows Capitalist society (which can be thought of as a religious assemblage that bestows a false sense of shared reality upon its subjects with logos and branding instead of crosses and thorns) its own face in a pure manner, disassembling the conjunction inherent in any such pseudo-religious space so as to reveal precisely that which the facialising mechanisms of all such systems strive to dissimulate, namely, its essential disjunction—which is to say its power to separate out individuals and render communication impossible. Something similar is suggested by Marc Katz who writes,

Hotel lobbies are notoriously charged with narrative possibility. The hotel, as microcity, is a site of exchanges of all sorts—information, money, services, goods. And among these we might include identity as well, since as sites of displacement, hotels tend to magnify that sense of the performative that is concomitant with urban anonymity. This is what gives the lobby its particularly promiscuous energy. Open to dispersal, the lobby invites guests into the scrambling of identity codes and deterritorialization of desire that Deleuze, for one, associates with the euphoria of capital. (Katz 2000, 138–139)

It is precisely this sense of euphoria and concomitant loss of self that comes from the hyperperformativity on display in the hotel lobby that make of it not an "inverted image of the house of God" (Kracauer 1995, 175) but, rather, an intensified house of God, a sacred space without conjunctive shrouds of mystery, a space in which the disjunctive devices of 'civilisation' are laid bare, a space that consumes civilised man (who was never intended to seek) and that has no function other than to consume him.

The hotel lobby, then, is hell. Not the kingdom of Satan in which the wicked toil for all eternity, but a transparent space of transcendent absolutes, an all-consuming space composed entirely of flames which feeds on all that enters into its realm, the disjunctive synthesis itself—Kracauer's 'mere gap'.[2] It is for this reason that the lobby can be exploited aesthetically, as Kracauer goes on to note when he writes,

> But if a sojourn in a hotel offers neither a perspective on nor an escape from the everyday, it does provide a groundless distance from it which can be exploited, if at all, *aesthetically*—the aesthetic being understood here as a category of the nonexistent type of person, the residue of that positive aesthetic which makes it possible to put this nonexistence into relief in the detective novel. (Kracauer 1995, 177)

To infer from this, however (as do both Kracauer and Tallack to differing degrees), that the hotel lobby in and of itself—in reality, outside of the realm of the aesthetic—is a space which provides a groundless distance from the everyday, a space which needs to be subjected *to* critique and which also provides the perspective or distance required *by* critique, as Tallack puts it (2002, 142), is to desanctify its space and to deny it its dissimulative or revelatory role. For the hotel lobby is precisely that space which does not provide a groundless distance from the everyday, but which subjects the individual in its space to an intensified experience of the everyday. Far from being a space "waiting to be given meaning by purposeful narratives and minimal signs of activity" (Tallack 2002, 146), the hotel lobby—as a concrete (not fictional) space—provides its inhabitants with an everyday narrative of its own making, and therefore spatialises narrative only as do the faint blue lines and figures on a painting-by-numbers canvas. The hotel lobby, then, comes to behave like a *socius*, a quasi-cause for all those drawn into its space through a revolving door—a constantly infolding boundary between an aleatory outside, the flux of the street, and the hotel's internal void. In it, individual desire is relinquished, for the fulfilment of desire in the space of the lobby is dependent on its surrender. In order to feel at home (*chez soi*) in this pretend home away from home, you must check in your self (*soi*) along with your coat—even if your cell is to be themed. It is from this aspect that the hotel lobby acquires its sacred nature, existing only to be consumed by the consumer who is in turn consumed by the product.[3]

The hotel lobby, then, is a space in which the disjunctive syntheses that govern the civilised Capitalist machine are laid bare, it is a kind of inverted panopticon where the guests/inmates willingly succumb to the apparatus of capture on open display. As a space in itself, regardless of its artistic manifestations and representations as figured in various narratives, the hotel lobby performs an erasure of its contents, territorialising the individual in its own constructed artifice. Not so much "displac[ing] people from the unreality of the daily hustle and bustle" (Kracauer 1995, 176) as placing them in a hyper-accelerated (albeit static) unreality, not so much "an upholstered substitute for the reality of the street" (Tallack 2002, 144) as a negation of desire/the real, the hotel lobby is a void, a space constituted by the reterritorialisation of absolute deterritorialisation. In the hotel lobby—and the rooms to which the lobby acts as a portal—, every individual is interchangeable. And yet, in the spaces of the hotel, there is no accession to a higher plane of organisation, no auto-objective/supra-subjective mode of organisation, which is to say that the hotel lobby *does not* constitute a plane of consistency on which each individual becoming is linked by connective syntheses (truly immanent lines of communication in other words) to an infinite number of possible connections—the ideal of desubjectified desire envisaged by Deleuze and Guattari—, since every one of its spaces is a *generic simulacrum of private spaces*. In the hotel lobby, the desubjectified individual actually aids in her own capture, since it is the deterritorialized spaces of the hotel which perform the reterritorialization. The giving of a 'false' name along with the briefest of personal histories, for instance, in actuality erases individual narrative and facilitates the axiomatization of the individual into the pseudo-private spaces of the hotel. Inscribed on the very surface of the hotel (in the register), the guests are miraculated to the hotel which serves as a limitative body without organs on whose surface only disjunctive syntheses can take place. No autonomy is possible from this point on. Every communication (dial 0) and every movement is governed according to a strictly regimented pre-existing code, and this is the case whether the individual is in stasis (Kracauer's concept of the lobby as a purposeless space (Kracauer 1995, 176–177), Tallack's (2002) 'waiting, waiting') *or* in movement towards a pre-defined destination through approved channels with a bellhop as guide. In the hotel lobby, every Smith,

Jones, John, Brown, Black and White becomes grey, blending into an anonymous undifferentiated mass, a collection of faceless consumers even without a dissimulative newspaper, irreconcilably separated in their proximity.

Performing an explicit foregrounding and deshrouding of the axiomatics governing the Capitalist machine, the hotel lobby is a disjunctive space, and as such can be exploited aesthetically as a space of narrative spatialisation. Douglas Tallack has enumerated many instances of such usage of the lobby in various art forms, especially the cinema (Tallack 2002). One of the main objects of Tallack's study is Edmund Goulding's *Grand Hotel* of 1932, a film in which, as he rightly points out after Kracauer, the disjunction of the hotel lobby, its mere gap, is exploited aesthetically. If one is to examine the use made of the space of the hotel in the Coen Brothers' *Barton Fink* and Stanley Kubrick's *The Shining*, however, the hotel can be seen no longer merely to serve as an aesthetic tool produced in the very constitution of the narrative for which it provides a space, but rather as an agent of erasure, consuming the narratives that enter into its space—symbolised in both cases by the onset of writer's block—to replace them with its own violent, destructive narratives.

BARTON FINK

"Why's it so goddamn hot out here?"

The Coen Brothers' 1991 film, *Barton Fink*, tells the story of its eponymous hero's journey from small-time New York political playwrite to contracted Hollywood hack, his time spent suffering from severe writer's block in his self-appointed prison (a small room in the seedy and rundown downtown Hotel Earle) and his even more agonising times spent with those he meets. Soon after his arrival in the Hotel Earle—motto: THE HOTEL EARLE: A DAY OR A LIFETIME—it becomes clear that Barton has checked into hell. This is apparent even before he enters into his room—which is so hot that the walls sweat until their coverings peel off—, before he discovers that he has a very thirsty mosquito for a roommate, and before his neighbour turns out to be a homicidal psychotic who murders Barton's one-night-stand whilst he is asleep next to her, only to entrust him with a package probably containing her head. Cutting from the paradisiacal vision of waves crashing against the Pacific shore, Barton is seen entering a hotel lobby with "*wilting potted palms, brass cuspidors turning green, ratty wing chairs,*" a style described as "*deco-gone-to-seed*" (Coen 2002, 407). The very epitome of faded grandeur, this hotel lobby has lost its capacity to dazzle those entering into its space with the

seductive spectacle of opulent surface. As a result, the disassembling of the
conjunctive synthesis and the revelation of the disjunctive synthesis that is the
preserve of the lobby is all the more marked. The directions continue:

> *Barton Fink enters frame from beneath the camera and stops in the middle
> foreground to look across the lobby.*
> *We are framed on his back, his coat and his hat. The lobby is empty. There is a
> suspended beat as Barton takes it in.*
> *Barton moves toward the front desk.*
>
> THE REVERSE
>
> *As Barton stops at the empty desk. He hits a small silver bell next to the register.
> Its ring-out goes on and on without losing volume.*
> *After a long beat there is the dull scuffle of shoes on stairs.*
> *Barton, puzzled, looks around the empty lobby, then down at the floor behind
> the front desk.*
>
> A TRAP DOOR.
>
> *It swings open and a young man in a faded maroon uniform, holding a shoe-
> brush and a shoe—not one of his own—climbs up from the basement.*
> *He closes the trap door, steps up to the desk and sticks his finger out to touch
> the small silver bell, finally muting it.* (Coen 407–408)

Totally alone in an empty space, Barton follows the prescribed order of the
lobby to the letter, miraculating himself to its surface, inscribing himself in
its disjunction. Since the dazzling, dissimulating glare of this surface is long
since tarnished, it is this very disjunction and its attendant consumption of the
individual entering into the disjunctive space which is apparent in this scene.
The intensified disjunction of this space is reinforced even in the soundtrack,
for the bell that Barton strikes (a summons to the desk clerk, the master of
inscription) rings on and on and on, creating a soundscape which highlights
the inherent nature of the space of the lobby (which—being disjunctive—
cares little for the individual passing through and is concerned ultimately
only with its own processing of that individual) since—up until the clerk's
appearance—there is no other noise to divert the auditor's attention away
from this sound of pure function. This lobby truly is hell, then, not because
its keeper appears from its depths, that is just a clue, but because it is a space
in which Barton has no choice but to set in motion this space's sole function,
to participate in those very transparent processes of territorialisation and inscription which consume him.

It is by no means solely the lobby which serves this purpose in the film,
however, for the hotel as a whole—as well as the formulaic Hollywood film-

making machine for which Barton has moved to Los Angeles—serves only to be consumed and to consume. Just as the hotel lobby explicitly foregrounds and deshrouds the axiomatics governing the apparently banal Capitalist machine, allowing access to a vision of hell, so the Hotel Earle, a seemingly innocuous space of the everyday, intensifies the everyday until the disjunction at its core is revealed in scenes of abjection. For Kristeva, abjection brings about a "massive and sudden emergence of uncanniness, which, familiar as it might have been in an opaque and forgotten life, now harries me as radically separate, loathsome" (Kristeva 1982, 2); for Barton, however, the abjection that he experiences, that which puts him "literally beside himself" (Kristeva 1982, 1), comes from the supposed everyday, the generic simulacrum of private space he has checked in to. In this manner, the 'home comforts' of Barton's room become persecutory: his bed is so soft that his suitcase is almost swallowed whole by it, his artificially ventilated room (the film is full of fans) is infernally hot, his window is so stiff that he almost falls through it as he yanks it open, and the decorative coverings that adorn his room slowly peel away from the walls to reveal their viscid mucous mucilage.

However, although this last aspect of his room comes close to a scene of true abjection, it is not until Barton meets his neighbour, Charlie Meadows (aka Karl Mundt, aka Madman Mundt), that abjection truly takes hold of Barton. The very epitome of the everyday, common man that Barton's 'real theatre' purports to be written about and for, the function of Charlie Meadows (the Hotel Earle's seemingly permanent resident, despite his frequent 'business' trips) is much like that of the hotel itself—and, indeed, Joel Coen has actually stated in interview that the hotel itself is "an exteriorization of the John Goodman character" (cited in Bergan 140). An archetype of the congenial working-class-salt-of-the-earth type, Charlie Meadows' actions frequently place Barton in the face of abjection. It is Charlie, a large, sweaty man approximately three times Barton's size and with a large wad of cotton wool in his ear to soak up the flow of pus from an ear infection, who shows Barton the basic wrestling moves in person, throwing and pinning him in two seconds flat; it is Charlie's cotton wool that Barton discovers in his overflowing sink shortly after this incident; and it is Charlie who thrusts Barton into the otherworldly space of abjection by slaughtering his bed partner.

It is not only Barton's love life that is dealt a serious blow by Charlie, however, for his creative life also suffers. This is not immediately apparent to Barton, for his conviction in his own artistic vision is so strong that he totally disregards the narrative of the everyday he is given the opportunity to explore—his original intention in checking into this downtown hotel being, of course, to get closer to and be inspired by the common man. This is clearly

illustrated in a scene where Barton discusses his profession as a writer with
Charlie:

BARTON: I'm a playwright. My shows've only played New York. Last one got
a hell of a write-up in the *Herald*. I guess that's why they wanted me here.

CHARLIE: Hell, why not? Everyone wants quality. What kind of venue, that is
to say, thematically, uh . . .

BARTON: What do I write about?

Charlie laughs.

CHARLIE: Caught me trying to be fancy! Yeah, that's it, Bart.

BARTON: Well, that's a good question. Strange as it may seem, Charlie, I guess
I write about people like you. The average working stiff. The common man.

CHARLIE: Well, ain't that a kick in the head!

BARTON: Yeah, I guess it is. But in a way that's exactly the point. There's a
few people in New York—hopefully our numbers are growing—who feel we
have an opportunity now to forge something real out of everyday experience,
create a theater for the masses that's based on a few simple truths—not on
some shopworn abstractions about drama that don't hold true today, if they
ever did . . .
He gazes at Charlie.
. . . I don't guess this means much to you.

CHARLIE: Hell, *I* could tell you some stories —

BARTON: And that's the point, that we all have stories. The hopes and dreams
of the common man are as noble as those of any king. It's the stuff of life—why
shouldn't it be the stuff of theater? Goddamnit, why should that be a hard pill
to swallow? Don't call it *new* theater, Charlie; call it *real* theater. Call it *our*
theater.

CHARLIE: I can see you feel pretty strongly about it.

BARTON: Well, I don't mean to get up on my high horse, but why shouldn't we
look at *ourselves* up there? Who cares about the Fifth Earl of Bastrop and Lady
Higgingbottom and—and—and who killed Nigel Grinch-Gibbons?

CHARLIE: I can feel my butt getting sore already.

BARTON: Exactly, Charlie! You understand what I'm saying—a lot more than
some of these literary types. Because you're a real man.

CHARLIE: And I could tell you some stories —

BARTON: Sure you could! And yet many writers do everything in their power
to insulate themselves from the common man—from where they live, from

where they trade, from where they fight and love and converse and—and—and
. . . so naturally their work suffers, and regresses into empty formalism and—
well, I'm spouting off again, but to put it in your language, the theater becomes
as phony as a three-dollar bill.

CHARLIE: Yeah, I guess that's a tragedy right there.

BARTON: Frequently played, seldom remarked.
Charlie laughs.

CHARLIE: Whatever that means.

Barton smiles with him. (Coen 2002, 423–425)

In this scene, Barton's discourse and his art are seen to be at a point of ultimate remove from the common man for whom he claims to speak. No matter
how much celebrity Barton's intellectualised conception of the function of
his art and of its service to the common man brought him in New York—the
epicentre of cultural (non-pragmatic) activity in the United States—, his artistic
manifesto ultimately crumbles beneath him in the spaces of the Hotel Earle and
Hollywood because they are spaces in which the everyday is intensified. The
erasure of Barton's narrative is manifold, therefore, for not only does he lose
himself in the anonymity of the hotel and become a cog in the Hollywood system, he is also robbed of his ability to write, the very same lines that made his
name in New York seeming hollow in his present context (Coen 2002, 444).

In the Hotel Earle and its spaces of generic simulacra, of an intensified version of the everyday, the fallacy on which Barton has based his career is thus
revealed. Barton, in turn, becomes unable to write, and it is only once he has
been informed—in the hotel lobby—of Charlie Meadows' true identity and
of the nature of his 'business trips' that he overcomes his writer's block in a
burst of frenetic creativity. An allegory for the violence inherent in the life of
the common man, Charlie's murders bring home to Barton for the first time
ever the downside of the existence he had idealised from his own privileged,
naïve, intellectual perspective. This news—as well as the comment concerning
Barton's Jewish origins from the harbinger of this revelation, "'I didn't think
this dump was restricted'" (Coen 2002, 496)—finally allows Barton to see that
commonality and the everyday are synonymous with divisive disjunction, and
to take Charlie up on his offer: "'Make me your wrestler. Then you'll lick that
story of yours'" (Coen 2002, 488). No longer attempting to write a generic
tale of everyday folk but an existential narrative of an individual's struggle,
Barton's screenplay does not go down well within the disjunctive space of
the Hollywood film system, as might be expected. On the contrary, the studio
boss Lipnik tells him in no uncertain terms that "'This is a wrestling picture;
the audience wants to see action, drama, wrestling and plenty of it. They

don't wanna see a guy wrestling with his soul—well all right, a little bit, for the critics—but you make it the carrot that wags the dog. Too much of it and they head for the exits and I don't blame 'em'" (Coen 2002, 518). More than this, however, when Barton protests "'I tried to show you something beautiful, something about all of *us*'" (Coen 2002, 519), Lipnik explodes:

> LIPNIK: You arrogant sonofabitch! You think you're the only writer who can give me that Barton Fink feeling?! I got twenty writers under contract that I can ask for a Fink-type thing from. You swell-headed hypocrite! You just don't get it, do you? You still think the whole world revolves around whatever rattles inside that little kike head of yours. Get him out of my sight, Lou. Make sure he stays in town, though; he's still under contract. I want you in town, Fink, and out of my sight. Now get lost. There's a war on. (Coen 2002, 519)

Like the Hotel Earle, the Hollywood film industry as seen here is a space of generic simulacra in which any writer under contract can, upon request, produce a facsimile copy of an individual narrative, a 'Fink-type thing'. Like the Hotel Earle, therefore, Hollywood is also, for Barton, a space of revelation. Barton's revelations lead not only to the completion (and rejection) of his script, however. They also lead to the culmination of *Barton Fink*'s, the film's, narrative, which is itself a revelation for the viewer of what has been implicit up until this point, namely, that the disjunctive spaces of the hotel and the common man's condition in Capitalist society are hell. As the following scene makes apparent, at the climax of the film, the Hotel Earle is transformed before the viewer's eyes into hell, a self-consuming space composed entirely of flames and abject horror which consumes everything within its realm:[4]

BARTON: Charlie's back. It's hot . . . He's back.
[. . .]
THE WALL
Tacky yellow fluid streams down. The walls are pouring sweat. The hallway is quiet.
[. . .]
Smoke is beginning to drift into the far end of the hall.
We hear a muted rumble.
[. . .]
LOW STEEP ANGLE ON ELEVATOR DOOR
The crack where the floor of the elevator meets that of the hall. It flickers with red light from below. Bottom-lit smoke sifts up.
[. . .]
The rumble and crackle of fire grows louder.

THE HALLWAY
More smoke.

PATCH OF WALL
Sweating.
A swath of wallpaper sags away from the top of the wall, exposing glistening lath underneath.
With a light airy pop, the lathwork catches fire.
[...]
The hallway. Its end—facing—wall slowly spreads flame from where the wall-paper droops.

LOW STEEP ANGLE ON ELEVATOR DOOR
More red bottom-lit smoke seeps up from the crack between elevator and hall-way floors.
With a groan of tension-relieved cables and a swaying of the elevator floor, a pair of feet crosses the threshold into the hallway.

JUMPING BACK
Wide on the hallway. Charlie Meadows has emerged from the elevator and is hellishly backlit by the flame.
His suit coat hangs open. His hat is pushed back on his head. From his right hand his briefcase dangles.
He stands motionless, facing us. There is something monumental in his posture, shoulders thrown back.
[...]
He straightens up from the briefcase, a sawed-off shotgun in his hands.
BOOM! The shotgun spits fire.
Mastrionotti's face is peppered by buckshot and he is blown back down the hallway into Deutsch.
Bellowing fills the hallway over the roar of the fire:

CHARLIE: LOOK UPON ME! LOOK UPON ME! I'LL SHOW YOU THE LIFE OF THE MIND!!

THE HALLWAY
The fire starts racing down the walls on either side.

CLOSE STEEP ANGLE ON PATCH OF WALL
Fire races along the wall-sweat goopus.

TRACK IN ON DEUTSCH
His eyes widen at Charlie and the approaching fire; his gun dangles forgotten from his right hand.
HIS POV
Charlie is charging down the hallway, holding his shotgun loosely in front of his chest, in double-time position. The fire races along with him.
He is bellowing:

CHARLIE: LOOK UPON ME! I'LL SHOW YOU THE LIFE OF THE MIND!
I'LL SHOW YOU THE LIFE OF THE MIND!

DEUTSCH
Terrified, he turns and runs.

REVERSE PULLING DEUTSCH
As he runs down the flaming hallway, pursued by flames, smoke, and Karl Mundt—who, also on the run, levels his shotgun.
BOOM!

PUSHING DEUTSCH
His legs and feet sprout blood, paddle futilely at the air, then come down in a twisting wobble, like a car on blown tires, and pitch him helplessly to the floor.

PULLING CHARLIE
He slows to a trot and cracks open the shotgun.

PUSHING DEUTSCH
Weeping and dragging himself forward on his elbows.

PULLING CHARLIE
He slows to a walk.

BARTON'S ROOM
Barton strains at his handcuffs

HIS POV
Through the open doorway we see Charlie pass, pushing two shells into his shotgun.

PULLING DEUTSCH
Charlie looms behind him and—THWACK—snaps the shotgun closed.
Deutsch rolls over to rest on his elbows, facing Charlie.
Charlie primes the shotgun—CLACK.
He presses both barrels against the bridge of Deutsch's nose.

CHARLIE: Heil Hitler.

DEUTSCH
Screams.

CHARLIE
Tightens a finger over both triggers. He squeezes.
BLAM. (Coen 2002, 506–512)

Far from being a gratuitous scene of Hollywood ultraviolence with a flippant reference to the very epitome of horror in the Twentieth Century, the end of this scene invokes Hannah Arendt's ideas on the banality of evil, establishing an equivalence between the ultimate evil of the Nazi régime and its attempts to create a uniform master race through the obliteration of the (primarily Jewish) Other, and the ultimate banality of the life of the common man within Capitalism, a banality which also attempts to dissimulate the infinite potential and diversity of humanity, to reduce the individual to a generic type.[5] That such is the case is clearly indicated by the final exchange between Barton and Charlie in which the latter is presented as the very epitome of the everyday man who suffers in that condition:

CHARLIE: . . . They say I'm a madman, Barton, but I'm not mad at anyone. Honest I'm not. Most guys I just feel sorry for. Yeah. It tears me up inside, to think about what they're going through. How trapped they are. I understand it. I feel for 'em. So I try to help them out . . .
He reaches up to loosen his tie and pop his collar button.
. . . Jesus. Yeah. I know what it feels like, when things get all balled up at the head office. It puts you through hell, Barton. So I help people out. I just wish someone would do as much for me . . .
He stares miserably down at his feet.
. . . Jesus, it's hot. Sometimes it gets so hot, I wanna crawl right out of my skin.

Self-pity

BARTON: But Charlie—why me? Why —

CHARLIE: Because you DON'T LISTEN!
A tacky yellow fluid is dripping from Charlie's left ear and running down his cheek.
. . . Jesus, I'm dripping again.
He pulls some cotton from his pocket and plugs his ear.
. . . C'mon Barton, you think you know about pain? You think I made your life hell? Take a look around this dump. You're just a tourist with a typewriter, Barton. I live here. Don't you understand that . . .
His voice is becoming choked:
And you come into *my* home . . . And you complain that *I'm* making too . . . much . . . noise.
He looks up at Barton.
There is a long silence.
Finally:

BARTON: . . . I'm sorry
Wearily:

CHARLIE: Don't be.
[. . .]
CHARLIE: I'm getting off this merry-go-round.
He takes his shotgun and walks to the door.
[. . .]
THE HALLWAY
As Barton emerges. Flames lick the walls, causing the wallpaper to run with the tacky glue sap. Smoke fills the hallway. Barton looks down the hall.

HIS POV
Charlie stands in front of the door to his room, his briefcase dangling from one hand, his other hand fumbling in his pocket for his key.
With his hat pushed back on his head and his shoulders slumped with fatigue, he could be any drummer returning to any hotel after a long hard day on the road. (Coen 2002, 513–515)

A descent into the *Inferno* constituted by the disjunction at the heart of the modern human condition, *Barton Fink*, in spite of its (black) humour, is by no means a *Commedia*, the *Paradiso* the main protagonist reaches at the end of the film being merely an exact replica of the paradisiacal picture postcard vision that has haunted him from his hotel-room wall throughout the film. A simulacrum of paradise, a holiday brochure image of manufactured pleasure, this scene would appear to have all the necessary ingredients to bring about an Adornian state of noetic anaesthesia and the ability to forget about everyday suffering. For Barton, such a luxury is no longer possible, however, for in the Hotel Earle, he has been privy to the disjunction that lies behind the conjunctive synthesis of all such apparent h(e)avens, and he is thus condemned to remain forever in the inferno.

THE SHINING

There are many respects in which Stanley Kubrick's 1980 film *The Shining*—adapted from the novel of the same name by Stephen King—is very similar to the Coen Brothers' film, for Jack Torrance also leaves his familiar surroundings to spend time in a hotel where he suffers from writer's block, meets a series of persecutory figures (although phantasmic in his case) and experiences the very depths of horror. What is more, Kubrick's *The Shining* can be seen to conceive of the space of the hotel lobby in a very similar way to the Coen Brothers' *Barton Fink*, for despite the fact that Jack Torrance occupies the hotel as an employee and not as a guest, his own narrative is, nonetheless, consumed by the hotel, overtaken by the history of the Overlook which becomes a setting for scenes of abjection that participate in the erasure of personal narrative.

Situated in the depths of the Colorado mountains, the Overlook Hotel closes for seven months of the year due to the extreme winter weather conditions. Jack Torrance and his family move into the hotel for these winter months, Jack having been hired as the winter caretaker. The isolation that comes with this job is, as he informs his future employer at the job interview, precisely what he is looking for since he is outlining a new writing project. This same isolation, however, also has the effect—as was the case in *Barton Fink*—of intensifying the conjunctive space of the hotel to reveal its essential disjunction. Emptied of its guests—its living, non-phantasmic guests, that is—the spaces of the Overlook are concentrated solely on Jack Torrance and his family over a prolonged period, rather than on a multitude of transient residents for short periods of time. Intensified in this way, rather than provide a 'home away from home' for Jack Torrance and his family—the conjunctive intent of any hotel's anodyne interiors, even when, as is the case in Kubrick's film, those interiors are shining examples of garish '70s interior design—, the family unit is ripped apart by the hotel's pseudo-familial spaces, the exclusive disjunctive syntheses of the latter replacing the connective syntheses of the former, the Overlook imposing a new order of hyper-dysfunctional family relations. Something similar is suggested by Thomas Allen Nelson when he writes,

> Symbolically, the Overlook Hotel becomes Jack's other Home and other Family, a nightmare world of dismemberment and alienation (where 'sliced peaches' and 'Heinz Ketchup' recall family massacres, not family meals), in which the mother and child are victims of the father's desire to cannibalize one family to ensure the 'survival' of another, to violate one home to resuscitate the corpse of another. (Nelson 1982, 217–218)

What is perhaps most remarkable and, indeed, most disturbing about this imposition of an apparently new family order characterised by disjunction and dysfunction, is the extent to which Kubrick portrays the violence of this new familial order in the original family unit. For Jack's descent into destructive madness is, although clearly delineated, a gradual one, perceived by the viewer privy to Jack's confession of violence against his son to a phantasmic bartender as merely the re-actualisation and intensification of a *pre-existing* destructive bent which, in itself, is fundamental to an understanding of the dynamic governing relations in the initial manifestation of the Torrance family. Within the intensified spaces of the hotel, therefore, it is not only the essential disjunction at the heart of the hotel which comes to light, but that at the heart of the modern-day family. The revelatory space of the hotel does not limit itself to deshrouding only these axiomatics of the everyday, however, for in Jack's final (and infamous) mania, as well as ironically mimicking an ideal of domestic bliss as he axes his way through a door to his wife ("Wendy, I'm *home*"), he also 'becomes' the Big Bad Wolf ("Little pigs, little pigs, let me in, not by the hair on your chinny chin chin; then I'll huff and I'll puff and I'll blow your house in") and Johnny Carson ("Heeeeeeere's Johnny"), thereby revealing the violent, divisive disjunction inherent in the conjunctive spaces of nursery rhymes and the corporate-run media.[6]

As in *Barton Fink*, this demystification of everyday axiomatics and its subsequent replacement of individual narratives with pseudo-individuated narratives is symbolised by a severe case of writer's block. Jack is rarely seen in the grip of his muse seeming to spend most of his time either sitting on his bed, staring blankly and threateningly into space, or throwing a tennis ball around in the Overlook's Colorado Lounge. Even when he does thrash away at the keys of his typewriter, it is revealed, in one of the late, revelatory passages of the film, that his 'writing' has consisted merely of the obsessive repetition of the mantra-like phrase, "all work and no play makes jack a dull boy"—a phrase which in itself highlights the disjunctive nature of Capitalism with its attendant commodification of human labour. Nelson sees the obsessive nature of Jack's manuscript as indicative of his denial of existential time in search of private time, surmising that, "in the end, *The Shining* concerns old projects and unfinished journeys, secret longings and frustrated desires, movements in reverse rather than movements forward, 'interviews' with the Self's dark but hardly imaginary friends" (Nelson 1982, 213). However, in light of the present argument, it would seem rather that it is not so much private time that is sought by Jack as it is pseudo-individual time, that *The Shining* is concerned not so much with interviews with the self as with the self's struggle with the imposition of surrogate selves and the erasure of personal narrative that the adoption of such identities entails.

This aspect of the film becomes most apparent in scenes containing supernatural events, somewhat unsurprisingly perhaps since the supernatural or uncanny might be thought of as an intensification of the everyday in which the ordinarily banal, its disjunction revealed, loses its anaesthetic effect. Indeed, as Freud has suggested, the conversion of *das Heimliche* into *das Unheimliche* "is in reality nothing new or foreign, but something familiar and old-established in the mind that has been estranged only by the process of repression" (Freud 1925, 394). In one such scene, Jack enters room 237's green bathroom to find a naked young woman who climbs out of her bath to embrace him, only to be transformed in his arms into an old woman covered in putrid green sores—a transformation which reveals the disjunction at the core of the banal act of love-making, a romantic dissimulation of the reproductive necessity of man's organic nature. Jack's initial reaction to this transformation is, as might be expected, to recoil in abject horror from this cackling hag. What is slightly more puzzling is his subsequent disavowal of these events, an act which erases personal narrative not only through denial, but also through the internalisation and sublimation of an abject reality.

Another supernatural event (which functions as a *leitmotif* throughout the film) can be found in the torrents of blood that are seen gushing out of the elevator door at various points in the narrative—an abject image if ever there was one. Although these rivers of blood may, as Bill Blakemore (1987; 1999) suggests, symbolise the colonial massacre of Native Americans—one of History's most extreme instances of narrative erasure—, Kubrick also employs this image to bring about the dissolution of the film's visual space, the spaces of the hotel being employed, therefore, not to spatialise narrative so much as to destroy it. Indeed, the blood that spills from between the (red) elevator doors not only consumes the space of the hotel as it sweeps away all in its wake, it also, as it surges, crests and splashes up against the camera, filling the entire frame, dissolves the visual space of the film—in which contrast and definition are pre-requisites for the construction of narrative—in a pure wash of colour.

The most significant supernatural event linked to narrative dissolution, however, comes as Jack and Grady (a waiter) retire to the Gold Room's red bathroom to clean some spilled advocaat off Jack's jacket. In this bathroom, there is some confusion as to the identity of the former caretaker, for whereas Jack thinks Grady is the caretaker (because of the coincidence of surname), Grady is categoric in his affirmation that, on the contrary, Jack is the caretaker and has always been. This confusion arises, of course, because there is no single caretaker, anybody is capable of being overtaken by the Overlook, of adopting the identity and function necessary for its maintenance—and, indeed, that of the Capitalist (or Imperial in Blakemore's analysis) machine for which the hotel is an intensified allegory. To do so, however, to take on such an identity is effectively to convert the self into a generic simulacrum, to erase individual narrative and history, a process which, in *The Shining*, results in the complete conflation of past and present temporalities. For the closing shot of the film shows Jack at the forefront of a group photograph taken at the Overlook Hotel's July 4th ball, 1921, over fifty years previous, that is to say, to the main diegesis.

LOBBY MUSIC

Ending with this revelatory image, *The Shining* does not, as Nelson suggests, enclose its audience aesthetically (Nelson 1982, 206). It does not leave the spectator—as it does Jack—a frozen, petrified figure trapped in a maze. Like the picture postcard image at the end of *Barton Fink*—a banal idyll displaced by the introduction into this scene of the package entrusted to Barton by Charlie—the close-up shot of the photograph with which *The Shining* closes—showing Jack's inimitable smile, both charming and diabolical— does not allow the viewer to lose him/herself in a space of reminiscence, this very image contravening the immutable laws of temporality on which the act of remembering is premised. Thus, in both *Barton Fink* and *The Shining*, the all too often banal space of the hotel is not merely an empty stage, a blank canvas waiting to be given meaning by a purposeful narrative, for its conjunctive space is intensified until its essential disjunction is revealed, a process which results in the onset of abjection and a subsequent annihilation of personal narrative. Rather than being filled with narrative, therefore, the space of the hotel in these films is genetic, the revelation with which both films end being produced by the very erasure of narrative effectuated in that space. Being produced in and by the intensified space of the hotel, however—a space which has been said to constitute the very disjunctive synthesis itself—, the narratives produced by these films are themselves narratives of disjunction, providing none of the answers or easy conclusions normally proffered by the invariably banal products of Hollywood. For these films' conclusions, whilst appearing to provide a conjunctive resolution, an interpretive key with which retrospectively to piece together the puzzle, utterly subvert such an expectation, refusing the pure function of a tidy ending, that 'feelgood factor'.[7]

Serving to reveal rather than reinforce or dissimulate the disjunctive synthesis on which the space of the hotel lobby is founded, it is perhaps significant that no music is heard in the Hotel Earle, whilst the music heard in the Overlook Hotel is not that which is usually associated with such spaces, namely, Muzak or 'elevator music',[8] but the discordant, atonal, syncopated strains of Béla Bartók, György Ligeti, Krzysztof Penderecki, Wendy Carlos and Rachel Elkin. For Muzak/elevator music might be said to create a space akin to that of the hotel lobby—when the latter is apprehended in its conjunctive role. A generic anodyne simulacrum stripped of individuality, an apparently banal everyday soundscape which hides an essential disjunction, Muzak is music as pure function, existing only as a means to convert the individual into consumer. As Bill Gifford notes:

> Business music must never aspire to be art. Business music functions as a design element, like a desk or a chair or a mural. Ideally, it makes workers work harder and shoppers buy more, without their noticing it. Muzak is meant to be heard but not listened to. 'If your head goes up to the ceiling' because of something you hear, says Muzak VP Bruce Funkhouser, 'we've blown it'. (Gifford 1995)

Similarly, Joseph Lanza writes:

> Muzak distinguished itself as an emotional buffer in otherwise intimidating environments by combining motivational psychology with the aesthetics of 'cash flow'. Instead of making music with the science of notation, scale, and time signatures in mind, Muscio used marketing terms that measured bottom-line impact over everything else. In 1967, he told the *Christian Science Monitor*: 'Muzak no longer thinks of itself as just nice, bland background music with no commercials. Today, we think of music as our raw material. Our service actually lies in its sequential arrangement to gain certain effects and to serve a functional purpose'. (Lanza 1995, 155)[9]

Muzak, then, like the hotel lobby, erases individual narrative to inscribe those within its space on its own surface, miraculating the individual to itself as a limitative body without organs, a Fascist attractor, "a weapon of total war", as Nick Groom has put it (1996, 11). Like the space of the hotel lobby in *Grand Hotel* which is pervaded by Muzak-like music (Lanza 1995, 55–56), the space of Muzak—when not intensified as it is in the work of Brian Eno, Angelo Badalamenti and the Aphex Twin, to name but a few—is, due to its very nature, stripped of intensity, the job of a Muzak arranger being to create a product "purified for mass-consumption", "not a single piece of music but a component of a larger whole, a brick in Muzak's wall of sound, [t]he differences between individual bricks [being] minimal, at best" (Gifford 1995). As Gifford notes:

> Arranging a song for Muzak is like cooking for 50 people. Suzuki [a Muzak arranger] has to please everyone to some degree, but it's more important that he offend nobody. His job is to take the edges off of songs. Vocals are removed and replaced by a suitably anonymous instrument, usually piano, guitar, woodwinds or vibes. Punchy rhythm parts are deflated a bit; distorted guitars and overly brassy horns are filed down. High, squeaky passages are lowered an octave, and dissonant chords are sweetened. (Gifford 1995)

Erasing narrative, inscribing the individual within its own disjunctive synthesis, Muzak—which, for Groom, is "necrophiliac", "more than a parasite [since it] smothers noise, reanimates it in a disgusting semblance of life" (Groom 1996, 11)—dissimulates its essential disjunction with a conjunctive synthesis, disallowing, like the hotel lobby, a critical perspective,[10] claiming to provide a sense of communality and shared experience. Lanza talks of this function in reverential tones, stating, "Years after surviving the golden age of 'individualism', we no longer have Huxley's luxury of bleating about the excesses of capitalist greed and centralized power. They are a fact of life: a fact that we are learning not only to accept but to enjoy" (Lanza 1995, 232). The most striking concrete example of this erasure of critical distance can be found in Lanza's description of the opening of the Empire State Building. He writes:

> All of the monstrous visions of gargoyle-lined skyscrapers (perfected in Fritz Lang's 1919 [sic] film *Metropolis*) came to life on May 31, 1931, when New York City unveiled the 102-story Empire State Building. Music had to be piped into the elevators, lobbies, and observatories to give people at least some illusion of continuity amid the disorder. (Lanza 1995, 39)

Intensifying the space of the hotel lobby to deshroud its divisive disjunction, refusing the 'feelgood factor' and preferring to revel in the abjection that these spaces should arouse, there is no room in *Barton Fink* or *The Shining* for Muzak or elevator music. Indeed, according to the findings of Cardinell's research into Muzak, it might be said that the aesthetic of Muzak (if this is not an oxymoron) constitutes the very antithesis of that of the Coen Brothers and especially that of Kubrick. Cardinell writes:

> Factors that distract attention—change of tempo, loud brasses, vocals—are eliminated. Orchestras of strings and woodwinds predominate, the tones blend-ing with the surroundings *as do proper colors in a room*. The worker should be no more aware of the music than of good lighting. The rhythms, reaching him subconsciously, create a feeling of well-being and eliminate strain. (Cardinell in Lanza 1995, 48; my emphasis)[11]

As similar as this may appear to Kubrick's view that "an audience should respond to a film through 'its feelings, not through any conscious analysis of what it has seen'", and that "film can only achieve the ambiguity and 'subconscious designating effect of a work of art' by communicating visually and through music rather than words" (Nelson 1982, 7), the difference be-tween the two lies in their respective intentions. For whereas Kubrick wishes to establish out of disjunction a connective synthesis between product and consumer, stating that "to deprive [the audience] of an intensive experience would be a sin" (Nelson 1982, 7), Muzak's very *raison d'être* is to provide a semblance of identification and communication, to establish a conjunctive synthesis that disables the individual, distracting her from her inscription on the surface of the Capitalist machine, "sopping up our random, private thoughts like super-efficient sponges. Thoughts which, it sometimes seems, are too much to bear," as Gifford puts it. Lanza seems to welcome such noetic anaesthesia, concluding his book in the following manner:

> Elevator music (besides just being good music) is essentially a distillation of the happiness that modern technology has promised. A world without elevator music would be much grimmer than its detractors (and those who take it for granted) could ever realize. This is because most of us, in our hearts, want a world tailored by Walt Disney's 'imagineers', an ergonomical 'Main Street U.S.A.', where the buildings never make you feel too small, where the act of paying admission is tan-tamount to a screen-test—and where the music never stops. (Lanza 1995, 233)

This utopian dream will hopefully seem to some more akin to a vision of hell, for if the hotel lobby is hell, then Muzak is its soundtrack. It is true, therefore, that the devil gets all the best tunes, but look what he does to them!

NOTES

1. Whilst brief explications of Deleuze and Guattari's disjunctive, conjunctive and connective syntheses will be attempted here, readers unfamiliar with these terms

might wish to refer to Brian Massumi's excellent explanations (Massumi 1992, 47–52).

2. Kracauer (1995, 176) writes: "The lobby, in which people find themselves *vis-à-vis de rien*, is a mere gap that does not even serve a purpose dictated by *Ratio* (like the conference room of a corporation), a purpose which at the very least could mask the directive that had been perceived in the relation."

3. "The body without organs is not God, quite the contrary. But the energy that sweeps through it is divine, when it attracts to itself the entire process of production and serves as its miraculate, enchanted surface, inscribing it in each and every one of its disjunctions" (Deleuze and Guattari, 1984, 13).

4. Abjection can be said to provide a space of consumption since, as Kristeva (1982, 10) writes, by entering into the space of the abject, the subject enters into that reality which, "si je la reconnais, m'annihile".

5. Arendt (1958; 1963). There are, of course, further invocations to Arendt's work in Charlie Meadow's demonic mantra as he charges down the hotel corridors (see above, p. 265) which recalls the title of Arendt's 1978 work, *The Life of the Mind*.

6. Most nursery rhymes have a cautionary function, serving to repress certain modes of behaviour in children, and one need only turn to Chomsky or Barthes to understand that the corporate media and its attendant banality is designed to perform the same function on adults and children alike.

7. This is perhaps why Kubrick refuses to give his film the same ending as the King novel in which the hotel, as in *Barton Fink*, is consumed by flames, this ending being prepared for throughout the novel and the film by repeated mention of the old boiler's pressure problem. Even with Kubrick's altered finale, however, the hotel can still be said to consume itself, to sink into its own disjunction, since having fully erased his own personal narrative and internalised that of the hotel, Jack is effectively killed by the hotel, being unable to find his way out of its maze.

8. It is pointless squabbling over exact terminology and the fact that Muzak is in fact a trademarked company title since, as Gifford (1995) notes, "within a decade after Muzak, Inc. was founded in 1934, its name had entered general usage as a [common] noun, the way Kleenex, Xerox, and Rollerblade have since."

9. Lanza (1995, 48) also quotes the results of Cardinell's research which states that, "'In some cases, it is possible to achieve a direct production increase by playing a program which completely ignores employee preferences and concentrates on the functional aspects only.'"

10. On the hotel lobby as a space which does not allow a groundless distance from the everyday, see *infra.*, p. 257. The similar function of Muzak is talked of by Nick Groom (1996, 10) in the following terms: "Muzak has created an architecture for us, it has engineered cities of sound. Silence is unthinkable—the absence of Muzak, but because Muzak has no end, no critical perspective is possible."

11. Some may contest the opposition made here to Kubrick's aesthetic in light of the director's comment that, as Nelson (1982, 7) notes, "'a preoccupation with originality of form is more or less a fruitless thing' and that if he had to choose between a film maker like Eisenstein ('all style, no content') and one like Chaplin ('all content, no style'), he would take Chaplin'." However, even the most cursory

examination of any of Kubrick's films cannot but reveal such comments to be utterly disingenuous.

REFERENCES

Arendt, Hannah. *The Human Condition*. Chicago: University of Chicago Press, 1958.

——. *Eichmann in Jerusalem: A Report on the Banality of Evil*. London: Faber and Faber, 1963.

——. *The Life of the Mind*. 2 vols. London: Secker & Warburg, 1978.

Bergan, Ronald. *The Coen Brothers*. London: Phoenix, 2001.

Blakemore, Bill. 'The family man' *The San Francisco Chronicle* (July 29, 1987), reproduced at http://www.visual-memory.co.uk/amk/doc/0052.html (accessed 22 February 2008).

Coen, Joel and Coen Ethan. *Collected Screenplays Volume 1: Blood Simple, Raising Arizona, Miller's Crossing, Barton Fink*. London: Faber and Faber, 2002.

Deleuze, Gilles and Guattari, Félix. *Anti-Oedipus: Capitalism and Schizophrenia* (trans Robert Hurley, Mark Seem and Helen R. Lane). Minneapolis: University of Minnesota Press, 1983.

Freud, Sigmund. 'The Uncanny.' pp. 219–252 in *The Standard Edition of the Complete Works of Sigmund Freud, Volume XVII*, edited by James Strachey. London: Hogarth Press/Institute of Psychoanalysis, 1953–1974.

Gifford, Bill. 'They're playing our songs' *FEED* (Oct 1995) http://www.feedmag .com/95.10gifford1.html (accessed March 1 2001)

Groom, Nick. 'The Condition of Muzak' *Popular Music and Society* 20 no. 3 (1996): 1–17.

Katz, Marc. 'The Hotel Kracauer' *differences: A Journal of Feminist Cultural Studies* 11 no. 2 (July 1999): 134–152.

Kracauer, Siegfried. 'The Hotel Lobby.' pp. 173–185 in *The Mass Ornament: Weimar Essays*. Translated by Thomas Y. Levin. Cambridge: Harvard University Press, 1995.

Kristeva, Julia. *Powers of Horror: an Essay on Abjection* (trans. Leon S. Roudiez). New York: Columbia University Press, 1982.

Lanza, Joseph. *Elevator Music: A Surreal History of Muzak, Easy-listening and Other Moodsong*. London: Quartet Books, 1995.

Massumi, Brian. *A User's Guide to 'Capitalism and Schizophrenia': Deviations from Deleuze and Guattari*. Cambridge, MA: MIT Press, 1992.

Nelson, Thomas Allen. *Kubrick: Inside a Film Artist's Maze*. Bloomington: Indiana University Press, 1982.

Tallack, Douglas. '"Waiting, Waiting": The Hotel Lobby, in the Modern City,' pp. 139–151 in *The Hieroglyphics of Space: Reading and Experiencing the Modern Metropolis* edited by Neil Leach. London: Routledge, 2002.

Chapter Ten

Parallel Hotel Worlds

Yvette Blackwood

Mike/Gerard: A large house made of wood surrounded by trees.
The house is filled with many rooms, each alike.
But occupied by different souls, night after night.

Dale Cooper: The Great Northern Hotel!

Twin Peaks (1990)

If we consider the structure of the hotel—a structure with the communal space of the lobby, then individual rooms connected via walls and a corridor—we are already presented with the framework of parallel worlds. For some time, the idea of the hotel existing as a miniature world or parallel universe in either tension or symmetry with the city outside has been articulated in theory, literature, and film. Through the films examined in this chapter, I argue that the hotel is the exemplary model for contemporary narratives that require multiple stories. There are two parts to this argument. Firstly, films such as Jim Jarmusch's *Mystery Train* (1989) use the structure of the hotel's rooms to tell stories of multiple lives. The 'hotelization' of narrative is the way in which multiple stories and disconnected lives can be housed within a single, connecting framework. Sofia Cappola's *Lost in Translation* (2003) similarly uses the hotel for the organising arc of a story about two lonely Westerners in Tokyo. Secondly, the chapter focuses on David Lynch's television series *Twin Peaks* (1990) and his film *Lost Highway* (1997), which use the hotel to express postmodern concerns with identity, text, location, and subjectivity. The struggle to navigate the hotel in Lynch's work is emblematic of the struggle to locate the self in postmodernity, where self is not seen as reflection, but via proximity.

It can be argued that what we see through the dominance of hotels in film is the death of character, and the birth of space. The hotel becomes a character in its own right. Conversely, individual characters become increasingly abstract, multiple and difficult to grasp. Both Lynch's characterisation and Bill Murray's character in *Lost in Translation* demonstrate this depersonalisation. Thus, new spaces not only give rise to new narratives, as Franco Moretti concludes in *Atlas of the European Novel*, but also to a new form of characterisation. Both the psychic and social structure of the hotel make it a vital organising principle of multiple, parallel narratives.

Lynch emphasises space over personalised characterisation. At the same time, space—particularly hotel space—is an allegory of contemporary subjectivity. Space and subjectivity have long been entwined, and de Certeau (1984) argues that each successful negotiation of space is a renegotiation of the mirror stage (Lacan, 1977). But what happens when space is not successfully negotiated? What impact does this have on subjectivity? Postmodern spaces, particularly hotel spaces, articulate the new form of the mirror stage Anthony Vidler writes of in *Warped Space*. No longer, Vidler claims, is the contemporary self

> committed to split identity, not only as between imago and I, but also between two imagos, so to speak, blurred and morphed into a distorted physiognomy that is far from transparent or clear, but rather opaque and translucent. It would be as if this subject were truly lost in space, wandering vaguely in a state of continuous psychasthenia, disguising itself as space in space, ready to be devoured by the very object of its fear. (Vidler 2001, 245)

He argues that Lacan's mirror stage can no longer be taken at face value (pun intended): the replacement for the Lacanian mirror today is the screen—the omnipresent flat surface in postmodernity. Thus, Vidler (2001, 245) argues, "We [are] dealing with a subject whose imago was screened and projected back to it, not as reflection but as scanned image." The split in subjectivity, where the subject sees itself as scanned image, not reflection, does not belong solely to the world of postmodern science fiction such as *The Matrix*. It is present in slipstream narratives, and the hotel, as a consequence of its social and architectural structure, is the apparatus in which this new kind of parallel (asymmetrical) subjectivity is contained.

Kracauer (1999, 290) raises the image of the hotel as housing parallel worlds when he describes the hotel lobby in detective fiction as a "negative church." He argues that "togetherness in the hotel lobby has no meaning" (Kracauer 1999, 291) because the hotel distances individuals both from "actual life" and from other human beings. The hotel as inversion of the church means that not only are individuals detached from one another, they are coming together not to worship God as in a church, but to serve the self:

> This limit case "we" of those who have dispossessed themselves of themselves—a "we," realised vicariously in the house of God owing to human limitations—is transformed in the hotel lobby into the isolation of anonymous atoms. (Kracauer 1999, 295)

The many unfamiliar faces and disconnected people in the hotel lobby (but united by space) raise the image of the hotel as a space that gathers disconnected souls together. It is a microcosm where an infinite number of individual worlds collide, but Kracauer argues that these worlds remain alienated from each other.

Kracauer's argument concurs with Marc Augé's (1995) theory of non-places as characteristic of supermodernity. In his opening vignette, Augé refers to exactly the same convergence of individuals at the airport: "thousands of individual itineraries converged for a moment, unaware of one another" (1995, 3). Together, Kracauer and Augé's theories of disconnected individuals in non-places (spaces such as airports, highways, and hotels—spaces designed for moving through) point towards the idea of individual monads, individual worlds that sit together, and are sometimes forced to connect, like guests dwelling in hotel rooms. Kracauer's reference to anonymous atoms in an inverted church is akin to the Deleuze's idea that "Every monad thus expresses the entire world, but obscurely and dimly because it is finite and the world is infinite" (2004, 86). Augé's account of "thousands of individual itineraries converged for a moment" is also homologous with Deleuze's monad. Yet, because of the structure of hotel, the individual itineraries of each monad are frequently forced to open up, to connect with another life or another world: this is precisely what is at work in *Lost in Translation*.

Ideas of parallel lives and parallel narratives certainly predate postmodernity. The polyphonic novel (Bakhtin's term) has long been a dominant narrative form in both literature and film. As Ian Buchanan points out, the polyphonic novel may have been the inspiration for Deleuze's concept of the assemblage:

> The assemblage is a structure, which, like the novel, is able to articulate the slide into oblivion of one model of thought together with the rise to dominance of another without having to explain it in terms of either succession or negation, but can instead stage it as a co-adaption. (Buchanan 2000, 118)

The structure of parallel hotel narratives operates in the same way: we see the slide between narratives in *Mystery Train*, for example, operating via place (hotel) and sounds within the hotel.

David Harvey argues that fragmentation of subjectivity through shifting space is a significant part of postmodern theory and narratives, and quite frequently films project these concerns of fragmented subjectivity onto the hotel (*Barton Fink* and *The Shining* are examples of these). Harvey (1989, 291) also reminds us of the time-space compression that accompanies post-modernity, where the "temporal contract in everything . . . then becomes the hallmark of postmodern living." Harvey sees this temporality affecting everything, "from novel writing and philosophizing to the experience of la-bouring or making a home." Fragmented thought, anxiety over place-identity, and a compression of space and time mean that the hotel is a principal space in which these complexities and shifts are played out. And the hotel space provides the framework, the beginning and the end, for these complexities.

The influence of space on narrative construction is also considered by Franco Moretti. Moretti (1999, 5) describes "literary maps" that highlight the "place-bound nature of literary forms: each of them with its particular geom-etry, its boundaries, its spatial taboos and favourite routes. And then, maps bring to light the internal logic of narrative: the semiotic domain around which a plot coalesces and self-organises." Moretti argues that certain spaces give rise to certain kinds of narratives. A new space encourages paradigm shifts because "it poses new problems—and so asks for new answers" (Moretti 1999, 196). Whilst the hotel is not, strictly speaking, a new space, Moretti's analysis of the influence of space in narrative concurs with my own argument that hotel narratives are shaped by the hotel, that narratives are 'hotelized' by the space. Hence parallel lives and parallel narratives are ideally framed by hotels. Parallel lives have been depicted in compartmentalised spaces prior to postmodernism. The opening scene of Hitchcock's *Rear Window* reveals parallel lives in one clear shot: the viewer follows James Stewart's gaze as he watches the multiple lives of the apartment building next door.

Slavoj Žižek (2005, 205) argues that the "natural progression" of the paral-lel worlds found in Hitchcock—the individual apartments in the block James Stewart gazes on in *Rear Window*—is towards science-fiction narratives like *The Matrix* (2005, 205). This argument is refuted in this chapter. Rather, the multiple narratives and worlds found in Lynch's hotel-based films sit between the Hitchcockian parallel worlds and science-fiction. The parallel worlds have moved from Hitchcock's apartment block to the hotel—this is movement by the smallest margin, but movement nonetheless. Rather than the apartment block, the hotel, with its emphasis on the mobilized and virtual gaze, and its centrality to postmodern everyday life, is the natural home for two kinds of multiple narratives: first, it houses the multiple worlds and lives of the polyphonic story; second, it houses multiple subjects and multiple realities. In Lynch's stories, the hotel is a space that is at once real and unreal — that is, a space in which the characters are physically present and sometimes disembodied, sometimes someone else entirely. The hotel in Lynch's work is folded space, in accordance with Deleuze's and Leibniz's notion of the fold. It is space that is placed onto other spaces, is entered 'unnaturally' and is interior through and through. Importantly, the kinds of parallels that are presented in these hotel worlds are asymmetrical ones. This suggests a rhizomic understanding of self and other, reality and unreality. But this complication of reality and unreality is clearly framed by the hotel.

MYSTERY TRAIN'S PARALLEL NARRATIVES

Jarmusch's *Mystery Train* operates as a 'hotelized' narrative. *Mystery Train* is divided into three stories, located in three rooms of a run-down hotel. Each narrative is connected in both space and time by pictures of Elvis in the guest rooms, the sound of the song *Blue Moon* on the radio late at night, and the sound of a gunshot in one of the hotel rooms early the next morning. These noises and images run like a spine through the narrative, like a corridor that connects the disparate stories for the viewer and to some extent the other characters. Each character is like a monad, experiencing disconnection from those closest to them. Knowledge and understanding of others is like the hotel itself, where meaning lies just behind the wall.

The search for connectedness in contemporary culture is present throughout *Mystery Train*, and is simultaneously contained and undone via the hotel. The first strand of *Mystery Train* follows two teenage Japanese tourists travelling to Memphis as Elvis fans. They arrive on the train and slowly make their way to a run-down hotel in the city. Slow, wide shots depict the couple walking the dirty streets of Memphis. Many of the shots are taken up by the wide sky and linear footpaths, emphasising the emptiness of the space, which in turn serves as a contrast to the dark, confined, dingy hotel room the couple eventually reach. They comment on the similarities between Memphis and Yokohama: "You know, Memphis does look like Yokohama. Just more space. If you took away sixty percent of the buildings in Yokohama, it would look like this." This statement expresses the urge to find connections between space abroad and at home, regardless of the tenuousness of the link between the two. In the hotel room, the couple find parallels between images of Elvis, Buddha, Madonna and the Statue of Liberty. Again, these searches for connections between vastly disconnected icons highlight the complex

Figure 10.1 *Mystery Train*
© 1989 Mystery Train Inc.; photo Sukita

relations in postmodernity between the universal and the particular (Figure 10.1).

This tendency towards facialisation, finding faces in abstract or inanimate objects (or in this case, finding the same facial features in icons), is symptomatic of a search for the universal. This takes place in a city that is filmed as alienating, uninteresting, disappointing, and fundamentally *dis*connecting.

Isolation permeates the three stories in *Mystery Train*, despite the close proximity in which friends, lovers, and strangers find themselves. Connectedness is sought out through external objects such as the landscape and the iconic images, but there is a vast gulf between the two teenagers in the hotel room, as they lie together after unexciting sex, with the boy asking the girl about hairstyles. At this point, *Blue Moon* is heard on the radio for the first time for the audience. The lyrics of *Blue Moon* are heard three times in the diegesis of the film, as though the content points directly to the isolation experienced in all three narratives: 'You saw me standing alone, without a dream in my heart, without a love of my own.' The smooth tones of Tom Waits as the radio announcer emphasises the paradox of intimacy in postmodernity: his voice is present, tender, directly connecting to the listener, but he is simultaneously connecting with everyone and no one. This complex, depersonalised relationship that is present between radio announcer and listener is emblematic of the other relationships in the hotel: they are intimate because of proximity, but metaphysically distant.

In the first story Jun takes a picture of the hotel room from several angles. Mitzuko asks:

> Jun, why do you only take pictures of the rooms we stay in and never what we see outside while we travel?

> *Jun:* Those other things are in my memory. The hotel rooms and the airports are the things I'll forget.

Jun's comments here unconsciously refer to Benjamin's early modernist argument that architecture is rendered invisible by everyday usage (Vidler, 2001, 64). The sameness and blandness of the hotel rooms are emphasised as the forgettable moments of travel.

Like the first story, the other two stories in the film emphasise disconnection. In the second story, two women are forced together in a hotel room. An Italian tourist has an overnight stop in Memphis on the way back to Rome with her recently deceased husband. The woman she shares a room with (Dee Dee) is on the run from her husband, Johnny, who is in the next room of the hotel. In this room lies the third story: Johnny, Charlie and Will are drunk, and take the room for the night after accidentally holding up a liquor store, at one point listening to *Blue Moon* on the car radio. Escaping from the police, the men seek refuge in the hotel. It is their gun that is accidentally fired in the hotel room early in the morning, finally solving the mystery of the gunshot heard in the first two stories. The gunshot wounds one of them, causing them to leave the hotel and flee in their truck. In the hotel Johnny laments his estrangement from Dee Dee, and as the night progresses, and the men drink more and commit a crime, they alienate themselves from society.

In the final scene of *Mystery Train* we see the double articulation of the intersection of the three stories, where they are all interconnected in the one place (again) at the same time: the characters in the third story speed off in a red truck that drives through an underpass, over which the train containing the characters in the first and second stories speeds out of Memphis. A police car, searching for the red truck, sails past, heading in the opposite direction. Thus the road, train, and hotel serve as chronotopes: the road at the end of the film confirms the way in which the hotel is able to house a polyphonic narrative. For a moment, the road is able to contain all the narratives in one space, but for an entire night, the hotel has done this.

Present in Jarmusch's film is a continuous spatial experience, but disconnected characters. The hotel forces the film's three narratives to intersect, but only at the level of space. There is an absence of intimacy and meaningful relationships in between both the lovers and strangers in this film. Displaced souls are forced at various points to interact (in the second story, for example), but the only real connection experienced is through space and sound in the hotel.

INTIMACY IN SUPERMODERNITY:
LOST IN TRANSLATION

Lost in Translation reverses *Mystery Train*'s East/West tourist story, and, indeed, reverses the absence of intimacy in the hotel. The two protagonists in *Lost in Translation*, Bob (Bill Murray) and Charlotte (Scarlett Johansson), are Western outsiders in an Asian country. Both Charlotte and Bob feel alienated in Tokyo. Charlotte is a philosophy graduate in her mid 20s and Bob is a tired TV star in his early 50s/late 40s. Both are reluctant visitors to Tokyo, and as they form a friendship, they analyse their own lives in a place they seem to loathe—the hotel. Yet it is only in a hotel that such characters are able to be on an equal footing, because the hotel does not confer identity. In this way, the hotel deterritorializes Charlotte and Bob, removing them from their homes, the possessions that surround them (particularly relevant to Bob and his material wealth), their families (even though Charlotte's husband is present in Tokyo, the point of the film is that he is emotionally and physically absent), and their standing in their respective communities. The same absence of territory is present in the Tokyo hotel. Both Charlotte and Bob have the neutral but elevated grounding of guest; theirs is an encounter that would be impossible without the space of the hotel.

The plot of *Lost in Translation* is not particularly complex. Rather, the emphasis lies on space and character in this film. The story is simple: Bob arrives in Tokyo to film a whisky commercial for two million dollars. Charlotte is a young philosophy graduate staying in the same hotel, killing time while her husband works as a photographer. The distance between Charlotte and her husband, and Bob and his wife (on the phone), is acute throughout the film. Bob and Charlotte meet in the hotel bar, both unable to sleep, and they begin their intimate 'affair,' their friendship. It is certainly an unusual friendship, just as the film in its quietness and lack of climax, lack of sex and 'big' story, is an unusual narrative. This old-fashioned narrative is, however, located in supermodernity, using the paradigm of the hotel as an allegory of isolation and loneliness. At the same time, the film contains sentiments that are in many ways modern rather than supermodern. The kind of chance meeting/ instant attraction is played with in this film, as are the Benjaminesque moves through phantasmagorical spaces.

The chance meeting in the hotel occurs between two unlikely characters: the characterisation of Bob confirms the idea that place and identity (or the lack of these) are entwined. In this film, non-place houses non-personal protagonists. Bob is not an individual character, corresponding to Jameson's (1995, 176) argument that the category of individual character is now "outmoded." The hotel is in a sense, then, a character-system assemblage, a single object that is able to articulate an image of a certain kind of characterisation, or rather, an absence of it. Similar depersonalisation is at work in Lynch's narratives.

Bill Murray's character in *Lost in Translation* confirms the idea that the hotel is a character-system assemblage. This idea is another way of expressing a wider argument, that the hotel is an analogon of postmodernity. The assemblage is able to co-adapt the apparent contradictions of the traditional and the modern. The complex hotel space in *Lost in Translation*, with its parallel depiction of old and new, and its depiction of physical discomfort yet emotional awakening, can be aligned with Bob. Just as Bob is deindividualized, the hotel is personalised. As a character-system assemblage, the hotel space provides the organising arc for a film that does not contain a thrilling, twisting plot. The film embodies Augé's idea of solitude in supermodernity but then turns the hotel, a non-place, into a space that contains the possibility of intimacy between two people who would otherwise not meet. Given that Sofia Coppola's narrative is so gentle (exploring partly her own marriage breakdown and partly her obsession with Bill Murray), the hotel is the only aspect of the film that lends it shape and consistency. It organizes the plot as well as the lives of Bob and Charlotte, much like the hotels that frame the narratives of *Barton Fink* and *The Shining*. In the end, both characters in *Lost in Translation* leave the hotel: Bob is returning to America, and Charlotte is exploring the streets again. Bob sees Charlotte from his taxi and runs to her. They kiss in the crowded street with the sun setting in the background, and then he returns to his taxi. It is an old-fashioned ending to a supermodern tale. Whilst the final scenes of the film do not take place in the hotel, it is the hotel that has provided the framework for the beginning and the end — the arrival and departure — of the narrative.

Cinematic convention often dictates opening a scene with a brief establishing shot. However, the audience is not granted an establishing shot of the hotel at the beginning of *Lost in Translation*. An establishing shot would place the hotel firmly and clearly in the city, and would outline the building for the audience. We do not see a clear external shot of the Park Hyatt Tokyo as Bob enters it. Whilst the narrative begins and ends with his arrival, this arrival is shot much like the arrival of the central character in Godard's *Alphaville*: all we see is the car pull up to the door of the hotel. *Barton Fink* also avoids an external shot of the Hotel Earle. The effect of the absent establishing shot is that it creates the hotel as assemblage. Indeed, the hotel is not even located on the ground floor in *Lost in Translation*. Bob is greeted on both the ground floor of the building and the hotel floor, with gifts and formalities.

There are multiple ways of entering the hotel. This enables rhizomic possibilities and connectedness to the city, which on the surface is alienating, but the characters and camera delight in it, just as they delight in the contradictory and historical Japan that lies around the corner from the hotel. The rhizomic city adheres to Barthes' description of Tokyo, which "offers this precious paradox: it does possess a centre, but this centre is empty. The entire city turns around a site both forbidden and indifferent" (1982, 30). The hotel in *Lost in Translation* becomes much more entwined with the city when not filmed as a separate entity. Like the cityscape outside, the hotel in this film sets itself up (or is set up) to be alienating, but it ends up not being alienating at all. The hotel indeed mimics the parallel worlds of supermodern and traditional Tokyo, beautifully conveyed when Charlotte wanders around the hotel, finding in one room a shallow American actress giving a press conference, and in the other, Japanese women doing traditional flower arranging. Again, the hotel provides the model for parallel worlds and parallel lives through its architecture that is freely moved through, corresponding to the concept of the assemblage, where one mode of existence can slide freely into another.

The hotel in this and countless other modern and postmodern films flattens the differences that would typically occur between the two protagonists. Two characters that would never normally meet now find themselves running into each other in robes heading to and from the pool, or in the bar, or in the lobby. So the hotel space throws them into intimacy. This is something both Charlotte and Bob find surprising, as their initial encounters with the hotel are alienating, but it is only through this supermodern space that intimacy between the two can occur, through the passageways, bars, and rooms. The fascination of this encounter stems from the presumption of solitude in nonplaces. Whilst destiny is a common Hollywood theme, the intimacy that occurs between Bob and Charlotte is strictly emotional and conversational, and it is a relationship based on a span of ten days. Their surprise at this unusual encounter comes from an occidental Western attitude, where there is little expectation of being in company in a foreign country. Thus there is a reversal of expected alienation in the hotel.

The protagonists struggle to reterritorialize space and find homeliness in supermodernity. Prior to the encounters and exchanges with Bob, Charlotte has led a solitary existence in Tokyo. At one point she cries when recounting her day to a friend on the phone because she was unable to feel anything when she saw an ancient Buddhist ceremony being performed. Charlotte cries because she is unable to feel deeply and meaningfully at an apparently 'authentic' spiritual moment. Charlotte attempts to create a home in her hotel room, confirming Augé's argument that non-places are alienating. She spends a great deal of time in her room; many shots are repeated of Charlotte sitting around the hotel room in her underpants, smoking cigarettes and gazing out of the window at the city beneath her. She is watching it but is not able to participate in it. Early in the film she tries to create territory, to create home in the hotel room through decorating it with plastic pink cherry blossoms, but when her husband returns, he does not seem to notice. And rather than create a comfortable space, it just seems to add to the mess in the hotel room. It certainly does not make Charlotte any more comfortable about being in Tokyo. This does not happen through the pink cherry blossom, but through an exchange of sightseeing, drinks and meals with Bob. They reterritorialise Tokyo in this way.

When Bob arrives he has his defences up and he loathes Tokyo, and does not seem interested at first in reterritorialising the hotel space. He loathes home too. This is quickly established through the faxes and phone calls between him and his wife that revolve around her ideas for redecorating his study. Whilst Bob is disappointed by home, he is also initially alienated by Tokyo and the hotel. He is truly in a non-place, a state of existence where he is not comfortable at home or away. His face gestures towards nostalgia, but for what? For what hasn't been? He poses nostalgically at the camera when filming the whisky commercial in a dinner suit, saying "For relaxing times, make it Santori times." Bob, however, does not seem nostalgic for much at home, except of course his children, he tells Charlotte. Bob's physical and emotional alienation is manifested in his first few hours in the hotel. Initially, nothing sits comfortably. The television, usually a source of comfort and solace in hotel rooms, usually some marker of sameness (at least American-ness, via CNN), is alienating. The television channels range from an in-house channel of tulips in a field, to a talk show with a crazy host, to repeats of Bob's infamous '70s television show. Bob goes to the hotel bar at 4 a.m. as he can't sleep, and is recognised by two drunken businessmen who want to talk to him about his old show. When they ask him what he's doing in Tokyo, Bob tells them he is "visiting friends"—hardly the reality of his overpaid, but apparently humiliating, job of shooting a whisky commercial. In telling the businessmen he's "visiting friends," Bob is attempting to create a territory around him within Tokyo, within the hotel, but he lacks strength to do so effectively. It is only when he meets a similarly displaced figure, Charlotte, that he is able to draw a territory around himself, and also reterritorialise his space through his relationship with her. They are able to exchange insights and intimacies and they reterritorialise the hotel rooms and indeed Tokyo by this exchange. This is shown cinematically in the frequent close-ups on the bed. A middle-aged man and young woman (both unhappily married) chat on a hotel-room bed, drink saké and watch television. But they don't have sex. Bob and Charlotte exchange various details about their lives, their ambitions, how Bob feels about his wife and children, how Charlotte feels about her husband and her future. In this way, Bob and Charlotte exchange not only self-knowledge, but their worlds. They exchange not gifts or sexual pleasure but information. This shared information comes to stand for the home they create together in an alienating city.

Small spaces—particularly the elevator and the bed—operate as miniature versions of the hotel, reinforcing the possibilities of intimacy. It is appropriate that in an encounter located in supermodernity the first glances between Charlotte and Bob happen in the hotel elevator. An elevator is always the ultimate chronotope. It is a space about time (hopefully just minutes), and a space about other spaces: it is one of the smallest and fastest forms of Bakhtin's chronotope. It compresses both time and space. The scene where Bob and Charlotte meet also gestures towards racism: Bob (being head and shoulders above the others in the elevator) glances over at the only other white person in the elevator and smiles at her. This is a break in the silent starring ahead that usually occurs in elevators. Those in the elevator are like the individual monadic supermodern characters to which Augé refers, on the same silent journeys through non-place. As if to compound the artificiality of supermodern space, the whoosh of the suction of the hydraulic doors is emphasised, sounding like a science-fiction effect. Bob's smile to Charlotte is a break in flat, immobile elevator experience. The "profound immobility in the technological world" usually depicted in science fiction, according to Vidler (2001, 246), is unexpectedly also depicted here. This immobility and flattening of reality is present for Vidler in air-conditioned, muffled offices, but is also clearly evident in the elevator in *Lost in Translation*. Yet despite the absence of apparent intimacy in the elevator, or perhaps because of it, Bob and Charlotte have their first, brief encounter in this space.

The protagonists' search for meaning and authenticity is made difficult by the seeming absence of individualisation in both Bob and Charlotte. When Charlotte is listing all the things she could be, or has tried to be, she sets herself up as a kind of non-person, an 'everygirl' who has tried all the things a white middle-class arts-oriented American girl tries. As noted earlier, Bob also has some attributes of a non-person, or at least a person depersonalised. Bob is an 'inauthentic' character of the highest degree: a once-successful actor whose old TV shows are still big in Japan, and he is now being paid two million dollars to appear as the face of a brand of whisky. In the photo-shoot the photographer tries to ask him to be James Bond (and they argue over whether it is Sean Connery or Roger Moore) or do a Rat Pack signature face. Bob complies with these requests, with irony unseen by the Japanese photographer but clear to the Western cinemagoer, creating the racist undertone that is present at various moments in the film. At the same time, the duality of Bill (a name close to Bob) Murray playing this character is present too. For some time he has been a fading star, and has the facial expression of a weeping clown. He 'does' this face too in the photo shoot for the whisky commercial. Bob can be read as a non-person, confirming the corollary that non-places produce non-people. Bob functions as a non-person insofar as he is already virtual: the character is an actor, and Bill Murray himself is a tired actor playing a tired actor. Bob as a non-person corresponds to the non-place of the hotel: he is a non-person in a non-place trying to become personalised; to reterritorialize the space. Only through another person, Charlotte, does Bob achieve this.

The characters move around the city, sometimes with a map, always finding their way, mirroring the way in which their sense of friendship develops as they both help each other map their futures. It also mirrors the plot, which ambles along, punctuated by a few incidents, but is only clearly mapped or framed by the arrival at and departure from the hotel. Thus the hotel is the central chronotope through which a perception of and movement in nomadic space is articulated. Indeed, through the camera we have the Deleuzean experience of the creation of space through the mobilized and virtual gaze, both in terms of movement around the hotel and Tokyo, and in Charlotte and Bob's unusual relationship, which defies the borders (if that is the right term) of gender, sexuality, and age. Their relationship, like the camera, moves in unexpected ways.

The sense of unmappable space referred to by Jameson (1999, 39) in relation to the Bonaventure Hotel is present in this film. Whilst the hotel lighting and the absence of establishing shots connote in cinematic logic postmodern alienation, there is also the playfulness present in exploring Tokyo's other spaces, both physical and psychic. Ceremony is the breath that holds together old and new Tokyo (e.g., Bob bringing a gift to a crazy television host, the bowing and presents when Bob arrives in Tokyo). It enables the parallel worlds of the old and the supermodern to exist in almost absolute proximity to each other, manifesting themselves in something like the same way as the hotel function rooms visited by Charlotte. The hotel's parallel structure, where tradition and supermodernity exist side by side, is also seen in the surrounding city: Charlotte watches a Buddhist ceremony around the corner from supermodern, neo-lit sections of Tokyo. The proximity of the ancient and supermodern is articulated in a street shot, where Charlotte is crossing the road and looks up to watch a giant screen with a dinosaur walking across it.

Much like the parallel lives of Barton Fink and Charlie Meadows in *Barton Fink*, we have the same dynamic in this film, the dynamic that is inherent to the structure of the hotel. In this respect, Tokyo, like the hotel, is filmed as an assemblage, in which Charlotte and Bob are able to slide freely between one kind of world and another.

DAVID LYNCH'S ASYMMETRICAL WORLDS

In 1993, David Lynch experimented with a hotel-based polyphonic narrative similar to *Mystery Train*, with the defunct television series *Hotel Room*. This story focuses on guests in one hotel room, from 1936 to 1993. The hotel staff never age as various guests come and go. The guests' experiences are divided into three stories. Rather than being connected by space and time, like those in *Mystery Train*, the characters in *Hotel Room* are connected by the room. *Hotel Room* has been widely regarded as a huge failure for Lynch, and did not get television release, but it is mentioned here because it confirms Lynch's obsession with hotels, an obsession that is better articulated in *Twin Peaks* and, to a lesser extent, *Lost Highway*.

Twin Peaks was a groundbreaking television series focusing on the town of Twin Peaks and following the rhizomic connections of the town that begin with the death of Laura Palmer. FBI agent Dale Cooper comes to town and stays at the Great Northern Hotel. The Great Northern Hotel becomes the focus of a labyrinthine, polyphonic narrative that operates much like the unmappable hotel. The Great Northern Hotel is also folded into parallel, unreal worlds, forming the anchor point between real and unreal. Similarly, the incest theme that runs through the show is abstracted in various dream realities and unreal characters. The absence of reality in this noir series is seen in many ways, through the space, the depersonalised characters, and the various methods used to find clues (such as dreams and Tibetan rituals), as well as through the folding of one character onto another.

Lynch uses the hotel as a slipstream space—a space between the real and the virtual. Lynch never bothers to create a sense of reality in his dream worlds. The fake, *Mary-Poppins*-like robin singing at the end of *Blue Velvet* epitomises this on a micro level. Lynch avoids an attempt at reality through space as well: the external shots of the Great Northern Hotel in no way 'match' the inside space. The external shots of the hotel are filmed with a different grade and colour film, and the camera never tracks from outside to inside the hotel. The establishing shots serve as guideposts for the Great Northern Hotel, but its 'reality' lies elsewhere, in the corridors and in its parallel world in Dale Cooper's dreams.

Gaston Bachelard could have designed the inside of the hotel, with its wood-lined corridors and appearance of a cosy home. However, despite its apparent homeliness, the organic, corrupt, incestuous underworld of Twin Peaks is condensed in the hotel. Presented here is the rhizome or root system as this is alluded to in the tree-truck beams and wood panelling that lines the hotel and other spaces in *Twin Peaks* (the log cabin, the messages from the log lady, One Eyed Jack's). Whilst it might seem that the trees would indicate an arborescent system, the way in which the trees in the woods and in the hotels have no beginning and end strongly suggests that they constitute a rhizomic system. The system of this assemblage operates via the spatial displacement of the red curtains. Red curtains in the hotel are present in many of the 'evil' spaces in the town of Twin Peaks. They map out the movement between reality and virtual and provide the portal to parallel worlds—the Black Lodge, the White Lodge, One Eyed Jack's. The red curtains together with the hotel provide the organising frame for both the narrative and the structure of parallel worlds. The disjunction between outside and inside, and real and virtual, emphasises that *Twin Peaks* is a narrative aware of its fictionality, and means that the viewer is unable to map the space and locate it in 'reality.'

As though Lynch were following instructions for following the construction of Leibniz's baroque chapel, curtains are never opened in *Twin Peaks*. All is interior. As a parallel to this, if we consider Leibniz's idea that the soul is the darkened room, like a monad, then we might ask whether we are seeing the interior of someone's soul within these closed-off curtains. Is it Dale Cooper's? Laura Palmer's? Evil Bob's? Not everything needs to be reduced to an individual psychology, however; what we have through the connected spaces that stem from the hotel, coupled with the detective work done via dreams and Tibetan rituals, *is* a presence of a kind of rhizomic mindscape. In this narrative, the parallel worlds entered through dreams that contain the hotel's red curtains confirm this: Dale Cooper on several occasions dreams that he is finding answers to Laura Palmer's murder by walking down a corridor shrouded in red curtains. Meaning for Cooper always lies just behind the curtain but is rarely understood. Curtains, rather than doors, provide a folding, multiple reality; they are at once a solid and fluid structure, much like the parallel worlds that co-exist throughout the narrative, and much like the fluid identity that perpetuates this and other Lynch stories.

It is the red curtains throughout the hotel that provide the connection between the various worlds in the town of *Twin Peaks*. Folding curtains in turn are mirrored in other spaces, thus folding the hotel onto other spaces. Curtains act like a tunnel that connects the other spaces to the hotel; it is as though, if you dug through the hotel, you would somehow be connected to other spaces, such as One Eyed Jack's (the casino/brothel) or the Black

Lodge. The red curtains provide the connecting clue for Dale Cooper time and time again. Cooper is told about the red curtains in a dream, and, believing in the power of his dreams, presumes that when he stumbles across the cabin in the woods that his target is reached. But in fact it is Leland Palmer, Laura's father, dancing in front of the red curtain in the hotel who is the 'real' Bob. The red curtains not only recall the image of the Leibnizian/Deleuzian Baroque chapel, but also provide the portal to other realities. Wherever there are red curtains in *Twin Peaks*, Laura and corruption have dwelt there. The spiritual evil (along with the incest story between Leland and Laura) in the narrative is folded onto the closed hotel curtains, which in turn are folded out into many other 'infected' spaces in the town. This is played out on a micro level when Audrey works as a prostitute at One Eyed Jack's and, hiding behind the red curtains surrounding the bed, narrowly avoids sex with her first client: her father.

The Great Northern Hotel always provides the intersection between the real and other worlds. As the momentum of *Twin Peaks* progresses through its seemingly endless episodes, space and subjectivity no longer become either real or unreal. As Deleuze writes of the film *Last Year at Marienbad*, things are no longer real or unreal because we do not have a place from which to ask that question. Thus the hotel serves as what Deleuze would term a "crystal image:" "the uniting of an actual image and a virtual image to the point where they can no longer be distinguished" (1989, Glossary). The Great Northern Hotel thus contains both the virtual and actual worlds of *Twin Peaks*.

Lynch's film *Lost Highway* also uses the hotel space (albeit briefly) in its parallel narratives. The hotel again provides the intersection between parallel worlds. *Lost Highway* (like Lynch's subsequent film, *Mulholland Drive)* is divided into two halves, in which identity is multiple. The Lost Highway Hotel provides the space whereby the twin identities of Fred Madison and Pete Dayton, and Alice and Renee come together. But doubles in *Lost Highway* are not quite doubles: Pete becomes Fred but different actors play the characters; Renee and Alice are played by the same actor (Patricia Arquette) but are emphasised (by Alice) as being different women. In classic film noir tradition, one femme fatale is blonde, the other (Renee, the victim) is brunette. Pete sees a photo of Alice and Renee together, and asks Alice which of the two she is. Alice points clearly to herself (the blonde Arquette) and says *"that's me."* Thus the two Arquette characters are not quite one, just as Pete's and Fred's characters are not quite two. Aparallel identities abound in Lynch's work, reinforcing Vidler's argument that the Lacanian mirror stage needs to be revised. Here we are presented with the post-Lacanian 'screen stage:' identity is not located through a mirror image but is always asymmetrical.

Even the space of the hotel is not clearly a separate space. In the last half of the film, the hotel is seen only as a single floor, but it is entered via the stairway of someone's home. Thus it is neither a completely separate hotel entity, nor is it a home. The use of space, subjects, and narrative technique in *Lost Highway* confirms my reading of *Twin Peaks*: just as one space is folded onto another, so too is subjectivity. Thus, the intersection of the real and virtual spaces of the hotel resonates with the formation of identity in *Lost Highway*. The hallucinatory nature of experience is expressed cinematically via the shaking camera, and the strobe lighting in the hotel corridor. These are clear indicators of another reality and a fractured self.

The effect of this is the presentation of folded space in the film: Pete goes up stairs after murdering Dick Laurant and finds himself in a hotel corridor. At the end of the film, Fred goes up the stairs of the Mystery Man's house in the desert and finds himself in the same hotel. Revealed in this hotel, behind the various doors, are the dark aspects of his/their lives. Two forms of space—psychic and social—are conjoined, folded onto each other through the metaphysical and real spaces of hotel and home. The hotel in *Lost Highway* penetrates other spaces and appears as the manifestation of the unspeakable aspects of the mind. The moments of Pete/Fred walking up the stairs to the hotel echo the ideas of Leibniz's Baroque house united by "two stories, one material, one spiritual, joined by a stair of infinite folds" (Vidler, 2001, 233). This is the way in which parallel worlds are presented in contemporary slipstream narrative: through a space—the hotel—that is at once virtual and actual.

The unstable self that is central to postmodern noir is epitomised by the moment in *Lost Highway* when Fred Madison drives down the road at night. The yellow lines on the road slip under the car as he drives, then his hand begins to shake and his face streaks like Francis Bacon's painting of *Pope Innocent X*. So in a space of utter containment—the image Deleuze sees as the new monad—in a car travelling down an isolated highway, this character becomes someone else. The blurred close-up shaking camera is again the way in which Lynch conveys this impossible, virtual concept. Is this a postmodern schizophrenia? The same movement towards someone else's identity happens to Dale Cooper at the end of *Twin Peaks* too, where he stares in the mirror and realises that he has become Bob, just as Leland Palmer did earlier. This kind of narrative, where one becomes someone else (but not entirely, not completely), operates as an exploration of multiple realities in postmodernity, and the hotel becomes the central organising figure for these parallel realities.

In these slipstream hotel narratives, characters become depersonalised— the expression of ideas rather than individual subjects. Characters for Lynch are not self-contained subjects. They can easily and illogically become someone else. Two men play one split male character in *Lost Highway*; one woman plays two female characters. Leland in *Twin Peaks* is Bob, but then Dale Cooper also becomes Bob. Sherilyn Fenn plays the dead Laura Palmer, but also plays her cousin who arrives in town. Not only is this depersonalisation present in Lynch's narratives, but also in acting styles in all of Lynch's films. The dialogue is delivered often in a stagy, stilted manner. There are long pauses in conversation, as in daytime soap operas (which, incidentally, are frequently played on televisions in Lynch's films). This is not wooden acting; this is a deliberate Lynchian style. Similarly, Bob in *Lost in Translation* lacks individualisation, moving through the non-place of the hotel as a non-person. Personalised character ends and space takes over as the vessel through which the impossibility of negotiating the self is presented. These are slipstream narratives that are not science fiction but more like a dream reality (or rather, a nightmare reality) framed through the hotel.

CONCLUSION

In all the films considered here, the way to express an absence of a system, of totality, is to present multiple or parallel worlds. These worlds are not entered in a conventional manner by any means, and the confusion about outside and inside, entry and exit, adds to the bewildering, unsystematic labyrinth of self, space, and reality in supermodernity. Kevin Lynch's (1960) argument that, as Jameson (1999, 415) puts it, "urban alienation is directly proportional to the mental unmappability of local cityscapes," is evident in these films set in the microcosmic world of the hotel. The confusion in these hotel narratives that occurs for both the viewer and characters has to do with the confusion of inside and outside, entry and exit. These uncertainties in turn impact on comprehension of the self—the subject in Lynch's films is fractured into several subjectivities, but these are not entirely split or parallel identities. Following de Certeau's idea that every spatial negotiation is a renegotiation of the mirror stage, this unsuccessful negotiation indicates a rethinking of the mirror stage as a movement away from identification as reflection to identification understood through proximity, through something or someone sitting slightly beside oneself.

Whether the parallel worlds of the hotel are used to explore many characters' lives or to depict slipstream realities, recurring in the narratives discussed in this chapter is the search (and failure) to understand identity. This failure, rather than being articulated by the characters themselves, is displaced onto the hotel: comprehension lies in the adjoining room.

As the hotel space articulates discontinuities between self and other, body and space, characters are depersonalised and become figures through which concepts are expressed, but are not complete, contained characters in their own right. The hotel space in *Lost Highway* is folded onto other spaces—Dick Laurant's home and the house in the desert—much like the folding subjectivity of the characters themselves. It is not comprehensive space. Similarly, the parallel worlds of the traditional and the supermodern exist side by side in the Tokyo hotel in *Lost in Translation*.

Lynch's red curtains provide a portal to other realities, but beyond this portal lie other worlds where nothing is particularly clear. The image of Dale Cooper wandering through the red-curtained hallway in the Black Lodge, opening another curtain to find no more understanding than he already had, is a prime example of this. The hotel here provides a graspable framework for parallel (or rather, quasi-parallel) worlds that slip between virtual and actual worlds, and presents for us—in a form or space that we can recognise—multiple subjectivity in postmodern conditions. The hotel, then, confirms Moretti's argument that space shapes narrative. Operating as it does in culture as well as film, the hotel slips between being a real and a virtual world, thus it is the slipstream text's privileged vehicle (or space), so what we see in hotel films is the death of character and the birth of space, "where people come and people go, and nothing ever happens" (*Grand Hotel*, 1932).

FILMOGRAPHY

Alphaville. Dir. Jean-Luc Godard. Prod. André Michelin. Janus Films, 1965.

Barton Fink. Dir. Joel Coen. Prod. Ethan Coen. Colombia TriStar Home Video, 1991.

Four Rooms. Dir. Alison Anders, Alexandre Rockwell, Robert Rodrigeuz, Quentin Tarantino. Prod. Lawrence Bender. Miramax Films, 1995.

Grand Hotel. Dir. Edmund Goulding. Prod. Paul Bern. MGM,1932.

Last Year at Marienbad. Dir. Alain Resnais. Prod. Pierre Couran. Fox Lorber, 1961.

Lost Highway. Dir. David Lynch. Prod. Deepak Nayar. REP, 1997.

Lost in Translation. Dir. Sofia Coppola. Prod. Sofia Coppola. Focus Features, 2003.

Mystery Train. Dir. Jim Jarmusch. Prod. Jim Stark. MGM Home Entertainment, 1989.

The Matrix. Dir. Andy and Larry Wachowski. Prod. Joel Silver. Roadshow Entertainment, 1999.

Rear Window. Dir. Alfred Hitchcock. Prod. Alfred Hitchcock. Universal Home Entertainment, 1954.

Twin Peaks. Dir. David Lynch, Mark Frost et al. Prod. Gregg Fienberg. Artisan Entertainment, 1990.

REFERENCES

Augé, Marc. *Non-places: Introduction to an Anthropology of Supermodernity.* London: Verso, 1995.

Bakhtin, Mikhail Mikhailovich. *The Dialogic Imagination: Four Essays* (ed. Michael Holquist.; trans. Caryl Emerson, and Michael Holquist). Austin: University of Texas Press, 1981.

Barthes, Roland. *Empire of Signs* (trans. Richard Howard). New York: Hill and Wang, 1982.

Buchanan, Ian. *Deleuzism: A Meta-commentary.* Durham, NC: Duke, 2000.

de Certeau, Michel. *The Practice of Everyday Life* (trans. Steven Rendall). Berkeley: University of California Press, 1984.

Deleuze, Gilles. *Cinema 2: The Time-Image* (trans. Hugh Tomlinson and Robert Galeta). London: Athlone, 1989.

———. *The Fold: Leibniz and the Baroque* (trans. Tom Conley). Minneapolis, Minnesota: 2004.

Harvey, David. *The Condition of Postmodernity: An Enquiry into the Origins of Cultural Change.* Oxford: Blackwell, 1989.

Jameson, Frederic. *The Geopolitical Aesthetic: Cinema and Space in the World System.* Bloomington, Indiana: Indiana University Press, 1995.

———. *Postmodernism, or, The Cultural Logic of Late Capitalism.* London: Verso, 1999.

Kracauer, Siegfried. 'The Hotel Lobby' *Postcolonial Studies* 2 no. 3 (1999): 289–297.

Lacan, Jacques. *Écrits: A Selection.* London: Routledge, 1977.

Lynch, Kevin. *The Image of the City.* Cambridge, MA: MIT Press, 1960.

Moretti, Franco. *Atlas of the European Novel, 1800–1900.* London: Verso, 1999.

Vidler, Anthony. *Warped Space: Art, Architecture, and Anxiety in Modern Culture.* Cambridge, MIT Press, 2001.

Žižek, Slavoj. *Enjoy your Symptom! Jacques Lacan in Hollywood and Out.* London: Routledge, 2001.

Chapter Eleven

No Quarter(s), No Camel(s), No Exit(s): *Motel Cactus* and the Low Heterotopias of Seoul

David Scott Diffrient

There is no denying that Korean movies have changed for the better over just the past year. Only two years ago, many critics were complaining that Korean movies were nothing but a collection of scenes filmed secretly at tawdry yŏgwan hotels. Many decried these so-called "yŏgwan room genre" Korean movies, but with a series of new-style melodramas produced last year, domestic films have shown significant improvement. Meaningless erotic scenes are no longer used to spice up Korean films as in the past. Directors now believe there is no need to insert sex scenes into their films in order to woo Korean viewers.

Yu Ji-na[1]

In her short, informal article extolling the virtues of *Shiri* (*Swiri*, 1999), an espionage thriller whose box-office success and international distribution helped to reinvigorate South Korean cinema during a time of economic uncertainty (the immediate aftermath of the IMF crisis), film scholar Yu Ji-na sums up some of the widely held suspicions about a genre deemed aesthetically deficient (by formalist critics), ideologically bankrupt (by feminist critics), and politically disengaged (by neo-Marxist critics). The "yŏgwan room genre" of films popular from the mid-1970s to the mid-1990s, although a vital link between South Korea's cinematic Golden Age of the 1960s and the industry's artistic and commercial renaissance in 1998, strikes many today as an embarrassing blot on the nation's otherwise distinguished track record of cultural productions—something to be overlooked or brushed aside so as to make way for less dubious objects of study.

Most critics, in fact, share Yu Ji-na's cynicism toward older sexploitation films and optimism about the future of South Korean cinema, which nevertheless remains shackled to patriarchal discourses and predicated on a system of visual pleasure that posits females as objects of the male gaze (one need only watch the intoxicating period pieces of Im Kwon-t'aek—the country's most celebrated filmmaker—to witness this fetishistic disposition). They believe that, by venturing outside the cheap, claustrophobic motel rooms that had for so long characterized South Korean film and symbolized the country's stereotypical status as a 'hermit kingdom,' the new millennium's vibrant comedies, compelling melodramas, visionary sci-fi epics, and visceral war movies not only bring a breath of fresh air into what once was a stuffy and stultifying arena of sexual exploitation, but also attest to the nation's heightened awareness of itself as a prominent player on the world stage. After all, unlike their regressive predecessors, recent blockbusters like *Shiri*, *Joint Security Area* (*Kongdong gyŏngbi guyŏk*, 2000), *Friend* (*Ch'in'gu*, 2001), and *Taegukgi* (*T'aegŭkgi hwinallimyŏ*, 2004) show off South Korea's technological advancements while highlighting its geopolitical ascendancy in East Asia as a modern, militarized, urbanized, democratic, and capitalistic society. However, what critics often fail to reconcile are the structural continuities and semantic consistencies that see yŏgwan iconography and its attendant tropes (insularity, immobility, sexuality) carrying over to ostensibly forward-looking, contemporary films—from crowd-pleasing comedies like *My Sassy Girl* (*Yŏpgijŏk kŭnyŏ*; 2001) and *Sex is Zero* (*Saekjŭk sigong*, 2002) to female-directed melodramas like *Ardor* (*Milae*, 2002), which all feature at least one scene set in a 'love motel.'

Ironically, the recent blockbuster phenomenon sparked by *Shiri*, which thrust South Korean cinema into the international spotlight, now affords Western spectators an unprecedented peek beneath the neon exterior of modern-day Seoul—a teeming metropolis frequently depicted by the most politically-engaged filmmakers as a collection of drab and claustrophobic interiors. Several New Wave *auteurs* such as Kim Ki-dŏk and Hong Sang-su have continued to put emphasis on the heterotopic 'non-places' scattered in the shadows and along the periphery of the cinematic cityscape, from nightclubs, strip-joints, and karaoke bars to flophouses, pharmacies, and photo-shops. In this urban landscape of commerce and consumption, amidst the highrise offices and apartment buildings of the capital city, one particular space has achieved a high degree of cinematic visibility, to the dismay, no doubt, of Korea's Ministry of Culture and Tourism. On view in festival-friendly films such as *Birdcage Inn* (*P'aran taemun*; 1998), *The Power of Kangwon Province* (*Kangwŏn-do ŭi him*, 1998), *Peppermint Candy* (*Pakha sat'ang*, 2000), and *Oldboy* (2003), the so-called 'love motel' (a variant of the more neutral Korean term yŏgwan, which literally means 'inn') is a polymorphous space signifying the physical entanglements and spiritual bankruptcies behind South Korea's modernization drive. Reserved for liaisons between the sexes, the ubiquitous love motel is where upwardly mobile men and downhearted women enact gender-coded rituals in a space that is marginal yet central to the understanding of sexual mores in a patriarchal society. Indeed, no other site of social and sexual intercourse is so integral to the situational poetics of South Korean cinema.

By 'situational poetics' I mean the rhetorical and narrative maneuvers undertaken by cinematic texts and other cultural productions whose principle settings—in this case, hotels and motels—provide a kind of critical commentary on the social conditions and the general state of a given nation at a particular moment in history. Because the word 'situation' can itself be doubly situated to denote both place and predicament, position and plight, it proves useful as a description of film's unique chronotopic abilities to consolidate seemingly disparate material while placing thematic content into a structural form or stylistic expression amenable to political allegory. When converted into an adjectival marker and hitched to the Aristotelian nomenclature 'poetics,' the term 'situation' radiates outward in several directions at once, conjuring the spatial, temporal, social, and ideological implications of dramas set primarily or exclusively in motels and designed—like classic Greek tragedies—to arouse pathos and fear. This essay scrutinizes these implications vis-à-vis contemporary Korean cinema, and seeks to address the convergence of personal and national agendas at this paradoxical site of transience and escape, intimacy and aggression, hourly rates and prolonged sorrows. Taking as my centerpiece Pak Ki-yong's award-winning *Motel Cactus (Motel Sŏninjang*, 1997), a multi-episode film in which a single fleabag room serves the libidinous needs of four couples, I explore one of the most prevalent, if understudied, iconographic elements in a national cinema that has itself functioned in an allegorical capacity.

I have chosen *Motel Cactus* as a case study for a number of reasons. Set almost entirely in one motel room, the film chronicles fleeting moments in the lives of six main characters who form four different couples. Each of its four episodes focuses on a man and a woman undergoing an emotional crisis, one that is negotiated through sexual intercourse yet—unlike classic Greek tragedies (which offer cathartic endings)—is not purgatively expunged from the narrative. Indeed, by the conclusion of the film, the mounting sense of ennui and frustration that has accrued episode-to-episode in the limited confines of a yŏgwan cannot be fully cleansed from *our* systems, for *we too* have inhabited that claustrophobic room for nearly ninety minutes (an amount of time only slightly in excess of what is typically allotted for clandestine meetings in love motels rented by the hour). *Motel Cactus* would thus seem to be a phenomenologically engaging if apolitical text largely concerned with disintegrating personal relationships and failed romances. However, in foregrounding these disparate couples and the motel they momentarily occupy, the film puts forth a composite, microcosmic image of Korea as a space of transience, transformation, and cohabitation; peopled with strangely inert drifters who—like the nation-state—are caught between opposing forces.

Theatrically released only a few months before South Korea's artistic and commercial renaissance in the fall of 1998 (not to mention newly elected President Kim Dae-Jung's sweeping reorganization of executive and legislative branches), the film itself was sandwiched between contrasting industrial and economic motivations. It was both the last gasp of the industry's earlier predilection for sexploitation fare set within motel rooms and a harbinger of what was to come at the dawn of the new millennium, when modes of production became streamlined and certain art-house directors (including Pak Ki-yong) attained cultural cachet in the international arena. Thus, as a liminal moment in the country's film history, as a barometer of the conflicting domestic attitudes toward increasingly global products, *Motel Cactus* is important on a variety of fronts. Not only did it foretell the subsequent wave of *auteur*-driven vehicles in which pretensions to art or social critique outweighed financial motives; but—in providing an image of liminality in the guise of a degraded yet fetishized motel room—it also self-reflexively comments on its own status as an object of both critical scorn and admiration, a film ferociously attacked and passionately defended by reviewers inside and outside South Korea.

This inner/outer dialectic of reception—a dialectic in which cultural insiders may draw upon different aesthetic traditions, evaluative criteria, and hermeneutic assumptions than outsiders yet still arrive at a critical consensus in which differences are negated—becomes a convenient extradiegetic paradigm for understanding the film's own diegetically inscribed emphasis on interiors and exteriors; spaces delineated by the walls of the motel room and indicative of the tension between South Korea's national and international agendas. In an effort to extend my metaphor of situational poetics into the socioeconomic realities of the country as well as into the realm of political discourse, and in hopes of illustrating the metaphor's usefulness as a critical tool, I situate *Motel Cactus* within a variety of cultural and historical contexts in this essay. After framing its relationship to earlier sexploitation features as well as to other films set within the spatial confines of a motel/hotel room, I move on to a textual analysis that accounts for its savvy manipulation of interior and exterior spaces. Before concluding the essay with a nod to the film's transnational viability (as a text that speaks to audiences in other East Asian markets), I ruminate on the ways in which love motels figure differently in Japanese and Chinese-language films. And, drawing on information that I gathered during my 2003 interview with director Pak Ki-yong, I gesture beyond this particular film to his 'sequel' of sorts: *Camel(s)* (*Nakt'a[dŭl]*, 2001). This latter film, Pak's sophomore feature, may be radically different from its predecessor in terms of visual style and narrative (s)pacing; but it likewise puts emotionally estranged yet physically entangled lovers under a kind of unforgiving microscope that only a motel room—in all of its focused intensity—could provide.

SOUTH KOREAN SOCIOECONOMIC AND CULTURAL CONTEXTS

Besides Seoul and its satellite suburbs, today there are several cities—from Pusan in the southeast to Inch'on in the northwest—where one might find love motels and hotels in South Korea. Here, 'love motel' is simply used to refer to any yŏgwan that advertises two different rates: 'to stay' and 'to rest.' The first rate, referring to overnight occupancy, is no different from that of a typical business hotel. The second, hourly rate is designed for people with just enough time to squeeze in a little sex between other activities or obligations. Because its rooms can be rented by the hour, a love motel fosters a deeper sense of ephemerality among its guests than other establishments renting rooms strictly by the night.

Like those in Japan, love motels in South Korea were initially linked to prostitution and situated "on the edges of entertainment districts," offering "inexpensive, private space" for married or unmarried couples "in cities where apartments [were] cramped and often uninviting, and a suburban home and bedroom [was] a long commute away."[2] However, unlike Japan's Vegas-style theme hotels sprinkled throughout Tokyo and Nagoya, kitschy inns modeled after Greco-Roman castles, cruise ships, space rockets, hot-air balloons, and Moorish harems that give married couples and adventurous singles a momentary break from job and home,[3] the love motels in South Korea are linked neither to tourism nor to imagined travel. Serving a more utilitarian, less aesthetic, function, these often seedy venues suggest paralysis and alienation in South Korean cinema, and are surrogate homes in which the inconveniences of limited space oftentimes force a direct confrontation between patrons of different social classes.

The modern Korean yŏgwan business—of which the love motel is only the most recent manifestation—dates back to the late nineteenth century, a period of social, economic, and industrial transformation that laid the groundwork for the country's subsequent shift into modernization under the Japanese colonial government (1910–1945).[4] The development and increased visibility of the yŏgwan runs parallel to the consolidation and strengthening of Japan's colonial power through urbanization projects, launched in the wake of its 1910 annexation of Korea. By 1930 there were nearly 400 yŏgwans in Seoul alone (approximately 85% of which were run by Koreans rather than Japanese), not to mention many such establishments built near outlying hot-springs resort areas, where both foreign and domestic tourists flocked to escape the tedium and strife of urban life.

The notion of escape (from the city and from the responsibilities associated with work and family) came to be a motivating force behind the emergence of love motels in South Korea throughout the 1980s and 1990s. That period of increased commerce, consumption, and democratic freedoms—following decades of political turmoil and authoritarian rule under the postwar governments of Syngman Rhee (1948–1960) and Park Chung Hee (1961–1979)—has been characterized as a 'golf boom' by economic analysts who see the nation's burgeoning middle-class aspirations as a kind of consumer-driven corrective to preexisting social problems, which were not completely rectified by the 1988 election of President Roh Tae Woo. As James Cotton and Kim Hyung-a van Leest mention in their study of the so-called golf republic's hedonistic, middle-class leisure activities and consumer patterns, an increase in the number of pleasure resorts, massage parlors, and love hotels is one notable outcome of this economic boom.[5]

Of course, one cannot ignore the altered perceptions of sexuality and gender among the latest generation of South Koreans, who seem just as eager to cast off the shackles of Confucian ideology as they are in putting the country's poverty-stricken past behind them. In formulating a "new sexual subjectivity and morality" within the spatial confines of love motel/hotel rooms, contemporary cultural producers are not only challenging hidebound notions of chastity and fidelity that have dictated the social realities of Korean women for centuries; but also revealing a paradox at the heart of paradigm-altering attempts at social change.[6] For, with the loosening of moral strictures over the past decade, not to mention a de-politicizing of youth culture, an attendant increase in market-driven consumption patterns has underwritten liberationist discourses, thus creating new, equally confining (and life-defining) codes of normative behavior for the supposedly upwardly mobile man and (especially) woman.[7]

One of the most important cultural producers of the revitalized 1980s and 1990s was poet, novelist, and painter Ma Kwang-su. Ma was at the forefront of the anti-authoritarian movement, publishing controversial works that challenged conformist attitudes toward sexuality and which were frequently set in yŏgwans. Three years before writing his notorious 1992 novel, *Happy Sara* (which landed the author in jail for two months because its storyline—

concerning the sexual adventures of an unmarried female college student—was deemed obscene), Ma had published a book of poetry entitled *Let's Go to the Rose Inn*. Between its 1989 publication and its filmic adaptation one year later,[8] much debate swirled in the popular press; not about its artistic merits, but rather about its 'immoral' libertinism. Peopled with fingernail fetishists and foot-smellers, the collection touched a nerve simply by shifting focus away from spiritual love to physical attraction and the pleasures of the flesh, played out in spaces that became sanctuaries for those seeking solace from the political corruption and social injustices outside. The title poem, 'Let's Go to the Rose Inn,' rhapsodizes about coffee and conversation as well as the act of combing a woman's hair, rendered in fetishistic detail that ultimately tips the balance toward full-blown carnality. By putting instant gratification and hedonistic sensuality above the Confucian tenets of patience and moderation, Ma Kwang-su (often called 'the D. H. Lawrence of South Korea') presents the spatial confines of the motel room as a relatively emancipatory—if still potentially stagnating—alternative to the parochial limitations beyond its walls. This provocateur's work epitomized the era as few cultural productions—in print or onscreen—did; and would serve as a template for *Motel Cactus* and other yŏgwan-centered films ostensibly fixated on sex, fetishism, and voyeurism.

Although motels and hotels have frequently appeared in South Korean films dating back to the cinematic Golden Age of the 1950s and 1960s, when such representative works as *Third Class Hotel* (*Samdŭng hot'el*, 1958) and *Third Class Inn* (*Samdŭng yŏgwan*; 1967) were released,[9] it was not until the 1970s and 1980s that a significant number of productions utilized such settings in an exploitative manner, beginning with director Chŏn Cho-Myŏng's *A Hotel Room* (*Yŏjang*, 1971). Even before the hugely unpopular leader of South Korea's Fifth Republic, President Chun Doo Hwan (1980–1988), launched a 'Three 'S' Policy' (promoting Sports, Screen, and Sex as a means of both diverting public scrutiny away from governmental corruptions and appeasing powerful representatives of the entertainment industry in the months leading up to the 1988 Olympics), dozens of titillating melodramas had been produced in South Korea. Typically filled with nymphomaniacs and peeping toms, such sex-themed films as *The Parrot Cries with Its Body* (*Aengmusae mom ŭro ulŏtda*, 1981), *The Married Woman* (*Yubunyŏ*, 1981), *Lost Youth* (*Pŏryŏjin ch'ŏnch'un*, 1982), *Hotel at 00:00* (*0 si ŭi hot'el*, 1983), and *Heaven Night After Night* (*Pam mada ch'ŏnguk*, 1984) were ostensibly designed as cinematic distractions, crowd-anaesthetizing alternatives to nightly news programs about student demonstrations, labor disputes, and social unrest. Thus, these outwardly exploitative and commercial products served a political purpose in the immediate aftermath of the 1980 Kwangju

Massacre, and in many ways were harbingers of the more sexually explicit cinematic diversions of the early-to-mid-1990s, such as *Love Hotel Exit* (*Lŏbŭ hot'el pisanggu* 1993) and *Yellow House '96* (1996), which are set in Seoul's red-light districts and peopled primarily with nightclub patrons, prostitutes, and pimps.

Despite their often tacky façades, many of the commercial motion pictures made during the Chun Doo Hwan era revolve around serious themes, including extortion, kidnapping, prostitution, male impotence, rape, death due to drug overdose, overseas adoption, and the plight of children born out of wedlock. Not coincidentally, yŏgwan imagery dominates the semantic terrain of these and other sexploitation films, all of which feature fatalistic females either trapped inside their own crumbling psyches or killed as a result of natural, self-inflicted, or murderous circumstances. In fact, few spaces of sexual and social interaction occupied so central a position in the textual unfolding of desire (whether libidinal or material) during the 1980s as the motel/hotel room. This phenomenon can be linked to two specific historical moments prior to the publication of Ma Kwang-su's *Let's Go to the Rose Inn*, each providing a contextual basis for understanding the deeper implications of cultural transformation in South Korea and thus demanding at least a cursory overview prior to my critical analysis of *Motel Cactus*—a film that simultaneously deconstructs and reconstructs sexploitation tropes of the 'yŏgwan room genre' criticized by Yu Ji-na and other theorists.

First, on January 6, 1982, and as a gesture of liberalization to silence his critics, President Chun Doo Hwan officially abolished the night curfew in Seoul, which had been in effect since the end of World War II. The effect that this had on businesses, particularly those staked out in entertainment or red-light districts, was enormous. Hourly and overnight accommodations in flourishing areas such as Kangnam benefited the most from this lifting of the curfew; and owners of such establishments suddenly found themselves able to afford decent furnishings, such as beds (as opposed to floor mats), color televisions, and VCRs—not to mention an array of porno films on Beta videotape. These amenities made all the difference in the world to the politically oppressed working classes, who could momentarily escape from the realities of the day into the secret seductions and carnal intoxications of the affordable yŏgwan at night. Thus, the inn came to function in much the same way as the third-tier movie theater, showing ostensibly mindless sex films and giving audiences a temporary escape hatch from the daily grind, not to mention a kind of safe haven from the threats posed to livelihood and life during a time of social unrest, political protest, human-rights violations, and prisoner-torture scandals.

The second historical touchstone contributing to the increased cinematic visibility of motel/hotel rooms came one month after Chun Doo Hwan's lifting of the national curfew, when the first X-rated Korean motion picture was theatrically released, setting a precedent not only in terms of what was permissible on screen but also as an enormously popular box-office hit that was responsible for a series of official and unofficial sequels—each one kinkier than the last. Directed by Chŏng In-yŏp, the film—*Madam Aema* (*Aema puin*)—created a stir unlike any before, its story of a thirtysomething married woman indulging her fantasies with a younger man hyped to the point of saturation in the weeks before its February 6, 1982 debut at Seoul Theater.[10] Hundreds of men and women traveled to the capital city from as far away as Inch'on and Suwŏn, only to be turned away from the box-office once tickets were sold out. A few of the non-ticket-holders became so infuriated and unruly that they broke the theater's windows, instigating a riot and bringing even more publicity to the film. Fortunately for them, the lifting of the curfew system enabled theater owners to tack on midnight screenings, enabling a greater number of movie patrons to discover for themselves what all of the fuss was about.[11]

The fuss, it seems, grew from *Madam Aema*'s unique approach to female sexual desire and liberation, expressed in a way that directly contradicted Confucian moral codes and ethical standards (which demanded that women be sacrificial wives, daughters, and mothers).[12] In the film, a married woman named Ae-ma patiently awaits the release of her philandering husband who was jailed for involuntary homicide.[13] After two years, however, her patience has begun to wear thin, and she engages in a polymorphously perverse relationship with an old boyfriend before finding her true love in the person of a young student of art, who promises her a trip to France. And yet, as potentially attractive as *Madam Aema*'s storyline may have sounded to contemporaneous female audiences, its titular heroine remains positioned before the camera as an *object* of desire, visually fetishized through fragmenting close-ups designed solely to attract the heterosexual male gaze. Indeed, for all of its outward focus on a liberated woman who exerts sexual agency as the main protagonist, *Madam Aema* culminates with a conservative realignment of the narrative within the parameters of patriarchal values, showing Ae-ma—once a "model housewife before the start of the affair"—returning to her husband, who has been released from jail.[14]

Moreover, its many images of copulation unleashed what critic Kim Ji-seok calls a "visual hedonism" during the 1980s; one directed toward the fetishized figures of female characters—from prostitutes and bar hostesses to college girls and married women—in other films.[15] In opting *not* to cut away from copulating bodies, *Madam Aema* was a bridge, then, between the soft-core imagery of 1970s 'hostess films' (such as *Winter Woman* [*Kyŏul yŏja*, 1977] and *I am Number Seventy-Seven Woman* [*Nanŭn 77bŏn agassi*, 1978]), and the full frontal nudity and intercourse on view in subsequent erotic films set primarily in motel/hotel rooms (such as *Prostitution* [*Maech'un*, 1988] and *Cow Breast Madam Commits Adultery* [*Chŏtso puin param natnae*, 1996], not to mention the spate of *Madam Aema* sequels—ten in all—whose ever-dwindling production costs were in inverse proportion to the actresses' increasing bust sizes).

Although the top-grossing Korean film of 1982, one that seduced some 300,000 curious spectators into a single theater over the course of four months, *Madam Aema* only ranked sixth at the box-office that year, behind such steamy Hollywood fare as *Body Heat* (1981) and *The Postman Always Rings Twice* (1981). Besides being a contradictory period in which executive power became even more centralized and authoritarian, yet moral restrictions were being dismantled, the 1980s was a decade when Western attitudes toward sexuality firmly took root in the Korean psyche thanks to American cultural products like the J. Geils Band's hit single "Centerfold" and the Sylvia Kristel vehicle *Private Lessons* (1980)—both of which were imported into South Korea in 1982. In fact, coming right behind *Madam Aema*—at the number seven box-office spot—was *Private Lessons*, a juvenile sex comedy featuring the star of such soft-porn classics as *Emmanuelle* (1974) and *Lady Chatterley's Lover* (1980). With this influx of sexually explicit cultural productions came certain negative attitudes about motel/hotel rooms—attitudes that are thus not unique to South Korean cinema but are in fact widespread among American and European films and television series, and which I would now like to turn to as a preamble to my discussion of *Motel Cactus*.

COMFORT, CORRUPTION, AND VICE: WESTERN ATTITUDES TOWARD MOTEL/HOTEL ROOMS

At first glimpse, the Korean love motels and hotels on view in the above-mentioned sexploitation films seem like a cross-cultural manifestation of the so-called "no-tell motels" and "hot-sheet joints" that began to dot the American landscape from Phoenix to Philadelphia during the 1960s. These stateside love-nests rented by the hour, where a Gideon's Bible might be bookmarked with used condoms, not only gave couples the opportunity to "consummate their clandestine affairs" in the rarefied world of Magic Fingers massaging beds, ceiling-affixed mirrors, and Jacuzzi bathtubs, but also served as places where, in the words of Michael Witzel, "criminals hid from the law and strong-arm men brewed their plans."[16] In his overview of the American motel, Witzel briefly discusses the historical roots of the no-tell motel, which is similar to the 'Functional Motel' that Vladimir Nabokov writes about in *Lolita* ("To any other type of tourist accommodation I soon grew to prefer the Functional Motel—clean, neat, safe nooks, ideal places for sleep, argument, reconciliation, insatiable illicit love"). As an outgrowth of prewar motor cottages and "seedy cabin camps and courts" renting out "temporary mattress space" (what Witzel describes as "illegitimate businesses that sanctioned promiscuity and promised prostitution"), the no-tell motel was simply the newest haven "for vice and corruption" during the postwar era. As he states,

> For a single hour, two hours (and in a minority of cases, the entire night), liberal-minded motel customers could check in—with nary a single bag of luggage—and enjoy the anonymous comforts of a motel room. Later, when their recreational needs were satiated, they merely left the key on the bed stand (the bill was settled up in advance), slipped into their automobile, and motored down the road, unnoticed. With the mattress still warm, maids rushed in to perform a quick once-over, change the sheets and the pillowcases, and prepare the bed chambers for the next flock of lovebirds.[17]

Not coincidentally, when represented on screen in American and European productions, the motel/hotel room is where one is likely to find "a lot of heavy drinking, a lot of fast women, and a lot of loose talk," to borrow a quote from Michael Nesmith in an episode from the hit TV show *The Monkees* (1966–1968). The very sight of a motel or hotel is enough to inspire knee-jerk associations based on this sensationalistic premise. For example, in writer-director Tony Richardson's adaptation of the John Irving novel *The Hotel New Hampshire* (1984), Lilly, the youngest member of the incestuous Berry clan, accurately predicts that "there's going to be sex and violence" upon first seeing the Viennese establishment that lends the film its title. More recently, such motion pictures and television programs as the raunchy comedy *Road Trip* (2000) and the recently revived *Family Guy* (1999, 2005) have shown motel/hotel rooms to be particularly prone to negative stereotyping, as when a desk clerk in the former film sarcastically asks one of the dopehead protagonists, "Is there anything else I can help you with? Perhaps you'd like an eleven-year-old prostitute sent to your room. We can do that. Or maybe we can 'off' someone for you."[18] In an episode from the latter animated TV series, Brian and Stevie try to sleep while an audible drug deal plays out in the next room.

Apart from its connections to violence, drugs, sex, and prostitution, a motel/hotel room serves other communal functions, as evidenced in Martin Ritt's social-problem film *Norma Rae* (1979), a whistle-blowing drama in which textile-industry worker Reuben Warshowsky implores his fellow peons to sign their union cards in a room at the Golden Cherry Motel, a site of both privacy and congregation, momentary confinement yet projected emancipation. The motel/hotel room is thus a contradictory space of personal desire and utopian potential (bringing together disparate individuals under a single roof); one in which divergent attitudes (toward politics, religion, sex, gender, etc.) can be addressed and racial or ethnic differences can be minimized if not completely erased. Moreover, it often serves to illustrate the underlying appeal of social mobility—of moving up in the world (in the case of hotel verticality and hierarchical architecture) or passing beyond boundaries (in the case of motel horizontality and integrated architecture).

In American cinema, social mobility is often linked to the spatial paradigm of the open road, the ease with which men and women might venture off the beaten track to roadside inns and honeymoon hideaways. Self-determination and individual choice, two thematic mainstays of Hollywood's dream factories, are thus allied with the rise of the automobile; and in fact an entire film genre—the road-movie—came into being partially as a response to the call for increased democratic freedoms, and has made frequent use of family-run motels and trackside hotels as iconographic stopovers not only for gumshoe detectives, migratory laborers, auto-gypsies, and other representatives of the working-class, but also for middle-class characters seeking personal meaning and professional success amidst the 'familiar otherness' of the roadside inn. Although Charlie, the prickly, put-upon protagonist in Barry Levinson's Oscar-winning road-movie *Rain Man* (1988), complains that his business is going down the toilet while he and his autistic brother Raymond are stuck at the Honeymoon Haven Motel in "Bumblefuck, Missouri," his temporary immobility only underscores the socioeconomic leverage he was able to exert before this *temporary*, ultimately life-enriching setback. Indeed, just as automotive tourism in the United States during the first two decades of the twentieth-century contributed to the advent of municipal auto-camps, cabin courts, country inns, shotgun shacks, and other predecessors of what is today known as the motel, so too have road films supplied many of the perennial clichés about individual mobility and democratic freedom that remain at the heart of America's neon highway folklore and contemporary car culture.

Combining 'motor' and 'hotel,' the portmanteau word "motel" itself has built-in motility, an ambulatory freedom that casts in comparative relief the stuffiness and stasis permeating South Korean cinema. Only by escaping the homeland, many South Korean films suggest, can one achieve more than a modicum of conjugal privacy. This point is illustrated in *Lies* (*Kŏjitmal* 2000), a film in which two sadomasochistic vagabonds move from one motel to the next in search of the perfect tryst only to ultimately leave the exigencies of extended families behind for the more upscale environs of a Paris hotel.[19] Tellingly, the most perverse aspect of Chang Sŏn-u's controversial sex drama is the iconoclastic director's decision to keep his camera—along with the December-May couple—claustrophobically confined to the interior of the Parisian hotel in the film's closing moments, leaving the City of Lights as an offscreen and intangible source of personal yearning during the dénouement. I would now like to turn to another Korean film, *Motel Cactus*, in which this sense of stasis, confinement, and interiority takes on allegorical, perhaps even political, meaning over the course of its four episodes.

MOTEL CACTUS AND THE 'PRICKLY' POLITICS OF PERSONAL LONGING

Motel Cactus begins with a curious three-minute prologue in which a young woman named Hyŏn-ju lectures an associate about the pitfalls of love, advising the recently jilted, heartbroken girl not to "cave in to men" anymore. The unnamed recipient of Hyŏn-ju's admonition can be heard crying offscreen, yet at no point during this prologue does her presence become visible. As we shall see, this absent presence, this telling omission, gradually informs our understanding of the film's subsequent four episodes, each of which pivots on a dialectical axis of interior/exterior, onscreen/offscreen spaces. Only in the episode that immediately follows the prologue, "Summer," do we begin to grasp the ironic implications of Hyŏn-ju's words; for it is *she* who gives in to her own sentimentality during an all-day marathon of loveless intercourse in the motel room with her brooding lover, a distracted TV-addict named Min-gu.

The first images of this episode—Hyŏn-ju peering into the bathroom mirror—express the self-reflexive disposition of the film, and underline the ways in which spectatorial awareness of such ironies is lost on this self-delusional and contradictory character. Having been tear-gassed by riot police at a demonstration, Hyŏn-ju now finds herself struggling to rub the stinging chemicals from her eyes. The unseen political protest is an event 'outside' the diegetic space of the motel room; yet, when clips of the event are broadcast on the television later in the episode, it becomes an enigmatic touchstone that invites certain questions about its relevance to the narrative. When and where did this volatile demonstration take place? And what was Hyŏn-ju's role in it? We soon learn that she and Min-gu were only casual eyewitnesses to a student rebellion. Yet the reasons behind their passive participation go unanswered throughout the episode, which is content to usher in details about the characters' lives only to frustrate attempts at deciphering their meanings through elisions and omissions—two narrative conventions of the loosely episodic yet severely condensed anthology/omnibus form. If anything, Hyŏn-ju's momentarily impaired vision—an outcome of her spectatorial position vis-à-vis an offscreen demonstration against the government—signifies the audience's own discombobulation throughout *Motel Cactus*, a film that is filled with the kind of intentionally 'blotchy' visuals for which Australian cinematographer Christopher Doyle has become world-famous.

As in his collaborations with Hong Kong *auteur* Wong Kar-wai, Doyle's smearscreen effects bring an impressionistic abstraction to these tales of disconsolate lovers, their emotional restlessness conveyed through a fidgety yet fetishistic camera. Besides *Motel Cactus'* color palette, which consists of saturated reds, neon pinks, and aquamarine blues (all bleeding into one another and suffusing the environment with a sense of sexual anticipation, danger, and allure), the film's mottled mise-en-scène—its watery mélange of textures and surfaces—not only challenges our ability to accurately see characters' actions, but also metaphorically underscores the difficulties involved in intuiting or understanding their motivations.[20] Occasionally, the beautiful decay of the room's weathered wallpaper vies against out-of-focus faces and pixilated bodies. This attention to supposedly extraneous surface details would seem to counteract our ability to plumb the depths of a character's psychosis, to extract meaningful reasons for his/her meaningless flings or self-destructive behavior. However, even as it functions as a visual correlative to a narratological feature of this and other episode films, in which there is a surplus of surface (thanks to the multifarious nature of the genre) and a dearth of character depth (due to the brevity of the sequentially told tales), this stylistic decision also reveals a great deal about the "situation" of these and other men and women in South Korea.

For example, the disorienting second shot of this episode—an *in medias res* extreme close-up of Hyŏn-ju's face reflected in the bathroom mirror—translates extreme proximity into emotional distance, her abstracted features muddling the hermeneutic quest of the spectator. During Hyŏn-ju and Min-gu's first act of lovemaking, Doyle's camera freely oscillates between different spaces, going from inside to outside the bathtub and back again. Significantly, these sweeping lateral movements of the camera introduce the theme of *partitions*—physical as well as emotional—deployed throughout the entire film. As an expression of this thematic motif, Min-gu grows increasingly concerned that their neighbors in the next room can hear their screams of ecstasy through the walls. The emphasis here on setting, on situational context, evokes more than a self-conscious fear of prying ears. It provides the material metaphors necessary to sustain a spatial poetics, one constructed along a frontier separating the claustrophobic confines of the motel room and the vast unseen that is the outside world. In *Motel Cactus*, the 'outside world' is not simply one's immediate surroundings, but an imaginative space that encompasses the concentrically ringed communities (neighborhood, city, province, nation) implicit in South Korea's postwar industrial and economic shift from local to regional to global markets.

While those communities remain invisibly offscreen throughout the four hermetically enclosed narratives of *Motel Cactus*, they exert sway over the characters in oblique ways (sonically, for instance; or through the presence of material objects). Moreover, one can imagine this suggestion of outward expansion in less political, more poetic terms by turning to Georges Perec's *Espèces d'espaces*, in which the foremost purveyor of "literary architecture" and the "world's concreteness" zooms-out from a sheet of paper—past bedroom, apartment, neighborhood, town, country, continent, and world—to the infinite reaches of space (a void not unlike the primal space of a blank page). As a kind of anti-*Wavelength* (1967) meditation on scale,[21] Perec's text takes the reader to the farthest reaches of domestic, urban, and even cosmic space, yet—like *Motel Cactus*—is no less concerned with the material objects that split space in two. In a paragraph devoted to doors, which "stop and separate" people, the French author writes,

> On one side, me and my place, the private, the domestic . . . on the other side, other people, the world, the public, politics. You can't simply let yourself slide from one into the other, can't pass from one to the other, neither in one direction nor in the other. You have to have the password, have to cross the threshold, have to show your credentials, have to communicate, just as the prisoner communicates with the world outside.[22]

In a sense, similar demands are placed on spectators of episode films, the 'doors' of which swing open only at those in-between moments—the interstitials that separate one story from another and provide momentary release from the paradoxically pleasant prison of narrative.

While Min-gu's consciousness of his surroundings might initially suggest that he is attentive to the needs of others, he in fact fails to perceive Hyŏn-ju's desires, and becomes increasingly bored, uncomfortable and distant after their second and third attempts at sex. He wants to leave the motel and venture outdoors, but the heavy downpour of rain visible through the cracked and bandaged window puts a damper on this. His noncommittal attitude and lack of enthusiasm, which are only exacerbated once Hyŏn-ju begins to hypothesize about having a baby, are denoted by a bunch of deflating balloons. Bearing the logo of Baskin Robbins (one of the many American specialty food chains to make inroads in South Korea),[23] these remnants of the sentimental woman's birthday celebration could be said to represent not only the exhausted male's dwindling interest, but also the beguiling effects of American cultural capital within an East Asian nation that has itself been historically characterized as the 'product' of U.S. or Western intervention.

Given the film's insistent fixation on a single interior setting, much of its meaning could be said to reside in the nooks and crannies of the episodic narrative, in the material objects (such as the Baskin Robbins balloons) that in other films would appear to be little more than props. Among the many metaphor-imbued details in the motel room (including a spinning pinwheel and a condom dispenser in the last episode) is an electric waterfall print hanging on one of the walls, a framed image of movement and stasis that Min-gu bought for Hyŏn-ju as a birthday gift. Saying that the kitschy image of the waterfall might be better suited for a barbershop, she appears noticeably unimpressed by his small gesture of kindness—a reaction that helps to explain the forsaken gift's reappearance in the following episodes. The recurring image of the electric print episode-to-episode secures a semblance of order and coherence for the fragmented film, reining in whatever differences there may have been among the six characters for the sake of structural synchronicity and psychological affinities. Like the neon sign outside the motel (an entangled set of glass tubes, inside of which electrified gasses are trapped in a circuitous flow), the image of the waterfall gives the impression of *contained motion*. As an objective correlative, it represents the characters' inability to fully free themselves from the socioeconomic constraints of South Korea's calcified class system as well as the emotional deadlock that too often characterizes heterosexual relations in its cinema. Also, the picture's artificial rendering of the natural world, later recalled by a fleeting shot of silk flowers in the third episode, hammers home the idea that such contrivances have supplanted authentic experience, which can only be gestured toward through fabricated versions of reality.

Moreover, as an image familiar to most patrons of Chinese restaurants as well as viewers of Mandarin and Cantonese-language films, the electric painting situates the film's thematic interests within a broader transnational context.[24] In 1997, the same year *Motel Cactus* was released, another Christopher Doyle-lensed film—Wong Kar-wai's *Happy Together* (*Cheun gwong tsa sit*)—highlighted the visual iconography of an almost identical waterfall print so as to provide a (false) Edenic image of escape and allegorize the cultural hegemony faced by the film's border-crossing protagonists during a time of national euphoria and apprehension (Britain's landmark handover of the city to China). Holed up in Buenos Aires' Hotel Riviera, Po-wing and Yiu-fai occupy a liminal position in Chinese society, and their exclusion from the political process back 'home' is an extension of their outsider status in Argentina as an Asian gay couple. The creative redeployment in *Motel Cactus* of an icon ensconced within the Chinese cultural imagination is just one of the ways in which the film transcends its spatio-temporal confines and gestures toward other national contexts in which dysfunctional couples (gay or straight) might similarly be construed as allegorical figures in times of transformation or crisis.

Significantly, the emergent discourse of homosexuality in South Korea slips into the proceedings of *Motel Cactus*. During another curious outdoor prelude—this time sandwiched between the first and second episodes—a teenage girl is questioned by an offscreen interviewer about marriage between two people with the same family-clan name (a persistent problem in the land of Kims, Lees, and Parks). Confusing *tongsŏng* (same last name) with *tongsŏng* (same sex), the girl responds that gay Koreans deserve respect and equal rights. While her openness to queer sensibilities is laudable, the fact that it serves as a source of comic misunderstanding (slippage between homonym and homosexual) says much about the status of gays and lesbians in South Korea, a nation that—despite increased socioeconomic liberalization—is rife with the kinds of cultural stereotypes that 'otherize,' rather than normativize, oppositional discourses and posit homosexuality as the butt of politically incorrect jokes. If nothing else, the emphasis in this prelude on *sameness* gestures toward the overarching uniformity (some might say monotony) of the film's four episodes—all of which hinge on similarly bleak depictions of male–female relations. Again, much of this thematic and visual overlap is generated through the reappearance of the electric waterfall print—one of the many 'leftovers' strewn about the room in episode two.

Titled 'Spring,' the second episode is perhaps the most self-reflexive of the four narratives due to its focus on filmmaking (or, rather, video-making) as both an exercise in futility and a means toward (hetero)sexual consummation. When the two main characters of this narrative—college students Chun-gi and Sŏ-gyŏng—first enter Room 407, they find that it has not yet been attended to by the maid, whose neglect in picking up the garbage left by the previous occupants casts in relief the ongoing slippage between past and present, between preceding and ensuing episodes. Traces of the past infringe on the present, much like the way in which the motel-room ceiling, stained with yesterday's mildew, is a palimpsestic reminder of the post-coital moment (later denoted by virginal Sŏ-gyŏng's blood-stained panties, which Chun-gi attempts to wash in vain).[25] Having made a reservation two days earlier, Chun-gi complains to the motel proprietor, "I paid 10,000 won in advance," and insists, "It has to be this room." Despite the debilitating state of debris, he and Sŏ-gyŏng intend to shoot a softcore porn video there, not in the hope of cashing in on the success of the erotic film industry, but rather as a school project to be turned in to their teacher the following Monday.

However, the shoot is delayed indefinitely due to the no-show of cameraman Chong-p'yo.

While waiting for their AWOL classmate (who, we later learn through a telephone conversation, was arrested by police the previous night), the young man and woman order Chinese delivery, play videogames, and hesitantly begin to kiss and caress one another after hearing a couple in the next room making love. Once again, this emphasis on the permeability of partitions, on the collapsible time-space of the motel room, conveys the reverberation of thematic material across the film's porous narrative divisions—interstitial markers delineating one episode from another. Moreover, it gestures toward the outside world, a sonically articulated space of continuous construction. Throughout the episode, the persistent sound of drilling and machine work filters into the claustrophobic (yet, according to Sŏ-gyŏng, "spacious") motel room, as if to illustrate how insidiously South Korea's late-twentieth-century industrial development has encroached upon the lives of its increasingly privatized citizens.

Exterior sounds similarly seep into the third episode. Entitled 'Fall,' this episode is largely silent save for the caterwaul singing of the drunken male protagonist, Sŏk-t'ae; the quiet, non-diegetic strumming of a guitar during a slow-motion shot of lovemaking; and the occasional wail of police sirens (a sound which evokes the offscreen presence of suppression forces in the first episode, as well as the arrest of the delinquent videographer in the second episode). The sirens likely remind many Korean viewers beyond a certain age of the *minjung* (people's) movement of the 1980s, when labor unionists, leftist students, progressive intellectuals, and other supporters of the urban proletariat took to the streets to demonstrate against their government's corrupt policies and collaboration with foreign powers (namely the United States and Japan). To most non-Korean viewers, such allusions remained buried.

Sŏk-t'ae's partner, Hyŏn-ju, was the female protagonist in the first episode. Her reappearance in the film breaks the chain of what might be called 'differentiated repetition' while visually manifesting some of the film's recurring thematic motifs. That is, the return of an already familiar yet exited character works against the ostensible logic of episodic dramaturgy by turning away from the structured difference of this narratological genre for the sake of sameness rather than similarity. As if to further underscore the irony of her own words in the first episode (a warning against getting involved with strange men solely for sex), Hyŏn-ju is shown being manhandled by Sŏk-t'ae (a stranger whom she just met in a bar). Dragging the woman across the motel floor, Sŏk-t'ae is a more misogynistic version of the patriarchy personified by Min-gu, her previous lover. Min-gu's fear of being heard by neighbors in the first episode seems reasonable in light of her new partner's loud singing. The people next door complain by beating on the thin wall, percussively setting the tone for Sŏk-t'ae's drunken and lecherous lunge toward her. After several bouts of aggressive sex (broken up by intermittent horseplay), the two gaze out of the cracked window as if searching for some ameliorative end to their longing and loneliness.

The final episode, 'Winter,' begins with a fortune-teller informing her customer that she hasn't changed a bit since their last session—words that once again transmit a condition of sameness. The woman, a recent divorcee named Hŭi-su, replies to her clairvoyant companion, "You were right about everything. . . . You said we weren't well-matched and that I shouldn't marry him." These cryptic words lead to another motel tryst, this time involving the divorced woman and her former lover, a man to whom we have already been introduced: Sŏk-t'ae. A bit more backstory fleshes out the female character, who—after the death of her father and the predicted end of her ill-fated marriage—left her home in Canada for Korea, where her ex-boyfriend continues to reside. Although she will return to Canada in a few days (an imminent departure that suggests the fleeting nature of narrative episodicity), this upper-middle class woman achieves momentary catharsis in the arms of Sŏk-t'ae. As in the earlier segments, lovemaking leads to browbeating, although in this case the couple's heated argument (in which they yell at one other through the frosted partition of the bathroom's glass doors) evokes more than the petty squabbles of their predecessors (who engaged in more ferocious, less loquacious acts of sex). Indeed, the partition itself might remind us of the interstitial dividers that not only separate one story from another in an episode film, but also pit those stories against one another as objects of potential fetishism competitively vying for the spectator's interest.

Competition is diegetically inscribed through the presence of an American basketball game, which Hŭi-su and Sŏk-t'ae watch on TV before switching the dial to a soccer match between Korea and Japan. Their spectatorial act, which recalls the favored pastime of Min-gu in the film's first episode, is brought to an end when the motel's electricity shuts off (something that happens in each of the four episodes), but not before bringing *Motel Cactus* full circle. Indeed, this return to an act of television viewing—as a self-reflexive moment—prepares us for a passage of dialogue in the penultimate scene of the film, which draws to a close just after Hŭi-su asks Sŏk-t'ae why the yŏgwan is called 'Cactus.' His reply, that "a cactus has thorns," is a simultaneously roundabout and direct way of saying that they must reside in pain if they are to pursue libidinal desires—a bleak pronouncement driven home when he thereafter poses the question, "Does that mean we will get pricked?"

By invoking the landscape of the American Southwest, *Motel Cactus* ushers in yet another transcultural signifier. The title of the film not only ironically counterposes the arid conditions of the desert with the wet ambience of the motel room, but also inverts the name of a famous establishment in Tucumcari, New Mexico: the Cactus Motel.[26] The final, enigmatic image of the film, showing waves breaking along an unidentified beach, brings together sand and water motifs and provides a fitting (orgasmic) climax to a film literally and figuratively filled with miniature climaxes. As the only scene of *Motel Cactus* shot on video in black-and-white, it also sets the stage for Pak Kiyong's subsequent feature *Camel(s)*, a minimalist road movie-cum-chamber drama in which the interior of a car and the interior of a love motel serve as the principle settings for a middle-aged couple who travel to a coastal city to act out an illicit affair. Indeed, the washed out, pebbly texture to the latter film's black-and-white digital imagery recalls the final shot in *Motel Cactus* and suggests that it is a sequel of sorts, a post-coital coda that deposits the viewer once again into the claustrophobic confines of a motel room, thus rendering the notion of freedom as something necessarily fleeting.

DIVIDING TIME, BLURRING BOUNDARIES

Like so many anthology and omnibus films, *Motel Cactus* features four episodes, each roughly twenty-five minutes in length. It therefore invites us to erect a kind of critical scaffolding around the concept of 'quarter'—a word whose various meanings are registered in the film. Not only does 'quarter' denote temporary housing, a place where one momentarily drops anchor, but it also suggests dismemberment, the cleaving or cutting up of a whole into separate parts. The narrative fragmentation of this particular episodic film, which is (not coincidentally) divided into four quarters, resonates with the idea of cutting emotional and familial ties. Significantly, the motel room number (407) conjures fatalistic associations in the minds of many Koreans, who— because the Chinese character representing 'four' also means 'death'—are wary of fourth-floor apartments and hotel rooms.[27] The negative implications of both the motel room number and the number of episodes gathered together in *Motel Cactus* inform the spectatorial positions of domestic audiences who may 'see' the film differently than Western viewers (for whom no such fear of four exists).

Four has been a numerical mainstay of episodic cinema throughout the world, as evidenced by the titles of such anthology, compilation, and omnibus films as *Four Love Stories* (*Yottso no koi no monogatari*, Japan, 1947), *The Four Truths* (*Las cuatro verdades*, Spain, 1962), *Love in 4 Dimensions* (*Amore in 4 dimensioni*; France/Italy, 1964), *Four Women* (*Quatre d'entre elles*; Switzerland, 1967), *Four Clowns* (U.S., 1970), and *The Four Faces of Eve* (*4 Si Mian Xiawa*, 1996). This latter film, a Hong Kong production, was shot by Christopher Doyle one year before he served as director of photography on *Motel Cactus*—a contribution that was often cited in reviews as the sole reason to see the film. This privileging of visual over thematic and narrative material is indicative of the critical fetishism that often attends readings of East Asian films in the West. Nevertheless, because Doyle himself has been a frequent contributor to anthology and omnibus films, from the two-episode *Chungking Express* (*Chunghing Samlam*, 1994) to multinational co-productions like *Three . . . Extremes* (2004) and *Eros* (2004), schematic delineations between form and content, style and structure, are problematized or blurred (not unlike the cinematographer's intentionally smudgy visuals).

The fact that *Motel Cactus* has sometimes been referred to as a recycled pastiche of Doyle's Wong Kar-wai films should remind us that recycling itself is linked both to episodic narrativity (wherein each segment after the first salvages and processes themes or images from previous segments) and to the material as well as temporal conditions of hotel/motel occupancy, which is divided by the intervals of maid service (refreshing what has been worn-out if not completely used-up). This theme of recycling also animates the Chinese film *Happy Times* (*Xingfu Shiguang*, 2001), one of Zhang Yimou's rare departures from epic period pieces. In this contemporary comedy set near the port city of Dalian, the out-of-work male protagonist—armed with a can of red paint and aided by a pal—transforms a dilapidated bus into a love hotel that, as another character says, looks a lot like "a public toilet." "Beat-up places are all the rage these days," our enterprising protagonist rationalizes, providing us not only with a visualization of the (im)mobility bound up in motel/hotel narratives (the broken-down bus as stationary sign, or unfilled promise, of transportability), but also with a metaphor of the increased predilection these days for a cinematic space amenable to both the utopian projection of an imagined future and the nostalgic longing for a fabricated past (a 'simpler time' that, in reality, was just as fraught, perhaps more so, with socioeconomic constraints and civil rights violations).

Such a contradictory space can be found in numerous East Asian films produced over the last fifty years.[28] Indeed, love motels/hotels have been an architectural fixture of Japan's cinematic landscape for decades. From casual references to or glimpses of such places in Akira Kurosawa's *Stray Dog* (*Nora inu*, 1949) and Takeshi Kitano's *Kikujiro no natsu* (1999), to their more emphatic foregrounding in New Wave classics like Nagisa Oshima's *Cruel Story of Youth* (*Seishun zankoku monogatari*, 1960) and *Pleasures of the Flesh* (*Etsuraku*, 1965), Japanese love motels/hotels (*tsurekomi hoteru* or *rabu hoteru*) often blur "the borderline between prostitution, seduction, and liaison;" but they do so by exploiting the sexual fantasies of the nation's business class.[29]

As suggested earlier in this essay, those sexual fantasies tend to be more highly wrought when transposed onto the fanciful façades and interiors of Japanese love motels/hotels, which—besides being typically identified by heart-shaped neon signs on the roofs (as opposed to the 'flowing waters' bath signs atop Korean yŏgwans)—today often feature outrageous architectural embellishments (medieval turrets, shark fins, etc.), theme décor ("S&M, Versailles, safari, warzone, shuttle, samurai"),[30] and soothing background environmental sounds, not to mention names like "Little House on the Prairie" and "Anne of Green Gables."[31] Perhaps the epitome of this postmodern mélange and kitschy excess is the Meguro Emperor love-hotel in downtown Tokyo, whose exterior, as Nick Perry points out in his book *Hyperreality and Global Culture*, is a replica of Ludwig's Neuschwanstein castle in Bavaria, an "original fake" in its own right.[32]

Regardless of surface differences, the love motel/hotel is an accepted facet of both Korean and Japanese cultures, a space where couples can rent rooms for private purposes without fear of social stigma. It is "looked upon benignly, as a fact of life in [cities] where living space is so limited."[33] It has furthermore become a prominent fixture throughout East and Southeast Asia, most notably in the *lorongs* (alleyways) of Singapore's infamous red-light districts, catering to foreign businessmen and tourists. Of course, love hotels/motels are not unique to these national and regional settings. The population explosions of many South and Central American countries, combined with the cramped housing conditions and limited means of either physical or class mobility faced by their citizens, have led to an increased need for the privacy offered by such establishments. In Argentina, for example, there are what are called *amoblados*, hotels in which rooms can be rented at hourly rates. Likewise, in Chile, one can find love hotels west of the Andes—places like the Hotel Valdivia, a "Disneyworld for couples" that, according to Sara Wheeler, features dozens of themed rooms and is "disguised as a private mansion" filled with "inscrutable and silent" patrons.[34] Cuba has likewise seen a spike in the number of thatched-roof cabanas known as *posadas*, austere settings open round-the-clock and where, for the cost of around five pesos, *hombres* and *mujeres* might find temporary relief from familial constraints and engage in "one of the few aspects of life not controlled by the state": sex.[35]

This transnational spread of love-motel/hotel culture runs parallel to the increased proliferation of anthology and omnibus films since the 1997 release of *Motel Cactus*, including *Hotels* (*Hoteles*, 2003), a five-episode film written and directed by Argentine filmmaker Aldo Paparella and shot in five different cities: Shanghai; Asuncion; New York; Buenos Aires; and Chernobyl. If lacking the epic sweep and global diversity of Paparella's film, Pak's *Motel*

Cactus nevertheless charts a compelling course through South Korea's recent past, subtly showing how the history of previous occupants encroaches on each new couple's amorous encounter while gesturing toward political events outside its claustrophobic setting. Given its compactness, the room at the heart of *Motel Cactus* would appear to be ill equipped to contain the expansiveness of history, yet—like the fingernail scratch that Hyŏn-ju leaves on Min-gu's back in the first episode—it reveals deep rifts in Korean society while providing palimpsestic traces of the country's cultural and political pasts. With pleasure and consumption, the film seems to say, comes an inevitable, intensified feeling of loneliness and longing.

While I yield to Yu Ji-na's academic expertise in matters of gender discrimination and sexual exploitation, and fundamentally agree with her that South Korean cinema is undergoing an artistic and commercial renaissance, I feel compelled to disagree on one significant point: erotic scenes in South Korean cinema have *never* been, as she says in the opening quote of this essay, "meaningless." Gratuitous, yes. Degrading to women, often. A barometer of the social and political climate, certainly. But always, and most importantly, congested sites of meaning and ideological convergence. If critics of South Korean cinema have thus far failed to examine this lexicon of limbs, this syntax of sweaty bodies, this hotbed of hermeneutic activity set primarily in hotels and motels, we should not simply attribute this shortsightedness to the relative 'newness' of the sexploitation genre (which has been around since the 1982 release of *Madame Aema*); instead, we should see this absence of critical discourse as an opportunity to re-evaluate the very evaluative criteria that we bring to cultural productions like *Motel Cactus*, and ask why yŏgwan imagery continues to proliferate in this new millennium.

NOTES

1. Yu Ji-na, "Glory days of Korean Movies," *Korea Focus on Current Topics*, vol. 7, no. 2 (March–April 1999): 150.

2. Sandra Buckley, ed., *Encyclopedia of Contemporary Japanese Culture* (London: Routledge, 2002), 291.

3. There is also a rich tradition of theme motels/hotels in the United States, one that has begun to fade from America's cultural landscape thanks in part to the steam-rolling effect of commercial enterprises. There remain, however, vestiges of these weird and wild expressions of local color. Throughout the Southwest, for instance, there are theme motels modeled after wigwams, adobe huts, and Spanish missions. Travelers to the Northeast might chance upon multistory hotels in the shape of light-houses and windmills. The Red Caboose Motel in Strasburg, Pennsylvania, collapses mobility and stability in the form of a stationed locomotive. However, these quirky

establishments differ significantly from love motels/hotels in Japan, where programmatic styles reign supreme.

4. In the years following the 1876 signing of the Kanghwa Treaty, which saw
Japan's opening of three Korean ports (Inch'on, Iksan, and Wŏnsan) where commercial interests could be exploited, there was an increase in the number of foreigners
traveling to Korea. This demographic spike necessitated the establishment of cheap
accommodations for visitors from other East Asian nations as well as from parts of
Europe and the Americas. According to historian Yi Tong-jin, the yŏgwan industry
grew from a mere four establishments near Seoul's Japanese quarter at the end of the
1890s to eight overnight inns in 1900 to 123 yŏgwan in or around the capital city just
eight years later. This increase has been partially attributed to the signing of the First
Korea–Japan Treaty in 1904 and the Ulsa Treaty in 1905, which brought diplomats,
politicians, and traders to Korea in droves. Many of these establishments were merely
cement buildings lacking architectural ornament if not structural integrity, and were
oftentimes conveniently located near train stations (such as Namdaemun, Yongsan,
and Sodaemun). Yi Tong-jin, "Research on the Transformation of Korean Accommodation Facilities," Master's Thesis in Hotel Management (Sejong University, 1992).

5. Drawing upon a "study carried out by the Seoul City Hall" in examining this increase in pleasure-seeking among South Koreans, Cotton and van Leest state, "While
there were 713 pleasure resorts in 1983, there were 1,211 by 1986. In the same period
the number of hotels increased from 658 to 853, and massage parlours from 57 to
122." James Cotton and Kim Hyung-a van Leest, "The new rich and the new middle
class in South Korea: the rise and fall of the 'golf republic'," in Richard Robison and
David S. G. Goodman, eds., *The New Rich in Asia: Mobile Phones, McDonald's and
Middle-class Revolution* (London: Routledge, 1996), 191.

6. See Laura Kendall's Introduction to her edited anthology, *Under Construction:
The Gendering of Modernity, Class, and Consumption in the Republic of Korea* (Honolulu: University of Hawai'i Press, 2002), for a more elaborate description of some
of the paradoxes born out of this "new sexual subjectivity and morality."

7. Elaine H. Kim speaks of the "complex, contradictory tangle of the residual and
emergent" that characterizes gender relations in South Korea's class-stratified consumer culture. Moreover, she singles out the recent appearance of love hotels near
Seoul's college campuses as one particular "element of extremism" in the nation's
reconfigured conceptions of sexuality, marriage, and dating. Elaine H. Kim, "Men's
Talk: A Korean American View of South Korean Constructions of Women, Gender,
and Masculinity," in Elaine H. Kim and Chungmoo Choi, eds., *Dangerous Women:
Gender and Korean Nationalism* (New York: Routledge, 1998), 103.

8. In 1990, a movie adaptation of Ma Kwang-su's title poem, "Let's Go to the
Rose Inn," was produced, simply titled *The Rose Inn* (*Changmi-yŏgwan*; 1990).

9. Throughout South Korea's cinematic Golden Age of the 1960s, the Park Chung
Hee government enforced film laws that controlled motion picture content with re-
gards to politics and ideology as well as sexuality. Although a few directors, such
as Yu Hyŏn-mok and Yi Man-hŭi, incorporated subversive political statements into
their social melodramas and war pictures during that era, only one—Kim Ki-yŏng
(aka "Mr. Monster")—really challenged industry standards and government poli-

cies dealing with screen sexuality; as illustrated in *The Housemaid* (*Hanyo*, 1960), a hothouse chamber drama about female aggression, male impotency, and 'abnormal' expressions of heterosexual desire.

10. Director Chŏng In-yŏp, South Korea's version of French filmmaker Roger Vadim, initially established himself as a purveyor of soft-focus female sexuality. Co-incidentally, Chŏng—who had nothing to do with the last seven of the ten remakes—made an official sequel to *Madame Aema* in 1998, a few months after the release of Pak Ki-yong's *Motel Cactus*. Titled *Paris Aema*, this sexploitation film is not to be confused with *Madame Aema in Paris*, a 1991 installation art piece by Yook Tai-jin consisting of poster images from the "Madame Aema" series of films.

11. *Madam Aema* was in fact South Korea's first midnight movie.

12. The Korean-language journal *Cine 21* celebrated the twentieth anniversary of *Madam Aema* in an attempt to critically recuperate this pivotal if overlooked piece of film history. See "Special: The Twentieth Anniversary of *Madam Aema*," *Cine 21* (February 19, 2002).

13. Although the title of the film might suggest—at least to English-speaking audiences—a connection between Aema's sexual indiscretions and those of Emma, the titular protagonist in Gustave Flaubert's *Madame Bovary*, when literally translated "Aema puin" means "Horse-Loving Woman." This title was changed to "Marihuana-Loving Woman" due to censorship concerns, yet the film itself was released without cuts. Ibid.

14. Kim Ji-seok, "Confucian Confusion: Understanding Sexuality in Korean Cinema," *Cinemaya* 51 (Spring 2001): 40–41.

15. Ibid., 160.

16. Michael Witzel, *The American Motel* (Osceola, WI: MBI Publishing Company, 2000), 152.

17. Ibid., 160.

18. Although made during a comparatively more conservative era, Claude Autant-Lara's black comedy *The Red Inn* (*L'Auberge Rouge*, 1951) concerns a couple of proprietors who murder the various guests staying at their titular establishment (a storyline similar to the one in Kim Ji-Woon's horror-comedy, *The Quiet Family* [*Joyonghan gajok*]).

19. Adapted from a controversial novel banned in South Korea (its author, Jang Jung-il, jailed on charges of obscenity), *Lies* is your average boy-meets-girl, boy-loses-girl story set in the claustrophobic, sadomasochistic world of whippings. The "boy" in this case is a 38 year-old married sculptor, known only as J, whose taste for kinky hijinks swells after his first rendezvous with an 18 year-old high-schooler who goes by the appropriately quizzical nickname Y. Interspersed throughout their sexual odyssey, which literally flings them across the globe, are glimpses of the intervening camera-crew and clips of the unseen director interviewing his two auditioning non-actors; this footage, like the skin abrasions left after the couple's intense floggings, are permanent traces of a momentary obsession—the blister-marks of an honesty and reality soon to be concealed by lies.

20. The incessant pouring of rain outside the motel, plus the overriding focus on sex as communicative process (in lieu of actual conversation), makes *Motel Cactus*

a kind of sequel to one of Christopher Doyle's collaborations with Wong Kar-wai: *Days of Being Wild* (*A Fei jing juen*, 1991).

21. An avant-garde 'suspense film,' Michael Snow's *Wavelength* consists of a 45-minute zoom-in that takes the viewer from the interior of one Manhattan loft to another before culminating with a close-up of a photograph of ocean waves on a wall.

22. Georges Perec, *Espèces d'espaces: Journal d'un usager de l'espece* (Galilee, 1974). The translated text is taken from *Species of Spaces and Other Pieces*, ed. and trans. John Sturrock (New York: Penguin, 1997), 37.

23. The Baskin Robbins logo also makes an appearance in Park Chan-wook's savage social allegory *Sympathy for Mr. Vengeance* (*Poksu nŭn na ŭi gŏk*, 2002).

24. Besides being a fixture of contemporary Hong Kong and Chinese cinemas, the electric waterfall painting can be seen in such European and American films as *Augustin: King of Kung Fu* (*Augustin: Roi du Kung-Fu*, 1999) and *Femme Fatale* (2002).

25. The shot of Chun-gi washing the bloodstained panties recalls a similar post-coital moment in Hong Sang-su's *Virgin Stripped Bare by Her Bachelors* (*O! Su-jŏng*), when a young man named Chae-hun jokes that he will keep the motel-bed sheets that Su-jŏng has just stained.

26. Desert iconography of the American Southwest is also suggested by the name of a struggling establishment taking center stage in director Pak Sŏng-ho's Golden Age classic *Excuse Me* (*Sillye haet sŭpnida*, 1959): the Hotel Arizona.

27. A scene in Song Il-gon's *Flower Island* (Kkotsŏm) (2001) includes a reference to this superstition.

28. Images of love motels/hotels are not unique to East and Southeast Asian cultural productions, and can be found in European films and television series. In the German film *Das Love Hotel in Tirol* (1978), for example, a sibling spat is precipitated by two brothers' inheritance of a hotel. As the film's title discloses, one brother's goal of transforming the hotel into an educational institute is nixed, leaving the way open for the second brother's proposal (which involves prostitutes imported from Bangkok).

29. Maureen Cheryn Turim, *The Films of Oshima Nagisa: Images of a Japanese Iconoclast* (Berkeley: University of California Press, 1998), 38. According to Turim, Oshima, in *Pleasures of the Flesh*, furthermore utilizes the gleaming modernist interior of a love hotel as the "backdrop for a male character whose pursuit of pleasure is framed and ultimately annihilated by his connections and debts to the illegal and violent capitalism of Japan's Mafia," thus suggesting a link between "the yakuza, pornography, and prostitution" (265–266).

30. Sandra Buckley, ed., *Encyclopedia of Contemporary Japanese Culture* (London: Routledge, 2002), 291. This encyclopedia includes a useful entry on love hotels, putting forth the case that they "are closely linked to essential elements of Japan's modernisation—urban crowding, commuting and motorisation. Though now primarily associated with short-stay liaisons and roadside prostitution rings, the phenomenon of short-stay hotels initially developed as accommodation for a new breed of car commuters, traveling salesmen and truckers in the wake of the expansion of commercial road transport and the *ŏnaaduraibaa* (owner-driver) boom of the 1960s.

These roadside hotels vied with one another through extravagant façades to capture the eye of weary travelers" (291).

31. Elise K. Tipton, *Modern Japan: A Social and Political History* (London: Routledge, 2002), 205.

32. Nick Perry, *Hyperreality and Global Culture* (London: Routledge, 1998), 48. Perry goes on to say that Tokyo's Meguro Emperor love-hotel "literally signals a cementing in place of the discursive interdependency of what are, respectively, these manic and Magic Kingdoms. It is a localized material confirmation of a globalized conjuncture of images, ideas and practices whose nodes are sited in Hollywood and in Germany, in cinema and in tourism, in theme parks and in national imagining."

33. David Rakoff, *Fraud: Essays* (New York: Broadway Publishing, 2002), 191.

34. Sara Wheeler, *Travels in a Thin Country: A Journey Through Chile* (New York: Random House, Inc., 1999), 5–8.

35. Emily Hatchwell writes about the importance of these "spartan love hotels" in her travel book, *In Focus Cuba: A Guide to the People, Politics and Culture* (Northampton, MA: Interlink Publishing; 1999), 56.

Chapter Twelve

Off the Highway: Some Notes on Stopping Places in Cinema

Rob Lapsley

Everything good is on the highway

Emerson

And, whereas the National Geographic is on its way somewhere, we're not

John Berryman

How long are we going to live in stuffy cabins, doing filthy things and never behaving like normal people?

Lolita

CREATURES OF DISTANCE

"Saigon. Shit I'm still only in Saigon." When Captain Willard looks through the blinds of his room in Francis Ford Coppola's *Apocalypse Now*, he just wants to be out of there, to be anywhere but its cramped confines. In the absence of a mission, a destination, he is despairing and disorientated. A camera pan reveals his apparent choices: nostalgia (the photograph of home), violence (his gun) and oblivion (alcohol). But there is no choice. He has become a stranger in his own home—when he was in Nam he wanted to be home, when he was at home he wanted to be back in Nam. As for violence, in this context it offers no release; it can only be self-directed. He reaches for the glass.

Of course, Willard gets what he thinks he wants: a mission. Within days he is on his way to terminate "with extreme prejudice" the command of

Colonel Kurtz. But this is not the mission dreamed of in that room. Rather than bringing him the desired consistency it confronts him with "The Horror. The Horror."

Insofar as there is ineradicable disparity between where he is and where he wants to be Willard is an emblematic figure of modernity: a nomad who longs to return home only to find he has none. Unable to come into his own, condemned to self-dispersion and incompletion, he wanders. This homelessness makes for a tension between the impulses of the subject and any stopping place and it is this tension I will explore in what follows.

Hotels, motels, and the like can, of course, function in very different ways in different movies. They can be sites of adultery (*The English Patient*), writer's block (*Barton Fink*), family reunion (*Kill Bill 2*), witness protection (*Bullitt*), disease (*Death in Venice*), shoot-outs (*True Romance*), prostitution (*Alphaville*), score-settling (*Heat*), temptation (*Romeo is Bleeding*), resignation (*A One and a Two*), havoc (*The Bellboy*), romance (*Out of Sight*), rape (*5 x 2*), battles with zombies (*Shaun of the Dead*), truancy (*Igby Goes Down*), swimming practice (*Kikujiro*), etc, etc. In *Pretty Woman* the hotel is Prince Charming's castle, in *Pulp Fiction* a sanctuary, in *Fear X* a perilous labyrinth, in *Tequila Sunrise* a crime scene, in *The Shining* the trigger for a psychotic homicidal breakdown, and so on.

Plainly it would be ridiculous to generalize about such diversity. However, all stopping-off places by definition have one feature in common: they are approached and entered in the context of a larger journey. Now, as Lévinas (1986, 348–9; cf. 1987, 91) reminds us, journeys can assume one of two forms. Like that of Ulysses returning to Penelope, a journey can be circular, a homecoming. Alternatively a journey can be Abrahamic, a voyage into an unknown land from which no return is possible.

In modernist culture the second conception has prevailed. Thus, famously for, at least, the early Eliot the only available truths are those of the desert. For Kafka, the castle when approached loses all of its allure. Most famously in the emblematic modernist novel, James Joyce's *Ulysses*, Leopold Bloom is an exile in his own city. 7 Eccles St. may be his house but it is no longer home. Molly, his twentieth century Penelope, is not faithfully awaiting his return but impatiently looking forward to four o' clock and the arrival of her lover, Blazes Boylan. Hence Bloom in his wanderings is ultimately going nowhere; he is concerned not to return but rather to delay his return. His journey, despite his arrival back at Eccles St. in the early hours, is only apparently circular, for, this side of death, it will never be over. Following Lévinas, Derrida (1992, 7) writes of Odysseus that he "returns to the side of his loved ones or to himself; he goes away in view of repatriating himself, in order to return to the home from which the signal for departure is given and

the part assigned, the side chosen, the lot provided, destiny commanded."
Bloom, by contrast knows only destinerrance. We are told at the end of the
chapter known as 'Nestor' that the nomadic Bloom once lived in a hotel, the
City Arms. In a sense, on 16 June 1904, he still does.

Similar thematic patterns are prominent in cinema. To cite just three examples. In Antonioni's *The Passenger* the death of the protagonist, David Locke,
behind the iron bars of an anonymous hotel room figures his exilic condition.
Dying unknown, in the middle of a desert, he is, as he always has been, in a
nowhere without exit. More recently in Peter Haneke's *Hour of the Wolf* refugees gather by a railway line for a train that never comes. Their rescue is as
impossible as it is desired. As they struggle to survive, quarrel over resources
and bait each other, as they grapple with trauma and suicidal despair, their
only consolation is art in the form of audio-tape played on a cassette machine
with failing batteries. The setting of the diegesis is supposedly that of some
future, unspecified post-catastrophic situation but the final tracking shots from
the train (which they will never board) reveal their world is our world.

Finally, in an obvious echo of Bloom's wanderings, Dr. Harford's sexual
odyssey in Stanley Kubrick's *Eyes Wide Shut* is similarly only apparently
circular. Horrified and panicked by his wife's confession that she has fantasised about sex with an irresistibly attractive stranger, Harford Bolts. As his
apartment is suddenly no longer home, he just wants out of there. Bereft like
Bloom of any desired destination, he stops off time and again to postpone his
return for, like Bloom, he wishes to avoid a further encounter with the real
of feminine desire.

ALWAYS ELSEWHERE

Homelessness is also a central theme of modern philosophy, most notably
in the work of Martin Heidegger. While Hegel described man as separating
himself from himself and thereby transcending himself in order to return to
himself, Heidegger, at least in his more radical moments, denied the possibility of any such return. Although Heidegger at times spoke of thought
as homecoming and suggested the possibility of self-appropriation, he elsewhere wrote of a constitutive homelessness. "Homelessness," he wrote "has
become a world destiny in the form of world-civilisation" (cited in Mehta,
1987, 21). As Žižek notes, for Heidegger man is out of joint. Not only is man
thrown into the world and never fully at home in it but there was no previous
home from which he was deported. Dislocation is "the primordial condition,
the very horizon of our being" (Žižek, 2001, 6). Hence, in this same tradition,
Badiou's aphorism: "courage has no other definition: exile without return"

(cited in Hallward, 2003, 38). In brief, the notion of man as homeless is such a commonplace in twentieth-century thought and art that, when the film director, Friedrich, in *The State of Things* cites Murnau's 'I'm not at home anywhere', it seems a bathetic cliché.

So, in this tradition, between a human being and where he or she wants to be there is always a gap, in which all stopping-off places are to be situated. The question is what are we to make of this space and the stopping places within it? How are we to think them? It has become fashionable recently to question whether theory is equal to this or any other task. What such talk misses is, firstly, the task's ineluctability—we have of necessity to try to understand our situation—and, secondly, the resources afforded by theory to re-describe our situation in alternative vocabularies. As an example of such an approach, I wish to explore the usefulness of two possible theoretical re-descriptions of stopping places in journeys without destinations.

At its simplest our homelessness can be envisioned in one of two ways: as exile or opportunity. On the first account all journeys end in an encounter with impossibility. The desired destination is never attained and stopping places are either more of the same, sites of dereliction, or fantasmatic refuges from the real as impossible. In the alternative perspective, the absence of home is our chance. If, as Nietzsche (1961, 213) claims, "*the* way does not exist", then many ways become possible: the ocean lies open before us. Just as, for Nietzsche, the death of God is grounds for cheerfulness in that it opens up "our new infinite" (cited in Ansell Pearson, 2001, 141), so the absence of the way is our opportunity to find new ways. In the context of such journeys stopping places become what travellers make of them: a deferral of adventure or adventures in themselves.

Within current thinking about cinema, the first approach is perhaps best represented by a particular reading of Lacanian psychoanalysis, a reading that conceives of the desiring subject as constitutively lacking "its own place", while the second would be represented by Deleuze in his Nietzschean vein.

SUBJECTIVITY AS UNREST

So, to begin, a brief detour through some of the fundamentals of Lacan's teaching. To function the human infant must organise a relationship to the real; it must acquire a stable sense of self and a framework within which to comprehend experience. Language, or more precisely the symbolic order, provides both; it introduces a sense of order and affords the child a means of organising its experience. For example, the child faced with the anxiety-provoking situation of determining what others want identifies with the signifier that is the specular image of the mirror phase. In so doing, it seeks to achieve security and mastery by becoming the ideal they demand it be.

But this recourse to language and concomitant sense of control comes at a cost for the Other of language is lacking. Put simply, the crucial signifiers are missing, that is the signifiers which would enable the subject to express both his identity and his desire. The subject cannot coincide with the signifier of any socially assigned identity and cannot find the words to enunciate his desires. Always between signifiers, the subject ineluctably seeks the signifier affording completion. Hence the subject is vehicled along the chain in search of what can never be found.

Furthermore it divides the subject from something of life. Although language affords a measure of order and unity, it also separates the subject from something of being. The object a, the remainder of the process of subject constitution, falls and becomes the lost object of desire. Consequently, the subject is again impelled forward in quest of what can never be attained.

Thus the signifier promises more than it delivers. It is Janus-faced, promising a solution to the child's problems only to bring new problems in its wake. On the one hand, it is indispensable to the subject's existence, the prosthesis without which it cannot function, but, on the other hand, it is the agent of alienation and mortification, the locus of exile and desire.

These intrasubjective divisions have profound consequences for intersubjective relations. If the Other of language is lacking, then the subject is afflicted by a lack, a lack no other can make good. Consequently, the desire which is the unspecifiable signified of every demand addressed to others can never be met: the Other is lacking. By the same token, when demands are made of the subject by others, s/he too is necessarily found wanting. Neither can make good the lack in the other; desire is unfulfillable and discordant. Hence encounters with the real of the Other's desire are always traumatic.

Crucially for what follows, this entry into and constitution within the signifying chain is not achieved once and for all. In trying to articulate a relationship between the real of the body and the real of the Other (subject) the human infant has recourse to a signifier. But, as the signifier is never *the* signifier, this is the beginning not the end of the process, for the subject is seeking its place and there is no such place. While a place is assigned to the subject, it is never *the* place and in consequence the subject in its *ek-stasis* is always at a non-place.

Thereafter the subject is caught up in the circuit set out by Lacan (1998, 83) in the schema of the three vectors. In response to each encounter with the real, say the real of another's desire, the subject seeks to resolve matters with a signifier. Hence the subject approaches the Other of language along the vector in the direction of the symbolic. As the crucial signifiers are missing, the subject encounters the real that is the lack in the Other. In a bid to fend off the real, the subject then seeks refuge in the imaginary, in idealised images. But as the imaginary is structured by the symbolic, the subject discovers that it too is holed. To repair the image, the subject again turns to the symbolic to find the appropriate signifier only to find there is no such signifier. The process is then repeated for the duration of the subject's existence. This circuit is therefore the matrix of all journeys.

The implication is clear: insofar as the object of a journey is the object of desire, no journey can succeed. If, in Heidegger, Dasein is irreversibly moving towards death, in Lacan the subject is just as inexorably moving towards yet another encounter with the lack in the Other. Whatever border, boundaries or frontiers a journey traverses, it will never cross the internal limit that divides the subject. To journey is to encounter an impasse.

Home is the pretence that there is no such limit, the fantasy that the lack in the Other can be overcome, the dream that there is a place where the subject can come into its own and achieve self-consistency. Once at home, the subject would no longer be a stranger to itself and others but only to alienation and separation. Although no such place exists, we are fated to seek it.

Art is response not illustration. We go to art, whether as artists or audiences, for something unavailable elsewhere; we go to have our situation altered not rendered. Art is always performative, seeking to accomplish what cannot otherwise be accomplished. Consequently, to understand the nature and valency of a filmic element, say stopping places, we must consider its role within the textual operation.

So how does art respond to our homelessness? An obvious answer is that it affords the shelter of fantasy. In its absence, the temptation is to fantasise that home exists. Two variants on this fantasy are particularly salient in cinematic stopping places. In the first, stopping places anticipate our arrival home; they are stepping stones to a future home. For example, the hotel in *Pretty Woman* is a foretaste of the palace to which Vivien will shortly be translated. In the second variant, home exists but is unattainable because of some contingent circumstance. Texts in this category can be further divided into two sub-categories. In the first, an obstacle separates the protagonists from any permanent home but experience testifies to its existence for it is experienced in temporary form (*Casablanca*, *Brief Encounter*, *Lost in Translation*, *Last Life in the Universe*, etc). The execrable *Million Dollar Baby* affords a recent example. When Frankie Dunne and Maggie Fitzgerald stop at a diner to sample what is claimed to be "the best lemon meringue pie in the world," they are not disappointed and the implication is, that but for her tragic accident, surrogate father would have found surrogate daughter and their reconciliation would have been a homecoming.

In the second category stopping places are where things go awry. In such films, everything would have been all right if the protagonist had not taken a wrong turning. *Psycho*, on a narrow reading (and one on which we will seek to improve later), provides the classic example. If only Marion had not left *the* highway, she would not have not stopped at the Bates Motel and . . .

So on a first approach, stopping places in many films are to be understood in the context of narratives which hold out the promise of homecoming and mask its impossibility by either postponing it to a beyond of the narrative or providing an alibi explaining away its inaccessibility. But quite simply this will not do. As an account of stopping-off places in cinema it is inadequate for at least two reasons. Firstly because there are many films which obviously fall outside this account. For example, there are many films that acknowledge our exile to be structural rather than contingent. In contrast to Frankie and Maggie, when Bobby Dupee stops of at a diner in *Five Easy Pieces* he cannot get what he wants. Homeless and going nowhere, stopping places for Bobby offer no respite. Orson Welles' *Touch of Evil* is a further example. This could be described in terms of the third of the above categories. It could be argued that, but for their enforced stay in Los Robles, Vargas and Suzy, after an idyllic honeymoon of chocolate sodas and the like, would have returned home to live happily ever after just like other idealised Hollywood couples of the '50s. But the tenor of the film suggests otherwise. Despite their passionate embrace as they are reunited in the final scene, the implication is that both have been permanently marked by Suzy's ordeal at the hands of the "dope fiends" at her motel and that the world is such that some such traumatic encounter was inevitable. All of us are destined to be touched by "evil." For every ET who returns to a fantasmatic home there are many other Hollywood characters who will never know home again. Not least those whom ET leaves behind.

Secondly the typology sketched above is inadequate because the operation of filmic texts is much more complex than that model allows. Texts do not simply hold out the promise of homecoming and find ways of disguising its impossibility. Their "progress" is more complex than that. As the significance of stopping places can be understood only within the context of textual functioning, it is to those complexities I shall now turn.

"WITH NO DIRECTION KNOWN"[1]

As an example, let's consider a Hollywood favourite, Alfred Hitchcock's *North by Northwest*, a film whose entire length is given over alternately to travel and stopping places. On one level the film is a typical Hollywood fantasy, in which the hero, Roger Thornhill, thwarts the villains, solves the

crime, and gets the girl. In terms of the categories outlined above, it appears
to be an instance of a narrative where home exists and is attained at the
moment of narrative closure; stopping places in the film function either as
anticipations of home or interruptions of his progress.

Read in these terms the film appears to be a conventional linear narrative.
However, on further examination more complex narrative patterns emerge.
In an initial approach, consider the means of transport that bring Thornhill
to the various stopping places. The salience of transportation in the text was
first highlighted by Raymond Bellour in his canonic study, 'The Symbolic
Blockage' (see Bellour, 2000). However, where Bellour's concern was with
their participation in rhyming patterns, our focus is their metaphoric status.
At first sight the modes of transport are easily interpreted: they represent the
symbolic. The planes, cars, taxis, trains etc. are metaphors for the diverse elements of the signifying chain which vehicle the vagabond subject along the
metonymic line of desire. At the inception of the narrative, the protagonist
Roger Thornhill is abducted, bundled into a waiting car and thereafter is in
transit, a process figuring the way in which the subject is taken up into the
signifying chain and transported along it for the remainder of his existence.

Of course it is more complex than this. As always in psychoanalysis, no
signifier has a fixed value; it is all a matter of context: modes of transport
have different valencies at different times. However, preponderantly they can
be read as the elements of the signifying chain to which the subject, in his
straits, necessarily has recourse.

If they are metaphors for the elements of the signifying chain we would expect them to be Janus-faced and this is exactly what we find. On the one hand
they promise deliverance; on the other they threaten death. For example, a
stolen pick-up truck enables him to escape death at the Prairie Stop but where
does this truck take him? To Eve's hotel and another betrayal.

A similar pattern is discernible in the portrayal of women and, most perti-
nently for this piece, stopping places. Women first. From the masculine, heterosexual perspective of the film, they at once promise salvation and imperil
Thornhill. For example, under arrest he appeals to his mother only to be put
at further risk by her scepticism and lack of faith. Later, with police in close
pursuit, he believes he has been rescued by a guardian angel, Eve, only to
discover that she is the mistress and accomplice of his would-be assassin.

Similarly stopping places are Janus-faced. They too figure in an oscillating pattern holding out a promise only to betray it and further endanger
Thornhill. At the beginning, he stops off at a hotel for a few relaxing drinks
before the theatre only to be abducted. Later, on the train, finding himself
seated opposite Eve in the dining car, he imagines he is safe only for the train
to make an unscheduled stop allowing his pursuers to board. But the train as

site of danger then metamorphoses into an approximation of paradise when the detectives' incursion prompts Eve to usher him all the more quickly into her sleeping compartment. Here another supposed sanctuary transforms into its opposite for he falls in love with Eve only to be despatched by her to a rendezvous with his would-be murderers. This is, of course, the famous Prairie Stop, where, once more, the anticipated resolution proves a mirage and annihilation again threatens.

So in the figuration of women and stopping places there is a reversal of promise into danger. Indeed their equivalence is overtly established at the end of the scene where Eve sends him to his intended death: the final shot of her face dissolves into the Prairie Stop, signifying that both embody a lethal threat. And it is easy to see why for, in this context, both promise a final and therefore impossible resolution.

In this perspective, the oscillating rhythm of the narrative's progress is better described in terms of the schema of the three vectors. Thornhill seeks the signifier (figured as transport, woman or stopping place) which will simultaneously rescue him and unlock the mystery, only to encounter the real as impossible. Taking refuge in the imaginary he discovers that while he may seek to forget the real it does not forget him. Expelled from his imagined sanctuary he is impelled forward.

The text is therefore in difficulties. How is an ending to be found? If, to adopt a phrase of Judith Butler's (1999, 8), the subject "is its travels", how is a stopping place to be located? This is a problem not just for *North by Northwest*. Most works of art are in search of a stopping place and experience difficulties in locating one. In the case of *North by Northwest* Hitchcock "solves" his problems by an act of violence: a *deus ex machina* in the form of a CIA marksman magically appears to save the romantic couple. This sets at nought the inexorable forward logic of the narrative as outlined above but it provides the semblance of an ending.

MISSING THE BUS

Why, outside of fantasy, are we never at home? Why is there always a gap between where we are and where we want to be? One reason is alterity. We can never be at one because any form of unity is indebted to otherness. We have already encountered three forms of irreducible alterity: firstly we are always other than our assigned identity; secondly we are always separated from the other, the lost object which will supposedly complete us; and, thirdly, it follows that the other (subject) is never our lost complement. Thus a non-appropriable space always separates us from the place we would inhabit.

So how does Hitchcock respond to this dilemma? Like most human beings, in different ways at different times. For example, on occasion he appreciates that our situation is less tragic than comic and responds with humour. At the beginning of *North by Northwest* he seeks to board a bus and the doors close in his face. As will be apparent from the above, we always miss the bus. We may catch a bus and reach a destination but it is never *the* bus and never *the* destination. Now this has, as Hitchcock appreciates, its comic side, hence his jokey cameo.

It is when he becomes more straight-faced that the problems set in. One particular inhabitant of non-appropriable space preoccupies him: the desire of the Other. In Hitchcock's case that desire is the infinite of feminine desire. Five of the films in which stopping places have a prominent role can be read as attempts by Hitchcock to negotiate the non-appropriable space of female desire: *Vertigo*, *North by Northwest*, *Psycho*, *The Birds*, and *Marnie*.

Let's start with *Vertigo*. Here the concern with the desire of the other, the desire of woman is presented at the outset. The film opens with a close-up of a woman's eye. In other words, it begins with the gaze of the woman, a gaze inscribing her enigmatic and infinite desire. For Hitchcock this encounter with the alterity of the Other is traumatic. Hence it is figured in the opening credits as equivalent to the abyss. Why does the hero suffer from vertigo? Because he fears that, if he opens himself to the alterity and infinity of the Other's desire, he will be engulfed. How is this to be dealt with? Scottie has two clinically-related strategies: phobia and fetishism. Both set limits to avoid confronting the limits inherent in the real as impossible. In this instance the intention is to keep the woman and the real of her desire at a distance thus evading the impossibility of a sexual relation.

Phobia places certain areas off-limits. It organises space in such a way as to establish uncrossable boundaries; it creates no-go areas. Thus Scottie has to avoid heights and this avoidance is echoed in the way he has to hold back when following Madeleine. The problem is that life lived at too great a distance is no life at all. Significantly when Madeleine enters the McKittrick Hotel she vanishes. This disappearance is never explained but it prefigures her later disappearance at the mission where Scottie, unable to climb the stairs, cannot join her and she departs his life. So, although Scottie burdens himself with a phobic inability (to ascend to any height) in a bid to evade the real as impossible, the real finds him out.

In the second part of the film Hitchcock essays another strategy to articulate a sexual relationship: fetishisation. Judy is discovered in a hotel and Scottie persuades her to undergo a makeover transforming her into Madeleine. Where in the earlier hotel he had suffered Madeleine's disappearance, in this new hotel he wants to make Judy disappear so that Madeleine can reappear. This strategy is no more successful than its predecessor. Through the fetishisation of Judy, through dressing and styling her on the pattern of Madeleine, he takes refuge from the real (of her own impossible desires) in the imaginary. But the real again finds him out: Judy's desires do emerge and his imaginarisation is punctured.

Scottie is in search of what he conceives to be the right distance, that is, the distance from which he can at once relate to the woman as a subject and remain at a safe distance. He is, dare one say it, in search of a stopping place. Briefly that appears to be the hotel which he tries to turn into a home where, through fetishisation, he can insulate himself from Judy and the real of her desires. The problem with this strategy, as Mulvey (1975) pointed out, is that it brings the narrative itself to a standstill. "Life" in the confines of that room is inevitably as deadly and suffocating as that of which Lolita complained in the epigraph. If the narrative is not to stall, Scottie must leave but his departure propels him from the imaginary into the real.

Consequently the circuit begins anew, leaving Hitchcock, once again, at a loss as to how to call a halt. So, as in *North by Northwest*, he has recourse to a *deus ex machina*. The CIA marksman becomes a nun whose appearance triggers Judy's fatal fall. Her death solves Scottie's problem with the real of her desire (a dead Judy is not a desiring Judy) but leaves him nothing to live for. Having failed to find the appropriate distance his world disintegrates.

OFF THE COMPASS: *NORTH BY NORTHWEST* AGAIN

As we have seen *Vertigo* is two films in one, two attempts to find a way of articulating a relation to the real of the Other's desire. With *North by Northwest* Hitchcock has another go. As applying the brakes got him nowhere, Hitchcock now presses the accelerator. His new stand-in, Thornhill is despatched in headlong quest of a better solution. But again he encounters an impasse.

To travel, to leave the security of a circumscribed space like that which Scottie tried to construct, is to be open to experience, and experience, as Derrida (2002, 93) reminds us, is always "experience of the other." Here, as we have seen, the other is the femme fatale Eve Kendall. So Thornhill now faces the same task as Scottie: the appropriation of the infinite space of feminine desire. As this task is impossible, as Hitchcock can find no way of appropriating the woman without also losing her, he resorts to violence. Earlier I described the intervention of the CIA marksman as one such act but an altogether more significant violence precedes it: the transmutation of Eve from alluring femme fatale into would-be American housewife. Eve is transformed into a Penelope whose desires perfectly accord with those of Thornhill. Ithaca, it seems, can be an express train entering a tunnel.

THE UNCROSSABLE BORDER

In the trilogy which comprises *Psycho*, *The Birds*, and *Marnie* Hitchcock adopts another strategy: he identifies with his female protagonists; he attempts to appropriate the non-appropriable along the axis not of desire but of identification.

In the present context, the three films are of particular interest because of the salience in each of stopping places. Marnie uses hotels while in flight from the law, Melanie rents a room from Annie, and Marion visits the most famous motel in cinema. In each case the stopping places are associated with transgression. This is obviously the case in *Psycho* and *Marnie*: both Marion and Marnie hole up in their rooms like the outlaws in a myriad Hollywood crime movies. It is less obvious but no less the case in *The Birds*. While it is true that Melanie, in contrast to Marion and Marnie, gives rather than steals, she is still their sister in crime. Where, as Deleuze implies, they steal on behalf of another (Marion on behalf of Sam to pay off his alimony, Marnie on behalf of her handicapped mother) she gives on behalf of another (she gives the love-birds to Jessica on behalf of her brother Mitch). Moreover her gift is intended to steal Mitch from Lydia and involves criminal trespass. Finally like Marion and Marnie her journey requires her to rent a room under false pretences. So instead of three different narratives we have three attempts by Hitchcock to articulate a relationship to the real as impossible.

The repetition of his attempts to find a resolution attests to their failure. Once he has launched these excitingly transgressive young women on their journeys he is at a loss where to go. He cannot imagine a future for them. Were this the world according to Hegel, Hitchcock, in identifying with his women, would have divided himself only to re-appropriate himself but on the current Lacanian reading no such sublation is possible. Any re-appropriation would destroy what makes him wish to re-appropriate them. Their desirability stems from their independence and initiative but in Hitchcock's restricted world-view that cannot survive the only resolution he can envisage: romantic union and domesticity. His dilemma is that of the master as outlined by Sartre: if he fails to control them he is no master but if he does control them they are no longer the subjects he wished to control. Thus his attempted appropriation ends in his expropriation. At a loss, his only recourse is to bring in the roof upon them: each is savagely attacked.

So what exactly is Hitchcock trying to say about journeys and stopping places, women and desire? It is impossible to say and that is why he repeatedly tries and, as repeatedly, fails to say it. If the Other is lacking, there is, at once, an impossible-to-say and an imperative to make the attempt. The temptation is to find the truth in an isolated moment. For example, to claim that the truth of what happens in the hotel room in Phoenix is the murder in the Bates motel: one man makes love to her, another murders her but both are following their own desires at her expense. But, if the Other is lacking, the truth can only be half-spoken. Hence, like every subject, Hitchcock is between signifiers: in his case, between the Marnie who steals and the Melanie who gives, the Scottie who cannot climb the tower and the Scottie who can. In Joyce's (1964, 583.07) phrase his art is "two thinks at a time." Consequently, every stopping place in Hitchcock's films is divided.

HISTORY AND JOUISSANCE

Of course, the above account is immediately open to a number of objections. In the space available we can consider only two: the apparently ahistorical nature of the account and its theoretical omissions. Let's take each in turn.

At first glance the initial objection seems damning. A principal concern of the present volume is to theorise the present social configuration in which, as Marc Augé (1995) points out, people circulate more than ever and, in the course of their travels, increasingly frequent non-places. If for psychoanalysis the journey is always the same circuit, then it can neither describe nor explain particular journeys in their specificity. As such it cannot start to do justice to subjects in their specificity, not least those who have suffered less metaphysical varieties of homelessness, exile and dislocation.

Such a dismissal would be unjust. No body of thought is more sensitive to historical and cultural differences than psychoanalysis. To appreciate at least something of this, consider one of the stations on the subject's way: the symbolic. This is never given in itself; *the* symbolic order is nowhere to be found. It is transmitted to the subject only by the utterances of others and as these are different for each subject, the symbolic is, to varying degrees, different for each subject. The symbolic is, consequently, both historically and culturally specific. It follows that, as the imaginary is structured by the symbolic, it too is contingent. The terms of the subject's idealisations and imaginarisations are again those of particular cultural forms.

The real as impossible is, of course, historically invariant—for Lacanians there is no conceivable culture in which subjects would either coincide with a signifier or attain the object of desire (they are homeless)—but the subjective experience of these impossibilities is individual. Although, by definition, the real can be neither symbolised nor imaginarised, subjects will, of necessity, attempt both symbolisation and imaginarisation and these attempts will mediate the experience of the real. For example, although sexual rapport is impossible except in evanescent moments, not all sexual relationships are the same. On the contrary, they are manifestly very different and constantly changing.

Before coming to the second objection, let's see if the claim that history enters at every turn of the subject's circuit can be cashed in relation to the present discussion. Using the broadest of brushstrokes, the historical nature of the symbolic can be illustrated by the distinction between traditional and post-traditional societies. Within any symbolic order not all signifiers are equal. Certain so-called master-signifiers possess a privileged status; unlike other signifiers, their meaning does not appear to endlessly shift; they seem to be given in themselves. Hence they have an unquestioned authority. Signifiers acquire meaning only within a context and these master-signifiers do much of the work of contextualisation. As such they anchor the signifying chain, provide a stable framework of intelligibility and orientate the subject.

Historically the foremost example was the Name-of-the-Father. As the cornerstone of the patriarchal symbolic order it assigned identities and roles and thereby organised a framework in which the different sexes could relate to one another. Hence Lacan's (1977, 276) infamous pronouncement at the end of Seminar XI that a sexual relation was only possible under the aegis of the Name-of-the-Father. On this account it secured a coordination of otherwise colliding desires through the provision of a common symbolic framework.

Now, of course, the effects of this social organisation were less happy than this formulation suggests: the supposed coordination was nothing other than repression in the interests of powerful heterosexual males and its 'success' a myth. Despite the ideological mystification, desires still clashed and impasses still obtained. Indeed, as we have seen, Hitchcock's dilemma in the trilogy is directly attributable to the impasses associated with the patriarchal order. His female antagonists excite him because they transgress the Law of the Father but, as he is bound to the Law, he can envisage no realisation of their desires within patriarchy. Their appeal depends on their inhabiting non-places as sites of transgression but where are they to go from there? How are the desires they embody to be reconciled with the law? Hitchcock can find no answer. The second part of *Psycho* exists to distract spectators from the fact that he could not imagine anywhere for Marion to go after the Bates Motel. Back in the arms of Sam and with the money repaid she would no longer be Marion and no longer be of any interest. Similarly a Melanie transformed into a devoted wife and dutiful daughter-in-law would no longer be the attractively intrepid trespasser and a Marnie, coerced into marriage with a rapist, would no longer be the outlaw playing fast and loose with her identity in hotel rooms while getting away with daylight robbery.

However, while it is obvious that we are well rid of the patriarchal structures of traditional societies, for Lacanians the contemporary eclipse of the Name-of-the-Father bequeaths a problem: namely how in its absence is the subject to organise a relationship to the real as impossible? If subjects require master-signifiers as stars by which to steer, which signifiers are to assume this status? To function, subjects need a framework organising their relationship to the real. In particular they need a framework to organise a relationship to the real of the other's desire, a pre-structuring framework of shared misrecognitions to introduce a measure of harmony where otherwise there is discord.

It would be altogether too crude to argue that, while in traditional societies the framework came ready-made, in forms with collective authority, today each individual has to construct one as he or she goes along. Insofar as the Other is lacking, subjects have always had to construct part of the frame themselves. The difference between traditional and post-traditional societies is one of degree not kind. That said, the difference is significant. If, in traditional societies, the problem for all was how to live up to the impossible socially imposed ideals and the problem for the oppressed was how to endure or combat their oppression, the problem today is how to formulate a schema in accord with those of others. At least in much of the west, we have moved from a cultural economy where repression (in the guise of the coordination of desires) largely silenced dissonance to one in which the all-too-apparent conflictual nature of desire has become the pre-eminent problem in social relationships.

This is the drama enacted by *Memento*. At first sight the film is just another take on the modernist theme of exile, just another film about an uprooted subject haunting non-places. The protagonist, an ex-insurance investigator called Leonard Shelby, is trying to identify and exact revenge on the murderer of his wife. In, what he believes to be, close pursuit he moves from one anonymous motel room to another. It is plain he will never go home again. As the ending makes clear, he is condemned to an endless quest; the earlier domestic idyll can never be regained. The only home he now knows is the series of indistinguishable motel rooms. As in Hitchcock, subjectivity is without resting place.

However, on a more interesting reading, Leonard is a postmodern subject whose first priority is to make sense of events in a post-traditional society, where in the absence of any overall framework, he has to make it up as he goes along. As there are no 'resources,' such as those afforded by the Name-of-the-Father, with which to make sense, he is condemned to improvisatory strategies. And these fail him. As the dénouement makes clear he may think he knows what he is doing but he does not. When, at the end, he returns to his car and asks himself, "Now where was I?" perhaps the spectator's only certainty is that Leonard, for all his confidence, will never know where he is.

This is allegorised by his disability: the absence of a short-term memory. Since the trauma of his wife's death he has become incapable of retaining any new memory for much more than ten minutes. To cope with this handicap, he has developed a number of strategies: he makes extensive notes, takes polaroids and even tattoos the most significant "facts" on his body. Thus he is an emblematic figure of postmodernity trying to make good the lack in the Other, by installing his own master-signifiers. Moreover, as such signifiers are never enough (the Other of language is lacking), he supplements them with fantasy structures to further frame and order his world. It is, for example, unclear whether his *idée fixe*, the death of his wife, is more than a delusion designed to assure him that he has his bearings when he does not.

His amnesia is a metaphor for the inevitable failure of attempts at totalizing knowledge which rely on others no more reliable than himself. The efficacy of his belief system is consequently limited. Its lack of congruence with those of others leaves him vulnerable to exploitation and manipulation. In a world where 'man is a wolf to man' and where each is in some degree blind and uncomprehending, the clash of desires issues in an omnipresent and anarchic violence.

So while Hitchcock and his female protagonists were struggling with the problems, impasses, and contradictions associated with a particular institution, namely a symbolic order governed by the Name-of-the-Father, Leonard is struggling to institute an order. Whereas for the Hitchcock of the trilogy, the non-places, the hotels and motels are sites of transgression, in *Memento* they are the norm, stations on the way to somewhere that will always be other than the desired destination. If for Hitchcock the problem is the articulation of desire, for Leonard the problem is to establish a measure of permanence and stability.

The second objection, that from within psychoanalytic theory, is much more serious. Within a psychoanalytic perspective to suggest that subjects wish to go home is the grossest of simplifications. Firstly it ignores the ambivalence of the subject towards any putative home. It ignores all within the subject that opposes any home, all in the subject that is in insurrection against any supposed completion. Plainly Hitchcock was deeply ambivalent about home: he did and did not want his characters to make their way home. Home attracts insofar as it promises resolution and harmony but it repels insofar as it is the end of desiring and hence the end of life.

Ultimately the desire for home, insofar as it is a desire to be done with desire, constitutes a version of the death drive. If the subject is its journey, arrival at its destination is a form of death. Life, as Freud observed, is a detour (Freud, *S. E.*, 39).

Secondly, and more importantly, it fails to take account of the satisfactions of the drive. As Žižek has stressed, the drive is to be distinguished from desire. While desire encounters an impasse the drives do not (Žižek 2001, 63; cf. 1999, 82). Whereas desire never attains its sought-after satisfaction (there is no home) the drive is always satisfied. Freud's most disconcerting discovery was that although on one level his patients suffered to the extent that they sought treatment, on another level they enjoyed their symptoms. So, at one and the same time, they were distressed by their failure to lead lives free of their symptom and found jouissance in that failure. Thus it seems doubtful if any sense of failure weighed on Hitchcock. It is much more probable that, but for his, shall we say, 'falling out' with Tippi Hedren, he would have happily gone on making films in which she followed her (i.e., Hitchcock's) desires before suffering some terrible outcome until the end of his career.

Of course everyone enjoys differently. To illustrate this, before coming back to Hitchcock and by way of a contrast, consider the work of Wong Kar-wai. Like Hitchcock's, many of his films concern couples' missed encounters in hotel rooms. In *Chungking Express*, *Happy Together*, *In the Mood for Love*, and *2046* couples both homosexual and heterosexual try and fail to make their relationships work. Yet the tone of the films is anything but desolate. Maggie Cheung, the female lead of *In the Mood for Love* reportedly formed the impression during the film's protracted shooting that Wong did not want the filming to end. He was happy to film his lovers time and again failing to achieve a romantic union. The sequel, *2046*, similarly endlessly circles the void that is figured by that eponymous room. On one level the failure of the couples in both films to achieve romantic union in their various hotel rooms occasioned Wong pain but, on another level, it afforded him jouissance for the narrative secreted the fantasy that, but for contingent circumstances, it could all have worked out. Perhaps he enjoyed the failure because any imaginable consummation would have disappointed. Whatever the reason, Wong enjoys life at his heartbreak hotel.

Hitchcock, like Wong, endlessly circles the void but he enjoys differently. Where Wong's jouissance has a melancholic cast, Hitchcock's is perverse. He enjoys the absence of resolution, the failure of his women to find a place in patriarchy. He can at one and the same time identify with them as figures enacting his own illicit desires and imagine himself the instrument of the Law which punishes them. Their crimes license him to engage in the voyeuristic practices and sadistic punishments famously identified by Laura Mulvey (1975).

What holds for directors holds equally for spectators. They too enjoy in ways of which they may not be wholly conscious. For example, part of the pleasure of watching *Memento* obviously derives from occupying a position of supposed knowledge. At the end the spectator is afforded the narcissistic pleasures of the imaginary. Briefly occupying the apex of the triangular schema he can imagine that he knows, in contrast to Leonard, the existentialist sap. But in the course of the film a very different form of pleasure is on offer: ignorance. As Žižek (2002, 61) observes, for Lacan, "the spontaneous attitude of a human being is that of 'I don't want to know anything about it.'" Subjects do and do not want to know and *Memento*'s reversal of linear narrative structure allows the spectator to inhabit a labyrinth of illegible signs where he can indulge his passion for ignorance. So for the audience, as for the artist, the text in its articulation of contradictory impulses can be 'two thinks at a time.'

Of course, there is no necessity for the spectator to occupy such a position. The trajectory of the spectator is never wholly pre-programmed; ultimately it is his unfathomable decision. While the text proposes the reader disposes. Thus there is an ethics of reading. Each spectator must take a stance in relation to the text, deciding how he will interpret and enjoy. For psychoanalysis, as for Deleuze in Nietzschean vein, every spectator experiences the text he deserves.

DELEUZE AND LACAN

This brings me to the second of the two perspectives: that associated with the Nietzscheanism and Bergsonianism of Deleuze. It will already be apparent that the initial opposition posed between Lacan and Deleuze is less clear-cut than suggested above. To cite just three instances. Both think of our relationship to the world in terms of organisations which are finally always open to alteration and hence impermanent. There can be no insulation from the real. Marion and Marnie may imagine themselves safe in their hotel rooms but they are en route to catastrophe. For both, following Heidegger, if the subject never fully inhabits a place, it is equally never fully inhabited by that place. It is futural, open. Secondly, both Deleuze and Lacan conceive of reality as continually changing; every repetition involves difference. In *2046* a series of women inhabit the hotel room but all are different and all are different at different times: none is identical to the longed-for (mythical) woman whom Chow Mo Wan met earlier in another hotel room with that number. Thirdly for both, again following Heidegger, human subjectivity is always already underway and what counts is how one is underway. For Lacan there are only modes of jouissance: what matters is how one enjoys. For Deleuze what matters is how one desires. Are the desires active or reactive? While reactive desires tend to imprison the subject, active desires open the subject to the new and transformative affects that are life itself. Thus, for both, the significance of anything, whether a stopping place or a work of art, depends on the forces, drives and desires that take hold of it. This is another lesson from Joyce: Bloom's situation could be portrayed as desolate but *Ulysses* is an affirmative comic novel.

That said, there is a significant difference on the question of impossibility. As we have seen, for Lacan the real is the impossible: it is impossible to attain the object of desire, etc.; there are internal limits. Now, of course, Deleuze also recognises the existence of impossibilities. For example, as just mentioned, he insists that no organization can be totally closed upon itself; no territorialization is immune from deterritorialization. But there are no internal limits. Any conception of such a limit is a hypostatization which is a function of a particular historical moment. We do not know what a body can do. For Lacan we know that the body is hedged by impossibilities; for example, it can never coincide with its specular image, never join with the object a, etc. Deleuze, on the other hand, is reluctant to specify any such limits to what the body can become. Only cowards and obsessional neurotics dwell on impossibilities.

Within this perspective, Hitchcock's problems with the real as impossible are not solved, rather they simply disappear. If Hitchcock could not think of an alternative for his women, a Deleuzian would have no such difficulty. As desire is not lack but productive energy, the desires of others are not a threat but the opportunity for self-transformation. We do not know what a body can do and the only way to find out is by experimenting, by, for example, conjoining the forces in one's own body with those in others. Only those afraid of the risks involved in life and change wish to appropriate the desires of the other. There is no necessity to reterritorialize deterritorialized desire in the paranoid manner of Hitchcock. Those with a greater capacity to affect and be affected seek, on the contrary, to open up to the other, to undergo transformation.

Thus for Deleuze journeys neither end nor begin with an impasse. We do not know in advance where we can go or what we can become. It is no accident that the notion of home barely features in his work. The absence of home, like the death of God, is our chance to become something new. "The real," he insists, "is not impossible; on the contrary, within the real everything is possible, everything becomes possible" (Deleuze and Guattari, 1983, 27).

To illustrate this there is time for only one example but it is a marvellous example: Raul Ruiz's film of Proust's *Time Regained*. In Proust all journeys are fated to end in disappointment and the narrator's final visit to the Faubourg is no exception. He discovers all the major characters from the earlier volumes dreadfully altered: each is now painfully at odds with his youthful idealisations. The lustrous world to which he had once so ardently aspired now seems bankrupt and empty; in close-up the aura of the *beau monde* has entirely and irreversibly dissipated. But, like the book, the film does not end on a note of disillusion and despair. Instead the narrator and, by implication, the spectator is transported back to the hotel terrace at Balbec where he first saw Albertine and the little band on the sea-shore.

Crucially, for our purposes, this is not a neurotic escape into nostalgia. The hotel is not recalled as a fantasised shelter from the disappointments of the present or the uncertainties of the future. On the contrary, it is a celebration of the possibilities of creation. This Balbec had no prior existence; the Grand Hotel is not regained but remade and reshaped in the imagination as a new beginning. It is not the recovery of a lost paradise or the promise of a future home but the proclamation, in their absence, of the opportunities for artistic creation. The journey of Proust's narrator is only apparently circular. In reality it is oriented to a future where the possibilities for transformation, for being otherwise, for going beyond known forms of the human condition, are inexhaustible. Hence the film ends with an affirmation of universal variation: a sunlit image of the sea.

DO THE LOCOMMOTION

For Deleuze the pre-eminent question is: what can we become? As he writes in his book on Foucault, "the question that constantly returns is therefore the following: if the forces within man compose a form only by entering into a relation with forms from the outside, with what new forms do they now risk entering into a relation, and what new form will emerge?" (Deleuze, 1988a, 130). As we do not know what a body can do, Deleuze calls on us to experiment, to explore how we can affect and be affected.

One obvious form of experiment is the journey. But, if a journey involves self-transformation, the mere traversal of space does not constitute a journey. In other words, as Deleuze emphasizes, it is possible to journey while sedentary and possible to travel without journeying. Catherine Malabou, from a Derridean perspective, has made a rather similar point. "The very thing one always expects of a voyage," she writes "is that it will deliver 'the other' — the unexpected, a type of defamiliarization if not adventure or exoticism. One can always travel afar, but if there is not this sudden emergence of otherness, whatever form it may take, the voyage isn't accomplished, it doesn't really take place" (Malabou, 2004, 2). There is, she continues, "no true voyage without an event . . . that abducts the traveller's identity and allows an opening to alterity to become experience of the world in general." For both Deleuze and Derrida, if a journey is to be a journey, translation must involve transmutation.

James Bond offers a cinematic proof of the thesis. Bond, while an indefatigable traveller never journeys for he is unaffected by his foreign adventures. In the course of his missions he may be surprised, shaken, even stirred but ultimately he always remains the same; everything happens to him and nothing. When like a modern Odysseus he returns home to flirt with his Penelope, Miss Moneypenny, he is indistinguishable from the Bond who flirted and left. Of course, Bond encounters strangers but he is never affected; the villainous males are eliminated, the attractive females bedded. While he appropriates, he is never expropriated; his self-possession remains absolute. Hence a favoured trope is his self-announcement: "My name's Bond, James Bond". In that moment it seems he names himself. He is able to do so because he pre-exists this baptism and is the master of the naming process. As such he is the subject as conceived by neither Lacan nor Deleuze.

For Lacan the subject is named through interpellation by the Other and never coincides with his name, consequently he is always en route to an identity with which he will never coincide. As coincidence with a signifier would be a form of death, the impossibility of self-identity is the possibility of his voyaging in the temporal and spatial gap opened up by the irreducible incompletion of self and symbolic. Bond in his integrity, on the other hand, is self-identical and self-contemporaneous: errancy is the fate of others. If life is experience, and if experience is always experience of a transformative encounter with alterity, then, from a Lacanian perspective, the apparently vigorous, vital Bond is as dead as the corpses he leaves in his wake.

For Deleuze, as we have seen, the subject is more event than entity: it has no essence—rather it is constituted by pre-individual forces and as such endlessly reconstituted by the forces which it encounters. When the energies which produce a particular form of subjectivity connect with heterogeneous energies in what Deleuze terms a machinic assemblage, something new can be produced. Programmed, calculating and murderous, Bond is machinic in a very different sense: the slaughter and copulation are so mechanical he functions rather than lives.

In *Une Liaison Pornographique*—yet another film about a couple in a hotel room—there is a moment when the Nathalie Baye character's eyes suddenly fill with tears. What had been an arrangement to fulfil her transgressive erotic fantasies has become, at least on her side, the most intense of romances. Surprised by the force of her passion, she no longer knows where the affects will carry her. At once elated and frightened, she realises that she is no longer in control of her destiny. She knows neither where she will be transported nor what she will become and the prospect both scares and enthralls her. Bond never experiences such moments; he is being not becoming. Derrida (cited in Malabou 2004, 36) writes that "to travel is to give oneself over to commotion: to the unsettling that, as a result, affects one's being down to the bone, puts everything up for grabs." "Nothing," he continues, "is more frightening, nothing more desirable. Whatever the pretext, place, moment, vehicle, so many mediations, I would nickname them means of locommotion." From this perspective, Nathalie Baye travels further crossing the street to her hotel than Bond on all of his missions.

TIME AS THE OPEN

Drawing on Bergson and in accord with Nietzsche, Deleuze elaborates this theme of becoming in relation to cinema. On this model, he conceives of the cosmos as an open-ended dynamic system in which everything interacts with everything else. Out of this flux organisations emerge. One such is what he terms a "living centre," which for present purposes can be taken as approximating to the subject. Whereas in the cosmic flux everything perceives everything else, living centres perceive only what is of interest to them. Perception is subtraction. Subjects perceive according to their utilitarian concerns. This pragmatism of perception is most apparent in sensory-motor situations where subjects respond to clearly recognisable situations and act to meet the problems identified. Bond wakes in his Jamaican hotel room, appraises his situation—he is at mortal risk from a deadly tarantula—and responds by overcoming the threat—he kills it. Here the reactions to situations and the ensuing actions are automatic or habitual. In consequence, the novel and the different are held at bay.

On this basis Deleuze (1986; 1989) distinguishes two forms of cinema: the cinema of the action-image and the cinema of the time-image. The former is organised by sensori-motor situations. The protagonist perceives a situation in terms of his needs, desires and interests and reacts to it in such a way as to alter or modify the inaugural situation. Perception is recognition and is automatically extended into action. Bond enters his hotel room, sees a girl wearing only a choker and immediately joins her in bed for another bout of implausible sex (*From Russia with Love*) or, in his suite, recognises the aftershave of the supposed waiter, realises it is an assassination attempt and goes into sadistically lethal action (*Diamonds are Forever*).

In the cinema of the time-image the sensori-motor situation breaks down and, consequently, the protagonists are often at a loss. Unlike Bond who can always locate himself—he invariably knows where he has come from, where he is going and how to get there—they possess no such assurance. Confronted by a situation which is difficult to decipher, the subject is uncertain how to behave and proceed. Although on the one hand this experience can be insupportable, on the other it is their chance; it is the possibility that something may happen. Where time ceases to be a pre-given framework or horizon within which characters were destined to behave in their accustomed fashion, there is the opportunity for exploration and discovery. When destinations are no longer given from the outset, when Odysseus cannot return home, it becomes possible to think and become otherwise.

Thus hotels figure in films organised by the time-image very differently from the way they function in the cinema of the movement-image. In the latter they either constitute a site prompting an action or their nature is disclosed by the action. In both cases they form part of a well-defined and recognisable milieu. With the cinema of the time-image, by contrast, hotels, like all other places, elude recognition within pre-established schemas. Obvious examples would be the hotels in Rossellini's *Viaggio in Italia* and Antonioni's *L'Avventura* where, in each case, the female protagonist confronts a situation she cannot encompass and is consequently uncertain how to react. In both cases a situation befalls them where matters are undecidable yet they have to decide.

While nothing happens to Bond something is happening to them. Where Bond quickly takes the measure of the most novel of situations—Jill Masterson has been murdered by the application of gold paint, etc.—and thereby consigns everything to the realm of the same, these women have to proceed without any such supposed knowledge. Unlike Bond they are not the masters of their environment and that is their opportunity. No longer enchained by habit, they can enter into new relations with the forms and forces of the Outside, jump the tracks and take off in different directions. Opened up to what Deleuze (1988b, 28) terms "the inhuman and the superhuman" they can go beyond what is taken to be 'the human condition' and create new forms of life.

THE SHADOW OF HER SMILE

To expand on this, and by way of a conclusion, three films by Claire Denis which all turn upon hotels. In *Dialogues* Claire Parnet claims, presumably with Deleuze's approval, that "Beckett's characters are in perpetual involution . . . already en route," "always in the middle of a path [which] has no beginning or end" (Deleuze and Parnet, 1987, 30). A similar claim could be advanced in relation to the characters in the films of Denis. Each is on a journey. But more significantly Denis herself can be seen as always in the middle, always in between. For Denis, as for Deleuze's Proust, art is a new beginning: departure not homecoming.

Let's start with *Trouble Every Day*, one of the most powerful statements in modern cinema of the discordance of desire and the dereliction of originary exile. June's honeymoon in her Paris hotel has not gone as she had hoped. Her husband, Shane, refuses to come when they have sex and there are mysterious bloodstains on the shower curtain. What the audience knows but she does not is that orgasm renders him a cannibal—the blood comes from the chambermaid he has just seduced and butchered. So when Shane announces "I want to go home", and June says "OK" she senses and the audience is certain that "home" will be no less horrific than this stopping place.

But, although extraordinarily compelling, this figuration of individuals as isolated by their violently appropriative desires is far from Denis's last word on the 'human condition'; it is a perspective not a summation. As her other films make clear, if there is 'this' there is also 'that'; no determination is final. Consider the second text: *Beau Travail*. Originally the narrative was destined for a conclusion as bleak and anguished as the dénouement of *Trouble Every Day*. Denis intended to end with the scene in which Galoup, lying on the narrow hotel bed he has made in accordance with the rigorous prescriptions of the Legion, cradles his automatic and considers suicide. At that juncture, expelled from the regiment because of the attempted murder of his rival, yearning for what now seems a lost paradise, Galoup believes death preferable to the futility of his exilic existence. But Denis decided against this strategy and opted instead to conclude with what had been an earlier scene. So the film now ends with a cut to Galoup alone, motionless on a dance-floor. As the music, 'The Rhythm of the Night,' begins, he starts to move and then dance. Is this memory or fantasy? Is this the recollection of a happier time or what he did after deciding against suicide? The spectator cannot know. But what becomes apparent is that exile can be the possibility of invention and a Nietzschean self-overcoming: the absence of the way is the existence of the dance-floor.

From this Deleuzian vantage point the works of Denis are not, as the earlier Lacanian reading might have had it, so many inevitably failed responses to the real as impossible, but explorations of our possibilities. If, on a Nietzschean account, there are many eyes and consequently many truths, our task is not to determine a final truth but to make new eyes for ourselves and multiply the perspectives available, thereby both doing justice to the plurality of the world and testifying to the intensity of the life of which we are capable. This is the task Denis undertakes. In that sense she could be seen as exemplifying what Deleuze variously terms the "method of Between" or the "method of And." This logic of conjunction and relation dispels "the cinema of the one," the "cinema of Being-is," for the concern is no longer to determine once and for all the nature of "x" but to explore what happens when "x" is combined with "y." If, as Proust (1992, 212) observed, there is not one universe but millions, the nature and multiplicity of the universes one perceives depends on who and how one is.

If the perspective does not exist it is possible to create new ones. Similarly with sexuality, if our ways of relating to others are not ordained and constrained by the Name-of-the-Father, it is possible to invent different modes. For example, modes where desire in hotel rooms, or anywhere else for that matter, is not the attempt to make good an irreparable lack but expenditure as an end in itself. This brings me to the third film: *Vendredi Soir*.

Laure's path is mapped out: she is about to move in with Francois. All her belongings are packed away in carefully labeled cardboard boxes. She is even on the point of selling the symbol of her freedom, her car. With nothing further to do until the arrival of the removal men the following morning, she sets off to meet her friends only to become ensnarled in the immense traffic jam caused by a public transport strike. She cannot attain her planned destination but that apparently frustrating circumstance opens her to an encounter with the Outside. Just when life seemed to have stalled, it takes off in an entirely unexpected direction: her enforced 'exile' allows her to meet a stranger, Jean. Abandoning the car, they adjourn to a hotel.

If this were a scene from Hitchcock's trilogy, Laure would now be waylaid by the real as impossible. Not here. Instead, in Deleuze and Guattari's (1983, 294) wonderful phrase, they "make love with worlds." Desire in this hotel room is not the violent, because failed, appropriation of the non-appropriable space of the other but the nuptials of the newly created.

In the early morning, without waking him, she leaves to look for her car. And can't find it. She becomes desperate—the removal men will be there at 8—she starts to run. Street after street is lined with cars but none is hers; anxiety turns to panic. . . . Then, as at the end of *Beau Travail*, a reversal. Suddenly all that matters is what she recalls of her night in that room with Jean. It was a night on a road leading nowhere (life will continue as planned), a night when no destination was reached (the hotel was just a stopping place, just another detour). And yet. . . . In the discovery that "love's movement counts no less than its having arrived at its destination"[2] she is surprised and overtaken by joy. As the memories come back, the film goes into slow motion to accentuate the brightness of her smile on that otherwise ordinary Parisian Saturday morning. Denis ends with that smile and so will I.

NOTES

1. Bob Dylan, 'Like a Rolling Stone'
2. The phrase is from Derrida (1986, 26)

REFERENCES

Ansell Pearson, Keith. 'Pure Reserve: Deleuze, Philosophy and Immanence.' pp. 141–155 in *Deleuze and Religion* edited by Mary Bryden. London: Routledge, 2001.

Augé, Marc. *Non-places: Introduction to an Anthropology of Supermodernity*. London: Verso, 1995.

Bellour, Raymond. 'The Symbolic Blockage' pp. 77–192 in *The Analysis of Film* edited by Constance Penley. Bloomington: Indiana University Press, 2000.

Butler, Judith. *Subjects of Desire: Hegelian Reflection in Twentieth Century France*. New York: Columbia University Press, 1999.

Deleuze, Gilles. *Foucault* (trans. and ed. Sean Hand). Minneapolis: University of Minnesota Press, 1988a.

——. *Bergsonism* (trans. Hugh Tomlinson and Barbara Habberjam). New York: Zone Books, 1988b.

——. *Cinema 1: The Movement-Image* (trans. Hugh Tomlinson and Barbara Habberjam). London: Athlone, 1986.

——. *Cinema 2: The Time-Image* (trans. Hugh Tomlinson and Robert Galeta). London: Athlone, 1989.

Deleuze, Gilles and Guattari, Félix. *Anti-Oedipus: Capitalism and Schizophrenia* (trans. Robert Hurley, Mark Seem and Helen R. Lane). Minneapolis: University of Minnesota Press, 1983.

Deleuze, Gilles and Parnet, Claire. *Dialogues II* (trans. Hugh Tomlinson and Barbara Habberjam). London: Athlone, 1987.

Derrida, Jacques. *Memoires: For Paul de Man* (trans. Cecile Lindsay, Jonathan Culler and Eduardo Cadava). New York: Columbia University Press, 1986.

——. *Given Time: II. Counterfeit Money* (trans. Peggy Kamuf). Chicago: University of Chicago Press, 1992.

——. *Negotiations*. Stanford: Stanford University Press, 2002.

Freud, Sigmund. *Beyond the Pleasure Principle* in *The Standard Edition of the Complete Psychological Works of Sigmund Freud Volume XVIII* edited by James Strachey. London: Vintage, 1953–1974.

Hallward, Peter. *Badiou: A Subject to Truth*. Minneapolis: University of Minnesota Press, 2003.

Joyce, James. *Finnegan's Wake*. London: Faber, 1964.

Lacan, Jacques. *The Four Fundamental Concepts of Psychoanalysis* (ed. J.–A. Miller, trans. A. Sheridan). Harmondsworth: Penguin, 1977.

——. *The Seminar of Jacques Lacan Book XX: On Feminine Sexuality, The Limits of Love and Knowledge, 1972–73 (Encore)* (ed. J.–A. Miller, trans. B. Fink). New York: W. W. Norton, 1998.

Lévinas, Emmanuel. 'The Trace of the Other' (trans. Alphonso Lingis) in *Deconstruction in Context: Literature and Philosophy* (ed. M. C. Taylor). Chicago: University of Chicago Press, 1986.

——. *Collected Philosophical Papers* (trans. Alphonso Lingis). Dordrecht: Martinus Nifhoff Publishers, 1987.

Malabou, Catherine. *Counterpath* (trans. David Wills). Stanford: Stanford University Press, 2004.

Mehta, Jarava Lal. 'Heidegger and Vedanta: Reflections on a Questionable Theme' pp. 15–46 in *Heidegger and Asian Thought* edited by Graham Parkes. Honolulu: University of Hawaii Press, 1987.

Mulvey, Laura. 'Visual Pleasure and Narrative Cinema', *Screen* 16 no. 3 (Autumn 1975): 6–18.

Nietzsche, Friedrich Wilhelm. *Thus Spoke Zarathustra* (trans. Reginald John Hollingdale). Harmondsworth: Penguin, 1961.

Proust, Marcel. *In Search of Lost Time Volume V: The Captive* (trans. C. K. Scott Moncrieff and Terence Kilmartin; revised D. J. Enright), London: Chatto and Windus, 1992.

Žižek, Slavoj. *The Ticklish Subject.* London: Verso, 1999.

——. *On Belief.* London: Routledge, 2001.

——. *Welcome to the Desert of the Real.* London: Verso, 2002.

Chapter Thirteen

The Real of the Screen:
Atom Egoyan's *Speaking Parts*

Maria Walsh

I have worked in a hotel for five years. I have worked in film for ten. Both of these professions involve the creation of illusion. In one, the territory of illusion is a room. In the other it is a screen. People move in and out of rooms. Actors move in and out of screens; *Speaking Parts* explores a terrain that moves between rooms and screens; a terrain of memory and desire. Somewhere in the passage from a room to a screen, a person is transformed into an image. I am fascinated by this crucial moment, and by the contradictions involved in making images of people.

(Atom Egoyan, in Desbarats et al, 1993, 119)

In Atom Egoyan's *Speaking Parts* (1989), set in the Windsor Arms Hotel, Toronto, a series of video screens create a filmic architecture that stretches beyond the labyrinth of the hotel. This filmic architecture of rooms and screens is imbued with multifarious psychic investments, which range from fantasies to possess another, to merge with another, to become another, and to remember and preserve another. These fantasies are indulged in via particular screens, e.g., the video-conferencing screen in the hotel and a video-mausoleum screen in a crematorium, both of which are used to link characters so that they might appear to be with one another in the present moment. While Egoyan's use of the hotel in this and other films, e.g., *The Adjuster* (1991), can be read against the backdrop of how hotels "allegorize exilic and diasporic transitionality" (Naficy 2001, 253), *Speaking Parts* does not investigate this condition as such but focuses on a more general form of psychic displacement through the global mediation of images.[1]

Although Egoyan's having worked in the Empress Hotel in Victoria over several summers sorting laundry before becoming a filmmaker is not the reason why hotels appear in his films, Egoyan has remarked on a connection

353

between the professions. Referring to working in a hotel he says: "I was fascinated by the process of preparing a room for someone to come into, so that the guest would believe it was virgin territory. When I began to make films, I became aware of parallels: both professions have systems to support illusions" (Egoyan, in Naficy 2001, 252–3). This statement and others that Egoyan makes about his critical attitude towards how events and memories are mediated by images in a media-saturated culture evoke a familiar set of distinctions in classical film theory and contemporary cultural studies between illusion and the real. The film image and film narrative are considered as ersatz copies that seduce and veil us from the real of experience. As opposed to Hollywood and mainstream cinema, avant-garde and alternative film practice aim to distance the viewer from the spectacle and force us to question connections between things. While Egoyan's filmmaking background is in experimental film, he has always combined a critical attitude with an interest in telling stories, therefore inventing a peculiarly emotional form of distanciation. His strategy in making the viewer feel how they traverse the different spaces in a film rather than taking this movement for granted is never at the expense of a deep attachment to the image.[2] In *Speaking Parts*, which critics surprisingly found extremely cold, but Egoyan describes as dealing with operatic emotions such as unrequited love, this emotional distanciation is filtered through the numerous video screens that occur within the film. The film, as do others in Egoyan's *oeuvre* such as *Family Viewing* (1987), deals with how in a media-saturated culture experience and memory are recorded and preserved.[3] Intense experiences may be memorialized by a hackneyed or clichéd image culled from the repertoire of media images as if these impersonal, global forms embodied the local and personal. These ephemeral images stand in place of what has disappeared in time. Out of the ruins of these mediated image fragments we construct our identities and invent the narrative fictions necessary for survival. Needless to say, due to the shared ubiquity of such image fragments, what we call our identities are not necessarily our own preserve but stem from or at least transverse an exterior symbolic apparatus from which we borrow our means of personal expression.

Speaking Parts exemplifies this symbolic and social interconnection in its use of English subtitles (the dialogue is already in English) which underscores the lack of coincidence between a character and his or her 'speaking' part.[4] Also, on a more imaginary level, the physical resemblances between all four main protagonists—they all four have long curly hair and rather patrician features—accentuates their psychological interconnectivity. Three of the main characters use video and film images to play out deeply personal fantasies and desires which further threaten to abolish the differences between them. The impetus to abolish difference stems from the characters' paranoid desires, but rather than reading this in a psychoanalytic register, it can be viewed against the backdrop of diasporic cinema where "paranoid structures also serve the comforting and critical functions of embodying the exiles' protest against the fluid and hostile social conditions in which they find themselves" (Naficy 2001, 5). This is particularly true of the character Lisa (Arsinée Khanjian), who appears to be of Armenian descent and whose irrational pursuit of Lance (Michael McManus), her object of desire, culminates in a final sequence in the film where their images dissolve and form an indistinct black silhouette. Rather than reading this dissolution in a negative way, this scene arguably offers a sense that the image can indeed generate something which transcends the proliferation of images that threaten to extinguish difference. Lisa's faith that the image is a vehicle to something beyond the sway of seduction yet, at the same time, uncannily dependent on it, preserves an alternative to the ubiquitous ungrounded flow of images in a media-saturated culture. I shall link this resistant preservation of faith in the image to a non-productive but affective creativity. In other words, rather than producing rooms of fantasy as in a hotel or a film, Lisa's faith in the image to deliver something real creates a sensation that affects or moves the viewer beyond the encryption of the screen.

AN ACCIDENTAL HEROINE

Speaking Parts features three main characters, Lance (McManus), Lisa (Khanjian), and Clara (Gabrielle Rose), whose destinies are bound up with the space of the hotel and the filmmaking business. The film script suggests that Clarence, Clara's brother (Frank Tata), who we see on screen in the video mausoleum where Clara repeatedly plays some footage she shot of him before he died, should also be considered as a main character (Figure 13.1).

All four character's names resonate phonetically, as, in the film, resemblances circulate between Lisa and Lance, and Lance and Clara, both of whom he is involved with, while the script also suggests a resemblance between Lance and Clarence. Clara is an academic who has written a screenplay about the true-life story of her bother's donation of a lung, which saved her life. A film of the screenplay is being planned and the film crew comes to stay at the hotel where Lisa and Lance work in housekeeping. Lisa, who works in the laundry room, is suffering from unrequited love for Lance, who works as a bellboy and is also a bit-part actor. She spends her free time watching the films he appears in. Lance also provides sexual services for clients who stay at the hotel. He begins an affair with Clara hoping to get a speaking part in the film. She suggests him to the Producer (David Hemblen) who casts him

Figure 13.1.   Clara (Gabrielle Rose) in the video mausoleum
Courtesy of Johnnie Eisen, © Ego Film Arts

to play her brother Clarence in the film being made of her tragic life-story. While Lisa and Lance do occasionally encounter one another at work in the hotel, their minimal interactions are at cross purposes not least because both of them seem to be sleep-walking through their parts, Lance blankly expressionless, Lisa hypnotically fascinated.

Throughout the film, video technology is used for the purposes of communication, remembrance, and fantasy. The Producer uses the video screen in the hotel conference room to communicate with his film crew. When Clara leaves the hotel to meet with the Producer, Clara and Lance use the same screen as an interface to continue their affair, each masturbates in front of the camera, apparently reaching simultaneous orgasm. Clara preserves the memory of Clarence by obsessively watching the video footage she shot of him on the mausoleum screen at the crematorium (Figure 13.2). Lisa rents home videos starring Lance for her fantasy productions. And surveillance monitors which act as windows onto events occurring simultaneously in different hotel rooms pervade and define the labyrinthine space of the hotel itself. Part of Egoyan's interest in the quality of this hotel was its capacity to combine up-to-the-minute technology with an old-world style.

> I was drawn to the colonial-style hotel and its old-world paneling because they suggested the sophistication of an earlier time. By placing the main action there,

Figure 13.2. Lance (Michael McManus) video conferencing in the hotel; Clara is on screen
Courtesy of Johnnie Eisen, © Ego Film Arts

> I created a counter-effect to the video technology so a viewer was not able to apply the usual reaction to seeing high tech in film, which is that it's somehow futuristic. In order to get that dichotomy across it was important that the environment seemed lush. (Egoyan 1993, 55)

In effect, video acts as a thread that links all the characters in a kind of dance macabre which culminates in the film's final fast-cutting montage sequence where we are frenetically moved between Lisa in hotel room 106 (earlier in the film one of Lance's clients committed suicide there) to a studio where a sequence from Clara's script, revised by the Producer, is being filmed. As this montage sequence precedes the final shot in the film that I want to focus on, I shall give an account of it here which demonstrates the complicated proliferation of narrative fragments that comprise *Speaking Parts*.

The Producer directs the sequence, which is being shot in the format of a TV chat show. The Producer also hosts the chat show. He introduces Lance as the brother of David the transplant patient in the operation under discussion in the show. (In the Producer's re-writing of Clara's script, her character has been changed to a brother.) David, seen in a hospital bed, turns out to be Ronnie, a minor character encountered previously as a bridegroom at a wedding Lisa went to help video-store owner Eddy record. This is followed by a flash insert of the video footage of Clarence, Clara in the mausoleum, Lance in the audience, Lisa in room 106. The point of view in room 106 is from the surveillance monitor, which, as Lisa moves towards it hand outstretched as if to touch or penetrate the image, turns from film to video with horizontal interference breaking up her image. Suddenly, we see Clara in the studio audience. She lifts a gun to her head. Lisa replaces the nurse tending Ronnie who in turn is replaced by Lance. As Jonathan Romney (2003, 73) puts it, "Events that we expect to see on film appear in video and vice versa, dissolving all divisions between the two media." As well as this, the substitution of one person for another underscores the physical resemblances and links between the main characters that have been developed and played with throughout the film. As if in response to Clara's threatened suicide, Lance screams "No!" and we end with the video image of Lisa dissolving to snow followed by a shot of the now empty mausoleum, its video screen left blank. In a sense, it could be said that it is Lisa, logically still in the hotel room, who 'causes' the montage frenzy to stop as she moves towards the video monitor and the image fades to snow.

The notion that Lisa is the ultimate controller of the proliferation of images is underscored in the film script in a scene that was never filmed, but which resonates with the final sequence of the film which follows the montage frenzy. After the rapid montage sequence, we see Lisa returning to her apartment and finding Lance waiting outside. He follows her in. They kiss, their bodies silhouetted in black against the faint glow of a TV screen in the apartment. In the script, a scene with Lance and Lisa sitting on the couch in her apartment watching the Producer's film follows. Lance, catching sight of himself in the extras crowd and Clara staring back at him, gets upset and Lisa comforts him saying "It's just the stupid television. I turned it off." In not filming this scene, Egoyan allows Lisa's gesture to be implied rather than literal. She is the only one throughout the film whose capture by the image does not lead her into a web of deceit and lies. She believes Lance not only has feelings for her but that when she looks at his image, he has the capacity to feel her internal state of being in the same way as she feels it herself. Her faith in this, which might be seen as perverse in some respects, saves both of them from being reduced to a 'speaking part.' Lisa's belief in the power and 'liveness' of the image makes her almost akin to a primitivist film spectator whose belief in the image to provide an intimacy missing in modern life is characterised by Rachel O. Moore (2000, 20) in the anthropological terms of "close contact," i.e., an animistic relation to the image. Moore (2000, 20) notes that, for early film theorists such as Vachel Lindsay and Béla Balázs, the cinema allowed for an access to gesture that "could reveal the secrets of things and souls inexpressible in the impoverished language of mere words." Similarly, Lisa has no faith in words. "There's nothing special about words," she says, and indeed throughout the film she uses them minimally, her character being motivated by the intensity of her hypnotic and compelling gaze. When in the final sequence, Lisa and Lance's images, which they have employed to mimic and seduce, dissolve into a black silhouette, the underlying affective currents that have been struggling for a channel of communication throughout the film come to the fore. In my first viewing of the film, I found this shot moving in a way that could not be explained by recourse to the narrative of a happy ending. The image itself seemed to generate the force of a sensation that spiraled beyond the frame of the image, incorporating my viewing in a manner that transcended the boundaries of spectator and screen. In what follows, I shall explore this sensation in relation to some of Gilles Deleuze's ideas in his book on the philosophy of Henri Bergson, *Bergsonism*, rather than his ubiquitous books on cinema. Focusing on Lisa, I shall read her character as an intercessor that, in preserving the real of intimate experience in the face of its atrophy in the proliferation of mediated images, allows the viewer access to a sensation that exceeds the surface of the image. In this trajectory, Lisa is an accidental heroine. She moves about the film in a semi-hypnoid, almost paralytic state but the force of her emotion and belief in something real—intimacy—causes a caesura in the film that posits another value in the image.

In relation to this, it is worth noting that Lisa is the character in this film whose ethnicity is most pronounced. While all the characters are outsiders in the sense of being ensconced in social and linguistic structures that predetermine their existence, Lisa is doubly outside the economy of exchange and circulation that unites the characters in the film business. For Hamid Naficy, *Speaking Parts* differs from other 'accented films' in that in its use of the hotel as a border site, transitory identities are not celebrated as they are in much postcolonial filmmaking. Referring to *Speaking Parts*, Naficy (2001, 252) says:

> The hotel as a site of exchange relations and video as an instrument of voyeurism, recording, and remembering drive the characters' deceitful behaviors and transgressive crossing of identity and sexuality. However, these performative strategies—unlike what is suggested in much of the literature on hybridity and border crossing—do not free the participants. In fact, they make the participants extremely self-conscious and uncomfortable.

This echoes Egoyan's view that, "In the case of *Speaking Parts*, people are basically lying to each other all of the time, setting up stratagems all based on deceit. [. . .] They're very aware of what comes out of their mouths and how it's interpreted or distorted in some way in order to fulfill someone

else's motivations" (Egoyan, in Naficy 2001, 252). However, I would maintain that while Lisa could be said to be a deluded, captivated film spectator in
her pursuit of Lance, unlike Clara and Lance, who compromise their desires
for the sake of the film being made of Clara's story, she sticks to her resolve.
In this she acts as a counterfoil to the only other character who sticks to his
desire: the Producer, who tells Lance that he knows what makes a good film,
that is, whatever he himself would want to watch—"people have always
watched what I'd like to watch." But where the Producer is fully bound up
with the economy of exchange that underpins the filmmaking business, Lisa
is outside it. It is perhaps this position as an outsider that allows her to act
as a conduit for something that cannot be registered within the economy of
representation and thereby either celebrated or negated. This 'something,'
which is mediated or triggered by the image, gives way onto the realm of
affect and sensation, types of emotive experience that can only ever be intuited, rather than verified or guaranteed. Both Lisa's status as an outsider and
her irrational belief in a love that has no basis other than her own conviction
positions her in a liminal, intervallic, space between social exchanges. She is
suspended in this interval, neither able to procure the object of her desire nor
seize the means of producing his image, i.e., video and film technology. (Her
attempt to be Eddy's assistant in making videos of weddings and club or-
gies fails due to what Eddy refers to as her "lack of objectivity.") However,
it is Lisa's 'close contact' to the image that, as Romney (2003, 67) claims,
"pushes her to go beyond surfaces, to infiltrate forbidden territory both figuratively and literally—to penetrate the video image, to enter the 'forbidden'
hotel room." Contrary to Egoyan's suggestion that both Clara and Lisa fail
to understand the production of images, I would maintain that by means of
her intervallic existence, Lisa is the intermediary in the film for the production of something akin to what Deleuze (1988, 111) calls "creative emotion."
For Deleuze (1988, 111), creative emotion "no longer has anything to do
with the pressures of society, nor with the disputes of the individual. It no
longer has anything to do with an individual who contests or even invents,
nor with a society that constrains, that persuades or even tells stories. [. . .]
It is instead a transindividual force that gathers us in its unfolding as it leaps
from one soul to another, [. . .] crossing deserts." Where the hermetically
sealed site of the hotel resembles a studio in "purveying artificial luxury"
and creating fictional narratives that "apparently [cater] exclusively to the
outside world" (Romney 2003, 65; 63), the 'creative emotion' generated by
the force of Lisa's will is outside all exchange values be they economic
or cultural. In this transindividual act, she goes beyond the nomadic confines
of diasporic identity and intercedes in the creation of an imaginary space in
which anyone can potentially find a quality of being.

Before exploring this further, it is worth mentioning that in her discussion of 'hybrid cinema,' which includes Egoyan's films, *Calendar* (1993) in particular, Laura U. Marks, while borrowing extensively from Deleuzian concepts, also raises questions about the limits of Deleuze for considering diasporan cinema.[5] Deleuze, while addressing the question of the collective, simultaneously insists on the autonomy of a perception, memory or affect that extends beyond the known or received. Marks takes Deleuze to task for divorcing the act and object of perception from the collective memory of a (diasporic) community, where the recovery or excavation of tactile memories is essential to the preservation and construction of identity. "[T]actile (and other sense) memories are most important to those who do not have access to conventional speech in film" (Marks 1994, 259). As we shall see in what follows, the final scene of *Speaking Parts* has been read in terms of how the physical touching of the protagonists redeems the deceptions inherent in the circulation of images. The problem with these types of reading is the binary distinction made between the senses where touch and, for Marks, smell, are deemed more authentic and true than the supposed artifice of the visual register. This is in contrast to Deleuze for whom sensory distinctions and the hierarchies that subtend them need to be overridden for the sake of producing a new affect or sensation.

> To describe the relationship of the eye and the hand, and the values through which this relation passes, it is obviously not enough to say that the eye judges and the hands execute. The relationship between the hand and the eye is infinitely richer, passing through dynamic tensions, logical reversals, and organic exchanges and substitutions. [. . .] Finally, we will speak of the *haptic* whenever there is no longer a strict subordination in either direction [. . .] but when sight discovers in itself a function of touch that is uniquely its own, distinct from its optical function. (Deleuze 2003, 154–55)

While the image I am focusing on in *Speaking Parts* is indeed one where the protagonists touch without the aid of screens, I do not want to situate their encounter in terms of a dichotomy between the real and the artificial. The merit of persisting with Deleuze's deposing of both the visible and the tactile is to establish another kind of surface which does not recover the senses as such but incorporates the viewer in a screen relation that goes beyond the distinction between surface and depth. While there are indeed problems in how Deleuze's categorization of something that exceeds identity might be taken up by individual agents in the world of social relations, I nonetheless want to persist in using his notion of a transindividual creative emotion, which, in bypassing sensory hierarchies, allows for an engagement with the image beyond the visible realm of ownership.

SURFACE SPECTATORSHIP

> It is a strange prejudice which sets a higher value on depth than on breadth,
> and which accepts 'superficial' as meaning not 'of wide extent' but 'of
> little depth,' whereas 'deep,' on the other hand, signifies 'of great depth,'
> and not 'of small surface'. (Tournier, cited in Deleuze 1993, 261–2)

Deleuze's revaluation of the extensive nature of surface resonates with
Egoyan's discussion of surface in relation to the screen.

> The idea of surface, when associated with the depiction of character, suggests
> superficiality and lack of dimension. We tend to think of a surface as something
> that is without depth, something that offers nothing more than what is imme-
> diately visible. On a closer reading, however, the concept of surface proves to
> be the most complex and intriguing aspects of any rendering of personality.
> (Egoyan 1993, 25)

Egoyan's notion of surface can be related to Moore's classification of primitivist spectatorship in the sense that, for theorists such as Balázs and Lindsay, surfaces lend themselves to the secrecy not of a hidden depth but to the
"scarcely perceptible and yet immediately obvious nuance" (Moore 2000,
70). The physiognomy of the image renders visible the otherwise invisible
sense of "emotions, moods, intentions and thoughts" (Moore 2000, 71). In
accounts of spectatorship based on semiotic and psychoanalytic theory, the
viewer is generally thought to take up a credulous position whereby his or
her production of fantasy and desire is largely determined by the cinematic
apparatus. Hence the goal, in counter-cinema, to rupture the imaginary identifications that might be promulgated by the dream-machine of mainstream
cinema. However, Egoyan, in conjunction with his critical stance on the image, is interested in creating a connection between image and viewer. "When
the screen image *contains* something more immediate to the viewer (a loved
one for example) a true surface can be developed if the viewer breaks the
impassive nature of the screen identification process with a degree of involvement" (Egoyan 1993, 28). For Egoyan this involvement does not preclude a
critical dimension. In his filmmaking process, he incites the actor to "'frame'
his own performance, allowing once again a higher degree of interaction with
the viewer. Rather than inviting the viewer to lose himself in a screen presence, the actor asks the viewer to question what it is about the character he's
supposed to identify with. In this way, a more profound relationship can be
established" (Egoyan 1993, 33). What would it mean to consider this 'more
profound relationship' in terms of an exchange of surfaces? Although Egoyan
does not mention Deleuze, there are links between their ideas on the profun-

dity of surface communication which correspond to the emotional impact of the final scene in *Speaking Parts* without returning this scene to a humanism the film has put in question.

Speaking Parts opens with scenarios of pure spectatorship—female spectatorship to be precise. For the first eight minutes of the film, there is no dialogue. First we see shots of a graveyard, followed by shots of a piano recital which focuses in on Lance in the audience. We then see that this scene is happening on a television screen as the camera moves from a close-up of Lance to focus on Lisa's gaze as she stares transfixed in the direction of the television. We move from this private video viewing to another scene where Clara watches footage of her brother Clarence in the video mausoleum. Although this viewing takes place in public space, it has the air of privacy, as we never see anyone else at the mausoleum. What is of note in relation to the women's gazes is that they both trigger the camera's leap into the screen creating a particular kind of surface involvement. This is especially true of Lisa's gaze, which in this opening sequence and in other shots later in the film, eradicates the frame of the TV monitor honing in on Lance's image to such an extent that his face spreads across the screen in an array of coloured pixels. On one occasion, Clara's gaze also leaps, as it were, into the video screen. In one of the final mausoleum scenes, her gaze transforms the video footage of Clarence by not only eradicating the frame but also moving to the left of the image to show herself in the frame actually shooting the footage, which would logically imply the presence of another camera person. In these scenes, Egoyan makes us feel the presence of the camera as a type of character who also participates in the film. However, what is of interest to my argument in these scenes of female video-viewing is how their immersive looking resonates with Marks' notion that the medium of video as opposed to film "appeals to a tactile, or haptic, visuality" (Marks 1998, 332). While Marks' argument seems to rest in large part on the questionable contrasting of the blurry, flatness of video images to the depth-of-field clarity of film, it is the case that in *Speaking Parts*, proximity to the grainy quality of these video close-ups engages a particular surface sensibility. In the close-up of Lance in the aforementioned opening scene, the degrading of the video image by augmenting and isolating it causes it to become imbued with the temporality of the viewer's look as it scans the gaps between the coloured pixels for sense and meaning, this desire stemming from the viewer's identification with Lisa's emotional intensity. Egoyan states:

> The only avenues of emotional connection in the film are created during those moments when one of the women's fantasy images matches the image she is witnessing on the screen. When Lisa finds Lance in the crowd scenes of the

rented videos, when Clara gazes at the image of her brother in the mausoleum, or at Lance, an actor she wants to portray her brother, the women's faces express a sense of attachment and love. (Egoyan 1993, 36)

I want to suggest that this idea of an avenue of emotional attachment, which derives from the women's desires to merge with their love objects, is the means by which a different kind of surface, one that incorporates the viewer in the screen, emerges.

Egoyan discusses the film in terms of the production and reception of images. There are those who produce like the Producer and those who ostensibly consume but have the desire to produce images. However, the power mechanisms that the latter entails are not in the women's hands in the film. In fact, Egoyan goes so far as to claim that the lack of facility to create their own versions of these images results in the women's downfall.

> But these moments are fleeting, if only because they involve projected images that are time-based and must come to an end. The desire expressed by both these women to elaborate these images, to learn how to *make* their own image, will be the source of their personal *unmaking*. Their dream of gaining control over image production is doomed to failure because their relationship to images is not founded on the idea of the image as cultural artifact, but on the ideal of the image as an extension of fantasy and personal mythology. [. . .] Tragically (to use the Producer's expression), Clara and Lisa over invest themselves in the images of their dreams, and lose sight of themselves in the process. (Egoyan 1993, 37)

This view is shared by commentators on the film such as Ron Burnett (1993, 17), who states that Clara "does not understand that films are created through a process of negotiation between an industrial context and creative artists, and that the final product never looks like the original proposal or scenario. [. . .] These characters do not understand that images take the sacred and drain it of significance."[6] And in response to Lisa's attempt to help video-store owner Eddy to make videos, Burnett (1993, 11) states that "Lisa's experiment with video fails because she understands neither the medium nor the effects it has on the characters she interviews." For Burnett, Lisa's invasive questioning of the bride Trish at her wedding as to whether she can feel Ronnie feeling her the way she feels herself is seen by Burnett as naïve. However, through Lisa's faith that Lance does indeed love her despite all evidence to the contrary, she generates a crack or caesura in the economic logic of image production, which in turn produces an intensity that exceeds that logic. (As she says to Trish at her wedding, "Love is about . . . feeling someone else feel you, right, but sometimes you can feel someone else, and you can feel them feeling you, but they may not act that way.")[7] Contrary to his own analysis of the film in terms of the women's failure to understand image production Egoyan echoes this sentiment when he states that:

> A cinematic moment can transcend its limitations as an image and work its way into a viewer's subconscious only if the viewer is able to 'frame' the image in a manner similar to that of these two women. That is, the viewer must consciously acknowledge that he is observing an image, and must make an active, *self-conscious* decision to absorb it. By making this enormous conceptual leap, the viewer identifies with the image and forms a passage of exchange. The screen becomes a surface. (Egoyan 1993, 32)

In the final scene of the film, Lisa is the conduit that transforms the screen into a surface, which incorporates the viewer in its passage. What do I mean by this? As I've said, her character traverses the spaces of the hotel and the video store in a semi-hypnoid state. In this she is akin to Deleuze's 'seers,' characters who see rather than act, whose delayed and, in this case, inappropriate reactions to events, intimate an expansion of what Deleuze calls the affection-image, affection usually being the minimal intermediate zone between perception and reaction. Lisa's suspension of the linear logic of perception and reaction can be aligned with an exilic or diasporic identity, in the sense that being displaced from the homeland and suspended in the anonymity of the hotel, her habitual modes of (re)acting have reduced means of extension.[8] She suffers from what Deleuze (1988, 53) calls an "*affection-subjectivity* [where] perception does not reflect possible action," but is instead immobilized in a receptive passivity. Deleuze connects the "immobility of a purely receptive role" to pain, but rather than this being negative, it is the intensity of surrendering to pain (unrequited love) that allows Lisa to function as a figure through which something new can emerge. Interestingly, Marks (1998, 344) relates "haptic visuality" to the passive receptivity of the viewer, that is, a "masochistic identification, in which the film viewer gives herself over to an entire scene—sometimes literally a shimmering surface." When Lisa returns the videos of Lance's films to the video store, she says to the owner, Eddy: "I saw things, things I hadn't seen before." Eddy responds by asking: "What? Other meanings? [. . .] I guess that's normal." Lisa enigmatically replies: "And other scenes." Lisa's extra-vision—Deleuze might call this the optical dimension of the image which extends in time when action is suspended—acts as a performative rupture that releases the image from being considered an ersatz or false copy of reality. In losing herself in Lance's image, a risky business, Lisa effects a movement out of her individual dilemma to create a transindividual emotion that allows us as viewers to glimpse, like "passers-by that might be nudged in a dance [. . .] the nature of emotion as pure element" (Deleuze 1988, 110). While this may sound rather esoteric, what I am suggesting here is an alternative to the view that the recovery of a cultural memory or the confirmation of a preexisting fantasy of identity are the only kinds of pleasures to be gained from watching a film that deals with displacement. The pleasure of self-dispossession can also be a strong draw.

THE INTENSITY OF DISPOSSESSION

I am not alone in being moved by the final scene in *Speaking Parts*. In fact, most of the literature on the film focuses on the scene at the close of the film when Lance and Lisa kiss, silhouetted against the glow of Lisa's television. For Hamid Naficy (2001, 286) this scene is one of redemption.

> Even in the most radical of exilically accented films, there are moments of sedi-
> mentation, moments of so-called authenticity, when the copy corresponds more
> or less fully to the original, bringing to a temporary end the chain of repetition,
> signification, and mediation. In Egoyans' *Speaking Parts* [. . .] that moment of
> total correspondence or bliss [. . .] is reached through sincere and passionate
> love.

Ron Burnett (1993, 22) echoes this: "At the end of the film, Egoyan proposes that it is the physical contact between two human beings that will transform the role of the image and generate another space within which different questions of identity can be worked out. Lance and Lisa discover their need for each other. The image of their touching transmits the intensity of their feelings." These readings of this scene return it to an economy of closure where, within the conventions of film narrative, a heterosexual kiss pacifies rupture and signifies a happy ending. They also promulgate the hierarchy of physical and therefore by implication real contact over and above the deceptive artifice of images, a hierarchy that the film itself questions. In my reading of this scene as a productive opening out onto an intensive emotion that spirals beyond the protagonists' desires, I want to insist on the radical nature of the sensation that extends in time from this image.

In this scene, the flattened, silhouetted image of the couple, rather than sealing rupture by a physical coming together, instead produces a gap, a pulsating blackness, through which a raw state of sensation leaks. The notion of a gap resonates with the notion of surface contact that Egoyan refers to where a passage occurs between image and viewer, which blurs boundaries between the supposedly separate spaces they occupy. This in turn resonates with Deleuze's use of Henri Bergson's philosophy. For Bergson the body is also an image in the world, but one that effects a passage between different classes of images, in this case, film images. For the viewer, the affective dimension of the image appears in the gap between the double sense of moving in and being moved by the image, the image here becoming a surface of co-existing layers of time that exceed the present moment. In this double movement, the viewer has a choice. He or she can translate the chaotic array of sensations to which he or she is subjected in this moving passage and interpret the scene in terms of Lance and Lisa's discovery of their need for one another. However, this trajectory alone encrypts the force of the image in the form of a standard happy ending where tension is resolved by a kiss and we are back in the world of commonsense. If the black silhouetted image of Lance and Lisa enacts an image of love, then I would argue it would be love as a dynamic force that removes us from commonsense. Because of the double movement of being moved by and moving in the image, the translation we make of the image into sense, i.e., reciprocal love, is also being unseated by the forceful co-existence of sensations in themselves intimated by the pulsating blackness of Lance and Lisa's silhouetted bodies. The power of these subtle invisible movements unsettles the viewer's ability to simply contemplate or interpret this image in terms of Lance and Lisa living happily ever after.

For Deleuze (2001, 25) an image has the capacity to give us access to the underlying continuum of becoming that flows in the passage between one sensation and another, sensation being "only a break within the flow of absolute consciousness." Becoming, or 'creative emotion' is beyond sensation conceived of as bodily affect, although it depends on the body to realise, but not rationalize, its capacity.[9] This scene is so powerful because it intimates something that falls outside the image, yet whose invisibility is dependent on it. In this moment, the film most successfully answers Egoyan's provocative questions about what we want from images, a question that presented itself to him in relation to a primal image in Ingmar Bergman's *Persona* (1966). "Confronted with the composition of this very strange shot where the faces of two actresses merge into one, I found myself up against a host of questions. How do people look at images? What do we expect from them? What do we see in them?" (Egoyan 1993, 9–10). While it is perhaps spurious to speak of influence here, the resonance between Bergman's merging of two characters into one and Egoyan's is worth commenting on. There is also a scene in *Persona* where a boy's hand reaches out as if to touch the image of a woman's face, a gesture which is reminiscent of Lisa's reaching out to touch the monitor in the hotel towards the end of the film. In *Speaking Parts*, Lisa's gesture of reaching out to touch or turn off the monitor (it could be either) exacerbates the series of images that culminates in a dissolving of difference between the characters and ends with the final merging of her image with Lance's. I am arguing that this gesture of merging is the conduit for the viewer to effect a surface connection with the image, which extracts something from it that overrides the differential nature of linguistic forms of communication. Lisa, the vehicle for the transversing of individual identities and locations in the film, generates a gesture that composes an affective sensation that carries us away on the temporal folds of the image, which spiral to infinity. In the final scene, she no longer retains her identity nor acquires a new one but generates an image composite which is incredibly moving as a new kind of image—an image of sensation. In *Bergsonism*, Deleuze (1988, 74) states that a sensation "is the operation of contracting trillions of vibrations onto a receptive surface." For me, the final image of merging in *Speaking Parts* is just such a receptive surface. It contracts the viewer's sense of being moved by and moving in what is ultimately an image of an infinitely extensive hollow blackness. In the process, we encounter points of intensity that cannot be contained by the logic of image production in a media saturated environment. It is in this sense then that *Speaking Parts* reaches an operatic excess that paradoxically preserves the silence of the whole.

NOTES

1. Egoyan is a Canadian director born in Egypt in 1960 to two artists, who were descendants of Armenian refugees and who emigrated to Canada in 1962. In *The Adjuster*, Noah Render (Elias Koteas), an insurance adjuster, lives with his partner Hera (Arsinée Khanjian), who is a film censor, her sister Seta, (Rose Sarkisyan) and Hera's son, Simon (Armen Kokorian) in a model home built for an urban development that has never taken place. Working nights, Noah appears at the site of burned-down houses to help their owners process their insurance claims. Part of his job involves placing the victims in a motel while they await new housing. Noah also engages in sexual relations with his clients, male and female, in their motel rooms.

2. Egoyan's interest in making the viewer traverse the spaces in a film is literally extended in his turn to film installation in the mid 1990s. One of his best known film installations *Steenbeckett* (2002), commissioned by Artangel, London, is a meditation on memory and its recording by means of the degradable media of film and video.

3. In *Family Viewing*, the only remaining images of the young protagonist's (Aidan Tierney) Armenian mother, who is dead, are home movies that, having been transferred to video, have already lost resolution. This sense of loss is being further aggravated by the boy's father (David Hemblen), an Anglo-Canadian, who records sexual games with his mistress (Gabrielle Rose) over the family videotapes.

4. The copy of *Speaking Parts* that I saw at The Other Cinema, London in 2003 had English subtitles as well as English dialogue, but this is not mentioned in any of the literature on the film. The cinema has subsequently closed down.

5. *Calendar* is Egoyan's most personal film in the sense that it features a husband and wife played by himself and his real-life wife Arsinée Khanjian. The film explores

the gap that grows between them on a holiday to Armenia where the husband, a photographer, feels excluded by her contact with the language, the place and the people.

6. Interestingly, Elena del Rio's (1996, 109) reading of *Speaking Parts* insists on Clara's success "in writing and reliving this story according to terms that are not susceptible to commodification."

7. Coincidentally, Egoyan puts the question "To what extent can one trust one's identity to someone else feeling what that identity is about?" at the core of *Speaking Parts*, although, as opposed to Lisa's character, he does not believe it is possible (Egoyan, in Glassman, 1993, 56).

8. There are of course distinctions between exile and diaspora, which are beyond the scope of this essay: see Naficy (1999).

9. Deleuze emphasizes even more in *What is Philosophy?*, co-authored with Félix Guattari, that he is not talking about bodily sensation but sensation liberated from bodily co-ordinates. "Sensations, percepts, and affects are *beings* whose validity lies in themselves and exceeds any lived" (Deleuze & Guattari 1994, 164).

REFERENCES

Boundas, Constantin V. (ed.). *The Deleuze Reader*. New York: Columbia University Press, 1993.

Burnett, Ron. 'Speaking of Parts' pp. 9–22 in *Speaking Parts* edited by Egoyan Atom. Toronto: Coach House Press, 1993.

Deleuze, Gilles. *Bergsonism* (trans. Hugh Tomlinson and Barbara Habberjam). New York: Zone Books, 1988.

———. *Cinema 2: The Time-Image* (trans Hugh Tomlinson and Robert Galeta). London: Athlone, 1989.

———. *Pure Immanence: Essays on a Life*. New York: Zone, 2001.

———. *Francis Bacon: The Logic of Sensation* (trans. Daniel W. Smith). London: Continuum, 2003.

Deleuze, Gilles and Guattari Félix (1994). *What is Philosophy?* (trans. Hugh Tomlinson and Graham Burchill). London: Verso.

Del Rio, Elena. 'The Body as Foundation of the Screen: Allegories of Technology in Atom Egoyan's *Speaking Parts*' *Camera Obscura* 38 (May 1996): 92–115.

Desbarats, Carole, Danièle Rivière, Jacinto Lageira and Paul Virilio (eds.). *Atom Egoyan* (trans. Brian Homes). Paris: Editions Dis Voir, 1993.

Egoyan, Atom. 'Surface Tension' pp. 25–38 in *Speaking Parts* edited by Atom Egoyan. Toronto: Coach House Press, 1993.

Glassman, Marc. 'Emotional Logic,' pp. 41–57 in *Speaking Parts* edited by Atom Egoyan. Toronto: Coach House Press, 1993.

Harcourt, Peter. (1995) 'Imaginary Images: an Examination of Atom Egoyan's Films' *Film Quarterly* 48, no. 3 (Spring, 1995): 2–14.

Marks, Laura U. 'A Deleuzian politics of hybrid cinema' *Screen* 35 no. 3 (Autumn 1994): 244–264.

——. 'Video haptics and erotics' *Screen* 39 no. 4 (Winter 1998): 331–347.

——. *The Skin of the Film: Intercultural Cinema, Embodiment, and the Senses.* Durham, NC: Duke University Press, 2000.

Moore, Rachel O. *Savage Theory: Cinema as Modern Magic.* Durham, NC: Duke University Press, 2000.

Naficy, Hamid. *Home, Exile, Homeland: Film, Media, and the Politics of Place.* London: Routledge, 1999.

——. *An Accented Cinema: Exilic and Diasporic Filmmaking.* Princeton: Princeton University Press, 2001.

Polan, Dana. 'Francis Bacon: The Logic of Sensation' pp. 229–254 in *Gilles Deleuze and the Theater of Philosophy* edited by Constantin V. Boundas, and Dorothea Olkowski. London: Routledge, 1994.

Romney, Jonathan. *Atom Egoyan.* London: BFI, 2003.

Departures:
The 21st Century Hotel—
Your Media/Home Away from Home

James Hay

Raymond Williams's *Television: Technology and Cultural Form* (1974) introduced at least two key concepts that have been integral to the critical vernacular of media studies since the 1970s.[1] One concept was his description of TV's "flow"—the practice of programming TV as a continuous sequence, whereby individual programs, ads, and announcements bleed into one another. For Williams, flow was the "defining characteristic" of TV broadcasting as a communication technology and cultural form. It distinguished TV from prior communication systems and cultural production (e.g., books, magazines, plays, films) whose "essential items were discrete."[2] Through the 1980s and 90s, academic TV and media criticism in the UK and North America often used Williams's term to examine TV as a relatively distinct set of formal or signifying practices. One of TV/media criticism's primary pursuits—and fundamental contradictions and dilemmas—was how to define and study TV as a *discrete*, even distinctive, medium while acknowledging its organization as *flow*.

As a few purveyors of TV theory and criticism have noted, Williams introduced the term through one of the book's only anecdotal passages about watching a film on TV one night in Miami, Florida, "still dazed from a week on an Atlantic liner." According to Williams, watching TV in Britain had not prepared him for the experience of watching TV (particularly a film on TV) in the United States.[3] Aside from this brief confessional moment, however, he never quite acknowledges how much TV's flow qualities, or his recognition or discovery of flow, was a consequence or accident of tourism—how much his reflection about TV at home and in the United States had anything to do with travel and tourism. And this issue has certainly not been at the forefront of accounts or deployments of Williams's term by other TV/media theorists and critics. Many (following William's own emphasis) dwell on the formal and aesthetic implications of TV flow. To my knowledge, Mimi White has come to the closest to recognizing the relation between TV, travel, and tourism in her reading of Williams's anecdote, casting him as a "tourist-ethnographer" in order to underscore that the "unexpectedness" or "shock" of encountering TV's flow, and that understanding TV as flow, have everything to do with degrees of separation from Home and with the knowledge/baggage with which one travels. For White, Williams's anecdote offers a way of thinking about the difficulties and complexities of watching TV in "global locales." However, her explanation of the significance of Williams's encounter with TV in Miami leads her to emphasize (once again) the aesthetic, textual, and interpretive questions about TV over TV's mattering within routes and economies of travel and tourism.[4]

Among those who have cited Williams's anecdote, there has been a strange lore that has developed around his having watched TV in a hotel room. Williams's brief anecdote never states that he was watching TV in a hotel room. He could have been in a hotel, or he could have been at the house of friend or a house that he had rented. But over the years various invocations of Williams's anecdote have inferred that he was in a hotel, or they have embellished their description of his description by adding the hotel room as setting or prop. For instance William Uricchio conjures "images of Raymond Williams, sacked out in his own hotel room in Miami . . . watching a heavy dose of defamiliarized (read American) TV."[5] And Lisa Parks and Shanti Kumar, in their Introduction to the book in which White's essay was published, states that Williams's ideas about TV occurred when he "sat in his Miami hotel room." Whether Williams did encounter U.S. TV in a Miami hotel room, or whether the hotel room is a logical inference that everyone should draw from his anecdote, is less important than the almost inconsequentiality or triviality of the hotel room for nearly everyone who has benefited from Williams's thoughts about TV as flow. For all of White's interest in constructing Williams as an early "traveler/ethnographer," neither Miami nor the hotel room are particularly relevant for her argument about TV analysis as a "traveling theory." Hers is not primarily an account of TV/media through a theory and analysis of travel, or of how TV/media matter within the institutions, economies, networks, and sites of travel and tourism. As is typical of 'media studies,' the effects of media are everywhere; thinking about what travel, tourism, and hotels *require of* media and particular spheres of activity may be counterintuitive to the specialized knowledge of media analysis and criticism.

Whether Williams watched TV in a hotel room should pose a different set of questions about TV as technology and cultural form than has typically been posed by media criticism. And although Williams's failure to mention whether he was in a hotel room (either because he was not or because he considered it relatively unimportant) may suggest that his anecdote is not the place to begin; another dimension of his argument about TV does provide a way of thinking about how the hotel room matters. Getting to this perspective involves a brief detour through his (only slightly more elaborated) comments about television's formation and use within changing regimes of mobility and privacy—what he termed "mobile privatization." As Williams explains, television did not spring simply from a series of technical improvements upon earlier communication/media technologies but rather through a socio-spatial arrangement—one that situated domesticity (privacy) increasingly "at a distance" from other sites and from its earlier locations, even as it conjoined spheres of privacy to an outside through broadcasting and transportation networks.[6] "Mobile privatization," in this sense, refers to the changing and geographically uneven interdependencies between social space, transportation, and communication technology. The link between Williams's anecdote about TV as flow and his view that TV only became socially useful (a "social technology") through a regime of mobility and privacy reminds us that watching TV at home depends upon technologies of transport, and that feeling at home on the road depends upon technologies of communication.

To the extent that Williams's discovery of flow occurred away from home and 'on the road,' there are good reasons to think about that discovery (perhaps even TV as flow) as having occurred at an intersection between communication/media and travel/tourism, and between historically and geographically situated regimes of mobility and domesticity. In the early 1970s, an Atlantic liner like the one on which Williams traveled to the United States may have shown a movie, offered musical and dance performances, or allowed time for reading, but it certainly did not offer TV. Hotels (particularly those in the United States), however, did. In fact, TVs had been standard accouterments of many classes of hotels in the United States since the 1950s. For a particular class of traveler from outside the United States, entering the United States involved passing through the intersection between TV and the hotel room. The televisual hotel room was a *space of conversion* and a chamber designed to manage or channel the feeling of being (to invoke the title of Sofia Coppola's 2003 film) 'lost in translation.' But the hotel room has always been a space of conversion with a profound relation to Home (i.e., to the design and enactment of domesticity through regimes of mobility). If home is an idea or place arrived at by having gone somewhere else,[7] and if television developed by representing and enacting a place called home through communication and transportation networks, then the televisual hotel room is a technology and cultural form for transacting/converting 'home away from home.' The hotel room is a provisional home, where one brings a few things from home (clothes, photos, children's toys) but where TV and other communication technologies mediate the familiar and unfamiliar.

It is difficult to glean from Williams's anecdote whether he was watching a feature film or a television series (what in Europe are often referred to as 'telefilms'), or whether he was disturbed or excited by the way that a film was reprocessed to fit the requirements of televisual flow, but reconstructing Williams's encounter with TV in the United States involves recognizing the historical formation of the hotel room (and not just TV) as a technology and cultural form that materialized within a regime of mobility, privacy, and communication. And one way to think about the historical formation of the hotel room as televisual or mediated space is to begin with the transformation of the domestic sphere through technologies of transport—particularly TV's relation to *auto-mobility*.[8] Lynn Spigel has suggested that in the United States during the 1960s the portability of TV (and advertising's representation of portable TV) precipitated the "mobile home as cultural metaphor"—a representation of personal power through portability that supplanted earlier promotions of TV as part of the "family circle" and as the "home as theater."[9] However, rather than replacing a model of domesticity as private theater (and the accompanying ideal of home as insulated and secure from the outside), the naturalization of portable television at home[10] occurred concurrently with the emergence of domestic technologies that made it possible to watch commercially uninterrupted movies at home—a development that made it less necessary to 'go out' to see movies and that accelerated the design and use of 'living rooms' as private movie theaters.

The commercial and technical convergence of television and cinema was launched through satellite distribution, the first and most prominent ventures of which was Time-Life's subscription movie-service, Home Box Office (HBO) in 1975. Over the late 1970s, HBO was followed by other 'home-movie' TV networks such as Cinemax, Showtime, The Movie Channel as well as the para-subscription, 'commercial-free,' movie channels such as American Movie Classics and Turner Classic Movies.[11] The success of this trend not only contributed to the rapid expansion of the cable- and satellite-delivery of various TV channels (most of which were not subscription-based movie channels), but also to the rapid domestication of video play-back systems, to the attachment of domestic video systems to domestic audio systems, and to the proliferation of outlets renting and selling videos of movies for home consumption.

Even though the trend toward satellite distribution hastened the practice of watching commercial-free films at home, and of transforming the living room into a private movie theater, it also expanded the distribution of movies and TV movie-channels to hotel rooms—private movie theaters away from home.

Over the 1980s and 1990s, this occurred through the material overlapping of the technologies and economies of tourism, hospitality, and cable/satellite programming. As the business and technology of satellite delivery to both homes and hotels facilitated the movement of customers between these to spheres, de-differentiating the place of access to TV-movies, the hotel room became a site where customers could experiment with ('try on') new, mostly 'premium' services that could then be subscribed to or purchased at home as an 'upgrade' in cable/satellite service. The hotel room became not so much another extension of the movie theater but a site between the movie theater and home—a sphere for private screenings away from home. For film and video distribution, as well as for the hospitality industry, the video monitor became a way of adding commercial value to travel and tourism. On the one hand, the hotel guest room as private screening room was an amenity (even a luxury) for some customers; on the other hand, the hotel became a stage for naturalizing the home-entertainment center and the domestic bedroom as private screening room.

In the United States over the 1980s and 1990s, a number of companies were created primarily to provide communication and entertainment technologies for hotel guest rooms, and this industry has been integral to and sometimes drove the developments and practices of cable/satellite and broadband programming for the home. One of the oldest and largest of these distributors has been LodgeNet. Formed in 1980 as the Satellite Movie Company (SMC), it became one of the first U.S. providers of basic and premium cable TV programs to hotels. By 1986, SMC began offering pay-per-view in hotel rooms, at roughly the same time that the major cable companies were beginning to provide this service to their premium customers. Between 1988 and 1989, SMC introduced remote controls for TV interactive systems in the guest rooms of their client hotels—a technology that soon thereafter became available at home through cable/satellite providers. In 1992, SMC reinvented itself as LodgeNet, oriented toward providing broadband, local network systems for hotels, and hastening the development of 'on-demand' viewing/programming—another technology that moved from the hotel to everyday domestic usage. In 1993, LodgeNet entered into a partnership with Nintendo, a venture that made the partnership the first national in-room provider of video games. And in 1999, LodgeNet became the first national chain offering high-speed Internet access to hotel guest rooms.

Over the 1990s, the expansion of entertainment media/technologies in guest rooms has been accompanied by the growth of the hospitality entertainment-network industry. LodgeNet currently claims a network of 860,000 guest rooms in the United States and Canada. Its competition includes Guest-Tek (with a network of 3,400 hotels and 505,000 guest rooms), EthoStream

(1,589 mostly budget hotels with 117,000 rooms), Kool Connect, and the On Command Corporation (subsequently acquired by LodgeNet). These companies not only provide media content but they also work as design consultants to strategize with hoteliers about how to enhance guest rooms as entertainment and work centers. The reach of these companies is noteworthy (particularly as a network largely unexamined by film and media studies) less because they deliver multiple media than because their clients and networks are exclusively hotels—rather than movie theaters or the home.

Since the 1990s, the conversion of a 'satellite movie company' to a 'lodge-network' attests to a trend toward refashioning the hotel guest room into a multi-media space for 'multi-tasking,' wherein the delivery of movies becomes an amenity in menus of hospitality services—movie delivery as part of digital/broadband-mediated system of interactive, customizable, self-managed technologies of hospitality. Whereas prior to broadband systems, hotel guests' requests for films were made through a bank of video-cassette players at the hotel (a process that often involved the staggering of movie times), the transformation to broadband supported the ideal of self-managed work and leisure from the hotel and home. But the installation of these technical support and service systems in hotels has involved not only the expansion of spaces where movies and television could be consumed but also a deepening synergy between the home-based private movie theater and the hotel-based private movie theater—between the TV and personal computer as forms of transport from home, and the hotel room as technological apparatus for managing home (maybe even feeling at home) on the road. The running of households (the performance of domestic work and leisure) through matrices of communication technologies has also made it increasingly desirable for hotel guests to *carry* these comforts and technical requirements with them.

In some respects, there is nothing new about the instrumentality of cinema and television in a tourist economy; particularly in the United States, the current relation between the 'mediated' domestic sphere and hotel guest room has been developing for decades. The longstanding connection between cinema, tourism, and hotels is the subject of numerous essays in this book. TV in the United States emerged during the 1950s not only as a form of transport from home and but also as a technology of tourism-specific 'programs' for traveling beyond one's locality and for navigating tourist destinations. TV as 'tourist program' was implicated in mobile privatization but not explicitly in ways that Williams described. One of the most famous examples of TV's tourist program was the cooperation between Disney and the American Broadcast Company (ABC) during the 1950s.[12] ABC assisted Disney in financing its first theme park, Disneyland, while Disney gave ABC the exclusive rights to televise the building and opening of the park, made-for-TV children's series set at the park after it opened, and some of the company's old films and cartoons (exhibited on TV during the televised features about the theme park). However, during the 1970s, the period when Williams encountered and wrote about TV in the United States, TV, cinema and entertainment industries, and the urban hotel all became instrumental in projects of urban gentrification that would attract middle-class consumers, residents, and tourists to the downtown of cities that had undergone a prior period of flight to the suburbs.[13] By the 1990s, the design of homes and hotel guest rooms with 'multi-media centers' became crucial to maintaining the interdependence of the household as economy, the economy of communications media, and the tourist economy. A standard feature of the cable/satellite service in most downtown hotel rooms in the United States is a channel about attractions for tourists visiting the hotel's city. In this regard, the video-tour guide on the hotel TV menu becomes one of several technologies for navigating on the road (alongside, for instance, personal or car-based GPS units, or the city-based travel magazines provided in hotel guest rooms). In certain respects, the video-tour guide serves to correct the crisis of displacement that tourists/travelers such as Williams experienced decades ago.

Fashioning the contemporary hotel guest room as a space for 'interactive' services and entertainment also became instrumental to a 'Neoliberal' governmental rationality that values the maximization of self-sufficiency through personal forms of mobility.[14] Gaining control of one's environment, encapsulating oneself, and/or insuring one's safety through pre-designed menus and technologies of mobility and habitation (guides and resources for going and stopping) not only bespeaks the interdependencies of the current economies of cinema/media and tourism, but also their importance for a governmental rationality about personal freedoms and security as a mobile subject/traveler. The capacity of the current regime of communication technology to 'free' users is tantamount to their capacity (or promise) to offer a mobile, traveling subject greater self-control. In this respect, the contemporary hotel room, as a space of privacy and even secrecy, is designed as much to assure 'freedom of choice' as to shape self-responsible (ethical) travelers/tourists, able to provide for themselves and to look after their own needs without undue interference from hotel managers.

The greater availability of porn from hotel guest rooms is one example of the contradictions of the 'wired' guest room as a newly liberalized space of private indulgence and erotic pleasure. The 'mainstreaming' of porn that has occurred since the 1980s, when Playboy launched the first cable/satellite TV channel in the United States, has occurred through access to 'on-demand,' erotic technology as much at home as in the hotel guest room.[15] Even though the hotel room is generally thought of and marketed as an 'escape' from home, and thus from the restrictive apparatuses of domestic life, the contemporary hotel guest room provides many of the same self-censoring technologies that have become attached to the home entertainment center. Adult guests can monitor and regulate which movies, TV, and games can be accessed by other members of the family, and can choose between 'extreme,' 'erotic,' and 'couples',' porn.

Television and other media have not been, as Williams was prone to point out, simply the outcome of prior media technologies (the result of a techno-logical determinism), unless one thinks about the symbiotic relation between space and technology (technological zones and activity spaces) that enact regimes of mobility and the socio-spatial arrangements for living, acting, and governing oneself in certain ways. The utility of understanding cinema or other media through particular spheres of activity (such as the hotel guest room) is that doing so underscores what that performance space *requires of* particular networks, economies, and governmental rationalities. This is the problem with references to 'Williams's hotel room' or with accounts of me-dia that invoke the hotel guest room as a metaphor or an incidental site where media are encountered (as in Uricchio's personal anecdote of his hotel room as a multi-media space representative of 'life after TV'). How exactly is the mobile home technically enacted, valued, made to matter, and regulated on the road, as one travels—in these times and in one part of the world in rela-tion to others? The usefulness of this book is that it asks how media matter from the changing paths of movement and the places for stopping, and that it considers this process from one of those transit stops.

NOTES

For Meaghan, and *her* Henry Parkes Motel.

1. Raymond Williams (1974/1992) *Television: Technology and Cultural Form*, Hanover, Wesleyan University Press.
   2. Ibid., pp. 80–81.
   3. "I began watching a film and at first had some difficulty in adjusting to a much greater frequency of commercial 'breaks.' Yet this was a minor problem compared to what eventually happened. Two other films, which were due to be shown on the same channel on other nights, began to be inserted as trailers. . . . I can still not be sure what I took from that whole flow. I believe I registered some incidents as happening in the wrong film, and some characters in the commercials as involved in film episodes, in what came to seem—for all the occasional bizarre disparities—a singe irresponsible flow of images and feelings," Ibid., pp. 85–86.
   4. Mimi White (2002) 'Flows and Other Close Encounters with Television,' *Planet TV: A Global Television Studies Reader*, ed., Shanti Kumar and Lisa Parks,

New York, New York University Press. I agree with White's general emphasis on Williams's TV-encounter in the United States as a useful point of reference for recognizing that teaching, analyzing, or theorizing TV/media always occur from some place. However, I am less persuaded by her essay's interest in developing a phenomenology of the ethnographic encounter and with positing ethnography (and particularly a media ethnography sensitive to TV as aesthetic and semiotic form) as an antidote to the media- or cultural-imperialism thesis of political economy and to the empirical methodologies of social-scientific studies of media. In this regard, her perspective never moves too far from understanding the articulation of the televisual and flow as primarily a formal and aesthetic question, rather than as about the mattering of communication/media technology in the production of space, the production of mobility, the production of home, and the economies of travel and tourism. Engaging these latter issues involves, as I have argued elsewhere, seeking alternatives to the binarisms between political economy and textual analysis or ethnography, and between empirical research and critical studies of media. See for instance Hay, "Locating the Televisual," *Television and New Media*, vol. 2, no. 3, August 2001, and "Between Cultural Materialism and Spatial Materialism," *Thinking with James Carey: Essays on Communications, Transportation, History*, ed., Jeremy Packer and Craig Robertson, New York: Peter Lang, 2006.

5. William Uricchio, "Television's Next Generation: Technology/Interface Culture/Flow," *Television after TV: Essays on a Medium in Transition*, ed., Lynn Spigel and Jan Olsson, Durham, NC: Duke UP, 2004, pp. 163–182.

6. Williams, op cit., pp. 20–21.

7. See David Morley, "A Place Called Home," *Home Territories*, London: Routledge, 2002.

8. For more on my use of this term, in part in relation to 'mobile privatization,' see James Hay and Jeremy Packer, "Crossing the Media(-n): Auto-mobility, the Transported Self, and Technologies of Freedom," *Media/Space: Place, Scale, and Culture in a Media Age*, ed., Anna McCarthy and Nick Couldry, New York: Routledge, 2004. See also Mike Featherstone, Nigel Thrift and John Urry, eds., *Automobilities* London: Sage, 2005.

9. Lynn Spigel, "Portable TV: Studies in Domestic Space Travel," *Welcome to the Dreamhouse: Popular Media and Postwar Suburbs*, Durham, NC: Duke UP, 2001.

10. According to Spigel, citing the U.S. Bureau of the Census, "Manufacturer's Sales and Retail Value of Home Appliances, 1955–1969," "by 1969 over twice as many portable and table-top [TV] models were sold than were consoles (7,606,000 versus 3,442, 000)." Ibid., p. 67.

11. During the 1980s, American Movie Classics did not insert advertisements into its broadcasts, but that practice changed during the late 1990s. During the 1980s, Turner Classic Movies sometimes broadcast colorized versions of old black-and-white films, reasoning that TV viewers preferred color-TV, but that practice also changed during the 1990s. For more on how cinema and TV developed through one another in the U.S., see Hay, "Cinema and TV," *Storia del cinema mondiale*, vol. 2, ed. Gian Piero Brunetta, Torino: Giulio Einaudi, 2000.

12. See Michael Sorkin, "See You in Disneyland," *Variations on a Theme Park*, ed. Michael Sorkin, New York: Hill and Wang, 1992; Christopher Anderson, *Hollywood TV*, Austin: University of Texas Press, 1994.

13. For a discussion of media industries' involvement in these projects over the 1980s and 90s, see John Hannigan, *Fantasy City: Pleasure and Profit in the Postmodern Metropolis*, New York: Routledge, 1998.

14. See Hay, "Unaided Virtues: The (Neo-)Liberalization of the Domestic Sphere," *Television and New Media* vol. 1, no. 1, pp. 53–73, 2000; Hay and Packer, op cit.; and Hay, "Designing Homes to be the First Line of Defense: Safe Households, Mobilization, and the New Mobile Privatization," *Cultural Studies*, vol. 20, no. 4–5, July/September 2006.

15. For more on the contradictions surrounding the 'mainstreaming' of porn in the U.S., see Jane Juffer, "Sexual Technology and Domestic Technology: Porn as an Everyday Matter," *Contemporary Culture and Everyday Life*, ed. Tony Bennett and Elisabeth Silva, British Sociology Association, London: Sociology Press, 2005, pp. 71–85.

Index

13 rue Madeleine, *94*, *95*, 96,130n62, 133
2046, 4, 8, 236, 249–50, 252n10, 341–42

abjection, 3, 261, 264, 268, 272–73, 275n4
Ackerman, Chantal, 1
action-image, 224, 346
Adlon Hotel, Berlin, 17, 24, 46n16, 81
Adorno, Theodor W., 146; noetic anaesthesia, 268, 274
affect, 221, 223–26, 231, 343–46, 355, 360–61, 366–68, 369n9
affection-image, 224–25, 365
agoraphobia, 246
Alice in the Cities, 6, 185
Alphaville, 173n27, 179, 285, 295, 326
Amarcord (I Remember Fondly), 4, 13–14, 16, 44n2, 44n4
Ambassador Hotel, Los Angeles, 6, 7, 23, 209–10, 213–16, 216n5, 217n6
Andersen, Thom, 217n9
Antonioni, Michelangelo, 6, 171n1, 185, 327, 347
architecture, 4, 21, 46, 83, 119, 121, 123n10, 124nn21–22, 173n24, 210, 215, 275n10, 283, 286, 308; cinematic, 115; filmic, 353;

literary, 311; psychogeographic, 79; Rationalist, 22, 26, 28
Arendt, Hannah, 8, 266, 275n5
arrival, 3, 105, 156, 190, 236, 259, 285, 289, 326, 330, 341, 349
Art Deco, 21–22, 31–32, 64, 81
Asambhav, 143–45, 168, 172n18, 175
assemblage, 231, 256, 279, 285–86, 290–91, 345
atrium, 83, 124n22, 243
Augé, Marc, 2, 9, 127n44, 211, 237, 279, 285, 287–88, 337
auteur, 298, 300, 310
auto-mobility, 374, 379n8
avant garde, 156, 198, 216, 322n21, 354

Bachelard, Gaston, 291
Bakhtin, Mikhail Mikhailovich, 6, 45n9, 79, 123n13, 186, 194, 279, 286
Balázs, Béla, 358, 362
balcony, 58, 63
Bar at the Folies-Bergère, 92
Barthes, Roland, 275n6, 286
Barton Fink, 8, 251n1, 255–76 *passim*, 280, 285, 290, 326
bath, 73, 188, 270, 318
bathroom, 59, 88, 237, 251, 270, 309–310, 315
Baudrillard, Jean, 8, 222

Baudry, Jean, 46n19
Bauhaus, 21
Baum, Vicki, 25–26, 28, 45n13, 46n23, 83, 122n9, 124n19, 251n2
Bauman, Zygmunt, 2, 185
Bazin, André, 214
Beau Travail, 9, 173n29, 348–49
becoming 258, 345–46, 367, *see also* creative emotion
bed, 3, 73, 77, 88, 115, 219, 235, 237, 241, 261, 270, 288, 292, 304, 306–307, 322n25, 346, 348, 570
bedroom, 77, 155, 158, 161, 215, 301, 311, 375
Bellour, Raymond, 332
Benjamin, Walter, 283
bergfilm, 155, 172n21
Bergman, Ingmar, 101, 143, 156, 179, 367
Bergson, Henri, 10, 346, 359, 366
Berlin, 6, 16–17, 21, 24, 26, 31, 46n23, 81, 152, 160, 183–208 *passim*
Beyond the Clouds (*Au-delà des Nuages*), 6, 185, 187
Bhabha, Homi K., 127n42
Biograph, 76
The Birds, 9, 334, 336
Blanchot, Maurice, 1, 209, 213–14
The Blue Dahlia, 5, 89, 108–9, 111, 120, 125n23
body, 7, 96, 99, 114, 151, 219–33 *passim*, 240, 295, 329, 340, 343–44, 366–67
body without organs, 258, 273, 275n3
Bogart, Humphrey, 90–113 *passim*, 126n27, 126n31, 128n46
Bogdanovich, Peter, 143, 148, 176
Bollywood, 6, 144, 155, 157, 171n4
Bonaventure Hotel, Los Angeles, 2, 53, 250, 289
Bond, James, 154, 157, 288, 345–47
Boorstin, Daniel, 121n2, 129n60
Borderline, 156, 175
Bruno, Giuliana, 3, 78, 107, 115, 123n12, 126n30, 217n10
Bukowski, Charles, 159–61

The Business of Strangers, 8, 236, 241, 243
Butler, Judith, 333

Calle, Sophie, 3
Camerini, Mario, 4, 30, 32, 34, 39, 41
capitalism, 267, 270, 322n29; capitalist society, 256, 264, 298; capitalist machine, 258–59, 261, 271, 274
Capra, Frank, 5, 85–87
Casablanca, 63
Casablanca 112, 330
casino, 18–19, 24, 32, 38, 47n25, 166, 172n15, 250, 291
Casino, 239
Castelli in aria (*Castles in the Air*), 4, 42–43
Century Hotel, 8, 236, 245–46
Chabrol, Claude, 6, 143, 146–47
Chandler, Raymond, 111
Chaplin, Charlie, 24, 172n11, 197, 275n11
Chelsea Girls, 252n7
Chelsea Walls, 8, 236, 245–47, 252n8
Chŏng In-yŏp, 305, 321n10
chronotope, 6, 17–18, 79, 123n13, 186, 194–96, 202, 204, 206n7, 283, 288–89
Chungking Express (*Chunghing Samlam*), 317, 341
cinema vérité, 219
city, 5, 16–26 *passim*, 30–34 *passim*, 63–64, 73–78 *passim*, 81, 87, 89, 130n61, 153–54, 157–60, 163–64, 191, 193–96, 201, 205, 210, 215, 237, 240, 277, 281–82, 285–89, 298, 302, 310–11, 236, 377
Clark, Timothy James, 92–4
Clarke, David B., 217n9, 220–21, 252n5
class, 4, 5, 17–43 *passim*, 44n7, 45n14, 56–67, 76, 80–88, 107, 116, 119, 125n26, 199, 261, 288, 301–12, 320n5–7, 377
claustrophobia, 156, 190, 202, 243, 244, 245, 298, 299, 309, 310, 314, 316, 319, 321n19,

Cloak and Dagger, 153, 176

Coen brothers, 8, 255–76 *passim*

Cold War, 114–119 *passim*

Collateral, 215

Connery, Sean, 112, 289

Consequences of Love (*Le Conseguenze dell'amore*), 143, 156–57

consumption, 18, 51, 186, 197, 260, 273, 275n4, 298, 302, 319, 374

Coover, Robert, 3

Coppola, Francis Ford, 325

Coppola, Sophia, 1, 4, 285, 373

corridor, 22, 76, 79, 83, 90, 124n22, 156–61 *passim*, 170, 217n12, 248, 275n5, 277, 281, 290–91

creative emotion,10, 360–61, 367, *see also* becoming crime, 100–101, 105, 116–17, 238, 243–44, 247, 283, 326, 332, 336, 341

cruise-liner. *See* liner

curtain, 213, 219, 241, 292–92, 295, 348

D.O.A., 5, 89, *91*, 97, 101–105, *106*, 111, 120, 125

Daisy Miller, 148–50

Dali, Salvador, 210–11

de Certeau, Michel, 120, 127n44, 278, 294

Dead Reckoning, 89, *90*, 91, 94, 101, 111–12, 116, 124, 126n27, 126n31

Death in Venice, 45n13, 326

Decasia, 212

The Decay of Fiction, 9, 209–218

deferred interpretation [*Nachträglichkeit*], 216

Deleuze, Gilles, 9, 10, 212, 224–27, 230–31, 257–58, 274n1, 275n3, 279, 281, 292–93, 328, 336, 342–49, 359–62, 365–68, 369n9

Denby, Elaine, 2, 83, 125n25

Denis, Claire, 9, 173n29, 347–49

department store, 83, 84, 124n22

departure, 3, 156, 190, 205, 209, 315, 326, 335, 347

Der Himmel über Berlin. See Wings of Desire

Der Letzte Mann, 81, 134

Derrida, Jacques, 7, 103, 192, 210, 212, 326, 335, 344, 345, 349

desire, 5, 7–8, 16, 33, 35, 66, 77, 84, 87, 94, 98, 114–16, 155, 161, 184, 192–93, 195, 205n3, 214, 257–58, 269–70, 304–305, 308, 311, 315, 327–43, 346, 348–49, 353–66

destinerrance, 327

detective, 4, 19, 28, 45n13, 51, 63, 76, 88–90, 96, 99–101, 103, 105, 108, 111, 122n9, 125n26, 127n45, 152, 198, 215, 242, 256–58, 291, 308, 333

deterritorialization, 257–58, 284, 343, *see also* reterritorialization

Devil, 8, 161, 248, 256–76

dialectic, 9, 300, 309

diaspora, 353, 355, 360–361, 365, 369n8

difference, 214, 342

Dimendberg, Edward, 115, 122n10, 217n9

Dirty Pretty Things, 8, 236, 248, *249*–52

Disney, 6, 154, 155, 274, 318, 376

Disney, Walt, 143, 145, 154, 173n22

Doane, Mary Ann, 212

domesticity, 36, 44n7, 336, 373–74

door. *See* revolving door

doppelganger, 78, *see also* double

double, 3, 35, 37, 41, 78, 89, 104–105, 113, 247, 292, *see also* doppelganger

Douglas, Mary, 79, 120

Doyle, Christopher, 310, 312, 317, 321n20

dream, 160, 274, 290–92, 294, 364

Eastwood, Clint, 143, 145, 152, 155, 164, 176

Egoyan, Atom, 10, 353–70

Eisenstein, Sergei, 275n11

elevator, 8, 79, 264–65, 270–74

ethnicity, 53, 359

evil, 102–103, 236, 266, 291, 292, 331; evil, banality of (Arendt), 8, 266 exile, 107, 164, 166, 326–29, 331, 337, 339, 348–49, 353, 355, 365–66, 369n8

expressionism (Deleuze), 221, 226–30

Expressionism, 19, 26, 31, 193

Eyes Wide Shut, 327

Fallen Angel, 91, 92, 109, 133

fantasy, 7, 81, 83, 89, 113, 119, 155, 159, 160, 192, 240, 305, 317–18, 327, 330–31, 333, 340–41, 345, 348, 353–56, 362–66; escapist, 4, 18, 42–43, 65

fascism, Italian, 14, 22, 29, 34, 36, 37–43, 44n1, 44n5, 47n28, 47n31

Fellini, Federico, 4, 13, 14, 44n2, 44n4, 171n1

femme fatale, 111, 215, 223, 292, 335

fetish, 29, 298, 300, 303, 305, 310, 315, 317, 334–35

Figgis, Mike, 7, 235, 252n4

film festival: Locarno, 143–45, 174–75n44; Venice Biennale, 37, 40–41, 47n36; Berlinale, 196–97

film noir, 4, 5, 19, 85, 92, 100–102, 105, 110–12, 114–16, 119, 122n10, 123n13, 123n18, 125n23, 126n27, 129n57, 130n67, 215, 223, 228, 290, 292–93

Fitzgerald, F. Scott, 59, 149

flâneur, 216, 217n11

Flaubert, Gustave, 321n13

flophouse, 129n53, 298

flow, 2, 15, 26, 52, 237, 245, 248, 261, 312, 355, 367, 371–77, 378n3

fold, 9, 281, 290–93, 295, 368

Ford, John, 61, 191

Foucault, Michel, 6, 28, 43, 51, 58, 65, 78, 83, 127nn43–44, 128n47, 186, 202, 344

Frears, Stephen, 8, 135, 236, 248

Freud, Sigmund, 3, 117, 216, 220, 221, 270, 341

Frontier Hotel, Los Angeles, 197–98, 206n13

Gardies, André, 6, 185–87, 190, 192, 203, 204

gaze, 5, 55–9, 61–64, 74, 114, 280, 289, 298, 305, 315, 334, 359, 363–64

gender, 7, 53, 58–59, 85, 88, 107, 131n71, 163, 243, 289, 299, 302, 308, 319

Geneva, 6, 143–181

Genina, Augusto, 4, 39, 41–42

God, 28, 193, 237, 252n3, 255–57, 275n3, 279, 328, 343

Godard, Jean-Luc, 6, 143, 146, 156–65, 173n31–32, 174n33, 285

Goldfinger, 154, 157, 172n9

Gondry, Michel, 7, 210, 213

Goretta, Claude, 165

Goulding, Edmund, 1, 4, 13, 83, 132, 133, 235, 259, 295

Gramsci, Antonio, 18, 19, 45n11

Grand Hotel, 13–48 *passim*, 85–86, 119, 143–182 *passim*, 344, *see also hôtel de luxe*

Grand Hotel, 1, 4–5, 13, 15, 20, 23–28 *passim*, 33, 40, 45n13, 46n15, 76, 81, *82*, 84, 87, 89, 99, 120, 122n9, 123n18, 124n21, 235, 251n1, 259, 273, 295

Grand Hotel Esplanade, Berlin, 184, 193–96, 205

Groth, Paul, 2, 78, 80, 110–11, 121n2, 123n16, 125nn25–26, 129n53, 129nn60–61

Groupe 5, 165

Guattari, Félix, 224–31 *passim*, 258, 343, 349, 369n9

Gunning, Tom, 76

Gurevich, Georges, 186, 190–96

Happy Sara, 302

Happy Together (*Cheun gwong tsa sit*), 252n10, 312, 341

haptic, 10, 361, 363, 365

Harvey, David, 9, 184–86, 190, 194, 196, 203, 280

Hawke, Ethan, 8, 236, 244

Hegel, Georg Wilhelm Friedrich, 327, 336
Heidegger, Martin, 3, 9, 327, 330, 342
Heimlich, 8, 270
Hell, 8, 239, 257–74 *passim*
Hemingway, Ernest, 144, 149
Hesse, Hermann, 144–47, 156
Hesse-Rabinovitch, Isa, 144
heterotopia, 6, 9, 29, 58, 65, 78, 100, 119, 127nn43–44, 186, 202–205, 298
Hitchcock, Alfred, 1–9 *passim*, 49, 76, 109–10, 118, 124n23, 134–54 *passim*, 280, 331–49 *passim*
Hollywood, 7, 10, 19–40 *passim*, 46nn17–18, 46n20, 47n31, 47n35, 81, 91, 107, 123n18, 153, 172n16, 187, 197, 199, 204, 209, 214, 216, 259–60, 263–6, 272, 286, 306, 308, 323n32, 331, 336, 354
home, 16–41 *passim*, 44n7, 50–51, 58–59, 67–68, 75, 77, 79, 88, 100, 105, 109–10, 114–5, 120–21, 128n50, 131n71, 158, 160, 185, 188, 190–91, 206n6, 237, 239–40, 251, 258, 269, 281, 284, 287, 288, 310, 312, 325–26, 330–33, 340, 343–47, 348, 372–78 *passim*, 379n4
homecoming, 64, 114, 326, 330–31, 347
homelessness, 85–87, 107, 113, 121, 129n57, 191–92, 235, 326, 327–33, 337–39 *passim*, 343
honeymoon, 92, 100, 117–18, 127n43, 152, 155, 209, 308, 331, 348
Hong Kong, 236, 249, 250, 310, 317, 322n24
Hopper, Edward, 185, 192, 201–202
hospitality, 4, 375–76
hôtel de luxe, 15, 19, 23, 29, *see also* Grand Hotel
Hotel Napoleon, Paris, 17, 24
Hotel Room, 290
Hotel Waldhaus, Sils-Maria, 6, 146–68 *passim*, 171n5
Huston, John, 5, 112, 132, 133

hyperreality, 318
hysteria, 219–22, 229, 232n1

identity, 15, 16, 22, 35, 37, 40, 54, 59, 60, 64–65, 73–141 *passim*, 163, 183–203 *passim*, 216, 235–51 *passim*, 256–57, 271, 277–78, 280, 284–85, 291–94, 329, 333, 339, 344–45, 359–61, 365–68, 369n7
Il Signor Max, 4, 34–37, 42
Im Kwon-t'aek, 298
imaginary, 65, 83–84, 86, 93, 100, 105, 115–116, 120–121, 159, 160, 220, 250, 270, 330, 333, 335, 337, 342, 354, 360, 362
immigrant workers, 248–49
Impact, 5, 91, *93*, 96–120 *passim*, 126n28, 133
In the Mood for Love, 249–50, 341
individual, 22–23, 65, 79, 89, 99, 102, 221, 226, 230, 238, 245, 248, 255–76 *passim*, 278–80, 285, 294, 308, 338–39, 348, 360–61, 368
intensity, 36, 147, 163, 231, 238, 273, 301, 348, 359, 363–68
intervallic, 360
Irreversible, 212

Jakle, John A., 2, 121n1, 128n52
James, Henry, 77, 80, 143, 148–49, 153
Jameson, Frederic, 2, 53, 123n14, 285, 289, 294
Jarmusch, Jim, 8, 277, 281, 283
Jewish, 263, 266
journey, 9, 30, 33–35, 39, 50, 64, 66, 76, 187, 259, 270, 288, 326, 328, 330, 336–47
Joyce, James, 326, 337, 343

Kapoor, Raj, 155, 173n30
Katz, Marc, 2, 89, 122n9, 238, 256–57
key, 73, 102, 116–17, 220, 268, 307
Key Largo, 5, 107, 112–14, 119–20, 133
Killer Bait, 89, 91, *98*, 111, 133
Kluge, Alexander, 6, 145–47, 171n5, 180

Koestenbaum, Wayne, 3
Koolhaas, Rem, 78
Kracauer, Siegfried, 2, 5, 8, 28, 51–52,
    63, 84, 89, 99, 127n39, 238, 255–59,
    275n2, 278–79
Kristeva, Julia, 261, 275n4
Kubrick, Stanley, 1, 8, 134, 210, 251n1,
    259, 268–74, 275n7, 275–76n11, 327

L'Avventura, 347
La Cava, Gregory, 5, 132
labyrinth, 290, 294, 326, 342, 353, 356
Lacan, Jacques, 9, 115, 224, 278, 292,
    328–48 *passim*
Lady for a Day, 5, 85, 87, 90, 120, 132
Lang, Fritz, 100, 143, 153, 164, 273
Las Vegas, 47n25, 236, 239–40, 250, 301
Lascars, 5, 61
*Last Year in Marienbad (L'Année
    dernière à Marienbad)*, 1, 7, 165,
    209, 292
Lausanne, 148–160 *passim*
Lean, David, 154
Leaving Las Vegas, 7, 235, 239, 240
Lefebvre, Henri, 14, 28
Leibniz, Gottfried Wilhelm, 281,
    291–293
Let's Go to the Rose Inn, 303–304,
    320n8
Lévinas, Emmanuel, 9, 326
Life magazine, 105, 107, 115, 119,
    130n63, 131n72, 210–11
limbo, 236, 250
Lindsay, Vachel, 358, 362
liner, 4, 5, 13, 17, 21–23, 34, 45n9,
    45n14, 46n20, 49, 64, 66–67, 170,
    371, 373
Linklater, Richard, 8, 236, 241
livre d'or, 146, 171n7 *see also* register,
    hotel
lobby, 2, 8, 28, 51–52, 79–81, 83,
    88–89, 99–100, 113–14, 124n22,
    127n39, 200, 203, 215, 249, 251,
    259–61, 263, 268, 271–74, 275n2,
    275n10, 277–79, 286

locomotion, 344, 346
LodgeNet, 375–6
Lolita, 307, 325, 335
London, 17, 146–47, 153, 154, 168–70,
    236, 248
Los Angeles Plays Itself, 217n9
Lost Highway, 8, 277, 290, 292–95
Lost in Translation, 1, 4, 8, 277–79,
    284–88, 294–95, 330, 373
love motel, 9, 298–302, 306, 316–18,
    320n3, 322n28
Lubin, Arthur, 5, 133
luminal, 1, 25, 88, 300, 312, 360
Lynch, David, 8, 277–78, 280–81, 285,
    290–95
Lynch, Kevin, 294

Ma Kwang-su, 302–304, 320n8
MacCannell, Dean, 129n57
machinic, 345
Madam Aema (Aema puin), 305–306,
    319, 321nn10–12
The Magic Mountain, 45n13, 149–50
The Maltese Falcon, 89, 132
The Man Who Knew Too Much, 134,
    152, 177
Manet, Édouard, 92–94, 126n29
Mann, Michael, 215
Mann, Thomas, 45n13, 144, 146, 149,
    172n11
Marienbad, 115, 165
Marnie, 9, 112, 134, 334, 336–37, 339,
    342
Marshall, George, 5, 133
Marx Brothers, 84, 132
Massumi, Brian, 221–22, 225–27, 229,
    230–31, 274–75n1
Maté, Rudolph, 5, 102, 133
Méliès, Georges, 6, 143, 151–52, 154–
    55, 164, 172n14, 179
Memento, 7, 9, 210, 213, 219–33
    passim, 236, 241–43, 339–40, 342
memory, 6–7, 98, 105, 145–47, 156,
    165–67, 185, 191, 194, 200, 210–16
    passim, 219–32 *passim*, 235–51

passim, 283, 340, 348, 353–54, 361, 366, 368n2

Menschen im hotel (People in a Hotel), 25, 45n13, 124n19

Mexico City, 118

Meyerowitz, Joanne, 123n16, 130

microcosm, 5, 52, 61, 158–59, 215, 279, 294, 300

The Million Dollar Hotel, 6, 185, 196–98, *199*, 200–205

mirror, 9, 67, 78, 93–94, 114–15, 188, 200, 223, 225, 227, 231–32, 278, 289, 291–94 *passim*, 306, 309–10, 329

Mitchell, W. J. T., 211

mobile privatization, 373, 376, 379n8

mobility, 2–3, 16, 24–43 *passim*, 50–65 *passim*, 76–7, 105, 110–11, 162, 308, 317–18, 373–74, 377–79

modern, 2, 5, 14–15, 19, 21–32, 52–4, 60, 66, 73–74, 85, 99, 118–20, 158, 215, 237, 251, 268, 274, 284–86, 298, 301, 327, 348, 358

modernism, 16, 21, 26, 28, 46n18, 124n22, 185, 191, 215, 283, 322n29, 326, 339

modernity, 15, 18–20, 22, 50, 61, 65–67, 74, 80, 83–85, 118, 121n1, 131n70, 185, 326

Monte Carlo, 20, 32, 110, 154, 166

Moore, Rachel O., 358, 362

Moretti, Franco, 9, 278, 280, 295

Morris, Meghan, 3, 378

Morrison, Bill, 212

Motel Cactus, 9, 297–323

movie theatre, 14–27 *passim*, 42–43, 45n7, 45n15, 46n19

Mulholland Drive, 292

multiplicity, 349

Mulvey, Laura, 335, 341

murder, 4, 26, 49, 66, 84, 89, 101–109 *passim*, 111, 117–18, 198, 213, 219–32 *passim*, 242–46 *passim*, 249, 259, 263, 291, 293, 304,

321n18, 333, 337, 339, 345–348 *passim*

Murnau, F. W., 19, 81, 84, 191, 328

Mussolini, Benito, 40, 47n30

Muzak, 272–74, 275n8, 275n10

My Favorite Wife, 91, 125n27, 126n28

My Man Godfrey, 5, *85*, 87, 120

Mystery Train, 8, 277, 280–81, *282*, 283–84, 290

Nabokov, Vladimir, 144, 165–66, 174n39, 307

Name-of-the-Father, 338–40, 349

narrative: cinema, 76, 91, 123n18, 246; economy, 16, 19, 22; form of identity, 79; hotelization of, 8, 277, 280; multiple/multi-linear/parallel, 220, 245, 278–81; reverse/anti-chronological, 223, 243, 342; space, 80, 259

Nazi, 43, 46n23, 68n11, 96, 111, 266

neo-realism, 29–30, 38

New York, 17, 23, 25, 74–75, 80, 86, 88, 112, 246, 259, 262–63, 273, 318

Nietzsche, Friedrich, 147, 168, 328, 342, 346, 348

Nocturne, 143, 147, 150

Noé, Gaspar, 212

noir. *See* film noir

Nolan, Christopher, 7, 9, 210, 213, 219–34 *passim*, 236, 241

nomad, 2, 116, 185, 289, 326–27, 360

non-place, 2, 100, 127n44, 156, 190, 237, 279, 285, 287–89, 294, 298, 329, 337–40

North by Northwest, 9, 331, 333–36

O'Neill, Pat, 6, 209–218

object a, 329, 343

object of desire, 16, 244, 305, 329–30, 338, 343, 355

ocean, 322n21, 328, *see also* sea

Odysseus, 326, 345, 347

odyssey, 34, 321n19, 327

Oshima, Nagisa, 171n1, 317, 322n29

other, 5, 29, 53, 56, 86, 107, 127n44,
    186, 266, 281, 295, 308, 313, 329,
    333–35, 339, 343–44, 349
Other, 329–30, 334–35, 337, 339–40,
    345
Oxide Pang Chun, 8, 236

Pak Ki-yong, 9, 299–300, 321n10
parallel worlds, 8, 278, 280, 286, 289,
    291–95
Paris, 17, 21, 24, 41, 75–83, 116, 119,
    127n37, 151, 166, 173n27, 174n33,
    308–309, 348–49
Paris.Texas, 6, 184–85, 187, 192–93,
    220
passport, 22, 50, 76, 118, 239, 248
patriarchy, 9, 220–23, 232n1, 297, 299,
    305, 314, 338–39, 341
Penley, Constance, 126n28
perception-image, 224
Perec, Georges, 311, 322n22
The Persistence of Memory, 211
phobia, 334
Plattner, Patricia, 143, 157, 161, 178
Plaza Hotel, New York, 17
poetics, 9, 203, 299–300, 310
Polanski, Roman, 131n77, 135
pornography, 10, 304, 306, 313,
    322n29, 345, 377–78, 380n15
The Postman Always Rings Twice, 102,
    135, 306
postmodern, 2, 8, 184, 222, 256, 277–
    80, 286, 289, 293, 295, 318, 339
postmodernism, 184, 222, 280
postmodernity, 127n44, 184, 277–85,
    293, 340
Potsdamer Platz, Berlin, 184, 193
Preston brothers, 5, *53, 54*, 62, 64
Pretty Woman, 216n5, 326, 330
private space, 1, 58, 80, 116, 127n35,
    258, 261, 301, *see also* public space
prostitution, 40, 78, 123n16, 159, 229,
    239–40, 246, 248, 292, 301, 304–
    305, 307, 317, 322n28–30, 326
Proust, Marcel, 343–44, 347–48

Psycho, 1, 3, 9, 64, 73, *74*, 76, 93, 96,
    118, 331, 334, 336, 338
public space, 1, 45n7, 52, 58, 63, 80,
    120, *see also* private space
purgatory, 8, 235–51 *passim*, 252n3

queer, 313

race, 80, 266
rape, 225, 227, 231, 242–45, 304, 326
realism, 33, 43, 66, 166, 228
reception desk, 5, 73–141 *passim*, 156
register, hotel, 5, 22, 73–141 *passim*,
    258, 260, *see also livre d'or*
Resnais, Alain, 1, 115, 165, 215
reterritorialization, 37, 258, 286–87,
    289, 343, *see also* deterritorialization
revenge, 8, 114, 236, 240–46, 339
revolving door, 26–28, 43, 52, 124n19,
    257
rhizomic, 281, 286, 290–91
Ritz, César, 146–47
Riviera: French, 32, 119; Hotel Riviera,
    Buenos Aires, 312; Italian, 32;
    Swiss, 171n6
road movie, 4, 161, 220, 231, 232n1,
    308, 316
rooming house, 110, 130n61
Rossellini, Roberto, 347
Rotaie (The Rails), 4, 30–38, 47nn29–30
Roy, Jean-Louis, 157, 165

Sandoval-Strausz, Andrew, 74–5, 80,
    97, 116, 122n4, 124n23, 125n26,
    126n34, 127n35–36, 127n40
Sartre, Jean-Paul, 336
Sassen, Saskia, 249
The Savoy, 146–47, 167–70
Scarr, Dr. John Barker, 5, 60, 62–63
schizophrenic, 220, 293
Schmid, Daniel, 6, 143, 146–47, 164–
    67, *169*, 170
Schwartz, Vanessa R., 84
science fiction, 66, 250, 278, 280, 288,
    294

Scorsese, Martin, 239
sea, 49, 51–52, 56–58, 64, 66–67, 169–70, 188, 190–91, 248, 344, *see also* ocean
seduction, 32, 304, 317, 355
sensori-motor situations, 346
Seoul, 9, 298, 301–302, 304–305, 320n4
sexploitation, 297, 300, 304, 306, 319, 321n10
sexual relation, 312, 334, 338, 368n1
The Shining, 1, 8, 210, 259, 268–71, 273, 280, 285, 326
shower, 73, 348
signature, 73, 90, 96–104, 126n32, 127n38, 127n40, 128n48
signifier, 16, 43, 47n37, 63, 158, 192, 315, 328–30, 332–3, 337–40, 345
Signorell, Riccardo, 6, 143, 147, 150
Silverman, Kaja, 123n12, 126n28, 220
Simmel, Georg, 19, 45n12
simulacrum, 195, 258, 261, 263–64, 268, 271–72
Sirk, Douglas, 143, 153, 154, 164, 167
Sitwell, Edith, 59, 66
Snow, Michael, 322n21
Sorrentino, Paolo, 143, 156, 176
soul, 196, 235–50 *passim*, 264, 277, 279, 284, 291, 358, 360
Soutter, Michel, 143, *144*, 157, 164–67
Speaking Parts, 10, 353–54, *256*, *257–70*
St Moritz, 145, 148, 150, 152, 172n16, 174n42
stairs, 158, 161, 260, 293, 334
The State of Things (Der Stand der Dinge), 6, 185, 188–92, *193*, 196–98, 201–205 *passim*
Stettner, Patrick, 8, 236, 241
The Street with No Name, 89, *96*, 111, 126n32
subject, 123n11, 202, 220, 227, 230, 241–2, 256–57, 275n4, 278, 281, 293–94, 326, 328–46, 365, 377
subjectivity, 9, 56, 220, 245, 255, 277–78, 281, 292–95, 302, 320n6, 328, 345

suicide, 30, 150, 160, 198–99, 246, 348, 357–58
surface, 78, 102, 258, 260, 273–74, 278, 286, 310, 318, 359–68
surreal, 197, 209, 211, 217n12
surveillance, 52, 62, 75, 78, 89, 118, 199, 219, 223–24, 256, 258,
Svevo, Italo, 10
symbolic order, 328–45
synthesis: conjunctive, 256, 260, 268, 273, 274; connective, 258, 269, 274; disjunctive, 8, 257–58, 260, 269, 272–73

tactile, 213, 261, 263
Tallack, Douglas, 3, 124n22, 256–59
Tanner, Alain, 143, 156–57, 163–65, 170, 173n22, 174nn33–37
Tape, 8, 236, 241, 244–45
telegram, 102
telephone, 21–29 *passim*, 47n28, 50, 104, 114, 159, 190, 314
television, 8, 96, 149, 158, 160, 277, 287–90 *passim*, 294, 304–309 *passim*, 315, 358, 363, 366, 373–78 *passim*
The Tesseract, 8, 236, 245, 247–48
time-image, 212, 346–47
To Catch a Thief, 101, 110, 119, 134
Tokyo, 277, 284–90, 295, 301, 318, 325n32
Touch of Evil, 5, 107, 117–20, 125n18, 134, 331
tour, 30, 31, 33–34, 38, 39, 42–43, 117
tourism, 5, 15–45 *passim*, 45n9, 50, 67, 117, 121, 150–51, 155, 166, 168, 203, 248, 298, 301, 308, 323n32, 371–79
transience, 3, 6–7, 107, 110, 113, 115, 190, 237, 246, 299–300
transindividual, 10, 360–61, 365
transit, 2, 3, 127n44, 235, 332, 378
transition, 3, 8, 35, 59, 184, 193, 239, 248–51, 253
transitory, 131, 214–15, 236, 240, 243, 359

transnational, 9, 20–21, 158, 247, 251, 300, 312, 318
travel, 2, 5, 15–43 *passim*, 45n9, 49–68 *passim*, 73–77, 80, 94, 109–120 *passim*, 122n4, 127n44, 131n76, 151–52, 190, 195, 237–38, 248, 283, 301, 328–37 *passim*, 344–46, 371–79
travelling salesman, 75, 111, 152
travelogue, 151, 157
Trollope, Anthony, 77–80
Trouble Every Day, 9, 348
Twin Peaks, 8, 272, 290–94

Ulysses, 326, 343
uncanny 3–4, 104, 117, 270, *see also* Unheimlich
unconscious, 216, 217n12
underclass, 62, 169, 200
Unheimlich, 3, 6, 117, 270, *see also* uncanny
unreal, 65, 78, 258, 281, 290, 297
Urry, John, 2–3, 5, 62, 379n8
Usai, Paolo Cherchi, 211–12, 216n4
utopia, 29, 34, 43, 274, 308, 317

vacancy, 3, 73, 83, 94, 108, 113, 121
vacation, 18–20, 30–31, 42, 44, 51, 53, 65, 67, 103–104, 238
vagabond, 35, 308, 332
Vendredi Soir, 9, 349
Vertigo, 9, 134, 334–35
video, 10, 197–98, 201, 304, 313–16 *passim*, 353–365 *passim*, 368nn2–3, 374–77
Vidler, Anthony, 9, 123n11, 124n22, 278, 283, 288, 292
voyage, 31, 79, 326, 344
Voyage à travers l'impossible, 6, 151, 172n14
voyageur, 126n30, 79, 94

voyeurism, 5, 78–79, 94, 159, 217n11, 303, 341, 359

Waldorf-Astoria Hotel, New York, 17, 23, 80, 88, 125n25
Warburton, George, 5, 56–58, 62
Warhol, Andy, 252n7
warped space, 77–78, 123n11, 278
Waugh, Evelyn, 58–60, 62
Wavelength, 311, 322n21
Weaver, David, 8, 236
Weekend at the Waldorf, 89, 122n9, 133
Weimar Republic, 2, 29, 195
Welles, Orson, 5, 111, 117–18, 133–34, 174n38, 331
Wenders, Wim, 6, 10, 171n1, 182–208 *passim*, 220
Williams, Raymond, 371–74, 376–78
Williamson, Jefferson, 75–76, 121n3, 122nn7–8, 123n16
window, 31–32, 62, 115–17, 154–70 *passim*, 191, 201–202, 214, 261, 287, 305, 311, 315, 356
Wings of Desire (Der Himmel über Berlin), 6, 184–85, 187, 192, 193, *194*, 195, 196, 202, 204
Wong Kar-wai, 4, 8–9, 236, 249, 310, 312, 317, 321n20, 341

xenophobia, 118

Yersin, Yves, 165, 173n22
yŏgwan, 297–323 *passim*
You Only Live Once, 100, 121n1, 132
Yu Ji-na, 297, 304, 319

Zermatt, 148, 173n22
ziggurat, 81, 83, 124n21
Žižek, Slavoj, 9, 280, 327, 341–42
Zurich, 153, 165, 171n4, 172nn18–19
Zwischensaison, 147, 165, 167, 168, *169*, 170

Contributors

Stuart Aitken is Professor of Geography at San Diego State University in the USA. His research centres on film, space, masculinity, and fatherhood. He has co-edited, with Leo Zonn, *Place, Power, Situation and Spectacle: A Geography of Film* (Rowman and Littlefield, 1994); is the author of numerous book chapters and journal articles on geography and film; and is commissioning editor of the journal *Children's Geographies*.

Yvette Blackwood is an academic and a filmmaker. She completed a doctoral thesis on *Hotels in Postmodernity* in 2005, and is currently Lecturer in Gender Studies at the School of Philosophy, University of Tasmania, Australia.

David B. Clarke is Professor of Human Geography and Director of the Centre for Urban Theory at Swansea University in the UK. He is the editor of *The Cinematic City* (Routledge, 1997) and the author of *The Consumer Society and the Postmodern City* (Routledge, 2003). His research focuses on urbanism and social theory, consumerism, media, and film.

Valerie Crawford Pfannhauser is an independent scholar based in Austria. She has been interested in the significance of hotels and motels since completing a Master's thesis on the topic in 2001, and currently writes freelance about film for several publications in Vienna.

David Scott Diffrient is Assistant Professor of Film and Media Studies at Colorado State University. He has published articles in *Cinema Journal*, *Film Quarterly*, *The Historical Journal of Film, Radio, and Television*, *Film and History* and *Screening the Past*, and his essays can be found in such anthologies as *Horror Film: Creating and Marketing Fear* (University of Mississippi Press) and *New Korean Cinema* (NYU Press). His recently completed manuscript exploring the cultural history of *M*A*S*H*, from novel to film to award-winning TV series, was published in 2008 by Wayne State University Press (TV Milestones series).

Marcus A. Doel is Professor of Human Geography at Swansea University in the UK. He is the author of *Poststructuralist Geographies: the Diabolical Art of Spatial Science* (Edinburgh University Press, 1999) and has edited a number of books and authored numerous papers in the field of social and cultural geography.

Asbjørn Grønstad is a postdoctoral fellow at the Department of Information Science and Media Studies, University of Bergen, Norway. He has published numerous articles on film theory and history, and is co-editor of *To Become the Self One Is: A Critical Companion to* A Saloonkeeper's Daughter (Novus, 2005) and *Image–Music–Text: Discovering Album Aesthetics* (Museum Tusculanum Press, 2007). His current research project is the monograph *Nothing's Shocking: Film and the Poetics of Negation*, on images of transgression in contemporary European art cinema.

Greg Hainge is Reader in French at the University of Queensland, Australia. He has authored a monograph and numerous articles on Louis-Ferdinand Céline, and has published widely in the areas of film, critical theory, and contemporary music, both popular and experimental. He serves on the editorial boards of *Culture, Theory and Critique*, *Contemporary French Civilization*, and *Études Céliniennes*, and is the President of the Australian Society for French Studies.

James Hay is an Associate Professor in the Department of Speech Communication, the Graduate Program in Cultural Studies, the Unit for Criticism and Interpretive Theory, and the Unit for Cinema Studies at the University of Illinois in the USA. His books include *Popular Film Culture in Fascist Italy* (Indiana University Press, 1987); *The Audience and Its Landscape* (Westview, 1996); *Better Living Through Reality TV* (with Laurie Ouellette, Blackwell, forthcoming); and he is the author of numerous essays about communication, media, space, and governmentality.

Stan Jones is Senior Lecturer in Screen and Media at the University of Waikato, Hamilton, New Zealand/Aotearoa. He has published on 20th-century German literature (*Der Sturm. A Focus of Expressionism*, Camden House, 1986); Wim Wenders; and German and New Zealand film in volumes including *European Identity in Cinema* (1996), *Screening the Past* (1998), *Projecting a Nation* (1999), *Fifty Contemporary Filmmakers* (2001), *Writing Europe's Pasts* (2003), and *European Cinema: Inside Out* (2003). His current research interests include *The Lord of the Rings* trilogy (E. Mathijs ed., *Lord of the Rings* Wallflower, 2006) and cross-cultural influence and identity in contemporary cinema ('Germany' in *Schirmer Encyclopaedia of Film*, Thompson and Gale, 2006).

Roland-François Lack teaches French and film at University College London in the UK. His publications include *Poetics of the Pretext: Reading Lautréamont* (University of Exeter Press, 1998); *The Tel Quel Reader* (co-edited with Patrick ffrench, Routledge, 1998) and numerous articles on Jean-Luc Godard. He is currently preparing a book on ciné-tourism.

Rob Lapsley is a part-time lecturer in the Centre for Continuing Education at the University of Manchester, UK. He has completed, with Michael Westlake, the second edition of *Film Theory: An Introduction* (Manchester University Press, 2006) and a survey of psychoanalytic criticism and literature for the *Routledge Companion to Critical Theory* (2006).

Katherine Lawrie Van de Ven is a doctoral candidate in the Department of Film, Television and Digital Media at UCLA in the USA. Her primary research interests lie in the changing nature of the city film and in the intersections of film and spatial theories more broadly. She currently lives in Toronto and holds the position of Manager in the Editorial Department of the Toronto International Film Festival Group.

Jann Matlock has taught at Harvard University, the Université de Paris-VII, and currently teaches in the Department of French, University College London, UK. She has been a Getty Postdoctoral Fellow, a Whitney Humanities Center Fellow, and a Guggenheim Fellow. Her books include *Scenes of Seduction: Prostitution, Hysteria, and Reading Difference in Nineteenth-Century France* (Columbia University Press, 1993), a co-edited volume, *Media Spectacles* (with Marjorie Garber and Rebecca Walkowitz, Routledge, 1993), and the forthcoming *Desires to Censor: Spectacles of the Body, Aesthetics, and Reading Difference in Nineteenth-Century France*. She has recently been writing on justice, war, and representation, as well as on the institutions of modernity.

Heather Norris Nicholson is Research Fellow at the Manchester Centre for Regional History and Manchester European Research Institute, Manchester

Metropolitan University, UK. She works closely with the North West Film Archive on socio-cultural and landscape-related change in relation to the interpretation of visual evidence and the politics of representation. She is currently writing *Visual Pleasures: Britain's Amateur Film Movement, Leisure and Society, c. 1925–1977* (Manchester University Press). Her publications include *Screening Culture: Constructing Image and Identity* (Lexington, 2003), chapters in *Film and Landscape* (Routledge, 2006), *Mining the Home Movie* (University of California Press, 2007) and *Movies on Home Ground* (Cambridge Scholars Press, 2009), and articles in *Moving Image, Film History, History Workshop, GeoJournal, Area, Journal of Intercultural Studies, Tourist Studies* and *Landscapes*.

Maria Walsh is Senior Lecturer in Art History and Theory at Chelsea College of Art and Design, The University of the Arts, London, UK. She has published essays on film and video in journals such as *Screen, Angelaki, Senses of Cinema, filmwaves*, and *COIL*. She is currently working on a book on spectatorship, narrative, and embodiment in film installation.